A Legal Analysis of NGOs and European Civil Society

European Monographs Series Set

VOLUME 109

Editor

Prof. Andrea Biondi is Professor of European Law and Director of the Centre of European Law at King's College London

Introduction & Contents/Subjects

As the process of European integration assumes an increasingly complex character, the EU legal system continues to undergo sweeping changes. The European Monographs series offers a voice to thoughtful, knowledgeable, cutting edge legal commentary on the now unlimited field of European law. Its emphasis on focal and topical issues makes the series an invaluable tool for scholars, practitioners, and policymakers specializing or simply interested in EU law.

Objective

The aim is to publish innovative work appealing to academics and practitioners alike. The result is an original and ongoing library of detailed analyses, theories, commentaries, practical guides, and proposals, each of which furthers the cause of meaningful European integration. Cumulatively, the series may be regarded as a 'work in progress' engaged in building a sharply defined representation of law in Europe.

Readership

Academics and practitioners dealing with EU law.

The titles published in this series are listed at the end of this volume.

A Legal Analysis of NGOs and European Civil Society

Piotr Staszczyk

Wolters Kluwer

Published by:
Kluwer Law International B.V.
PO Box 316
2400 AH Alphen aan den Rijn
The Netherlands
E-mail: international-sales@wolterskluwer.com
Website: lrus.wolterskluwer.com

Sold and distributed in North, Central and South America by:
Wolters Kluwer Legal & Regulatory U.S.
7201 McKinney Circle
Frederick, MD 21704
United States of America
Email: customer.service@wolterskluwer.com

Sold and distributed in all other countries by:
Air Business Subscriptions
Rockwood House
Haywards Heath
West Sussex
RH16 3DH
United Kingdom
Email: international-customerservice@wolterskluwer.com

Printed on acid-free paper.

ISBN 978-94-035-1251-8

e-Book: ISBN 978-94-035-1252-5
web-PDF: ISBN 978-94-035-1253-2

Printed in the United Kingdom.

Table of Contents

List of Figures

List of Tables

Introduction

It appears that we live in a new era of democracy.[1] It is without doubt that the tools of democratic participation are presently more common than ever in the modern history. Still, the proliferation of egalitarian principles and measures encounters numerous obstacles on the way. For instance, in recent years, many organized and long-term protests have swept through the world.[2] However, the conducted studies indicate that these movements hardly materialized into significant political powers after the outcries had run out.[3] Furthermore, the postulates for giving voice to the citizens or democratizing the rulemaking procedures both at the national and the international levels have been especially noticeable in the last few years.[4] Still, these demands have often been misused by populists in order to promote the idea of direct democracy not as a tool of improving citizen participation but rather of imposing the "will of the people." This led

1. See e.g. J.-M. Moreno-Jiménez, W. Polasek, *E-Democracy and Knowledge. A Multicriteria Framework for the New Democratic Era*, Journal of Multi-Criteria Decision Analysis Vol. 12/2004, pp. 163-176, E. Vigoda-Gado, *Revitalizing Democracy? New Avenues for Citizen Participation in the Era of Information Technology*, Public Administration Review Vol. 4/2007, pp. 789-791, P. Parvin, *Democracy Without Participation: A New Politics for a Disengaged Era*, Res Publica Vol. 24/2018, pp. 31-52, M. Kilanowski, *Ku wolności jako odpowiedzialności. Dewey, Rorty I Habermas o nowej jakości demokracji*, Toruń 2013, pp. 279-290, M. du Vall, *Electronic Civil Disobedience (ECD) jako jedna ze współczesnych form obywatelskiego nieposłuszeństwa*, Państwo i Społeczeństwo Vol. 2/2010, p. 127.
2. E.g. The Occupy movements; see to this extent M. Balanguera Cuervo, *Public Space Without Demands: Understanding Traveling Theory and Practice in Occupy and Transnational Protests* in: *Arab Revolutions and Beyond. The Middle East and Reverberations in the Americas*, S. Alnasseri (ed.), New York 2016, pp. 95-117, J.S. Juris, *Reflections on #Occupy Everywhere: Social Media, Public Space and Emerging Logics of Aggregation*, American Ethnologist. Journal of the American Ethnological Society Vol. 39/2012, pp. 259-279, M. Chou, *From Crisis to Crisis: Democracy, Crisis and the Occupy Movement*, Political Studies Review Vol. 13/2015, pp. 46-58.
3. See I. Ortiz, S. Burke, M. Berrada, H. Cortes Saenz, *World Protests 2006-2013*, Initiative for Policy Dialogue. Working Paper #274, available at: http://policydialogue.org/publications/working-papers/world-protests-2006-2013/ (on February 9, 2019).
4. See e.g. B. Akinrinade, *Democratizing International Law-Making* in: *Shielding Humanity*, Ch. Jalloh, O. Elias (eds), Leiden 2015, pp. 144-162, S. Ratner, R. Goodin, *Democratizing International Law*, Global Policy Journal Vol. 2/2012, pp. 241-247.

to many problematic decisions made in various states in the form of referendums.[5] As it has turned out, democracy is very vulnerable to risks associated with the Internet and social media.[6] In particular, these new means give an illusion of participation, social inclusion and fighting for the right cause without actual and direct involvement in the given case or the decision-making.[7]

At the same time, agents of civil society face growing inequalities in treatment in many states around the globe, in both political and fiscal terms.[8] The problem of maintaining participation or advocacy instruments with their parallel and factual undercutting has been known as the "shrinking of civil space"[9] dilemma. Moreover, many grassroot movements have been accused of "astroturfing"[10] which undermines the public confidence in agents of civil society.

The above-listed issues are also very noticeable in the European Union and its Member States and are exceptionally urgent as grassroot civil movements should always play a prominent role in protecting the values of the Union, in particular the rule of law. In this dimension, another matter of great importance appears—the democratic deficit of the EU. It means that there is no sufficient democratic link between the EU institutions and the Member States societies. Subsequently, it may be arguable whether a "European civil society," i.e. a society which gathers around affairs of common, European interests across borders, is in fact possible. If so, it would definitely contribute to a solid ground of the EU democracy. Yet, its establishment appears as especially burdensome in the light of the presently varying Europe.[11]

The preliminary observations lead to a conclusion that the means of civil society participation require more structuring and independence. For this reason, nongovernmental organizations (NGOs) as legal entities will be the focal point of further deliberations because they are historically designed to meet these ends. The aim of this

5. The most apparent example is perhaps the European Union membership referendum held in 2016 in the UK, resulting in the so-called "Brexit."
6. See e.g. N. Confessore, *Cambridge Analytica and Facebook: The Scandal and the Fallout So Far*, New York Times 2018, available at: https://www.nytimes.com/2018/04/04/us/politics/cambridge-analytica-scandal-fallout.html (on February 9, 2019). However, new technologies deploy new possibilities for democracy as well. See, to this extent, e.g. *Can Civic Tech Save Democracy? How technology is renewing civic engagement*, L'Atelier BNP Paribas Report, available at: https://atelier.bnpparibas/uploads/file/20171208-Civic-Tech-Study-LAtelier-BNP Paribas-NA.pdf (on February 9, 2019).
7. See e.g. E.D. Hersh, *The Problem with Participatory Democracy Is the Participants*, New York Times 2017, available at: https://www.nytimes.com/2017/06/29/opinion/sunday/the-problem-with-participatory-democracy-is-the-participants.html (on February 9, 2019).
8. Shrinking space for civil society: the EU response. A study of Directorate-General for External Policies Policy Department, available at: http://bit.do/eg9Ac (on February 9, 2019).
9. See e.g. Challenges facing civil society organizations working on human rights in the EU. Report of the European Union Agency for Fundamental Rights, Luxembourg: Publications Office of the European Union 2017, available at: http://fra.europa.eu/en/publication/2018/challenges-facing-civil-society-orgs-human-rights-eu (on February 9, 2019), I. De Jesus Butler, *Participatory Democracy under Threat: Growing Restrictions on the Freedoms of NGOs in the EU*, Civil Liberties for Europe. August 2017, available at: http://bit.do/eg9By (on February 9, 2019).
10. I.e. the practice of masking the sponsors of a message or organization to make it appear as though it originates from and is supported by grassroot participants; P. Howard, *New Media Campaigns and the Managed Citizen*, New York 2005, p. 93.
11. I. Krastev, *After Europe*, Philadelphia 2017, pp. 17 et seq.

book is to discuss the legal role of these organizations in shaping European civil society. The two main hypotheses of this book read: (1) NGOs, as subjects acting in the interest of European civil society, can diminish the democratic deficit of the EU, (2) the legal instruments of forming European civil society are present in the EU law but are not sufficient. The collateral hypotheses can be worded as follows: (1) there is a tendency of increasing the role of NGOs not only in the EU legal system but also in other intergovernmental organizations; (2) European civil society, as a legal community, is possible; (3) NGOs have played a significant role in the history and theory of European integration; (4) the EU provides various democratic tools and arenas of cooperation between the institutions and the representatives of civil society; (5) the EU law also provides certain means of advocating for the collective interests of civil society; (6) these tools are often not effective; (7) as a result, other, frequently unofficial means of influencing the EU institutions are used by NGOs; (8) the EU law concerns numerous spheres of cross-border activities of NGOs; (9) there are spheres which might be regulated in order to ameliorate such enterprises.

Since this book focuses on legal matters, the appropriate methodology has been used. It includes dogmatic, analytical, explanatory, empirical, hermeneutic, instrumental and evaluative types of research. As part of the analysis concentrates on issues on which doctrinal debates are constantly ongoing, and the adopted or planned legal solutions are still in the evolutionary phase, it has also been indispensable to use the comparative method. Incidentally, supporting disciplines, comprising of legal history, legal sociology, theory of integration and, to some extent, statistics, have also been used.[12]

The book covers various aspects concerning the role of NGOs as subjects acting toward shaping European civil society. It consists of five chapters. The first one, "Defining NGOs and Setting Their Place in European Civil Society," discusses the notions of a "NGO" and a "European civil society." In doing so, it particularly invokes various modes of cooperation between NGOs and intergovernmental organizations and the theories of European integration. The second chapter, "NGOs in the EU Constitutional System," provides a general insight into the role of NGOs in the history of integration. Furthermore, it discusses the treaty basis for social cooperation and presents the areas of NGO participation at the EU level. The third chapter is entitled "The NGO Influence on Shaping the EU Law." It examines and evaluates access to documents and the European Citizens' Initiative as means of exerting pressure on the EU legislation. Moreover, it discusses legal basis and practices of relations between the EU institutions and NGOs, including lobbying activities. The fourth chapter, "NGOs as Entities Acting in the Collective Interest of European Civil Society," discusses the possibilities of bringing actions in the common good before courts and other institutions, which derive from the EU law. It also presents the special role of NGOs in environmental protection which was guaranteed by the Aarhus Convention. The fifth chapter, "The EU Law and the Cross-Border Activities of NGOs: Selected Aspects," examines the case law of the CJEU with reference to the transboundary operations of

12. For explanation of these types of research see M. von Hoecke, *Methodologies of Legal Research: Which Kind of Method for What Discipline?*, Oxford 2011, pp. 1-69.

NGOs. Furthermore, it presents the regulation proposals for a European Association and a European Foundation. It also indicates the possible areas of the EU legislation which could promote the operations of NGOs at the European level. Lastly, the book presents concluding remarks which consist of findings and implication of the conducted research.

To complete these introductory remarks, it should be noticed that the research carried out for the purposes of this book encountered certain difficulties. In particular, the chosen subject, even if concentrating primarily on the legal matters, often relates indirectly to other fields of science (for instance to political science). Also, the analyzed legal matter is frequently fragmented and not easily identifiable. Finally, the choice of national legislations which could be perceived as representative of referable ideas on the place of NGOs in the legal system was not always clear and required some selection. Nevertheless, the topic of this book was analyzed to the widest possible extent.

CHAPTER 1

Defining NGOs and Setting Their Place in European Civil Society

International law, including the EU Treaties[1] and other norms of the EU legislation, hardly ever define "nongovernmental organizations" or "civil society."[2] Additionally, there is no single legal interpretation of "European civil society." Therefore, it is crucial for further analysis to explain what will be understood under these notions. At this point, it should be notified that the definitions provided in the subsequent parts of this chapter are mere proposals and other understandings, based on different assumptions, could be justifiable as well.

The following paragraphs will not only concentrate on a definition attempt of the abovementioned terms. Thus, it will be indicated how other international organizations incorporate the representatives of civil society in their legal systems and day-to-day routines. Additionally, it will be argued that the concept of shaping European civil society has been present in the theory of integration since the beginning of the "European project." In this way, it will be maintained that the topic of this book is not detached from comparative law studies and theoretical basis.

§1.01 NONGOVERNMENTAL ORGANIZATIONS IN THE INTERNATIONAL SPHERE

In 2008, K. Annan, the former Secretary-General of the United Nations (UN), stated that the twenty-first century would be the era of NGOs.[3] These words turned out to be

1. The Treaty on European Union (consolidated version), Official Journal C 326, 26.10.2012, pp. 13-390 (hereinafter referred to as "TEU") and the Treaty on the Functioning of the European Union (consolidated version), Official Journal C 326, 26.10.2012, pp. 47-390 (hereinafter referred to as "TFEU").
2. See e.g. A.-K. Lindblom, *Non-governmental Organisations in International Law*, Cambridge 2008, p. 46.
3. S. Lang, *NGOs, Civil Society and the Public Sphere*, Cambridge 2012, p. 1.

foreshadowing as NGOs undoubtedly play a prominent role not only in the domestic spheres but also at the international and the EU levels. The significance of such entities ranges from decision-making to law enforcement, providing democratic standards in politics in general.[4] As a result, the multilevel governance in which the citizens can attribute to the decisions undertaken at the supranational level is being developed.[5]

The following paragraphs will be focused on defining the notion of NGOs in the legal context. Furthermore, as it has already been notified, the position of these organizations will be discussed in the framework of chosen intergovernmental organizations. Hence, some general remarks will be made for the purposes of further analysis of the position of NGOs in the EU system.

[A] Definition

The Charter of the United Nations (UN Charter)[6] was the first international legal act to adopt the notion of a "nongovernmental organization."[7] According to its Article 71, the Economic and Social Council may make suitable arrangements for consultation with nongovernmental organizations which are concerned with matters within its competence. Such arrangements may be made with international organizations and, where appropriate, with national organizations after consultation with the Member of the United Nations concerned.

Even though the discussed term was first used at the international level by the UN, it is important to point out that it did not discover NGOs as new species of civic actors, nor did it define it in any way, but rather labeled and categorized in a constructivist manner a broad set of previously active organizations.[8] Moreover, this constructivist labeling was not restricted to truly internationally operating organizations, as it was used to identify a very wide range of civic organisms, from transnational to national, regional and local associations. As it will be further argued, many concepts of defining NGOs have emerged since the first utilization of this notion by the UN. Additionally, there seems to be a growing negative connotation with the term "NGO" in some environments. Consequently, some attempts to replace it with the substitute

4. E.g. according to T. Alexander, the notion "politics" consists of four elements: "governing," "challenging," "supporting" and "submitting." NGOs should play a significant role in the "challenging" and "submitting" parts as they demand transparency in the lawmaking procedures and represent the opinions of grassroot civil society; see T. Alexander, *Practical Politics. Lessons in Power and Democracy*, London 2016, p. 6.
5. See also e.g. Ch. Bakker, L. Vierucci, *Introduction: A Normative or Pragmatic Definition of NGOs* in: *NGOs in International Law: Efficiency in Flexibility?*, P.-M. Dupuy, L. Vierrucci (eds), Cheltenham 2008, p. 1.
6. The Charter of the United Nations signed on June 26, 1945, available at: http://www.un.org/en/sections/un-charter/un-charter-full-text/index.html (on February 9, 2019).
7. Before that it was used by the US governmental institutions; for more see M. Olivo U., *Evolution of the Term Non Governmental Organization (NGO)*, Revista Venezoelana de Analisis de Coyuntura Vol. XIII/2007, pp. 97-121.
8. R. Sanchez Salgado, *Europeanizing Civil Society. How the EU Shapes Civil Society Organizations*, London 2015, p. 14.

notion of "civil society organizations" (CSOs)[9] are noticeable, especially in the last few years.[10]

The EU Treaties do not employ the notion of a "nongovernmental organization." Yet, Article 11 (2) of the Treaty on European Union (TEU) states that the institutions maintain an open, transparent and regular dialogue with representative associations and civil society. As it can be seen, according to this provision, it cannot be determined what a "representative association" is or even more interestingly—what makes an association (an NGO) representative. Nevertheless, as it will be often discussed in this book, the notion of a "NGO" appears in various acts of the EU law. Still, it is not defined anywhere but is rather used in a descriptive way, often in line with other representatives of civil society (e.g., trade unions).[11] As a result, the notion of an NGO at the EU level remains remarkably vague. However, there is one significant exception in the European law,[12] namely the European Convention on the Recognition of the Legal Personality of International Non-Governmental Organizations, proposed by the Council of Europe in 1986.[13] In Article 1 it is stated that this Convention shall apply to associations, foundations and other private institutions (hereinafter referred to as "NGOs") which satisfy the following conditions: (a) have a non-profit-making aim of international utility, (b) have been established by an instrument governed by the internal law of a party, (c) carry on their activities with effect in at least two states, (d) have their statutory office in the territory of a party and the central management and control in the territory of that party or of another party. The Convention entered into force on January 1, 1991, and has been ratified by 12 countries.[14] Its scope of application is therefore rather limited.

The term "nongovernmental organization" is also rarely defined at the national level.[15] One of the few exceptions is the definition in the Polish Public Benefit and

9. H. Johansson, S. Kalm, *Thinking Rationally: Questions, Themes and Perspectives for the Study of EU Civil Society* in: *EU Civil Society. Patterns of Coopeation, Competition and Conflict*, H. Johansson, S. Kalm (eds), Basingstoke 2015, p. 19, H. Yanacopulos, *International NGO Engagement, Advocacy, Activism. The Faces and Spaces of Change*, London 2016, p. 3.
10. E.g. M. Noortmann, C. Ryngaert, *Non-State Actor Dynamics in International Law. From Law-Takers to Law-Makers*, Oxford 2015, p. 3, A. Kutay, *Limits of Participatory Democracy in European Governance*, European Law Journal Vol. 21/2015, p. 816.
11. For more grounds of linking the present NGOs with trade unions and, historically, labor movements see J. Menkes, A. Wasilkowski, *Organizacje międzynarodowe. Prawo instytucjonalne*, Warsaw 2010, pp. 267-369.
12. It should be emphasized that the notion of "European law" cannot be equated with the EU law. The former one encompasses not only the EU *acquis* but also the legislation of other intergovernmental organizations operating in Europe. "European law" can also be linked with "Europeanization" of law, understood as a process of mutual influences between various legal system of European countries; for more information dealing with differences between these notions see S. Biernat, *Europejskie prawo administracyjne i europeizacja krajowego prawa administracyjnego (zarys problematyki)*, Studia prawno-europejskie Vol. VI/2002, pp. 71 et seq.
13. Available at: http://bit.do/eg9F6 (on February 9, 2019).
14. I.e. Austria, Belgium, Cyprus, France, Greece, Liechtenstein, Macedonia, the Netherlands, Portugal, Slovenia, Switzerland and the United Kingdom.
15. Even when national legislatures envisage specific provisions for NGOs, they tend to omit legal definitions. A good example is the Hungarian Act CLVI of 1997 on Public Benefit Organizations (*1997. évi CLVI. törvény a közhasznú szervezetekről*) which applies the notions of "pubic benefit organization" and "civil society organization" without defining them.

Volunteer Work Act.[16] In Article 2 (1) it interprets NGOs as corporate and noncorporate entities, which according to separate provisions have the capacity to perform acts in law, such as foundations and associations, and: (1) do not form part of the public finance sector as defined in the Act on Public Finance[17] or comprise companies, research institutes, banks and commercial companies that are national or local legal entities; (2) do not operate for profit.

As there is no single definition of "nongovernmental organizations," it is most effective to differentiate them from other legal entities on the basis of their unique qualities. Thus, on the most basic level, NGOs: (1) are not related to government, (2) are not for profit,[18] (3) are voluntary and (4) pursue activities for the common good instead of just for their members.[19] In broad terms, these activities can take the form of either providing services or advocating public policy.[20]

Furthermore, NGOs are part of a broader notion of nonstate actors (NSA) and "the third sector," in contrast to the public sector and the private sector.[21] NSAs include not only NGOs but also multinational enterprises (MNEs),[22] national liberation armies (MNEs),[23] intergovernmental organizations (IGOs),[24] indigenous peoples,[25] criminal and terrorist organizations[26] or social movements,[27] which, in simplification, can be defined as NGOs without legal capacity.

16. I.e. *Ustawa z dnia 24 kwietnia 2003 o działalności pozytku publicznego i o wolontariacie* (unified text: Dz. U. of 2016 item 239).
17. I.e. *Ustawa z dnia 27 sierpnia 2009 o finansach publicznych* (unified text: Dz. U. of 2016 r. item 1870).
18. Which, however, cannot be equated with the term "nonprofit." The latter one means that an organization cannot carry any economic activities, whereas a "not-for-profit" entity can conduct such activities but the potential profit shall be allotted to the organization's statutory aims. Furthermore, some legal system distinguishes a separate legal form of "charitable organizations" or "charities" which are nonprofit organizations whose primary objectives are philanthropy and social well-being. See P. Staszczyk, *Ustawa o fundacjach. Komentarz praktyczny*, Warsaw 2015, p. 23.
19. This feature is especially noticeable in the definition of "nongovernmental organizations" provided by the World Bank. Accordingly, it defines NGOs as "private organizations that pursue activities to relieve suffering, promote the interests of the poor, protect the environment, provide basic social services, or undertake community development" (Working with NGOs. A Practical Guide to Operational Collaboration Between The World Bank and Non-governmental Organizations. World Bank 2015, available at: http://bit.do/eg9Hy). See also H.K. Anheier, *The Nonprofit Sector: Introductory Remarks. What Kind of Nonprofit Sector, What Kind of Society? Comparative Policy Reflections* in: *Comparative Corporate Governance of Non-profit Organizations*, K.J. Hopt, T. von Hippel (eds), Cambridge 2012, pp. 4-5.
20. According to the definition by Britannica, http://www.britannica.com/topic/nongovernmental-organization.
21. Even though this notion may raise some doubts as it assumes a complete distinctiveness from the government which, as it was already pointed out, cannot be a valid statement. See, to this extent, e.g. R. Godin, *Democratic Accountability: The Distinctiveness of the Third Sector*, European Journal of Sociology Vol. 44/2003, pp. 357 et seq. Still, in this book the term "third sector organizations" will in some places be used interchangeably with "NGOs."
22. E.g. P. Muchlinski, *Multinational Enterprises and the Law*, Oxford 2007, p. 7.
23. E.g. M. Noortmann, C. Ryngaert, *Non-State...*, p. 5.
24. E.g. A. Kaasch, K. Martens, *Actors and Agency in Global Social Governance*, Oxford 2015, p. 108.
25. E.g. I. Brownlie, F. M. Brookfield, *Treaties and Indigenous Peoples*, Oxford 1990, pp. 4-5.
26. E.g. J. Tankebe, A. Liebling, *Legitimacy and Criminal Justice*, Oxford 2013, p. 17.
27. E.g. D. Meyer, N. Whittier, B. Robnett, *Social Movements. Identity, Culture and the State*, Oxford 2002, pp. 3-4.

NGOs at the international level are subjects of law because they are created by legitimate subjects of international or domestic law (i.e., individuals) under a typical principal–agent relationship as rational–legal bodies entrusted with certain functions.[28] It follows that (like other NSAs), NGOs do not compete with any states. They are legal organisms established by formal arrangements to perform the same type of issue-oriented task.[29] Nevertheless, the actual legal forms of NGOs are very diverse and depend upon legal cultures, norms and practices in various countries.[30] Yet, four main family groups of NGOs can be distinguished in the literature:[31] (1) unincorporated and voluntary associations; (2) trusts, charities and foundations; (3) companies not just for profit; (4) entities formed or registered under special NGO or nonprofit laws. As this group is very miscellaneous, a long catalog of other organizational types and, thus, acronyms can be found in the elaborations.[32] The subsequent remarks of this book generally embrace all of these types of NGOs.

This broad characteristic makes it possible to define NGOs in detail, both on the empirical and theoretical grounds. First, NGOs tend to operate at the intersection between traditional, mostly nation state and institutionally bound politics and newer forms of stronger identity-based, non-party driven civic engagement.[33] In fact, in legal terms, NGOs tend to limit their political engagement to what appears to be "nonpolitical" activities.[34] Thus, they often do engage in a form of politics "outside and beyond the representative institutions of the political system of nation-states."[35] Therefore, some authors claim that the nongovernmental sector is credited with playing a central part in establishing new geographies of political power at the intersection of civil

28. E. Szazi, *NGOs: Legitimate Actors of International Law*, Leiden 2012, p. 25, J. Menkes, A. Wasilkowski, *Organizacje...*, p. 364.
29. Globally, the most common spheres of NGO activity are culture, sport, education and social services; for specific information concerning chosen countries see: http://fakty.ngo.pl/wiadomosc/2079897.html.
30. Most commonly, these cultures of cooperation between the government and NGOs are divided into the "socio-democratic Scandinavian model" and "liberal Anglo-Saxon model"; for more see e.g. O. Berthoud, *NGOs: Somewhere Between Compassion, Profitability and Solidarity*, Envio Digital Vol. 241/2001, available at: http://www.envio.org.ni/articulo/1526 (on February 9, 2019).
31. G. Stillman, *Global Standard NGOs: The Essential Elements of Good Practice*, Geneva 2007, pp. 13-14, B. Weitemeyer, *Eine neue Gemeinnützigkeit? Organisations- und Rechtsformen von Nonprofit-Organisationen* in: *Forschung zu Zivilgesellschaft, NPOs und Engagement. Quo vadis?*, A.E. Zimmer, R. Simsa (eds), Wiedbaden 2014, pp. 41-62.
32. Including e.g.:

    - BINGO—"big International" NGO.
    - GONGO—government-organized NGO.
    - INGO—international NGO.
    - ENGO—environmental NGO.
    - TNGO—transnational NGO.

    Also, some authors distinguish the group of "affiliated NGOs," i.e. NGOs working in the framework of IGOs. See J. Menkes, A. Wasilkowski, *Organizacje...*, pp. 376-377.
33. R. Sanchez Salgado, *Europeanizing...*, p. 13.
34. T. Szawiel, *Tozsamości polskie a Europa*, Nowa Europa. Przegląd Natoliński Vol. 5/2007, p. 229.
35. H. Johansson, P. Kalm, *EU...*, p. 27.

society and institutional politics.[36] Second, NGOs have a certain "moral" purpose that orientates them toward problems and people outside their organization and thus distinguishes the sector's rationale from that of business and from reality lenses that focuses on profit or other self-serving individualist motives.[37] Third, NGOs can but do not have to be "territorial" as they are not bound by any nation states and they may engage in multiple levels of society (or governance) and act both locally and transnationally.[38] However, this does not mean that they are not affected by local or international laws. It can be stated that NGOs are influenced by norms at the levels on which they perform or at the levels where their activity is aimed at. Finally, NGOs may often play a role of "public" experts[39] (e.g., as amicus curiae).[40] They are focused (or should be focused) on lending their expertise to a greater public good. This characteristic is very evident in the field of providing legitimacy to the EU institutions, as described in the subsequent remarks of this book.

To complement the preceding observations, it should be acknowledged that the process of broad inclusion of NGOs at the international level has its followers and opponents. For some, it is an indicator of revitalized democracies across the globe[41] or a manifestation of "global associational revolution."[42] In contrast, for others, the increasing number of NGOs operating both nationally and internationally undermine the foundations of representative democracy as in fact they are self-proclaimed and nonrepresentative groups bolstered by an unelected activist elite[43] with the "potential to undermine the sovereignty of constitutional democracies."[44]

To sum up, for the purposes of this book, an NGO will be understood as a voluntary organization, grounded not-for-profit reasons, that is bound legally to be nonpolitical but can and often does engage in decision-making and lawmaking processes through consultations or lobbying activities. These activities generate normative claims about a common good that acts on these claims as public expert in variously scaled civic spaces.[45] On these bases, NGOs can be considered as a link between authority institutions and grassroot civil society. It should be once more emphasized that this explanation is not based solely on existing legal norms or definitions.

36. R. Sanchez Salgado, *Europeanizing...*, p. 7.
37. K. Kietlińska, *Rola trzeciego sektora w społeczeństwie obywatelskim*, Warsaw 2010, p. 91.
38. K. Kietlińska, *Rola...*, p. 93.
39. D. Moroń, *Organizacje pozarządowe—fundament społeczeństwa obywatelskiego*, Wrocław 2012, p. 94.
40. I.e. "friend of the court"—someone who is not a party to a case but who assists the Court by offering information that matters to the case; for more explanation see e.g. L. Bartholomeusz, *The Amicus Curiae Before International Courts and Tribunals*, Non-State Actors and International Law Vol. 5/2005, pp. 209 et seq.
41. E. Szazi, *NGOs...*, p. 31.
42. S. Lang, *NGOs...*, p. 10.
43. E. Sternberg, *NGOs v. Civil Society: Reflections on the Illiberal, the Illegitimate and the Unaccountable*, IEA Economic Affairs Vol. 10/2010, pp. 22 et seq.
44. S. Lang, *NGOs...*, p. 12.
45. J. Babiak, *Rola organizacji pozarządowych we współczesnym społeczeństwie* in: *Rola organizacji pozarządowych w kształtowaniu społeczeństwa obywatelskiego. Doświadczenia i praktyka*, J. Babiak, W. Sługocki (eds), Warsaw 2009, p. 29.

Having presented these preliminary observations, they can now be transposed to the existing legal matter at the international level. In this way, the importance of collaboration measures between NGOs and IGOs can be emphasized.

[B] NGOs and Chosen Intergovernmental Organizations

In the last few years, the idea of representation of affected individuals in international institutions through NGOs has become an important strand in conceptualizing more legitimate rulemaking and enforcement not just at the EU level,[46] but at the general international level as well.[47] The literature emphasizes two political developments that triggered this process. The first one is the successful role of NGOs in international treaty-making.[48] A good example of this practice is a fortunate lobbying of certain organizations in the elaboration of the Rome Statute of the International Criminal Court.[49] The second one is the critical role of some NGO networks in organizing protests against political projects run by international institutions, such as the World Trade Organization.[50] A good illustration of this phenomenon at the EU level is a very active role of certain NGOs in protesting against the TTIP agreement.[51]

Basing on these developments, many authors stressed out the power of a globally operating civil society to politicize and democratize international institutions.[52] However, the main fora for decision-making and lawmaking processes at the international level are intergovernmental organizations (IGOs). With few exceptions, full membership and the right to vote is exclusively reserved for nation states.[53] Consequently, NGOs and other types of NSAs are excluded from the actual participation in these mechanisms. However, many IGOs grant special rights for NGOs which include, e.g. the right of observation or of providing opinions and recommendations. This may

46. Which requires a new form of governance; for conceptual reasons see e.g. P. Herrmann, *Partizipationskulturen in der Europäischen Union*, Munich 1998, pp. 33-36.
47. A. von Bogdandy, *The European Lesson for International Democracy: The Significance of Articles 9-12 EU Treaty for International Organization*, The European Journal of International Law Vol. 23/2012, p. 321.
48. Especially during the so-called pre-diplomatic stage and during "conference stage." For more see R. Geiß, *Non-State Actors: Their Role and Impact on the Fragmentation of International Law* in: *Unity and Diversity in International Law*, A. Zimmermann, R. Hofmann (eds), Berlin 2006, pp. 66 et seq. For more information on the reasons of the increasing NGO engagement in treaty-making see also E. Riedel, *Questionnaire Human Rights and the Unity-Diversity Divide* in: *Unity...*, pp. 112-113.
49. S. Iglesias Sanchez, *Fundamental Rights and Citizenship of the Union at a Crossroads: A Promising Alliance or a Dangerous Liaison?*, European Law Journal Vol. 4/2014, p. 465.
50. A. von Bogdandy, *The European...*, p. 322.
51. Which is represented by, e.g. the proposal of STOP-TTIP European Citizens' Initiative, see more: https://stop-ttip.org/.
52. See e.g. S. Charmovitz, *Nongovernmental Organizations and International Law*, American Journal of International Law Vol. 100/2006, pp. 348-372, D. Thürer, *The Emergence of Non-governmental Organizations and Transnational Enterprises in International Law and the Changing Role of the State* in: *Non-State Actors as New Subjects of International Law*, R. Hofmann (ed.), Berlin 1999, pp. 57 et seq., S. Stroup, A. Murdie, *There's No Place Like Home: Explaining International NGO Advocacy*, The Review of International Organizations Vol. 7/2012, pp. 425-448, Ch. Mollers, *Multi-level Democracy*, Ratio Juris Vol. 3/2011, p. 248.
53. A.-K. Lindblom, *Non-governmental...*, p. 366.

sound like their role is utterly passive. However, NGOs engage in institutionalized cooperation with IGOs to an increasing extent and appear to have some influence on their decision-making and lawmaking procedures.[54] This may also include nonformal means of collaboration, especially through widely understood lobbying. In short, it can be said that the more access to legislative processes is given to NGOs and the more effective they are, the greater is the overall level of democratization of the given IGO.[55]

The subject matter of analysis in the subsequent paragraphs will be the legal and factual position of NGOs in selected IGOs (the United Nations, the International Labor Organization, the World Bank, the World Trade Organization and the Council of Europe). This choice is justified as these organizations provide different modes of cooperation with NGOs. Therefore, the aim of this part of study is to determine what are the patterns of including NSAs in the decision-making and lawmaking processes at the international level. In this way, certain general remarks and suggestions can be made, which will be advantageous for further establishing the importance of NGOs at the EU level.

[1] The United Nations

As a general rule, in the UN system, NGOs shall not have the same rights of participation as non-Member States and the specialized agencies.[56] Presently, the official institutional framework of the UN allows for a rather limited (yet still much wider than other IGOs) participation of NGOs in decision-making and lawmaking processes. An NGO may request accreditation for a special UN conference, establish working relations with special bodies of the UN, associate itself with the UN Department of Information (DPI) or ask, if it fulfills the below mentioned criteria, for consultative status with the Economic and Social Council (ECOSOC). Among these four options, having a consultative status with the ECOSOC results in the most far-reaching rights and privileges. Accordingly, this sphere of cooperation will be the center of analysis of the subsequent paragraphs.

The ECOSOC is one of the six principal organs in the UN system, responsible for coordinating the economic, social and related work of 14 UN specialized agencies (including, e.g. the International Labor Organization), their functional commissions and five regional commissions. It serves as the central forum for discussing international economic and social issues and for formulating policy recommendations addressed to Member States and the UN system in general.[57] As it has already been stated, according to Article 71 of the UN Charter, the Economic and Social Council (ECOSOC)

54. M. Prasad, *The Role of Non-governmental Organisations in the New Human Rights Procedures for Human Rights Complaints*, International Law and Politics Vol. 5/1975, p. 444.
55. Cf. T. Kubin, *Legitymizacja system instytucjonalnego Unii Europejskiej*, Katowice 2014, pp. 45 et seq.
56. B. Seary, *The Early History: From the Congress of Vienna to the San Francisco Conference* in: *The Conscience of the World*, P. Willets (ed.), Oxford 1996, pp. 26-27, R. Brett, *The Role and Limits of Human Rights NGOs at the United Nations*, Political Studies Vol. 1/1995, p. 96.
57. H.-M. Jaeger, *"Global Civil Society" and the Political Depolitization of Global Governance*, International Political Sociology Vol. 1/2007, p. 257.

may make suitable arrangements for consultation with nongovernmental organizations which are concerned with matters within its competence. Such arrangements may be made with international organizations and, where appropriate, with national organizations after consultation with the Member of the United Nations concerned. It can be seen that this provision enables the ECOSOC to make suitable arrangements for consultation with NGOs which are concerned with matters within its competence.[58] Such arrangements may be made with international NGOs and, where appropriate, with national organizations after consultation with the Member State concerned.[59]

Following the mandate given to the ECOSOC in the abovementioned legal norm, on July 25, 1996, it adopted Resolution 1996/31 on the Consultative Relationship Between the United Nations and Non-Governmental Organizations.[60] It replaced the previously applied Resolution 1296 (XLIV) of May 23, 1968.[61] The Regulation of 1996 provides for the granting of "consultative status" to NGOs. There are three types of this status: general consultative status, special consultative status and inclusion on the Roster.[62] It is upon the recommendation of the UN Committee on Non-Governmental Organizations (the NGO Committee—a standing committee of the ECOSOC) that consultative status is granted by the ECOSOC. What is both very appealing and important is that the recognition of consultative status to the ECOSOC should ensure, to the extent possible, participation of nongovernmental organizations from all regions, and particularly from developing countries.[63] Furthermore, greater involvement of nongovernmental organizations from countries with economies in transitions should be encouraged.[64]

General consultative status can be granted to an organization that is concerned with most activities of the ECOSOC and its subsidiary bodies and that is broadly representative of major segments of society in a large number of countries in different regions of the world.[65] Special consultative status, however, can be given to an organization that has a special competence in and is concerned specifically with only a few of the fields of activity covered by the Council and its subsidiary bodies.[66] Nevertheless, both types of NGOs have to fulfill 17 requirements provided by Part I of the resolution. In particular, these preconditions envisage that:

(1) the organization shall be concerned with matters falling within the competence of the Economic and Social Council and its subsidiary bodies;

58. S. Chesterman, I. Johnstone, D.M. Malone, *Law and Practice of the United Nations*, Oxford 2016, p. 474.
59. S. Chesterman, I. Johnstone, D.M. Malone, *Law...*, p. 475.
60. Available at: http://www.un.org/documents/ecosoc/res/1996/eres1996-31.htm (on February 9, 2019).
61. Available at: https://www.globalpolicy.org/component/content/article/177/31832.html (on February 9, 2019).
62. Part I para. 15 of Resolution 1996/31.
63. Part I para. 5 of Resolution 1996/31.
64. Part I para. 7 of Resolution 1996/31.
65. Part II para. 22 *in fine* of Resolution 1996/31.
66. Part II para. 23 of Resolution 1996/31.

(2) the aims and purposes of the organization shall be in conformity with the spirit, purposes and principles of the Charter of the United Nations;
(3) the organization shall undertake knowledge of its principles and activities, in accordance with its own aims and purposes and the nature and scope of its competence and activities;
(4) the organization shall be of recognized standing within the particular fields of its competence or of a representative character;
(5) the organization shall have an established headquarters, with an executive officer. It shall have a democratically adopted constitution, a copy of which shall be deposited with the Secretary-General of the United Nations, and which shall provide for the determination of policy by a conference, congress or other representative body, and for an executive organ responsible to the policy-making body;
(6) the organization shall have the authority to speak for its members through its authorized representatives. Evidence of this authority shall be presented, if requested;
(7) the organization shall have a representative structure and possess appropriate mechanisms of accountability to its members, who shall exercise effective control over its policies and actions through the exercise of voting rights or other appropriate democratic and transparent decision-making processes. Any such organization that is not established by a governmental entity or intergovernmental agreement shall be considered a nongovernmental organization for the purpose of these arrangements, including organizations that accept members designated by governmental authorities, provided that such membership does not interfere with the free expression of views of the organization;
(8) the basic resources of the organization shall be derived in the main part from contributions of the national affiliates or other components or from individual members. Any financial contribution or other support, direct or indirect, from a government to the organization shall be openly declared to the Committee through the Secretary-General and fully recorded in the financial and other records of the organization and shall be devoted to purposes in accordance with the aims of the United Nations.

As it can be seen, these provisions set requirements concerning structural and financial transparency of the organization that wishes to be given a consultative status with the ECOSOC. Although the financial requirements are rather obvious and state general demands providing that the NGO's contributors are both known to the public and generally not linked to any state authorities, the structural prerequisites may raise some doubts. The most questionable condition is the need for having a "democratically adopted constitution." It is not clear what is hidden under this statement. It seems that the constitution (or generally speaking—the statute) of an NGO should be adopted by its participants. However, what if the statute is adopted by a single person (or a small group of people) at the moment of forming a new organization? Such a situation is normal as far as foundations are concerned.[67] Does this mean that these organizations should not be given a consultative status with the ECOSOC as their constitution was not "democratically adopted?" There is no clear answer to this question, but it seems that they are not overall favored in these terms.

NGOs obtaining one of the types of consultative status are provided with a different set of rights. NGOs in general consultative status:

(1) are informed of the provisional agenda of the ECOSOC and may propose to the Council Committee on Non-governmental Organizations (NGO Committee) that the Committee request the UN Secretary-General to place items of special interest of the provisional agenda of the Council;[68]
(2) may orally present to the Council introductory statements of an expository nature on items included on the Council's agenda at the proposal of the NGO;[69]
(3) may submit written statements with a maximum of 2,000 words for circulation to the Members of the Council;[70]
(4) may make oral statements to the Council (at the recommendation of the NGO Committee and subject to the approval of the Council).[71]

NGOs in special consultative status enjoy most of the same rights granted to NGOs in general consultative status. Nevertheless, they cannot propose items for the agenda or the Council, nor can they make oral statements at meetings of the Council. However, they can make a statement at meetings of the Council's subsidiary bodies that deal with subject matters or specific interest to them.[72] They may also submit shorter written statements to the Council (consisting of maximum 1,500 words).[73]

NGOs on the Roster can make occasional contribution to the work of the ECOSOC. They are consulted at the request of ECOSOC and its subsidiary bodies.[74] The scope of their privileges is limited to the designation of UN representatives, attendance at UN meetings and invitation to UN conferences.[75] However, there are numerous NGOs enrolled on the Roster list not because they did not fulfill the ECOSOC requirements but because they have a consultative status with specialized agencies and other UN bodies.[76] This often results in problems as the criteria of establishing consultative relationships vary considerably with respect to different UN bodies.[77]

67. Cf. P. Staszczyk, *Ustawa o fundacjach...*, p. 49.
68. Part IV paras. 27 and 28 of Resolution 1996/31.
69. Part IV para. 32 (b) of of Resolution 1996/31.
70. Part IV paras. 30 and 31 of Resolution 1996/31.
71. Part IV para. 32 (a) of of Resolution 1996/31.
72. Part V para. 38 of Resolution 1996/31.
73. Part V paras. 36 and 37 of Resolution 1996/31.
74. Part V paras. 33 and 35 of Resolution 1996/31.
75. Part VII para. 42 of Resolution 1996/31.
76. J.D. Aston, *The United Nations Committee on Non-governmental Organizations: Guarding the Entrance to a Politically Divided House*, European Journal of International Law Vol. 12/2001, p. 943.
77. J.D. Aston, *The United...*, p. 945.

Particularly, some bodies require that an NGO has only one consultative status within the UN system.[78]

NGOs obtain consultative status with the ECOSOC upon their application. In most cases, the ECOSOC follows the recommendations of its consultative body (the NGO Committee) and grant such status to those who are positively evaluated.[79] NGOs in consultative status are obliged to submit a report on their activities every four years ("quadrennial report").[80] This obligation does not apply to NGOs on the Roster list. By this requirement the NGO Committee examines if the organizations continue to satisfy the abovementioned criteria. Accordingly, it can recommend reclassification or even withdrawal of consultative status with the ECOSOC.[81]

The number of NGOs in consultative status has significantly and rapidly increased for the last two decades as it can be clearly seen in Table 1.1.

Table 1.1 Number of NGOs in Consultative Status at the ECOSOC in Chosen Years in the Time Period 1948-2016[82]

Year	*General Consultative Status*	*Special Consultative Status*	*Roster*	*Total*
1948	13	26	1	40
1967	12	135	43	190
1980	10	205	373	588
1992	38	297	409	744
1995	65	406	415	886
1998	100	742	663	1,505
2000	122	1,048	880	2,050
2005	136	1,639	944	2,719
2011	144	2,408	984	3,536
2013	147	2,774	979	3,900
2014	142	2,926	977	4,045
2016	143	3,544	978	4,665

Undoubtedly, the number of NGOs in general consultative status is steady. However, the special consultative status has become lately the most popular way to participate in the UN system. This statement can be easily explained. First of all, the number of NGOs dealing with most spheres of the ECOSOC's activity and operating globally is limited. Such organizations need humongous budgets and operating staff. NGOs wishing to

78. *Ibid.*, p. 946.
79. *Ibid.*
80. Part IX para. 51 (c) of Resolution 1996/31
81. A.-K. Lindblom, *Non-governmental...*, p. 377.
82. Own elaboration, data based on the annual lists of nongovernmental organizations in consultative status with the Economic and Social Council available at the United Nations Digital Library, http://bit.do/eHWtW (on February 10, 2019).

obtain a special consultative status do not have to fulfill such demanding requirements and can act on a smaller scale. Therefore, it is easier for them to provide expertise and be more influential in the decision-making and lawmaking process in the fields they are specialized in. This remark is also supported by practice. It can be noted that the most active NGOs are those with a rather narrow range of specialization[83] (e.g., human rights[84] or environment protection). Moreover, as it was mentioned above, the privileges of NGOs in general consultative status do not vastly differ from the rights of NGOs in special consultative status.[85]

Nevertheless, the increasing number of organizations in special consultative status is also a subject matter of criticism.[86] It should be stressed out that it is very tough for "new" NGOs to actually take part in the cooperation process with the ECOSOC. Their voice is very rarely heard[87] and, in practice, organizations in general consultative status and those who have been active in the UN system for decades are more likely to influence the actual decision and lawmaking processes. Therefore, in some cases gaining special consultative status by an organization is aimed more at its internal policy rather than at the desire to be active in the UN system. This leads to a conclusion that the requirements of obtaining consultative status should be either restricted[88] or that the ECOSOC should encourage NGOs to form coalitions rather than to apply for a consultative status on their own.[89] It is also suggested that more emphasis should be put on the geographical diversity of NGOs in both general and special consultative status.[90]

Another criticism of the presented model of cooperation deals with the position and composition of the NGO Committee.[91] It consists of 19 Member States which are

83. Cf. NGO participation arrangements at the UN and in other agencies of the UN system, available at: http://bit.do/eg9JE (on February 9, 2019).
84. For more information concerning the importance of enhancing the role of NGOs in European human rights protection see e.g. E. Riedel, *Global Human Rights Protection at the Crossroads: Strengthening or Reforming the System* in: *Der Staat im Recht. Festschrift für Eckhart Klein zum 70. Geburtstag*, M. Breuer, A. Epiney, A. Haratsch, S. Schmahl, N. Weiß (eds), Berlin 2013, 1289-1306.
85. See also S. Ripinsky, P. van den Bossche, *NGO Involvement in International Organizations. A Legal Analysis*, Camberley 2007, p. 29.
86. K. Reimann, *A View from the Top: International Politics, Norms and the Worldwide Growth of NGOs*, International Studies Quarterly Vol. 50/2006, p. 58 and the literature mentioned there, J. Menkes, A. Wasilkowski, *Organizacje...*, pp. 382-383.
87. See e.g. *NGOs Blocked from Delivering Statement*, International Service for Human Rights, available at: https://www.ishr.ch/news/ngo-committee-ngos-blocked-delivering-statement (on February 9, 2019).
88. Cf. K. Martens, *NGOs and the United Nations*, New York 2005, pp. 125 et seq. Still, the formal obligations needed to obtain the consultative status remain quite rigorous, and the whole procedure can last up to two years. See J. Menkes, A. Wasilkowski, *Organizacje...*, pp. 382-383.
89. Cf. A. Gillespie, *Facilitating and Controlling Civil Society in International Environmental Law*, Review of European, Comparative and International Environmental Law Vol. 15/2006, pp. 332-333.
90. Nowadays, roughly 47% of NGOs in general and special consultative status operate in Europe and 32% of these organizations operate in North America. For more see J. Menkes, A. Wasilkowski, *Organizacje...*, p. 384.
91. See e.g. A.-K. Lindblom, *Non-governmental...*, pp. 386-387.

elected by the ECOSOC on the basis of equitable geographical representation.[92] It is often argued that the Committee is particularly close to NGOs dealing with human rights issues and, consequently, it diminishes their role in the UN system. As it is stressed in literature,[93] the key to understanding the policy of the NGO Committee is that those states that are frequently targeted by human rights NGOs are by the same token those that decide on what NGO shall be granted consultative status. For instance, NGOs known for strong criticism of human rights' conditions in undemocratic states are not likely to receive a favorable treatment of its application by those countries. Politically speaking it can be understood. However, this is obviously contrary to the basis of forming consultative status in the first place and opposite to NGOs capacity to support the work of the UN.[94]

Although the main forum for NGOs to cooperate in the UN system is the ECOSOC, there are some forms of opportunities for organizations wishing to contribute to the work of the General Assembly and the Security Council as well.

Article 9 (1) of the UN Charter provides that the General Assembly shall consist of all the members of the United Nations. The Rules of Procedure[95] do not contain any provisions regarding the participation of observers in the work of the Assembly. Decisions on the admission of new observers are taken in the form of resolution by the Assembly.[96] In practical terms, the observer status means that the organizations have access to the meetings of the General Assembly and its committees and that they can deliver statements on subjects within their competence.[97] Apart from the observers of non-Member States, the UN specialized agencies and other IGOs,[98] the General Assembly has accepted observers from a few liberation movements.[99] Consequently, NGOs do not have observer status with the UN General Assembly as a rule. However, there are three exceptions. The first one is International Committee of the Red Cross (ICRC)[100] which was granted observer status in 1990 with reference to the mandates conferred upon it by the Geneva Conventions of August 12, 1949,[101] and "its special role ... in international humanitarian relations." The second one is the International Federation of Red Cross and Red Crescent which was granted observer status in 1994 due to "the special functions of the member societies ... which are recognized by their

92. I.e. five members from African States, four members from Asian States, two members from Eastern European States, four members from Latin American and Caribbean States and four members from Western European and other states.
93. J.D. Aston, *The United...*, p. 950.
94. See the preamble to Resolution 1996/31.
95. Available at: http://www.un.org/en/ga/about/ropga/ (on February 9, 2019).
96. Rule 59 of the Rules of Procedure.
97. C. Koenig, *Observer Status for the International Committee of the Red Cross at the United Nations: A Legal Viewpoint*, International Review of the Red Cross Vol. 280/1991, p. 37.
98. I.e. African Union, Council of Europe, Hague Conference on Private International Law, for the full list see: http://www.un.org/ga/search/view_doc.asp?symbol=A/INF/70/5 (on February 9, 2019).
99. I.e. The State of Palestine.
100. Interestingly, the ICRS is an atypical NGO as it does not have legal capacity or an official legal status in any state. It is also referred to as a "legal entity *sui generis*." See also M. Huber, *Principles, Tasks, and Problems of the Red Cross in International Law*, Geneva 1946, p. 4.
101. Available at: https://www.icrc.org/eng/assets/files/publications/icrc-002-0173.pdf (on February 9, 2019).

respective Governments as auxiliaries to the public authorities in the humanitarian field on the basis of the Geneva Conventions."[102] The third exception is the Order of Malta which was granted observer status in 1994 because of its "long-standing dedication ... in providing humanitarian assistance and its special role in international humanitarian relations."[103] It means that, in comparison to the first two cases, the observer status was granted to the Order of Malta not regarding treaties or special status under international law, but rather its role in humanitarian assistance and relations.[104]

As the UN Charter does not provide any rules of procedure regarding the possibility of obtaining the observer status within the General Assembly and in the light of an increasing role of NGOs, it is plausible that some forms of formal arrangements for cooperation with NGOs will be adapted in the future. In fact, this possibility has been discussed on the ECOSOC forum for several years.[105]

As far as the Security Council is concerned, there are not any formal requirements concerning contacts with NGOs. However, informal consultations do take place. They are called "arria consultations" or "arria formula meetings" after the former Venezuelan representative who initiated the practice in 1992 during the crisis in former Yugoslavia.[106] In fact, there is a legal basis for such consultations. Rule 39 of the Council's Provisional Rules of Procedure[107] states that the Security Council may invite members of the secretariat or other persons, who it considers competent for the purpose, to supply it with information or to give other assistance in examining matters within its competence. Generally speaking, it allows the Council to be briefed by non-Council members, including NGOs, on issues of international peace and security.[108]

Apart from the "arria consultations," there a few additional semiformal channels for NGOs to communicate with the Security Council. One example is the NGO Working Group on the Security Council (WGSC). Its main goal is to hold meetings with the Security Council members to deliberate on matters of special interest to civil society. In fact, this initiative started from informal private meetings between different NGOs and the Council members and became systematic over time.[109] Even though the WGSC does not have any official status within the UN legal system, it seems highly influential and maintains close access to the officials and government delegates.[110] Nevertheless,

102. Resolution A/RES/49/2 of 19.10.1994; see also Ch. Lanor, *The Legal Status of National Red Cross and Red Crescent Societies*, International Review of the Red Cross Vol. 840/2000, p. 1053.
103. Resolution A/RES/48/265 of 24.8.1994.
104. A.-K. Lindblom, *Non-governmental...*, p. 371.
105. S. Chesterman, I. Johnstone, D.M. Malone, *Law...*, p. 478.
106. L.J. Shepherd, *Power and Authority in the Production of United Nations Security Council Resolution 1325*, International Studies Quarterly Vol. 2/2008, p. 387.
107. Provisional Rules of Procedure of the Security Council of 1983 (S/96/Rev.7), available at: https://www.un.org/ar/sc/pdf/rules.pdf (on February 9, 2019).
108. K. Martens, *NGOs in the United Nations System: Evaluating Theoretical Approaches*, Journal of International Development Vol. 18/2006, p. 697.
109. For briefings of the WGSC see: https://www.globalpolicy.org/about-gpf-mm.html (on February 9, 2019).
110. K. Martnes, *NGOs in the United Nations System...*, p. 697.

the "representativeness" of the Group is limited as it associates just about 30 large NGOs.[111]

To conclude, it should be emphasized that NGOs can play a significant role in the UN jurisdiction proceedings which may include issuing amicus curiae opinions[112] or complaining about human rights violations in individual communications procedures.[113] Yet, the presentation of complex procedural requirements in various proceedings exceeds the scope of this book.[114]

[2] The International Labor Organization

The International Labor Organization (ILO) was created in 1919 as part of the Treaty of Versailles.[115] In 1946, it became a UN-affiliated agency dealing with labor issues.[116] This agency is unique among other international organizations as it brings together representatives of governments, employers and workers (representing one of the groups of the organized civil society). This model is usually defined as "tripartism"[117] and is particularly interesting for this book as it formally materializes the cooperation between state and nonstate actors at the international level. Thus, the ILO does not simply collaborate with NGOs[118] but actually integrates sectors of civil society into its structure.[119]

---

111. Oxfam International or Medecins Sans Frontières.
112. E.g. according to Art. 50 of the Statute of the International Court of Justice (available at: http://www.icj-cij.org/en/statute), the Court may, at any time, entrust any individual, body, bureau, commission or other organization that it may select, with the task of carrying out an inquiry or giving an expert opinion. Thus, it is apparent that such an opinion may be requested from an NGO. For more see e.g. L. Bartholomeusz, *The Amicus...*, pp. 209-286, W. van Ginneken, *Zivilgesellschaft und sozialer Basisschutz*, Internationale Revue für Soziale Sicherheit Vol. 3-4/2014, p. 95.
113. K. Sękowska-Kozłowska, *The Role of Non-governmental Organisations in Individual Communication Procedures Before the UN Human Rights Treaty Bodies* in: *Czech Yearbook of International Law 2014. The Role of Governmental and Non-governmental Organizations in the 21st Century*, A.J. Belohlavek, N. Rozehnalova, F. Cerny (eds), New York 2014, pp. 367 et seq.
114. For more information see e.g. F.W. Stoecker, *NGOs und die UNO. Die Einbindung von Nichtregierungsorganisationen (NGOs) in die Strukturen der Vereinten Nationen*, Frankfurt am Mein 2000, pp. 193 et seq., I. Rossi, *Legal Status of Non-governmental Organizations in International Law*, Antwerp 2010, pp. 243-332.
115. See Part XIII of the Treaty of Versailles, available at: https://www.loc.gov/law/help/us-treaties/bevans/m-ust000002-0043.pdf (on February 9, 2019).
116. J.-M. Servais, *International Labour Organization (ILO)*, Alphen aan den Rijn 2011, pp. 7-8.
117. A. Vedder, *NGO Involvement in International Governance and Policy: Sources and Legitimacy*, Leiden 2007, p. 147, B. Deacon, *The Social Protection and Global Social Governance: Towards Policy Synergy and Cooperation Between International Organizations*, International Social Security Review Vol. 3-4/2013, p. 46, M. Kamminga, *The Evolving Status of NGOs under International Law: A Threat to the Inter-State System?* in: *Non-State Actors and Human Rights*, P. Alston (ed.), Oxford 2006, p. 101.
118. This statement is made on the basis that unions and other representative organizations of employees are considered one of the type of NGOs.
119. See: http://www.ilo.org/global/about-the-ilo/lang--en/index.htm (on February 9, 2019). Nevertheless, this "integration" is often criticized due to its reduction consultation mechanisms and not full participation. See, to this extent, E. Riedel, *The Development of International Law: Alternatives to Treaty-Making? International Organizations and Non-State Actors* in: *Developments of International Law in Treaty Making*, R. Wolfrum, V. Röben (eds), Berlin 2005, p. 307.

Although according to Article 1 (1) of the ILO Constitution[120] only states can be members of the ILO, its Article 3 (1) provides that the meetings of the International Labor Conference (or the General Conference) shall be composed of four representatives of each of the members, of whom two shall be government delegates and the other two shall be delegates representing respectively the employers and the workpeople of each of the members. On the basis of the third paragraph of this article, the members undertake to nominate nongovernment delegates and advisors chosen in agreement with the industrial organizations, if such organizations exist, which are most representative of employers or workpeople, as the case may be, in their respective countries.

In addition to the tripartism system in the ILO, there is an additional possibility for establishing a consultative status for certain NGOs. Article 12 (3) of the ILO Constitution states that the organization may make suitable arrangements for such consultation as it may think desirable with recognized nongovernmental organizations, including international organizations of employers, workers, agriculturists and cooperators. This provision resulted in practice in the development of three categories of consultative status for the interested NGOs:

(1) "NGOs with an Important Interest in a Wide Range of the ILO's Activities" that are gained either general or regional consultative status.[121]
(2) "Special List of Non-Governmental International Organizations" that was set up by the ILO Governing Body with a view to establishing working relations with international NGOs other than employers' and workers' organizations.[122]
(3) "NGOs that receive invitations from the ILO Governing Body" and which meet certain established criteria to attend ILO meetings in which they have demonstrated a particular interest.[123]

Representatives of NGOs in general or regional consultative status are permitted at the sittings of the Conference.[124] NGOs which have been invited by the governing body are also allowed to be represented at the Conference.[125] These NGOs may also, with the permission of the President, circulate statements for the information of the Conference on questions which are being considered with the exceptions of administrative and financial questions.[126] NGOs in general or regional consultative status and

120. Available at: http://bit.do/eg9Kh (on February 9, 2019).
121. There are currently 7 NGOs in general consultative status and 18 in regional consultative status; for full list see: http://www.ilo.org/pardev/partnerships/civil-society/ngos/WCMS_201411/lang--en/index.htm (on February 9, 2019).
122. There are currently about 150 NGOs on the Special List; for full list see: http://www.ilo.org/pardev/partnerships/civil-society/ngos/ilo-special-list-of-ngos/lang--en/index.htm (on February 9, 2019).
123. A. Vedder, *NGO...*, p. 149.
124. A.-K. Lindblom, *Non-governmental...*, p. 415.
125. *Ibid.*, p. 416.
126. A. Vedder, *NGO...*, p. 152.

organizations which have been invited by the governing body or the Conference may also be present at the meetings of the Conference Committees.[127]

[3] The World Bank

The World Bank (WB) is a part of the World Bank Group and the UN system. It is an international financial institution that, in particular, provides loans to developing countries for capital programs.[128] Although there is no official provision dealing with formal relations between the WB and civil society, in practice, the WB deploys a rather practical and instrumental approach toward the interested NGOs. As a result, the organizations are seldom directly involved in governing bodies or have any formal status.[129] Still, there are multiple semiformal networks of deliberation, cooperation and information.[130] Moreover, NGOs are frequently linked to the WB through cooperation on projects, critical advocacy on policy issues and invited consultations sponsored (usually) by the Bank.[131] Thus, three spheres of cooperation between the WB and NGOs can be distinguished: consultations, funding opportunities and influencing the domestic policy.

First, the WB pays an increasing attention to the role of consultation. As it is noticed in the doctrine, "the effort to introduce deliberative, participatory elements into the Bank's policy-setting processes advances both the Bank's interest in building the legitimacy that comes with such input from nonstate stakeholders, and in building the knowledge-based interaction that it now upholds as its pre-eminent contribution to global development."[132] In fact, the WB assures that the interested organizations engage in various advisory committees, ad hoc consultative meetings and public discussions or are involved in discussions on policy papers and research publications.[133] This practice means that hardly any act of law or other public document is developed without some form of prior hearing with the organized civil society.[134] This is especially visible in the Bank's biennial report on its interaction with civil society as its first eight pages are devoted to an array of consultative mechanisms, processes and topics.[135] Moreover, in 1993, in response to environmental and human rights campaigns, the WB established the Inspection Panel, an institution that accepts complaints from any affected party regarding the organization's projects and any failure of the

127. *Ibid.*, p. 153.
128. B. Cali, *International Law for International Relations*, Oxford 2010, p. 61.
129. P. Nelson, *The Varied and Conditional Integration of NGOs in the Aid System: NGOs and the World Bank*, Journal of International Development Vol. 18/2006, p. 706.
130. See: http://www.worldbank.org/en/about/partners/civil-society (on February 9, 2019).
131. P. Nelson, *The Varied...*, p. 706; see also K. Lavelle, *Legislating International Organizations*, Washington 2011, p. 191.
132. P. Nelson, *The Varied...*, p. 702.
133. M. van Huijstee, P. Glasbergen, *Business-NGO Interactions in Multi-stakeholder Context*, Business and Society Review Vol. 3/2010, p. 278.
134. S. Ripinsky, P. van den Bossche, *NGO...*, p. 134.
135. E.g. World Bank—Civil Society Engagement. Fiscal Report 2010-2012, http://siteresources.worldbank.org/CSO/Resources/228716-1369241545034/ENGLISH.pdf (on February 9, 2019).

Bank to follow its own rules.[136] Although it was supposed to be a forum for private citizens who believe that their rights or interests have been or could be directly harmed by a project financed by the Bank, in practice it is the most formal and most fully institutionalized mechanism for contacts with civil society in general. The Inspection Panel's operating procedures[137] are very detailed and define precisely the institutions' investigative powers, as well as a standard timetable for investigation decision and reporting by the Panel, management and the Board, specifying responsibilities more clearly than any other mechanism.[138] Still, it appears that the Inspection Panel is perhaps a little underutilized in terms of law enforcement control.[139] Other formalized mechanisms of consultations can be exemplified by the NGO-World Bank Committee, which was created in 1982. It is composed of the representatives of the Bank and 25 NGO participants.[140] Furthermore, the WB established more than one hundred Civil Society Focal Points with experienced social scientists and communication officers working in over 80 offices that act as liaison officers with civil society.[141] Additional formal platforms of consultation are "invited consultations about development policy issues and World Bank sector policies,"[142] which deal with the most controversial policy issues (including involuntary resettlement or dam constructions) and their technical interactions.[143]

Second, NGOs are frequent beneficiaries of the WB funds.[144] Yet, what is particularly compelling is that the funding patterns vastly differ from other similar financial opportunities as the Bank's funds are smaller and supposedly less significant in the daily life of civil society organizations. Thus, the possible thrust of the founder on the beneficiaries is perhaps less apparent.[145]

Finally, the WB's political influence attracts certain NGOs that seek to take part in decision-making and lawmaking processes at the domestic level. Quite frequently NGOs use the WB to influence the borrowing governments' behavior. It takes place, for instance, when NGOs advocate in issues (often environment-related) which are influenced by a WB-funded project.[146]

136. D. Bräutigam, M. Segarra, *Difficult Partnership: The World Bank, States and NGOs*, Latin American Politics and Society Vol. 4/2007, p. 151.
137. Available at: https://inspectionpanel.org/sites/ip-ms8.extcc.com/files/documents/2014%20Updated%20Operating%20Procedures.pdf (on February 9, 2019).
138. P. Nelson, *The varied...*, p. 710.
139. I.e. in 2016 and 2017, only three cases were pending before the Inspection Panel with three others under investigation; for more information see The Inspection Panel Annual Report July 1, 2016—June 30, 2017, available at: http://ewebapps.worldbank.org/apps/ip/Pages/Annual-Reports-2017.aspx (on February 9, 2019).
140. S. Ripinsky, P. van den Bossche, *NGO...*, p. 139, Ch. Pallas, *Transnational Civil Society and the World Bank. Investigating Civil Society's Potential to Democratize Global Governance*, London 2013, p. 44.
141. For detailed data see: http://bit.do/eg9KM (on February 9, 2019).
142. D. Bräutigam, M. Segarra, *Difficult...*, p. 154.
143. E.g. see: https://consultations.worldbank.org/consultation/review-and-update-world-bank-safeguard-policies (on February 9, 2019).
144. In fact, many organizations are heavily relied on these funds; see D. Bräutigam, M. Segarra, *Difficult...*, p. 156.
145. D. Bräutigam, M. Segarra, *Difficult...*, p. 157.
146. P. Nelson, *The varied...*, p. 711.

[4] The World Trade Organization

The World Trade Organization (WTO) is an intergovernmental organization which regulates international trade. The Marrakesh Agreement Establishing the WTO (the WTO Agreement)[147] explicitly empowers the organization to engage NGOs in consultation processes. According to its Article V:2, the General Council may make appropriate arrangements for consultations and cooperation with nongovernmental organizations concerned with matters related to those of the WTO. Although this provision seems comparable with Article 71 of the UN Charter, there are significant differences in how the WTO and the UN approach engagement with NGOs.[148]

On the basis of the abovementioned Regulation, in 1996 the General Council of the WTO adopted the so-called Guidelines on Relations with Non-Governmental Organizations.[149] In this document, it was emphasized that NGOs can play a role "to increase the awareness of the public in respect of WTO activities" and that they are "valuable resource" that can "contribute to the accuracy and richness of the public debate."[150] It was also stated that the interaction process with NGOs should be developed through the symposia on specific WTO-related issues, informal arrangements to circulate position papers and information NGOs may wish to make available among interested members, the continuation of the practice of the WTO Secretariat of responding to requests for general information and briefings about the WTO and participation of chairpersons of the WTO councils and committees in their personal capacity, in discussions and meetings with NGOs.[151]

The Guidelines make it very clear what the limits of NGO inclusion in the decision-making and lawmaking processes are. In the concluding paragraphs, it is stated that "as a result of extensive discussions, there is currently a broadly held view that it would not be possible for NGOs to be directly involved in the work of the WTO or its meetings."[152] Furthermore, it was added that "closer consultation and cooperation with NGOs can also be met constructively through appropriate processes at the national level where lies primary responsibility for taking into account the different elements of public interest which are brought to bear on trade policy-making."[153] Furthermore, in contrast to the requirements dealing with the possibility of obtaining a consultative status in the UN system, the WTO law provides virtually no rules to

147. Available at: https://www.wto.org/english/res_e/booksp_e/analytic_index_e/wto_agree_e.htm (on February 9, 2019).
148. P. Van Bossche, *NGO Involvement in the WTO: A Comparative Perspective*, Journal of Economic International Law Vol. 11/2008, p. 720.
149. Available at: https://www.wto.org/english/forums_e/ngo_e/guide_e.htm (on February 9, 2019).
150. Para. IV of the Guidelines.
151. *Ibid.*; these possibilities are often referred to as the "democratic control" of the WTO; for more see K. Dingwerth, M. Blauberger, Ch. Schneider, *Postnationale Demokratie. Eine Einführung am Beispiel von EU, WTO und UNO*, Wiesbaden 2011, p. 133, M. Knodt, *Zivilgesellscchaftliche Einbindung im Handelsbereich: der Einfluss der WTO auf die Europäische Kommission* in: *Europäische Zivilgesellschaft. Konzepte, Akteure, Strategien*, M. Knodt, B. Finke (eds), Wiesbaden 2005, pp. 223 et seq.
152. Para. VI of the Guidelines.
153. *Ibid.*

ensure that the WTO only engages with NGOs that "add value" to its lawmaking, policy implementation, compliance monitoring and dispute resolution activities.[154] In fact, when the WTO first confronted the problem of "choosing" proper NGOs,[155] the WTO Secretariat accredited all nonprofit NGOs that could indicate that their activities (factual and not even statutory) are to some extent associated to those of the WTO.[156] These NGOs did not have to submit any further examination of their objectives, membership, institutional structure or financing. The sole criterion was the "non-profit character" of the applicating NGO. Moreover, this practice has been continued ever since at the Sessions of the Ministerial Conference.[157] The WTO employs an ad hoc registration for these events. However, the General Council can issue specific information dealing with accreditation or registration before the Session.[158]

In addition, it should be acknowledged that NGOs (dealing mainly with human rights and environmental issues) frequently attempt to influence the outcomes of proceedings before the Appellate Body (which resolves disputes brought by the WTO members) by issuing amicus curiae briefs and opinions.[159]

[5] The Council of Europe

The Council of Europe (CoE) is an IGO focused on promoting human rights, democracy and the rule of law in Europe.[160] The CoE often dealt with the legal principles of NGO activity on the national scale. For instance, it proposed the European Convention on the Recognition of the Legal Personality of International Non-Governmental Organizations in 1986 (as already mentioned in the preceding remarks of this chapter), Fundamental Principles on the Status of Non-governmental Organizations in Europe and explanatory memorandum in 2002[161] and Recommendation of the Committee of Ministers to Member States on the legal status of nongovernmental organizations in

154. L. Casier, R. Fraser, M. Halle, R. Wolfe, *Shining a Light on Fossil Fuel Subsidies at the WTO: How NGOs Can Contribute to WTO Notification and Surveillance*, World Trade Review Vol. 13/2014, p. 623, see also P. Van Bossche, *NGO...*, p. 721, A. Qureshi, *Extraterritorial Shrimps, NGOs and the WTO Appellate Body*, International and Comparative Law Quarterly Vol. 48/1999, p. 201; see also S. Ripinsky, P. van den Bossche, *NGO...*, p. 192.
155. On the occasion of the first Session of the Ministerial Conference in Singapore in December 1996; for more see M. Slotboom, *Participation of NGOs Before the WTO and EC Tribunals: Which Court Is the Better Friend?*, World Trade Review Vol. 5/2006, p. 73, see also Van Bossche, *NGO...*, p. 723.
156. I. Odumosu, *Revisiting NGO Participation in WTO and Investment Dispute Settlement: From Procedural Arguments to (Substantive) Public Interest Considerations*, Canadian Yearbook of International Law Vol. 44/2007, p. 364.
157. P. van den Bossche, W. Zdouc, *The Law and Policy of the World Trade Organization*, Cambridge 2013, p. 145.
158. *Ibid.*, pp. 144 et seq., I. Odumosu, *Revisiting...*, p. 367.
159. For specific examples see P. van den Boschee, *NGO Involvement in the WTO: A Lawyer's Perspective on a Glass Half-Full or Half-Empty*, Maastricht 2006, pp. 17-18, available at: http://bit.do/eg9Lm (on February 9, 2019).
160. There are presently 47 Member States (all of the European states besides Belarus), http://www.coe.int/en/web/portal/47-members-states (on February 9, 2019).
161. Available at: https://www.coe.int/t/dghl/standardsetting/cdcj/ONG/Fundamental%20Principles%20E.pdf (on February 9, 2019).

Europe in 2007.[162] Moreover, in 2009, upon a recommendation of the Council of Europe's Forum for the Future of Democracy, the Conference of INGOs drafted a Code of Good Practice on Civil Participation in the Decision-Making Process.[163] The principle objective of the Code of Good Practice is the definition of a set of European principles and guidelines for NGO participation in decision-making processes that are to be implemented at local and national level in the CoE Member States. However, all of these acts do not concern NGOs operating at the international or European level.

As far as the cooperation between the CoE itself and NGOs is concerned, a resolution considering the relations with NGOs in 1951 should be mentioned. This act stated that the Committee of Ministers may, on behalf of the Council of Europe, make suitable arrangements for consultation with international nongovernmental organizations which deal with matters that are within the competence of the Council of Europe.[164] Further legal acts which established the basis of cooperation with NGOs were adopted in 1976[165] and 1993.[166] In November 2003, the Ministers' Deputies adopted Resolution 2003(8) on participatory status for INGOs[167] which was amended in 2016.[168] With installing this regulation, the Committee of Ministers wished to reflect the active and constructive role of NGOs and to clarify, facilitate and intensify the cooperation between the CoE and the international NGOs, in particular underlining its participatory character.[169] Thus, there is a possibility of obtaining participatory status with the CoE upon fulfilling certain requirements. Accordingly, an interested NGO should i.a.:

(1) respect and defend the values and principles of the CoE;
(2) be created on the basis of a constitutive act adopted according to democratic principles;[170]
(3) have a democratic structure and governance;
(4) already have working relations with the CoE;
(5) be particularly representative in the field(s) of their competence, which should correspond to the CoE's fields of action;

162. Recommendation CM/Rec (2007)14, available at: http://bit.do/eg9LB (on February 9, 2019).
163. Available at: http://bit.do/eg9LK (on February 9, 2019).
164. Ch. Bakker, L. Vierucci, *Introduction…*, p. 14.
165. I.e. the establishment of the Liaison Committee, a body made up of 17 INGOs elected by the "Plenary Conference of the INGOs enjoying consultative status with the Council of Europe."
166. Resolution 93(38) on Relations Between the Council of Europe and International Non-Governmental Organisations adopted by the Committee of Ministers on October 18, 1996, available at: http://bit.do/eg9L2 (on February 9, 2019).
167. Resolution (2003)8 on Participatory status for international nongovernmental organizations with the Council of Europe adopted by the Committee of Ministers on November 19, 2003 at the 861st meeting of the Ministers' Deputies, available at: http://bit.do/eg9Md (on February 9, 2019).
168. Resolution 2016(3) on Participatory status for international nongovernmental organizations with the Council of Europe adopted by the Committee of Ministers on July 6, 2016 at the 1262nd meeting of the Ministers' Deputies, available at: http://bit.do/ekxxY (on February 9, 2019).
169. S. Schmachl, M. Breuer, *The Council of Europe. Its Laws and Policies*, Oxford 2016, p. 128.
170. Doubts concerning the understanding of this condition are the same as in the case of the UN system, as discussed above.

(6) be represented at the European level, i.e. have members in at least five Member States;
(7) be able, through their work, to support the achievement of the closer unity mentioned in Article 1 of the CoE's Statute;
(8) be capable of contributing to and participating actively in CoE deliberations and activities;
(9) be able to make known the work of the CoE among European Citizens.[171]

Once an NGO is granted participatory status, it gains many rights. Notably, it may address memoranda to the Secretary-General, have access to the agenda and public documents of the Parliamentary Assembly, be invited to the public sittings of the Congress of Local and Regional Authorities, be invited to provide specific activity or expertise or be invited to attend seminars, conferences and colloquies of interest to their work.[172] However, NGOs that obtain a participatory status are tied to certain obligations as well. It means that they should:[173]

(1) promote the respect of the CoE' conventions and legal instruments in the Member States;
(2) contribute to the implementation of CoE standards and policies in collaboration with local, regional and national NGOs;
(3) participate actively in the sessions and the work of the Conference of INGOs;
(4) keep themselves regularly informed of CoE activities and developments in standards;
(5) furnish, either spontaneously, or at the request of the CoE's different bodies, information, documents or opinions relating to their own fields of competence on matters which are under consideration or which would be addressed by the CoE;
(6) work to promote the respect of the CoE standards, conventions and legal instruments in the Member States and assist in the implementation of these standards (and in close contact with local, regional and national NGOs);
(7) give maximum publicity to the initiatives and achievements of the CoE in their own fields of competence and disseminate information on CoE standards, instruments and activities;
(8) submit every four years a report to the Secretary-General specifying, among other things, their attendance at events organized by the Secretariat General and any action they have undertaken with a view to ensuring respect of CoE standards and to publicizing its work.

NGOs enjoying participatory status[174] make up, since 2005, the Conference of INGOs which constitutes the "civil society's pillar in the Council of Europe

171. See para. 2 of the Appendix to Resolution 2016(3).
172. See Art. 3 of the Appendix to Resolution 2016(3).
173. See Art. 4 of the Appendix to Resolution 2016(3).
174. Currently more than 300.

'quadrilogue' with the Committee of Ministers, the Parliamentary Assembly and the Congress of Local and Regional Authorities."[175] On June 24, 2016, the Conference applied its Rules of Procedure.[176] The main task of the Conference is signified in paragraph 1.3.3. According to this provision, it "adopts positions on fundamental issues and may submit them, in the form of recommendations or resolutions, to other Council of Europe bodies, to other international or national institutions, as well as to the media."

It can be stated that NGOs enjoying participatory status with the CoE enter into a partnership, in which both sides have obligations to each other. Actually, the NGOs' obligations seem more extensive than the obligations of the CoE[177]—while organizations with participatory status "shall" furnish the CoE with certain information, they only "may" be invited to provide expert advice.

To conclude, it should be emphasized that NGOs play a significant role in influencing the jurisdiction of the European Court of Human Rights (ECtHR). According to Article 34 of European Convention on Human Rights[178] (ECHR), the Court may receive applications from any person, nongovernmental organization or group of individuals claiming to be victim of violation by one of the High Contracting Parties of the rights set forth in the Convention or the Protocols thereto. The High Contracting Parties undertake not to hinder in any way the effective exercise of this right. In fact, some organizations "specialize" in the representation of individuals during litigation before the ECtHR. Others are active in monitoring the pending proceedings and in issuing amicus curiae briefs and opinions. It was noticed in the literature that if NGOs had not been pushing specific issues into the agenda of the Court, the underlying social conflicts would have been settled differently.[179] As a result, these organizations impact not only the actual content of each individual decision but also the overall shape of the human rights' case law.[180]

[6] The Modes for NGO Participation in IGOs

The above-presented legal grounds for NGO participation in the decision-making and lawmaking processes in the systems of various IGOs[181] can be summed up by a statement that there is no single model for such a cooperation. In fact, the models that

175. For more details see: http://www.coe.int/en/web/ingo/the-conference-of-ingos-in-a-nutshell (on February 9, 2019), see also para. 1.3.5 of the Rules of Procedure of 2016.
176. Available at: http://www.coe.int/en/web/ingo/rules-of-procedure (on February 9, 2019).
177. A.-K. Lindblom, *Non-governmental...*, p. 423.
178. I.e. Convention for Protection of Human Rights and Fundamental Freedoms, Rome, 4.11.1950, available at: http://www.echr.coe.int/Documents/Convention_ENG.pdf (on February 9, 2019).
179. For examples (concerning mainly Russia) see G. Cliquennois, B. Champetier, *The Economic, Judicial and Political Influence Exerted by Private Foundations on Cases Taken by NGOs to the European Courts of Human Rights: Inklings of a New Cold War?*, European Law Journal Vol. 22/2016, pp. 92 et seq.
180. G. Cliquennois, B. Champetier, *The Economic...*, p. 125.
181. Additionally, what exceeds the scope of this book, there are compelling means of cooperation between international and national NGOs. For more information see e.g. H. Elshorst, *Die Rolle der Nichtregierungsorganisationen—insbesondere Transparency International—bei der*

could be distinguished very often interpenetrate even in one organization. It is very noticeable that some institutions provide for legal basis for NGO participation in their works, whereas other institutions in the same IGO take a very informal approach for this type of cooperation. Therefore, it is more rational to differ some *modes* of NGO participation, instead of *models* of cooperation.

The first mode of participation is based on the direct involvement of NGOs in the decision-making and lawmaking processes. This mode can be most visibly seen in the ILO—the employees' representatives are one of the components in the tripartism system. However, such a mode of cooperation can be achieved only if the objective of the organization is very closely linked to the activity of certain groups of interests. Therefore, the workers associated with trade unions can and should present their opinions and recommendations in the field of labor law. Their position is based on their strong legitimacy in this sphere.[182] However, this mode could not be easily transferred into the system of IGOs dealing with more general matters. The reason for this statement is quite simple: there are no NGOs that have strong legitimacies in a wide range of legal matters.[183] If an IGO that deals with general objectives confessed such a strong position to certain NGOs, then it would definitely expose itself (and quite rightly so) to the critique why it had chosen those NGOs and not the other. This would mean that although an IGO widens the scope of actors in their legislative procedures, it closes the door in front of the others at the same time.

The second mode of participation is based on developing formal relations with certain NGOs which fulfill fixed requirements but at the same time are bound with certain obligations. These types of formal relations usually mean that an organization gains "consultative" (like in the UN system) or "participatory" (like in the CoE system) status. This mode of participation has obvious advantages. On the one hand, the IGO strengthens its democratic legitimacy, due to taking into account the views of the representatives of organized civil society, and receives specialized, technical knowledge in its legislative procedures from experts working in specific NGOs. On the other hand, the NGO in "consultative" or "participatory" status gains some level of influence on the decision-making and lawmaking processes at the international level. It can, therefore, conduct its policy more effectively, both nationwide and worldwide. However, this mode of participation is also vulnerable to many traps. First of all, it is hard to determine the conditions for gaining a formal status within the IGO system. If they are not particularly demanding, then there may be too many NGOs taking part in the legislative process, possibly hampering its outcomes. Thus, the IGO is unwittingly impelled to somehow limit the actual position of these organizations in lawmaking procedures. However, if the requirements are too strict, the IGO is exposed to critique

Bekämpfung der Korruption in: *Corporate Governance und Korruption. Wirtschaftliche und moralökonomische Perspektiven der Bestechung und ihrer Bekämpfung*, Berlin 2005, pp. 127 et seq.

182. Cf. S. Stroup, W. Wong, *The Agency and Authority of International NGOs*, Perspectives on Politics Vol. 14/2016, p. 138.

183. Cf. J. Tallberg, L. Dellmuth, H. Agne, A. Duit, *NGOs Influence in International Organizations: Information, Access and Exchange*, Oxford 2015, p. 14.

that it does not want to engage in deliberations with civil society.[184] Furthermore, formal accreditation or an official "status" does not guarantee that the relationship between the two parties is fluent, equal and fruitful.[185]

The third mode of participation, and practically the most common one, are informal consultations.[186] This mode is apparent in all IGOs. Even if they provide a legal basis for formal relations with NGOs, informal dialogue always takes place. Although it has numerous benefits, it usually lacks transparency. Generally speaking, the NGOs that are directly invited to such consultations and that can have a significant input into the legislative procedures are oftentimes those with biggest budgets and those with a history of prior cooperation with this specific IGO.[187] These NGOs often resemble large enterprises and are often remote from the needs of the civil society which they should represent. However, such informal consultations frequently transform into the mode of more or less formal lobbying practices.

The fourth mode of participation is based on a particular institution within the legal frames of specific IGO that is designed to represent the voices of NGOs or to be a common arena for dialogue with civil society. This mode of cooperation, as it will be discussed further, is especially visible in the constitutional system of the EU. However, to a certain level, it is also noticeable in other IGO systems as well. For instance, one of the main goals of the ECOSOC is to include the views of NSAs and other specialized groups in the UN system.[188] The most significant problem with this mode is its "artificiality" in terms of representing the organized civil society. Therefore, the democratic legitimacy of such an institution is very limited.

The legal construction of these modes of participation and the practice of their application are significant as exemplifications of the possible role NGOs can play at the international level. Moreover, they are not less important as a background for further analysis dealing with the position of NGOs in the EU constitutional system. This is also very compelling due to the fact that the EU developed quite autonomous modes of participation with the interested organizations that are not easily comparable with other IGO systems.

---

184. For more information see e.g. C. Kissling, *The Evolution of CSOs' Legal Status in International Governance and Its Relevance for the Legitimacy of International Organizations* in: *Civil Society Participation in European and Global Governance*, J. Steffek, J. Kissling, P. Nanz (eds), New York 2008, pp. 30 et seq.
185. M. Abad Castellos, *Accountability and Responsiveness of Governance Structures in the EU and Beyond: Is There a Role for Civil Society in EU Governance?* in: *The Changing Role of Law in the Age of Supra- and Transnational Governance*, R. Nickel, A. Greppi (eds), Baden-Baden 2014, p. 312; It appears that these are the main reasons why this mode was rejected in the EU system. In the Communication *An open and structured dialogue between the Commission and special interest groups* (Official Journal C 63, 5.3.1993), the Commission made an expressed pronouncement against the possibility of advisory statutes for NGOs.
186. Which, however, raises many concerns due to the lack of an explicit legal basis for such a form of cooperation. See S. Ripinsky, P. van den Bossche, *NGO...*, pp. 208-210.
187. Like in the "arria consultations" in the UN system.
188. G. Fox, B. Roth, *Democratic Governance and International Law*, Cambridge 2010, p. 91.

[C] Summary

As it can be noted, even though there is no general consensus regarding the definition of "nongovernmental organizations," this notion is commonly used both at the national and at the international levels. This tendency has been especially visible since the adoption of the UN Charter. Furthermore, many IGOs adopt various measures of including NGOs in their legal system and daily practices. These means are aimed not only at strengthening the democratic legitimacy of the transnational bodies but also at contributing to a better and more open decision-making at the international level. Thus, NGOs are the "natural" partners for many IGOs as they are ordinarily perceived as the representatives of civil society and advocates of its interests. Still, it would be difficult to evaluate which modes of cooperation between IGOs and NGOs are most favorable. It seems that everything depends on the IGO's specialization and its fields of activities. This statement is significant for further analysis as the EU has wide competences. Therefore, the appropriate means of cooperation with NGOs need to accommodate these peculiarities.

§1.02 EUROPEAN CIVIL SOCIETY

Defining "European civil society" is an even more challenging task than characterizing NGOs as there are much fewer indications of its constituting factors. Thus, the structuring of a definition attempt should begin with the approximation of the notion of "civil society." As there are hardly any indications of what constitutes "civil society" in international law, references to proper philosophical and sociological theories will be beneficial. By stating what should be understood under the term "civil society," it can be then transposed to the EU level, thus establishing constituents of "European civil society."

The following paragraphs will also present the importance of transboundary civil society in the theory of integration. As a result, it will be emphasized that the issue of shaping European civil society has been present since the outset of the "European project." Thus, since the EU integration faces many obstacles, it would be perhaps advantageous to find new means of strengthening civil society at the EU level.

[A] Definition Attempt

Like NGOs, the notion of "civil society" is used in international law in a very ambiguous way.[189] It is also not defined in any treaty. At the EU level, Article 15 (1) of the TFEU states that in order to promote good governance and ensure the participation

189. For instance, the World Health Organization seems to use notions of "civil society" and "NGOs" interchangeably while favoring the participation of nationally and internationally recognized NGOs in decision-making and law enforcement. In contrast, other IGOs (e.g., the WB) focus on the local civic associations in developing the capacity of citizens to participate in public life. Furthermore, there are instances where "civil society" is even equated with business and industry entities as well; for more information see L. Pedraza-Farina, *Conceptions*

of civil society, the Union's institutions, bodies, offices and agencies shall conduct their work as openly as possible. Noticeably, this provision mentions "civil society" without indicating what it means or rather what actors are part of this phenomenon. Yet, there are instances where this term is used in various acts of the EU law, often in parallel with the notion "NGO." They will be cited in the following parts of this book.

The hesitation in defining "civil society" in acts of international law is perhaps intelligible as this notion has been understood differently through the ages. Presently, it is a synthetic term that describes the status of individuals and social groups in current fields of codependency.[190] Most basically, "civil society" can be defined as a dense network of groups, communities, networks and ties that stand between individual and the modern state.[191] Other "present" (and nonlegal) definition proposals are centralized around the notions of "discourse,"[192] "self-constitution,"[193] "solidarity"[194] and "representation."[195]

Nevertheless, the understanding of "civil society" is far more grounded in philosophical and sociological theories than the notion of "NGOs." Therefore, in order to comprehend better how European civil society can operate, it is justified to refer to the roots of the modern comprehension of "civil society."[196]

---

of Civil Society in International Lawmaking and Implementation: A Theoretical Framework, Michigan Journal of International Law Vol. 34/2013, pp. 607-608.

190. H. Duszka-Jakimko, *Globalisation and Its Impact on Civil Society: Philosophical, Legal and Sociological Aspects*, Wrocław Review of Law, Administration and Economic vol. 1/2011, p. 21.
191. A definition proposed by Encyclopaedia Britannica; see: https://www.britannica.com/topic/civil-society.
192. "Civil society is composed of those more or less spontaneously emergent associations, organizations and movements that distil and transmit societal problems to the public sphere and are enhancing problem-solving discourses on questions of general interest"; a definition attributed to J. Habermas for: B. Kohler-Koch, *Die vielen...*, p. 53.
193. "Civil society defines a sphere of social interaction between economy, state and the intimate sphere of associations, social movements and forms of public communication. Modern civil society is created through forms of self-constitution and self-mobilization. It serves to stabilize social differentiation and self-government"; a definition introduced by J.L. Cohen and A. Arato for: B. Kohler-Koch, *Die vielen...*, p. 53.
194. "Civil society epitomizes such values as solidarity, horizontal social and institutional bonds, as well as civic activity which—one should add—implies responsibility and commitment to the well-being of the larger community"; a definition developed on basis of works of B. Barber for B. Kohler-Koch, *Die vielen...*, p. 53.
195. "Civil society includes all those voluntary and non-profit organizations which play an important role in giving voice to the concerns of citizens and in delivering services that meet people's needs. Civil society includes the following: trade unions, employers' and producers' organizations, nongovernmental organizations representing general interests such as environment, human rights, social welfare, health and culture, professional associations and grassroot organizations"; a definition proposed in B. Kohler-Koch, *Die vielen Gesichter der europäischen Zivilgesellschaft* in: *Die Entzauberung partizipativer Demokratie. Zur Rolle der Zivilgesellschaft bei der Demokratisierung von EU-Governance*, B. Kohler-Koch, Ch. Quittkat (eds), Frankurt am Mein 2011, p. 53.
196. Unfortunately, some substantial theories have been left out of the following analysis as they dealt with a rather different understanding of the modern concept of "civil society." For instance, for J.J. Rousseau, civil society resulted from the degeneration of a basically good state of nature. As a result, man's difficulties arose because of civil society; for more information see e.g. D. Pietrzyk-Reeves, *Idea społeczeństwa obywatelskiego*, Wrocław 2004, pp. 38 et seq. Furthermore, for T. Hobbes, civil society was the application of force by the state to uphold the obligations and concluded contracts. Consequently, civil society was developed by the state to

Aristotle was the first to use the term "civil society" (in his "The Politics" he used the Greek phrase *koinomia politike*).[197] For him, civil society was identified with the *polis* itself. He saw the political organization of the *polis* as natural, arising through the intermediate stages of the household and the village. In this concept, a man was naturally a political animal. Aristotle stated that there was an immanent impulse in all men toward an association of the *polis*, in which human life reached its highest social form. Therefore, all associations were purposeful.[198] They existed because their members had common ends. While many kinds of associations functioned, political associations were the highest form, encompassing and prevailing over all others as political ends were the highest ends of man.[199]

In the theory of G.F.W. Hegel, civil society was perceived as an opposite to the state.[200] Yet, the state was in many ways a realization of prior features of civil society, in particular of the universally acknowledged status of a largely voluntarist and commercialized association of self-interest individuals.[201] In the E. Durkheim's approach, civil society also existed outside the realm of the state, but it constituted the only organizational sphere through which ethical or social existence could exist.[202]

The liberal tradition was a clearer reflection of the insights of Aristotle. In "Democracy in America," A. de Tocqueville noted that due to the dynamic development of different types of organizations and associations appointed by the citizens themselves, a kind of "school of democracy" was formed, where citizens had the opportunity to freely exchange their views, as well as improve their ability of self-organization and strengthen their autonomy in the face of state institutions.[203] J.S. Mill echoed the idea of Aristotle that being a good citizen was a supreme civic virtue.[204] Furthermore, he insisted on the development of this virtue through private activity.[205] As a result, civil society was not seen as a contrast to the state. In fact, in some spheres, they were combined in mutual undertakings. It means that civil society offered models of conduct that could be used in service of the state.[206]

It seems that the idea of civil society has experienced a revival in the modern history. The peaceful transformation in Eastern Europe, the final triumph over the apartheid in South Africa and the return to democracy in Latin America have all been ascribed to the actions of civil society.[207] This is one of the main reasons as to why the

---

maintain law and order; for more information see e.g. J. Szacki, *Ani książę, ani kupiec: Obywatel. Idea społeczeństwa obywatelskiego w myśli współczesnej*, Kraków 1997, pp. 7 et seq.

197. Aristotle, *The Politics*, London 2000, p. 7.
198. W. Bokajło, *Społeczeństwo obywatelskie*, Wrocław 2001, p. 89.
199. B. DeWiel, *A Conceptual History of Civil Society: From Greek Beginnings to the Ends of Marx*, Past Imperfect Vol. 6/1997, pp. 9-10.
200. I.e. the contrast between *die Gesellschaft* and *der Staat*.
201. M. Freeden, *Civil Society and the Good Citizen: Competing Conceptions of Citizenship in Twentieth-Century Britain*, Oxford 2003, p. 282, D. Pietrzyk-Reeves, *Idea…*, pp. 129 et seq.
202. A. Seligman, *The Idea of Civil Society*, New Jersey 1992, p. 112.
203. A. de Tocqueville, *Democracy in America*, Washington 2004, pp. 1007 et seq.
204. Aristotle, *The Politics…*, p. 20.
205. M. Freeden, *Civil…*, p. 283.
206. *Ibid.*, D. Pietrzyk-Reeves, *Idea…*, pp. 97 et seq.
207. B. Kohler-Koch, Ch. Quittkat, *De-Mystification of Participatory Democracy: EU Governance and Civil Society*, Oxford 2013, p. 22.

concept of "European civil society" could be a good answer to the present political and legal problems of the EU, including the issue of the democratic deficit.[208] Civil society developed at the EU level and its positive public perception could overcome the distance between EU institutions and citizens of the Member States. This is a theory based on J. Habermas' discourse-theoretical approach with its connection between civil society and the political public view of realization of deliberative democracy.[209] Habermas argued that a European collectivity is possible, even though there is no "strong" common identity tied to territorial states and their membership. This collectivity could influence the political system at the EU level and, in this way, change the normative framework of political decisions.[210] Europe is therefore intended to be a pioneer in new governance, this time transnational rather than national, which gives some practical embodiment to the current extension of democratic thinking into conceptions of cosmopolitan democracy.[211] Still, even if there is a certain general agreement that the expression "European civil society" refers to a response to rising concerns about the need for a new social, economic and political deal at the EU level—a new governance model—there is no further consensus as to how this response should be[212] or what could be its constitutive elements.

In conclusion, it can be stated that there is no definition (or even an overall definition attempt) of "European civil society." For the purposes of this book, this notion will be understood as an organized aggregate of individuals that manifests its will and advocates for the collective interest in transboundary, European relations.[213] In order to do this, the individuals concerned use means of influencing and monitoring the EU institutions in the lawmaking procedures. Moreover, they utilize the existing instruments in the EU law to collaborate better with one another. As a result, there are three core points of European civil society: (1) transparency, (2) advocacy and (3) cooperation.[214] The starting point of this analysis is the supposition that European civil society is not merely the sum of the civil societies of Europe but rather a community

208. Cf. L. Graniszewski, *Deficyt demokracji w Unii Europejskiej a europejskie grupy interesu* in: *Deficyt demokracji w Unii Europejskiej*, K.A. Wojtaszczyk, J. Szymańska (eds), Warsaw 2014, pp. 215 et seq.
209. J. Habermas, *The Crisis of the European Union. A Response*, Cambridge 2013, p. 5.
210. *Ibid.*, p. 12.
211. *Ibid.*, p. 14.
212. E. Szazi, *NGOs...*, p. 25; see also B. Kohler-Koch, *The Three Worlds of European Civil Society—What Role for Civil Society for What Kind of Europe?*, Policy and Society Vol. 28/2009, p. 47.
213. In this regard, European civil society is a "product" of globalization. Globalization has highlighted the fact that the international community shares common public goods, such as the environment, and needs to address global challenges through globally concerted solutions; for more see P. van Amersfoort, *European Civil Society*, Asia Europe Journal Vol. 3/2005, p. 399.
214. Cf. A. Alemanno, *Unpacking the Principle of Openness in EU Law, Transparency, Participation and Democracy*, European Law Review Vol. 39/2014, pp. 72-90, F. Riemann, *Die Transparenz der Europäischen Union*, Berlin 2004, pp. 72-96, F. Furtak, *Nichtregierungsorganisationen (NGOs) im politischen System der Europäischen Union*, Munich 2008, p. 255. P. Nanz, J. Steffek, *Legitimation durch Deliberation? Die Rolle der Zibilgesellschaft in der supranationalen Politik* in: *Europäische...*, pp. 79 et seq.

that transcends boundaries[215] and which acts through their representatives, including NGOs, at the EU level.[216] And although there is a rich history of ideas of civil society, closely intertwined with the idea of European democracy, this category has never before referred as strongly to the EU as it does nowadays.

[B] The Basis of European Civil Society

As the concept of European civil society may appear vague, it is significant to embed it in firm prerequisites. Thus, the proposed approach to European civil society is based on European identity as its main contributing factor.

The subsequent remarks are based (yet not directly) on the main assumptions presented by F. Mayer and J. Palmowski[217] who argued that common European identity could be established either on the grounds of common history, culture or vastly speaking—law. However, only the latter one can be a solid foundation for developing European identity and—in this way—the European civil society, which, in fact, is a legal community.

[1] European Identity

It seems that the constituting factor of a well-functioning civil society is individuals interested in working for the common good. However, this is a rather simplistic approach. Individuals may cooperate to achieve some designated aims, but this does not always mean they will be eager to collaborate in the future. In other words, the sole fact that some individuals work together does not determine that they become a *community* and that they may be perceived as civil society. Therefore, there is a need to distinguish some determinants that could merge this group of individuals in a way that they feel connected to one another and to the common purpose. At the national level, it is obvious what factors constitute this feeling of identity. These are common history, language or the simple fact that some individuals live close to one another and that they are somehow destined to cope with the same or similar problems.[218] However, these foundations are not so clear if a construct of civil society at the EU level is considered, even though it is not difficult to argue that this sense of affiliation exists at the EU level by geographical and historical positions alone.[219] Furthermore, the

215. B. Finke, M. Knodt, *Einleitung: ZIvilgesellschaft und zivilgesellschaftliche Akteure in der EU* in: *Europäische Zivilgesellschaft. Konzepte, Akteure, Strategien*, M. Knodt, B. Finke (eds), Wiesbaden 2005, p. 16.
216. *Ibid.*, p. 15.
217. F. Mayer, J. Palmowski, *European Identities and the EU—The Ties That Bind the Peoples of Europe*, Journal of Common Market Studies Vol. 3/2004, pp. 573-598.
218. A. Maurer, D. Kietz, A. Crespy, *Der Europäische Verfassungkonvent und die "Zivilgesellschaft"* in: *Europäische Zivilgesellschaft. Konzepte, Akteure, Strategien*, M. Knodt, B. Finke (eds), Wiesbaden 2005, p. 199.
219. *Ibid.*, p. 200.

creation of a "transnational people" faces objective difficulties[220] as the individuals are not bound by common nationality. Yet, according to K. Deutsch, nationality is "a people striving to equip itself with power, with some machinery of compulsion strong enough to make the enforcement of its commands probable in order to aid in the spread of habits of voluntary compliance with them."[221] Furthermore, "nationality means an alignment of large numbers of individuals from the lower and middle classes linked to regional centers and leading social groups by channels of social communication and economic discourse."[222] This understanding is not reserved to national states and opens the possibility of a transboundary nationality which, still, is based on common identity.

European identity is commonly perceived as a necessary aspect to ensure the legitimacy of the EU and to foster solidarity among the citizens of the EU.[223] Furthermore, it is argued that the European people with collective identity is a prerequisite not only for developing European civil society but also to European democracy in general.[224] However, the question whether a real European identity exists or whether, in fact, it is possible, is subject to ongoing controversy. In this regard, the absence of a "strong" common European identity is referred to be the source of increasing Euroscepticism.[225] As a result, national identities, which have extensively developed over the past decades, are considered prone to posing an obstacle to a European identity by hindering the emergence of a further or all-encompassing European identity.[226]

Nevertheless, the survey conducted in 2016 by the Commission indicates that the majority of Member State citizens describe themselves as "Europeans" (66%).[227] Therefore, it can be concluded that there is a significant level of European identity. What is more, for the majority of EU citizens, national and European identities do not exclude each other. They are rather compatible.[228] A total of 51% of the EU citizens state that they have a multiple identity, which encompasses both their national and the European identities. However, this does not automatically mean that there is a "EU identity" or a strong attachment of the Member State citizens to the EU in general.[229]

---

220. For more see B. Moffitt, *Transnational Populism? Representative Claims, Media and the Difficulty of Constructing a Transnational People*, Journal of the European Institute for Communication and Culture Vol. 24/2017, pp. 409-425.
221. K. Deutsch, *Nationalism and Social Communication: Inquiry into the Foundations of Nationality*, Boston 1966, p. 104.
222. K. Deutsch, *Nationalism...*, p. 101.
223. D. Fuchs, I. Guinaudeau, S. Schubert, *National Identity, European Identity and Euroscepticism* in: *Euroscepticism: Images of Europe among Mass Publics and Political Elites*, D. Fuchs, R. Magni-Berton, A. Roger (eds), Leverkusen 2009, p. 91.
224. J. Roose, *Die Identifikation der Bürger mit der EU und ihre Wirkung für die Akceptanz von Entscheidungen* in: *Europäische Identität: Voraussetzungen und Strategien*, J. Nida-Rümelin, W. Weidenfeld (eds), Baden-Baden 2007, p. 123.
225. A. Kufer, *Images of Europe—The Meaning and Perception of "Europe" by Citizens of EU Member States* in: *Euroscepticism: Images of Europe among Mass Publics and Political Elites*, D. Fuchs, R. Magni-Berton, A. Roger (eds), Leverkusen 2009, pp. 35 et seq.
226. D. Fuchs, I. Guinaudeau, S. Schubert, *National...*, s. 95.
227. Standard Eurobarometer 85. Spring 2016. European citizenship, available at: goo.gl/7NFAu8.
228. What can be perceived as an outcome of "liberal patriotism." See M. Król, *Patriotyzm przyszłości*, Warsaw 2004, p. 129.
229. Cf. I.P. Karolewski, *Citizenship and Collective Identity in Europe*, Abingdon 2010, pp. 54 et seq.

There are two main approaches to the question what "Europe" means: one based on cultural aspects ("Europe as culture") and the other one defined by the common institutions ("Europe-as-EU").[230] The first one can be noticed in some instruments of the European law.[231] The second one has been promoted since the 1960s when it became clear that the "European project" was not on the radar of most citizens of the Member States.[232] The first years of integration produced no European *demos* as the whole process was, in fact, limited to the elites.[233] This is arguably one of the reasons why the European integration was further deepened with the extension on the issues dealing with rights of individuals and means of bringing the Communities' institutions closer to the grassroot societies.[234] In this way, it was believed that over time the integration process would gradually produce a convergence of beliefs, values and aspirations that would unite the peoples of the European Community and generate "new nationalism."[235] Thus, the future of Europe would be partly determined by the extent to which the Member States' citizens start to perceive themselves as citizens of broader Europe.[236]

Even though the European integration has obviously deepened since then, it can be stated that the development of European identity is still "in progress." In fact, in the last few years the sense of "Europeanness" has seemed to decline and citizens across Europe increasingly view their national governments as the main focus of their identities and political activity.[237]

It can be concluded that, indeed, there is some form of European identity (EU identity) which is the support for developing European civil society. This statement, however, does not provide a basis for further analysis. It should be determined what the actual foundation of European identity is, and in this way of European civil society. In this context, common history and culture are "natural" connotations.

230. C. Franzius, U. Preuß, *Die Zukunft der europäischen Demokratie*, Baden-Baden 2012, p. 63.
231. E.g. the Council of Europe's European Convention on Cinematographic Co-production of 2.10.1992 (available at: https://www.coe.int/en/web/conventions/full-list/-/conventions/treaty/220 (on February 9, 2019), European Treaty Series—No. 147; see Art. 9 (1) (c).
232. A. Utzinger, *Mythen oder Institutionen? Zur Bildung kollektiver Identität im postnationalem Europa* in: *Die EU und der Prozess ihrer Legitimation: Legitimationsgrundlagen der Europäischen Union*, F. Cheneval (ed.), Hamburg 2007, p. 235, E. Haas, *Beyond the Nation State: Functionalism and International Organisation*, Colchester 2008, p. 12.
233. M. Góra, Z. Mach, H-J. Trentz, *Situating the Demos of a European Democracy* in: *Rethinking Democracy and the European Union*, E.O. Eriksen, J.E. Fossum (eds), Devon 2012, pp. 159 et seq., D. Rucht, *Zivilgesellschaft oder zivile Inteaktionsformen in und jenseits von Europe?* in *Europäische Zivilgesellschaft. Konzepte, Akteure, Strategien*, M. Knodt, B. Finke (eds), Wiesbaden 2005, p. 32.
234. E.g., by establishing popular elections to the EP in 1979.
235. E. Haas, *Beyond...*, pp. 13-14.
236. U. Preuß, *Transformacja europejskiego państwa narodowego szansa na powstanie europejskiej opinii publicznej?*, Nowa Europa. Przegląd Natoliński Vol. 5/2007, p. 132.
237. N. Fligstein, A. Polyakova, W. Sandholz, *European Integration, Nationalism and European Identity*, Journal of Common Market Studies Vol. 50/2012, p. 107.

[2] Common History and Culture

The first half of the twentieth century in Europe can undoubtedly be described as an era of nationalism. Furthermore, the memory of the World War II and the national experiences of both heroism and tragedy fostered to differentiate, rather than to homogenize, the historical identities of the Europeans.[238] In fact, even the former allies were soon defeated as the French in Indochina in 1954, the British and French at Suez in 1956 or the Dutch in Indonesia in 1946-1947.[239] This is why many political and intellectual leaders seemed inspired to remold this common and calamitous background with a return to European humanist, enlightenment and democratic traditions. As a result, the west of Europe acquired an organized dimension in 1952 with the European Coal and Steel Community (ECSC), followed by the European Economic Community (EEC) in 1958. Consequently, the rise of the "European project" can be seen rather as an admittance of weakness rather than an expression of strength and undisputable historical identity.[240] This deficiency[241] has been visible ever since. The "Europe Day," celebrated on 9 May each year to honor the Schuman Declaration of 1950,[242] is not directly connected to any common European historical event. Thus, the EU as a whole cannot refer to a popular, historical founding myth similar to the US Declaration of Independence, Bastille Day or the Enactment of the Polish Constitution of May 3, 1791.[243] However, the absence of such an identity bolstered the vision of the European Communities as technocratic organizations that, according to J. Monnet, would bring a deeply "modernized" Europe, created by an "enlightened bureaucracy,"[244] encompassed with a certain degree of autonomy and cherishing the vastly understood "collective interest."[245] Furthermore, this was in line with Monnet's understanding of the European "course of history" (*cours de l'histoire*) which was oriented on the future and common aims that could be achieved by cooperation.[246] His famous words were: "we are not integrating states, we are uniting people."[247] This

238. F. Mayer, J. Palmowski, *European...*, p. 581.
239. *Ibid.*, p. 581., cf. A. Patek, J. Rydel, J.J. Węc, *Najnowsza historia świata 1945-1995. Tom I 1945-63*, Kraków 1997, p. 44.
240. A. Jaskulski, *Federalizm europejski początków integracji i doby kryzysu gospodarczego*, Rocznik Integracji Europejskiej Vol. 6/2012, p. 222, W. Schmale, *Eckpunkte einer Geschichte Europäischer Identität* in *Europäische Zivilgesellschaft. Konzepte, Akteure, Strategien*, M. Knodt, B. Finke (eds), Wiesbaden 2005, p. 63.
241. Sometimes referred to as a lack of "historic memory" (*die historischen Erinnerung*); cf. G. Kreis, *Die EU: legitimiert aud dem Gang der Geschichte* in: *Die EU...*, p. 69.
242. Full text available at: https://www.robert-schuman.eu/en/doc/questions-d-europe/qe-204-en.pdf.
243. Cf. H. Münkler, *Die politische Idee Europa* in: *Herausforderung Europa: Wege zu einer europäischen Identität* M. Delgado, M. Lutz-Bachmann (eds), Munich 1995, p. 133.
244. Cf. J.J. Węc, *Spór o kształt ustrojowy Wspólnot Europejskich i Unii Europejskiej w latach 1950-2010: między ideą ponadnarodowości a współpracą międzyrządową. Analiza politologiczna*, Kraków 2012, pp. 27-29.
245. S. Konopacki, *Dylematy federalizmu europejskiego*, Studia Europejskie Vol. 3/1988, p. 85.
246. G. Kreis, *Die EU...*, p. 71.
247. U. Guérot, *Now the EU Needs to Hand Power to Its Citizens. Here's Why*, The Guardian 2018, available at: https://www.theguardian.com/commentisfree/2018/feb/07/european-union-power-citizens-republic (on February 9, 2019).

approach is still current in the present EU as the preamble to the TEU directly recalls the historical importance of the ending of the division of the European continent and the need to create firm bases for the construction of the future Europe.

Due to the fact that there is no strong, common European identity, there appears a question of an overarching cultural identity. Practically speaking, it seems that one of the biggest obstacles in terms of developing this foundation is lack of a common language.[248] It has hindered the popular identification of Europeans with their politicians and with one another.[249] Consequently, if anything, the Europe's distinctive feature has been its heterogeneity and multiplicity.[250] These features have also been promoted by the EU in its cultural agenda since the beginning of the European integration.[251] At present, this approach is reaffirmed in the preamble of the TEU which "draws inspiration" from the cultural, religious and humanist inheritance of Europe, from which have developed universal values of the inviolable and inalienable rights of the human person, freedom, democracy, equality and the rule of law, and "desires" to deepen the solidarity between the peoples of Member States while respecting their history, their culture and their traditions. In this way, the cultural inheritance is combined with the sphere of law, which is especially interesting in the context of the following paragraphs of this book.

Consequently, it can be stated that the abovementioned foundations of European identity and, thus, European civil society are rather frail. Nevertheless, there is a much stronger basis for distinguishing European identity. As in their daily life the EU citizens are encompassed by the impact of the EU law, it becomes clear that the European identity substantially expresses itself by this ingredient.[252] According to K. Deutsch, if there is going to be a strong European identity, it will definitely arise from people who cooperate with one another across national borders. In other words, actual relations and corresponding spheres of law are the substantial part in binding the Europeans.[253] As a result, the best way to promote this kind of identification is to enhance common rights and to strengthen the position of individuals in lawmaking procedures at the EU level.[254] In this way, a common legal identity forms the basis for a European legal community.

248. F. Mayer, J. Palmowski, *European...*, p. 583; see also A. Kutay, *How Does the European Commission Create a European Civil Society with Words? A Discourse Theoretical Inquiry*, Journal of Common Market Studies Vol. 55/2017, pp. 1095 et seq.
249. C. Franzius, U. Preuß, *Die Zukunft...*, p. 64.
250. D. Rucht, *Zivilgesellschaft...*, p. 61, C. Semmelmann, *Legal Principles in EU Law as an Expression of a European Legal Culture between Unity and Diversity* in: *Towards a European Legal Culture*, G. Helleringer, K. Purnhagen (eds), Baden-Baden 2014, pp. 303 et seq.
251. Ch. Gaitanides, G. Grözinger, *Diversity in Europe*, Baden-Baden 2015, p. 10.
252. F. Mayer, J. Palmowski, *European...*, p. 588.
253. N. Fligstein, A. Polyakova, W. Sandholtz, *European...*, p. 107.
254. C. Franzius, U. Preuß, *Die Zukunft...*, p. 70.

[3] European Civil Society as a Legal Community

It appears that the principal way in which the EU institutions have transformed European relations is through the law.[255] Additionally, the notion of a community of law (*Rechtsgemeinschaft*) seems to capture the best feature of the European integration.[256] What will be argued in the subsequent paragraphs, in the light of the previous remarks, is that while a meaningful European historical identity or common culture (that could form some kind of European nationality) scarcely exist, law is the foundation of a real European identity.[257] Accordingly, European civil society should be perceived as a legal community.

Traditionally, national law, in line with the political, economic, cultural or social foundations, emanates from the supremacy of the national constitution. However, fundamental principles of the national legal systems also form a "philosophical, political and legal substratum common to Member States"[258] which contributes to the common, European legal heritage. For this reason, the EU law has always had strong foundations for further development. Accordingly, the CJEU, a judicial institution with a constitutional status, crucially affected the nature of the European integration.[259] With the rulings establishing the direct effect of the EU law at the national level[260] and the primacy of the EU over national law,[261] the CJEU precisely contributed to the legal status of individuals in terms of their rights and duties. In this way, it expressed what the EU is and what it aspires to be.[262] Furthermore, the CJEU, by the declaration of social, economic and cultural rights, has established[263] inalienable basis for an identity common to all people living in the EU.[264] Thus, its role has also been essential in developing consensus concerning common values and norms.[265] In this way, European

255. F. Mayer, J. Palmowski, *European...*, p. 590.
256. J. Nida-Rümeln, *Europäische Identität?—Das normative Fundament des europäischen Einigungsprozesses* in: *Europäische...*, pp. 29 et seq., F. Mayer, *Europa als Rechtsgemeinschaft*, Humboldt-Universität Berlin, Working Paper 8/05, Berlin 2005, p. 4, available at: http://whi-berlin.de/documents/whi-paper0805.pdf (on February 9, 2019).
257. Yet, it should also be emphasized that the distinctions between "culture" and "law" are sometimes perceived as vague. Thus, it is argued that the binding legal system is a *cultural* outcome; see e.g. L. Petrazycki, *Wstęp do nauki polityki prawa*, Warsaw 1968, p. 44.
258. See opinion of Advocate General Dutheillet de Lamothe in C-11/70, C-25/70, C-26/70, C-30/70, *Internationale Handelsgesellschaft mbH v. Einfuhr- und Vorratsstelle für Getreide und Futtermittel*, ECLI:EU:C:1970:100.
259. A.-M. Burley, W. Mattli, *Europe Before the Court: A Political Theory of Legal Integration*, International Organization Vol. 47/1993, p. 73.
260. C-26/62 *Van Gend en Loos*, ECLI:EU:C:1963:1.
261. C-6/64, *Costa*, ECLI:EU:C:1964:66, C-11/70 *Internationale Handelsgesellschaft*, ECLI:EU:C:1970:114.
262. A. Jaskulski, *Federalizm...*, s. 224.
263. See e.g. C-173/99 *The Queen v. Secretary of State for Trade and Industry, ex parte Broadcasting, Entertainment, Cinematographic and Theatre Union (BECTU)*, ECLI:EU:C:2001:356, C-303/98 *Sindicato de Médicos de Asistencia Pública (Simap) v. Conselleria de Sanidad y Consumo de la Generalidad Valenciana*, ECLI:EU:C:2000:528, C-131/04 *Robinson-Steele and Others*, ECLI:EU:C:2006:177.
264. F. Mayer, J. Palmowski, *European...*, p. 590; see also P. Craig, G. de Burca, *The European Court of Justice*, Oxford 1999, pp. 55 et seq.
265. J. Barcz, *Rzecz o przyszłości Europy*, Warsaw 2005, p. 74.

identity based on the EU law has become meaningful and identifiable, often in opposition to the egoistically perceived "national interest."[266]

The foundations of a legal community (on both the national and the EU level) are oriented on assuring standards of democracy. They ensure that the rule of law in which freedom, dignity and equality before the law are perceived as primary values.[267] Furthermore, the standards of justice and rightness should recognize the principles of social existence.[268] Finally, the legal community enables individuals to take part in the lawmaking procedures, both directly or indirectly, through their representatives (elected or, like NGOs, unelected).[269] Thus, in a well-functioning legal community, decisions of the public authority, deprived of arbitrariness are seen as a result of compromise and cooperation, are able to meet the needs of individuals and their communities.[270]

Certainly, there are doubts if the EU fulfills these requirements entirely. Nevertheless, there are strong foundations for assessing the EU as a legal community or a community of values.[271] The very existence of fundamental rights illustrates the particular nature of the EU law, as no other international organization provides for such a broad protection against its own acts.[272] This development and the association of European identity with the EU law have been especially noticeable since the 1990s.[273] At that time, the EU placed greater emphasis on social issues. Thus, as it is stressed out in the literature, the EU has established a "European ideal" in the "market ethic" which is oriented toward the individuals.[274] Furthermore, the Maastricht Treaty not only incorporated the notion of "European identity"[275] but also established the EU citizenship and, thus, created the "citizens Union"[276] which was an amplification of the

266. P. Cottrell, M. Nance, D. Trubek, *"Soft Law," "Hard Law" and European Integration: Toward a Theory of Hybridity*, New York 2005, p. 7.
267. H. Duszka-Jakimko, *Globalisation...*, p. 21.
268. *Ibid.*
269. S. Ripinsky, P. van den Bossche, *NGO Involvement in International Organizations*, London 2007, p. 10.
270. *Ibid.*, p. 14.
271. T. Biernat, *Wspólnota prawa. O osobliwościach systemu europejskiego*, Toruń 2002, pp. 49-53, Ł. Pikuła, *Aksjologia Unii Europejskiej w świetle źródeł, wykładni i instytucji*, Toruń 2015, pp. 17-23.
272. F. Mayer, J. Palmowski, *European...*, p. 589.
273. Still, first concepts of the European citizenship were designed in the 1970s. For more information see K. Kowalik-Bańczyk, *Komentarz do art. 20 Traktatu o funkcjonowaniu Unii Europejskiej* in: *Traktat o funkcjonowaniu Unii Europejskiej. Komentarz, t. I. Art. 1-89*, D. Miąsik, N. Półtorak, A. Wróbel (eds), Warsaw 2012, lex.pl.
274. G. Delanty, *Inventing Europe: Idea, Identity, Reality*, London 1995, p. 157, F. Jasiński, *Znaczenie Karty Praw Podstawowych UE dla tozsamości europejskiej* in: *Narody wobec Europy. Negocjowanie tozsamości*, J. Mikułowski-Pomorski (red.), Kraków 2002, pp. 125 et seq.
275. I.e., Treaty on European Union, Official Journal C 191, 29.7.1992; in the preamble it reads i.a.: "RESOLVED to implement a common foreign and security policy including the eventual framing of a common defense policy, which might in time lead to a common defense, thereby reinforcing the European identity and its independence in order to promote peace, security and progress in Europe and in the world"; this wording is repeated in the presently binding version of the TEU.
276. A. Kirsch, *Demokratie und Legitimation in der Europäischen Union*, Baden-Baden 2008, pp. 193-194, F. Sudre, *Droit européen et international des droits de l'homme*, Paris 2016, pp. 139-143, R. Kovar, D. Simon, *La citoyennété européenne*, Cahiers de droit européen Vol.

existing concept of integration between European nations.[277] The citizenship of the Union builds a special relationship between the individuals and the EU (based on rights and not any obligations), but it does not replace national citizenship.[278] The EU citizen, like any other person entitled to citizenship at the Member State level, can be described as "an individual who is a member of a democratic political community and is, based on its legal status, entitled to certain rights."[279] What is particularly omitted in the EU citizenship are identity-related concepts that require, for instance, a shared history, culture, religion or language .[280] At the beginning, the introduction of the EU citizenship was often perceived as purely symbolic[281] with rather weak prerogatives.[282] However, it appears that the CJEU has significantly amplified the scope of these rights.[283] Thereafter, the catalog of fundamental rights was set up in 2000 in the Charter of Fundamental Rights of the European Union (EUChFR),[284] which became legally binding[285] with the entry into force of the Treaty of Lisbon.[286] Presently, the EU

3-4/1993, p. 288. Previously, this concept could be noted in the judgments of the CJEU. See J.D. Mather, *The Court of Justice and the Union Citizen*, European Law Journal Vol. 11/2005, p. 723.

277. Which was established in the Treaty of Rome (Treaty establishing the European Economic Community) which referred to an "ever closer union among the peoples of Europe"; this invocation is also present in the preamble of the present wording of the TFEU. See also R. Putnam, *Społeczny kapitał a sukces instytucji* w: *Socjologia. Lektury*, P. Sztompka, M. Kucia (eds), Kraków 2005, p. 134.
278. According to Art. 9 of the TEU, in all its activities, the Union shall observe the principle of the equality of its citizens, who shall receive equal attention from its institutions, bodies, offices and agencies. Every national of a Member State shall be a citizen of the Union. Citizenship of the Union shall be additional to and not replace national citizenship.
279. S. Walter, *EU Citizens in the European Public Sphere*, Wiesbaden 2017, p. 34.
280. *Ibid.*, p. 34.
281. See e.g. D. Kostakopoulou, *Ideas, Norms and European Citizenship: Explaining Institutional Change*, Modern Law Review Vol. 68/2005, p. 234.
282. These prerogatives are currently established in Art. 20 (2) of the TFEU. Accordingly, citizens of the Union shall enjoy the rights and be subject to the duties provided for in the Treaties. They shall have, *inter alia*:
    (a) the right to move and reside freely within the territory of the Member States;
    (b) the right to vote and to stand as candidates in elections to the European Parliament and in municipal elections in their Member State of residence, under the same conditions as nationals of that state;
    (c) the right to enjoy, in the territory of a third country in which the Member State of which they are nationals is not represented, the protection of the diplomatic and consular authorities of any Member State on the same conditions as the nationals of that state;
    (d) the right to petition the European Parliament, to apply to the European Ombudsman, and to address the institutions and advisory bodies of the Union in any of the Treaty languages and to obtain a reply in the same language.
283. See e.g. C-224/98 *d'Hoop*, ECLI:EU:C:2002:432, C-148/02 *Garcia Avello*, ECLI:EU:C:2003:539, C-501/01 and C-31/02 *Silke Gaumain-Cerri and Maria Barth*, ECLI:EU:C:2004:413, C-499/06 *Nerkowska*, ECLI:EU:C:2008:300. Cf. also R. Grzeszczak, *Dwie narracje o obywatelskie unijnym—obywatel rynku i obywatel Unii Europejskiej* in: *Współczesne koncepcje ochrony wolności i praw podstawowych*, A. Bator, M. Jabłoński, M. Maciejewski, K. Wójtowicz (eds), Wrocław 2013, pp. 179 et seq.
284. Official Journal C 326, 26.10.2012.
285. I.e., for the institutions and bodies of the Union with due regard for the principle of subsidiarity and to the Member States only when they are implementing Union law (Art. 51 (1) of the EUChFR).
286. Official Journal C 206, 17.12.2007.

articulates its values in Article 2 of the TEU. They consist of human dignity, freedom, democracy, equality, the rule of law and respect for human rights including rights of persons belonging to minorities. These values are common to the Member States in a society in which pluralism, nondiscrimination, tolerance, justice, solidarity and equality between men and women prevail. Moreover, the preamble to the TEU confirms the attachment of Member States to the principle of liberty, democracy and respect for human rights and fundamental freedoms and the rule of law. The Treaty of Lisbon also introduced the express principle of participatory democracy at the EU level in Article 11 of the TEU. These provisions, which are legal basis for social participation in the EU, will be further discussed in the second chapter of this book.

In conclusion, it can be stated that the EU ensures the legal basis for shaping European civil society, which can be understood as a legal community. The EU is and always has been a complex structure where norms, land boundaries and economic factors change the qualities of civil society. Still, the EU law is in practice the cornerstone of building the identity between individuals and the EU as a whole. In this way, European civil society is an example of globalization in the traditional understanding of "civil society."[287] Furthermore, the outcomes of the European integration process do not result in a uniform legal system but they do influence the existing normative systems, penetrate national cultures and therefore require new patterns of behavior for participants in this constantly developing legal system. This opens complex and significant possibilities for activities of European civil society, which will be discussed in the following parts of this book.

[C] European Civil Society in the Theory of Integration

The dilemma of establishing European civil society and an active role of NGOs in this process have been a subject matter for analysis since the earliest theories of integration. Although this problem was named differently in the papers of the most acknowledged integrationists, it has always been obvious that an institutional integration has its limits and if the grassroot integration of the Member States societies does not follow, then the aims of the "European project" will not last.

The subsequent remarks concentrate on the views of four integration theories (neofunctionalism, constructivism, sociological approaches and multilevel governance) on European civil society and the role of NGOs.

[1] Neofunctionalism

Neofunctionalism emphasized the possibility of self-supporting social processes that start modestly, gain dynamics and may over time produce resounding outcomes for the integration procedure. It also draws attention to the relevance of subnational actors in

287. S. Peers, T. Hervey, J. Kenner, A. Ward, *The EU Charter of Fundamental Rights*, Baden-Baden 2014, p. 364.

this operation.[288] E. Hass, the founder of neofunctionalism in integration theory, perceived integration as a product of transactions across borders, European institutions and pluralist politics.[289] The process itself consisted of two stages. First of all, the "interest and values" of an emerging transnational society would be "defended by major groups involved in the process"[290] (like political parties, industrial associations, Member State governments and representatives of the civil society, in particular labor federations and trade unions). Then, the supranational organs of governance would possess "the formal attributes necessary to make them an agent of integration."[291] The full integration would be achieved if: (1) transnational activity and economic interdependence proceeded, revealing the potential both to reap joint gains and to deal with the negative externalities created by transnational activity, (2) European elites (public authorities and public actors, including NGOs as representatives of the civil society) were led to seek regional—rather than national—solutions to shared problems and (3) supranational organs of governance supplied rules (laws and procedures) which satisfied these needs.[292]

It can be seen that in this theory the emerging European, supranational power leads to changes in both expectations and behaviors of private actors (including NGOs) who are supposed to act at the transnational level in order to fulfill the anticipations of the civil society which, due to the common goals and interest with civil societies of other Member States, form a "transnational society"[293] which could be very well defined as European civil society. These goals were mainly orientated at cross-border transactions, involving exchange of goods, services, ideas, information or funds. Those who seek such transactions, experience the absence of European-level rules as a cost or an obstacle to the realization of greater gains.[294] Therefore, transnational transactions exert pro-integration pressure on both national governments and the EU institutions. That is one of the main reasons why a steadily increasing number of lobbying groups could be observed at the Communities' level throughout the 1960s and 1970s.[295]

As neofunctionalists predicted, the course of further integration will depend on the quotas of transnational exchange, the strength of the EU authority and, consequently, supranational lawmaking.[296] The empirical sphere of this theory consists of regular treaty revisions, regular extension of new competencies to the EU institutions and decision-making according to established legislative standards.[297] Furthermore,

288. T. Gehring, *Integrating Integration Theory. Neofunctionalism and International Regimes*, Florence 1995, p. 4.
289. P.J. Borkowski, *Polityczne teorie integracji międzynarodowej*, Warsaw 2007, p. 145, S. Konopacki, *Neofunkcjonalistyczna teoria integracji politycznej Ernsta Haasa i Leona Lindberga*, Studia Europejskie Vol. 3/1998, ss. 105 et seq., E. Fahley, *The Actors of Postnational Rule-Making*, London 2015, p. 12; cf. also A. Niemann, P. Schmitter, *Neofunctionalism* in: *European Integration Theory*, A. Wiener, Th. Diez (ed.), Oxford 2009, p. 47.
290. E. Jones, A. Menon, S. Weatherill, *Oxford Handbook of the European Union*, Oxford 2014, p. 74.
291. *Ibid.*, p. 76.
292. A. Arnull, D. Chalmers, *The Oxford Handbook of European Union Law*, Oxford 2015, p. 11.
293. *Ibid.*, p. 13.
294. E. Jones, A. Menon, S. Weatherill, *Oxford...*, p. 77.
295. S. Konopacki, *Neofunkcjonalistyczna...*, p. 107.
296. *Ibid.*, p. 111.
297. A. Arnull, D. Chalmers, *The Oxford...*, p. 114.

the course of integration cannot be restricted to narrowly understood "technical" participants or "low politics" areas of intergovernmental control.[298] A good mode of integration means that intergovernmental modes of governance should be always included and executed. In this regard, neofunctionalism demonstrates how and to what extent transnational bargaining and decision-making processes should be embedded in integration on the larger scale, including institutionalization of the supranational authority[299] which is provided with the means to cooperate with the supranational civil society.[300]

[2] Constructivism

In short, constructivists claim that social ideas and discourses, transferred both by governments and individual actors including NGOs, do matter for European integration.[301] The most important questions dealing with the integration process are formulated as to whether a European identity or public sphere exist and how strong they are. In this perspective, European integration is at its core a process of community building.[302] The outcome of this process would therefore mean establishing a form of European civil society. Communities are understood as groups or associations based on shared ideas—common identity, causal and normative beliefs, structures, etc.[303] As a result, over the years, community building and institutional integration have mutually influenced and reinforced one another.[304] Thus, the activity of civil society and NGOs influence the further integration process.

The main assumption of this concept is that the speed and depth of institutional integration depends on the actual strength of common European identity.[305] It is possible to reformulate this assumption to the statement that the integration is influenced by the process of developing collective European civil society. Weak European identity leads therefore to general resistance to further institutional integration. This statement may be seen as an aftermath of the works of K. Deutsch who stimulated compatible social values (together with mutual responsiveness) as essential conditions of functioning international communities.[306] Hence, integrated policy-making generates increased and frequent contacts which take place in a distinct, transnational environment structured by community norms.[307] These surroundings influence integration-friendly decisions that promote social learning processes (like imitation, persuasion and social influence). They can also transform identities, restructure discourses that aim at common meanings, values and beliefs.

298. E. Jones, A. Menon, S. Weatherill, *Oxford...*, p. 79.
299. Cf. B. Rosamond, *Theories of European Integration*, New York 2010, pp. 69-72.
300. E. Jones, A. Menon, S. Weatherill, *Oxford...*, p. 80.
301. P. Cottrell, M. Nance, D.M. Trubek, *"Soft...,"* pp. 11 et seq.
302. E. Jones, A. Menon, S. Weatherill, *Oxford...*, p. 92.
303. L. Woods, P. Watson, *Steiner & Woods EU Law*, Oxford 2014, p. 45.
304. P.J. Borkowski, *Polityczne...*, p. 176.
305. S. Konopacki, *Dylematy...*, p. 81.
306. K. Deutsch, *Nationalism...*, p. 77.
307. L. Woods, P. Watson, *Steiner...*, p. 47.

According to this theory, it is evident that thick identity is predominantly national and strongest at the mass level. It is a latent constraint on European integration, which becomes a manifest obstacle under conditions of mass politization and mobilization, for example during elections, campaigns or referenda on the EU treaties. In contrast, a thin, postnational identity based on liberal values and norms is compatible with and conducive to European integration. Its positive effects of European integration in general are most likely to materialize when the EU negotiations and policy-making take place at the elite and supranational level and remain insulated from mass politics.[308] This level of deliberation could be reached by NGOs operating, if possible, for the good of the European society as a whole.

NGOs can and should be a very significant factor in the transnational, European environment. There are numerous qualities that make them proper actors in this field, i.e.: (1) they possess the authority to act on behalf of a community which a particular organization identifies with, (2) they have a rather high legitimacy in which they perform, (3) their role is to encourage deliberation in the absence of external and political constraints.[309]

Of course, while this theory agrees with the assumption that ideas and discourses among not only states and institutional actors but also NSAs like NGOs do matter a great deal for further European integration, it lacks some crucial questions. There is no common meaning of "Europe" or to what extent the EU should integrate. Constructivism does not offer a definition of "European identity" and, consequently, "European civil society." The main opposition is between European, transnational identity and national identities which have a slightly unfavorable connotation, although in many papers they are seen as multiple, layered and nested.[310] This shifts the issue to how exclusive these multiple identities indeed are and how they can relate to each other. One interesting approach is presented by O. Waever who states that there is no harmonized vision of Europe or European community and there should not be any.[311] Instead, it is sufficient if these visions are compatible and included in the European project as a part of national identity. Thus, it seems that these visions could be transformed and performed in the deliberation processes by NGOs. It would be therefore understandable that in general preferences of the national actors performing on the EU level, they generally mirror their national constitutional traditions and ideas. Individuals that come from federally organized Member States are more likely to advocate supranational institutional solutions than unitary states.[312] S. Gstöhl argues[313] that the reluctance of Scandinavian counties in general and Switzerland to join the EU cannot be properly explained by solely economic costs or benefits but rather it should be analyzed in reference to their traditions of neutrality, direct democracy or ethnolinguistic cleavages in the Swiss case. As a result, the integration preferences are influenced by the ideational factors of both individual and state actors. Although this

308. A. Arnull, D. Chalmers, *The Oxford...*, p. 17.
309. *Ibid.*, p. 18.
310. L. Woods, P. Watson, *Steiner...*, p. 49.
311. P. Craig, G. de Burca, *The Evolution of EU Law*, Oxford 2011, p. 54.
312. *Ibid.*, p. 55.
313. E. Jones, A. Menon, S. Weatherill, *Oxford...*, p. 81.

theory helps to explain why some countries are more EU orientated than the other ones, it does not seem to have any explanations to the Euroscepticism which is an increasing tendency in these countries as well.

However, what is the highlight of this theory is that the more complex the EU and its law become, there is more need for including NSAs in decision- and policy-making processes. Accordingly, the EU cannot take a next step in its integration without shaping a stronger form of European civil society, which could be beneficial both for democratic and technocratic reasons.

[3] Sociological Approaches

One of the most recent tendencies in European integration theories is sociological perspectives. There is no common theory in this field, and the remarks mentioned below are some basic foundations for particular approaches.

Sociological theory followers view European integration as "grassroot" in contrast to the "top-down" logic. S. Hoffman explains this approach in short: "groups articulate preferences, governments aggregate them."[314] Politicians are therefore seen as solely "agents" of societal "principals" who seek interest group and electoral support by selecting policies that appeal to the best represented and most intensely expressed societal interests. Society is the basis for integration—EU obeys state control, but the states obey societal control.[315] NGOs are seen as agents who can and should explicate the needs and ideas of the grassroot civil society.

Recent sociological approaches analyze the foundations of European civil society in the media, public opinion, social mobility or cooperation programs between European cities.[316] This process is based on the perspective of "Europeanization" effect understood as a process "out-there" in European societies.[317] Sociological approaches, rather than advancing "bottom-up thinking" against the "top-down" perspective, analyze the spatial and interpretive context of action within the EU. Their novelty lies in posing questions about networks and "fields" of action within the EU integration. Consequently, they examine the perception of political arenas of activity by European actors, including NGOs.

Although these approaches are scattered, they provide one significant remark. European civil society cannot be shaped by the EU institutions themselves; the process of its development should be "grassroot." EU institutions cannot decide what is important for the civil society. Only when the individuals, including NGOs, are agreeable to conjointly take part in democratization of the EU, will this process will have chances for success.

314. A. Arnull, D. Chalmers, *The Oxford...*, p. 23.
315. E. Jones, A. Menon, S. Weatherill, *Oxford...*, p. 83.
316. L. Woods, P. Watson, *Steiner...*, p. 53.
317. *Ibid.*, p. 54.

[4] Multilevel Governance

Multilevel governance (MLG) does not explain why European integration happens and what its limits are.[318] It should be rather regarded as a middle-range approach for the day-to-day working of the EU in general.[319] It is perhaps one of the most acknowledged explanation to the processes taking place at the EU level.[320] Not only some European leaders have defined the EU as a multilevel governance structure[321] but also even the critics admit that the EU operates at several different administrative levels and exhibits features of "governance."[322]

The sole notion of "governance" is described as rules or practices of governing which generally approach power as exceeding or distinct from the centralized authority of the modern state.[323] In the White Paper on European Governance of 2001[324] (which will be thoroughly discussed in the second chapter) this term was defined as "rules, processes and behavior that affect the way in which powers are exercised at European level, particularly as regards openness, participation, accountability, effectiveness and coherence." The term multilevel governance, however, was introduced by G. Marks in the late 1980s to conceptualize and explain the evolving structure of EU policy after its reform, which was aimed to render the internal market compatible with the wider regional disparities resulting from Southern enlargement.[325] In his papers, G. Marks defined the new notion as "supranational, national, regional and local governments ... enmeshed in territorially overarching policy networks."[326] He then argued that while liberal intergovernmentalism could account for the 1988 decision to double the size of the European Communities' funds, the implementation of these funds gradually ended up escaping state control in many various ways. In order to ensure the effective use of the funds, governments (either willingly or reluctantly) agreed with the Commission to administrate them through partnership programs, comprising representatives of not only supranational actors (the Commission) but also regional and local agents.[327]

Based on the principle of partnership as one of the most substantial rules of integration, subnational parties (like local authorities) with the support of NSAs (including NGOs) were supposed to form alliances with supranational bodies, in order to circumvent and operate outside the competences of national governments. In this

318. In consequence, it is sometimes referred to as an "umbrella term." See R. Grzeszczak, *The Challenge of Good Governance: An Introduction* in: *Challenges of Good Governance in the European Union*, R. Grzeszcak (ed.), Baden-Baden 2016, p. 10.
319. A. Arnull, D. Chalmers, *The Oxford...*, p. 25, P.J. Borkowski, *Polityczne...*, p. 161, G. Peters, J. Pierre, *Governance Approaches* in: *European Integration...*, p. 95.
320. Cf. B. Rosamond, *Theories...*, pp. 109-112.
321. Cf. L. Hooghe, G. Marks, *Types of Multi-level Governance*, available at: https://core.ac.uk/download/files/153/6564108.pdf (on February 9, 2019), p. 4.
322. H. Enderlein, S. Walti, M. Zurn, *Handbook on Multi-level Governance*, Chaltesham 2012, p. 19.
323. This is why "good governance" means the elimination of an excessive administrative burdens or overregulation, R. Grzeszczak, *The Challenge...*, p. 13.
324. Communication from the Commission of 25 July 2001 "European governance—A white paper" [COM(2001) 428 final—Official Journal C 287, 12.10.2001].
325. G. Marks, L. Hooghe, *Multi-level Governance and European Integration*, London 2011, p. 55.
326. *Ibid.*, p. 57.
327. E. Jones, A. Menon, S. Weatherill, *Oxford...*, p. 90.

way, other forms of communication (e.g., autonomous Brussels representation offices) and pressure (e.g., taking part in pan-European lobbying groups) have been developed. It is important that the needs of subnational parties are expressed in a proper way. NGOs are responsible for transferring these needs on a European level. With NGOs operating in other Member States they could therefore establish the common views of European civil society.[328] What is more, the new channels of cooperation linking subnational and supranational actors could not be easily controlled by national governments, assuming a life of their own in order to promote interests and preferences often vastly diverging from those of national governments.[329]

According to the MLG theory, the EU is polycentric, states are not unitary and national governments are fragmented due to the loss of control to other actors (mostly nonstate) of different levels. The plurality of collective interests and actors is thus compatible with the pluralist conceptualization presented by neofunctionalism, as well as the statement that state and NSAs could form alliances with their counterparts in other Member States, transnational network potentially promoting the agenda and preferences of other supranational actors like the Commission.

In this approach, the EU still has a sui generis status. While it is much more than any international organization, it lacks proper government. Therefore, MLG focuses on different systems of governance involving transnational, national and subnational institutions and actors. The EU structure should be analyzed through negotiation processes and networks, instead of legal or constitutional frameworks. The capacity of governments to control the flows of goods, capital, services and people within and across their borders is declining. That proliferates with the emergence of various forms of governance.

NGOs play a very significant role in this perspective, being one of the "satellite organizations," among other NSAs, all of which are not formally part of the governmental framework.[330] They take part in sharing authority. This is the "supply side" of their role in MLG. However, they also participate in the "demand side" which can be explained as "simultaneous, diverse and contradictory forces that can be summarized in the clash between globalization, centralization and integration" and "localization, decentralization and fragmentation."[331] It means that NGOs are to be seen as the representatives of civil society in expressing their opinions in the decision and lawmaking processes.

The MLG theory raises important issues which are relevant to this book and the broader inclusion of NGOs at the EU level, leading to shaping European civil society. On the positive side, it brings a universal dissatisfaction of hierarchical policy-making authority and the monopoly of power by central governments and the EU institutions.[332] However, it heightens the risks on democratic accountability, meaning that with the spatial diffusion of power and control it makes political legitimacy harder to

328. *Ibid.*, p. 91.
329. G. Marks, L. Hooghe, *Multi-level...*, p. 113.
330. A. Arnull, D. Chalmers, *The Oxford...*, p. 44.
331. *Ibid.*, p. 46.
332. G. Marks, L. Hooghe, *Multi-level...*, p. 119.

pursue.[333] Given the inherent power asymmetry in multilevel relations and general preference of flexible, informal interaction above formal constraints, the deepening of this tendency may end up depriving the less powerful of the institutional guarantees aimed at controlling and offsetting the power of national powers.[334] It means that in contradiction to formal institutions, NGOs do not have the general advantage of being an institutional subject of hardly any democratic control. Moreover, the tendency of promoting informal capacity, the emerging role of NGOs and public–private networks may also serve as a strategy for various political interest to escape or bypass legal regulations.[335] NSAs players are not always neutral, and their participation does not imply equal influence. This raises concerns about the possibility of shaping an effective European civil society.

[D] Summary

The notion of "European civil society" is hard to define. Yet, basing on traditional philosophical theories and referring to the grounds of European identity, it can be characterized as an organized aggregate of individuals that manifests its will and advocates for the collective interest at the EU level. The basis of this approach can be most notably found in the general framework of the EU law which encompasses a vast scope of individual activities. By doing so and by providing democratic standards of openness, transparency and cooperation, it builds a common legal identity between individuals in different Member States.

The concept of European civil society is noticeable in various theories of integration. Even if this notion was named in different ways, it was obvious that grassroot organizations and civic movements were crucial for the eventual success of the "European project." This proves that European civil society is nothing contrived and it can, indeed, be a remedy to the dilemmas of the EU. The subsequent remarks of this book are not based on a single theory presented above. However, it should be mentioned that the main hypothesis can be attributed mainly to the MLG theory, as it is in some way mentioned in legal acts which will be further discussed in the subsequent chapters.[336] The concept of MLG is also significant for acknowledging NGOs as partners in the European governance in general.[337]

---

333. *Ibid.*, p. 120.
334. E. Jones, A. Menon, S. Weatherill, *Oxford...*, p. 91.
335. *Ibid.*, p. 92.
336. In fact, Ph. Schmitter, one of the main representatives of neofunctionalism, acknowledged the MLG theory as one of the main theories of integration. See J. Ruszkowski, *Problem wielopoziomowego zarządzania (Multi-level Governance) w Unii Europejskiej w świetle prakseologii I heurystyki* in: *Multi-legel Governance w Unii Europejskiej*, J. Ruszkowski, L. Wojnicz (eds), Szczecin 2013, p. 20.
337. Nevertheless, it should be emphasized that this theory has its drawbacks as well. It is sometimes argued that in practice it leads to *fuzzy governance* and *fuzzy accountability* (for more see J. Czaputowicz, *Wielopoziomowe zarządanie a deficyt demokracji w Unii Europejskiej* in: *Problem...*, p. 129). It is also argued that the MLG theory is rather an amalgam of theories than a single theory (A. Jordan, *The European Union: An Evolving System of Multi-level Governance... or Government?*, Policy & Politics Vol. 29/2001, pp. 201-202) and can even

§1.03 CONCLUSION: NGOs AND EUROPEAN CIVIL SOCIETY

At this point of analysis, it becomes clear that NGOs are an essential part of European civil society. What is more, if civil society at the EU level is to be further developed, it must be even more firmly based on NGOs involvement. NGOs are agents of citizens' interests at the national level, and their role at the supranational level, although not easily transmitted, is similar.[338] While it may sometimes raise some doubts, NGOs enjoy high levels of trust among Member States.[339] This credence can be transmitted to providing a better input and output legitimacy for the EU institutions[340] which, with regard the role of civil society, are also often jointly referred to as "throughput" legitimacy.[341]

As far as acting for the benefit of input legitimacy is concerned, it can be presumed that if NGOs have more opportunity to participate in the EU governance, they may act as a "transmission belt" between grassroot, national civil societies and an emerging European public sphere.[342] This transmission belt might operate in two directions. First, NGOs can give voice to citizens' concerns and channel them into the deliberative process of the EU. Second, they can make internal decision-making processes of the EU more transparent to the wider public and formulate technical issues in accessible terms.[343] In this way, they could provide means of transnational, EU structures of interest aggregation and representation. Therefore, NGOs could reassure that the decisions taken at the EU level are more accessible and understandable to the individuals.

NGOs could also provide a stronger output legitimacy for the EU institutions. As they often specialize in the EU-relevant spheres (e.g., environmental protection or

encourage corruption (D. Treisman, *Causes of Corruption: A Cross-National Study*, Journal of Public Economics Vol. 76/2000, pp. 399-457).

338. Nevertheless, it should be emphasized that some authors argue for a change in methodology while discussing democracy at the EU level. It follows that the EU is a "demoicracy"—a polity of multiple *demoi*—and has to be evaluated as such. For more see e.g. F. Cheneval, F. Schimmerfenning, *The Case for Demoicracy in the European Union*, Journal of Common Market Studies Vol. 51/2013, pp. 334-350, F. Wolkenstein, *Demoicracy, Transnational Partisanship and the EU*, Journal of Common Market Studies Vol. 2/2018, pp. 1-16.
339. F. Furtak, *Nichtregierungsorganisationen...*, p. 12.
340. Input legitimacy relates to the functioning rand machinery of an institution, e.g. how the procedures by which decisions are made and power are being exercised. Output legitimacy refers to the public assessment of the relevance and quality of the institution's performance. For more see e.g. V. Schmidt, *Democracy and Legitimacy in the European Union Revisited: Input, Output and "Throughput,"* Political Studies Vol. 61/2013, pp. 2-3.
341. The concept of "throughput" legitimacy depends on both input and output legitimacies. Moreover, it consists of governance processes with the people, analyzed in terms of their efficacy, accountability, transparency, inclusiveness and openness to interest consultation. In other words, "output" can be described as "for" the people, "input" as "by" and "of" the people and "throughput" as "with" the people. See also e.g. V.A. Schmidt, *Democracy and Legitimacy...*, pp. 2-22.
342. P. Nanz, J. Steffek, *Legitimation...*, pp. 69 et seq.
343. J. Steffek, P. Nanz *Emergent Patterns of Civil Society Participation in Global and European Governance* in: *Civil...*, p. 8.

consumer rights), they possess specialized knowledge[344] that could be used for the benefit of the EU law quality. Indeed, the EU institutions need "external" resources to improve various matters relevant to policy-making.[345] This tendency is obviously not unique only to the EU but is evident in other spheres of international governance. As it was observed, most IGOs have indeed adopted some (narrower or larger) means of cooperating with the representatives of the organized civil society.[346]

In fact, both of these opportunities interpenetrate as NGOs and European civil society can be of a great significance for diminishing the democratic deficit of the EU.[347] This issue can be defined as a structural remoteness between the EU institutions and the citizens of Member States.[348] This issue has basically been around since the beginning of European integration. It should be stated that this "connecting" function should be in theory primarily performed by the European Parliament (EP). Nevertheless, the Parliament itself suffers from the lack of social legitimacy.[349] Since the first general elections to the EP in 1979, participation has been constantly decreasing—from 62% in 1979 to 43% in 2009 and 2014.[350] This evidently proves the weakening confidence that the EP is capable of exerting rational influence and deliver proper democratic legitimacy on decision-making and lawmaking processes at the EU level.[351]

However, the problem of democratic deficit seems even more complex.[352] It appears that the instruments of party competition, elections and parliamentary representation, proven within the national framework, fall too short to democratically link decision within the multilayered system of the EU.[353] This means that the parliamentary control of the EP cannot fully develop due to an underdeveloped transnational

344. See also M. Menkes, *Governance gospodarczy—stadium prawnomiędzynarodowe*, Warsaw 2016, p. 47.
345. G. Randi, *Environmental Democracy and Law*, Groningen 2014, p. 26.
346. E. Szazi, *NGOs...*, p. 45.
347. Nevertheless, it should be observed that the dilemma of democratic deficit at the EU level is very complex. Some spheres of the EU law are specific, need more efficiency and, therefore, suffer from an even greater democratic deficit. This is the case of, e.g. undertaking actions during financial crises. However, such "undemocratic" (even though necessary) actions further undermine the trust in the EU democratic principles. See also V.A. Schmidt, *The Eurozone's Crisis of Democratic Legitimacy: Can the EU Rebuild Public Trust and Support for European Economic Integration?*, European Commission Discussion Paper 015/2015, available at: https://ec.europa.eu/info/sites/info/files/dp015_en.pdf (on February 11, 2019).
348. J. Steffek, P. Nanz, *Emergent...*, p. 9, A. Verhoeven, *The European Union in Search of a Democratic and Constitutional Theory*, The Hague 2002, pp. 60-62.
349. P. Huber, *Der Beitrag des Europäischen Parlaments zur demokratischen Legitimation der EU* in: *Die Europäische Demokratie in guter Vergassung?*, K. Hofmann, K. Naumann (eds), Baden-Baden 2010, p. 35.
350. See: http://www.europarl.europa.eu/elections2014-results/en/turnout.html (on February 9, 2019).
351. F. Cheneval, F. Schimmelfennig, *The Case...*, p. 335.
352. For further information see also O. Hołub-Sniadach, *Obywatel Unii Europejskiej w europejskiej przestrzeni publicznej* in: *Ochrona praw obywatelek I obywateli Unii Europejskiej. 20 lat—osiągnięcia i wyzwania na przyszłość*, G. Baranowska, A. Bodnar, A. Gliszczyńska-Grabias (eds), Warsaw 2015, pp. 82-84.
353. Cf. L. Vesnic-Alujevic, R. Castro Nacarino, *The EU and Its Democratic Deficit: Problems and (Possible) Solutions*, European View Vol. 11/2012, pp. 63 et seq., A. Follesdal, S. Hix, *Why There Is a Democratic Deficit in the European Union. A Response to Majone and Moravsik*, Journal of Common Market Studies Vol. 44/2006, pp. 533 et seq.

public.[354] As such, the EU not only suffers from democratic deficit understood in the strict sense (which could theoretically be remedied by further institutional reforms) but also is caught in a fundamental dilemma of democracy inextricably linked with the European integration. Some authors propose a review of the federative development as a way out of this dilemma,[355] whereas others draw attention to the so-called postnational constellation[356] or the importance of rethinking the EU institutional system to the post-parliamentary age, which would require new forms of democracy.[357] Nonetheless, civil society organizations and participation are considered the "royal road" to democratic self-determination[358] and the "symbiosis of civil society and Europe" is even elevated to the central political or legal theme of "cosmopolitan Europe."[359]

The EU, like any other intergovernmental organizations, along with their Member States seem to incur the mistake when they tried to monopolize the public sphere.[360] If NGOs and other social movements can be acknowledged as legitimate voices of plural civil society and, thus, contribute to the general democratization of the public sphere, then they can also play an analogous role at the international and the EU level.[361] This is why the emphasis of democratic standards (openness, transparency and cooperation) in the EU system and their "tools" are so relevant.

Yet, it should be remembered that some authors claim that the EU, like any other intergovernmental organization, cannot be really democratic.[362] These arguments are based on an assumption that even though the EU provides protection of fundamental rights, they can be effectively performed only at the national and not the supranational level. They also deepen the line of reasoning presented above concerning the lack of strong historical or national basis for the collective identity. Thus, as it is emphasized, the EU is deficient in any acceptable threshold of democracy.[363]

There is no doubt, however, that the EU is unique as it provides measures of bringing its institutions closer to the citizens. Even though these instruments are limited, often do not function properly and are subject to criticism,[364] their mere

354. B. Kohler-Koch, *De-Mystification...*, p. 18.
355. J. Anderson, *Regional Integration and Democracy*, Lanham 1999, p. 42.
356. J. Habermas, *The Crisis...*, p. 20.
357. J. Anderson, *Regional...*, p. 43.
358. F. Furtak, *Nichtregierungsorganisationen...*, p. 22.
359. J. Steffek, P. Nanz, *Emergent...*, p. 11.
360. M. Musiał-Karg, *Instytucje demokracji bezpośredniej w procesie integracji europejskiej—od referendum ogólnonarodowego do europejskiej inicjatywy obywatelskiej*, Rocznik Integracji Europejskiej Vol. 6/2012, p. 203.
361. Cf. B. Kohler-Koch, *Regieren mit der europäischen Zivilgesellschaft* in: *Die Entzauberung*, p. 20.
362. R. Dahl, *On Democracy*, Yale 1999, p. 152; cf. S. Bredt, *Prospects and Limits of Democratic Governance in the EU*, European Law Journal Vol. 17/2011, pp. 35 et seq. Cf. also A.J. Menéndez, *The European Democratic Challenge: The Forging of a Supranational Volonté Générale*, European Law Journal Vol. 3/2009, pp. 279-283.
363. R. Dahl, *On...*, p. 156.
364. It is sometimes argued that these instruments "are only designated to stimulate the involvement of active citizens and groups in some precise procedures and not to enhance the general level of civic consciousness and participation." See I. De Jesus Butler, *Non-governmental Organisation Participation in the EU Law-Making Process: The Example of Social Non-governmental Organisations at the Commission, Parliament and Council*, European Law Review Vol. 14/2008, p. 562. See also S. Smismans, *European Civil Society: Institutional*

existence proves that the EU attempts at enabling European civil society in the decision-making procedures.[365] This is why NGOs and European civil society have significant amount of space for further development.

Interests and the Complexity of a Multi-level Polity in: *Democracy and the Role of Associations: Political, Structural and Social Contextsm*, S. Rossleutshcer (ed.), Abingdon 2005, p. 503.

365. Or even at electing the EU highest officials. For the EU *Spitzenkandidat* model see e.g. F. Pothier, *Why Europe Needs US-Style Primaries*, available at: https://www.politico.eu/article/europe-needs-us-style-primaries-spitzenkandidaten/ (on February 9, 2019). See also P. Guasti, *The Politics of Inclusion: Comparing the Contribution of Civil Society Actors to EU Legitimacy* in: *The EU Economic and Social Model in the Global Crisis. Interdisciplinary Perspectives*, D. Schiek (ed.), Abingdon 2013, pp. 141 et seq.

CHAPTER 2

NGOs in the EU Constitutional System

Having discussed the general notions of "NGOs" and "European civil society," as well as the legal measures existing in the selected IGOs to include the representatives of civil society in their systems, the observations made in the first chapter can be transposed to the EU constitutional system at this point of analysis. Therefore, the following remarks will concentrate on three issues. First, the role of NGOs in European integration will be analyzed from a historical perspective. These observations will be based mainly on various EU documents which emphasized the capacity of social and civil partners in policy and lawmaking, as well as, indirectly, in diminishing the democratic deficit of the EU institutions. Second, the Treaty basis for social participation in the EU system will be discussed. These provisions range from general ones, which establish fundamental rights and the common rules of the EU, to those explicitly naming the prerogatives of civil society and "representative associations." Third, the actual arenas of NGO participation in the EU system will be examined. They can overall be divided into the EU institutions which were founded specifically to present the voice of civil society at the EU level and various types of organizations which are present in Brussels and pursue their own policy.

As a result, the following chapter will provide a general insight into the position of NGOs in the EU constitutional system[1] which can be later deepened with regard to specific means of collaboration and tools of influencing the EU lawmaking.

1. For the purposes of this book the notion "EU constitutional system" is understood as the whole legal system which "constitutes" the basic governance structure of the EU. As the EU itself does not have a constitution, the term "EU constitutional system" is often replaced in the doctrine with notions that are, in fact, identical in scope, e.g. with "EU institutional system" or simply with "EU system"; cf. e.g. D. Schiek, *Economic and Social Integration. The Challenge for EU Constitutional Law*, Cheltenham 2013, pp. 53 et seq. For the grounds of using the term "constitutionalization" in relation to the EU see also N. Bernard, *Multilevel Governance in the European Union*, The Hague 2002, pp. 242 et seq.

§2.01 A HISTORICAL REVIEW

The importance of involving civil society has been present since the early days of European integration. Still, the explicit role of NGOs had not been articulated until the emergence of the social dimension of the EU policy. Even then, their position was in the shadow of trade unions. Only later was the value of NGO participation acknowledged in other EU-related spheres as well. Nevertheless, this affirmation did not easily translate into "hard" legal measures attributed to the representatives of civil society.

[A] The Significance of "Social Partners" in the History of European Integration

Since 1957 the EU has been centered around the "institutional triangle," i.e. the Commission, the Council and the EP.[2] At the same stage of European integration, the European Communities' system has provided a unique institution that was supposed to be an arena for representing the views of civil society in the legislative procedures—the Economic and Social Committee.[3] Still, the Communities did not then envisage any other significant position for NGOs. They were not officially included anywhere outside the scope of the Economic and Social Committee. This has changed gradually since the 1990s. There were a couple of reasons for this development. First of all, the democratic deficit became very distressing, even despite the introduction of direct elections to the EP is the late 1970s.[4] Thus, the EU institutions remained remote from the nations of Member States.[5] Second, the Maastricht Treaty[6] established the "social dimension" of the Community.[7] As a result, NGOs as key actors operating in the area of social issues at the local level were to be included in this new dimension and make it more effective.[8] They were one of the "social partners," understood as organizations representing the interest of European workers and employers.[9] However, the possible role of NGOs was limited to a narrow range of subject matters. Also, their inclusion was more a declaration than a legal postulate as it was proposed only in the nonbinding acts of law. This position is also visible in Declaration 23 to the Maastricht Treaty on cooperation with charitable associations. It reads that the Conference stresses the importance in pursuing the objectives of Article 117 of the Treaty establishing the European Community, of cooperation between the latter and charitable associations and foundations as institutions responsible for social welfare establishments and services. Third, it became more evident that NGOs can strongly influence the EU institutions. This led to the

2. D. Ferri, *Participation in EU Governance: A "Multi-Level" Perspective and a "Multifold" Approach* in: *Citizen Participation in Multi-level Democracies*, C. Fraenkel-Haeberle, S. Kropp, F. Palermo, K.-P. Sommermann (eds), Leiden 2015, p. 336.
3. Which will be closely presented in the ensuing paragraphs of this chapter.
4. A. Warleigh, *"Europeanizing" Civil Society: NGOs as Agents of Political Socialization*, Journal of Common Market Studies Vol. 39/2001, p. 621.
5. D. Ferri, *Participation...*, p. 337.
6. Official Journal C 191, 29.7.1992.
7. R. Sanchez Salgado, *Europeanizing...*, p. 35.
8. E. Szazi, *NGOs...*, p. 27.
9. D. Ferri, *Participation...*, p. 340.

discovery of civil society and its agents as not only a source of legitimization but also a basis for administrative reform.[10]

The process of broader acknowledgment of the position of NGOs and other social partners began in 1993 when the Commission of the European Communities published the Green Paper on European Social Policy.[11] Its main purpose was to propose new channels of cooperation in the light of the entry into force of the TEU which opened new possibilities for the Community action in the social field.[12] The Green Paper stressed that the role of the Union in relation to the common policy is to mobilize the efforts of the Member States and civil society. It pointed out that the social dialogue in the field of social policy should be strengthened and broadened, assuming the willingness of the partners.[13] This could be achieved by: (1) new possibilities for European-wide collective bargaining; (2) broadening of the agenda on issues which will influence the future of industry: health and safety at the workplace, demographic trends including the role of older workers, social protection, equal opportunities, integration of migrant workers, preventing and combating exclusion, measures to facilitate the free movement of workers (mutual recognition of qualifications, transnational training, portability of occupational pensions, etc.); and (3) possible partnership with other bodies on some issues (e.g., with "NGOs on equal opportunities and the integration of disabled persons in the labors market, and with NGOs and local authorities on exclusion").[14]

These recommendations were later generally confirmed in the Commission's White Paper on European Social Policy of 1994, entitled "A Way Forwards for the Union."[15] The role of NGOs, alongside community bodies, local authorities, the social and economic partners and the private, as well as the public sector, is underlined in the sphere of developing a broader partnership in order to increase efficiency and

10. One example of this process is the outcome of C-106/96 *United Kingdom of Great Britain and Northern Ireland v. Commission of the European Communities*, ECLI:EU:C:1998:218, in which the CJEU annulled a Commission Decision to fund 86 European projects seeking to overcome social exclusion. To avoid other condemnations, the Commission decided to suspend temporarily several funding projects which lacked a clear legal basis. This caused serious problems for many European NGOs—not only did they get project funding from the EU, but also many of them depended on EU funding to keep their organizational structure alive. This crisis motivated the social NGOs to join forces, specifically under the coordination of the Platform of European Social NGOs. Moreover, an alliance with the development NGOs and human rights NGOs was made. This brought the NGO sector to the attention of MEPs, Council representatives, national governments and parts of the Commission that had previously neglected its role. By the end of the year 1998 most budget sources were unblocked. Still, the financial position of the NGOs remained uncertain in the following years, given the absence of strong legal basis. The Platform, therefore, linked the funding crises to a request for a solid institutionalization of civil dialogue. This included a Treaty basis and a list of accredited NGOs to be compiled by the Commission, on the basis of which it would structure its consolidation. For more see S. Smismans, *European...*, p. 63. See also V. Cuesta Lopez, *The Lisbon Treaty's Provisions on Democratic Principles: A Legal Framework for Participatory Democracy*, European Public Law Vol. 1/2010, p. 123.
11. Available at: http://bit.do/ehaqn (on February 9, 2019).
12. T. Grosse, *Dialog Społeczny a dialog w Unii Europejskiej*, Trzeci Sektor Vol. 4/2006, p. 21.
13. See points 20-21 of the Green Paper of 1993.
14. See point 21 of the Green Paper of 1993.
15. Available at: http://aei.pitt.edu/1118/1/social_policy_white_paper_COM_94_333_A.pdf (on February 9, 2019).

transparency not only in granting of knowledge and expertise but also in funding decisions.[16] The latter one was especially important in the PHARE programs (Poland and Hungary: Assistance for Restructuring their Economies) and the reformed Social Fund. The role of NGOs in the first aspect was to include support of regional development to promote an integrated approach to industrial reconversion support for an autonomous civil society, structures for social dialogue, and the promotion of SMEs (small and medium enterprises) and local job creation programs.[17]

Moreover, according to the White Paper of 1994, the position of NGOs can also be used in the integration policy of migrants. The Commission stated that it would make a periodic evaluation of integration projects and projects against racism carried out by NGOs, in order to develop guidelines which could be used at national, regional or local level.[18]

In 1996 the Commission's Directorate-General responsible for social policy presented the concept of "civil dialogue" to plead the increased interaction with civil society organizations.[19] It was stated that while the social dialogue had been strongly institutionalized since the Maastricht Treaty, the dialogue with other associations in the social policy arena lacked formal recognition and well-established structures.[20] However, in dealing with such issues as gender, youth, social exclusion, disability and racism, the EU intervened in policy sectors, in which NGOs played a crucial role. Therefore, the consultation and involvement of these organizations in decision-making and lawmaking became a very important issue. As a result, the Directorate-General responsible for social policy founded an ally with the EP's Committee of Social and Employment Affairs.[21] Their common initiative was the European Social Policy Forum. It was first held in March 1996 bringing together over 1,000 representatives of NGOs dealing with social issues.[22]

The role of social partners was also highlighted in 1997 in the "Social Chapter"[23] of the Amsterdam Treaty.[24] It emphasized that the Commission facilitates dialogue between the social partners and consults them on the content of proposals in the social field before presenting them and that the social partners are involved throughout the legislative process, and this allows them to play a substantial role both in drafting and

16. See point 21 of the White Paper of 1994.
17. See point 46 of the White Paper of 1994.
18. See point 30 of the White Paper of 1994.
19. S. Smismans, *European...*, p. 61.
20. S. Smismans, *"Civil society" in European Institutional Discourses*, Paper presented to the ECPR Joint Sessions on March 22-27, 2002, Torino, available at: http://bit.do/ehatT (on February 9, 2019).
21. For more see: http://www.europarl.europa.eu/committees/pl/empl/home.html (on February 9, 2019).
22. S. Smismans, *European Civil Society: Shaped by Discourses and Institutional Interests*, European Law Journal Vol. 9/2003, p. 483.
23. I.e., the modified version of the Protocol on Social Policy and the Agreement on Social Policy which was initially annexed to the Treaty of Maastricht. In contrast to the Protocol, the Agreement was signed by 11 Member States (without the UK). Both texts were almost identical and they proposed a constitutionally recognized role for the social partners in the legislative process.
24. Official Journal C 191, 29.7.1992.

implementing new measures. It was concluded that "indeed each Member State can leave it to the social partners to implement the new directives."[25]

Moreover, Declaration 38 of the Amsterdam Treaty recognized the significance of the voluntary sector, stating that the Community "will encourage the European dimension of voluntary organizations with particular emphasis on the exchange of information and experiences." This was followed by the Communication from the Commission on "Promoting the role of voluntary organizations and foundations in Europe"[26] which was drafted by its Directorate-General for social policy and the Directorate-General for social economy, small and medium-sized enterprises and tourism. In this paper, the role of NGOs was, for the first time, extended to the spheres of democratization. Voluntary organizations are precisely distinguished in this document from cooperatives and mutual societies.[27] Trade unions, employers' organizations, religious congregations and political parties are also excluded from the scope of the Communication. The role of "voluntary organizations" is to foster a sense of solidarity and citizenship and to provide the essential underpinnings of European democracy.[28] These functions were said to be more vital "in the light of the challenges now facing the European Community."[29] The Communication, however, does not provide any explanation of how the "voluntary organization" could actively take part in the lawmaking at the EU level. It mainly provides a survey of the voluntary sector in the Member States and presents the problems and challenges it is facing rather than looking at to the role of NGOs in a multilevel policy and providing a framework for the further institutionalization of "civil dialogue" at the European level.[30] The Communication had a very limited impact—it did not receive any support from other institutions, and it provoked rather limited reaction from the representatives of the civil society.[31]

As it can be seen, the abovementioned documents recognized NGOs as important actors at the EU level but their actual role in the EU governance was not specifically formulated.[32] Social NGOs were in the center of attention as they were to become crucial players in developing European Social Policy.

Nonetheless, these acts of law, although nonbinding, were the ground for establishing more formalized relations between NGOs and the EU institutions that will be deeply examined in the successive chapter. However, at this stage of analysis it is

25. For the full text see: http://eur-lex.europa.eu/legal-content/PL/TXT/?uri=URISERV:a14000 (on February 9, 2019).
26. Communication from the Commission of 6 June 1997 on promoting the role of voluntary organisations and foundations in Europe, COM(1997) 241 final.
27. According to the Commission, while "mutual societies" are enterprises providing life and nonlife insurance services, complementary social security schemes and small value services of social nature (see: https://ec.europa.eu/growth/sectors/social-economy/mutual-societies_pl); "co-operatives" are autonomous associations of persons united to meet common economic, social and cultural goals (see: https://ec.europa.eu/growth/sectors/social-economy/cooperatives_pl, available on February 9, 2019).
28. Point 7.1 of the Communication of 6 June 1997.
29. Point 9 of the Communication of 6 June 1997.
30. Point 9.7 of the Communication of 6 June 1997.
31. E. Lundberg, *Changing Balance: The Participation and Role of Voluntary Organisations in the Swedish Policy Process*, Scandinavian Political Studies Vol. 35/2012, p. 370.
32. S. Smismans, *European...*, p. 487.

worth mentioning that the Commission was the first institution that noticed the need for steady cooperation with NGOs. In the Discussion Paper from the year 2000,[33] it pointed out the value of NGOs in developing stronger European Governance. Consequently, the Paper specified five considerations for the rationale behind the cooperation between the Commission and NGOs:

(1) "Belonging to an association provides opportunity for citizens to participate actively in new ways other than or in addition to involvement in political parties or trade unions. Increasingly NGOs are recognized as a significant component of civil society and as providing valuable support for democratic system of government." Although "the decision-making process in the EU is first and foremost legitimized by the elected representatives of the European people, NGOs can make a contribution fostering a more participatory democracy both within the European Union and beyond."
(2) NGOs have the ability to reach out to the poorest and most disadvantaged and to provide for those not sufficiently heard through other channels.
(3) NGOs provide the EU with expert input.
(4) NGOs can manage, monitor and elevate projects financed by the EU.
(5) NGOs contribute to the European integration. By encouraging national NGOs to work together, the European NGO networks make an important contribution to the formation of a European public opinion.

As it can be noted, these considerations are rather an expression of the already presented merits of involving the representatives of civil society at the EU level than being innovative in their approach. Still, it is commendable that these benefits were officially presented in an EU document.

[B] The Main Postulates of the White Paper on European Governance

The shape of relations between NGOs and other representatives of the organized civil society with the EU institutions was later discussed by the Commission in 2001 in its White Paper on European Governance.[34] The Paper's main goal is to make EU's decision-making and lawmaking processes "more transparent and less top-down."[35] The White Paper states that "policies should no longer be decided at the top and the legitimacy of the EU should lie with the participation of its citizens." Europe, it declares, faces a "real paradox": on the one hand, the Europeans want it to find solutions confronting our societies and, on the other hand, people increasingly distrust institutions and politics or are simply not interested in them.[36] The problem is that

33. The Discussion Paper *The Commission and NGOs: building a stronger partnership* adapted on January 18, 2000 (COM(2000) 11).
34. Communication from the Commission of 25.7.2001 "European governance—A white paper" COM(2001) 428 final—Official Journal C 287 of 12.10.2001.
35. See "Proposals of change" in the White Paper of 2001.
36. See "Executive Summary" in the White Paper of 2001.

despite having delivered "fifty years of stability, peace and economic prosperity," many Europeans "feel alienated from the Union's work" and "do not understand who takes the decisions that affect them."[37] The White Paper continues that "Europeans expect the Union to take the lead in seizing the opportunities of globalization for economic and human development."[38] As a result, the challenge for the Commission is "to open up policy-making to make it more inclusive and accountable."[39] A better use of powers should connect the EU more closely to its citizens. According to the Commission, the impetus for giving the EU greater powers comes from below—from ordinary Europeans who, rather than looking to their own elected governments to act on their behalf, now "expect the Union to take the lead in dealing with the major problems of our times."[40] Thus, the White Paper proposes opening up the policy-making process to get more people and organizations involved in shaping and delivering the EU policy which would promote greater openness, accountability and responsibility for all those involved. Accordingly, this should help people to see how Member States, by acting together within the Union, are able to tackle their concerns more effectively.[41]

To attain these goals, the Commission proposes five principles of good governance:[42]

(1) "Openness"—the institutions should work in a more open manner. Together with the Member States, they should actively communicate about what the EU does and the decisions it takes. They should use the language that is accessible and understandable for the general public.
(2) "Participation"—the quality, relevance and effectiveness of the EU policies depend on ensuring wide participation throughout the policy chain—from conception to implementation. Participation crucially depends on central governments following an inclusive approach when developing and implementing EU policies.
(3) "Accountability"—roles in the legislative and executive processes need to be clearer. Each of the EU Institutions must explain and take responsibility for what it does in Europe. There is also a need for greater clarity and responsibility from Member States and all those involved in developing and implementing EU policy at whatever level.
(4) "Effectiveness"—policies must be effective and timely, delivering what is needed on the basis of clear objectives, an evaluation of future impact and, where available, past experience. Effectiveness also depends on implementing EU policies in a proportionate manner and on taking decisions at the most appropriate level.

37. See "Why reform European governance" in the White Paper of 2001.
38. See "Executive Summary" in the White Paper of 2001.
39. See "Why reform European governance" in the White Paper of 2001.
40. See "Refocused policies and institutions" in the White Paper of 2001.
41. See "Executive Summary" in the White Paper of 2001.
42. See "Principles of good governance" in the White Paper of 2001.

(5) "Coherence"—policies and action must be coherent and easily understood. The need for coherence in the Union is increasing as the range of tasks has grown. Coherence requires political leadership and a strong responsibility on the part of the Institutions to ensure a consistent approach within a complex system.

Although all of these principles interpenetrate, "participation" and "openness" (understood jointly as grounds for "Better Regulation")[43] are most relevant for the purposes of this book as they concentrate on stronger cooperation with civil society. At the same time, the White Paper focuses on a broader meaning of civil society while the previous documents applied mainly to "social partners." As it was acknowledged in the doctrine, the White Paper on European Governance, although in a rather limited range, "does not only include NGOs but also trade unions and employers' organizations, professional associations, charities, grassroots organizations, organizations that involve citizens in local and municipal life with a particular contribution from churches and religious communities."[44] In the part entitled "involvement of civil society," the Paper states that "European political parties are an important factor in European integration and contribute to European awareness and voicing the concerns of citizens" and even that "the involvement of national parliaments and their specialized European affairs committees ... could also be encouraged."[45] However, the proposal of defining civil society in the White Paper is not free from ambiguity.[46] On the one hand, it refers to the existence of nearly 700 ad hoc consultation bodies, yet on the other hand, it does not explain which of them should be involved in consultation processes on a daily basis. Thus, there seems to be a tension between the general tendency to define civil society very widely (including in this notion not only NGOs but almost every consultative forum at the EU level) and the proposals to institutionalize contacts with it.

One of the main statements of the White Paper is that participation depends on people being able to take part in public debate.[47] To make it happen, the general public needs to be more actively informed about European issues. Therefore, the Commission calls on national and local networks and authorities in order to present information which is adapted to the concerns of European citizens. Accordingly, the Commission considers that civil society plays an important role in the development of the Community (EU) policies.[48] It continues to encourage the activities of NGOs, the social partners and civil society in general. That is why the Commission declared to set up an online database of civil society organizations by the end of 2001.[49] Moreover, the White Paper

43. See "Proposals for change" in the White Paper of 2001.
44. S. Smismans, *European...*, p. 490.
45. See "More effective and transparent consultation at the heart of EU policy-shaping" in the White Paper of 2001.
46. S. Smismans, *European...*, p. 491.
47. J.D. Giuliani, *La bonne gouvernance*, available at: http://www.jd-giuliani.eu/fr/article/cat-4/33_La-bonne-gouvernance.html.
48. See "Confidence in expert advice" in the White Paper of 2001.
49. See "Involving civil society" in the White Paper of 2001.

announces a list of standards considering consultations between the Commission and the representatives of civil society. In this field, the document's intention is to emphasize the need of producing an overview of existing consultative structures and of consulted NGOs in order to increase transparency and to formulate a code of conduct that sets minimum standards for consultation (meaning what to consult on, when, whom and how to consult).[50] The minimum standards were issued as a follow-up to the White Paper and will be presented in the third chapter of this book.

A very interesting aspect of the White Paper are the recommendations for organizational change in the EU. The document suggests that other EU institutions, apart from the Commission, should reinterpret their position toward the organized civil society. Thus, a reinforced culture of consultation and dialogue should be developed—a culture which is adopted by all EU institutions and which associates particularly the EP in the consultative process, given its role in representing the citizens. The EP should play a prominent role, for instance, by reinforcing its use of public hearings.[51] Also, a very noticeable critique toward the functioning of the Economic and Social Committee can be seen in the White Paper. The document states that this institution, created to be a voice of the organized civil society on the EU level, must play a role in developing a new relationship between the institutions and grassroot organizations. Although there is no detailed recommendation on how to manage it, the White Paper suggests that the role of the Economic and Social Committee should be reconsidered—like the Committee of the Regions, it should be more active by developing opinions and explanatory reports in order to help shape policies at a much earlier stage.[52] The White Paper also requests the Member State to make an effort to promote the exchange of information and views between the European and the national, regional and local authorities and the organizations of the civil society.[53]

As far as the Commission is concerned, the document advocates that a genuine participation is based on partnership. This should result in the Commission's commitment for additional consultations compared to the minimum standards. In return, the arrangements would prompt civil society organizations to tighten up their internal structure, furnish guarantees of openness and representativeness, and prove their capacity to relay information or lead debates in Member States.[54] Thus, the Commission sees NGOs as proper partners in the decision and lawmaking processes but at the same time urges that they should seek more democratic legitimacy in the area they work in. In other words, NGOs representing civil society should apply themselves the principles of good governance as a presentation of their responsibility and openness.[55] Only in this way, once they achieve a desirable level of transparency and equality in

50. See also S. Smismans, *European...*, p. 491.
51. See "More effective and transparent consultation at the heart of EU policy-shaping" in the White Paper of 2001.
52. See "Involving civil society" in the White Paper of 2001.
53. *Ibid.*
54. See "More effective and transparent consultation at the heart of EU policy-shaping" in the White Paper of 2001.
55. See "Better involvement and more openness" in the White Paper of 2001.

their actions, can they be a significant player in diminishing the democratic deficit of the EU.

There seems to be a practical problem with the approach presented by the Commission in the White Paper. It strongly emphasizes the important role played worldwide by NGOs in development policy, but at the same time, it omits to mention organizations active at the EU level in the fields of environment, social and consumer protection, human rights and culture in the widest senses.[56] This is a quite relevant issue as NGOs are actually most active in these spheres and, arguably, have the strongest democratic legitimacy (and expertise) in these areas. This omission is perhaps due to the lack of clear distinction between "social dialogue" and "civil dialogue." The White Paper, in line with the previously discussed documents, seems to focus mainly on the first scope of cooperation.

The White Paper suggests that the partnership between the Commission and NGOs should not concentrate solely on the EU level but also at the regional, local and international level. Therefore, the Commission should ensure that the regional and local knowledge and conditions are taken into account when developing policy proposals. For this purpose, it should organize a systemic dialogue with European and national associations of regional and local governments, while respecting national constitutional and administrative arrangements.[57] Moreover, the Commission is supposed to improve the dialogue with governmental and nongovernmental actors of third countries when developing policy proposals with an international dimension.

These arrangements for participation can be seen as quite detailed, but at the same time, it must be kept in mind that the White Paper is in its core a declarative and nonbinding act of law—it does not easily translate to the actual rights of the organizations in the EU legislative procedures. What can also be seen is that the White Paper concentrates on two overlapping agendas. The first one can be described as a political program of institutional reform that aims at making the EU decision-making more open, participatory and accountable to European citizens.[58] The second one is a piece of information and public relations strategy designed to counter growing public indifference toward the EU and boost the legitimacy of its institutions.[59] Three major flaws of this agenda were discussed in the doctrine.

First, it was pointed out that the EU was not designated to "reach out" to the public at large. As a result, democratic engagement might be one of the Commission's aims, but it was never something it was actually expected to do.[60] As it was argued "dirigisme and distance from the public were embodied in the very fabric of the European Community."[61] Second, it was observed that while democratizing the EU and drawing citizens more closely into the decision-making and lawmaking procedures are important goals for legitimizing the EU and its institutions, the Commission's approach

56. S. Smismans, *European...*, p. 491.
57. See "Reaching out to citizens through regional and local democracy" in the White Paper of 2001.
58. C. Shore, *"European Governance" or Governality? The European Commission and the Future of Democratic Governments*, European Law Journal Vol. 17/2011, p. 291.
59. *Ibid.*
60. *Ibid.*, p. 292.
61. P. Lamy, cited in G. Ross, *Jacques Delors and European Integration*, Cambridge 1995, p. 194.

to this issue was to recast these problems as technical matters to be solved through information and communication policy.[62] Hence, this dilemma was seen as a quite easily solvable problem to be rectified through the use of PR or marketing techniques of information campaigns designed to "educate" the public about what the EU is doing for them.[63] Third, it was asserted that in the White Paper the Commission treated civil society almost like a *deus ex machina* for all kinds of problems. At the same time, the concept of widening the EU governance to grassroot organizations did not go beyond mere recommendations or vague proposals.[64]

Although the second and the third criticisms may appear reasonable,[65] the first one does not seem to be justified. The Commission, as an executive power in the EU system, is obviously authorized to propose solutions to the democratic deficit. As it was discussed in the first chapter, this deficit is not something that can be treated as a normal phenomenon and it rebounds negatively on the functioning of the EU. The EU, through the Commission, should, therefore, *reach out* to a large public, meaning to European civil society.

Some appealing remarks concerning these controversies come from the opinion of the Economic and Social Committee considering the White Paper.[66] This document stresses the role of developing European identity and, consequently, of European civil society. This process cannot be *artificial* and must be grounded on solid, common values. In the Committee's regard, deficits in the EU's political objectives and measures have been responsible for people's skepticism of the European integration.[67] Thus, the EU should avoid creating too high expectations, which cannot be met, thus generating mistrust and harming its credibility. A European identity can emerge but will not unless the common values shared by its citizens are translated into effective EU policies and tangible benefits across-the-board. The opinion states that Europeans wish for Europe that is stable, with a social profile, a sound economic performance, which respects the environment, creating healthy living and working conditions and which ensures that basic goods and services are available to all members of society at a fair price.[68] These

62. C. Shore, *"European Governance"...*, p. 293. Thus, it was also argued that the White Paper did not, in fact, define the concept of governance in any meaningful way. See R. Grzeszczak, *The Concept and Practice of Good Governance in the European Union*, World Academy of Science, Engineering and Technology. International Journal of Social, Behavioral, Economic, Business and Industrial Engineering Vol. 9/2015, p. 450.
63. T. Börzel, Th. Rosse, *Governance Without a State: Can It Work?*, Regulation & Governance Vol. 4/2010, p. 134.
64. J.R. Grote, B. Gbikpi, *Participation and Metagovernance: The White Paper of the EU Commission* in: *Participatory Governance. Political and Societal Implications*, J.R. Grote, B. Gbikpi (eds), Cham 2002, p. 272.
65. Even though, obviously, White Paper is by nature a nonbinding act of law and takes a rather inconclusive approach to the development of the EU politics. Yet, the critique in this scope seems justified as the White Paper was not followed by any concrete legal proposals concerning the positions of civil society actors in the EU governance.
66. C. Shore, *'Government Without Statehood?' Anthropological Perspectives on Governance and Sovereignty in the European Union*, European Law Journal Vol. 6/2006, p. 113.
67. Opinion of the Economic and Social Committee on "European Governance—a White Paper" (COM(2001) 428 final), Official Journal C 125, 27.5.2002, point 2.2.
68. Opinion of the Economic..., point 2.3., see also A. Maurer, D. Kietz, A. Crespy, *Der Europäische Verfassungkonvent und die „Zivilgesellschaft"...*, p. 201.

comprehensive objectives, which also include respect for the Member States' cultures, must be recognized as common values, defined—and, if need be, extended—and pursued as such. Only then will it be possible for Europe's citizens to recognize the benefit of a common European identity and declare their support for it.

In addition, the Committee reasonably mentions that apart from the five principles of good governance discussed in the White Paper (i.e., "openness," "participation," "accountability," "effectiveness" and "coherence"), "subsidiarity" is the basic and the most important principle in this field. The Committee reiterates that subsidiarity is not merely a principle of administrative technique and distribution of powers but the expression of a certain conception of the individual, its freedom, its responsibilities and the society it lives in.[69] Thus, society would work better if citizens had the feeling that the decisions concerning them are taken at the most appropriate level.[70] This level is not only determined by territorial criteria (European, national, regional and local) but also by functional criteria according to specific expertise (public authorities, economic community, social partners and other NGOs).[71] In other words, deciding who is to be involved in decision-making ("functional, horizontal subsidiarity") must be taken into account alongside "territorial (vertical) subsidiarity."[72] These two spheres guarantee greater responsiveness to people's concerns and greater efficiency.

As it can be noticed, the White Paper brought the issue of governance and involvement of civil society at the EU level to the center of discussion on the future of Europe. This single observation lets this document to be assessed in a positive way.

[C] Further Developments

The White Paper on European Governance is often seen as the hallmark of the debates concerning the inclusion of NGOs and European civil society at the EU level. It illustrates the EU's aspirations and desires to experiment with new types of governance mechanisms and NGOs involvement in deliberation, debates and policy-making processes at the EU level.[73]

As it will be discussed in the succeeding chapters of this book, since the publication of the White Paper on European Governance there have been various legal

69. Opinion of the Economic..., point 3.2, see also B. Kohler-Koch, Ch. Quittkat, *De-Mystification...*, p. 122.
70. Cf. J. Maśnicki, *Good Governance Through Better Regulation. Looking for the Impact Analysis to the Proportionality Principle* in: *Challenges of Good Governance in the European Union*, R. Grzeszczak (ed.), Baden-Baden 2016, pp. 214-217.
71. Opinion of the Economic..., point 3.2, see also R. Balme, D. Chabenet, *European Governance and Democracy: Power and Protest in the EU*, Plymouth 2008, p. 104, N. Kerschen, M. Sweeney, *Participation Democracy and European Governance in Social Policy*, Working paper series FVeP 26, p. 4, available at: http://bit.do/ehauV (on February 9, 2019).
72. Opinion of the Economic..., point 3.2.
73. J. Almer, M. Rotkirch, *European Governance—An Overview of the Commission's Agenda for Reform*, Stockholm 2004, p. 32, available at: http://www.sieps.se/en/publications/2004/european-governance-an-overview-of-the-commissions-agenda-for-reform-20041u/Sieps-2004-1.pdf? (on February 9, 2019).

improvements concerning NGO participation at the EU level. They include both procedural norms (referring especially to the lobbying aspect of NGOs activity) and proposals that could facilitate the third sector enterprises in transnational relations. However, since the White Paper, there has been no systemic document of any EU institution that stressed out the role of NGOs in declining the democratic deficit or that extensively proposed the inclusion of the representatives of civil society in the decision and lawmaking processes at the EU level. Further developments in these aspects were focused on the broadly understood issue of democratization. Thus, the focal points of analysis and institutional proposals were the improvements of the democratic legitimacy and accountability of the institutions and the EU as a whole or determining the powers and roles of institutional actors and national parliaments.[74]

A good example is that in 2001, a few months after issuing the White Paper on European Governance, Declaration No. 23 on the future of the EU annexed to the Treaty of Nice[75] addressed the democratic challenge of the EU and acknowledged "the need to improve and to monitor the democratic legitimacy and transparency of the Union and its institutions, in order to bring them closer to the citizens of the Member States." As it can be seen, this is a general conclusion which does not mention how or by whom this *need to improve the democratic legitimacy* could be achieved.

It is puzzling that the role of NGOs, after releasing the White Paper on European Governance, was not strongly emphasized in the Laeken Declaration from December 2001.[76] This document was supposed to be the foundation for the future Constitution for Europe and was adopted committing the EU to greater democracy, transparency and efficiency.[77] This was to be achieved by a convention, which was intended to comprise the main "stakeholders," in order to examine questions about the future direction of the EU.[78] Accordingly, the Convention was said to be "a major boost to the further development of democracy in Europe as for the first time citizens and their representatives will participate in the decision-making on the future shape of the European system of governments, in the spirit of a more open and participative governance."[79] The Declaration pointed out that "in order for the debate to be broadly based and involve all citizens, a forum will be opened for organizations representing civil society (the social partners, the business world, nongovernmental organizations, academia, etc.). It will take the work of a structured network of organizations receiving regular information on the Convention's proceedings."[80] As it can be seen, the meaning of "organizations representing civil society" is quite odd as it combines both NGOs and

74. B A. Armstrong, *Rediscovering Civil Society: The European Union and the White Paper on Governance*, European Law Journal Vol. 8/2002, p. 103.
75. Official Journal C 080, 10.3.2001.
76. Available at: http://www.consilium.europa.eu/en/european-council/conclusions/pdf-1993-2003/european-council-meeting-in-laeken--presidency-conclusions-14-15-december-2001/ (on February 9, 2019).
77. R. Sanchez Salgado, *Europeanizing...*, p. 15. T. Grosse, *Komisja Europejska wobec trzeciego sektora na przykładzie strategii lizbońskiej*, Trzeci Sektor Vol. 20/2009, p. 34, F. Furtak, *Nichtregierungsorganisationen...*, p. 112.
78. T. Grosse, *Komisja...*, p. 35.
79. Opinion of the Economic..., point 1.2.
80. See point I.3 of the Laeken Declaration.

the business organizations—organisms which come from two separate worlds and most often have contradictory interests. Also, although the Declaration underlines the need of democratization, it does not repeat the need of deepening the dialogue with NGOs or of any other representatives of the civil society in decision-making or lawmaking procedures at the EU level on a daily basis.

Nevertheless, the draft for the Treaty Establishing a Constitution for Europe[81] set fundamental grounds for elevating the role of European civil society (and its representatives, including NGOs) at the EU level:

- Article I-46 (which is now—after the Treaty of Lisbon—repeated in Article 11 of the TEU),
- Article I-47 entitled "The social partners and autonomous social dialogue" which reads that the European Union recognizes and promotes the role of the social partners at Union level, taking into account the diversity of national systems; it shall facilitate dialogue between the social partners, respecting their autonomy (which was later adopted in a slightly modified manner in Article 152 of the TFEU).

The Constitution for Europe also replicated the previously binding provisions concerning the role of the civil society, meaning Article I-49 (1)[82] which reads that in order to promote good governance and ensure the participation of civil society, the Union institutions, offices and agencies shall conduct their work as openly as possible. This regulation is now repeated in Article 15 (1) of the TFEU.

After these developments, the need for conducting a regular dialogue with NGOs was rather suggested than strongly advocated for. For instance, in the Commission's strategy entitled "Europe 2020"[83] it was outlined only that "all national, regional and local authorities should implement the partnership, closely associating parliaments, as well as social partners and representatives of civil society, contributing to the elaboration of national reform programmes and to its implementation."[84] Additionally, the role of NGOs or civil society in general was not accentuated in the White Paper on the

81. Available at: https://europa.eu/european-union/sites/europaeu/files/docs/body/treaty_establishing_a_constitution_for_europe_en.pdf (on February 9, 2019).
82. Previous Art. 255 of the Treaty establishing the European Community.
83. I.e., Communication from the Commission of 3.3.2010 COM(2010) 2020—"Europe 2002. A strategy form smart, sustainable and inclusive growth." This document sets goals to be achieved by the EU economy by 2020 as follows:

    - 75% of the population aged 20-64 should be employed.
    - 3% of the EU's GDP should be invested in R&D.
    - The "20/20/20" climate/energy targets should be met (including an increase to 30% of emissions reduction if the conditions are right).
    - The share of early school leavers should be under 10% and at least 40% of the younger generation should have a tertiary degree.
    - 20 million less people should be at risk of poverty.

84. See Europe 2002..., p. 27. This "consultative" and vague approach to civil society was also used in, e.g. the Council's "Renewed EU Sustainable Development Strategy" of 2006 (10917/06) (see paras. 32, 43) or the Commission's EU Citizenship Report 2010 "Dismantling the obstacles to EU citizens' rights" COM(2010) 602 final (pp. 3, 21).

Future of Europe of 2017[85] which presented five possible scenarios for further EU integration.[86] Even though a couple of months later a special report (yet unofficial) on the need of "reaching out to the citizens" was issued,[87] it did not change the primary impression that the Commission somewhat neglected the possibility of encouraging civil society at the EU level.[88]

Consequently, since the entry into force of the Treaty of Lisbon, there have been no further proposals for Treaty reforms concerning civil society (and NGOs) participation at the EU level. Nonetheless, individual institutions adopted respective provisions concerning their relations with the representatives of civil society or—more broadly speaking—with groups of interests. This technocratic approach can be perceived as insufficient. The omission (or lack of proper mentioning) of the role of NGOs in current developments concerning the democratic deficit should be seen as a major issue in the debate about the future of the EU.

[D] Summary

The issue of involving NGOs and enabling civil society at the EU level has been noticeably present in the considerations of the EU institutions for quite some time. The emergence of NGOs as proper partners in lawmaking and promoting European values was primarily an outcome of the new competences attributed to the EU. The new "social dimension" of the Union and the establishment of "social dialogue" led to the recognition of trade unions and NGOs as they represent the employees. Afterwards, the need of conducting a regular dialogue with the representatives of civil society was also recognized in other dimensions. Thus, the notion of "civil dialogue" was deployed into various EU documents. Still, there seems to be a distinctive difference between "social dialogue" and "civil dialogue." It is noted in the literature that while the actors in the first one accomplish specific functions in the decision-making, the intention of the latter one is only to ensure that the views of NGOs are taken into account by the EU legislators.[89]

The White Paper on European Governance of 2001 remains the most specific EU document on reasons, means and implications of engaging NGOs and other representatives of civil society at the EU level. Even though it raised some controversies in the

85. European Commission COM(2017) 2025 of 1.3.2017.
86. Without going into details, the presented scenarios were entitled as follows: (1) Carrying on, (2) Nothing but the Single Market, (3) Those who want more do more, (4) Doing less more efficiently, (5) Doing much more together.
87. Reaching out to the EU citizens: A new opportunity. "About us, with us, for us." A report by L. Van den Brande, Special Adviser to the President of the European Commission, J.-C. Juncker, October 2017, available at: https://ec.europa.eu/commission/sites/beta-political/files/reaching-out-to-citizens-report_en.pdf.
88. See e.g. K. Aiginger, *Juncker's missing scenario: Empower the member states*, available at: http://www.euractiv.com/section/future-eu/opinion/junckers-missing-scenario-empower-the-member-states/, T. King, *Juncker's White Paper: More Style than Substance*, available at: https://www.politico.eu/article/junckers-white-paper-more-style-than-substance/ (on February 9, 2019).
89. D. Obradovic, *Civil Society and the Social Dialogue in European Governance*, Yearbook of European Law Vol. 24/2005, pp. 322 et seq.

literature, it still brought the issue of the need for expanding consultation obligations and empowering civil society with certain participatory tools to the EU agenda. Sadly, this nonbinding document was not followed by any further "hard" legal provisions. Still, the Treaty of Lisbon introduced norms that at the first sight seem as strongly authorizing NGOs at the EU level. These provisions, among others, will become the center of analysis in the following part of this chapter.

§2.02 TREATY BASIS FOR SOCIAL PARTICIPATION IN THE EU

The ensuing paragraphs will focus on the Treaty basis for social participation at the EU level. Accordingly, the norms discussed further include the already mentioned new provisions of Article 11 of the TEU and Article 152 of the TFEU, introduced by the Treaty of Lisbon. These rules may be perceived as "specific" as they directly refer to "representative associations" and "social partners." However, the legal foundations of the need of involving NGOs at the EU level can be found in more general Treaty provisions as well. They particularly invoke the common grounds for democracy, the rule of law and freedom of assembly and freedom of association.

Obviously, the catalog of the Treaty basis for social participation at the EU level is open, and proper regulations could also be sought in other general principles and norms of primary law. In addition to the listed treaty provisions, one could, for example, indicate the general principle of subsidiarity, which in the traditional sense provides the basis for the development of civil society.[90] Nevertheless, the EU understanding of this principle is based in particular on the division of tasks between the EU institutions and the Member States, and concerns the scope of EU legislation, both as regards the subject matter of the regulation and its nature.[91] Therefore, the principle of subsidiarity will not be discussed further in the context of the topic of this book.

[A] Basic Values

The basis for social participation at the EU level is first and foremost envisaged in Article 2 of the TEU. It states that the Union is founded on the values of respect for human dignity, freedom, democracy, equality, the rule of law and respect for human rights, including the rights of persons belonging to minorities. These values are

90. Cf. P. Wilczyński, *Pomocniczość jako zasada udziału podmiotów niepublicznych w realizacji zadań administracji publicznej*, Acta Universitatis Lodziensis. Folia Iuridica Vol. 69/2009, pp. 125 et seq.
91. I.e., according to Art. 5 (3) of the TEU, under the principle of subsidiarity, in areas which do not fall within its exclusive competence, the Union shall act only if and in so far as the objectives of the proposed action cannot be sufficiently achieved by the Member States, either at central level or at regional and local level, but can rather, by reason of the scale or effects of the proposed action, be better achieved at Union level. The institutions of the Union shall apply the principle of subsidiarity as laid down in the Protocol on the application of the principles of subsidiarity and proportionality. National parliaments ensure compliance with the principle of subsidiarity in accordance with the procedure set out in that Protocol. For more see e.g. J. Barcik, A. Wentkowska, *Prawo Unii Europejskiej*, Warsaw 2014, p. 246.

common to the Member States in a society in which pluralism, nondiscrimination, tolerance, justice, solidarity and equality between women and men prevail. As it can be seen, democracy and the rule of law are included as foundational principles of the EU, even though the Treaty does not provide for their definition. These two qualities are the most crucial components of Article 2 of the TEU in the context of this book.

At elementary level, democracy as a value means that the law is an outcome of open discussion with respect to fundamental rights of all citizens.[92] The latter part of this description means that the citizens are able to demand the protection of their rights and liberties not only from the public institutions but also from other individuals.[93] This also means that they should have an effective access to justice and be able to exercise their fundamental civil rights, including freedom of association. Thus, democracy as a value creates legal environment for a "participative individual."[94] The rule of law can be perceived as an overlapping principle, even though it is rather difficult to construe it in detail.[95] Still, there is no doubt that the rule of law in the TEU sets a legal restriction which constraints not only the EU institutions[96] but also authorities at the national level and ensures that the EU law is secure and effective.[97] In other words, the rule of law can be encapsulated in a statement that only when the institutions are effectively held accountable, which guarantees the protection of individual freedom and rights, a genuine democracy is possible. This, in turn, ensures the necessary conditions for the development of a free and active civil society.[98] To attain this, the rule of law provides that the actions of all authorities remain transparent[99] and means of participation are attributed to individuals and their organizations.[100]

Such understanding of the discussed values is shared by the EU institutions. For instance, the CJEU sees access to the EU documents as a direct tool of ensuring

92. S. Freiberg, *Nowy traktat o Unii Europejskiej*, Warsaw 2015, p. 3.
93. *Ibid.*
94. P. Pszczółkowski, *Jednostka partycypatywna i jej prawa* in: *Ochrona praw jednostki*, B. Drzewiecka, K. Malinowska, P. Pszczółkowski, A. Siejka (eds), Warsaw 2003, p. 10.
95. R. Baratta, *Rule of Law "Dialogues" Within the EU: A Legal Assessment*, Hague Journal on the Rule of Law Vol. 8/2016, p. 358.
96. Which is referred to as an "internal dimension" of the rule of law at the EU level. See L. Pech, *Rule of Law as a Guiding Principle of the European Union's External Action*, The Hague 2012, pp. 9-10.
97. R. Baratta, *Rule...*, pp. 358-359. In addition, the Commission recently calls for a broader involvement of civil society in the debate on the state of the rule of law in the EU. See, to this extent, European Commission Press release of 3.4.2019 – Rule of Law: The Commission opens a debate to strengthen the rule of law in the EU.
98. D. Mineshima, *The Rule of Law and EU Expansion*, *Liverpool Law Review* Vol. 24/2002, p. 77. See also O. Burlyuk, *Variations in EU External Policies as a Virtue: EU Rule of Law Promotion in the Neighbourhood*, Journal of Common Market Studies Vol. 53/2015, p. 518.
99. See e.g. D. Curtin, H. Hofman, J. Mendes, *Constitutionalising EU Executive Rule-Making Procedures: A Research Agenda*, European Law Journal Vol. 19/2013, p. 9, R. Leal-Arcas, *Essential Elements of the Rule of Law Concept in the EU*, Queen Mary University of London, School of Law Legal Studies Research Paper No. 180/2014, p. 5, available at: http://bit.ly/2lrpszc (on February 9, 2019).
100. Cf. J. Mendes, *Delegated and Implementing Rule Making: Proceduralisation and Constitutional Design*, European Law Journal Vol. 19/2013, p. 39.

democratic standards and the rule of law at the EU level.[101] This instrument of executing the principles of democracy and the rule of law by NGOs, among others, will be discussed in the following chapters of this book. Nevertheless, it should also be remembered that the standards of democracy and the rule of law set out in Article 2 of the TEU are required not only at the EU level but also at the national level. Thus, the Commission distinguishes a safe civil society, operating in legal surroundings without excessive restraints (including financial), as one of the elements of the rule of law.[102] In case of compromising these standards, a Member State may be subject to the procedure determining a clear risk of a serious breach of the values referred to in Article 2 (Article 7 (1) of the TEU)[103] or the existence of a serious and persistent breach of the values referred to in Article 2 (Article 7 (2) of the TEU).[104] This, in consequence, can lead to the suspension of certain rights deriving from the application of the Treaties of the Member State in question, including the voting rights of the representative of the government of that Member State in the Council (Article 7 (3) of the TEU).[105]

The rule of law and democracy, together with other standards referred to in Article 2 of the TEU, especially those invoking respect for human rights, freedom, pluralism and tolerance also imply that individuals should be able to freely associate and assembly. These freedoms are expressly provided in other Treaty norms.

[B] Freedom of Assembly and Association

In the light of the prior remarks, the right to participate in the EU democratic life can be recognized as a fundamental right.[106] What should be also highlighted is the fact that this participation can (and sometimes should) be performed through the representatives of the civil society (in particular NGOs), for instance in consultations conducted by the EU institutions. These requirements match the standards of the EU as a legal

101. See, to this extent, e.g. C-41/00 P *Interporc Im- und Export Gmbh*, ECLI:EU:C:2003:125, paras. 38-39, 41.
102. See Proposal for a Council Decision on the determination of a clear risk of a serious breach by the Republic of Poland of the rule of law, COM(2017) 835 final, para. 69; cf. also W. Sadurski, *How Democracy Dies (in Poland): A Case Study of Anti-Constitutional Populist Backsliding*, Sydney Law School Legal Studies Research Paper No. 18/01, pp. 47-49, available at: http://ssrn.com/abstract=3103491 (on February 9, 2019).
103. On a reasoned proposal by one-third of the Member States, by the European Parliament or by the European Commission, the Council, acting by a majority of four-fifths of its members after obtaining the consent of the European Parliament, may determine that there is a clear risk of a serious breach by a Member State of the values referred to in Art. 2. Before making such a determination, the Council shall hear the Member State in question and may address recommendations to it, acting in accordance with the same procedure.
    The Council shall regularly verify that the grounds on which such a determination was made continue to apply.
104. The European Council, acting by unanimity on a proposal by one-third of the Member States or by the Commission and after obtaining the consent of the European Parliament, may determine the existence of a serious and persistent breach by a Member State of the values referred to in Art. 2, after inviting the Member State in question to submit its observations.
105. See also A. Sikora, *Sankcje finansowe w razie niewykonania wyroków Trybunału Sprawiedliwości Unii Europejskiej*, Warsaw 2011, p. 311.
106. J. Barcz, F. Jasiński, A. Łazowski, K. Podstawa, *Fundamental Rights Protection in the European Union*, Warsaw 2009, p. 22.

community. Hence, freedom of assembly and of association, seen as one of the general rules of the EU law, becomes of interest at this point of the analysis. This freedom is ensured in both the EU Charter of Fundamental Rights[107] (EUChFR) and the ECHR. This distinction is important due to the fact that the EU has not yet acceded to the ECHR (on the basis of the opinion 2/13 of the CJEU).[108] However, according to Article 6 (3) of the TEU Fundamental rights, as guaranteed by the European Convention for the Protection of Human Rights and Fundamental Freedoms and as they result from the constitutional traditions common to the Member States shall constitute general principles of the Union's law.

According to Article 12 (1) of the EUChFR, everyone has the right to freedom of peaceful assembly and freedom of association at all levels, in particular in political and civic matters, which implies the right of everyone to form and to join trade unions for the protection of his or her interests. According to Article 11 (1) of the ECHR, everyone has the right to freedom of peaceful assembly and freedom of association with others, including the right to form and join trade unions for the protection of his interests. In the second paragraph of this article, it is stated that no restrictions shall be placed on the exercise of these rights other than such which are prescribed by law and are necessary in a democratic society in the interests of national security or public safety, for the prevention of disorder or crime, for the prevention of health or morals or the protection of the rights and freedoms of others. This Article shall not prevent the imposition of lawful restrictions on the exercise of these rights by members of the armed forces, the police or of administration of the state.

Both acts of law recognize the freedom of association[109] in a generic and a specific way. The generic way means that the cited provisions enable individuals to gather and collectively articulate, promote, defend and advocate for those interest that they have in common.[110] The recognition of this freedom by all public authorities and its persistent performance by the society in general are crucial for the purpose of establishing genuine democracy and ensuring that, once achieved, it remains healthy.[111] The specific way is related to political matters, trade unions and civic matters. The latter one tends to honor the role of NGOs.[112] The distinction with trade unions, made in the ECHR, may appear unfortunate, since they include some of the oldest NGOs.[113]

---

107. Official Journal C 326, 26.10.2012.
108. ECLI:EU:C:2014:2454.
109. Which is also sometimes referred to as "associative democracy" or "associationalism." These concepts make a central normative claim that individual liberty and human welfare are both best served when as many of the affairs of the society as possible are managed by voluntary and democratically self-governing associations. For more see P. Hirst, *Associative Democracy. New Forms of Economic and Social Governance*, Oxford 1994, p. 19.
110. M. Eliott, R. Thomas, *Public Law*, Oxford 2014, p. 4.
111. J. McBride, *International Law and Jurisprudence in Support of Civil Society* in: *Enabling Civil Society: Practical Aspects of Freedom of Association*, Public Interest Law Initiative, New York 2003, p. 22, available at: http://www.pilnet.org/public-interest-law-resources/30-enabling-civil-society-practical-aspects-of-freedom-of.html (on February 9, 2019).
112. A. Kirsch, *Demokratie...*, p. 33.
113. D. Kornobis-Romanowska, *Europejska Konwencja Praw Człowieka w systemie prawa Wspólnot Europejskich*, Warsaw 2001, p. 109.

The foregoing observations do not solve the problem of a possible collision of the freedom of association with other fundamental rights.[114] According to the CJEU, the principle of freedom of association which is enshrined in Article 11 of the ECHR and stems from the constitutional traditions common to Member States is one of the fundamental rights protected in the EU legal order.[115] Nevertheless, this principle is not absolute. Restrictions may be imposed, for legitimate reasons, on the exercise of freedom of association, provided that they do not constitute, with regard to the aim pursued, disproportionate and unreasonable interference undermining the very substance of that right.[116] The CJEU has evaluated the correlations and possible derogations of freedom of association (and of assembly) in order to restrict or exclude the application of competition rules and free movement rules. It also dealt with the cases of collisions of freedom of association and other fundamental rights like freedom of expression.

For instance, in C-112/00 *Schmidberger*[117] the Austrian state argued that ecological activists blocking the motorway[118] were exercising their right to freedom of peaceful

114. As a side note, it should be observed that at the national level the full exercise of the freedom of assembly and of association often raise concerns and, thus, face some debatable legal obstacles. This is the case of the recent proposal of the French *La loi "anti-casseur"* of 2019 *(Proposition de loi visant à renforcer et garantir le maintien de l'ordre public lors des manifestations)*, available at: http://www.assemblee-nationale.fr/15/ta/ta0226.asp (on February 9, 2019).
115. See e.g. C-415/93 *Bosman*, ECLI:EU:C:1995:463, par. 79, C-235/92 P *Montecatini v. Commission*, ECLI:EU:C:1999:362, para. 137.
116. See e.g. C-5/88 *Wachauf*, ECLI:EU:C:1989:321, para. 18, C-292/97 *Karisson and Others*, ECLI:EU:C:2000:202, para. 45. See also J. Meyer, *Charta der Grundrechte der Europäischen Union*, Baden-Baden 2014, p. 285.
117. ECLI:EU:C:2003:333.
118. According to the file in the main proceedings, on May 15, 1998, the Transitforum Austria Tirol, an association "to protect the biosphere in the Alpine region," gave notice to the Bezirkshauptmannschaft Innsbruck (Innsbruck provincial government) of a demonstration to be held from 11.00 on Friday June 12, 1998 to 15.00 on Saturday June 13, 1998 on the Brenner motorway (A13), resulting in the fact that motorway was closed to all traffic on the section from the Europabrücke service area to the Schönberg toll station (Austria). On the same day, the chairman of that association gave a press conference following which the Austrian and German media disseminated information concerning the closure of the Brenner motorway. The German and Austrian motoring organizations were also notified, and they too offered practical information to motorists, advising them in particular to avoid that motorway during the period in question. On May 21, 1998, the Bezirkshauptmannschaft requested the Sicherheitsdirektion für Tirol (Directorate of security for Tyrol) to provide instructions concerning the proposed demonstration. On June 3, 1998, the Sicherheitsdirektor issued an order that it was not to be banned. On June 10, 1998, there was a meeting of members of various local authorities in order to ensure that the demonstration would be free of trouble. Considering that that demonstration was lawful as a matter of Austrian law, the Bezirkshauptmannschaft decided not to ban it, but it did not consider whether its decision might infringe Community (EU) law. The demonstration took place at the stated place and time. Consequently, heavy goods vehicles which should have used the Brenner motorway were immobilized from 09.00 on Friday June 12, 1998. The motorway was reopened to traffic on Saturday June 13, 1998 at approximately 15.30, subject to the prohibition on the movement of lorries in excess of 7.5 tons during certain hours on Saturdays and Sundays applicable under Austrian legislation. Schmidberger was an international transport undertaking based at Rot an der Rot (Germany). Its main activity was the transport of timber from Germany to Italy and steel from Italy to Germany. Its vehicles generally used the Brenner motorway for that purpose. Schmidberger brought an action before the Landesgericht Innsbruck (Innsbruck Regional Court, Austria) seeking damages against the

assembly as well as freedom of expression. The CJEU recognized that freedom of assembly and of expression constitute general principles of the EU law. Therefore, there is a need to reconcile the requirements of the protection of fundamental rights in the Community (the EU) with those arising from a fundamental freedom enshrined in the Treaty and, more particularly, the question of the respective scope of freedom of expression and freedom of assembly guaranteed by Articles 10[119] and 11 of the ECHR and of the free movements of goods, where the former is relied upon as justification for a restriction of the latter one. As a result, the application of the proportionality test proved to be beneficial to the Austrian state. It was not held liable for authorizing its citizens to exercise their freedom of assembly.[120] Although there is an obvious positive outcome of the case implicitly for the organized civil society and to freedom of assembly in general, the reasoning of the Court met partial disapproval. The most problematic part of the judgment is that despite the seemingly deferential attitude toward the autonomy of activists in defining the objectives and the goals of their demonstration, the Court insisted on the fact that the activists manifested an opinion which they considered to be of importance to the society.[121] The CJEU also held that the purpose of the demonstration was not to restrict trade of any particular goods or coming from any particular source.[122] For these reasons, it was even suggested in the literature that the Court outlawed the exercise of freedom of assembly and of expression in case when it sought to contest the economic foundation of the Common Market.[123] However, this impression is quite misleading as the CJEU came to a different conclusion in case C-265/95 *Commission of the European Communities v. French*

Republic of Austria on the basis that five of its lorries were unable to use the Brenner motorway for four consecutive days because, first, Thursday June 11, 1998 was a bank holiday in Austria, while June 13 and 14, 1998 were a Saturday and Sunday, and second, the Austrian legislation prohibits the movement of lorries in excess of 7.5 tonnes most of the time at weekends and on bank holidays. That motorway was the sole transit route for its vehicles between Germany and Italy. The failure on the part of the Austrian authorities to ban the demonstration and to intervene to prevent that trunk route from being closed amounted to a restriction of the free movement of goods. Since it could not be justified by the protesters' right to freedom of expression and freedom of assembly, the restriction was a breach of Community (EU) law in respect of which the Member State concerned incurred liability. The Republic of Austria contended that the claim should be rejected on the grounds that the decision not to ban the demonstration was taken following a detailed examination of the facts that information as to the date of the closure of the Brenner motorway had been announced in advance in Austria, Germany and Italy and that the demonstration did not result in substantial traffic jams or other incidents. The restriction on free movement arising from a demonstration is permitted provided that the obstacle it creates is neither permanent nor serious (paras. 11-17 in Case C-112/00).

119. I.e., (1) Everyone has the right to freedom of thought, conscience and religion. This right includes freedom to change religion or belief and freedom, either alone or in community with others and in public or in private, to manifest religion or belief, in worship, teaching, practice and observance.

(2) The right to conscientious objection is recognized, in accordance with the national laws governing the exercise of this right.

120. Paras. 51-82 in C-112/00.
121. S. Peers, T. Hervey, J. Kenner, A. Ward, *The EU...*, p. 360.
122. Para. 85 in C-112/00.
123. S. Peers, T. Hervey, J. Kenner, A. Ward, *The EU...*, p. 361.

Republic[124] where the freedom of association and of assembly was perceived as misused and, therefore, was judged as unlawfully restricting the free movement of goods in the EU.[125]

Clearly, the CJEU provides protection of the freedoms of association and assembly, but their borders can be disputable. Although the collision of these fundamental rights with other rights have raised many more questions in the doctrine,[126] it must be stated that generally speaking the CJEU sees these freedoms as integral to ensuring democratic standards in the EU and, therefore, they may be given supremacy over other principles. This observation, in turn, means that the democratic principles in the context of encouraging civil society to express their view, also at the EU level, have solid grounds and potential for further development.

[C] The Principle of Participatory Democracy

It would be a mistake to understand the Union's general principle of democracy only in the scope of its citizens. This rule is also important for the citizen organizations like

124. ECLI:EU:C:1997:595. The case was based on the fact that from 1993 certain groupings of French farmers, including an organization known as "Coordination Rurale," launched a systematic campaign to restrict the supply of agricultural products from other Member States, which mainly took the form against threats to wholesalers and retailers in order to induce them to stock exclusively French products, the imposition of a minimum selling price for the products concerned and the organization of checks to verify whether those traders are complying with the instructions given. The same type of action, involving threats against shopping centers and destruction of goods and means of transport, was directed against Spanish strawberries in particular (paras. 3-5).Consequently, the interception of means of transport and the damaging of agricultural products originating in other Member States, and also the climate of insecurity caused by the threats made by various farmers' organizations against distributors of fruit and vegetables from those states, which had been found to took place in France, constituted an obstacle to intra-Community (EU) trade in those products, which the Member States are required to prevent by adopting appropriate measures, including measures against private individuals who imperil the free movement of goods (para. 17). According to the CJEU, the fact that a Member State abstains from taking action or, as the case may be, fails to adopt adequate measures to prevent obstacles to the free movement of goods that are created, in particular, by actions taken by private individuals on its territory aimed at products originating in other Member States is likely to obstruct intra-Community (EU) trade as is a positive act. The EU law requires the Member States not merely themselves to abstain from adopting measures or engaging in conduct liable to constitute an obstacle to trade but also to take all necessary and appropriate measures to ensure that that fundamental freedom is respected on their territory. In the latter context, the Member States, which retain exclusive competence as regards the maintenance of public order and the safeguarding of internal security, unquestionably enjoy a margin of discretion in determining what measures are most appropriate to eliminate barriers to the importation of products in a given situation. It is therefore not for the Community (EU) institutions to act in place of the Member States and to prescribe for them the measures which they must adopt and effectively apply in order to safeguard the free movement of goods on their territories (paras. 31-34). Nevertheless, the acts of violence committed in France and directed against agricultural products originating in other Member States, such as the interception of lorries transporting those products, the destruction of their loads and violence toward drivers, as well as threats to wholesalers and retailers and the damaging of goods on display, unquestionably created obstacles to intra-Community (EU) trading of those products (para. 38).
125. See also S. Peers, T. Hervey, J. Kenner, A. Ward, *The EU...*, p. 362.
126. E.g. J. Meyer, *Charta...*, p. 287.

NGOs. Alongside the EU citizens, the Member States' democratically organized people are acting in the Union decision-making process as organized associations.[127] Consequently, engaging in grassroot organisms by the citizens can be an expression of their rights to participate in lawmaking and law-execution. Hence, the Union's principle of participatory democracy is based on two elements: on the one hand, the treaties refer to the peoples of the Member States, and on the other hand, to the Union citizens. In other words, the Union rests on a dual structure of democratic legitimization: the peoples in the EU as organized by their respective Member States and the totality of the Union's citizens.[128]

Yet, for many decades, European democracy was not an issue in terms of legal provisions as it was understood as part of the general rule of law.[129] This changed fundamentally by introducing Title II, called "Provisions on democratic principles," to the TEU after the Treaty of Lisbon. Thus, the general, nonwritten rule of democracy became a treaty regulation. It now consists of two elements. While Article 11 establishes the principle of "participatory democracy," Article 10 of the TEU[130] sets up the rule of representative democracy. Both provisions should be seen as a remedy for the remoteness between the EU and its citizens.[131]

In general, participatory democracy as a rule is a set of instruments and procedures to include citizens in public policy-making and to increase their influence in this process.[132] Accordingly, the provision follows an alternative legitimacy concept of "democracy by association"[133] which means that the EU citizens wishing to take part in consultations at the EU level should use the legal forms of existing national NGOs.[134] As mentioned in the first chapter, Article 11 of the TEU reads that the institutions shall, by appropriate means, give citizens and representative association the opportunity to make known and publicly exchange their views in all areas of the Union action.

127. A. von Bogdandy, *The European...*, p. 322.
128. A. Peters, *Elemente einer Theorie der Verfassung Europas*, Berlin 2011, p. 209.
129. S. Iglesias Sanchez, *Fundamental...*, p. 474.
130. This provision reads as follows:

(1) The functioning of the Union shall be founded on representative democracy.
(2) Citizens are directly represented at Union level in the European Parliament.
Member States are represented in the European Council by their Heads of State or Government and in the Council by their governments, themselves democratically accountable either to their national parliaments or to their citizens.
(3) Every citizen shall have the right to participate in the democratic life of the Union. Decisions shall be taken as openly and as closely as possible to the citizen.
(4) Political parties at European level contribute to forming European political awareness and to expressing the will of citizens of the Union.

131. Ch. Mollers, *Multi-Level...*, p. 249.
132. G. Moro, *Citizens in Europe. Civic Activism and the Community Democratic Experiment*, Rome 2012, p. 54.
133. M. Ruffert, *Artikel 11 [Bürgerbeteiligung]* in: *EUV/AEUV. Das Verfassungsrecht der Europäischen Union mit Europäischer Grundrechtekarta. Kommentar*, Ch. Calliess, M. Ruffert (eds), Munich 2011, p. 187.
134. C.R.M.. Versteegh, *Civil Society under the Treaty of Lisbon: Relationship Between National Public Benefit Organizations and European Union Policy?*, Nonprofit Policy Forum Vol. 2/2011, p. 3.

Moreover, as stated in paragraph (2) of this regulation, the institutions shall maintain an open, transparent and regular dialogue with representative associations and civil society and—in paragraph (3)—the European Commission shall carry out broad consultations with parties concerned in order to ensure that the Union's actions are coherent and transparent. Paragraph (4), which will be discussed in the subsequent chapter of this book, refers to the new legal institution—the European Citizens' Initiative.

Article 11 of the TEU provides two basic standards of the EU democratic principle—participation and transparency[135]—which, as noted in the previous paragraphs of this chapter, have been present in the postulates concerning the EU governance at least since the White Paper of 2001. Both can be put into a complex of forms of political deliberation that goes beyond elections.[136] In other words, the democratic legitimacy of the EU after the Treaty of Lisbon seems to be based on the links it establishes with its citizens—both through representation in the EP and Member States democratic accountability, and through direct participation, as provided by Article 11 of the TEU which is based on an assumption that participation of interested and affected parties might be a further avenue to realizing the democratic principle.[137] This provision is inspired by a conception of participation that goes beyond the mere connection between participation and improved policy outcomes.[138] However, it is very difficult to divide the notions of "consultations," "public exchange of views" and "dialogue." It can be generally stated that the EU has hardly ever experienced popular consultations.[139] These types of consultations are reserved to the state level. The consensus achieved on this level can be later transmitted by Member States to the EU level. Yet, the EU system enables individuals to intervene in the political processes. This implies that the instruments of participation should be intended to refrain from political gridlock or the so-called agency capture by strong, organized groups.[140] It means that participation of citizens in the EU lawmaking process is no more a declarative postulate but a legislative norm. As a consequence, participation practices should no longer be regarded solely as an expression of participatory governance (like in the White Paper of 2001) but be rather evaluated in the light of the wider meaning of the principle of participatory democracy.[141] Thus, participatory democracy became a legal principle instead of being a political aspiration and acquired normative founding for the EU constitutional system as a whole.[142] Such

135. A. von Bogdandy, *The European...*, p. 323, D. Curtin, J. Mendes, *Transparence et participation: Des principes démocratiques pour l'administration de l'Union européenne*, l'E.N.A. Revue française d'administration publique Vol. 1/2011, pp. 101 et seq.
136. A. Peters, *Elemente...*, p. 210.
137. B. Kohler-Koch, Ch. Quittkat, *De-Mystification...*, p. 35.
138. Ch. Bertrand, *La démocratie participative dans le système institutionnel de l'Union européenne*, Siècles. Cahiers du Centre d'histoire "Espaces et Cultures" Vol. 37/2013, p. 7, I. Karolewski, *Pathologies of Deliberation in the EU*, European Law Journal Vol. 1/2011, p. 72.
139. The exceptions are, e.g. protests against TTIP and CETA agreements, see: http://www.euractiv.com/section/trade-society/news/thousands-across-europe-protest-against-ttip/ (on May 24, 2019).
140. A. von Bogdandy, *The European...*, p. 326.
141. *Ibid.*, p. 324.
142. *Ibid.*, p. 326.

an understanding of Article 11 of the TEU would require reforms, both in political and legal matters, aimed at ensuring the "representative associations" with stronger rights in the decision and lawmaking procedures.

Article 11 (1) of the TEU generally refers to "soft" rather than formal tools of consultation.[143] Still, it seems that it requires changing the approach from the instrumental usages of participation typical for participatory governance to participation conceived as a basis of participatory democracy.[144] Respectively, participation privileges should be primarily conceded to representative associations and not to the EU citizens directly.[145] This opens the possibility of expanding the position of NGOs at the EU level because they are perceived as holders of rights or legally protected interests affected by the legislative process.[146] It means that the "representative associations" should be also further included in procedures, in which they had been previously frequently absent, e.g. in informal consultations. However, this does not close the possibilities of enabling NGOs at the EU level. The wording "by appropriate means" allows a broad range of capabilities, varying from general participatory tools directed at citizens without distinction to policy-oriented instruments.[147] As participation also means control,[148] the cited phrasing implies more means of civic supervision of the EU institutions which closely relates to the principle of transparency. Nevertheless, as it was mentioned in the first chapter, Article 11 (1) of the TEU does not provide any definition of a "representative association" and, thus, it does not determine what association is legally offered the rights to participate in the lawmaking process at the EU level. It appears that this notion hints a requirement of somehow selecting the interested NGOs.[149] As a result, this term is likely to appear in litigation before the CJEU concerning a more prominent role of access to participation.

Generally speaking, all these remarks signify that the EU institutions should take a more citizen-oriented approach as far as their policy-making is concerned. This could mean, for instance, a need for more social campaigns of the EU institutions to inform civil society about legal initiatives and their possible consequences. This understanding can also be attached to the wording of "public exchange of views" which has no clear definition, and no clear boundaries can be traced between this exchange and dialogue or consultation. However, this does not seem to include the obligation to conclude regular consultations in the first place.[150] This is perhaps the main difference between "social dialogue" and "civil dialogue." While the first one provides that

143. S. Ozcurumez, J. Hoxha, *Conditional Deliberation: The Case of Joint Parliamentary Committees in the EU*, Journal of Common Market Studies Vol. 3/2015, p. 644.
144. A. Crespy, *Deliberative Democracy and the Legitimacy of the European Union: A Reappraisal of Conflict*, Political Studies Vol. 62/2014, p. 88.
145. I. Karolewski, *Pathologies...*, p. 73.
146. A. von Bogdandy, *The European...*, p. 326.
147. Ch. Geiger, D.-E. Kahn, M. Kotzur, *Commentary...*, p. 69.
148. F. Riemann, *Die Transparenz der Europäischen Union. Das neue Recht auf Zugang zu Dokumenten von Parlament, Rat un Kommission*, Berlin 2003, pp. 60-62, Ch. Sobotta, *Transparenz in den Rechtsetzungsverfahren der Europäischen Union*, Frankfurt am Main 2000, pp. 79-81.
149. J. Mendes, *Participation and the Role of Law after Lisbon: A Legal View on Article 11*, Common Market Law Review Vol. 6/2011, p. 1849.
150. M. Ruffert, *Artikel 11...*, p. 188.

consultation with social partners is compulsory and systemic, the latter one does not establish such an obligation when it comes to consultations with NGOs.[151] The requirement of conducting regular consultations is apparent in Article 11 (3) of the TEU but is, however, reserved to the Commission which could indicate its roots back to the policy-driven practices and acts presented in the previous paragraphs (including the White Paper of 2001). Yet, the Commission is equally bound by the first two paragraphs of this article which establish a general rule of giving voice by other forms of participation.[152] Nevertheless, it seems that the Commission's approach to NGOs and their participation in the lawmaking is not as engaging as it ought to be.[153] Still, this attitude is the most far-reaching in comparison to other EU institutions, as it will be presented in the third chapter of this book.

As far as the general rule of transparency is concerned, as provided in Article 11 (2) of the TEU, it requires knowledge of the motives of the undertaken decisions by all EU institutions[154] as they are obliged to "maintain an open, transparent and regular dialogue with representative associations and civil society." Moreover, as it reads in Article 11 (3) of the TEU, the duty of the Commission to consult parties concerned has a specific purpose: to ensure that the "Union's actions are coherent and transparent." Yet, it is really ambiguous to settle how consultation can enhance the coherence of the Union's actions as it may be problematic to limit consultation to parties concerned if transparency is one of its goals, too.[155] This dilemma will be discussed further in the following chapter as it is particularly crucial for the lobbying process.[156]

The rule of transparency is applicable to all EU civil servants[157] and is strictly related to access to documents.[158] This institution, as one of the main "tools" of NGO activity at the EU level, will also be presented in the third chapter of this book.

151. D. Obradovic, *Civil...*, pp. 318 et seq.
152. A. von Bogdandy, *The European...*, p. 327.
153. The biggest development being the introduction of "Better Regulation Guidelines," SWD (2017) 350)—a nonbinding proposal of rules governing the legislation procedure in general. The package urged for the following components: (1) *ex post* evaluation of the existing legislative framework, (2) public consultation, (3) *ex ante* impact assessment, (4) draft of the proposal, (5) legislative procedure, (6) transposition and implementation, (7) enforcement. As it can be seen, public consultation remains an essential constituent of organizing the agenda of the Commission. See also G. Luchetta, *Impact Assessment and the Policy Cycle in the EU*, European Journal of Risk Regulation Vol. 3/2012, pp. 561-562, J. Maśnicki, *Good...*, pp. 201-202.
154. Ch. Geiger, D.-E. Kahn, M. Kotzur, *Commentary on the TEU/TFEU*, Oxford 2014, p. 67.
155. *Ibid.*, p. 69.
156. This dilemma is also at the center of interest for the current Commission—see e.g. State of the Union 2017, available at: https://ec.europa.eu/commission/sites/beta-political/files/state-union-2017-brochure_en.pdf (on February 9, 2019).
157. In June 2012, following a public consultation, the Ombudsman published a high-level distillation of the ethical standards to which the EU public administration adheres. These took the form of five public service principles. According to the fifth principle (entitled Transparency), civil servants should be willing to explain their activities and to give reasons for their actions. They should keep proper records and welcome public scrutiny of their conduct, including their compliance with these public service principles. See The European Code of Good Administrative Behaviour with the foreword of the European Ombudsman E. O'Reilly, 2005, available at: https://www.ombudsman.europa.eu/en/resources/code.faces#/page/1.
158. For more see e.g. opinion of Advocate General Sharpston in case C-562/14 P, ECLI: ECLI-:EU:C:2016:885, T-306/12 *Darius Nicolai Spirlea and Mihaela Spirlea v. European Commission*, ECLI:EU:T:2014:816, T-111/11 *ClientEarth v. European Commission*, ECLI:EU:T:2013:482.

Nonetheless, this principle is apparent in other treaty provisions as well. Consequently, according to Article 15 (1) of the TFEU, in order to promote good governance and ensure the participation of civil society, the Union's institutions, bodies, offices and agencies shall conduct their work as openly as possible, and according to its paragraph (2), the European Parliament shall meet in public, as shall the Council when considering and voting on a draft legislative act. Pursuant to Article 15 (3) of the TFEU and Article 42 of the EUChFR, any citizen of the Union and any natural or legal person residing or having its registered office in a Member State shall have a right of access to documents of the Union's institutions, bodies, offices and agencies, whatever their medium.

As it appears, Article 11 of the TEU lacks further implementing measures. A good example for legal development in this matter can be found in the ReNEUAL[159] Model Rules on EU Administrative Procedure,[160] even though their recommended scope is quite limited.[161] According to paragraph (1) *in fine* of the Introduction, the purpose of the Model Rules proposed is to ensure a higher degree of legitimacy of rulemaking activities, in accordance with Article 11 (1) TEU. Greater transparency of input into the procedure as well as the possibility for public debate and deliberation on alternatives will ensure more fully that all the relevant facts and legally protected interests are taken into account, which will contribute to the overall quality of rulemaking. An amplification of this motive can be found in Article II-4 (1) of the Model Rules. Accordingly, the EU authority in charge of drafting, amending or withdrawing the act shall give effect to the obligations in Article 11 of the TEU by consultation in accordance with the following paragraphs.[162] Pursuant to paragraph (38) of the Explanations to the Model Rules, this provision specifies what the general principles listed in Article 11 (1) of the TEU mean with respect to executive rulemaking in the EU and restates that the principles of Article 11 (1) of the TEU apply in the process of drafting a legally binding

159. Research Network on EU Administrative Law—an academic project funded by the Commission.
160. The so-called ReNEUAL 1.0, available at: http://www.reneual.eu/index.php/projects-and-publications/reneual-1-0 (on February 9, 2019).
161. According to Art. II-1 (1), the rules apply to the procedures leading to the establishment, amendment and repeal of legally binding nonlegislative acts of general application, including:
    (a) acts adopted by the Commission or the Council under Articles 290 and 291 of the TFEU;
    (b) legally binding nonlegislative acts of the EU institutions, bodies, offices and agencies adopted on the basis of Treaty provisions or legislative acts.
162. I.e.:
    - the draft act and the explanatory memorandum shall be published on a central EU website for consultations and accompanied by specific information laid down in Article II-4 (2);
    - the EU authority in charge of drafting the act may identify and address persons who are likely to be affected by the draft act and invite them to comment (Article II-4 (3));
    - comments should be made public in a way that allows public exchange of views (Article II-4 (4));
    - where the comments lead to the necessity of substantial revision of the initial draft act, the EU authority in charge of drafting the act must consider whether a new phase of consultation (Article II-4 (5);
    - after consultation, the EU authority in charge of drafting the act shall create a reasoned report (Article II-5 (1)).

nonlegislative act of general application. However, the Commission and other institutions and bodies of the Union can obviously develop additional means of exchanging ideas and including the public in their activities. Moreover, Article II-4 (in its paragraph (4)) also requires—in the interest of ensuring that under Article 11 (1) of the TEU citizens and representative associations have the "opportunity to make known and publicly exchange their views" that subsequent commentators be able to comments on comments made earlier. This exchange of views ought to allow for alternative approaches to be developed in a comment section and ensure a more lively and vivid exchange on a Commission proposal than would have been possible if earlier comments were not accessible to later commentators.[163]

Even though the recommended legal solution is an interesting approach to Article 11 of the TEU, it ought to be remembered that the ReNUAL project remains more a field for academic discussion and ideas shaping than an actual legal proposal for the EU institutions.

To conclude, it can be stated that Article 11 of the TEU is based on the previously analyzed assumptions of the Commission (especially referred to in the White Paper on European Governance) on how to link the EU institutions with civil society (and NGOs as agents operating on its behalf) and on an attempt to transform this linkage into duties, also of other institutions.[164] Still, it would be beneficial to introduce further legal developments in order to transform this "soft" proclamation on the need for wider consultation with civil society into "harder" prerogatives of specific individuals. As for now, it is argued that Article 11 of the TEU leaves a "corporatism" and "utopian" impression of an equal dialogue between all parties concerned, whereas, in fact, the practice is far from ideal.[165] It is also asserted that the discussed provision does not indicate a clear distinction between dialogue and lobbying which leaves a "gray area" in the field of advocacy at the EU level.[166] These issues will be further discussed in the following parts of this book.

[D] Acknowledgment of the Role of Social Partners

According to Article 152 of the TFEU, the Union recognizes and promotes the role of the social partners at its level, taking into account the diversity of national systems. It shall facilitate the dialogue between the social partners, respecting their autonomy. The Tripartite Social Summit for Growth and Employment shall contribute to social dialogue.

As it has already been stated, this article is a new provision, introduced by the Treaty of Lisbon. The mentioning of the Tripartite Social Summit in the EU primary law represented a remarkable political step, for it recognizes the role of the tripartite

163. See also para. (46) of the Explanations.
164. J. Mendes, *Participation...*, p. 1851.
165. M. Ruffert, *Artikel 11...*, p. 189.
166. L. Versteegh, *Civil...*, p. 4.

consultation (EU institutions—employers[167]—representatives of the employees)[168] at the highest level of the EU decision-making.[169] This condition fulfills the standard introduced in the ILO system as discussed in the first chapter of this book. Still, the Tripartite Social Summit itself was established much earlier, in 2003,[170] under the Council Decision 2003/174/EC.[171] According to Article 2 of this decision, the task of the Summit shall be to ensure, in compliance with the Treaty and with due regard for the powers of the institutions and bodies of the Community, that there is a continuous concentration between the Council, the Commission and the social partners. It will enable the social partners at European level to contribute, in the context of their social dialogue, to the various components of the integrated economic and social strategy, including the sustainable development dimension as launched at the Lisbon European Council in March 2000 and supplemented by the Gothenburg European Council in June 2001. For that purpose, it shall draw on the upstream work and discussions between the Council, the Commission and the social partners in the different concertation forum on economic, social and employment matters.

The official enactment of the Tripartite Social Summit into Treaty regulations can be seen as an aftermath of communitarization of the social policy in the Maastricht Treaty. As it has been discussed in the previous remarks, it became a cornerstone for establishing the notions of "social dialogue" and "social policy." In fact, since 1997 the Council presidency has invited the social partners to meet the "troika"[172] ahead of the European Councils and since the Nice Summit in 2000 it has been decided that these meetings should be held annually, before the spring European Council.[173] Thus, the *social* sphere of the EU law was the first one in which the role of European civil society has been so significantly noticed.

It seems that since then the role of "social dialogue" has not transformed drastically. Even though it is now a constitutional provision, the capacity of social partners in the tripartite dialogue is not to influence directly the content of the EU law but rather to participate in the creation of the main objectives of social policy.

167. Represented at the EU level by the Union of Industrial and Employers' Confederations of Europe (UNICE).
168. Represented at the EU level by the European Trade Union Confederation (ETUC).
169. S. Nakano, *Maastricht Social Protocol Revisited: Origins of the European Industrial Relations System*, Journal of Common Market Studies Vol. 5/2014, p. 1054.
170. Which superseded the Standing Committee on Employment in the European Communities established by the Council Decision of 14 December 1970 (70/532/EEC).
171. Official Journal L 070, 14.3.2003. The decision was amended in 2016 by Council Decision (EU) 2016/1859 of 13 October 2016 on the Tripartite Social Summit for Growth and Employment and repealing Decision 2003/174/EC, Official Journal L 284, 28.10.2016.
172. Currently, while talking about the troika (especially in the media) one refers to a decision group formed by the European Commission, the European Central Bank and the International Monetary Fund—for more see e.g. B. Keller, *Social Dialogues—The State of the Art a Decade after Maastricht*, Industrial Relation Journal Vol. 5/2003, p. 416.
173. The Summit takes place once a year, before the spring meeting of the European Council. It is chaired by both the President of the Council of the EU and the President of the Commission—for more information see J.J. Węc, *Spór...*, p. 317.

Therefore, the tripartite dialogue is a body which gives certain urges (a meta-purpose)[174] and the EU institutions should then take them into considerations while establishing acts of secondary law. In fact, the dialogue itself is a considerable value in the EU social policy. Being able to take part in such a dialogue for social partners is under protection, just like protecting other interest of the employees.[175]

The TFEU does not define what should be understood under the notion of "social partners." Therefore, it has to be interpreted in the same way as in previous, nonbinding acts of law (for instance, like in the Green Paper on European Social Policy of 1993). Furthermore, although the notions of the EU law are independent and should be defined autonomously,[176] the usage of national law could be useful to understand the scope of "social dialogue" and "social partners." These terms are used for example in Article 20 of the Polish Constitution.[177] According to this provision, a social market economy, based on the freedom of economic activity, private ownership and solidarity, dialogue and cooperation between social partners shall be the basis of the economic system of the Republic of Poland. Under this provision, "social partners" are the bodies representing the two sides of industry: the employers and the employees.[178] The representatives of employees could consist of trade unions or individual employees as a whole.[179] As it was noted in the first chapter, this remark is important for the hypothesis of this book as trade unions were historically one of the first NGOs and are considered an important part of NSAs. Accordingly, "social partners," both at the national and at the EU level, as a part of the organized civil society, remain to have a crucial role in reaching out to workers and owners of enterprises and in increasing the representation of their members in the field of public advocacy, its formulation and implementation to ensure broader social benefits.[180]

Continuously, "social dialogue" at the EU level is a type of negotiation conducted by the social partners in order to defend the interest of their members. This issue is also underlined in Article 154 and Article 155 of the TFEU. According to Article 154 of the TFEU, the Commission must consult the social partners prior to taking action in the field of social policy. Then, the partners can negotiate agreements that may be implemented independently according to their national practices or request their implementation through a Council decision (Article 155 of the TFEU). Moreover, the Commission should promote the consultation of bipartite dialogue between social partners and take any relevant measure to facilitate it by ensuring balanced support to

174. K. Complak, *Komentarz do art. 20* in: *Konstytucja Rzeczypospolitej Polskiej. Komentarz*, M. Haczkowska (ed.), Warsaw 2014, lex.pl.
175. T. Fashoyin, *Coopération tripartite, dialogue social et développement national*, Revue international du Travail Vol. 4/2004, p. 375.
176. See e.g. J.W. van Rossem, *The Autonomy of EU Law: More is Less?* in: *Between Autonomy and Dependence. The EU Legal Order under the Influence of International Organisations*, R.A. Wessel, S. Blockmans (eds), The Hague 2013, pp. 14 et seq.
177. As published in Dz. U. of 16.7.1997.
178. K. Complak, *Komentarz...*, lex.pl.
179. E.g., the working crew—for more see Z. Hajn, *Związkowe przedstawicielstwo pracowników zakładu pracy w Polsce—ewolucja, stan obecny, przyszłość* in: *Związkowe przedstawicielstwo pracowników zakładu pracy*, Z. Hajn (ed.), Warsaw 2012, pp. 34 et seq.
180. T. Fashoyin, *Coopération...*, p. 376.

the parties (according to Article 154 (1) of the TFEU). As a result, the notion of "social dialogue" consists of three different types of activities:[181]

(1) tripartite consultation—which describes the exchanges between the social partners and the European public authorities (provided by Article 152 of the TFEU);
(2) consultation of the social partners—which covers the activities of the consultative committees and the official consultations in the spirit of Article 153 of the TFEU;
(3) the European social dialogue—which is the name given to the bipartite work of the social partners, whether or not it stems from the official consultations of the Commission based on Articles 154 and 155 of the TFEU.

As it can be seen, "social dialogue" at the EU level covers both consultations between the social partners themselves and between them and the EU institutions. Moreover, the implications of "social dialogue" in the EU law can also be found in specific norms at the national level.[182] Social partners are, therefore, involved in establishing social policy in an appreciably vast scope. This conclusion and the fact that the social dialogue has a considerably long (and successful) history of being acknowledged by the EU institutions as a key element in consulting the shape of the EU social law makes it one of the pillars of establishing European civil society.

[E] Summary

There are four main Treaty bases for social participation at the EU level: Article 2 of the TEU, Article 12 of the EUChFR (Article 11 of the ECHR), Article 11 of the TEU and Article 152 of the TFEU. While the first two can be perceived as general rules of the EU law, the latter ones directly refer to "representative associations" and "social partners," thus engaging the role of NGOs and the representatives of civil society in the EU system. Still, it should be observed that the involvement of NGOs in the EU law is

181. Ch. Geiger, D.-E. Kahn, M. Kotzur, *Commentary...*, p. 683.
182. This statement refers specifically to the basis for consultation of the EU documents at national level. For instance, according to Art. 19[1] of the Polish Act of 23 May 1991 on Trade Unions (*Ustawa z dnia 23 maja 1991 r. o związkach zawodowych*, tekst jedn. Dz. U. of 2015 r. item 1881):

    (1) A Trade Union Organization, which is representative within the meaning of the law on the Council of the social dialogue, has the right to comment the consultation documents of the European Union, in particular white papers, green papers and messages, and draft legislation of the European Union in the field of the tasks covered by the tasks of trade unions.
    (2) The authorities and the state administration direct the European Union consultation documents and draft legal acts referred to in para. 1, to the appropriate statutory authority therefore, specifying the term submit reviews.
    (3) The consultation documents of the European Union and the draft legislation referred to in para. 1 shall be transmitted by government authorities and the state administration to the appropriate e-mail address, indicated by the appropriate statutory body.

provided on multiple levels. The general rule of democracy and the rule of law ensure that there ought to be conditions for developing a healthy and unbiased civil society not only at the EU level but also at the national level. The freedom of assembly and of association implies that the citizens who are members of grassroot organizations have the possibility to express their opinions. According to the CJEU, this freedom has to be understood very widely and can be given precedence above other general rules of the EU law, even those establishing the freedoms of the Common Market. After the Treaty of Lisbon, the representatives of civil society are also given express prerogatives when it comes to participation in consultation procedures in the EU lawmaking. Unfortunately, these privileges have not so far translated to other executive and binding norms in the EU law. Still, the principle of "participatory democracy" introduced a new measure of directly influencing the EU legislature, i.e. the European Citizens' Initiative. The specific aspects of the abovementioned means will be discussed in the following chapter of this book. Finally, the Treaty ensures that "social dialogue" is conducted not only at the EU level. The aim of this standard is to ensure that the voice of employees is taken into consideration in the "social dimension" of the Union.

All of these principles provide not only that NGOs have legal basis for acting at the EU level but also that there is considerable amount of space for further developments in this area. The actual and possible spheres of activity will be referred to in the ensuing parts of this book.

§2.03 THE OFFICIAL ARENAS OF NGO PARTICIPATION AT THE EU LEVEL

This part of analysis concentrates on presenting the *actual* (formal and informal) arenas of NGO participation at the EU level. As far as the formal channels are concerned, there are two institutions which have been created to ensure the voice of the grassroot civil society in the decision and lawmaking processes: the Economic and Social Committee and the Committee of the Regions. Due to the fact that these institutions are frequently ineffective, NGOs repeatedly seek other informal paths of representing their interests. Therefore, various structural types of NGOs operating at the EU level can be observed. All of these action arenas have considerable drawbacks which will be also discussed in brief.

[A] The European Economic and Social Committee

The Economic and Social Committee (or as it is commonly called European Economic and Social Committee (EESC)) was established in the Treaty of Rome as a body with advisory power across a wide range of policy areas dealt with at the European level.[183] At present, its legal status is determined by Article 13 (4) of the TEU, which describes it as "acting in an advisory capacity," and Article 300 (2) of the TFEU. According to the latter regulation, the Economic and Social Committee shall consist of representatives of

183. J.J. Węc, J.J. Węc, *Spór...*, p. 423.

organizations of employers, of the employed and of other parties representative of civil society, notably in socioeconomic, civic, professional and cultural areas.

The EESC describes itself as "a bridge between Europe and organized civil society"[184] and a "unique forum for consultation, dialogue and consensus among representatives of the various economic, social and civil components of organized civil society,"[185] aiming at "promoting the development of a more participatory European Union which is closer to its citizens, by acting as organized civil society's institutional forum for representation, information, expression and dialogue"[186] and "promoting the values on which European integration is founded and advancing, both within the European Union and in the whole world, the role of civil society organizations and participatory democracy."[187] The Council has 350 members (Councillors) who are drawn from all Member States from economic and social interest groups. The Councillors are nominated by national governments and appointed by the Council of the European Union for a renewable five-year term of office.[188] The territorial dimension officially remains "hidden" in the EESC internal organization. Therefore, national groups are disaggregated and reaggregated on the basis of what interests they represent.[189] Moreover, the Councillors are not based full-time in Brussels, but rather have their own jobs in their home countries, ensuring that they maintain direct contact with their grass roots.[190]

It may be argued that the EECS is a representative body in the sense that it is designed to represent the interests of the EU citizens, even though its members are not elected[191] as it seems obvious that it is and has always been considered in terms of an institutional representation of civil society. Yet only since the end of the 1990s the EESC has changed its focus from "representation of the European citizens" to representation of the "organized civil society," as it started to claim a role of "forum of organized civil society."[192]

Two-thirds of the EESC Councillors are representatives of employers and employees, and only one-third of their membership is left to "various other economic and social components of organized civil society."[193] Therefore, as it is reasonably stressed out in the doctrine, even if the representatives are not bound by any mandate,

184. See: http://www.eesc.europa.eu/?i=portal.en.home (on February 9, 2019).
185. The EESC from The Inside Out. Annual Activity Report 2015, p. 8, available at: http://www.eesc.europa.eu/?i=portal.en.about-the-committee (on February 9, 2019).
186. The EESC..., p. 8.
187. *Ibid.*
188. According to Art. 302 para. 1 of the TFEU, see also E. Jones, A. Menon, S. Weatherill, *Oxford...*, p. 274.
189. I. De Jesus Butler, *Non-governmental...*, p. 568, Cf. P. Birkinshaw, *Freedom of Information and Openness: Fundamental Human Rights?*, Law Review Vol. 58/2006, p. 256.
190. The EESC..., p. 9.
191. Ch. Marxsen, *Open Stakeholder Consultations at the European Level—Voice of the Citizens?*, European Law Journal Vol. 2/2015, p. 259.
192. S. Smismans, *European...*, p. 492.
193. Rule 27 of the EESC Rules of Procedure of July 2010, Official Journal L 324/52, 9.12.2010.

two-thirds of EECS represent only two particular categories of socioeconomic interest.[194] Of the remaining one-third, the EESC has established four subcategories: 36 belong to cooperatives, mutual, associations, foundations and social NGOs; 28 to the agricultural sector; 23 to consumer and environmental organizations; 19 to small and medium-sized enterprises, crafts and the professions.[195] Thus, NGOs[196] are represented only by roughly 20% of the Councillors, which cannot be seen as sufficient to be treated as an appropriate representation.

The EESC itself is aware of the fact that it does not represent the full spectrum of the organized civil society and NGOs from Member States. As it was stated, "EESC membership does not fully reflect the diversity and ongoing development of organized civil society."[197] Thus, the EESC tries to make arrangements on their legitimacy. For instance, in February 2014, the EECS opted to "move closer" to the EP and to consolidate its relations with the Committee of the Regions through an interinstitutional agreement.[198] The aim of this agreement was to reinforce the "democratic pillar" of the EU, achieving two objectives: making legislative action more effective and making the best possible use of available resources. Unfortunately, this agreement does not seem to have any significant outcomes.[199]

Yet, it should be mentioned that in 2004 the EESC established a "Liaison Group" whose objective was to formalize relations with various European civil society interests that are not formally represented within the EESC in a structured dialogue.[200] The Liaison Group has been active since then and has met regularly with representatives of various sectors of organized civil society at the EU level.[201] Due to these meetings, the EESC is seeking to deepen its input from the interested NGOs. Therefore, their opinions (i.e., those which are not directly represented by a Councillor) may be included in the recommendations presented by the EESC.[202] However, the very existence of the Liaison Group illustrates the problems of NGOs representation within the scope of the EECS. This issue is arguably one of the main reasons why NGOs, rather than being active in the forum of this institution, develop their own channels of communication with the lawmaking institutions of the EU, especially with the Commission.

194. S. Smismans, *European...*, p. 493, see also N. Perez-Solorzano, S. Smismans, *Representativeness: A Tool to Structure Interest Intermediation in the European Union?*, Journal of Common Market Studies Vol. 3/2012, p. 413, A. Armstrong, *Rediscovering ...*, p. 105 and O. De Schutter, *Europe in Search of its Civil Society*, European Law Journal Vol. 8/2002, p. 200.
195. Rule 29 of the EESC Rules of Procedure.
196. I.e., NGO and the specifically distinguished "consumer and environmental organizations."
197. Evaluation report of the Liaison Group with European civil society organisations and networks of 26.6.2006, available at: http://www.eesc.europa.eu/resources/docs/evalutation-report-en.doc (on February 9, 2019).
198. Cooperation Agreement between the European Parliament and the Economic and Social Committee, available at: http://www.eesc.europa.eu/resources/docs/cooperation-agreement-betweeen-the-eesc-the-ep-and-the-cor.pdf (on February 9, 2019).
199. Ch. Marxsen, *Open...*, p. 258.
200. I. De Jesus Butler, *Non-governmental...*, p. 270.
201. See The EESC Liaison Group Promoting civil dialogue and participatory democracy, available at: http://www.eesc.europa.eu/resources/docs/qe-04-15-637-en-n.pdf (on February 9, 2019).
202. I. De Jesus Butler, *Non-governmental...*, p. 271.

Still, the EESC, an as institution, forms an arena of participatory democracy in the sense that it groups different components of European civil society.[203] As stated in Article 304 of the TFEU, the EESC shall be consulted by the EP, by the Council or by the Commission where the Treaties so provide. The EECS may be consulted by these institutions in all cases in which they consider it appropriate. In fact, the EESC is consulted in most market-oriented subject matters (which include internal market, environment and sustainable development, agriculture, employment, social policy, cohesion policy, youth and education, vocational training, research and innovation, culture, health, transport and energy, consumer policy and trade).[204] It may also issue an opinion on its own initiative in cases where such action is considered appropriate. Therefore, the EESC plays the role of intermediary between citizens and the EU institutions. Even though it is undoubtedly pluralistic since its members are preselected at national level, its influence on the EU decision-making process is rather hard for unequivocal evolution.

The number of opinions presented by the EESC is steady and amounts to about 80-100 a year.[205] What is worrying is that the volume of opinions adopted on referral from the EP is notably declining[206] and just a few opinions are adapted every year on the specific request of the Commission.[207] It seems that these institutions very often decide to conduct dialogue with NGOs on their own without the "mediation" of the EESC.[208] However, what is worth mentioning is that since 2013 the Committee has introduced an approach which can be described as "project-based." Its aim is to transform certain recommendations—expressed through opinions—into concrete actions. This practice has involved external partners and the combination of several instruments to achieve practical policy outcomes.[209] Also, it organizes about 40 "special events" annually, addressing the most important issues of the EU policy.[210]

If the EESC issues an opinion, then it produces a certain outcome. According to the research conducted by Ch. Hönnige and D. Panke,[211] it can be generally summarized that the EESC can influence the lawmaking at the EU level, even though their recommendations are not binding for their addressees. Yet, this influence capacity is rather limited as 40% of the addresses fully ignore the advice given by the EESC.[212] Furthermore, the impact of the EESC on the outcomes of the lawmaking procedures is affected by several factors. For instance, the recommendation is more likely to be taken

203. Ch. Marxsen, *Open...*, p. 259.
204. Ch. Hönnige, D. Panke, *The Committee of the Regions and the European Economic and Social Committee: How Influential are Consultative Committees in the European Union?*, Journal of Common Market Studies Vol. 3/2013, p. 454.
205. 2015—86, 2014—88, 2013—103, 2012—105; for more see *The EESC...*, p. 14.
206. 2015—19, 2014- 61, 2013-84, 2012- 122; for more see *The EESC...*, p. 14.
207. 2015—4; for more see *The EESC...*, p. 17.
208. F. Furtak, *Nichtregierungsorganisationen...*, p. 44.
209. See The EESC..., p. 18; there were four projects in 2015.
210. 2015: TTIP, Digital Single Market, Urban Matters, see The EESC..., pp. 20-27.
211. Ch. Hönnige, D. Panke, *The Committee...*, p. 464.
212. According to the survey conducted by Ch. Hönnige and D. Panke; The 528 contacted MEPs returned 150 surveys (response rate: 28.41%) and the 755 staff of the Permanent Representations returned 323 surveys (response rate: 42.78%, see Ch. Hönnige, D. Panke, *The Committee...*, pp. 458-459.

into consideration if it is delivered early in the legislative process. Likewise, the possible influence of the recommendation tends to be limited if it is "delayed," meaning that other institutions have already formulated their opinions.[213] Also, it appears there is a regularity that if the addressee considers that the EESC has a high expertise in the given subject matter (relative to its own knowledge in the given field) then the recommendation becomes increasingly persuasive.[214] As a result, the quality of the recommendation enables the EESC to be heard in the lawmaking procedure. Moreover, it is noticeable that the opinions issued by the EESC are taken into consideration more frequently by the EP than by other institutions.[215] At the same time, the opinions tend to have the same leverage whether they are required by the Treaty, requested by an institution or prepared on its own initiative by the EESC.[216]

Obviously, the EESC is excluded from the "trilogue" procedure between the EP, the Council and the Commission, as it has no formal vote in the legislative process.[217] In consequence, the ability to formulate recommendations promptly and with high level of expertise is practically the only way for the EESC to influence other EU institutions.[218] Unfortunately, it is not always possible due to the limited access to expert knowledge ensured by the Councillors. As it was stated above, two-thirds of the EESC are linked with the social sphere, leaving the remaining one-third to all of the other fields of the EU competences. Frequently, the EESC does not have enough *inside*[219] knowledge and cannot produce a recommendation swiftly due to the fact that it has to *commission* the preparation of a draft to a different entity (e.g., a study group that consists of the members of NGOs active in the field where the recommendation is needed).[220] The drafts are then discussed and adopted by the Plenary Session. However, it is not unusual that the drafted opinions deal with specific matters, not even closely related to social policy. Thus, the discussion cannot always be as effective as desired.[221] A significantly higher number of Councillors representing NGOs could radically diminish this problem.

As a consequence, the current position of the EESC is often criticized. It is sometimes even pointed out that the Committee could, without much harm, be abolished and replaced, for example, by the system of granting consultant status to interested representatives of interest groups in the spirit of the UN system. Although some of this criticism is not unfounded (and, in fact, many initiatives or opinions regarding attempts to involve civil society at the EU level presented by the Committee

213. Ch. Hönnige, D. Panke, *The Committee...*, p. 461.
214. *Ibid.*, p. 463.
215. *Ibid.*, p. 462.
216. *Ibid.*, p. 466.
217. Similar to small states with very limited capacities; for more see D. Panke, *Small Stated in the European Union: Coping with Structural Disadvantages*, Farnham 2010, pp. 1-5.
218. C. Jeffery, *European Social Committee and Committee of Regions* in: *The Institutions of the European Union*, J. Peterson, M Shackleton (eds), Oxford 2002, p. 373.
219. I.e., provided by the Councillors themselves.
220. See The EESC..., p. 5.
221. Ch. Hönnige, D. Panke, *The Committee...*, p. 467.

are, at most, superficial[222]), it seems that it would be practically impossible to abolish the EESC.[223] First of all, the EU would face the accusation that it would further restrict civil dialogue by selecting partners to take part in it. Second, although the EESC's position is indeed quite weak, it is difficult to underestimate its attempts to involve the representatives of civil society in the decision-making processes at the EU level through various debates, conferences or promotional campaigns. Third, the EESC is a cooperation platform for European civil society and NGOs at the EU level that is developing around the aforementioned Liaison Group.[224]

[B] The Committee of the Regions

According to Article 4 (2) of the TEU, the EU shall respect regional and local self-government in the process of legislation. Despite the undoubted prominence of subnational public authorities in the post-Lisbon constitutional framework, they are still conceived as "vertically" and territorially organized civil society to be involved in European Governance through channels of participation, rather than as constitutional entities to include in the multilevel institutional decision-making process.[225] In order to provide such an official channel of participation, the Committee of the Regions (CoR) was established in 1993 by the Maastricht Treaty in the model of the EESC. Its task was to strengthen the role of regions and local authorities within the EU decision-making process, to which they previously had no access.[226]

Similarly to the EESC, the role of the CoR is formulated in Article 13 (4) of the TEU which states that it should assist the EU institutions in an advisory capacity. It means that the Commission, the Council and the EP must consult the CoR before adopting legislation in the fields relevant to local and regional competences. It can also submit voluntary opinions in response to the Commission's legislative proposals or produce recommendations on its own. As stated in Article 300 (3) of the TFUE, the Committee of the Regions shall consist of representatives of regional and local bodies who hold either a regional or local authority electoral mandate or are politically accountable to an elected assembly. The CoR consists of 350 members from all Member States who are elected by local or regional authorities. The internal organization is subordinated into political groups according to transnational party orientations.[227]

---

222. A good example is the EESC Opinion of 20.3.2019 – The Future of the EU: Benefits to citizens and respect for European values, SC/052. It does not present any new or in-depth conclusions about the role that civil society can play in the changing EU.
223. Cf. EESC President statement on ALDE's position paper about the future financial perspectives of 20.1.2011, available at: https://bit.ly/2TMTbTk (on February 12, 2019).
224. Cf. M. Westlake, *The European Economic and Social Committee* in: *Lobbying the European Union: Institutions, Actors and Issues*, D. Coen, J. Richardson (eds), Oxford 2009, p. 139.
225. J. Loughlin, *Representing Regions in Europe: The Committee of the Regions* in: *The Regional Dimension of the European Union: Towards a Third Level in Europe?*, C. Jeffery (ed.), London 1997, p. 121.
226. J. Loughlin, *Representing...*, p. 119.
227. According to the current wording of Rule 9 of the CoR Rules of Procedure, Official Journal L 65/41, 5.3.2014.

Unfortunately, the CoR remains particularly silent on the issues of civil dialogue and participation of the civil society in terms of lawmaking in the EU.[228] This is particularly visible in its practice of consultations. It prefers to make use of a discourse on "subsidiarity," "proximity" and "closeness to the people," rather than stress the role of intermediary organizations.[229] This is especially curious as local and regional authorities often have very well-established relations with intermediary organizations since they are the most natural direct interlocutors for grassroot organizations. Also, as it was noticed in the doctrine, the CoR has looked with reserve on civil dialogue practices which involve associations of regional and local authorities. In turn, the CoR tried to affirm its exclusive legitimacy as the institutional discussion partner for the local and regional authorities of the Union.[230] As a result, subnational entities' participation in EU governance has not been particularly facilitated by the Committee.[231]

This means that, regrettably, the CoR does not play the role it could play for enabling the capacity of European civil society. However, what is not surprising is the fact that there is little difference between both consultative committees (i.e., the EESC and the CoR) in terms of their actual influence on decision-making and lawmaking processes. Both institutions have a similar influence capacity on the addresses of the recommendations and the final outcomes of the lawmaking procedure.[232] The only significant difference seems to be the more proactive role of the EESC in terms of engaging in dialogue with the organized civil society.[233]

[C] Organizations Operating at the EU Level

The complexity of organizational possibilities for NGOs wishing to advocate at the EU level is much wider than often assumed. Originally, mainly trade unions and various lobby organizations were present at the EU institutions to impact political issues and speak for grassroot interests.[234] Nevertheless, the relocation of numerous competences in a wide number of policy areas from Member States to the EU implied that NGOs had become more aware of the processes taking place in Brussels.[235] Nowadays, they seek access and engage in various civil dialogue models with the EU institutions.[236] Consequently, the number of EU-based civil society actors is continuously growing. A brief review of the Transparency Register[237] (which will be discussed further in the

228. S. Smismans, *European...*, p. 493.
229. *Ibid.*, p. 494.
230. C. Jeffery, *European...*, p. 375.
231. E. Borghi E., *The Development of the Committee of the Regions* in: *Governing Europe under a Constitution*, H.J. Blanke, S. Mangiameli (eds), London 2006, p. 217.
232. Ch. Hönnige, D. Panke, *The Committee...*, p. 466.
233. Displaying itself in, e.g. the establishment of the Liaison Group.
234. E. Borghi E., *The Development...*, p. 218.
235. G. Cliquennois, B. Champetier, *The Economic...*, p. 93.
236. M.I. Neshkova, *The Impact of Subnational Interests on Supranational Regulation*, Journal of European Public Policy Vol. 8/2010, pp. 1201.
237. According to the EU Transparency Register, available at: http://ec.europa.eu/transparencyregister/public/homePage.do?locale=en#en (on February 9, 2019).

subsequent chapter) for early February 2019 indicates 3,161 NGOs (out of a total of 11,890 subjects) running activities in relation to the EU institutions. The actors who have funding or seek consultation of the EU officials and institutions are expected to register in this database.

What should be mentioned at this point of analysis (but what will be also the subject matter for investigation in the subsequent parts of this book) is that NGOs tend to take a different approach to particular EU institutions. The main reason for this is that the institutions themselves seek dialogue with NGOs to achieve diverse goals. The Commission has especially institutionalized various channels of "dialogues with civil society," in which a wide range of groups are able to participate in a variety of activities described as "decision shaping."[238] However, the unfortunate general statement that can be flagged at this point is that the composition of NGOs participating in dialogue at the EU level is repeatedly dictated by which groups and associations the Commissions choose to fund and often create.[239] It is why, contrary to the concept of civil society presented in the first chapter, as rooted in independence from political institutions, it seems that, until now, the Commission's effort to create a transnational civil society has ended up in undermining NGOs independence.[240]

Nevertheless, the scope of NGOs operating at the EU level is very wide. It can be generally observed that they tend to follow a "Russian Doll" pattern, with smaller units enclosed to ever-larger ones.[241] It seems that this analogy may be taken even further by recognizing that individual EU-level NGOs can be made of numerous national organizations, many of which are in turn composed of several groups. While the specifics vary with different settings, three levels of organization can be identified: (1) individual EU-level NGOs, (2) NGO platforms and (3) NGO meta-networks:[242]

(1) Individual EU-level NGOs[243] generally represent a particular interest and concentrate their activities on the EU institutions and sometimes also on (particular) Member States. Accordingly, they are usually registered under Belgian Law or have permanent representations in Brussels.[244] This level of organization is the most diversified as far as the objectives, resources and managements conditions are concerned. Some individual EU-level NGOs are well established with offices and employed staff members in central locations in Brussels and tend to follow the organization pattern of large enterprises.[245]

238. T. Risse, *"Let's Argue!" Communicative Action in World Politics*, International Organization Vol. 1/2000, p. 5.
239. R. Sanchez Salgado, *Europeanizing...*, p. 47.
240. Ch. Dany, *Civil Society Participation under Most Favourable Conditions: Assessing the Deliberative Quality of the WSIS* in: *Civil Society Participation in European and Global Governance*, J. Steffek, J. Kissling, P. Nanz (eds), New York 2008, p. 64.
241. D. Ferri, *Participation...*, p. 337.
242. *Ibid.*, p. 339.
243. I.e., Amnesty International, Care International, ClientEarth, Danish Refugee Council, Greenpeace, Handicap International, ILGA-Europe, International Rescue Committee, Médecins Sans Frontières International, Oxfam International, WWF EU.
244. D. Ferri, *Participation...*, p. 339.
245. E.g., the Memorial Society, see Cliquennois, B. Champetier, *The Economic...*, pp. 102-103.

In fact, there are some organizations that carry out campaigns, present positions papers, organize conferences or deliver press releases.[246] Still, others are less established or formalized and may lack professional personnel or have insufficient budget. This, however, does not change the fact that they may take advantage of all the possible participation tools available at the EU level. It is also important to emphasize that both small and large-scaled organizations provide the EU citizens and other individuals (including domestic NGOs) with information about the EU policy and possible means of cooperation in transnational relations.[247]

(2) NGO platforms organize individual EU-level NGOs in large networks on the basis of an issue area.[248] In fact, most NGOs of this type are associations of other associations. In this way, a highly organized system of coordinated "families" of thematic NGOs emerged, partly due to the initiative of the EU institutions[249] as they sought NGOs partners with whom they could consult different issues.[250] For instance, the establishment of Social Platform, which gathers organizations active in the fields of social policy and antidiscrimination, was intensively promoted in the mid-1990s especially by the Commission.[251] The main idea behind this process was a purposeful search for partners capable of acting as liaisons and agents of civil society in the new and meaningful sphere of the EU competences.[252] As such, it can be perceived as an outcome of the EU nonbinding papers issued in the 1990s on the possible role of NGOs, as discussed in the preceding paragraphs of this chapter. Still, most NGO platforms at the EU level have a far more "grassroot" origin and are an outcome of the "Europeanization" process of civil society.[253] In fact, some of the largest organizations of this type started to emerge in the 1970s, and they have been active ever since.[254] This level of organization is also

246. J. Greenwood, *Interest Representation in the European Union*, London 2011, p. 187.
247. D. Ferri, *Participation...*, p. 350.
248. F. Furtak, *Nichtregierungsorganisationen...*, pp. 79 et seq.
249. J. Greenwood, *Interest...*, p. 189. This governance strategy introduced by the Commission was said to be based on the confidence in "the malleability of society"; for more see B. Kohler-Koch, B. Finke, *The Institutional Shaping of EU-Society Relations: A Contribution to Democracy via Participation?*, Journal of Civil Society Vol. 3/2007, pp. 205 et seq.
250. C. Ruzza, *Changes in the Field of EU Civil Society Organisations: Institutionalisation, Differentiation and Challengers* in: *EU Civil...*, p. 36.
251. A. Classen, *Interessenvertretung in der Europaischen Union. Zur RechtmaBigkeit politischer Einflussnahme*, Wiesbaden 2014, p. 116.
252. It is often evaluated that the relationship between the EU institutions and various interest groups could be described as being "clientele" with the Commission selecting a few groups with which it felt "comfortable." See D. Obradovic, *Civil...*, 266.
253. T. Jansen, *Zur Europäisierung der "organisierten Zivilgesellschaft: ein Bericht aus der Praxis* in *Europäische...*, pp. 153 et seq., K. Borońska-Hryniewiecka, *Europeanization of Non-state Actors: Towards a Framework for Analysis* in: *Civil Society and International Governance. The Role of Non-state Actors in Global and Regional Regulatory Frameworks*, D. Armstrong, V. Bello, J. Gilson, D. Spini (eds), Abingdon 2011, pp. 73 et seq.
254. Some examples are Concord (i.e., European NGO Confederation for relief and development, active in the field of development aid; it was founded in 2003, but its predecessor, CLONG-EU, was created in 1976; for more see: http://concordeurope.org/who-we-are/) or the EEB (i.e., European Environmental Bureau, which was set up in 1974 to provide a focal point for its

attributed to "umbrella organizations." They can be described as associations that work together formally to coordinate activities or pool resources.[255] Umbrella organizations provide resources and often an identity to the smaller organizations. Moreover, they are often not specifically concentrated on one issue but are determined by the country of their origin.[256]

(3) NGO meta-networks are various mechanisms of cooperation, dialogue and ad hoc liaison between NGO platforms.[257] They are also sometimes referred to as "horizontal networks."[258] One example is the EU Civil Society Contact Group which gathers NGO platforms from eight sectors and aims at bringing together "the voices of hundreds of thousands of organizations across the Union."[259] Another one is the already mentioned Liaison Group, which groups representatives NGO platforms interacting with the EESC. Its goal is to provide a framework for dialogue and cooperation between the EESC and European organizations and networks and thus to maintain "a unique bridge between civil society and the European institutions."[260]

These three levels of organizations deliver a certain insight into the EU-based NGOs. Nevertheless, it should be borne in mind that civil society actors operating at the EU level can take many forms.[261] Even though some cannot be easily sorted into hierarchical structures, most of them are in fact, at least to some extent, connected with wider networks. Moreover, organizations performing at the EU level also include social movements which are more activist or grassroot oriented or are simply much less formalized.[262]

Without going into details, as they exceed the subject matter of this book, it should be notified that the present representativeness of European civil society in Brussels is strongly criticized in the literature. This criticism is based on two crucial

members to monitor and respond to the EU's emerging environmental policy; for more see: http://eeb.org/homepage/about/).

255. D. Ferri, *Participation...*, p. 352.

256. A good example of such an umbrella organization is Grupa Zagranica—a platform of Polish NGOs engaged in development, cooperation, democracy, support, humanitarian aid and global education (for more details see: http://zagranica.org.pl/en, on February 9, 2019).

257. D. Ferri, *Participation...*, p. 347.

258. P. Swieboda, P. Zerka, *Aktywność polskich organizacji pozarządowych na szczeblu europejskim. Ekspertyza przygotowana na zlecenie Urzędu Komitetu Integracji Europejskiej*, Warsaw 2009, p. 30, available at: http://kalendarz.ngo.pl/files/prezydencja.ngo.pl/public/aktywnosc_pol_ngo_szczebel_UE.pdf.

259. I.e., culture, environment, education, development, human rights, public health, social and women; for more information see: https://cultureactioneurope.org/projects/civil-society-contact-group/ (on February 9, 2019).

260. For more information see: http://www.eesc.europa.eu/en/sections-other-bodies/other/liaison-group (on February 9, 2019). Other examples are the European Migration Forum, run by European Commission's Directorate-General HOME, the Frontex Consultative Forum, the Fundamental Rights Agency's Fundamental Rights Platform; see also M. Thiel, *European Civil Society and "Participatory" Governance Tools: The Impact of the EU Fundamental Rights Agency and Platform* in: *Democratic Legitimacy in the European Union and Global Governance*, B. Pérez de las Heras (ed.), Cham 2017, pp. 104-105.

261. D. Ferri, *Participation...*, p. 347.

262. *Ibid.*, p. 347.

issues. First, it is argued that due to the corporate character of most influential NGOs and their further systems of cooperation, the existing environment of EU-based NGOs forms a "Brussels-oriented civil society"[263] which is almost utterly detached from the grassroot civil societies in Member States.[264] It follows that even though some NGOs compose a counter-elite,[265] their participation in the EU governance can widen the division between the EU institutions and the EU citizens by inserting an extra elite structure into the policy and lawmaking practices.[266] Second, it is argued that the present NGO schemes in Brussels privilege organization from the Western Europe as a result of their long history with EU institutions, larger budgets and better know-how.[267] The situation is also somewhat solidified by platforms of NGOs which usually gather organizations which have been present at the EU level for some time.[268] Thus, it is quite challenging for smaller and unknown NGOs to make their way in the Brussels environment. Although this assertion seems justified, it should be noted that organizations from "newer" Member States are also partly responsible for the present situation. They often neglect the advocacy possibilities at the EU level and usually abstain from joining international or European platforms of cooperation.[269] This, in turn, forms a vicious circle. The absence in various means of cooperation translates into a relatively low awareness of the EU agenda. Thus, the feeling of the EU "exclusiveness" and the indifference toward making one's own voice heard at the EU level deepen.[270] Though the present system is vulnerable to obvious criticism, the fact is that the only way to perform effectively in Brussels is to be present and to seek contacts and possible allies.[271]

[D] Summary

The official arena of NGO participation in the EU constitutional system is the EESC which even describes itself as "bridge between Europe and organized civil society." Additionally, another channel of participation is the CoR which functions as a representative arena for local and regional representatives. Still, their actual influence in the lawmaking is somewhat restricted. Moreover, even though the EESC is created

263. D. Obradovic, *Civil...*, pp. 318 et seq., A. Kutay, *Limits...*, p. 816.
264. Thus, the organizations operating at the EU level are often blamed for lack of accountability. For more see e.g. G. Moro, *Citizens...*, p. 62.
265. C. Quittkat, B. Finke, *The EU Commission Consultation Regime* in: *Opening EU Governance to Civil Society—Gains and Challenges*, B. Kohler-Koch, D. De Biévre, A. Maloney (eds), Mannheim 2008 (The CONNEX Report Series Nr 5), pp. 183 et seq.
266. A. Kutay, *Limits...*, p. 816.
267. See e.g. H. Cooper, G. Hervey, E. Bauvir, I. Antypas, *Big East-West Skew in Record EU Lobbying Bonanza*, available at: https://www.politico.eu/article/transparency-register-analysis-lobbying-east-west-skew-european-union/ (on February 9, 2019).
268. P. Cullen, *The Platform of European Social NGOs: Ideology, Division and Coalition*, Journal of Political Ideologies Vol. 15/2010, pp. 317 et seq.
269. In Poland only about 10% of organizations declare membership in an international platform of cooperation. In fact, this percentage has not really changed for years. See P. Swieboda, P. Zerka, *Aktywność...*, p. 42.
270. P. Swieboda, P. Zerka, *Aktywność...*, p. 61.
271. *Ibid.*, p. 49.

as a representative institution of civil society, only a minority of its members are assigned to NGOs. Therefore, the largest NGOs tend to operate on their own at the EU level, frequently forming platforms, meta-platforms and other means of ad hoc cooperation. This results in many problems of smaller organizations which face many entry barriers into the institutional environment in Brussels.

In reference to the remarks on the *modes* of participation existing in various IGOs presented in the first chapter, it should be emphasized that the EU developed means of NGO participation that are both unique (the existence of the EESC and the CoR) and similar to the ones existing in other systems (organizations operating on their own at the transnational level). However, the institutional channels of participation very often have limited influence on the actual outcomes of the legislative procedures. It is also remarkable that their position in the EU constitutional system is quite frail as their recommendations do not have any binding powers. On this account, NGOs regularly pursue an access to the EU institutions on their own. The paths of participation have different conditions depending on the particular institution. These requirements and the concerns they may raise will be examined in the subsequent chapter.

§2.04 CONCLUSION

The significance of the grassroot organizations in European integration has been important since 1957 when the EESC, a consultative institution for voicing the opinions of "social partners" and the representatives of civil society, was introduced to the system of the Communities. However, a stronger acknowledgment of citizens was endorsed much later, in the early 1990s, with the inclusion of the "social dimension" into the competences of the EU. Thus, a need for involving "social partners" into the "social dialogue" emerged. In this way, NGOs began to be mentioned as potential "partners" in various EU documents related to the social policy. Afterwards, a new notion of "civil dialogue" appeared at the EU level, this time encompassing various organizations and the representatives of civil society. The aim of this idea was to open the EU lawmaking to grassroot organizations in order to provide better input and output legitimacy of the Union. The most far-reaching conclusions were presented in the White Paper on European Governance of 2001 which proposed a new approach to the EU decision-making. Unfortunately, the concepts presented therein were not followed by any "harder" legislative means.

Nevertheless, the newly introduced[272] Article 11 of the TEU explicitly establishes the principle of "participatory democracy" at the EU level. Thus, the rules of participation and transparency are provided in order to make the activity of the EU institutions more open and to contribute to a stronger involvement of European civil society in decision-making and lawmaking procedures at the EU level. Moreover, the requirements of social participation, as well as freedom of assembly and of association, are provided in other Treaty provisions. All these preconditions are encapsulated in the rule of law and democratic standards which are expressly named as one of the "values"

272. I.e., after the Treaty of Lisbon.

of the EU in Article 2 of the TEU. The rule of law particularly requires that NGOs operate in a healthy and impartial civil society not only at the EU level but at the national level.

As discussed above, the EU constitutional system sets up separate consultative institutions that were designed to present the voice of the grassroot society in the EU lawmaking. However, due to their vulnerable competences, many NGOs seek to conduct their own policy in Brussels. As practice indicates, in order to be influential, the organizations have to group in platforms of cooperation and form coalitions. These circumstances, as well as the lack of know-how and adequate budgets, make it difficult for smaller-scaled organizations, particularly from the newer Member States, to function effectively at the EU level.

In conclusion, it can be stated that the position of NGOs in the constitutional system of the EU is a rather complex issue. The additional difficulty in discussing this subject matter arises from the fact that the EU does not simply adopt the most common *modes* of participation existing in various IGOs, as presented in the first chapter, but rather introduces unique forms of cooperation with NGOs. Therefore, no clear solutions from the experience of other IGOs can be easily transposed to the EU system. Nevertheless, the impact of NGOs on the functioning of the EU is evident. The EU law provides some direct legal "tools" of participation but in practice much depends on relatively informal factors. Legal and actual conditions of the dialogue between the EU institutions and NGOs, as well as other means of influencing the EU lawmaking, will be presented in the following chapter of this book.

CHAPTER 3

The NGO Influence on Shaping the EU Law

One of the main aspects of the EU-level direct democracy refers to the need of governing *with* the people, which "opens decision-making up to citizens *qua* organized interests."[1] In contrast to democratic participation *by* the people which is performed through voting,[2] government *with* the people depends on the inclusion of individuals (and NGOs as their representatives) in the EU lawmaking and implementation. This form of participation increases the transparency of the Union, and it enhances the EU legitimacy on the input side.[3] Nevertheless, as it was argued in the doctrine,[4] democracy *with* the people, as practiced across the EU, is hindered by the low involvement of individual citizens (rather than by their organized groups) in the EU procedures. Yet, it seems that this feature has great potential for strengthening supranational democracy.[5]

As it has already been mentioned in the previous chapters, there is no single route for NGOs to gain access to the EU institutions. Moreover, there is no formal recognition of NGOs which would allow them to be a formal actor in the EU lawmaking. In particular, there is no official "consultative status" (like in the UN system) that such organizations could obtain. Apart from that, the existing treaty regulations on democratic participation are short of proper executive norms. Moreover, even though the EESC was conceived as an institution having a purely advisory function, deprived of an active role in directly shaping the EU law, it has, in practice, a too limited capacity to effectively influence the EU decision and lawmaking even in an indirect manner.[6]

1. V. Schmidt, *Democracy in Europe: The EU and National Polities*, Oxford 2006, p. 25.
2. Apart from elections, ECI, for more see A. Leininger, *Direct Democracy in Europe: Potentials and Pitfalls*, Global Policy Vol. 6/2015, pp. 17 et seq.
3. P. Kostandinova, *Improving the Transparency and Accountability of EU Institutions: The Impact of the Office of the European Ombudsman*, Journal of Common Market Studies Vol. 5/2015, p. 1079.
4. V. Schmidt, *Democracy...*, p. 26.
5. P. Norris, *Democratic Deficit: Critical Citizens Revisited*, Cambridge 2011, p. 11.
6. Ch. Hönnige, D. Panke, *The Committee...*, p. 454.

Furthermore, although the creation of the CoR and the formalization of social dialogue,[7] both issuing from the Maastricht revision, were undoubtedly a significant change in addressing NGOs in the EU institutional system, they lacked subsequent actions in providing those organizations with strong, legal instruments to be a crucial partner in the lawmaking procedures.

The following paragraphs will aim at analyzing other, possibly more effective, means of access to the EU lawmaking by interest groups that continue to proliferate and increasingly gain importance. Thus, the first part of this chapter will concentrate on the grassroot legal tools of civil participation in the EU lawmaking, meaning access to documents and the European Citizens' Initiative. The second part will discuss the relations between NGOs and the EU institutions which, quite often, depend on both legal and nonlegal determinants. To complete the picture of the NGO influence on shaping the EU law, the third part will present lobbying regulations and practices.

§3.01 THE GRASSROOT TOOLS OF CIVIL PARTICIPATION IN THE EU LAW-MAKING

The subsequent paragraphs will concentrate on two legal tools that can be treated as incentives for active participation of grassroot civil society at the EU level:[8] access to documents and the European Citizens' Initiative. Even though the first one enables individuals to request for all EU documents (i.e., also those not directly linked to the lawmaking), it is most often used to exercise control over lawmakers in order to make their activities transparent and generally known to the public.[9] The latter one is a new instrument, introduced by the Treaty of Lisbon. Its main goal is to influence the EU law in a direct matter, i.e. by delivering a "grassroot" proposal for a legal act to the Commission.[10]

These two instruments will be first elaborated from a general perspective. After that, some practical references toward the NGO activity will be presented.

[A] Access to Documents

The essential part of direct democracy is the rule of transparency. It can be described as a rule enabling citizens to participate more closely in the decision-making process and guaranteeing that the administration enjoys greater legitimacy and is more effective and more accountable to the citizens.[11] Transparency is often used as a synonym for "access to documents" as it is the most evident element of the institutions'

7. Followed by the concept of "civil dialogue."
8. Cf. Ch. Marxsen, *Open Stakeholder Consultations at the European Level—Voice of the Citizens?*, European Law Journal Vol. 2/2015, p. 259.
9. Cf. J. Czerw, *Dostęp do informacji publicznej w Polsce*, Przegląd Prawa Publicznego Vol. 11/2013, p. 7.
10. A.J. Pichler, B. Kaufmann, *The European Citizens' Initiative: Into New Democratic Territory*, Oxford 2010, p. 11.
11. C-41/00 P *Interporc Im- und Export Gmbh*, ECLI:EU:C:2003:125, para. 39, C-28/08 P *European Commission v. The Bavarian Lager*, ECLI:EU:C:2010:378, para. 54.

transparency obligations. However, it should be remembered that it is a much wider notion which includes:[12]

- public access to documents,
- public access to information,
- openness of the decision-making system,
- institutional transparency and quality of drafting, and
- transparency of involvement of third-party actors.

The EU debate concerning transparency was undertaken only in the 1980s and early 1990s and resulted in developments introduced by the Maastricht Treaty. They proved the need for a different approach to contacts between the EU institutions and the Member States societies.[13] The incorporation of transparency obligations was primarily due to a greater involvement of the EP in the co-decision procedure.[14] Moreover, Declaration No. 17 on the right of access to information was added to the Maastricht Treaty. It reads: "the Conference considers that transparency on the decision-making process strengthens the democratic nature of the institutions and the public's confidence in the administration. The Conference accordingly recommends that the Commission submit to the Council no later than in 1993 a report on measures designed to improve public access to the information available to the institutions." In 1993 the Council issued Decision 93/731/EC on public access to its documents[15] which was followed by Decision 94/90/ECSC, EC, Euratom on public access to Commission documents[16] a year later. Both decisions enabled "the public" to have access to documents of these institutions under the conditions laid down.[17] The EP documents were made available under Decision 98/632/EC, ECSC, Euratom.[18] Subsequently, the Treaty of Amsterdam introduced a general right of public access to EP, Council and Commission documents in Article 255 of the TEC.[19]

12. B. Driessen, *Transparency in EU Institutional Law. A Practitioner's Handbook*, Aalphen aan den Rijn 2012, p. 4; Some authors associate "transparency" with the general rule of openness; see e.g. I. Kawka, *Zasady dobrego rządzenia w prawie Unii Europejskiej. Sektory infrastrukturalne*, Kraków 2011, pp. 61 et seq.
13. P. Craig, *EU Administrative Law*, Oxford 2018, pp. 388 et seq.
14. Which was previously not considered to be a strong institution, capable of representing citizens' interests effectively, see B. Driessen, *Transparency...*, p. 4. See also K. Kowalik-Bańczyk, *Komentarz do art. 24 Traktatu o funkcjonowaniu Unii Europejskiej* in: *Traktat o funkcjonowaniu Unii Europejskiej. Komentarz, t. I. Art. 1-89*, D. Miąsik, N. Półtorak, A. Wróbel (eds), Warsaw 2012, lex.pl.
15. Official Journal L 340/43, 31.12.1993.
16. Official Journal L 46/58, 18.2.1994.
17. These conditions were challenged in Case C-58/94 *Kingdom of the Netherlands v. Council of the European Union* (ECLI:EU:C:1996:171) as not transparent enough.
18. Official Journal L 263, 25.9.1997.
19. I.e., the Treaty establishing the European Community; see also A. Alemanno, O. Stefan, *Openness at the Court of Justice of the European Union: Toppling a Taboo*, Common Market Law Review Vol. 1/2014, pp. 97 et seq.

Nowadays, transparency is seen not only as democratic standard of the EU[20] but also as a key to the effectiveness and legitimacy of the EU institutions.[21] It also constitutes one of the general rules of the EU law.[22] Transparency is continuously amplifying in those spheres of the EU law where it has been absent so far.[23] Unfortunately, this general inclination is often undermined by informal "trilogues"[24] between the Commission, the Council and the EP in the lawmaking[25] or by the complexity of comitology procedures.[26] In general, the EU institution assumes that the documents[27] from the "trilogue" negotiations are precluded from disclosure.[28] However, the recent judgment of the General Court in T-540/15 *De Capitani v. European Parliament*[29] may limit this practice. In this judgment, the Court observed that "trilogue" meetings form an "established practice by which most EU legislation is adopted" and are therefore regarded as "decisive phases of the legislative process." Currently, between 70% and 80% of the EU legislative acts are adopted following a "trilogue."[30] At the same time, the EU primary law establishes a close relationship between legislative procedures and the principles of openness and transparency.[31] In

20. See opinion of Advocate General Tesauro in Case C-58/94 (ECLI:EU:C:1995:409), para. 19; see also J. Czaputowicz, *Administracja publiczna. Wyzwania w dobie integracji europejskiej*, Warsaw 2008, s. 15.
21. Which is also attributed to the need of "good quality of the services" provided by the EU institutions; see G. Krawiec, *Europejskie prawo administracyjne*, Warszawa 2009, s. 23.
22. Initially, legal doctrine was hesitant to recognize transparency as a new principle of EU law. It seems that its recognition as a general principle was heavily influenced by procurement law; for more see A. Buijze, *The Principle of Transparency in EU Law*, Vianen 2013, pp. 7 et seq.
23. This issue concerns, e.g. a new tendency of publishing position papers before trade negotiations. See, to this extent, e.g. Trade Package issued by the Commission in 2017, available at: http://trade.ec.europa.eu/doclib/press/index.cfm?id=1715. The need of transparency has also been raised in the context of negotiating the terms of the so-called Brexit; see e.g. E. Zalan, E. Maurice, *Transparency Is Key EU Tactic in Brexit Talks*, available at: https://euobserver.com/uk-referendum/137444.
24. A trilogue is understood as a tripartite, informal meeting between the Commission, the Council and the EP taking place in order to agree upon the amendments in the legislative procedure. See also e.g. T. Delreux, *Concluding Early Agreements in the EU: A Double Principal-Agent Analysis of Trilogue Negotiations*, Journal of Common Market Studies Vol. 2/2018, pp. 300 et seq.
25. See also, to this extent, e.g. Investigation of informal trilogue negotiations since the Treaty of Lisbon—Added value, lack of transparency and possible democratic deficit. Study by the EESC, 2017, available at: http://www.eesc.europa.eu/en/our-work/publications-other-work/publications/investigation-informal-trilogue-negotiations-lisbon-treaty-added-value-lack-transparency-and-possible-democratic-deficit.
26. P. Craig, *Comitology, Rulemaking and the Lisbon Settlement: Tensions and Strains* in: *Rulemaking by the European Commission. The New Systems for Delegations of Powers*, C.F. Bergstrom, D. Ritleng (ed.), Oxford 2016, pp. 174-175; see also P. Craig, *EU...*, pp. 111 et seq.
27. In fact, they consist of tables containing four columns: the first contains the text of the Commission's legislative proposal, the second the position of the Parliament as well as the amendments that it proposes, the third the position of the Council and the fourth the provisional compromise text or the preliminary positions of the Presidency of Council in relation to the amendments proposed by the Parliament. See also para. 75 in T-540/15.
28. On the basis of Art. 4 (3) of Regulation 1049/2001, as discussed in the following paragraphs. Cf. the European Ombudsman decision in Case OI/8/2015/JAS.
29. ECLI:EU:T:2018:167.
30. Para. 70 in T-540/15.
31. See, to that effect, Opinion of the Advocate General Cruz Villalón in C-280/11 P *Council v. Access Info Europe*, C-280/11 P, EU:C:2013:325, paras. 39-40.

particular, Article 15 (2) of the TFEU lays down that "the Parliament shall meet in public, as shall the Council when considering and voting on a draft legislative act." In addition, it is precisely openness in the legislative process that contributes to conferring greater legitimacy on the institution in the eyes of the EU citizens and increases confidence by allowing divergences between various points of view to be openly debated. It is, in fact, a lack of information and debate which is capable of giving rise to doubts in the minds of citizens, not only as regards the lawfulness of an isolated act but also as regards the legitimacy of the decision-making as a whole.[32] Therefore, openness contributes to strengthening democracy by allowing citizens to scrutinize all the information which has formed the basis of a legislative act. The possibility for citizens to find out the considerations underpinning legislative action is a precondition for the effective exercise of their democratic rights.[33] In general, giving the public the widest possible right of access entails that it must have the right to full disclosure of the requested documents, the only means of limiting that right being the strict application of the exceptions envisaged in the access to documents provisions.[34] Accordingly, the Court found that no general presumption of nondisclosure can be upheld in relation to the "trilogue" documents.[35]

The rule of transparency in its wide scope is provided by the already discussed Article 11 of the TEU and Article 15 of the TFEU. Nevertheless, as the conditions of consultations conducted by various EU institutions and their institutional openness will be a subject matter for analysis in the subsequent parts of this chapter, the following remarks at this stage of study will, in fact, concentrate on public access to documents. This right is ensured Article 15 (3) of the TFEU. Accordingly, any citizen of the Union, and any natural or legal person residing or having its registered office in a Member State, shall have a right of access to documents of the Union's institutions, bodies, offices and agencies, whatever their medium, subject to the principles and the conditions to be defined in accordance with this paragraph. General principles and limits on the grounds of public or private interest governing this right of access to documents shall be determined by the European Parliament and the Council, by means of regulations, acting in accordance with the ordinary legislative procedure.[36] Each institution, body, office or agency shall ensure that its proceedings are transparent and shall elaborate in its own Rules of Procedure specific provisions regarding access to its documents, in accordance with the regulations referred to in the second subparagraph. The Court of Justice of the European Union, the European Central Bank and the European Central Bank and the European Investment Bank shall be subject to this paragraph only when exercising their administrative tasks. The European Parliament and the Council shall ensure publication of the documents relating to the legislative procedures under the terms laid down by the regulations referred to in the second

---

32. Paras. 78-79 in T-540/15.
33. See, to that effect, C-39/05 P and C-52/05 P *Kingdom of Sweden and M. Turco v. Council of the European Union*, ECLI:EU:C:2008:374, para. 46, T-710/14 *Herbert Smith Freehills v. Council*, ECLI:EU:T:2016:494, para. 35.
34. Para. 80 in T-540/15.
35. Para. 84 in T-540/15.
36. This provision is the Treaty basis for Regulation 1049/2001.

subparagraph. The right of access to documents is also provided by Article 42 of the EUChFR. According to this regulation, any citizen of the Union, and any natural or legal person residing or having its registered office in a Member State, has a right of access to European Parliament, Council and Commission documents. As it can be seen, it is a repetition of the main premises of Article 15 of the TFEU.

Specific conditions dealing with public access to documents[37] are determined by Regulation (EC) No 1049/2001 of the European Parliament and of the Council of May 30, 2001, regarding public access to European Parliament, Council and Commission documents.[38] What is particularly significant for further analysis and what has been emphasized in the preamble:

- openness enables citizens to participate more closely in the decision-making process and guarantees that the administration enjoys greater legitimacy and is more effective and more accountable to the citizen in a democratic system;[39]
- in order to bring about greater openness in the work of the institutions, access to documents should be granted by the European Parliament, the Council and the Commission not only to documents drawn up by the institutions but also to documents received by them;[40]
- in principle, all documents of the institutions should be accessible to the public. However, certain public and private interests should be protected by way of exceptions. The institutions should be entitled to protect their internal consultations and deliberations where necessary to safeguard their ability to carry out their tasks. In assessing the exceptions, the institutions should take account of the principles in Community legislation concerning the protection of personal data, in all areas of Union activities.[41]

According to the Regulation, access to the EU documents is based on the following principles:[42]

(1) the access should be as wide as possible,
(2) the competent institution should ex officio consider partial access and overriding public interest,
(3) the exceptions should be interpreted in a strict manner,[43]
(4) the reasons for refusal must be presented thoroughly.

The very definition of a "document" is set out in Article 3 (a) of the Regulation. Accordingly, this notion shall mean any content whatever its medium (written on

37. Often referred to as "FOI requests" (i.e., Freedom of information requests).
38. Official Journal L 145, 31.5.2001.
39. Point 2 of the preamble to Regulation 1049/2001.
40. Point 10 *in principio* of the preamble to Regulation 1049/2001.
41. Point 11 of the preamble to Regulation 1049/2001.
42. B. Driessen, *Transparency...*, pp. 41-58.
43. For instance, the EU institution cannot refuse access to documents due to the fact that they are numerous and making them available would be burdensome (see T-2/03 *Verein für Konsumenteninformation v. Commission of the European Communities*, ECLI:EU:T:2005:125).

paper or stored in electronic form or as a sound, visual or audiovisual recording) concerning a matter relating to the policies, activities and decisions falling within the institution's sphere of responsibility.

The right of citizens' access to documents is an exercise of their democratic rights.[44] According to Article 2 (1) of the Regulation, any citizen of the Union, and any natural or legal person residing or having its registered office in a Member State, has a right of access to documents of the institutions, subject to the principles, conditions and limits defined in this Regulation. As it can be seen, NGOs, both having a statutory office in one of the Member States and foreign-based organizations operating in the EU, are included in the catalog of subjects with a right of access to the EU documents.[45] As a general rule, all documents held by the EP, the Council and the Commission should be made available to the public. Moreover, according to Article 12 of the Regulation, wider access should be granted to documents in cases where these institutions are acting in their legislative capacity, including under delegated powers, while at the same time preserving the effectiveness of the institutions' decision-making process.[46] Such documents should be made directly accessible to the greatest possible extent. In contrast, other EU institutions and bodies (e.g., the CJEU, the EESC or the EU agencies) are not encompassed by the scope of Regulation 1049/2001. This means that they provide their own rules for access to their documents[47] which is frequently a subject matter of controversies.[48]

Applications for access to a document should be made in any written form, including electronic form,[49] in one of the official languages of the EU. The applicant is not obliged to state reasons for the application. The request should, however, be formulated in a sufficiently precise manner in order to enable the institution to identify

44. Which is also referred to as "rights-based approach to access to documents." See M. Szwarc, *Dostęp do dokumentów instytucji Wspólnot Europejskich* in: *Unia Europejska. Prawo instytucjonalne i gospodarcze*, A. Łazowski (ed.), Warsaw 2005, p. 375.
45. Still, according to the European Ombudsman, the Commission should stop requiring requesters to provide their postal addresses. See Decision in Case 682/2014/JF on the European Commission's requirement that persons who ask for public access to documents provide their postal address.
46. According to the CJEU: "Openness in that respect contributes to strengthening democracy by allowing citizens to scrutinize all the information which has formed the basis of a legislative act. The possibility for citizens to find out the considerations underpinning legislative action is a precondition for the effective exercise of their democratic rights"; C-39/05 P and C-52/05 P *Kingdom of Sweden and M. Turco v. Council of the European Union*, ECLI:EU:C:2008:374, para. 46.
47. See e.g. Decision of the Court of Justice of the European Union of 11 October 2016 concerning public access to documents held by the Court of Justice of the European Union in the exercise of its administrative functions (2016/C 445/03), Official Journal C 445/3, 30.11.2016, Decision of the European Economic and Social Committee of 1 July 2003 on public access to European Economic and Social Committee documents (2003/603/EC), Official Journal C 205/19, 14.8.2003.
48. For instance, the CJEU, in contrast to, e.g. the ECHR does not provide access to transcripts, audio or video recordings of the hearings. See, to this extent, A. Alemanno, O. Stefan, *Openness...*, pp. 131-132. Still, it should be observed that the CJEU is not obliged to provide such access under Article 15 of the TFEU as it does not concern administrative tasks.
49. In fact, there are platforms that enable to lodge a request for access to a document using predefined templates (see e.g. https://www.asktheeu.org/).

the document (Article 6 (1) of the Regulation). The EU institutions are requested to assist the applicant. Thus, if an application is not sufficiently precise, the institution shall ask the applicant to clarify the application and shall assist the applicant in doing so, for example, by providing information on the use of the public registers of documents (Article 6 (2) of the Regulation). Moreover, the application for access to documents should be handled "promptly." Article 7 (1-3) of the Regulation sets the time frame of 15 days for the institution to either grant such access or refuse it. This period of time can be exceeded to 30 days in "exceptional cases." If the access to the requested document is refused (either in full or in part), the applicant can lodge a confirmatory application to the same EU institution. If the access remains defied, the decision can be appealed to the General Court or be subject of a complaint to the European Ombudsman, as discussed in the fourth chapter of this book. However, at this point of analysis, it is significant to outline that the utilization of the concrete measure depends on the applicant and the characteristics of a specific case. If the request deals with administrative issues (e.g., keeping minutes by the EU institution), it would be advantageous to lodge a complaint on account of maladministration.[50] There is also no time period to file a case before the Ombudsman and, in practice, this procedure is handled much quicker than the court proceedings.[51] However, the opinions issued by the European Ombudsman after the conducted inquiries are not binding for the EU institutions. Even though the institutions tend to recognize them, it is perceivable that in the most ambiguous cases the answer to the request would still remain negative.[52] The General Court does not have a direct competence of ordering access to the requested document either. However, it can require the proper EU institution to exhibit the document to the Court in order to evaluate the reasons for refusal.[53] Therefore, the authority of the CJEU in cases of access to documents is more compelling. Nevertheless, it should be also borne in mind that court proceedings are longer than the cases handled by the European Ombudsman and take approximately 15 to 24 months.[54]

The appeal procedures are important in practice as granting or refusing access to a document relies heavily on the discretion of the proper institution.[55] The exceptions to the general right of access to the EU documents are determined in Article 4.[56]

50. According to Art. 228 (1) of the TFEU, complaints to the European Ombudsman can be lodged only in cases of maladministration in the activities of the EU institutions.
51. P. Kostandinova, *Improving...*, p. 1088.
52. H. Kranenborg, W. Voermans, *Access to Information in the European Union: A Comparative Analysis of EC and Member State Legislation*, Amsterdam 2005, p. 37.
53. *Ibid.*, p. 22.
54. Cf. The CJEU 2017 Annual Report on Judicial Activity, available at: https://curia.europa.eu/jcms/upload/docs/application/pdf/2018-04/_ra_2017_en.pdf (on February 9, 2019), pp. 206 et seq.
55. In fact, even the disclosures of documents oftentimes cast doubts as in many cases they are limited to, e.g. references to press releases.
56. Narrower exceptions are provided in case of access to environmental information. This issue will be discussed in Chapter 4.

According to its paragraphs (1) and (2), the institutions shall refuse access to a document where disclosure would undermine the protection of:[57]

- the public interest as regards: public security, defense and military matters, international relations,[58] the financial, monetary or economic policy[59] of the Community (the EU) or a Member State;
- privacy and the integrity of the individual, in particular in accordance with Community (the EU) legislation regarding the protection of personal data;[60]
- commercial interests of a natural or legal person,[61] including intellectual property;
- court proceedings and legal advice;
- the purpose of inspections, investigations and audits—unless there is an overriding public interest in disclosure.

These are the so-called absolute exception of access to documents, in contrast to the relative exceptions which will be discussed afterwards. Nevertheless, in accordance with well-established case law,[62] in order to justify refusal of access to a document the disclosure of which has been requested, it is not sufficient, in principle, for that document to be covered by an activity mentioned in Article 4 (1) or (2). The institution concerned must also supply explanations as to how access to that document could specifically and effectively undermine the interest protected by an exception laid down in this provision.[63]

Many doubts concern the meaning of an "overriding public interest." What is significant for NGOs operating at the EU level is that their statutory aims, even if

57. For further information concerning the frequency of application of the specific exceptions see: http://blog.asktheeu.org/category/statistics/ (on February 9, 2019).
58. This exception is understood very widely by the EU institutions and the CJEU. See e.g. T-529/09 *S. in't Veld v. Council of the European Union*, ECLI:EU:T:2012:215, T-301/10 *S. in't Veld v. European Commission*, ECLI:EU:T:2013:135, T-331/11 *L. Besselink v. Council of the European Union*, ECLI:EU:T:2013:419.
59. For more information on the understanding of these conditions with reference to disclosure obligation of documents deriving from the pesticide companies see e.g. C-673/13 P *Commission v. Stichting Greenpeace Nederland and PAN Europe*, ECLI:EU:C:2016:889.
60. Which is commonly understood very extensively by the CJEU (see, to this extent, e.g. C-28/08 P *European Commission v. The Bavarian Lager Co. Ltd.*, ECLI:EU:C:2010:378). Still, there are cases there this exception is interpreted quite strictly as well (see, to this extent, e.g. T-115/13 *G.-J. Dennekamp v. European Parliament*, ECLI:EU:T:2015:497).
61. In particular, however, it cannot have an overriding value over the general presumption of disclosure of information which "relates to emission into the environment" (see, to this extent, T-716/14 and T-329/17 *Anthony C. Tweedale v. European Food Safety Agency (EFSA) and Hautala and Others v. EFSA*, ECLI:EU:T:2019:141).
62. E.g., Case C-139/07 P *European Commission v. Technische Glaswerke Ilmenau GmbH* (ECLI:EU:C:2010:376), Case T-677/13 *Axa Versicherung AG v. European Commission* (ECLI:EU:T:2015:473), T-306/12 *Darius Nicolai Spirlea and Mihaela Spirlea v. European Commission* (ECLI:EU:T:2014:816).
63. E.g., Case C-39/05 P *Sweden and Turco v. Council* (ECLI:EU:C:2008:374), para. 49; C-139/07 P *Commission v. Technische Glaswerke Ilmenau* (ECLI:EU:C:2010:376), para. 38, C-514/07 P, C-528/07 P and C-532/07 P *Sweden v. Association de la presse internationale ASBL (API)*, ECLI:EU:C:2010:541, para. 72, C-404/10 P, *Commission v. Éditions Odile Jacob* ECLI-:EU:C:2013:808, para. 116, C-477/10 P *Commission v. Agrofert Holding* (ECLI:EU:C:2012:394), para. 57.

directed at protecting specific spheres dealt by the EU law, do not per se constitute such an exception. As the General Court stated in T-424/14, 425/14 *ClientEarth*,[64] the interest of an applicant in supplementing the information held by the institution concerned and the participation in an ongoing procedure did not constitute an overriding public interest, even though the applicant was acting as an NGO, in accordance with the objects stated in its governing documents which consisted in the protection of the environment.[65] By analogy, it must be held that the interest of stakeholders who have taken part in a consultation organized by the Commission as part of the completion of an impact assessment does not automatically constitute an overriding public interest, even where the party is a not-for-profit organization whose object is the protection of the environment.[66]

Another example of this reasoning can be found in case C-514/11 P, C-605/11 P *Liga para Protecçāo da Naturez* (LPN).[67] LPN is a Portuguese NGO whose objective is the protection of the environment. In April 2003 it lodged a complaint with the European Commission in which it claimed that the dam construction project on the River Sabor in Portugal infringed Council Directive 92/43/EEC of May 21, 1992, on the conservation of natural habitats and wild fauna and flora[68] (Habitats Directive). Following the complaint, the Commission initiated an infringement procedure against the Portuguese Republic and contracted the Portuguese authorities in order to establish the extent to which the dam project was liable to infringe the Habitats Directive and Council Directive 79/409/EEC of April 2, 1979, on the conservation of wild birds.[69] In March 2007 LPN applied to the Commission for access to information on the processing of the complaint and asked to consult the documents drawn up by the "Commission working group" and those exchanged between the Commission and the Portuguese authorities. On the basis of the third incident of Article 4 (2) of Regulation 1049/2001, the Commission rejected that application by letter of May 22, 2007.[70] In particular, the Commission stated that in an infringement procedure, a climate of mutual trust needed to prevail between the Commission and the Member State concerned in order to enable them to start a process of negotiation and compromise with a view to an amicable settlement of the dispute without the need to bring proceedings before the Court of Justice. It also observed that, first, the process of negotiation between the Commission and the Portuguese authorities was still in progress and, second, several exchanges of views and meetings had taken place or were still due to take place for the purpose of assessing the impact of the dam project.[71] Moreover, so far as any "overriding public interest" is concerned within the meaning of the last phrase of Article 4 (2) of Regulation 1049/2001, the Commission considered there was none. Still, according to

64. ECLI:EU:T:2015:848.
65. See, to that effect, T-424/14 *LPN and Finland v. Commission*, ECLI:EU:C:2013:738, para. 95; see also, to that effect and by analogy, order in T-603/11 *Ecologistas en Acción v. Commission*, ECLI:EU:T:2014:182, paras. 75 and 121.
66. Para. 151 in T-424/14, 425/14.
67. ECLI:EU:C:2013:738.
68. Official Journal L 206, 22.7.1992.
69. Official Journal L 103, 25.4.1979.
70. Para. 8 in C-514/11.
71. Para. 20 in C-514/11.

Article 6 (1) of Regulation 1049/2001, an overriding public interest in disclosure must be deemed to exist where the information requested relate to emissions into the environment did not apply to investigations relating to possible infringements of the Community (EU) law, as in this case. It stated that the risk of the existence of a serious infringement of the Habitats Directive did not constitute such an interest since the CJEU alone had jurisdiction to establish that the Member State concerned had failed to fulfill its obligations under the EC Treaty. According to the Commission, disclosure of the requested documents would not provide any clarification in that regard until the Court of Justice had definitively resolved that issue.[72]

The Court of Justice stated that the requirement that an applicant relies on specific circumstances to show that there is an overriding public interest to justify the disclosure of the documents concerned is in accordance with the case.[73] However, even though LPN, as an NGO, is acting in accordance with its statutory aims, which consist of the protection of the environment and it may take an active part in that procedure,[74] that fact does not show that there is an "overriding public interest" within the meaning of Article 4 (2) of Regulation 1049/2001. Also, the Court of Justice stated that "the disclosure of the documents concerning an infringement procedure during its pre-litigation stage would, in addition, be likely to change the nature and progress of that procedure. In those circumstances, it could prove even more difficult to begin a process of negotiation and to reach an agreement between the Commission and the Member State concerned putting an end to the infringement alleged, in order to enable the European Union law to be respected and to avoid legal proceedings."[75]

Regulation 1049/2001 also deals with the access to legislative documents produced during the lawmaking procedure.[76] Thus, Article 4 (3) states that access to a document, drawn up by an institution for internal use or received by an institution, which relates to a matter where the decision has not been taken by the institution, shall be refused if disclosure of the document would seriously undermine the institution's decision-making process, unless there is an overriding interest in disclosure. In cases of closed procedures, the refusal of access to documents is justified if they contain opinions drawn up as part of deliberations or preliminary consultations.

Although the restriction established in the quoted paragraph seems rigorous, access to documents is most commonly declined on the grounds of possibly undermining the decision-making.[77] Furthermore, it is perhaps the most controversial exception due to its enhancing interpretation by the EU institution.[78] In case C-280/11 P *Council v. Access Info Europe*,[79] the CJEU had the opportunity to interpret the

---

72. Para. 21 in C-514/11.
73. See C-139/07 para. 62, Case C-514/07, para. 103, C-404/10, para. 126, C-447/10, para. 68.
74. Para. 95 in C-514/11
75. Para. 63 in C-514/11.
76. Which is basis for handling with the "trilogue" documents as mentioned before.
77. As noticed, this particularly concerns the "trilogue" documents. Cf. P. Konstandinova, *Improving...*, p. 1086.
78. Cf. *Guide on Access to EU Documents. Accessing Information from the European Union*, AccessInfo 2013, p. 35, available at: https://www.access-info.org/wp-content/uploads/EN_ONLINE_Guide_on_access_to_EU_Documents.pdf.
79. ECLI:EU:C:2013:671.

relevance of this "space to think" exception,[80] relating to situations where a decision has not yet been taken by the institution, in the legislative context. AccessInfo Europe, an NGO promoting freedom of information in the EU, requested access to the Council's legislative document including footnotes indicating the positions of individual Member States. The central question was whether access to Member State positions impacts negatively the effectiveness of the decision-making process and if so, which of the two rules—effectiveness or openness—should take priority. The ruling of the General Court, which confessed the primacy to the rule of openness, was appealed to the Court of Justice. The Council argued that the ruling had attached "undue and excessive weight to the transparency of the decision-making process, without taking any account of the needs associated with the effectiveness of that process."[81] Moreover, it disregarded the balanced approach laid down both in primary and secondary law to the relationship between the two objectives and argued that "its legislative process is very fluid and requires a high level of flexibility on the part of Member States so that they can modify their initial position, thus maximizing the chances of reaching an agreement."[82] Thus, in the Council's view identifying the delegations was not necessary for ensuring a democratic debate.[83]

The Court of Justice rejected the appeal on the assumption that full access can be limited only if there is a genuine risk that the protected interest might be undermined.[84] The high standard of proof required to establish that level of harm makes it almost impossible to rely on Article 4 (3) in this context. In particular, according to the Court: "the various proposals for amendment or re-drafting made by the four Member States delegations which are described in the requested document are part of the normal legislative process, from which it follows that the requested documents could not be regarded as sensitive—not solely by reference to the criterion concerning the involvement of a fundamental interest of the European Union or the Member States, but by reference to any criterion whatsoever."[85]

Further restrictions concerning the right of access to documents are provided in paragraphs (4), (5) and (6) of Article 4. Accordingly, as regards third-party documents, the institutions shall consult the third party with a view to assessing whether an exception in paragraph (1) or (2) is applicable, unless it is clear that the document shall or shall not be disclosed. A Member State may request the institution not to disclose a document originating from the Member State without its prior agreement. If only parts of the requested document are covered by any of the exceptions, the remaining parts of the document shall be released.

80. As it is commonly referred to in the literature. See e.g. Openness, Transparency and the Right of Access to Documents in the EU. In-depth analysis for the PETI Committee 2016, p. 8, available at: http://www.europarl.europa.eu/RegData/etudes/IDAN/2016/556973/IPOL_IDA(2016)556973_EN.pdf (on February 9, 2019).
81. Para. 23 in C-280/11.
82. Para. 24 in C-280/11.
83. Para. 15 in C-280/11.
84. Para. 40 in C-280/11.
85. Para. 63. in C-280/11.

These provisions were a basis of interpretation in the case C-135/11 P *Internationaler Tierschutz-Fonds gGmbh* (IFAW).[86] IFAW is a German NGO active in the field of the protection of animal welfare and nature conservation. Since it objected to an industrial project being carried out on a protected site in Germany, it requested access to a number of documents the Commission had received in connection with the examination of the industrial project, in particular certain documents originating from various authorities of the Federal Republic of Germany.[87] On June 19, 2008, the Commission adopted a decision relating to IFAW's request. By that decision, the Commission disclosed all the documents requested by IFAW, namely eight documents originating from the City of Hamburg and the Federal Republic of Germany but refused to grant access to the German Chancellor's letter because the German authorities had objected to disclosure of that document.[88] According to the decision, first, the German authorities had stated that disclosure of the Chancellor's letter would undermine the protection of the public interest regarding international relations and the economic policy of the Federal Republic of Germany within the meaning of the third and fourth indents of Article 4 (1) (a) of Regulation 1049/2001.[89] Moreover, the German authorities had stated that the disclosure of the Chancellor's letter would seriously undermine the protection of the Commission's decision-making process within the meaning of the second subparagraph of Article 4 (3) of Regulation 1049/2001.

The Court of Justice stated that unlike Article 4 (4) of Regulation 1049/2001, which gives third parties only a right to be consulted with respect to documents originating from them, by the institution concerned as regards the application of one of the exceptions in Article 4 (1) and (2), Article 4 (5) makes the prior agreement of the Member State a necessary condition for disclosure of a document originating from it, if that states so request.[90] It follows, conversely, that an institution which does not have the agreement of the Member State concerned is not entitled to disclose the document.[91] Yet, Article 4 (5) of Regulation 1049/2001 does not confer on the Member State concerned a general and unconditional right of veto,[92] so that it can oppose, in an entirely discretionary manner and without having to give reasons for its decision, the disclosure of any document held by an institution simply because it originates from that Member State.[93] Thus, the exercise of the power conferred on the Member State concerned by Article 4 (5) of Regulation 1049/2001 is delimited by the substantive exceptions set out in Article 4 (1)-(3) which the Member State merely being given in this respect a power to take part in the institution's decision. Accordingly, the prior agreement of the Member State referred to in Article 4 (5) resembles not a discretionary

86. ECLI:EU:C:2012:376.
87. Para. 10 in C-135/11.
88. Para. 24 in C-135/11.
89. Para. 25 in C-135/11.
90. Para. 54 in C-135/11.
91. Para. 56, in C-135/11, see also C-64/05 *Kingdom of Sweden v. Commission of the European Communities*, ECLI:EU:C:2007:802, para. 44.
92. See also, to this extent, C-64/05, para. 44.
93. Para. 57 in C-135/11 see also para. 58 in C-64/05.

right of veto but a form of assent that none of the groups of exception under Article 4 (1)-(3) is present.[94]

As far as the topic of this book is concerned, perhaps the most important statement of the Court of Justice in this case is a conclusion that from the point of view of a person requesting access, the Member State's intervention does not affect the nature of a European Union act of the decision subsequently addressed to him by the institution in reply to the request he has made for access to a document in its possession.[95] The institution to which the request is made, as the maker of a decision to refuse access to documents, is therefore responsible for the lawfulness of the decision[96] and must examine whether that state has based its objection on the substantive exceptions in Article 4 (1)-(3) of Regulation 1049/2001.[97]

Additionally, as it has already been noted, Article 15 of the TFEU currently establishes that the CJEU is subject to ordinary access to documents provisions only when exercising its administrative tasks. In August 2003, API, an NGO of foreign journalists based in Belgium applied to the Commission under Regulation 1049/2001 for access to the written pleadings lodged by the Commission before the General Court and the Court of Justice in proceedings relating to 15 cases at different stages.[98] The Commission granted access only in respect of the pleadings lodged in two preliminary ruling cases. Access to two pleadings was refused essentially because cases were pending. The same exception also applied to the pleadings of a closed case that was closely connected with another pending case. The Commission found that there was no overriding interest in disclosure.[99] Yet, clearly, the document applied for did fall within the scope of application of Regulation 1049/2001, in that they were documents either drawn up or received by the Commission and in its possession, and belonged to an area of activity of the EU.[100]

However, the Court of Justice confirmed in its ruling that an institution may base its decisions on a general presumption that apply to certain categories of documents. Thus, "it is clear, both of the wording of the relevant provisions of the Treaties and from the broad logic of Regulation 1049/2001 and the objectives of the relevant EU rules, that judicial activities are as such excluded from the scope, established by those rules, of the right of access to documents."[101] While the exclusion of the documents from the scope of public access was, in principle, acceptable, the Court argued for a temporal limitation: "the exclusion of judicial activities from the scope of the right of access to documents, without any distinction being drawn between the various procedural stages, is justified in the light of the need to ensure that, throughout the

94. Para. 58 in C-135/11 see also para. 76 in C-64/05.
95. Para. 60 in C-135/11.
96. Para. 61 in C-135/11.
97. Para. 62 in C-135/11.
98. In joined Cases C-514/07 P, C-528/07 P and C-532/07 P *Sweden v. Association de la presse internationale ASBL (API)*, ECLI:EU:C:2010:541.
99. For more see also P. Leino, *Just a Little Sunshine in the Rain: The 2010 case law of the European Court of Justice on Access to Documents* CML Rev Vol. 48/2011, p. 1215; D. Curtin, *Judging EU Secrecy*, Cahiers de Droit Européen, Vol. 2/2012 pp. 459 and 481.
100. Para. 73 in C-514/07, C-528/07 and C-532/07.
101. Para. 79 in C-514/07, C-528/07 and C-532/07.

court proceedings, the exchange of argument by the parties and the deliberations of the Court in case before it takes place in an atmosphere of total serenity."[102] For this reason, the Court judged it appropriate that there should be "a general presumption that disclosure of the pleadings lodged by one of the institutions in court proceedings would undermine the protection of these proceedings ... while those proceedings remain pending."[103] In the Court's view, "disclosure would flout the special nature of that category of documents and would be tantamount to making a significant part of the court proceedings subject to the principle of transparency." Consequently, "the effectiveness of the exclusion of the Court of Justice from the institutions to which the principle applies ... would be largely frustrated."[104]

As regards pleadings that had been lodged in closed cases, the Court pointed out that once the proceedings have been closed by a decision of the Court, there are no longer grounds for presuming that disclosure of the pleadings would undermine the judicial activities of the Court and the "general presumption" thus no longer applied.[105] The Court then pointed out that the procedures provided for under Articles 258 and 260 of the TFEU constitute two distinct proceedings, each with its own subject matter. Accordingly, as the General Court had found, it could not be presumed that disclosure of pleadings lodged in a procedure which ultimately led to the delivery of a judgment under Article 258 of the TFEU undermined investigations which could lead to proceedings being brought under Article 260 of the TFEU.[106] The Court's conclusion in this case deferred to public pressure with reference to equality of arms: "if the content of the Commission's pleadings were to be open to public debate, there would be a danger that the criticism levelled against them, whatever its actual legal significance, might influence the position defended by the Commission before the EU Courts."[107] Moreover, the Court proceedings would be at risk because "disclosure of the pleadings in question would have the effect of exposing judicial activities to external pressure, albeit only in the perception of the public, and would disturb the serenity of the proceedings."[108]

Basing on the discussed judgment and the existing legal provisions, it appears that there are no reasons to assume that the CJEU will provide broader access to documents related to ongoing procedures in the near future, even if wider access could be used for a broader collective good and the current situation is subject to criticism in the doctrine.[109]

As far as the practice of access to the EU documents is concerned, it should be observed that most of the requests are addressed to the Commission.[110] Applications to

102. Para. 92 in C-514/07, C-528/07 and C-532/07.
103. Para. 94 in C-514/07, C-528/07 and C-532/07.
104. Para. 95 in C-514/07, C-528/07 and C-532/07.
105. Para. 107 in C-514/07, C-528/07 and C-532/07.
106. Para. 122 in C-514/07, C-528/07 and C-532/07.
107. Para. 86 in C-514/07, C-528/07 and C-532/07.
108. Para. 93 in C-514/07, C-528/07 and C-532/07.
109. See e.g. A. Alemanno, O. Stefan, *Openness...*, pp. 97 et seq.
110. In 2016 6.077 initial applications were registered by the Commission; see Report from the Commission on the application in 2016 of Regulation (EC) No 1049/2001 regarding public access to European Parliament, Council and Commission documents, COM(2017) 0738 final.

the Council and to the EP are less frequent.[111] In fact, access to documents is granted in most cases.[112] Still, all applicants face many hurdles while seeking access to the EU documents. For instance, there are specific disclosure regimes in some spheres of the EU law.[113] Additionally, in certain instances, the EU institutions tend to opt for a general presumption of nondisclosure[114] or introduce internal rules of handling documents which raise doubts about their compatibility with Regulation 1049/2001.[115] Furthermore, the case law of the CJEU concerning access to documents can be inconsistent.[116] For this reason and based on the democratic and transparency provisions from Article 11 of the TEU, it seems that some modifications to Regulation 1049/2001 would be beneficial. Of course, general clauses (like "overriding public interest") limiting this access cannot be omitted. It is obvious that in some cases, a general access to documents should be restricted (yet, even then only temporarily).[117] This concerns, for instance, information obtained during negotiations with other parties or which affect public security. However, it appears that the application of exceptions should be restricted, especially when they are interpreted by the lawmakers themselves.[118]

Even though there is no official database regarding the applicants' profiles, it seems that NGOs and other agents of the organized civil society lodge a considerable number of requests for disclosure of documents to the EU institutions.[119] However, it should be also noted that the access to the EU documents is oftentimes overused. The

111. In 2015 a total of 2.784 initial applications were registered by the Council (see Fourteenth annual report of the Council on the implementation of Regulation (EU) No 1049/2001 of the European Parliament and of the Council of 30 May 2001 regarding public access to European Parliament, Council and Commission documents, 9308/16, p. 10). The EP received 499 applications via the online application form or by e-mail in 2016 (see Public Access to Documents 2016. European Parliament's Annual Report, PE 605.750/BUR/ANN, p. 8).
112. In 2016 only 4.8% requests were denied by the Commission (Report...), 17% request were denied by the EP (Public Access..., p. 8) and in 2015 14% request were denied by the Council (Fourteenth..., p. 10). However, it is important to emphasize that most request concern documents which are already available to the public (e.g., in online registers). These applications are "automatically" positively examined.
113. See e.g. Art. 8 of Commission Regulation (EC) No 773/2004 of 7 April 2004 relating to the conduct of proceedings by the Commission pursuant to Arts. 81 and 82 of the EC Treaty, Official Journal L 123, 27.4.2004. Furthermore, according to the EU data protection rules, in order to disclose personal data, the applicant has to provide proof of necessity (cf. C-28/08 P *European Commission v. The Bavarian Lager Co. Ltd*, ECLI:EU:C:2010:378).
114. Cf. e.g. T-424/14 and T-425/14 *ClientEarth v. Commission*, ECLI:EU:T:2015:848.
115. Cf. Handling of documents internal to the Council of 9.6.2011, 11336/11 which use the main principle of "nondisclosure, unless." See also, to this extent, Report of the Dutch parliamentary attorney Nieuwe Commissievoorstellen en initiatieven van de lidstaten van de Europese Unie 2016-2017, available at: https://goo.gl/4bd1Sz (on February 9, 2019).
116. Cf. C-28/08 P *European Commission v. The Bavarian Lager Co. Ltd*, ECLI:EU:C:2010:378 and T-166/05 *Borax Europe Ltd v. Commission of the European Communities*, ECLI:EU:T:2009:65, T-346/10 *Borax Europe Ltd v. European Chemicals Agency (ECHA)*, ECLI:EU:T:2011:510. See also, to this extent, D. Adamski, *Access to Documents, Accountability and the Rule of Law—Do Private Watchdogs Matter?*, European Law Journal Vol. 20/2014, pp. 520-543.
117. I. De Jesus Butler, *Non-governmental...*, p. 570.
118. Ch. Quittkat, *The European Commission's Online Consultations: A Success Story?*, Journal of Common Market Studies Vol. 49/2011, p. 653.
119. Basing on the data provided by the AskTheEU platform, it appears that academics are lodging requests most frequently (35.2% of all requests), followed by the civil society actors (24.8%).

case law demonstrates that, in some instances, Regulation 1049/2001, intended to secure the right of the general public to gain access to documents held by the institutions, is occasionally misused by parties for the purposes of individual administrative or judicial proceedings.[120]

[B] European Citizens' Initiative

The instruments of direct democracy have recently gained popularity around the world. Their main objective is to provide the public with means of direct influence on the decision and lawmaking procedures. Still, even if the rising role of citizen impact is accepted as enhancing democratic legitimacy in general, "the crucial normative question is the extent to which there should be an institutional capacity for the public at large to have a final say on issues of public policy."[121] In other words, it is not clear at which stage of the legislative process the citizens should be able to directly contribute to its outcomes, nor is it settled what ability should they have in the context of proposing the agenda in the first place.[122] On the one hand, it is often argued that the greater the scope of citizen influence (rather than political representatives or bureaucrats), the stronger the democratic legitimacy of the given policy.[123] On the other hand, it is indicated that if citizen influence is deprived of a certain degree of bureaucratic control, it is more likely to be ignored by the elected lawmakers.[124] The European Citizens' Initiative (ECI) is an instrument that tries to accommodate both approaches as it is generally designed to pass some control to citizens over the subject matter that is discussed as part of the legislative agenda at the EU level[125] under the assumption that this grassroot voice concerns the most important issues of the public at large.[126]

Nevertheless, it should be emphasized that the term "direct democracy" is usually referred to citizens directly voting on substantive issues that elected representatives normally vote on.[127] Perhaps the most common form of this concept is a facultative referendum, also called as a popular vote. Its aim is to put to a general vote a subject matter which may concern either a positive (e.g., a possibility of establishing

120. N. Persez-Solorzano, S. Smismans..., p. 413.
121. A. Leininger *Direct...*, p. 18, see also M. Marczewska-Rytko, *Idea demokracji bezpośredniej od okresu antycznego do czasów Internetu I globalizacji* in: *Demokracja bezpośrednia. Wymiar globalny i lokalny*, M. Marczewska-Rytko, A. Piasecki (eds), Lublin 2010, p. 13.
122. A. Leininger *Direct...*, p. 19.
123. S. Ahmed, *The Impact of NGOs on International Organizations: Complexities and Considerations*, Brooklyn Journal of International Law Vol. 36/2011, p. 819.
124. M. Setala, T. Schiller, *Citizens' Initiative in Europe. Procedures and Consequences of Agenda-Setting by Citizens*, London 2012, p. 73.
125. J. Organ, *Decommissioning Direct Democracy?, A Critical Analysis of Commission Decision-Making on the Legal Admissibility of European Citizens. Initiative Proposals*, European Constitutional Law Review Vol. 10/2014, p. 424, see also A. Warleigh, *On the Path to Legitimacy? The EU Citizens Initiative Right from a Critical Deliberativist Perspective* in: *Governance and Civil Society in the European*, C. Ruzza. V. Della Sala (eds), Manchester 2007, p. 55.
126. T. Hieber, *Die Europaische Bürgerinitiative nach dem Vertrag von Lissabon*, Tübingen 2014, p. 30.
127. M. Setala, T. Schiller, *Citizens'...*, p. 77.

a new law) or a negative measure (e.g., a recommendation of repealing an existing law). Still, it usually does not propose an introduction of a specific act of law.[128] In turn, the citizens' initiative is the most far-reaching form of direct democracy as it involves the citizens in terms not only of proposing a policy but also of subsequently voting on it.[129] Thus, if a group of citizens registers an initiative and collects a prescribed number of signatures in a prearranged time period, its proposal is put to a general (popular) vote.[130] Hence, some authors claim that the ECI cannot be treated as an instrument of direct democracy because of the fact that it is not followed by a popular vote of the EU citizens.[131] However, given that it is the only institutional possibility of directly influencing the EU law by European civil society, the above-presented statement should be treated with carefulness. For the purposes of this book, the ECI is considered the only instrument of direct democracy at the EU level, apart from the elections to the EP. Still, it should be remembered that overall it produces weaker legal consequences than national citizens' initiatives.[132]

The ECI is the first instrument of *transnational* citizens' initiative.[133] Its introduction was under consideration during the Convention on the Future of the EU in 2003-2004. In fact, it gained more supporters that the simultaneously deliberated idea of instituting a European referendum which eventually was considered to be possibly dangerous for the EU.[134] Thus, the ECI was designed as an agenda-setting tool which would enable the EU citizens to propose subject matters for further legislation.[135] It was also conceived as a direct participatory means that would invite grassroot initiatives to be put forward at the EU level, which would further deepen European identity.[136] This characteristic was set as a contrast to the existing institutionalized dialogue between the EU institutions and Brussels-based civil society.[137]

The ECI is established in Article 11 (4) of the TEU and is said to be the most innovative feature of participatory democracy introduced by the Treaty of Lisbon.[138]

128. J. Organ, *Decommissioning...*, p. 425.
129. A. Leininger *Direct...*, p. 18.
130. M. Setala, T. Schiller, *Citizens'...*, p. 80.
131. A. Leininger, *Direct...*, p. 19.
132. Cf. J. Organ, *Decommissioning...*, p. 438.
133. Or "supranational level," See J. Organ, *Decommissioning...*, p. 422, E. Hedling, A. Meeuwisse, *The European Citizens' Initiative Stage: A Snapshot of the Cast and Their Acts*, in: *EU Civil Society. Patterns of Cooperation, Competition and Conflict*, H. Johansson, S. Kalm (eds), Basingstoke 2015, p. 211.
134. As it is easier to engage citizens in negative campaigns (i.e., to stop something). See S. Hug, *Möglichkeiten und Grenzen direkten Demokratie in der EU* in: *Die EU und der Prozess ihrer Legitimation: Legitimationsgrundlagen der Europäischen Union*, F. Cheneval (ed), Hamburg 2007, pp. 111 et seq., M. Musiał-Karg, *Instytucje...*, pp. 203-220. In fact, in recent years, almost all popular votes on EU matters ended up with the same answer: no. See e.g. K. Lowe, K. Suter, *The Trouble With Referendums*, available at: https://www.politico.com/magazine/story/2016/07/brexit-trump-referendums-political-exclusion-214014 (on February 9, 2019).
135. See also J. Barcz, *Inicjatywa obywatelska—aspekty prawne i instytucjonalne*, Europejski Przegląd Sądowy Vol. 10/2011, p. 20, M. Dougan, *What Are We to Make of the Citizens' Initiative?*, Common Market Law Review Vol. 6/2011, p. 1807, T. Hieber, *Die Europäische...*, p. 15.
136. T. Hieber, *Die Europäische...*, p. 90.
137. Meaning NGOs based and operating in Brussels.
138. See e.g. J. Pichler, B. Kaufmann, *The European...*, p. 11.

According to this provision, not less than one million citizens who are nationals of a significant number of Member States may take the initiative of inviting the European Commission, within the framework of its powers, to submit any appropriate proposal on matters where citizens consider that a legal act of the Union is required for the purpose of implementing the Treaties. The procedures and conditions required for such a citizens' initiative shall be determined in accordance with the first paragraph of Article 24 of the Treaty on Functioning of the European Union.[139]

This provision could have been understood very broadly as allowing the EU citizens to choose the subject matter of proposals and seek popular support in relation to almost any issues that they, not the Commission, deem worth taking legislative action with the evaluation of the proposals only taking place when they are submitted to the Commission.[140] Nonetheless, it seems that Regulation (EU) No 211/2011 of the European Parliament and the Council on the citizens' initiative[141] took a much more restrictive approach by making registration of the initiatives subject to an admissibility test. This restraint seems to omit the reference to the ECI as an instrument of making "any appropriate proposals" of the EU citizens.[142]

In short, Regulation 211/2011 establishes two requirements for the registration of an ECI: admissibility test and procedural criteria.[143] The conditions for evaluating the admissibility test are set in Article 4 (2) (b), (c) and (d) of Regulation 211/2011. They require, respectively, that the proposed initiative is not "manifestly abusive, frivolous or vexatious" and "not manifestly contrary to the values of the Union as set out in Article 2 TEU." Moreover, the Regulation requires that the proposed citizens' initiative is not "manifestly outside the framework of the Commission's powers to submit a proposal for a legal act of the Union for the purpose of implementing the Treaties." The procedural criteria are provided in Article 2 of the Regulation. Thus, citizens living in at least a quarter of Member States should establish a "citizens' committee" which then becomes the subject responsible for the collection of at least one million signatures from at least seven countries.[144] The minimum number of signatories depends on the population of the given state.[145] The initiative must fall within the scope of the Commission's power to submit a proposal for the purpose of implementing the Treaties. Once the Commission receives a proper initiative with the required number of signatures, it should organize a hearing in order to enable the organizers to explain their proposal in detail. The citizens' committee should also be given an opportunity to present their initiative at a public hearing in the EP. Eventually, the Commission should officially respond to the initiative. It is not obliged to propose a legislative proposal even if it considers the initiative reasonable. In any case, the Commission is required to

139. I.e. in the already adopted Regulation 211/2011.
140. J. Organ, *Decommissioning...*, p. 427.
141. Official Journal L 65/1.
142. J. Organ, *Decommissioning...*, p. 427, E. Hedling, A. Meeuwisse, *The European...*, p. 214.
143. J. Organ, *Decommissioning...*, p. 425.
144. I.e., one quarter of all Member States, see Art. 2 point 1 of Regulation 211/2011.
145. E.g. Poland—37.500, Germany—74.250, Belgium—16.500, France—54.000, see Annex I to Regulation 211/2011.

explain the reasoning behind its actions. If it decides to recommend an act of law in response to the citizens' initiative, the proposal follows normal legislative procedure.

The procedural demands concerning the registration of an ECI do not seem especially demanding. The organizers are only asked to provide limited information concerning the initiative. An actual draft of a legal act is not required. Yet, the Commission seems to require that the initiative has an identified, specific legal base and is not based only on general principles of the EU.[146] Proposing an ECI also entails specific time limits, as presented in Figure 3.1.[147]

Figure 3.1 The European Citizens' Initiative Process

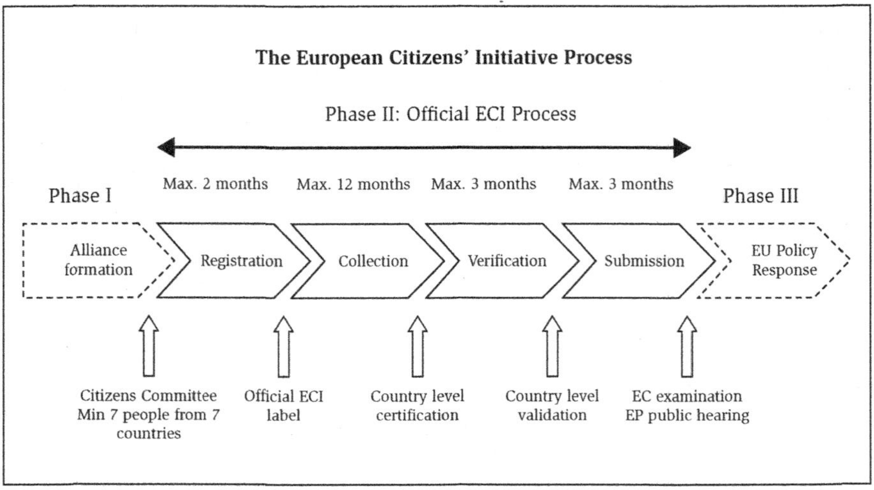

The prescribed time periods can be significantly burdensome as the "collection" period begins immediately after the registration of an ECI. While the registration depends on the discretionary power of the Commission, the organizers may be unprepared to start collecting signatures immediately after the decision is communicated to them. As 12 months is not an especially long time period for collecting one million statements of support, this can lead to a failure of the initiative.

Even more, problems are attributed to the admissibility test as in this phase the Commission has a wide range of discretionary power.[148] It is the interpretation and implementation by the Commission of Article 4 (2) (b) that have led to most of the refusals to register an initiative so far.[149] The Commission seems to apply this requirement very strictly and views most of the proposals as "manifestly outside the

146. J. Organ, *Decommissioning...*, p. 426.
147. As presented by C. Berg (The ECI Campaign, www.citizens-initiative.eu) in *How to launch a European Citizens' Initiative?*, a presentation during The Good Lobby Advocacy School 2017, 23.6.2017 in Brussels.
148. In practice, it is "judge and jury" while registering the ECIs.
149. J. Organ, *Decommissioning...*, p. 426.

framework of the Commission's powers."[150] Consequently, the difference between the "easiness" of registration and the actual requirements set by the Commission in the admissibility test often denies the organizers to receive a comprehensive or sufficient explanation of the reasons for the rejection of the initiative. Therefore, the possible input of the citizens' committees is often reduced in the actual decision-making process, allowing other factors to influence the registration of the initiatives at the same time.[151] This tendency, however, may be loosened by the case law of the CJEU. Recently, it even clearly indicated that "the aim of an ECI is to encourage participation by citizens and make the EU more accessible, so that ECIs must be easily accessible to citizens."[152]

For instance, in T-754/14 *Michael Efler v. European Commission*[153] the applicants instituted proceedings against a refusal of registering the ECI entitled "Stop TTIP." The ECI states that "the European Commission ... recommends that the Council cancel the negotiating mandate for the TTIP and not conclude the CETA." In respect of the aims pursued, the ECI proposal states that they consist in "preventing the TTIP and the CETA because they contain several critical issues such as procedures for the resolution of disputes between investors and the States and provisions on regulatory cooperation which threaten democracy and the rule of law ..., avoiding opaque negotiations leading to a weakening of the rules on employment protection, social protection, environmental protection, protection of private life and consumers and preventing public services and culture from being deregulated."[154] The Commission refused to register the ECI on the grounds that a Council decision authorizing the Commission to open negotiations with a view to conducting an agreement with a third country is not an EU legal act and that a recommendation relating thereto does not, therefore, constitute an appropriate proposal within the meaning of Article 11 (4) of the TEU and Article 2 (1) of Regulation 211/2011. The decision constitutes only a preparatory measure in the light of the subsequent decision of the Council to authorize the signing of the agreement, as negotiated, and to conclude that agreement. Such a preparatory decision would produce legal effects solely between the institutions concerned, without changing the EU law, contrary to the case of the decision to sign and conclude a specific agreement, which could be covered by an ECI. Moreover, the Commission evaluated that "destructive" acts (e.g., decisions not to sign or conclude the TTIP or the CETA) do not take effect for the purpose of "implementing the Treaties" and, therefore, cannot be covered by a proposal.[155]

The General Court did not share this reasoning. It stated that the objective of participation in the democratic life of the EU pursued by the ECI mechanism manifestly

150. See e.g. ec.europa.eu/citizens-initiative/public/initiatives/obsolete/details/2012/000009, ec.europa.eu/citizens-initiative/public/initiatives/non-registered/details/539 (on February 9, 2019).
151. J. Organ, *Decommissioning...*, p. 435, M. Dougan, *What...*, p. 1807.
152. See para. 64 in C-420/16 P *Balázs-Árpád Izsák and Attila Dabis v. Commission*, ECLI:EU:C:2019:177.
153. ECLI:EU:T:2017:323.
154. Para. 2 in T-754/14.
155. Paras. 4 and 40 in T-754/14.

includes the power to request an amendment of legal acts in force or their annulment, in whole or in part.[156] Therefore, nothing justifies excluding from democratic debate legal acts seeking the withdrawal of a decision authorizing the opening of negotiations with a view to concluding an international agreement, as well as acts whose object is to prevent the signing and conclusion of such an agreement.[157] The concept of a legal act, for the purposes of Article 11 (4) of the TEU and Regulation 211/2011, cannot, in the absence of any indication to the contrary, be understood as being limited only to definitive EU legal acts which produce legal effects vis-à-vis third parties.[158] Neither the wording of the provisions at issue nor the objectives pursued by them justify that a decision authorizing the opening of negotiations with a view to concluding international agreement, such as the TTIP and the CETA, should be excluded from the concept of a legal action for the purpose of an ECI.[159] Moreover, nothing precludes that the action that the Commission "intends to take, if any," for the purposes of Regulation 211/2011, may consist in proposing that the Council adopts the acts sought by the ECI proposal. Contrary to the Commission's contentions, nothing prevents, as the case may be, the institutions of the EU from negotiating and concluding new draft transatlantic free-trade agreements following the adoption of the Council of acts which are the object of the "Stop TTIP" proposal.[160]

Another complication concerns the fact that the Commission refuses to register ECIs unless they meet the criteria for admissibility for all aspects of their proposal. For instance, in the *Minority SafePack* Initiative,[161] the Commission stated that although some measures were within its power to submit a proposal for a legal act of the Union for the purpose of implementing the treaties, Regulation 211/2011 does not provide for the registration of part or parts of a proposed initiative.[162] However, in T-646/13 *Bürgerausschuss für die Bürgerinitiative Minority SafePack — one million signatures for diversity in Europe v. European Commission*,[163] the General Court annulled the decision of the Commission. It stated that the contested act of law did not contain sufficient elements to enable the applicant to ascertain the reasons for the refusal to register the proposed ECI. The Commission should have stated the grounds in support of its interpretation that a proposed ECI could not be registered if a part of the proposed measure did not fall within the framework of its powers.[164] It seems that this judgment implies that even if an ECI is considered as partially inadmissible, the Commission should expressly inform the applicant which elements of the proposal could be registered. This would give the organizers a feedback in order to "amend" the ECI.

156. Para. 42 in T-754/14.
157. Para. 43 in T-754/14.
158. Para. 35 in T-754/14.
159. Para. 36 in T-754/14.
160. Para. 48 in T-754/14.
161. Which proposed a wide range of measures to achieve progress toward its overall goal of improving the protection of persons belonging to national and linguistic minorities and strengthening cultural and linguistic diversity; for more see: http://www.minority-safepack.eu/assets/downloads/Pact_EN.pdf (on February 9, 2019).
162. See: http://ec.europa.eu/citizens-initiative/public/documents/1765 (on February 9, 2019).
163. ECLI:EU:T:2017:59.
164. Paras. 33-34 in T-646/13.

So far, only four initiatives have been registered by the Commission[165]—"Stop vivisection," "One of us," "Water and sanitation are a human right! Water is a public good, not a commodity! (Right2Water)" and "Ban glyphosate and protect people and the environment from toxic pesticides." The first two did not result in any form of legal action from the Commission's side.[166] The lack of outcome of the "One of us" initiative was unsuccessfully challenged before the General Court.[167] The "Right2Water" initiative produced, at first, a very limited legal activity, meaning that the Commission did not commit itself to adopt a specific act of law but instead took some actions leading to, e.g. reinforcing implementation of the EU water quality legislation, launching an EU-wide public consultation on the Drinking Water Directive, improving transparency for urban wastewater and drinking water data management and explore the idea of benchmarking water quality or bringing about a more structured dialogue between stakeholders on transparency in the water sector.[168] However, almost three years after the registration of the ECI, the Commission issued a proposal for a directive of the European Parliament and of the Council on the quality of water intended for human consumption[169] which directly refers in its explanatory memorandum to the

165. Until early February 2019. However, to this date another ECI—"Minority Safepack Initiative" (see: http://www.minority-safepack.eu) has fulfilled all the requirements and will eventually have to be met with a response of the Commission.
166. See the Commission's Communications available at: http://ec.europa.eu/transparency/regdoc/rep/3/2015/EN/3-2015-3773-EN-F1-1.PDF and http://ec.europa.eu/transparency/regdoc/rep/1/2014/EN/1-2014-355-EN-F1-1.Pdf (on February 9, 2019).
167. T-561/14 *European Citizens' Initiative One of Us v. European Commission*, ECLI:EU:T:2018:210. In this judgment, the Court recalls that the Treaties have conferred upon the Commission a near-monopoly on legislative initiative. According to the Court, the exercise of the right to the European citizens' initiative cannot require the Commission to submit a proposal for a legal act. A contrary interpretation would result in the Commission being stripped of all discretion in exercising its powers of legislative initiative following a European citizens' initiative. The Court takes the view, moreover, that the Commission's Communication is sufficiently reasoned. In particular, the Commission noted that, as all EU expenditure has to be in compliance with the EU Treaties and the Charter of Fundamental Rights, EU law ensures that all EU expenditure, including in the areas of research, development cooperation and public health, must respect human dignity, the right to life and the right to the integrity of the person. The Commission also explained that current EU legislation already meets numerous requests of the authors of the initiative, including that seeking to have the EU not fund the destruction of human embryos and to put in place appropriate controls. Last, the Commission argued that the support provided by the EU for the health sector in developing partner countries contributes substantively to a reduction in the number of abortions via access to safe and quality services and that a ban on abortion funding in developing countries would constrain the EU's ability to attain the objectives set out in the Millennium Development Goals, particularly that of maternal health. Finally, the Court notes that the Commission did not commit a manifest error of assessment. Thus, it is without committing such an error that the Commission took into account the right to life and human dignity of human embryos while also taking into account the needs of human embryonic stem cell research, which may result in treatments for currently incurable or life-threatening diseases, such as Parkinson's, diabetes, stroke, heart disease and blindness. Equally, the Commission demonstrated a link between unsafe abortions and maternal mortality so that it was able to conclude, without committing a manifest error of assessment, that the ban on abortion funding would constrain the EU's ability to attain the objective of reducing maternal mortality. (paras. 115-164).
168. See the Commission's Communication available at: http://ec.europa.eu/transparency/regdoc/rep/1/2014/EN/1-2014-177-EN-F1-1.Pdf.
169. COM(2017) 753.

"Right2Water" initiative. As for the "Ban glyphosate" initiative, it resulted, in part, in a direct commitment of the Commission to submit a legislative proposal in the future.[170]

Referring to the subject of this book, the statement that the ECI is an instrument for NGOs rather than for individual citizens seems quite obvious. The only initiatives to reach (or come close to) the support thresholds necessary for verification and then submission to the Commission are organizationally linked to NGOs.[171] Heavy burdens raised by the Commission on the organizers of initiatives result in the need of specialized knowledge, research capacity and resources which can be satisfied only by well-operating organizations. In fact, most initiatives had a strong support of national or transnational NGOs even if they were not directly identifiable with them.[172] Yet, it appears that the ECI is primarily a tool of fostering mass mobilizations around a specific proposal,[173] which may, however, be used by some organizations to become better established at the EU level. For example, it seems that the basic goal of the "One of Us" initiative was actually to launch a pan-European debate on abortion and to establish an organization advocating for restrictions in this area across the EU[174] and not to propose a concrete legal measure. In this respect, the initiative was used as a pure agenda-setting mechanism.[175] The ECI has also enabled new means of cross-sectoral partnerships. For instance, the "Right2Water" initiative was organized by a coalition of public service trade unions, environmental and social EU groups campaigning for the recognition of the rights to access to water.[176] As a result, the ECI can be seen as not only a strong instrument of direct influence on the EU law but also a field-transforming institution in various senses. Undoubtedly, it has increased the grassroot campaigning on EU-relevant issues.[177]

Even though it seems that the attitude of the Commission toward the ECIs has changed recently[178] and that the following proposals may be more successful in the

170. I.e., the commitment of a legislative proposal concerning transparency in scientific assessments and other aspects such as the governance of EFSA. Moreover, the Commission committed itself to strengthen efforts for the continuous and measurable reduction of risk from pesticide use. See the Commission's Communication available at: http://ec.europa.eu/transparency/regdoc/rep/3/2017/EN/C-2017-8414-F1-EN-MAIN-PART-1.PDF (on February 9, 2019).
171. The *Right to Water* initiative to Trade Unions and the *Stop Vivisection* initiative to animal rights groups and *One of Us* initiative is linked to the Roman Catholic Church.
172. P. Głogowski, A Maurer, *The European Citizens' Initiative—Chances, Constraints and Limits*, Vienna 2013, p. 14.
173. P. Głogowski, A. Maurer, *The* ..., p. 13.
174. "After collecting nearly two million signatures in support of *One of Us*, the coordinators of the initiative in the 28 European countries gathered in Krakow (Poland) last weekend, have agreed the implementation of a European federation to defend life before the EU institutions"; for more details see: https://www.pro-life.bg/en/2013/11/the-basis-for-the-foundation-of-a-european-federation-one-of-us-to-defend-life-in-the-eu-are-laid/ (on February 9, 2019).
175. J. Organ, *Decommissioning*..., p. 426.
176. J. Greenwood, *Civil*..., p. 194.
177. A. Warleigh, *On the Path*..., p. 56., M. Dougan, *What*..., p. 1811.
178. Which may be attributed to the "Democratic change" which is one of the priorities of the Commission for 2015-2019; for more see: https://ec.europa.eu/commission/priorities_en.

future,[179] the experience to date is anything but satisfactory. Some voices in the discussions suggest even that Regulation 211/2011 may not be compatible with the Treaties due to the fact that it disadvantages certain categories of the EU citizens in the process of collecting signatures.[180]

The ongoing debate concerning the ECI resulted in the Commission's proposal for the revision of Regulation 211/2011 of September 2017.[181] The main proposed changes include:

- a public hearing of the initiative at the EP followed by the "political assessment" on the support for the initiative (Article 14 of the proposal);
- improvements in the registration procedure, including the possibility of registering initiatives partially (Article 6 (4), (5) of the proposal);
- a help desk service by the Commission and an online collaborative platform for the ECI providing a forum for discussion and advice, as well as support to the organizers (Article 4 of the proposal);
- a central online collection system setup and operated by the Commission (Article 10 of the proposal);
- the simplification of the requirements concerning the signatories' data[182] (Article 9 of the proposal);
- the setting of minimum age for signatories at 16 years (Article 2 of the proposal);
- the free choice of the start date for the collection campaign (Article 8 (1) of the proposal);
- the commitment of the Commission to "raise public awareness about the existence of the ECI through communication activities and information campaigns" (Article 17 (1) of the proposal).[183]

Most of these changes follow the earlier demands of the doctrine and practitioners of the ECIs.[184] In particular, the introduction of public debates on the ECIs at the

179. It has been recently observed that the ECI is finally indicating some "signs of life." See J. Organ, *Signs of Life for EU "Citizens" Initiative*, available at: https://euobserver.com/opinion/137858 (on February 9, 2019).
180. For more see M. Dougan, *What...*, pp. 1807 et seq.
181. Proposal for a Regulation of the EP and of the Council on the European citizens' initiative 2017/0220 (COD), as determined in Provisional Agreement resulting from interinstitutional negotiations of 20.12.2018. It was adopted by the EP and by the Council and will apply from January 1, 2020. See Council of the EU Press release of 9.4.2019 – Updated rules on the European Citizens' Initiative adopted.
182. In particular, some legal systems demand too many personal data in order to support an ECI (e.g., ID numbers and father's name). See P. Merz, *End Ecocide in Europe: An ECI That Works! Learning from the First Two Years of the European Citizens' Initiative*, After 2014, available at: http://ecithatworks.org (on February 9, 2019), p. 38.
183. This is perhaps the most relevant proposal as in some Member States the ECIs receive hardly any coverage in media. See specific information in More Initiative for Europe's Citizens. Future of Democracy 02.2018, Bertelsmann Stiftung, p. 5, available at: http://www.bertelsmann-stiftung.de/fileadmin/files/BSt/Publikationen/GrauePublikationen/ZD_EINWURF_2_2018_EN_final2.pdf (on February 9, 2019).
184. See e.g. J.W. Pichler, *An Initiative Initiator's Experience* in: *The European Citizens' Initiative—Into New Democratic Territory*, J.W. Pichler, B. Kaufmann (eds), Wien-Graz 2010,

EP and their "political assessments" cannot only raise awareness about this instrument of direct democracy but also make the successful initiatives more "political" and, therefore, more impactful on the Commission in general. Yet, much will depend on the practice of the EP and the approach of the MEPs to the debates on the ECIs. Also, an introduction of a central online collecting system would be very valuable for the upcoming initiatives as most of the signatures are gathered via Internet, as presented in Figure 3.2 by the example of the "Right2Water" ECI.[185] A centralized platform, operated by the Commission, would possibly make this process easier and more reliable.

pp. 105 et seq., J.W. Pichler, *Recommendations to Initiatives—And to the EU as Well* in: *The European Citizens' Initiative – into new democratic territory*, J.W. Pichler, B. Kaufmann (eds), Wien-Graz 2010, pp. 57 et seq., J. Organ, *Reform ECI Registration and Expand Public Debate: Reconsidering Legal Admissibility* in: *An ECI That Works! Learning from the first two years of the European Citizens' Initiative, Alfter* 2014, available at: http://ecithatworks.org, pp. 97-100, R. Rustema, *Why the ECI Needs a Community-Developed Online Collection System* in: *An ECI That Works! Learning from the first two years of the European Citizens' Initiative, Alfter* 2014, available at: http://ecithatworks.org, pp. 104-106, B. Kaufmann, *An Infrastructure for People Power That Works* in: *An ECI That Works! Learning from the first two years of the European Citizens' Initiative, Alfter* 2014, available at: http://ecithatworks.org, pp. 107-110, A. Knaut, M. Conrad, *Making the ECI Work—A Social Science Perspective* in: *An ECI That Works! Learning from the first two years of the European Citizens' Initiative, Alfter* 2014, available at: http://ecithatworks.org, pp. 115-117, C. Berg, J. Thomson, *Lessons and Recommendations for an ECI That Works* in: *An ECI That Works! Learning from the first two years of the European Citizens' Initiative, Alfter* 2014, available at: http://ecithatworks.org, p. 118-122, A. Kavrakova, *Revising the ECI: How to Make It "Fit for Purpose,"* available at: https://www.euractiv.com/section/politics/opinion/revising-the-eci-how-to-make-it-fit-for-purpose/ (on February 9, 2019).

185. As presented by C. Berg (The ECI Campaign, www.citizens-initiative.eu) in *How to launch a European Citizens' Initiative?*, a presentation during The Good Lobby Advocacy School 2017, 23.6.2017 in Brussels.

Figure 3.2 The "Right2" Water Initiative Signature Collection from May 2012 to March 2013

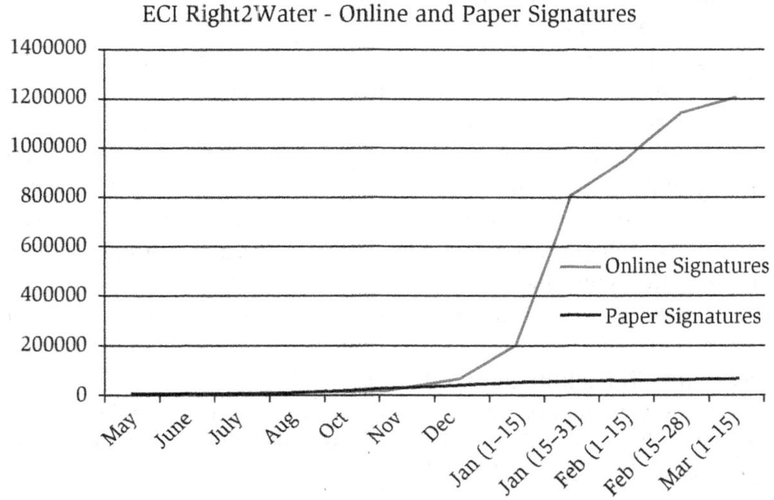

Still, additional provisions could have been proposed in order to oblige the EU institutions to decide on the registered ECI in a more thorough manner. For instance, the EP could not only organize public hearings on the initiatives' legislative proposals but also vote on them in plenary.[186] Moreover, some astonishment may also be caused by the fact that the final shape of the reform of one of the basic instruments of direct democracy at the EU level is established in a nontransparent process of trilogue.[187]

Nevertheless, the ECI, even as it stands, with its agenda-setting purpose, should be perceived as one of the main incentives for NGOs to act at the EU level. In fact, the issues brought by the ECIs to the EU agenda (like enhancing transparency in the activities of the EU institutions) seem to have spillover effects in more general spheres of the EU policies.[188]

186. Following, for instance, the measures of the Latvian Law on Online Signature Collection System and Its Technical Requirements (*Parakstu vākšanas tiešsaistes sistēmu drošības un tehniskās prasības*). See also J. Plottka, *The First Public Hearing on an ECI: Unclear Aims and Confusing Debates* in: *An ECI That Works! Learning from the first two years of the European Citizens' Initiative, Alfter* 2014, available at: http://ecithatworks.org, pp. 112-114; see also *Successful ECIs must be given a fair chance of having a political impact. The Commission proposal on ECI revision and what is crucially missing*, available at: http://www.citizens-initiative.eu/successful-ecis-must-given-fair-chance-political-impact/; M. Peñarubba, *Times of Change: The Public Consultation on the European Citizens' Initiative*, available at: http://www.thegoodlobby.eu/times-of-change-the-public-consultation-on-the-european-citizens-initiative/ (on February 9, 2019).
187. P. Staszczyk, *Zielone światło dla reformy Europejskiej inicjatywy obywatelskiej*, available at: http://bit.do/eH4he (on February 11, 2019).
188. For instance, in 2017 the Commission published its "Trade Package" which included the draft mandates to open trade negotiations with Australia and New Zealand (State of the Union 2017—Trade Package: Commission unveils initiatives for a balanced and progressive trade

[C] Summary

There are two main tools of social participation in the EU lawmaking: access to documents and the European Citizens' Initiative. The main characteristic of these measures is that they can be used by all EU citizens and NGOs operating in the EU, without having to be "Brussels-based," in contrast to consultations with specific EU institutions, as discussed in the following parts of this chapter.

It can be stated that the main objective of access to documents is to ensure transparency of the EU institutions and to make their decisions more accountable and understandable to the public. The deepening of this liability is crucial for the prospects of the EU. The aim of the ECI is quite different as it is designed as a measure of proposing subjects to the EU agenda by European civil society. Both of these tools are regularly used by NGOs wishing to impact the outcomes of the EU legislature. Although the practice of using these measures is ambiguous, the case law of the CJEU seems to push forward (although often very cautiously) the idea of wider openness and accessibility to the EU institutions and the EU lawmaking.

Access to documents and the ECI can also be seen as valuable incentives for advocating for the EU-relevant issues. This process makes European NGOs more aware of the EU policies and the impact they can have on them. Nevertheless, the use of these tools is often related to many hurdles, of both objective and subjective nature. The latter ones involve the actual handling of specific cases by the EU institutions. Thus, in order to reinforce these measures, not only legal amendments but also, if not primarily, the changes of attitude of the EU officials are needed.

§3.02 RELATIONS WITH THE EU INSTITUTIONS

The regular dialogue between the EU institutions and the representatives of civil society should be maintained in order to: (1) monitor, (2) analyze and evaluate, (3) propose agenda for the EU lawmaking.[189] Thus, the following paragraphs will concentrate on the relations between NGOs and particular EU institutions (the Commission, the EP, the Council and the CJEU) in the broad meaning of lawmaking. These relations, in contrast to the legal tools discussed in the previous part of this chapter, involve direct contacts with the EU officials.

Even at this stage of introductory remarks, it should be emphasized that such connections depend vastly on practice and features which are not precisely linked to legal provisions. Nevertheless, the latter ones are significant as they set the scope of NGO influence on the EU lawmaking. They also outline the crucial provisions on

policy, available at: http://trade.ec.europa.eu/doclib/press/index.cfm?id=1715 on February 9, 2019). Such openness seems to be one of the actual implications of the Stop-TTIP initiative.

189. M. Schlotmann, *Interessenvertretung bei der Europaischen Kommission*, Frankfurt am Mein 2005, pp. 55-58.

transparency which, however, are not rarely undermined by the "secret law-making" in the "trilogue" meetings between the Commission, the EP and the Council.[190]

[A] The Commission

Although the Commission often protests against its allegedly overrated role in the EU decision-making, it is without a doubt the most targeted institution by NGOs that wish their voice to be heard. The bilateral relations between the Commission and NGOs usually consist of regular or ad hoc consultations. This form of cooperation has great significance as it constitutes a direct communication tool between the institution setting a legislative agenda and the actors interested in its outcomes. In this way, the feasibility of policy choices, the legitimacy of adopted measures or the potential challenges in policy implementation can be communicated to the Commission.[191] Moreover, in case of disagreements between the EU institutions, open consultations, due to their potential source of information and legitimacy, can play a role in the interinstitutional balance of power.[192]

Thus, open consultations within the Commission level are ordinarily aimed at providing:

- certitude that the "Union's actions are coherent and transparent" as provided by Article 11 (3) of the TEU—since the Commission notifies the public about the proposals for policies or legal measures and invites the stakeholder to present their opinions, open consultation make the decision-making more transparent. In this way, the Commission enables democratic control over its activities.[193] Transparency is also provided within the subjects taking part in open consultations. Thus, the public should be able to verify who participates in such consultations;[194]
- democratic legitimacy of the EU—as the open consultations are aimed at empowering the citizens and grassroot organizations to take part and present their views in the lawmaking;[195]
- legislative initiative—according to the Commission itself, about 60% to 80% of the proposals are inspired by the ideas from the outside of the institution[196] (of

190. See P. Teffer, *EU "must lift lid" on secretive "deal-making,"* available at: https://euobserver.com/institutional/134340 (on February 9, 2019).
191. A. Bunea, *Designing Stakeholder Consultations: Reinforcing or Alleviating Bias in the European Union System of Governance?*, European Journal of Political Research Vol. 11/2016, p. 4.
192. A. Bunea, *Designing...*, p. 5.
193. C. Mahoney, *The Power of Institutions: State and Interest Group Activity in the European Union*, European Union Politics Vol. 5/2014, p. 451.
194. B. Kohler-Koch, B. Finke, *The Institutional...*, p. 207.
195. R, Eising, *Clientelism, Committees, Pluralism and Protests in the European Union: Matching Patterns?*, West European Politics Vol. 31/2008, p. 1167.
196. M. Hartlapp, J. Metz, C. Rauh, *Which Policy for Europe? Power and Conflict Inside the European Commission*, Oxford 2014, p. 11.

course, these proposals are being altered during the decision-making process, even though the final act often preserves the main ideas of the original one);[197]
- external expertise, technical details, regulation and settings introduced by the Commission implementing acts.

The ensuing paragraphs will discuss the Commission's overall solutions in respect of involving NGOs in the decision-making process on the basis of its commitments outlined in selected documents and the practice of the most common instruments of consultations.

[1] The Documents on NGO Participation: The Consultation Policy of the Commission

As already noticed, the Commission has been placing increasing emphasis on the need for enhanced democratic participation in the EU since the 1990s.[198] Apart from proposing documents which offered a structural approach toward NGO participation in the EU system (as presented in the second chapter of this book), the Commission has also issued a series of nonbinding acts of law which concerned its specific relations with European civil society. The most important ones will be presented at this point of analysis. It was argued that in these documents the Commission self-described itself as the guardian of representation by European civil society.[199]

The role of civil participation was first emphasized in 1993, in the Communication of the Commission entitled "An Open and Structured Dialogue with Interest Groups."[200] This document made a distinction between "nonprofit making organization (European and inter(national) associations/federations)" and "profit-making organization (legal advisers, public relations and public affairs firms and consultants)."[201] It indicated two forms of dialogue between the Commission and these interest groups: (1) through advisory committees and expert groups which can assist the Commission in the exercise of its own competences, (2) through contact with interest groups on an unstructured, ad hoc basis.[202] The Communication also provided the "Guiding principles" which would rule future contacts between both actors. They pointed out the need of the organizations to self-regulate themselves with regards to this area.[203]

197. R. Eising, *The Access of Business Interests to EU Institutions: Towards Elite Pluralism?*, Journal of European Public Policy Vol. 14/2007, p. 387.
198. I. De Jesus Butler, *Non-governmental...*, p. 572.
199. H.-J. Trenz, *European Civil Society: Between Participation, Representation and Discourse*, Policy and Society Vol. 28/2009, p. 37.
200. Official Journal C 63, 5.3.1993.
201. See Section II (Special Interest Groups).
202. *Ibid.*
203. See Point 2 (Transparency).

This document was followed by the Communication concerning the application of the Agreement on Social Policy[204] which emphasized the role of social partners and their demands in the social dialogue. Paragraph 31 of the Communication, in the section entitled "From consultation to negotiation" stated that "in their independent negotiations, the social partners are in no way required to restrict themselves to the content of the proposal in preparation within the Commission or merely to making amendments to it, bearing in mind, however, that Community action can clearly not go beyond the areas covered by the Commission's proposal. The social partners concerned will be those who agree to negotiate with each other. Such agreement is entirely in the hands of the different organizations." As it can be seen, two aspects were emphasized in this provision: first that the proposals recommended by the social partners should be as wide as possible and second that the social partners should coordinate their works between one another. Still, as it was pointed out by the CJEU, the Agreement on Social Policy and the Communication, due to their unbinding character, did not confer on any representative of management and labor a general right to take part in any negotiations in the first place.[205] Therefore, these acts of law could not form direct legal basis for actions brought by individuals before the CJEU in case of their breach or misuse.[206]

In 1994 the Commission proposed the Citizens First initiative[207] which was designed to encourage citizens and companies to turn to national courts when their EU rights are infringed upon. The Commission stated: "the adoption and implementation of legislation must be accompanied by an active information policy in order that citizens and companies are aware of their rights and obligations and can act quickly whenever they are infringed." The Commission perceived this document as its most ambitious information initiative ever taken.[208] However, this statement seems very questionable as the initiative was not followed by other significant acts of law or, in fact, a detailed information campaign.

The actual duty of consultation within the Commission was emphasized in the Amsterdam Treaty. Its Protocol 7 (on the application of the principles of subsidiarity and proportionality) stated in paragraph 9: "Without prejudice to its right of initiative, the Commission should ..., except in cases of particular urgency or confidentiality, consults widely before proposing legislation, and whenever appropriate, publish consultation documents." Still, this provision did not have a binding character, as it was not directly introduced in the text of the Treaty.

Basing on these foundations and following the remarks included in the White Paper on European Governance, in 2000 the Commission published a Discussion Paper

204. Official Journal C 397, 31.12.1994 P; the Agreement on Social Policy, as already discussed, proposed a constitutionally recognized role for the social partners in the legislative process. The Communication issued by the Commission had a more descriptive character.
205. See e.g. T-135/96 *Union Européenne de l'artisanat et des petites et moyennes entreprises (UEAPME) v. Council of the European Union*, ECLI:EU:T:1998:128, paras. 78, 90.
206. Cf. also e.g. C-104/97 *Atlanta AG and others v. Commission of the European Communities and Council of the European Union*, ECLI:EU:C:1999:498, paras. 71-72.
207. Available at: http://europa.eu/rapid/press-release_IP-97-1035_en.htm (on February 9, 2019).
208. See also R, Eising, *Clientelism...*, p. 1171.

focusing on its relations with civil society—"The Commission and Non-Governmental Organisations: Building a Stronger Partnership."[209] This document was aimed at emphasizing the significant role of NGOs in the decision-making processes. Their function was described as: "fostering participatory democracy," "representing the views of specific groups of citizens to the European Institutions," "contributing to policy making," "contributing to project management" and "contributing to European integration."[210] The document also pointed out difficulties in bilateral communication (caused especially by the lack of transparency and mutual information, the lack of legally established framework for contacts and the complexity of European institutions structures)[211] and included some solutions to these problems (e.g., regarding guidance for best practice, improving transparency and information, as well as pointing out the need for establishing legal basis for formal consultations).[212]

Another document worth mentioning is the Commission's Communication entitled "European Governance: Better Lawmaking."[213] In this document, published in 2002, the Commission once again stressed the overall need to improve the decision-making process and dealt, although in a rather brief manner, with general proposals on how to solve them. Thus, the importance of the Community method in the legislative procedure was highlighted. It was described as a unique system "producing rules which can be applied in any national context and which have the backing of legal certainty."[214] At the same time, the Commission stated that in order to fully benefit from this framework, more emphasis should be put on accountability of both the EU and Member States, as well as effectiveness (e.g., through introducing impact assessment procedures) and proportionality of the Community measures (in accordance with the subsidiarity principle).[215] The main solutions included: simplification and improvement of the regulatory environment, introducing more transparent and systematic approach into dialogue and participation framework and taking into account regional and local context.[216] In these fields, the role of civic participation and the grassroot support for the EU actions were especially accentuated.

In the same year, the matter of consultation and inclusion of social actors into decision-making and lawmaking processes was referred to in another document—a Communication entitled "General Principles and Minimum Standards for consultation of interested parties by the Commission"[217] (which will be hereinafter referred to as "General Principles"). This document had been earlier "announced" in the White Paper on European Governance. The main goals of this Communication were to "encourage more involvement of interested parties through a more transparent consultation process, which will enhance the Commission's accountability," "provide

209. COM(2000) 0011 final.
210. See point 1.3.5. (Contributing to European integration).
211. See point 1.1. (Purpose of the Discussions Paper).
212. See point 2 (Dialogue and consultation).
213. COM(2002) 275 final.
214. See remarks on Accountability, effectiveness, proportionality.
215. *Ibid.*
216. *Ibid.*
217. COM(2002) 704 final.

general principles and standards for consultation that help the Commission to rationalize its consultation procedures, and to carry them out in a more meaningful and systematic way," "build a framework for consultation that is coherent, yet flexible enough to take account of the specific requirements of all the diverse interests, and of the need to design appropriate consultation strategies for each policy proposal" and "promote mutual learning and exchange of good practices within the Commission."[218] Involving civil society actors into the decision-making is described as a "win-win situation" with NGOs as "facilitators of a broad policy dialogue."[219] This role was also linked to the fundamental right to form associations in order to pursue a common purpose.[220] Finally, the Communication stated the general principles for consultation,[221] which correspond with the principles proposed in the White Paper on European Governance:

- "participation"—an inclusive approach in developing and implementing the EU policies ("consulting as widely as possible on major policy initiatives");
- "openness and accountability"—the principle of transparency and full information;
- "effectiveness"—consultations starting as early as possible while taking into account certain framework and Treaty obligations;
- "coherence"—consistency and transparency in the way the Commission departments operate their consultation processes, inclusion of mechanisms for feedback, evaluation and review.

These principles were also reflected in the set of minimum standards which were provided in the same Communication:[222]

- "clear content of the consultation process"—"all communications relating to consultation should be clear and concise, and should include all necessary information to facilitate responses";
- "consultation target groups"—"when defining the target group(s) in a consultation process, the Commission should ensure that relevant parties have an opportunity to express their opinions";
- "publication"—"the Commission should ensure adequate awareness-raising publicity and adapt its communication channels to meet the needs of all target audiences. Without excluding other communication tools, open public consultations should be published on the Internet and announced at the 'single access point'";
- "time limit for participation"—"the Commission should provide sufficient time for planning and responses to invitations and written contributions. The

218. See point I (Introduction).
219. See remarks on The Specific Role of Civil Society Organizations.
220. *Ibid.*
221. See General Principles.
222. See Minimum Standards.

Commission should strive to allow at least 8 weeks for reception of responses to written public consultations and 20 working days notice for meetings";
- "acknowledge and feedback"—"receipt of contributions should be acknowledged. Results of open public consultations should be displayed on websites linked to the single access point on the Internet."

Despite its generally worded statements, the analyzed Communication is worth studying on numerous grounds. It can be summarized that the General Principles ensure that the consultations are open to all those with a potential interest, clearly organized and easy to follow. However, they do not envisage the obligation to launch consultations in the first place.[223] Also, they do not equate the idea of civil society to NGOs. On the contrary, they are clear that consultations should include all those that are affected by the policy, those who will be involved in the implementation of the policy, and bodies that have stated objectives giving them a direct interest in the policy.[224] Most notably, the discussed document refers to "wider constituencies (e.g., churches and religious communities) and specific target groups (e.g., women, the elderly, the unemployed or ethnic minorities)."[225] The consulted groups are to be selected on the basis of their perceived expertise for the specific case, and there is no obligation to consult a given group or organization, even if its interest is apparent.[226] Thus, the General Principles leave a significant discretion in terms of choosing partners for consultation purposes. They only require the inclusion of "targeted groups" while ensuring "adequate awareness-raising publicity."[227] In practice, the consultations conducted on the basis of the General Principles have taken place in two ways. The first one could be described as a closed consultation in which the Commission has approached specific stakeholders with potential concerns or opinions on a policy in order to include their views into the lawmaking process.[228] The second one has been opened to all willing parties which means that each EU citizen or NGO operating in the EU is welcome to participate.[229] However, the Commission itself has stressed that the Principles are not legally binding and that their objective was not to establish procedural rights, the respect of which would be subject to judicial control and review.[230] Therefore, it appears that the legislation introduced without regard to these standards could not be challenged before the CJEU solely on this ground.[231] Still, some

223. H. Johansson, S. Kalm, *Thinking...*, p. 19, I. De Jesus Butler, *Non-governmental...*, p. 567.
224. R. Uruena, *No Citizens Here: Global Subjects and Participation in International Law*, Leiden 2009, p. 253.
225. See Consultation Target Groups.
226. R, Eising, *Clientelism...*, p. 1174.
227. See Consultation Target Groups.
228. Ch. Marxsen, *Open...*, p. 261.
229. *Ibid.*
230. D. Obradovic, *EU Rules on Public Participation in Environmental Decision-Making Operating at the European and National Levels* in: *Aarhus Convention at Ten. Interactions and Tensions between Conventional International Law and EU Environmental Law*, M Pallemaerts (ed.), Groningen 2011, p. 162.
231. As it is a nonbinding act of law. However, in Case C-5/67 *Beus*, ECLI:EU:C:1968:13, the Tribunal stated that a lack of proper consultation may result in a legislative measure failing to

authors claim that the breach of the General Principles could be challenged in legal proceedings.[232]

In 2006, following a Communication entitled "Action Plan to Improve Communicating Europe by the Commission,"[233] the White Paper on a European Communication Policy[234] was issued. In both documents, the Commission promised a "fundamentally new approach" aimed at narrowing the communication gap looming between the EU and its citizens and ultimately mapping a way toward the development of a European public sphere.[235] The Communication was designed for the Commission itself, while the White Paper was addressed to the EU as a whole, including other central institutions, Member States, European political parties and civil society.[236] Although the White Paper lacked concrete policy proposals and did not result in any further legal developments, its texts can be characterized by a sense of realism and long-term perspective.[237] This approach seems to be fundamentally new as the Commission was seriously asking the other institutions and the European public at large for proposals to develop better communication on the EU matters.[238] Furthermore, the Commission introduced for the first time two new notions—"Communication Policy" and "European Public Sphere," although without defining them.[239] It appears that the watchword of "Communication Policy" encompassed the Commission's claim for the introduction of a new field of policy, as well as a new objective for the area of communication.[240] Yet, while no one would dispute the EU's competence to inform citizens about policy results, the creation of a "European public sphere" occurs as a much more ambiguous goal.[241]

In short, according to the White Paper on a European Communication Policy, the Commission wished to move from information to communication by establishing communication as a policy in its own right with the ultimate aim of developing a "European public sphere where the European debate can unfold."[242] The Commission put forward the principles of the right to information and freedom of expression, inclusiveness, diversity and participation of the citizens as the basis of public debate

---

contain sufficient reasons as required by Art. 235 of the Treaty of the EC. See also the already evoked Cases C-104/97 P and T-135/96.

232. D. Obradovic, *EU Rules....*, p. 162.
233. Available at: http://ec.europa.eu/transparency/regdoc/rep/2/2005/EN/2-2005-985-EN-F-0. Pdf (on February 9, 2019).
234. COM(2006) 0035 final.
235. See Part I (Putting Communication at the Service of Citizens) Point 1 (Communication as a Policy in Its Own Right).
236. See Part II (Taking Work Forward).
237. S. Kurpas, M. Brügemann, Ch. Meyer, *The Commission White Paper on Communication Mapping a Way to a European Public Sphere*, CEPS Policy Brief Vol. 101/2006, p. 2.
238. See Introduction: "Closing the Gap."
239. See Part I. Putting Communication at the service of citizens: (1) Communication as a Policy on its own right. (2) Enhanced debate and dialogue—a European public sphere.
240. Previously, there was no communication policy but rather a *strategy* for information and communication, and there was no Commissioner for Communication and DG Communication was called DG Press.
241. S. Kurpas, M. Brügemann, Ch. Meyer, *The Commission...*, p. 3.
242. See Part I. Putting Communication at the service of citizens: (1) Enhanced debate and dialogue—a European public sphere.

about European integration and suggested that they should be further elaborated into a European Charter or Code of Conduct of Communication, which ought to engage not only the EU institutions but also national, regional and local governments and NGOs.[243] Although the first draft of the White Paper was more outspoken in its criticism of the institutions for merely holding a "monologue" instead of a "dialogue" with citizens,[244] the main symptoms of the problem with Communication were analyzed quite precisely: there was too little coordination among actors, too little focus on the actual citizens' concerns and insufficient involvement from national, regional and local actors.[245] On its side, the Commission did not clarify how the voices of the EU citizens could be taken into account in a systemic way.[246] As a result, it has not changed much in terms of enhancing the consultation duties of the Commission.

In 2017 the Commission published "Better Regulation Guidelines"[247] which provide development of the "Better Regulation Toolbox" of 2015.[248] The Guidelines set "key requirements" of consultations undertaken by the Commission. According to them, prior to consultation, "a simple consultation" strategy should be established in order to identify and target relevant stakeholders.[249] In fact, the Guidelines do not distinguish the various types of possible stakeholders. In particular, they do not incorporate the notions of "NGOs" or "civil society."[250] Relations with stakeholders should be governed by four general principles of participation, openness and accountability, effectiveness and coherence,[251] as provided in the General Principles of 2002. The Better Regulation Guidelines also repeat the five minimum standards that all consultations have to respect (i.e., "clear content of the consultation process," "consultation of target groups," "publication," "time limits for participation" and "acknowledgment of feedback").[252] What is perhaps most meaningful in the Guidelines is the fact that they emphasize the obligatory nature of consultation and stress that stakeholders should always be consulted when preparing a Commission legislative documents including questionnaires and background information.[253] According to the Guidelines, stakeholders must be able to give feedback on:

- road maps for evaluation and fitness or policy initiative or when performing an evaluation or fitness check and on Communications which launch a consultation exercise or Green Papers.[254] Moreover, consultations in these spheres should have an open character (primarily via Internet). This aspect is the

243. See Introduction: "Closing the Gap."
244. S. Kurpas, M. Brügemann, Ch. Meyer, *The Commission...*, p. 7.
245. *Ibid.*
246. *Ibid.*, p. 8.
247. Commission Staff Working Document "Better Regulation Guidelines," SWD (2017) 350.
248. SWD (2017) 350.
249. SWD (2015) 111.
250. The Guidelines define three types of stakeholders, i.e. those: (1) affected by the policy, (2) who will have to implement it and (3) who have a stated interest in the policy. See How to Prepare and Conduct a Consultation—Three Interacting Phases.
251. See Key Principles and Standards.
252. See General Principles and Minimum Standards for Stakeholder Consultation.
253. See When is Stakeholder Consultation Required?
254. *Ibid.*

biggest difference in comparison to the General Principles of 2002. Furthermore, stakeholder engagement can, in principle, take place throughout the policy cycle. However, formal stakeholder consultations can be only launched for initiatives which have received political validation by the appropriate political level.[255] Consultations should be based on consultation checks, and road maps and inception impact assessment for a period of four weeks after publication;

- draft delegated acts and implementing acts of general application and draft measures following the regulatory procedure with scrutiny (four weeks);
- legislative proposals adopted by the College and, where applicable, the accompanying impact assessment;
- how to improve existing legislation, at any time via the website "Lighten the load."[256]

According to the Guidelines, the choice of the consultation method should determine the consultation tools. The consultation tools to be most commonly used consist of written consultations via consultation documents or questionnaires, as well as direct interactions with stakeholders via meetings, conferences, hearing or other events.[257] Even though the Guidelines provide a large scope of open, online consultations, they still leave a wide discretion in terms of selecting the stakeholders to participate in other, e.g. supplementary, consultations. In this case, proper services should build up knowledge about who has an interest in the policy area. They should also identify the persons and groups with expertise or technical knowledge in a given field and keep track of inputs made in earlier consultation exercises or less formal contacts and exchanges. Member States could also be invited to provide a list of interest groups for the concerned policy area within their countries.[258] Furthermore, the Guidelines confirm the actual practices of selecting the stakeholders as they refer to "existing contacts (e.g., in mailing or distribution lists), subscriptions in the 'Commission at work notifications' and 'Transparency register'" as "starting points" for inviting interest groups to consultations.[259] Also, "advisory or expert groups or standing groups of stakeholders, established by Directorates-General[260] around a specific policy area might be considered, in particular for targeted consultations."[261]

The Guidelines seem a valuable extension of the existing internal regulations dealing with consultations. Most importantly, they examine the circumstances under which consultations need to take place. Still, the Guidelines do not have a legally binding nature and, therefore, could not form direct basis for a legal action before the CJEU. Yet, after the entry into force of the Treaty of Lisbon, it is clear that if consultations were not conducted at all in a given case, then it would comprise a

255. *Ibid.*
256. *Ibid.*
257. See How to Prepare and Conduct a Consultation—Three Interacting Phases.
258. *Ibid.*
259. *Ibid.*
260. I.e., consultative committees, as presented in the following part of this chapter.
261. See How to Prepare and Conduct a Consultation—Three Interacting Phases.

breach of the already discussed Article 11 (3) of the TEU.[262] Certainly, an NGO which would feel unjustifiably left out in consultations may also request the European Ombudsman to examine the case.[263]

Despite the publication of the Guidelines, it seems that the introduction of Article 11 of the TEU did not have a profound implication on the Commission and its actual dialogue with interested NGOs. It seems that Article 11 of the TEU is, in fact, not more than recognition of existing practices, instead of a landmark for changed relationships between European civil society and the EU.[264] Moreover, the doctrine points out that in many cases both the nonbinding, internal regulations on consultation requirements and Article 11 (3) are perhaps not *violated* but rather *misused*.[265] In practice, the Directorates-General are often engaged in a more or less regular dialogue with those organizations which have a history of prior consultations with the EU institutions and which might be interested in being further consulted.[266] Thus, even if the Commission did not open consultations, some interested parties would still be aware of proposals recommended by the EU officials.[267]

Nevertheless, because the Commission paid particular attention to online consultations and special consultative committees in the Guidelines of 2017, it is worth analyzing them a bit closer. As a side note, it should be also observed that the Commission provides other rather informal channels of moving closer to the EU citizens. For instance, it carries out regular "Citizens' Dialogues."[268] However, they cannot be perceived as means of consultations but rather as information campaigns of the Commission.[269]

[2] Online Consultations

For the last few years, the use of the Internet has been especially promoted by the Commission as an interactive means to facilitate the participation of citizens and NGOs in the decision-making process.[270] This tool of participation in the EU legislative

262. Having examined the judicature of the CJEU, it appears that such an infringement has not yet occurred.
263. P. Kostandinova, *Improving...*, p. 1090.
264. S. Kalm, H. Johansson, *EU Civil...*, p. 12.
265. D. Panke, *Lobbying Institutional Key Players: How States Seek to Influence the European Commission, the Council Presidency and the European Parliament*, Journal of Common Market Studies Vol. 50/2012, pp. 133 et seq.
266. Cf. P. Kotzian, Ch. Quittkat, *Konsultationsprozess der Kommission: Steuerung von EU-Lobbying?* in: *Lobbying in der Europaischen Union. Zwischen Professionalisierung und Regulierung*, D. Dialer, M. Richter (eds), Wiesbaden 2014, pp. 76, 87.
267. I. De Jesus Butler, *Non-governmental...*, p. 571.
268. For more information see: https://ec.europa.eu/info/events/citizens-dialogues_en (on February 9, 2019).
269. Cf. L. Bouza Garcia, *Participatory Democracy and Civil Society in the EU*, London 2015, pp. 2 et seq., J. Greenwood, *Civil Dialogue and the Citizens' Initiative: Accounting for Collaboration and Competition Using the Advocacy Coalition Framework and the Strategic Action Field* in: *EU Civil Society. Patterns of Coopeation, Competition and Conflict*, H. Johansson, S. Kalm (eds), Basingstoke 2015, pp. 193 et seq.
270. Cf. P. Kotzian, Ch. Quittkat, *Konsultationsprozess...*, p. 76.

process was announced for the first time in the White Paper on European Governance[271] and the General Principles[272] and became a "default" instrument of conducting obligatory consultations in the Guidelines of 2017.[273]

Like any participation tools, online consultations are aimed at enhancing democratic qualities of the EU decision-making by enabling the general public to present their opinions on the given legislative proposals.[274] The most noticeable characteristic of online consultations is their apparent convenience and accessibility. Nevertheless, their use by the Commission often faces skepticism. Online consultations are frequently regarded as means of giving civil society the impression of contribution to the lawmaking while not much is done with this input afterwards.[275] Some critics argue that even though this instrument is portrayed by the Commission as a tool of integrating expert knowledge from various environments, it is, in practice, dominated by business interest representatives.[276] Others, including NGOs, dismiss many online consultations as mere "box-ticking exercises."[277] Unfortunately, very little is known about the actual outcomes of online consultations.[278]

The Commission conducts regular consultations through the "Consultations" website.[279] It invites citizens, NGOs, business associations and also public authorities and private companies to present their views on a given subject matter. Online consultations are usually carried out as follows. In the beginning, the Commission publishes the opening of a consultation on its Internet site and invites all citizens, including particular groups of stakeholders with special interest in the subject, to submit contributions in a prescribed time period. In most cases, written submissions are asked for, but occasionally the Commission invites stakeholders to hearings or special meetings. Consultation documents that introduce the issues at stake and relevant existing legal framework are also provided by the Commission. Apart from that, those stakeholders who maintain regular contact with specific Directorates-General are often expressly informed about the upcoming consultations.[280]

Although online consultations have become a regular instrument of consultation, not all Directorates-General use it and certainly not all Directorates-General apply it to the same extent and in the same way. The most active Directorates-General are Internal

271. See Involving Civil Society in the White Paper on European Governance.
272. See Minimum Standards point C Publication in the General Principles.
273. A 12-week Internet-based public consultation must be part of the consultation strategy for initiatives supported by impact assessments, evaluations and fitness checks as well as for Green Papers (unless an exemption has been granted). See Guidelines on Stakeholder Consultation in the Guidelines.
274. Ch. Quittkat, *The European...*, p. 654.
275. B. Cammaerts, *Civil Society Participation in Multistakeholder Processes: In Between Realism and Utopia* in: *Making Our Media: Global Initiatives Toward a Democratic Public Sphere*, L. Stein, D. Kidd, C. Rodriguez (eds), New Jersey 2009, p. 83.
276. Ch. Quittkat, *The European...*, p. 654.
277. *Ibid.*, p. 655.
278. J. Steffek, C. Kissling P. Nanz, *Civil...*, p. 69.
279. I.e., https://ec.europa.eu/info/consultations_en which replaced the "Your Voice in Europe" website (on February 9, 2019).
280. Ch. Marxsen, *Open...*, p. 261. See also e.g. B. Cammaerts, *Civil...*, pp. 84 et seq., Ch. Quittkat, *The European...*, pp. 653 et seq.

Market,[281] Enterprise and Industry,[282] Health and Consumer Protection[283] and Environment.[284] There are also some Directorates-General which hardly ever use the possibility of online consultations (e.g., Economic and Financial Affairs,[285] Enlargement[286] or External Relations).[287] Apparently, not all Directorates-General consider this type of consultation as an appropriate one for achieving proper input in their decision-making.

Online consultations can be generally divided into three categories: open, selective and closed.[288] Open online consultations are the most common.[289] They are aimed at all interested stakeholders without further need for distinguishing them. In contrast, selective online consultations are mainly directed at defined groups of interest, even though the Commission sometimes allows other interest parties to participate as well.[290] This type of consultations is less popular, yet not rare.[291] Finally, closed online consultations are very limited,[292] and they tend to gather the opinions of public authorities and business organizations. Although selective and closed consultations are rather exceptional, their very existence is still noteworthy as this instrument, when introduced, was originally "framed" as a mechanism for a wide civil society inclusion in the process of decision-making and lawmaking.[293]

A practical criticism concerning online consultations deals with their format,[294] representativeness and feedback.[295] It is even argued that they provide an "illusion of participation."[296] They are often perceived as simple surveys or, even worse, as instruments by which the Commission asks for approval for its policies without

281. A total of 81 consultations in the years 2009-2016 (based on data from https://ec.europa.eu/info/consultations_en).
282. A total of 80 consultations in the years 2009-2016 (based on data from https://ec.europa.eu/info/consultations_en).
283. A total of 69 consultations in the years 2009-2016 (based on data from https://ec.europa.eu/info/consultations_en).
284. A total of 58 consultations in the years 2009-2016 (based on data from https://ec.europa.eu/info/consultations_en).
285. Zero consultation in the years 2009-2016 (based on data from https://ec.europa.eu/info/consultations_en).
286. One consultation in the years 2009-2016 (based on data from https://ec.europa.eu/info/consultations_en).
287. Five consultations in the years 2009-2016 (based on data from https://ec.europa.eu/info/consultations_en).
288. Ch. Quittkat, *The European...*, p. 655.
289. I.e., 90.37% of all conducted consultations (based on data from https://ec.europa.eu/info/consultations_en).
290. They are often related to specific, technical issues covered by the Directorates-General or Enterprise and Industry and Taxation and Customs. See also Ch. Marxsen, *Open...*, pp. 265-266.
291. I.e., 6.04% of all conducted consultations (based on data from https://ec.europa.eu/info/consultations_en).
292. I.e., 3.59% of all conducted consultations (based on data from https://ec.europa.eu/info/consultations_en).
293. Ch. Quittkat, *The European...*, p. 660.
294. *Ibid.*, p. 661.
295. See the conclusions of the EESC study of 2017 entitled *EU public consultations in the digital age: Enhancing the role of the EESC and civil society organisations*, available at: https://www.eesc.europa.eu/sites/default/files/files/qe-07-17-001-en-n.pdf (on February 9, 2019), pp. 30 et seq.
296. P. Kotzian, Ch. Quittkat, *Konsultationsprozess...*, p. 74.

requesting for elaborated input.[297] As far as NGOs are concerned, it should be emphasized that even though online consultations do not involve any resources at first sight, the practice is not so obvious. In order to prepare an extensive reply to the consultation process, proper personnel and budgetary means are needed.[298] Participation in online consultation is considered a resource-consuming exercise.[299] Ironically, this is why this type of dialogue has further deepened the difference between business actors and NGOs in their actual influence on the EU institutions.[300] As it was pointed out in the literature: "the reason is that the doors have opened, but civil society does not have the resources to step up."[301]

[3] Consultative Committees

As it has already been acknowledged, the Commission often lacks specific knowledge on the given legislative proposal. This is why one of its most important institutional features is an extensive use of consultative committees.[302] The so-called committee governance[303] is a supplementary mechanism of institutionalized dialogue between the Commission[304] and private subjects, including representatives of the organized civil society.[305] This mechanism consists of selecting the policy areas where consultative committees are established with chosen participants. The Commission usually initiates such panels in those policy domains (e.g., environment, agriculture or human rights) where the stakeholders are most active.[306] The formation, composition and responsibilities assigned to consultative committees are utterly upon the discretion of the Commission.[307] This is the main difference between these bodies and the comitology

297. Ch. Quittkat, *Neue Medien im Dienste der Demokratie? Der zivilgesellschaftliche Gewinn von Online-Konsultationene* in: *Die Entzauberung partizipativer Demokratie. Zur Rolle der Zivilgesellschaft bei der Demokratisierung von EU-Governance*, B. Kohler-Koch, Ch. Quittkat (ed.), Frankurt am Mein 2011, p. 23.
298. Ch. Quittkat, *The European...*, p. 663.
299. Ch. Quittkat, *Neue...*, p. 27.
300. B. Kohler Koch, B. Finke, *The Institutional...*, p. 210.
301. *Ibid.*, p. 211.
302. A. Broscheid, D. Coen, *Lobbying Activity and for a Creation in the EU: Empirically Exploring the Nature of the Policy Good*, Journal of European Public Policy Vol. 14/2007, p. 348.
303. See e.g. Th. Christiansen, E. Kirchner, *Committee Governance in the European Union*, Manchester 2000, pp. 145 et seq., B. Flynn, *Postcards from the Edge of Integration? The Role of Committees in EU Environment Policy-Making* in: *Europe in Change. Committee Governance in the European Union*, T. Christiansen, E. Kirchner (eds), Manchester 2000, pp. 79 et seq.
304. Even though the Commission seems to organize consultative committees most often, it is significant to emphasize that other EU institutions establish various internal and interinstitutional committees as well. It may even seem that committees are some sort of aberration from a system that is sometimes viewed in terms of clearly delineated "separation of powers." For more see T. Christiansen, E. Kirchner, *Introduction* in: *Europe in Change. Committee governance in the European Union*, T. Christiansen, E. Kirchner (eds), Manchester 2000, pp. 5-8.
305. M. Schlotmann, *Interessenvertretung bei der Europaischen Kommission*, Frankfurt am Mein 2005, p. 27.
306. A. Broscheid, D. Coen, *Lobbying...*, p. 350, B. Ferrand, *Lobbying and Lawmaking in the European Union: The Development of Copyright Law and the Rejection of the Anti-Counterfeiting Trade Agreement*, Oxford Journal of Legal Studies Vol. 35/2015, pp. 487 et seq.
307. A. Broscheid, D. Coen, *Lobbying...*, p. 350.

committees and expert committees which are exclusively composed of Member State officials.[308]

In the phase of policy development, the Commission can establish consultative committees in order to obtain expert knowledge and legitimacy.[309] Usually, no formal competences are given to these committees. As a result, the outcomes of their deliberations have a purely advisory nature and are not binding for the Commission in any way.[310] Nevertheless, the influence of consultative committees on the EU legislative process is prominent. This is why participation in these bodies is often seen as a crucial access point for the private interest representation at the EU level.[311] Attempts to influence the topics deliberated at consultative committees are one of the main objectives of many interest groups in Brussels.[312]

The scope of consultative committees established by the Commission is very diversified. They cover such distinctive forms as small expert groups, large hearings or limited roundtables.[313] While small committee meetings are a more appropriate setting for obtaining detailed and expert knowledge, the larger ones are designed for discourses between broader groups of stakeholders.[314] The Commission also sets mixed committees comprised of representatives of Member States, private organizations and enterprises, scientists or experts.[315] Most of the consultative committees have a temporary nature. However, some of them have a more permanent character and are often referred to as "standing committees."[316] Counterintuitively, these committees are seldom the most influential ones. They are often very noticeable and persuasive upon inauguration but lose these characteristics over time. In contrast, ad hoc committees tend to focus the attention of their members on a precise problem for a limited time period which is usually far more effective.[317]

[4] Actual Influence of NGOs on the Commission

The above-presented remarks suggest that there are numerous ways for NGOs to gain access to the Commission and present their ideas during the lawmaking process. As the

308. S. Mazey, J. Richardson, *The Commission and the Lobby* in *The European Commission*, D. Spence (ed.), London 2006, p. 284.
309. P. Bouwen, *The Logic of Access to the European Parliament: Business Lobbying in the Committee on Economic and Monetary Affairs*, Journal of Common Market Studies Vol. 42/2004, p. 477.
310. Cf. P. Bouwen, *The European Commission* in: *Lobbying the European Union: Institutions, Actors and Issues*, D. Coen, J. Richardson (eds), Oxford 2009, p. 31.
311. R. van Schendelen, *More Machiavelli in Brussels: The Art of Lobbying the EU*, Amsterdam 2010, p. 117.
312. *Ibid.*, p. 121.
313. P. Bouwen, *The European...*, p. 35.
314. *Ibid.*, p. 37.
315. A. Broscheid, D. Coen, *Lobbying...*, p. 348.
316. A good example is Financial Services Action Plan (FSAP) organized by the Internal Market DG; for more information see: https://ec.europa.eu/info/business-economy-euro/banking-and-finance/financial-reforms-and-their-progress_en (on February 9, 2019).
317. P. Bouwen, *The European...*, p. 37.

surveys indicate,[318] the most common channels of cooperation between NGOs and the Commission are open consultations rather than advocating for own initiatives. Perhaps this is the reason why the Commission is sometimes reasonably open to NGO suggestions, even before launching the official lawmaking in course of other forms of dialogue, especially during committee deliberations or online consultations.[319]

The impact of NGOs can be very significant. Possibly the best-documented example of a legislative influence of NGOs on the Commission is the draft text for a directive combating discrimination on the basis of race, ethnicity and religion, proposed by the Starting Line Group (SLG) organization. The draft was initially produced in 1993, but the SLG was unable to persuade the Commission that the then binding EC Treaty accorded sufficient competence to legislate in this area.[320] This was one of the main reasons why the SLG, among other NGOs operating in Brussels, campaigned for an amendment of the EC Treaty provisions during the Amsterdam Intergovernmental Conference to grant the necessary competence in this area.[321] Accordingly, the new text of Article 13 of the EC Treaty (combined with an additional paragraph in Article 3) largely reflected the SLG proposals.[322] After this amendment of the EC Treaty, the SLG returned to the original proposal for a directive in 1998. The act of the Commission that appeared a year later—the Race Discrimination Directive[323]—reflected in many ways what the SLG had proposed. For instance, it prohibited discrimination on the basis of race and ethnicity in the field of employment and the delivery of certain services. It is said that during the lawmaking procedure, the Commission was in close and frequent contact with the SLG.[324] Another noticeable example of a legislative proposal brought by an NGOs is the draft for a Disability Specific Directive launched by the European Disability Forum[325] (i.e., a directive specifically addressing discrimination against people with disabilities). After several years of dialogue with the European Disability Forum, among other NGOs, the Commission presented a proposal to the Council.[326]

Another interesting example of cooperation between an NGO and the Commission in the legislative procedure are the International Financial Reporting Standards.[327] This is a regulation passed at the direct initiative of the International Accounting Standards Committee, which is an NGO consisting of various organizations working on financial standards across the world.[328] The initiative provided by the IASC is adopted

318. For more information see Ch. Quittkat, *The European...*, p. 667.
319. S. Wright, *A Virtual European Public Sphere? The Futurum Discussion Forum*, Journal of European Public Policy Vol. 14/2007, pp. 1167 et seq.
320. I. De Jesus Butler, *Non-governmental...*, p. 573.
321. F. Bannister, R. Conolly, *The Trouble with Transparency: A Critical Review of Openness in e-Government*, Policy & Internet Vol. 3/2011, p. 17.
322. I. De Jesus Butler, *Non-governmental...*, p. 571.
323. Council Directive 2000/43/EC of 29 June 2000 implementing the principle of equal treatment between persons irrespective of racial or ethnic origin, Official Journal L 180, 19.7.2000.
324. I. De Jesus Butler, *Non-governmental...*, p. 571.
325. A. Bunea, *Designing...*, p. 8.
326. COM(2008) 426 final. However, the proposal was eventually withdrawn.
327. For more information see: http://www.ifrs.org/About-us/Pages/What-are-IFRS.aspx.
328. H. Daske, L. Hail, Ch. Leuz, R. Verdi, *Adopting a Label: Heterogeneity in the Economic Consequences Around IAS/IFRS Adoptions*, Journal of Accounting Research Vol. 51/2013, pp. 495 et seq.

by the Commission (if required—with necessary amendments) and then it is proceeded as the Commission's initiative in the regular legislative procedure.[329] This special form of cooperation is often seen as a model that could be translated in other spheres of the EU law, especially where NGOs could provide for expert, specialist knowledge, e.g. in environmental law.[330] In such fields, organizations not directly connected with the Commission could create proposals for regulations which then would be proceeded as the Commission's own initiatives. This, however, although beneficial for both sides, would need an extensive modification at the basis of the EU lawmaking procedure.

Naturally, many (if not most) successful collaborations between NGOs and the Commission are not easily identifiable. In practice, many other, nonlegal factors play a significant role in this area.[331] Additionally, more effective outcomes can be attributed to lobbying rather than to formal consultations provided by the Commission. Still, the instruments discussed above cannot be neglected and are significant for advocating for the interests of European civil society.

[B] The EP

The second most affected EU institution by NGOs is the EP. It is understandable as the EP plays an important role in the EU lawmaking and is, at least in theory, the most democratic EU institution.[332] Nevertheless, it certainly does not constitute the axis of the EU's institutional system. Its actual position is partly a result of only a co-decision role in the lawmaking process and partly due to the continuous lack of full politicization.[333] Still, this institution consists of representatives from all Member States which often enables the interest groups to play the "nation card"[334] in contacts with various MEPs[335] while advocating for certain legal solutions. In general, the contacts of the EP with NGOs can be perceived as "quasi-formal"[336] as they combine only a few formal regulations and are mostly based on informal activities.[337] Still, some structural forms of cooperation can be distinguished, i.e. Intergroups and the right to petition.

---

329. *Ibid.*, p. 496.
330. Cf. M. Peeters, S Nóbrega, *Climate Change-Related Aarhus Conflicts: How Successful Are Procedural Right in EU Climate Law*, Review of European, Comparative & International Environmental Law Vol. 23/2014, p. 363 et seq.
331. I. De Jesus Butler, *Non-governmental...*, p. 572.
332. See e.g. M. Kenig-Witkowska, A. Łazowski, R. Ostrihansky, *Prawo instytucjonalne Unii Europejskiej*, Warsaw 2011, pp. 84 et seq.
333. See e.g. N. Scicluna, *Politization Without Democratization: How the Eurozone Crisis in Transforming EU Law and Politics*, International Journal of Constitutional Law Vol. 12/2014, p. 554.
334. A. Bunea, R. Thomson, *Consultations with Interest Groups and the Empowerment of Executives: Evidence from the European Union*, Governance: An International Journal of Policy, Administration and Institutions Vol. 28/2015, p. 520.
335. I.e., Members of the European Parliament.
336. A. Bunea, *Designing...*, p. 10.
337. For more see also A. Classen, *Interessenvertretung...*, pp. 52-60.

[1] General Rules: Intergroups

The first, obvious form of cooperation between the EP and NGOs are consultations. The provision of this form of collaboration is established in Rule 27 (Duties of the Conference of Presidents) (5) of the EP's Rules of Procedure of 2017.[338] According to this norm, the Conference of Presidents shall be responsible for organizing structured consultations with European civil society on major topics. This may include holding public debates, open to participation by interested citizens, on subjects of general European interest. The Bureau shall appoint a Vice President responsible for the implementation of such consultations, who shall report back to the Conference of Presidents. What is interesting is that this rule mentions the notion of "European civil society" (which, as it has already been noticed, is quite rarely used in the official EU documents), admitting that it should be the leading partner in developing the EU policy. It seems fully justified that in this type of dialogue the European civil society should be represented by its organizations, including NGOs.[339]

In practice, the most common form of NGO participation in the works of the EP is the so-called Intergroups. According to Rule 34 (Intergroups) (1) of the EP's Rules of Procedure, individual members may form Intergroups or other unofficial groupings of members, to hold informal exchanges of views on specific issues across different political groups, drawing on members of different parliamentary committees, and to promote contact between members and civil society. Again, the notion of "civil society" is mentioned (although without the prefix "European") which can signify the importance that the EP places in contacts with the third sector.[340]

In short, the EP Intergroup is an informal, cross-party collection of MEPs who form around a particular interest.[341] Its status is "informal" in the sense that it is not considered to be an organ of the EP, nor is it permitted to use, e.g. any names that might suggest its direct connection to the EP.[342] An Intergroup can be "registered" or "unregistered." A registered Intergroup should have the support of three political groups, provide a list of its members and declare any financial or material support received from third parties.[343] Although such an Intergroup does not receive any financial support from the EP, it is provided, e.g. with translation facilities or the ability to reserve meeting rooms[344] which, practically speaking, can be a noticeable benefit.

Intergroups may not use the name or logo of the EP and the political groups they are composed of or any name which might lead to confusion with the official bodies of the EP such as parliamentary committees, interparliamentary delegations and joint parliamentary committees. In case of breach of this principle, the Intergroup is not

338. Available at: http://bit.do/ekKKN (on February 9, 2019).
339. I. De Jesus Butler, *Non-governmental...*, p. 573.
340. Ch. Marxsen, *Open...*, p. 261.
341. A. Bunea, *Designing...*, p. 11.
342. I. De Jesus Butler, *Non-governmental...*, p. 574.
343. See Arts. 4 and 5 of Rules Governing the Establishment of Intergroups. Decision of the Conference of Presidents of the EP of 16 December 1991, available at: http://www.europarl.europa.eu/pdf/intergroupes/legislature_8/DecisionofCoPof16Dec1999-Rules_governing_the_establishment_of_integroupes.pdf (on February 9, 2019).
344. See Art. 9 of Rules Governing the Establishment of Intergroups.

entitled to use the EP's technical facilities.[345] In practice, Intergroups are run by a "Bureaus" or an "executive" consisted of one or more MEPs.[346] MEPs may become formal "members" of the selected Intergroups, or they may simply attend their meetings.[347] They are assisted by "secretariats" or "coordinators." These "bodies" are often provided from outside the EP by an entity interested in the work of the Intergroup.[348] Accordingly, for those Intergroups formed around human rights or social policy issues, it is typical for the secretariat or coordinator to be operated by an interested NGO or an NGO platform.[349]

Practically speaking, Intergroups are especially important as an informal channel of cooperation for NGOs in cases where they were not able to adequately participate in the official procedure of consultation with the Commission[350] or where the Commission did not incorporate their main postulates.[351] This form of cooperation can be also favorable in terms of raising the importance of given issues or exerting pressure on other institutions to take some form of action.[352] In addition, Intergroups form a particularly important channel for NGOs in cases where they have doubts about the content of the proposals launched by the Commission.[353] Furthermore, various

345. See Art. 2 of Rules Governing the Establishment of Intergroups.
346. I. De Jesus Butler, *Non-governmental...*, p. 574
347. S. Smismans, *European...*, p. 489.
348. I. De Jesus Butler, *Non-governmental...*, p. 574, A. Grigorescu, *Democratic Intergovernmental Organisations?*, Cambridge 2015, p. 201.
349. For instance, the coordinator of the Anti-Racism and Diversity Intergroup is usually provided by the European Network Against Racism, and the coordinator of the Disability Intergroup is generally operated by the European Disability Forum (see: http://www.enar-eu.org/About-us and http://www.edf-feph.org/about-us). See also I. De Jesus Butler, *Non-governmental...*, p. 575.
350. Like in the case of Services Directive. Cf. S. Bernhard, *Informational Capital: How It Is Developed and Used by CSOs and EU Institutions* in: *EU Civil Society. Patterns of Coopeation, Competition and Conflict*, H. Johansson, S. Kalm (ed.), Basingstoke 2015, pp. 43 et seq.
351. Like in the case of Regulation on air travel. Cf. S. Bernhard, *Informational...*, pp. 43 et seq.
352. Like in the case of SLG proposal. Cf. S. Bernhard, *Informational...*, pp. 43 et seq.
353. For example, the Disability Intergroup played a significant role in the lawmaking procedure of the Regulation concerning the rights of disabled persons and persons with reduced mobility when travelling by air (Regulation (EC) No 1107/2006—rights of disabled persons and persons with reduced mobility when travelling by air, Official Journal L 204, 26.7.2006). An analysis of the Commission's initial proposal (COM(2005) 0047 final—COD 2005/0007), the response paper from the European Disability Forum (among other NGOs, available at: http://www.accessibletourism.org/resources/edf_toolkit_eu_reg_1107_2006_rights_disabl_travelling_air_en.pdf [on February 9, 2019]), the EP's amendments (available at: http://www.europarl.europa.eu/oeil/popups/ficheprocedure.do?lang=en&reference=2005/0007(COD) [on February 9, 2019]) and the final version of the Regulation suggest that the EP took the view of the concerned NGOs into thorough consideration. A good example is the amendment of Art. 7 which exempted airports with annual traffic of less than two hundred million passengers per year from the standards of assistance to disabled passengers. The EDF's response paper indicated that there should be no such blanket exemption, but rather that the standards should be adopted according to the size of the airport, and this is the approach adopted by the EP's amendment. It seems that the Disability Intergroup allowed the European Disability Forum to play an influential role in these changes. For instance, it enabled discussions between NGOs and relevant EP Committee's shadow rapporteurs. It also organized roundtable meetings with MEPs and other interested parties. See also I. De Jesus Butler, *Non-governmental...*, p. 575.

Intergroups enable NGOs to influence the EP's Written Declarations.[354] In this regard, it should be emphasized that a declaration, even though it has no legally binding character, can have a very meaningful persuasive outcome.[355]

[2] Right to Petition

The second form of influencing the works of the EP by NGOs can be attributed to the right to petition. This right is a central figure of parliamentary systems and one which continues to be enjoyed in many jurisdictions. It is a classic means by which supervision can be exercised over the administration. Petitions which are lodged with the EP are, at least initially, referred to the Petitions Committee, a standing committee of the Parliament, another practice widely observed in parliaments worldwide.[356]

The right to petition was introduced by the Maastricht Treaty.[357] However, this instrument has practically existed since 1953 as it has been incorporated in the internal Rules of procedure of the Common Assembly of the European Coal and Steel Community.[358] Its present legal basis can be found in Articles 24[359] and 227 of the TFEU. Article 44 of the EUChFR provides, in effect, a common right to any citizen of the Union and natural and legal persons resident or registered in a Member State to address a petition to the Parliament on a matter within the Unions fields of activity and affecting him, her or it directly. The requirement of Article 227 of the TFEU that the petition addresses a matter within the EU field of activity encompasses matters within the purview of Member State authorities, provided that they fall under the Union law.

The EP has been much more generous in the interpretation of these preconditions than the CJEU has with respect to the similarly worded standing requirement for the annulment procedure under Article 263 (4) of the TFEU.[360] The Petitions Committee is expected to provide an appropriate response to each complaint, each request of

354. A written declaration is a text of a maximum of 200 words relating exclusively on a matter falling within the competence of the European Union. They do not, however, bind Parliament; that is, they cannot be considered as an act of the Parliament representing its position, but only those of its authors and signatories; for the full list of the EP's written declarations see: http://www.europarl.europa.eu/plenary/en/written-declarations.html (on February 9, 2019); a good example is the EP's written declaration on racism in football which was proposed by the Anti-Racism and Diversity Intergroup, available at: http://www.ardi-ep.eu/2016/06/17/written-declaration-on-homophobia-racism-and-discrimination-in-sports/ (on February 9, 2019).
355. J.J. Węc, *Spór...*, p. 317.
356. E. Hannah, *NGOs and Global Trade: Non-state Voices in EU Trade Policymaking*, London 2016, p. 44.
357. In its Art. 8D (1).
358. For more see also K. Kowalik-Bańczyk, *Komentarz do art. 24 Traktatu o funkcjonowaniu Unii Europejskiej* in: *Traktat..., t. I*, lex.pl/el., R. Grzeszczak, *Komentarz do art. 227 Traktatu o funkcjonowaniu Unii Europejskiej* in: *Traktat o funkcjonowaniu Unii Europejskiej. Komentarz, t. III. Art. 223-358*, D. Kornobis-Romanowska, J. Łacny, A. Wróbel (ed.), Warsaw 2012, lex.pl.
359. Which, according to A. Pilakos, has a more "symbolic" character. See A. Pilakos, *Les Conditions d'Exercice du Droit de Petition*, Cahiers droit europêen 1993, p. 319.
360. According A. Pilakos, these requirements, however, should be understood identically (see A. Pilakos, *Les Conditions ...*, pp. 328-330). Other authors claim that the preconditions in case of the right to petition should be interpreted in a more lenient manner (see e.g. K. Kowalik-Bańczyk, *Komentarz do art. 24...*, lex.pl).

position and each demand for action.[361] Considering technical matters, under Rule 202 of the Rules of Procedure of the EP, "an electronic register shall be set up in which citizens may lend or withdraw support to the petitioner, appending their own electronic signature to petitions which have been declared admissible and entered in the register." Petitions can be submitted electronically or in "paper" form.[362]

The investigation process consequent on a petition can be seen as falling into two broad parts: the establishment of the facts and the determination of the response.[363] The Petitions Committee is provided with three different investigative competences. It can request the Commission to provide information and access to documents and facilities, conduct hearings and carry out *in situ* factual inquiries, including on-the-spot visits in Member States. In the inquiry process, the Commission has the obligation to support the Petitions Committee.[364]

The Committee can prepare a report or in some other way express its opinion on petitions which it has accepted. The outcomes of inquiries have only the character of recommendations.[365] The Petitions Committee may involve the parliamentary committee relevant to the subject matter concerned in order to seek changes in existing law (by asking the Commission to exercise its right to initiate legislative measures). Where necessary, it proceeds by submitting motions for parliamentary resolutions or by requesting opinions to be forwarded to the Commission or the Council of the President of the Parliament.[366] The President informs petitioners of the decision taken.

In order to ensure that the Petitions Committee itself meets standards of accountability, the Rules of Procedure of the EP require the Committee to report each half-year to the EP and to submit an annual report on the petitions it receives.[367] It also informs the EP of the actions taken by the Council and the Commission in relation to petitions.[368]

As far as practice is concerned, the number of petitions has been rising constantly.[369] This growth may be a sign not only of the fact that the Petitions Committee is gradually becoming more significant but also that there is a growing awareness of the role of the EP itself.[370] However, the Petitions Committee's annual reports show that the petition process is in reality not a major instrument of political supervision of the EU administrative action.[371] In this way, other supervisory mechanisms, especially the

361. E. Hannah, *NGOs...*, p. 45.
362. A. Alemanno, *Lobbying for Change: Find Your Voice to Create a Better Society*, London 2017, p. 176.
363. See Rule 215 of the Rules of Procedure of the EP.
364. *Ibid.*
365. H. Hofmann, G. Rowe, A. Turk, *Administrative Law and Policy of the European Union*, Oxford 2011, p. 773. See also A.R. Schneider, *Petitionen zum Europaischen Parlament mit Berücksichtigung des Bürgeauftragten*, Frankfurt am Mein 2009, p. 152.
366. H. Hofmann, G. Rowe, A. Turk, *Administrative...*, p. 777.
367. See Art. 216 (7) of the EP's Rules of Procedure.
368. Cf. also E. Hannah, *NGOs...*, p. 47.
369. A total of 1.067 petitions (68% of those received) were submitted via the web portal in 2016, as compared to 992 in 2015. See Report under Rule 216 (7) on the deliberations of the Committee on Petitions during the year 2016, (2017/2222(INI)), point T.
370. E. Jones, A. Menon, S. Weatherill, *Oxford Handbook...*, p. 117.
371. Cf. Report under Rule 216 (7).

European Ombudsman, is said to play a more significant role.[372] In fact, there are strong similarities between petitions to the EP and the complaints to the European Ombudsman.[373] Although petitions may address both policy issues and individual grievances against the EU administration, the latter ones are often better placed before the Ombudsman.[374]

As the surveys indicate, the right of petition to the EP is regularly used by NGOs.[375] However, the actual influence of this instrument on the EU lawmaking is rather hard to estimate as it seldom results in clear legislative consequences.[376] It also seems that the right of petition is often used "besides" other forms of influencing the EP, while the most common forms of affecting this institution are either consultations or lobbying.[377]

[C] The Council of the EU

Even though the Council of the EU seems to steadily gain influence in the institutional system of the EU,[378] it is hardly accessible to NGOs wishing to advocate for the interests of European civil society. In particular, there is no formal channel for NGO participation.[379] The Rules of Procedure of the Council of 2009[380] do not provide any obligations or means of dialogue with the representatives of civil society. Moreover, informal relations are rather difficult to follow as much depends on national practices[381] and the "openness" of Member States missions in Brussels.[382] The majority of legislative proposals are discussed only within the preparatory bodies of the Council (also known as "working groups").[383] Access to those groups is generally closed to NGOs.[384]

Yet, some indirect channels of access to the Council and its working groups can be distinguished. First, NGOs can attempt to impact the Council by influencing the

372. H. Hofmann, G. Rowe, A. Turk, *Administrative...*, p. 774.
373. E. Fahley, *The Actors of Postnational Rule-Making*, London 2015, p. 12.
374. L. Woods, P. Watson, *Steiner & Woods EU Law*, Oxford 2014, p. 245.
375. E. Jones, A. Menon, S. Weatherill, *Oxford...*, p. 121.
376. R. Sanchez Salgado, *Europeanizing...*, p. 13.
377. H. Hofmann, G. Rowe, A. Turk, *Administrative...*, p. 778.
378. See e.g. D. Adamski, *Access...*, pp. 520 et seq., A. Classen, *Interessenvertretung...*, pp. 61-63.
379. In general, NGOs are not allowed to take part in the Council meetings. The exception to this practice are human rights NGOs which are invited to informal Council meetings. Moreover, since 2007 the Social Platform have been invited to take part in the Employment, Social Policy, Health and Consumer Affairs Council configuration (EPSCO), see P. Swieboda, P. Zerka, *Aktywność...*, p. 40.
380. Available at: https://europa.eu/european-union/sites/europaeu/files/docs/body/rules_of_procedure_of_the_council_en.pdf (on February 9, 2019).
381. P. Swieboda, P. Zerka, *Aktywność...*, p. 40.
382. Thus, national section or national NGOs belonging to a European NGO network would be urged by their EU-level counterparts to pressure their governments (via the relevant minister) to adopt particular stances within the Council negotiations (Cf. S. Bernhard, *Informational...*, pp. 43 et seq.). See also M.Z. Hillebrandt, D. Curtin, A. Meijer, *Transparency in the EU Council of Ministers: An Institutional Analysis*, European Law Journal Vol. 20/2014, p. 2.
383. It is estimated that there are ca. 250 groups within the Council, i.e. working groups, ad hoc groups, attaché groups, high-rank groups. For more information see M. Dondi, *Interesenvertretung beim Rat der Europäischen Union* in: *Lobbying in der Europäischen Union. Zwischen Professionalisierung und Regulierung*, D. Dialer, M. Richter (eds), Wiesbaden 2014, p. 92.

positions presented by Commission.[385] Second, they can try to contact with Member State representatives to discuss the state of legislative negotiations and present their views.[386] Both of these possibilities are in fact linked to the "trilogue" procedures and, therefore, their implications are extremely hard to estimate.[387] Third, NGOs can try to convince the Member State holding the Presidency of the Council (and thus chairing its meetings) to take their opinions into account or prioritize certain issues.[388] For instance, during its presidency in 2006, the Austrian government was very concerned with the creation of the EU Agency for Fundamental Rights and therefore successfully worked with many NGOs working in this sphere.[389] Yet, it seems that the general way of dealings between Member States representatives and groups of interests remain exceedingly opaque.[390]

The general "closure" of the Council is, in a narrow sense, not contrary to Article 15 (2) of the TFEU which states that it shall meet in public when considering and voting on a legislative act. However, it does not seem to be consistent with the general rule of transparency. In reality, the practice leaves a wide range of the Council activity in the lawmaking outside public control[391] which is even more troublesome given the fact that it is one of the most (if not the most) powerful of the legislative bodies. In order to change this situation, the Council should, for instance, provide more information on the positions presented during meetings by particular Member States. This demand was also strongly singled out by the European Ombudsman.[392] In this respect, it is quite interesting to indicate that NGOs have a wider access to the lawmaking intergovernmental fora of the UN than they do in the case of the Council, even though the UN

384. J. Cross, *Striking a Pose: Transparency and Position Taking in the Council of the European Union*, European Journal of Political Research Vol. 52/2013, p. 292. Cf. S. Bernhard, *Informational...*, pp. 43 et seq.
385. I. De Jesus Butler, *Non-governmental...*, p. 572.
386. *Ibid.*, p. 573.
387. Cf. E. Jones, A. Menon, S. Weatherill, *Oxford...*, p. 243. The normal legislative process starts with a bill from the Commission. The bill is then channeled through the EP and the Council to the EU, representing Member States. If no agreement is reached at first reading, a second reading is launched. However, according to figures provided by the EP, not a single bill ended up in the second reading in 2016; only the second time this has happened since the EP record keeping began in 2004. Second readings are important because they open up the debate to the public at large. Removing this phase means the details are being agreed behind closed doors and people have to rely on insider information to understand what is happening. Of course, well-connected lobbyists or specialized reporters may be able to follow the lawmaking process, but most people (apart from some small-scaled NGOs) will struggle to make sense of why or how decisions were made. Accordingly, rather than the lengthy and more transparent process, many bills are passed at first reading after closed-door negotiations between small groups of MEPs and national diplomats acting in the name of the Council with a Commission official as mediator (for more see N. Nielsen, *Secret Law Making Takes over Brussels*, available at: https://euobserver.com/institutional/136630 [on February 9, 2019]).
388. J. Cross, *Striking...*, p. 295.
389. M.Z. Hillebrandt, D. Curtin, A. Meijer, *Transparency...*, p. 4.
390. For more see e.g. P. Teffer, *EU embassies "shockingly" opaque about lobbyists*, available at: https://euobserver.com/institutional/144092 (on February 9, 2019).
391. Cf. K. Kowalik-Bańczyk, *Komentarz do Artykułu 15* in: *Traktat... t. 1*, lex.pl.
392. See Recommendation of the European Ombudsman in case OI/2/2017/TE on the Transparency of the Council legislative process, Case: OI/2/2017/TE.

system does not provide such direct democratic provisions as the EU does.[393] While the negotiations in the Council are generally closed to the public, within the UN (at least in the case of acts on human rights) they are habitually carried on within an "Open-Ended Working Group" allowing accredited NGOs to attend as observes and (where the chair permits so) to submit documents or make oral contributions.[394]

[D] The CJEU

Invoking the CJEU in the part dedicated to the impact of NGOs on the EU lawmaking may seem arguable as this institution does not take part in passing the generally binding acts of law. However, its judgments often take the form of legal precedents.[395] In fact, this phenomenon is also acknowledged in the case law of the CJEU.[396] Even though the position of the CJEU as a de facto lawmaker is often subject to criticism,[397] it is without any doubt one of the most persuasive institutions in shaping the EU law.

Still, it seems that there is a noticeable shortage of publications concerning the actual relations between the CJEU and NGOs. It is not until recently that the outcomes of the litigation undertaken by civil society litigants (especially NGOs) before the international courts have started to be intensely investigated. Some authors[398] argued that NGOs have the capacity to foster both judicial and political challenges through litigation actions. The analysis conducted in this field concentrated on specific relations between NGOs and courts in general. First, it was pointed out that the activity of nonprofit organizations is essential to evaluate the evolution of the human rights jurisprudence in general.[399] Still, the ability of these organizations to contribute to the development of human rights relies on diverse national legal cultures.[400] Second, it was stated that the possible impact of organizations concentrated on fundamental rights is correlated with their structure and financial resources.[401] As a result, it was argued that a "judicial lobby" can be successful only when the human rights organizations have various sources of financing in order to stay independent.[402] Finally, it was observed that achieving individual justice through human rights organizations is hardly ever the

393. J. Cross, *Striking...*, p. 295.
394. A.-K. Lindblom, *Non-governmental...*, p. 366.
395. See e.g. M. Jacobs, *Precedents and Case-Base Reasoning in the European Court of Justice*, International Journal of Constitutional Law Vol. 3/2014, pp. 832 et seq.
396. I.e., in the *acte éclairé* doctrine. See e.g. C-283/81 *CILFIT v. Ministero della Santà*, ECLI-:EU:C:1982:335.
397. Cf. e.g. M. Szabados, *"Precedents" in EU Law—The Problem of Overruling*, ELTE Law Journal Vol. 1/2015, pp. 125 et seq.
398. While, however, mainly concentrating on the US system; see e.g. J. Davis, *Justice Across Borders. The Struggle for Human Rights in U.S. Courts*, Cambridge 2008, pp. 75 et seq.
399. E.g. A. Sarat, S. Scheingold, *Cause Lawyering: Political Commitments and Professional Responsibilities*, Oxford 1998, pp. 11 et seq., G. Cliquennois, B. Champetier, *The Economic...*, p. 93.
400. For a different point of view see e.g. G. Rosenberg, *The Hollow Hope: Can Courts Bring About Social Change?*, Chicago 1991.
401. M.W. McCann, *Rights at Work: Pay Equity Reform and the Politics of Legal Mobilization*, Chicago 1994, pp. 7 et seq.
402. J.S. Migdał, *State in Society: Studying How States and Societies Transform and Constitute One Another*, Cambridge 2001, p. 45.

single predominating case before the international and EU courts as NGOs tend to advocate for "general" rather than "singular" rights.[403]

The CJEU does not confer any explicit rights on NGOs if they are not a direct party in the proceeding case. Neither the Statute of the Court of Justice of the European Union[404] nor the Rules of Procedure of the Court of Justice[405] or the General Court[406] mention amicus curiae briefs.[407] This omission may stem from the role given to Advocates General before the Court of Justice. They provide for a unique system to represent the public interest. According to Article 252 of the TFEU, it shall be the duty of the Advocate General, acting with complete impartiality and independence, to make, in open court, reasoned submissions on cases which, in accordance with the Statute of the Court of Justice of the European Union, require involvement. Yet, the Advocates General do not generally assist the General Court,[408] and a judge designated for the purpose of reasoned submissions may only perform the role of Advocate General in a limited number of cases. Nevertheless, there is no general right for a public interest group or any NGO for that matter to provide information and expertise to the General Court.[409]

That said, however, both the Court of Justice and the General Court have adopted a broad interpretation of Article 40 of the Statute[410] and the expression "an interest in

403. S. Ahmed, *The Impact...*, p. 818, S.K. Schmidt, *The Shadow of Case Law: The Court of Justice of the European Union and the Policy Process* in: *European Union. Power and Policy-Making*, J. Richardson, S. Mazey (eds), Abingdon 2015, pp. 159 et seq., R.A. Cichowski, *The European Court and Civil Society: Litigation, Mobilization and Governance*, Cambridge 2009, pp. 207-209.
404. The consolidated version of Protocol (No 3) on the Statute of the Court of Justice of the European Union, annexed to the Treaties, as amended by Regulation (EU, Euratom) No 741/2012 of the European Parliament and of the Council of 11 August 2012 (Official Journal L 228, 23.8.2012), by Art. 9 of the act concerning the conditions of accession to the European Union of the Republic of Croatia and the adjustments to the Treaty on European Union, the Treaty on the Functioning of the European Union and the Treaty establishing the European Atomic Energy Community (Official Journal L 112, 24.4.2012) and by Regulation (EU, Euratom) 2015/2422 of the European Parliament and of the Council of 16 December 2015 (Official Journal L 341, 24.12.2015).
405. Rules of Procedure of the Court of Justice of 25 September 2012 (Official Journal L 265, 29.9.2012), as amended on June 18, 2013 (Official Journal L 173, 26.6.2013) and on July 19, 2016 (Official Journal L 217, 12.8.2016), available at: http://curia.europa.eu/jcms/upload/docs/application/pdf/2012-10/rp_en.pdf (on February 9, 2019).
406. Rules of Procedure of the General Court of 4 March 2015 (Official Journal L 105, 23.4.2015), as amended on July 13, 2016 (Official Journal L 217, 12.8.2016) and on July 11 and 31, 2018 (Official Journal L 240, 25.9.2018), available at: https://curia.europa.eu/jcms/upload/docs/application/pdf/2018-11/tra-doc-en-div-t-0000-2018-201810296-05_01.pdf (on February 9, 2019).
407. As opposed to, e.g. the WTO system, see P. Van der Bossche, *The Law...*, p. 263. Still, nonofficial platforms of providing amicus curiae briefs do exist. See, to this extent, https://www.amicus-ecj.eu.
408. Yet, such a possibility is theoretically possible under Article 112 of the Rules of Procedure of the General Court.
409. R. Cichowski, *The European Court and Civil Society: Litigation, Mobilization and Governance*, Cambridge 2007, p. 56.
410. I.e., Member States and institutions of the Union may intervene in cases before the Court of Justice.

The same right shall be open to the bodies, offices and agencies of the Union and to any other person who can establish an interest in the result of a case submitted to the Court. Natural or legal persons shall not intervene in cases between Member States, between institutions of

the result of the case" in order to allow intervention by certain special interest groups (representative associations) whose purpose is to protect their members in cases raising questions of principle liable to affect those members.[411] Even if such a group has not taken part in the preliminary administrative procedure, it may intervene if:

- it represents an appreciable number of undertakings active in the sector concerned,
- its objects include that of protecting its members' interests,
- the case raises questions of principle affecting the functioning of the sector concerned,
- the interests of its members may, therefore, be affected to an appreciable extent by the forthcoming judgment.[412]

For instance, in the joint cases 16/62, 17/62 *Confédération Nationale des Producteurs de Fruits et Legumes and others v. Council,*[413] the Court of Justice granted leave for intervention to an association of producers on the basis of the mere fact that the regulation at issue was capable of affecting the interests of national producers of certain goods. The producers and, thus, their representative had a "direct, existing and undeniable interest in the continuation or annulment of the regulation at issue." Furthermore, in the joint cases C-241/91 P and C-242/91 P *Telefis Eireann v. Commission,*[414] the Court of Justice granted leave to intervene to a non-profit-making association whose interest was no more than an interest in establishing a general principle with which the original applicants hoped to persuade the Court.[415]

---

the Union or between Member States and institutions of the Union.

Without prejudice to the second paragraph, the states, other than the Member States, which are parties to the Agreement on the European Economic Area, and also the EFTA Surveillance Authority referred to in that Agreement, may intervene in cases before the Court where one of the fields of application of that Agreement is concerned.

An application to intervene shall be limited to supporting the form of order sought by one of the parties. See also Arts. 129-133 of the Rules of Procedure.

411. J. M. Almqvist, *The Accessibility of European Integration Courts from an NGO Perspective* in: *Civil Society, International Courts and Compliance Bodies*, T. Treves, M. Frigessi di Rattalma, A. Tanzi, Al. Fodella, C. Pitea, Ch. Ragni (eds), The Hague 2005, p. 278.
412. See e.g. T-87/92 *Kruidvat v. Commission*, ECLI:EU:T:1996:191, para. 14, T-18/97 *Atlantic Container Line AB and 15 other Liner Shipping Companies v. Commission*, ECLI:EU:T:2002:51, para. 18; for more information see K. Lenaerts, I. Maselis, K. Gutman, *EU Procedural Law*, Oxford 2014, p. 832.
413. ECLI:EU:C:1962:47.
414. J. M. Almqvist, *The Accessibility...*, p. 279.
415. See also e.g. C-84/17 P, C-85/17 P and C-95/17 P *Société des produits Nestlé SA v. European Union Intellectual Property Office (EUIPO)*, ECLI:EU:C:2018:16, C-104/16 P *Council of the European Union v. Front populaire pour la libération de la saguia-el-hamra et du rio de oro (Front Polisario)*, ECLI:EU:C:2016:973, C-248/15 P, C-254/15 P and C-260/15 P *Maxcom Ltd v. Council of the European Union*, ECLI:EU:C:2017:62, C-51/15 *Remondis GmbH & Co. KG Region Nord*, ECLI:EU:C:2016:985, C-249/14 P *Pêra-Grave — Sociedade Agrícola, Unipessoal Lda v. Office for Harmonisation in the Internal Market (Trade Marks and Designs) (OHIM)*, ECLI-:EU:C:2015:459, C-61/14 *Orizzonte Salute — Studio Infermieristico Associato v. Azienda Pubblica di Servizi alla persona San Valentino — Città di Levico Terme and others*, ECLI-:EU:C:2015:655.

NGOs may also intervene in preliminary rulings proceedings before the Court of Justice. However, only third parties which are also involved in the action before the national court making the request for a preliminary ruling have the right to submit statements or written observations to these kinds of proceedings.[416]

[E] Summary

Despite the introduction of Article 11 of the TEU and the "rights-based approach" to the participation of civil society in the EU-level lawmaking,[417] the practice of particular institutions in their contacts with the interested NGOs remains ambiguous.

The Commission seems to be the most open institution. In particular, it has referred to the need for involving grassroot organizations in its legislative consultations since the 1990s. In consequence, it is the only EU institution that provides substantive framework for consultation requirements. They were provided in the General Principles of 2002 and the Guidelines of 2017. The latter act of law envisages, specifically, the obligation to initiate consultations under the given circumstances. Nevertheless, the dialogues with civil society usually take the form of online consultation which are, in spite of their unquestionable outreach, often criticized as an "illusion of participation." Other forms of involving stakeholders in deliberations on the legislative proposals involve consultative committees. However, the scope of these bodies is quite limited.

Other EU institutions envisage noticeably fewer possibilities for NGO participation. The EP, apart from individual consultations conducted by various MEPs or MEP groups, provides the possibility of forming Intergroups which can include the representatives of civil society. Individuals also have the right to petition to the EP which, however, can produce rather "soft" outcomes. The Council provides no legal framework for NGO participation or any official consultations. Therefore, much depends on practices of specific Member States missions in Brussels. This lack of openness is rightly criticized, especially by the European Ombudsman. Finally, even though NGOs cannot officially present amicus curiae briefs in proceedings before the CJEU, they are entitled to intervene under certain conditions. However, the possible influence of NGOs on the judgments of the CJEU is rather hard to assess.

§3.03 LOBBYING THE EU INSTITUTIONS

As official channels of consultations are not always effective, NGOs repeatedly engage themselves in lobbying the EU institutions for their own initiatives or the amendments to the EU law which they find necessary. There is no consensus on what the notion of

416. See C-197-200/80, 243, 245 and 247/80 *Ludwigshafener Walzmuhle Erling KG v. European Economic Community*, ECLI:EU:C:1981:90.
417. J. Medes, *Participation in EU Rule-Making*, Oxford 2011, pp. 76-77.

"lobbying" means.[418] In general, lobbying[419] is a way of attempting to influence actions, policies or decisions of the lawmakers.[420] Lobbying is done by many types of organizations, including corporations, private sector and subjects acting not for profit.[421] It can be stated that the ethics and morality of lobbying are ambiguous. Lobbying is often attributed to overuse of economic power which implies that some stakeholders with bigger financial possibilities and political connections are corrupting the lawmaking procedures for their own interest.[422] Consequently, many critics point out that lobbying undermines the governments as institutions established to follow public interests.[423] However, lobbying can also have a far more positive aspect. It is often perceived as a reassurance that the grassroot interests have a voice in the lawmaking.[424] Clearly, the role of NGOs in lobbying fits in the latter part.[425] In fact, there has been a recent trend of "disenchanting" the concept of lobbying activity through grassroot movements at the EU level. Thus, "good lobbying" as a way to promote the interests of civil society is (rightly) portrayed as one of the ways to reduce the democratic deficit in the EU.[426]

The following paragraphs will focus on the legal grounds of lobbying in the EU institutional system and the shortcomings arising therefrom.

418. Private Interests, Public Conduct: The Essence of Lobbying in: Lobbyists, Governments and Public Trust, Volume 2. A report of the OECD, pp. 21-23, available at: http://bit.do/ej6LY (on February 9, 2019).
419. Historically, lobbying takes its name from the "lobbies" or hallways of Parliament where members gather before and after debates. However, today lobbying takes all kinds of forms. See *Lobbying the EU Institutions Library Briefing Library of the European Parliament 18/06/2013*, available at: http://bit.do/ej6M5 (on February 9, 2019).
420. P. Bouwen, *The European...*, p. 35, I. Michalowitz, *Warum die EU-Politik Lobbying braucht? Der Tauschansatz als implizites Forschungsparadigma* in: *Lobbying in der Europäischen Union. Zwischen Professionalisierung und Regulierung*, D. Dialer, M. Richter (eds), Wiesbaden 2014, pp. 17-19, S. Mazey, J. Richardson, *Shooting Where the Ducks Are: EU Lobbying and Institutionalized Promiscuity* in: *European Union. Power and policy-making*, J. Richardson, S. Mazey (ed.), Abingdon 2015, pp. 419 et seq., P. Kotzian, Ch. Quittkat, *Konsultationsprozess der Kommission...*, p. 87, J. Beyers, I. De Bruycker, *Lobbying Makes (Strange) Bedfellows: Explaining the Formation and Composition of Lobbying Coalitions in EU Legislative Politics*, Political Studies Vol. 10/2017, pp. 3 et seq., U. Kurczewska, M. Molęda-Zdziech, *Lobbing w Unii Europejskiej—zarys problematyki*, Studia Europejskie Vol. 2/1999, pp. 49 et seq.
421. K. Joos, *Lobbying in the New Europe*, Weinheim 2011, p. 87.
422. D. Panke, *Lobbying...*, p. 134.
423. *Ibid.*, p. 137.
424. Cf. A. Alemanno, *Lobbying...*, pp. 77 et seq., H. Klüwer, *Lobbying in the European Union*, Oxford 2013, p. 93.
425. For more see e.g. P. Bouwen, *The European...*, p. 37, A. Geddes, *Lobbying for Migrant Inclusion in the European Union: New Opportunities for Transnational Advocacy?*, Journal of European Public Policy Vol. 7/2000, p. 632, S. Mazey, J. Richardson, *Lobbying in the European Community*, Oxford 1993, pp. 10 et seq., B. Pijnenburg, *EU Lobbying by Ad Hoc Coalitions: An Exploratory Case Study*, Journal of European Public Policy Vol. 5/1998, p. 303.
426. For more see e.g. A. Alemanno, *Lobbying...*, pp. 70 et seq.

[A] The Background of Lobbying at the EU Level

Formalized lobbying in Brussels was initiated in the late 1970s due to the first direct elections to the EP.[427] Before that, informal campaigning for one's interest was basically reserved to diplomats.[428] Advocacy organizations were very rare and were not established at the Community level on daily basis.[429] After the first pan-European elections, many entities, including NGOs, began to track the legislative processes taking part in Brussels with the intention to influence them actively and effectively.[430] Lobbying was further developed because of the Single European Act of 1986[431] which instituted qualified majority vote for decision-making in the Council and enhanced the role of the EP. Both amendments made the legislation more complex and, thus, lobbying more important and attractive for stakeholders.[432] Still, up until the early 2000s, there were no structural norms concerning the admissibility of lobbying in the EU institutions.[433]

Basing on the premises of the White Paper on European Governance, in 2002 the database for Consultation, the European Commission and Civil Society (CONECCS) were created.[434] NGOs that took part in consultation processes with the Commission could enlist themselves in that database. The inclusion in the database was utterly voluntary although restricted to certain prerequisites. In order to be eligible, an organization must have been an active nonprofit representative body organized at European level, i.e. with members in two or more European Union or candidate countries, and had to have in one or more of the policy areas of the Commission, some degree of formal or institutional existence and be prepared to provide any reasonable information about itself required by the Commission, either for insertion on the database or in support of its requests for inclusion.[435] What was interesting in these provisions is that they explicitly envisaged an opportunity for lobbying activities held by organizations operating in candidate countries to the EU in order to allow them to represent their interests.[436]

However, "lobbying" itself was first officially referred to by the Commission in 2006, in the Green Paper on European transparency initiative.[437] For the purposes of this document, "lobbying" was understood as all activities carried out with the

427. A. Classen, *Interessenvertretung...*, pp. 37-38.
428. R. van Schendelen, *More ...*, p. 121.
429. *Ibid.*, p. 123.
430. J. Greenwood, *Interest Representation in the European Union*, London 2011, p. 187.
431. A. Vetulani-Cęgiel, *Lobbing w procesie kształtowania prawa autorskiego w Unii Europejskiej*, Warsaw 2014, pp. 62 et seq.
432. J. Greenwood, *Interest...*, p. 188.
433. Cf. A. Vetulani-Cęgiel, *Lobbing...*, p. 64.
434. For more information see: http://powerbase.info/index.php/European_Commission_CON ECCS_Database (on February 9, 2019); see also A. Colombo, *The Principle of Subsidiarity and European Citizenship*, Milan 2004, pp. 55 et seq.
435. See: http://powerbase.info/index.php/European_Commission_CONECCS_Database (on February 9, 2019), see also P.-M. Dupuy, L. Vierucci, *NGOs in International Law. Efficiency in Flexibility?*, Cheltenham 2008, p. 242.
436. J. Greenwood, *Interest...*, p. 189.
437. COM(2006) 194 final—Official Journal C 151, 29.6.2006.

objective of influencing the policy formulation and decision-making processes of the European institutions. Accordingly, "lobbyists" were defined as persons carrying out such activities, working in a variety of organizations such as public affairs consultancies, law firms, NGOs, think tanks, corporate lobby units ("in-house representatives") or trade associations.[438] The Green Paper underlined the merits of proper lobbying in the legislative process:[439]

- it is a legitimate part of the democratic system, regardless of whether it is carried out by individual citizens or companies, civil society organizations and other interest groups or firms working on behalf of third parties (public affairs professionals, think tanks and lawyers);
- lobbyists can help bring important issues to the attention of the European institutions. In some cases, the Community offers financial support in order to ensure that views of certain groups are effectively voiced at the European level (e.g., consumer interests, disabled citizens, environmental interests, etc.);
- at the same time, undue influence should not be exerted on the European institutions through improper lobbying;
- when lobby groups seek to contribute to the EU policy development, it must be clear to the general public which input they provide to the European institutions. It must also be clear who they represent, what their mission is and how they are funded.

However, certain problems concerning this phenomenon, dealing also with the position of NGOs, have been pointed out.[440] Thus, it has been acknowledged that the legitimacy of interest representation by European NGOs sometimes is questioned because some NGOs seem to rely on financial support from the EU budget as well as on political and financial support from their members.[441] This statement, as it will be discussed in the subsequent chapter of this book, is still partially true. Nonetheless, by contrast, according to many NGOs, up until now there has been no level playing field in lobbying because the corporate sector is able to invest more financial resources in lobbying.[442]

The Commission concluded that greater transparency in lobbying was necessary. The proposed system would consist of:[443]

- a voluntary registration system, run by the Commission, with clear incentives for lobbyists to register (the incentives would include automatic alerts of consultations on issues of interest known to the lobbyists);
- a common code of conduct for all lobbyists or at least common minimum requirements. The code should be developed by the lobbying profession itself, possibly consolidating and improving the existing codes;

438. Point II.1.—Transparency and Interest Representation. Definitions and basic framework.
439. *Ibid.*
440. Point II.1.—Transparency and Interest Representation. Potential problem areas.
441. Point II.1.—Transparency and Interest Representation. Definitions and basic framework.
442. Point II.1.—Transparency and Interest Representation. Potential problem areas.
443. See The way forwards.

- a system of monitoring and sanctions to be applied in case of incorrect registration and/or breach of the code of conduct.

Accordingly, it appears that the main reason for legal improvements was to strengthen transparency and to raise trust in the EU institutions. Basing on these declarations, in 2011 the EP and the Commission adopted an agreement on the establishment of a transparency register for organizations and self-employed individuals engaged in EU policy-making and policy implementation[444] which was amended in 2014.[445]

[B] The Transparency Register

The creation of the Transparency Register was based on an assumption that "European policy-makers do not operate in isolation from civil society, but maintain an open, transparent and regular dialogue with representative associations and civil society."[446] The register is an institution grounded on the rule of voluntary registration, as opposed to compulsory registration existing in many legal systems across the world.[447] It means that the individuals or organizations that would like to lobby for their interests in the EP or the Commission should, but are not obliged to, register prior to the beginning of such an activity. As it is stated in the agreement, "all organizations and self-employed individuals, irrespective of their legal status, engaged in activities, whether on-going or under preparation, covered by the register are expected to register."[448] Still, the registration entails certain privileges. Thus, only the registered lobbyists have the access to the highest officials of the Commission (i.e., Commissioners, their Cabinet and Directors-General) and the building of the EP. The shortcomings of the voluntary nature of this legal framework will be subject to further analysis in the subsequent part of this chapter. The Transparency Register currently[449] contains ca. 11,900 registrants, approximately 3,160 of which are NGOs (26.5%).[450]

The scope of the register covers all activities carried out with the objective of directly or indirectly influencing the formulation or implementation of policy and the

444. Official Journal L 191/29, 22.7.2011.
445. By the Agreement between the European Parliament and the European Commission on the Transparency Register for organizations and self-employed individuals engaged in EU policy-making and policy implementation, Official Journal L 277, 19.9.2014.
446. See the preamble to the Agreement.
447. E.g. in USA, Canada, German Bundestag; for more information see J. Greenwood, *Interest...*, pp. 11 et seq.
448. Point III (Scope of the Register) para. 7.
449. As of February 9, 2019.
450. Currently the registrants consist of:

- 5.812—in-house lobbyists and trade/business/professional associations;
- 1.284—professional consultancies/law firms/self-employed consultants;
- 920—think tanks, research and academic institutions.
- 593—organizations representing local, regional and municipal authorities, other public or mixed entities;
- 50—organizations representing churches and religious communities (see: http://ec.europa.eu/transparencyregister/public/homePage.do# [on February 9, 2019]).

decision-making processes of the EP and the Commission,[451] irrespective of where they are undertaken and of the channel or medium of communication used (e.g., via outsourcing, media contracts with professional intermediaries, think tanks, platforms, forums, campaigns and grassroots initiatives).[452] For the purpose of the agreement, "directly influencing" means influencing by direct contact or communication with the EU institutions or other action following up to such activities and "indirectly influencing" means influencing through the use of intermediate vectors such as media, public opinion, conferences or social events, targeting the EU institutions.[453] In particular, those activities include:

- contacting members and their assistants, officials or other staff of the EU institutions;
- preparing, circulating and communicating letters, information material or discussion papers and position papers;
- organizing events, meetings, promotional activities, conferences or social events, invitations to which have been sent to members and their assistants, officials or other staff of the EU institutions; and
- voluntary contributions and participation in formal consultations or hearings on envisaged EU legislative or other legal acts and other open consultations.

The agreement envisages some exceptions from its scope. First of all, activities in response to direct and individual requests from the EU institutions or MEPs, such as ad hoc or regular requests for factual information, data or expertise are not covered by the register.[454] Second, activities of the social partners as participants in the social dialogue (trade unions, employers' associations, etc.) are not covered by the register where those social partners perform the role assigned to them in the Treaties.[455] Third, activities concerning the provision of legal and other professional advice are not covered by the register so far as:[456]

According to the Transparency Register Factsheet: (available at: http://ec.europa.eu/transparency/docs/factsheet_transparency_register_en.pdf [on February 9, 2019]):

- an average of 50 organizations join the Register every week;
- one-fifth of all registrants have a head office in Belgium;
- 92% of registered organizations are EU-based. Every single EU Member State is represented.

The most represented countries are: Belgium (21%), Germany (12%), United Kingdom (11%), France (10%), Italy (7%), Spain (6%), the Netherlands (5%), United States (3.5%), Austria (2%), Sweden (1%).

451. It is estimated that lobbyists influence ca. 75% of the current EU legislation. See E. Korkea-Aho, *EU Lobbyists: Rule-Makers "In the Shadows"* in: *The Actors of Postnational Rule-Making. Contemporary Challenges of European and International Law*, E. Fahey (ed.), Abingdon 2016, pp. 207 et seq.
452. Point III (Scope of the Register) para. 7.
453. *Ibid.*
454. Point III (Scope of the Register) para. 12.
455. *Ibid.*, para. 11.
456. *Ibid.*, para. 10.

- they consist of advisory work and contacts with public bodies in order to provide better information to clients about a general legal situation or about their specific legal position, or to advise them whether a particular legal or administrative step is appropriate or admissible under the existing legal and regulatory environment;
- they consist of advice given to clients to help them ensure that their activities comply with the relevant law;
- they consist of analyzes and studies prepared for clients on the potential impact of any legislative or regulatory changes with regard to their legal position or field of activity;
- they consist of representation in the context of a conciliation or mediation procedure aimed at preventing a dispute from being brought before a judicial or administrative body; or
- they relate to the exercise of the fundamental right of a client to a fair trial, including the right of defense in administrative proceedings, such as activities carried out by lawyers or by any other professionals involved therein.

If a company and its advisers are involved as a party in a specific legal or administrative case or procedure, any activity relating directly thereto which does not seek as such to change the existing legal framework is not covered by the register. This exception applies to all business sectors in the EU.[457] However, the following activities concerning the provisions of legal and other professional advice are covered by the register where they are intended to influence the EU institutions, their members and their assistants or their officials or other staff:[458]

- the provision of support, via representation or mediation, or of advocacy material, including argumentation and drafting;
- the provision of tactical or strategic advice, including the raising of issues whose scope and the timing of communication of which are intended to influence the EU institutions and their assistants or their officials or other staff.

Therefore, it is possible that an NGO does not enlist itself on the Transparency Register but instead uses the services of other entities (especially law firms or individual lawyers) in order to be represented in the lobbying measures.

Annex I to the agreement explicitly names nongovernmental organizations, platforms, networks, ad hoc coalitions, temporary structures and other similar organizations as entities engaged in the EU policy-making and policy implementation and, thus, subject to registration. They are defined as not-for-profit organizations (with or without legal status), which are independent of public authorities or commercial organizations. It includes "foundations, charities, etc."

There are some problems with the quoted definition as it includes, contrary to the commonly functioning definition of NGOs, organizations without legal status. It means that a civic movement, as well as other forms of civil activity without legal personality,

457. *Ibid.*
458. *Ibid.*

could be enlisted on the Transparency Register. However, this results in a conclusion that an inclusion in the Transparency Register is not per se an evidence of existing legal personality for the purpose of action for annulment based on Article 263 paragraph 4 of the TFEU since the register is not subject to the existence of legal personality on the part of the body concerned.[459]

The registrants must provide some information considering their activity. According to Annex II of the agreement, this obligation includes:[460]

(a) organization name (names), address of head office and Brussels, Luxembourg or Strasbourg address where relevant, phone number, e-mail address, website;
(b) names of the person legally responsible for the organization and of the organization's director or managing partner or, if applicable, principal contact point in respect of activities covered by the register (i.e., head of EU affairs); names of the persons with authorization for access to the EP's premises;
(c) number of persons (members, staff, etc.) involved in the activities covered by the register and of persons benefiting from an access pass to the EP's premises and the amount of time spent by each person on such activities according to the following percentage of a full-time activity: 25%, 50%, 75% or 100%;
(d) goals/remit—fields of interest—activities—countries in which operations are carried out—affiliations to networks—general information falling within the scope of the register;
(e) membership and, if applicable, number of members (individuals and organizations).

Moreover, the registered organizations shall provide information concerning:

- links with the EU institutions;
- membership of high-level groups, consultative committees, expert groups, other EU supported structures and platforms, etc.;
- membership of, or participation in, the EP Intergroups or industry forums, etc.;
- their funding;
- an estimate of the annual costs related to activities covered by the register. Financial figures shall cover a full year of operations and refer to the most recent financial year closed, as of the date of registration or the annual update of the registration details;
- the amount and source of funding, received from the EU institutions in the most recent financial year closed, as of the date of registration or the annual update of the registration details. That information shall correspond to the information provided by the European Financial Transparency System.

459. See T-168/12, *European Platform Against Windfarms (EPAW) v. European Commission*, ECLI:EU:T:2014:47.
460. Point II (Specific Information) of Annex II.

As far as NGOs (alongside with think tanks, research and academic institutions or organizations representing churches and religious communities or representing local, regional and municipal authorities or mixed entities) are specifically concerned, they should also provide information concerning:[461]

(a) the total budget of the organization;
(b) a breakdown of the main amounts and sources of funding.

Moreover, if an NGO is a client of a company dealing with its lobbying interests, then this entity should also register in the Transparency Register.[462] The financial declaration made by professional consultancies/law firms/self-employed consultants concerning their clients (list and grid) does not exempt those clients from their obligation to include subcontracted activities in their own declarations, so as to avoid an underestimation of their declared financial outlay.[463]

Upon registration, the organizations and individuals concerned in particular:[464]

(a) agree that the information which they provide for inclusion in the register shall be in the public domain;
(b) agree to act in compliance with the Code of Conduct and, where relevant, to provide the text of any professional code of conduct by which they are bound;
(c) guarantee that the information provided for inclusion in the register is correct and agree to cooperate with administrative requests for complementary information and updates;
(d) agree to be subject to any measures to be applied in the event of noncompliance with the Code of Conduct;
(e) note that the parties hereto may, upon request and subject to the provisions of Regulation (EC) No 1049/2001 of the European Parliament and the Council, have to disclose correspondence and other documents concerning the activities of registrants.

The abovementioned Code of Conduct may be applied only in relations between interest representatives and the EU institutions. Therefore, it may not be used to regulate relations between third parties or between registrants.[465]

According to the Code of Conduct, in their relations with the EU institutions and their members, officials and other staff interest representatives shall:

(a) always identify themselves by name and, by registration number, if applicable, and by the entity or entities they work for or represent; declare the

461. Point II (Specific Information) para. C (Financial information related to activities covered by the register) of Annex II (Information to be provided by registrants).
462. *Ibid.*
463. *Ibid.*
464. Point IV (Rules applicable to registrants) para. 21
465. Point II (Complaints) of Annex IV (Procedures for Alerts and for investigation and treatment of complaints).

interests, objectives or aims they promote; and, where applicable, specify they clients or members whom they represent;

(b) not obtain or try to obtain information or decisions dishonestly or by use of undue pressure or inappropriate behavior;

(c) not claim any formal relationship with the European Union or any of its institutions in their dealings with third parties, or misrepresent the effect of registration in such a way as to mislead third parties or officials or other staff of the European Union, or use the logos of EU institutions without express authorization;

(d) ensure that, to the best of their knowledge, information, which they provide upon registration, and subsequently in the framework of their activities covered by the register, is complete, up-to-date and not misleading; accept that all information provided is subject to review and agree to cooperate with administrative requests for complementary information and updates;

(e) not sell to third parties copies of documents obtained from EU institutions;

(f) in general, respect and avoid any obstruction to the implementation and application of, all rules, codes and good governance practices established by EU institutions;

(g) not induce members of the institutions of the European Union, officials or other staff of the European Union, or assistants or trainees of those members, to contravene the rules and standards of behavior applicable to them;

(h) if employing former officials or other staff of the European Union, or assistants or trainees of members of EU institutions, respect the obligation of such employees to abide by the rules and confidentiality requirements which apply to them;

(i) obtain the prior consent of the Member or Members of the European Parliament concerned as regards any contractual relationship with, or employment of, any individual within a Member's designated entourage;

(j) observe any rules laid down on the rights and responsibilities of former Members of the European Parliament and the European Commission;

(k) inform whomever they represent of their obligations toward the EU institutions.

In the event of breaching the Code of Conduct by a registrant, a complaint procedure is provided. It consists of five stages:[466]

(1) submitting a complaint:
   - any person may lodge an alert to the JTRS (i.e., Joint Transparency Register Secretariat) by completing the standard contact form, available on the website of the register, with regard to information contained in the register and non-eligible registrations. The complaint shall specify the

466. According to Point II (Complaints) of Annex IV (Procedures for Alerts and for investigation and treatment of complaints).

clauses of the code of conduct which the complainant alleges have not been complied with;

(2) admissibility:
   - the JTRS shall acknowledge receipt of the complaint to the complainant within five working days, determine whether its falls within the scope of the register, verify any evidence adduced to support the complaint and decide on the admissibility of the complaint;
   - if the complaint is inadmissible, the JTRS informs the complaint in writing, stating the reason for the decision;
   - if the complaint is admissible, both the complainant and the registrant concerned shall be informed by the JTRS of the decision and of the following procedure.

(3) handling of an admissible complaint (examination and provisional measures):
   - the registrant concerned shall be notified by the JTRS of the content of the complaint and of the clauses allegedly not complied with and shall be invited to submit a position in response to that complaint within 20 working days; noncompliance with this deadline leads to a temporary suspension of the registrant concerned from the register until cooperation is resumed;
   - if examination of the material provided shows the complaint to be unfounded, the JTRS shall inform both the registrant concerned and the complainant of the decision to that effect, stating the reasons for the decision;
   - if the complaint is upheld, the registrant concerned shall be temporarily suspended from the register pending the taking of steps to address the issue and may be subject to a number of additional measures including removal from the register and withdrawal, where applicable, of any authorization for access to the EP's premises.

(4) handling of an admissible complaint—resolution:
   - where a complaint is upheld and problematic issues are identified, the JTRS will take all necessary steps in cooperation with the registrant concerned to address and resolve the issue;
   - if the registrant concerned cooperated, a reasonable period of time shall be allocated by the JTRS, on a case-by-case basis to achieve resolution;
   - where a possible resolution of the issue has been identified and the registrant concerned cooperated to give effect to that resolution, the registration pertaining to that registrant shall be reactivated and the complaint closed;
   - where a possible resolution of the issue has been identified and the registrant concerned does not cooperate to give effect to that resolution, the registration pertaining to that registrant shall be deleted;
   - where a possible resolution of the issue requires a decision from a third party, including an authority in a Member State, the final decision by the JTRS shall be suspended until such time as that decision has been taken;

- if the registrant does not cooperate within 40 working days of the notification of the complaint, measures for noncompliance shall be applied.

(5) handling of an admissible complaint—measures to be applied in the event of noncompliance with the code of conduct:

- where immediate corrections are made by the registrant concerned, the JTRS will provide written acknowledgment of the facts and their corrections;
- failure to react by the registrant concerned within the deadline of 40 days shall result in removal from the register and loss of access to any incentives linked to registration;
- where inappropriate behavior has been identified, the registrant concerned shall be removed from the register and shall lose any incentives linked to registration;
- in the abovementioned cases, the registrant concerned may reregister, if the grounds leading to the removal have been remedied;
- where either noncooperation or inappropriate behavior is deemed to be repeated and deliberate, or where serious noncompliance has been identified, a decision to prohibit reregistration for a time period of either one year or two years (pending on the gravity of the case) shall be adopted by the JTRS;
- in cases where a measure adopted by the JTRS results in a long-term removal from the register, the registrant concerned may—within 20 working days of the notification of the measure—submit a reasoned request for reexamination of that measure to the Secretaries-General of the EP and of the Commission;
- upon expiry of the 20 days deadline or after the Secretaries-General have taken a final decision, the relevant Vice President of the EP and the relevant Vice President of the Commission shall be informed and the measure shall be mentioned publicly in the register;
- where a decision on prohibiting reregistration for a certain time period entails a withdrawal of the possibility of requesting authorization to access the EP's premises as an interest representative, a proposal by the Secretary-General of the EP shall be submitted to the College of Quaestors, who shall be invited to authorize the withdrawal of the related access authorization held by the individual or individuals concerned for that time period;
- in its decisions on applicable measures, the JTRS shall have due regard to the principles of proportionality and good administration.

The measures that can be administered at the misbehaving registrant are presented in Table 3.1.[467]

Table 3.1 Measures Available in the Event of Noncompliance with the Transparency Register's Code of Conduct: Based on Annex IV of the Agreement

	Type of Noncompliance	*Measure*	*Publication of Measure in the Register*	*Formal Decision to Withdraw Access to EP Premises*
1	Noncompliance, immediately corrected	Written notification acknowledging the facts and their correction	No	No
2	Noncooperation with JTRS	Removal from the register, deactivation of the authorization for access to the EP premises and loss of other incentives	No	No
3	Inappropriate behavior	Removal from the register, deactivation of the authorization for access to the EP premises and loss of other incentives	No	No
4	Repeated and deliberate noncooperation or repeated inappropriate behavior and/or serious noncompliance	Removal from the register for one year and formal withdrawal of the authorization for access to the EP premises (as an accredited interest group representative);	Yes, by the decision of the Secretaries-General of the EP and the European Commission.	Yes, by the decision of College of Quaestors.

467. Table of measures available in the event of noncompliance with the code of conduct in Point II (Complaints) of Annex IV (Procedures for Alerts and for investigation and treatment of complaints).

	Type of Noncompliance	*Measure*	*Publication of Measure in the Register*	*Formal Decision to Withdraw Access to EP Premises*
		Removal from the register for two years and formal withdrawal of the authorization to the EP premises (as an accredited interest group representative).		

It seems that these sanctions are not particularly severe, as they do not result in either permanent exclusion from the EU lawmaking process[468] or any strict pecuniary fines. This observation is one of the main critiques of the present system of lobbying in the EU institutions.[469]

[C] The Disadvantages of the Present Lobbying Framework: Proposed Changes

The voluntary character of the current framework for lobbying at the EU level entails many loopholes. Although the scope of the Transparency Register seems very wide and covers both direct and indirect forms of influencing the EU lawmaking, in practice much depends on inner provisions of the MEPs and the Commission.[470] The first ones do not restrict the contacts of the MEPs to the registered lobbyists,[471] while the latter ones forbid meetings with nonregistrant lobbyists only at the highest level.[472] In fact, just about 1% of the Commission's staff is bound to meet only the registered

468. I.e., permanent exclusion of the right to reregister.
469. D. Panke, *Lobbying...*, p. 140.
470. I.e., Code of Conduct for Members of the European Parliament with respect to financial interests and conflicts of interest (available at: http://www.europarl.europa.eu/pdf/meps/201305_Code_of_conduct_EN.pdf) and Commission Decision of 31.1.2018 on a Code of Conduct for Members of the European Commission, C(2018) 700 final (available at: https://ec.europa.eu/info/sites/info/files/code-of-conduct-for-commissioners-2018_en_0.pdf [on February 9, 2019]).
471. The Code of Conduct only encourages the MEPs to meet with registered lobbyists. It also states that MEPs cannot be lobbyists while they belong to the EP (see Art. 6 of the Code of Conduct for the MEPs).
472. See, to this extent, Commission Decision of 25 November 2014 on the publication of information on meetings held between Members of the Commission and organizations or self-employed individuals, 2014/839/EU, Euratom, Official Journal L 343/22, 28.11.2014, Commission Decision of 25 November 2014 on the publication of information on meetings held between Directors-General of the Commission and organizations or self-employed individuals, 2014/838/EU, Euratom, Official Journal L 343/19, 28.11.2014.

lobbyists[473] and report all of those interactions.[474] Even though some informal and nonbinding guidelines for other officials do exist,[475] the current scheme leaves a wide margin for possible abuses. In fact, as the surveys indicate, most of the lobbyists work at a lower level. As the Directors-General are not likely to directly get involved in particular cases, they usually contact the "desk officers" who are responsible for a specific measure.[476]

Moreover, the Commission's decision on the mandatory reporting of meetings with lobbyists of 2014,[477] describes a "meeting" as a "bilateral encounter organized at the initiative of an organization or self-employed individual ... to discuss an issue related to policymaking and implementation in the Union." Yet, it adds that "encounters of a purely private or social character or spontaneous encounters are excluded from this." As a result, for instance, an exchange of business cards at a conference is not seen as a lobbying activity,[478] although it may result in establishing valuable contacts within the Commission or the EP. The transparency rules are also excluded from contacts established abroad (outside the EU) or out of the office.[479] This discharge is in force even for the highest EU officials, including Commissioners. In consequence, approximately 80% of the meetings of the Commission's lobbying meetings are not registered.[480]

A common practice in the EU lobbying procedure is not registering on its own, but rather hiring an individual lawyer. The reason for this is quite simple—lawyers can protect their clients' identities while lobbyists cannot.[481] In fact, in many European legal systems lawyers could be disbarred for revealing any information about the case

473. Only the most senior 250 employees of the estimated 30.000 Commission staff are covered. See *7,000 and counting. Lobby meetings of the European Commission. Transparency International EU Office Report. 1 December 2015*, p. 14, available at: https://transparency.eu/wp-content/uploads/2016/10/Lobby-Meetings-European-Commission.pdf (on February 9, 2019).
474. A. Geiger, *EU Lobbying Handbook*, Brussels 2012, p. 16.
475. See e.g. The European Ombudsman's Practical recommendations for public officials' interaction with interest representatives, SI/7/2016/KR.
476. J. Panichi, Q. Aries, *Beat the Betraymont. Five Easy Ways to Skirt the EU Lobbying Rules*, available at: http://www.politico.eu/article/know-your-eu-lobbying-loopholes/ (on February 9, 2019).
477. Commission Decision 2014/839/EU of 25 November 2014 on the publication of information on meetings held between Members of the Commission and organizations or self-employed individuals, Official Journal L 343/32, 28.11.2014; see also M. Korkea-Aho, *"Mr Smith Goes to Brussels": Third Country Lobbying and the Making of EU Law and Policy*, Cambridge Yearbook of European Legal Studies Vol. 18/2016, p. 55.
478. A.M. El-Agraa, *The European Union. Economics and Politics*, Cambridge 2011, pp. 421-422.
479. M. Korkea-Aho, *"Mr Smith...*, p. 56.
480. M. Silva, *The Biggest Loophole in the Commission's Lobby Transparency Efforts*, available at: https://www.euractiv.com/section/politics/opinion/the-biggest-loophole-in-the-commissions-lobby-transparency-efforts/ (on February 9, 2019). In order to analyze a specific case see e.g. P. Teffer, *Missing: Paper Trail of EU Meetings with Big Tech*, available at: https://euobserver.com/institutional/144082 (on February 9, 2019). Sadly, the lack of transparency seems to be neglected by the representatives of the Commission, cf. F. Timmermans, *Make Lobbying in the EU Truly Transparent*, available at: http://bit.do/eH3QB (on February 11, 2019).
481. See J. Panichi, Q. Aries, *Beat...*.

of their clients.[482] Nevertheless, this appears as an excessive privilege leading to an opportunity of providing all the services of lobbyists with none disclosure requirements. Therefore, it would be advantageous if the EU adopted a comparable approach to disclosure as the US system, where the lawyer–client disclosure privilege does not encompass lobbying activities.[483] Yet, basing on the present Treaty provisions and the general rule of institutional autonomy of the Member States, this revision would not seem admissible.

Furthermore, the rules concerning the Transparency Register are not applicable to the Council officials. However, most lobbyists do not even search for any contacts with them. The most valuable influence can be achieved through the permanent representatives[484]—the national offices of the Member States whose ambassadors and their staff attribute to the most of legislative work ahead of the Council meetings. These officials are also excluded from the scope of lobbying legal framework.

Of course, the Transparency Register itself does not ensure that the registrants always behave ethically in contacts with the EU institutions. This is one of the results of the abovementioned weak mechanism of sanctions in case of breaching the Code of Conduct. However, it should be mentioned that lobbyists are often bound to private, more demanding codes of conduct.[485] Yet, these regulations do not provide what enlisting on the Transparency Register should contribute to contacts with the EU officials in the first place—a certain level of prestige and recognition.[486]

All of these loopholes can lead to a conclusion that the presently existing legal framework for lobbying activities can often lead to political corruption, understood as the corruption of influence leading to the power of money determining political outcomes.[487] Even though the Transparency Register is an important development in making the contacts between lobbyists (including NGOs) and the Commission or MEP more transparent, it does not change the fact that some stakeholders can highly influence the EU agenda through different forms of "expert committees," thus contravening any democratic mandate.[488] Moreover, the steadily rising number of registered

482. See e.g. § 19 para. 1 of the Rules of Ethics for Advocates and the Dignity of the Profession (Code of Ethics for Advocates), adopted by the Polish Bar Council on Oct. 10, 1998 (Resolution No 2/XVIII/98), as amended by Resolution No 32/2005 of the Polish Bar Council of 19 November 2005 and resolutions of the Polish Bar Council Nos 33/2011-54/2011 of 19 November 2011, available at: http://www.ccbe.eu/NTCdocument/Code_of_Ethics_for_A1_1331278211.pdf (on February 9, 2019).
483. A. Geiger, *EU Lobbying…*, p. 15.
484. V. Pirker, *EU-Lobbying durch NGOs: Internationale Menschenrechtsorganisationen* in: *Lobbying in der Europäischen Union. Zwischen Profesinalisierung und Regulierung*, D. Diater, M. Richter (ed.), Brussels 2014, p. 200.
485. I.e., Bayer's Code of Conduct for Responsible Lobbying—http://www.bayer.com/en/code-of-conduct-for-responsible-lobbying.aspx (on February 9, 2019), Wienerberger's Code of Conduct for Lobbying Activities—http://www.wienerberger.com/investor-relations/corporate-governance/code-of-conduct-for-lobbying-activities (on February 9, 2019).
486. P. Kotzian, Ch. Quittkat, *Konsultationsprozess der Kommission: Steuerung von EU-Lobbying* in: D. Diater, M. Richter (ed.), *Lobbying…*, p. 74.
487. R. van Schendelen, *Trends im EU-Lobbying und in der EU-Forschung* in: *Lobbying. Strukturen. Akteure. Strategien*, R. Kleinfeld, A. Zimmer, U. Willems (eds), Berlin 2007, p. 56.
488. M. Säckl, *20 Jahre EU-Lobbying als Diensleistung* in: *Politikberatung und Lobbying in Brüssel*, S. Dagger, M. Kambeck (eds), Wiesbaden 2007, p. 161.

lobbyists is concealed by a presumably high level of unregistered lobbying at the EU level.[489] The voluntary nature of the register implies that many lobbyists can impact the EU lawmakers without having to appear on any publicly published lists. This mainly concerns entities of private interests who can quite easily overpower the representatives of civil society.

In the face of these shortcomings, it seems that one of the "strongest" advantages of registration in the Transparency Register is the possibility of being "alerted" in case of an "open" consultation. However, this is a feeble incentive as invitations to the "open" consultations are published on the Internet sites of particular Directorates-General as well. It appears that obliging the Directorates-General to call all registered organizations to participate in "targeted" consultations as well would be much more favorable.[490] As far as the transparency rule is concerned, the obvious superiority of the present system of registration above the previously binding CONECCS database is that the organizations that participate in the lobbying process are required to declare the amount of financial resources that they dedicate for their contacts with the EU institutions.[491] Nevertheless, it seems that the voluntary nature of registration and the lack of effective incentives resulting therefrom do not change the attitude of certain organizations that wish to retain a low profile in lobbying.[492] In fact, some organizations, especially NGOs with limited resources, often decide to leave the Transparency Register as they perceive it as too complex and too hard to follow as the rules are frequently changing.[493]

J.-C. Juncker, the current President of the Commission, promised during his campaign to tighten lobbying rules that were, according to his words, "too easily abused."[494] As a consequence, in 2016 the Commission proposed the introduction of a

489. See *Bursting the Brussels Bubble*, a study by LobbyControl, Berlin 2010, available at: https://www.lobbycontrol.de/wp-content/uploads/bursting-the-brussels-bubble.pdf (on February 9, 2019).
490. I. De Jesus Butler, *Non-governmental...*, p. 572.
491. See also V. Pirker, *EU-Lobbying...*, p. 203.
492. See I. De Jesus Butler, *Non-governmental...*, p. 572.
493. J. Panichi, Q. Aries, *Beat...*, see also A. Bunea, *Estimating Interest Groups' Policy Positions Through Content Analysis: A Discussion of Automated and Human-Coding Text Analysis Techniques Applied to Studies of EU-Lobbying*, European Political Science Vol. 10/2016, p. 15.
494. See J. Panichi, Q. Aries, *Beat...*; The focus on transparency came after a 2012 scandal that exploded after it was revealed that John Dalli, the commissioner for health, had held an unreported meeting in a Maltese café with a tobacco lobbyist when the Commission was drafting tobacco legislation. In consequence, the Commission has started a policy toward more transparency with its relations with lobbyists. For example, F. Timmermans, the Vice President of the Commission, told in May 2015 that companies that are dishonest about lobbying would not be welcome in his office. However, in the same month the press reported that Juncker's staff was not synchronizing his weekly activities with its table of disclosed meetings. After 10 days, the information had been updated to include all the meetings Juncker has had with the private sector, even those who met with the Commission President in their "personal capacities" (see *NGOs demand Timmermans make good on mandatory lobbying register*, https://www.euractiv.com/section/public-affairs/news/ngos-demand-timmermans-make-good-on-mandatory-lobbying-register/ [on February 9, 2019]). Still, the contacts with the Commissioners and lobbyists are unclear as the recent case of G. Oettinger in late 2016 (see *Hungary Asked Kremlin Lobbyist to Airlift Oettinger to Budapest*, http://www.euractiv.com/section/public-affairs/news/hungary-asked-kremlin-lobbyist-to-airlift-oettinger-to-budapest/ [on February 9, 2019]).

mandatory Transparency Register which would cover the Council as well.[495] Other EU institutions, bodies, offices and agencies would be encouraged to use the framework, created by the agreement, as a reference instrument for their own interactions with interest representatives.[496] The main objective of the proposal is to "win back the trust of the citizens," as they "have the right to know who tries to influence the EU law-making."[497] According to Article 3 (1) of the proposed agreement, it applies to activities which promote certain interests by interacting with any of the three signatory institutions, their members or officials, with the objective of influencing the formulation or implementation of policy or legislation, or the decision-making process within these institutions, unless an exception applies. However, an exception regarding legal and other professional advice in the context of a client–intermediary relationship is envisaged in Article 3 (2) of the proposed legal act, leading to possible misuses as mentioned above on the basis of the present lobby arrangements.

The most significant modification is introduced in Article 5 of the proposed agreement. According to this provision, the privileges of the registered lobbyists are expanded. Thus, only such subjects are entitled to take part in:

- meetings between interest representatives and members of the Commission, their Cabinet members and Directors-General;
- meeting between representatives and MEPs, the Secretary-General and Secretaries-General of political groups;
- meeting between interest representatives and the Ambassador of the current or forthcoming Presidency of the Council of the EU, as well as their deputies in the Committee of the Permanent Representatives of the Governments of the Member States of the EU, the Council's Secretary-General and Directors-General.

The agreement also introduces a new organ—the Management Board that will consist of the Secretaries-General of the three institutions and whose main goal will be to oversee the overall implementation of the proposed regulations.[498]

Although the proposed modifications seem to head in the right direction and provide a greater range of transparency in the activity of lobbyists, some major threats are still evident. First, the scope of the Transparency Register in respect to the Commission remains the same as the currently binding regulations. Thus, if the agreement is passed in its present form, it will still cover roughly 1% of the highest officials of the Commission. Second, the mandatory register should be followed by stricter ethical rules for the present and former members of the Commission so that all

495. Proposal for a Interinstitutional Agreement on a mandatory Transparency Register, COM(2016) 627 final, available at: https://ec.europa.eu/transparency/regdoc/rep/1/2016/EN/1-2016-627-EN-F1-1.PDF.
496. Art. 12 (1) of the proposal.
497. See the Commission's press release *Delivering on transparency: Commission proposes Transparency Register for all EU institutions*, available at: http://europa.eu/rapid/press-release_IP-16-3182_en.htm.
498. Art. 8 (1) (2) of the proposal.

contacts with lobbyists are more transparent.[499] Third, it is questionable if all the contacts between the stakeholders and MEPs will, in fact, be covered by the Transparency Register as this provision is considered a limitation in exercise of the free mandate by the members of the EP's constitutional affairs committee.[500] Even though this reasoning was criticized in the doctrine,[501] it may be shared by the EP.[502] Fourth, although the inclusion of the Council to the transparency framework is undoubtedly beneficial, the proposed regulations do not envisage that the actual and most common lobbying takes place at the level of permanent representatives and other national officials. This omission, unfortunately, will lead to an unavoidable bypass of the necessary character of Transparency Register in the EU lawmaking as the Council remains one of its main actors. Fifth, the new agreement does not eliminate the "lawyer loophole" in the lobbyist activity, meaning that it will be still possible to "hide" the actual identities of lobbyists by the hired lawyers. Finally, it would be beneficial to expand the scope of the register to other "exposed" EU institutions. This refers particularly to the President of the European Council.[503]

Unfortunately, contrary to the announcements of the President of the Commission, the reform of the Transparency Register seems unlikely in the near future, due to the fact that interinstitutional negotiations have stalled.[504] It also does not increase the overall picture of the EU decision-making as a nontransparent and unclear process.

To conclude, it is worth mentioning that perhaps the biggest problem arising from the present framework of lobbying at the EU level is the disparity between the particular Member States. It is estimated that 95% of the aggregated budget on the lobbying activities in Brussels is spent by entities from countries that joined the EU before 2004.[505] It is also noticed that the organizations coming from the "newer" Member States often neglect lobbying activities and, therefore, lack basic know-how and networking[506] which are crucial for being effective and influential.[507] Also,

499. See also, to this extent, Recommendations of the European Ombudsman in the joint inquiry into complaints 194/2017/EA, 334/2017/EA and 543/2017/EA on the European Commission's handling of post-mandate employment of former Commissioners, a former Commission President and the role of its "Ethics Committee."
500. See S. Guillaume, D. Hübner, *EU Parliament Should Befriend Transparency*, available at: https://euobserver.com/opinion/138363 (on February 9, 2019).
501. See A. Alemanno, *Legal Opinion on the Proposed Inter-institutional Agreement for a Mandatory Transparency Register in the European Union*, HEC Paris Research Paper No. LAW-2017-1218, pp. 10-13.
502. Still, some developments in enhancing transparency of the lobbying activities in the EP have been introduced recently. See C. Barbière, M. Flausch, *Les rencontres entre eurodéputés et lobbyistes sortent de l'ombre*, available at: https://bit.ly/2Sv7iA0 (on February 12, 2019).
503. For the grounds of this demand see the letter of the European Ombudsman to the President of the European Council entitled Administration of the European Council (SI/8/2017/KR). For more information on the need of more transparency in the activity of the European Council see also W. Wessels, *The European Council*, London 2016, p. 9.
504. Cf. The EP Press release of 27.9.2018—EP leaders call for negotiations on upgraded Transparency Register to continue, available at: http://bit.do/eH4kb (on February 11, 2019).
505. For more information see H. Cooper, G. Hervey, E. Bauvir, I. Antypas, *Big East-West....*
506. Which, however, can cause a "web of relationships." Cf. J.N. Victor, *Financing Friends: How Lobbyists Create a Web of Relationships Among Members of Congress*, Interest Groups & Advocacy Vol. 5/2016, pp. 224 et seq.
507. P. Swieboda, P. Zerka, *Aktywność...*, p. 9.

obviously, NGOs are not as influential as business stakeholders in their lobbying activities.[508]

[D] Summary

Due to the fact that official consultation tools provided by particular EU institutions remain rather opaque, NGOs, like other stakeholders, often engage in lobbying activities which, in practice, may be much more effective in influencing the outcomes of lawmaking.

The currently applicable legal framework for lobbying at the EU level is quite troublesome. It covers the Commission and the EP. The most crucial issue is associated with its voluntary character. Only the highest officials of the Commission are obliged to meet solely with the registered lobbyists. This leaves a large loophole for possible misuses of unregistered lobbying. In this way, the EU lawmaking is even less transparent and harder to follow. This is the reason why a mandatory Transparency Register is proposed by the Commission. Even though its improvements seem advantageous (especially considering the extension of the register on the Council), its scope is still troublesome as it leaves a vast extent of lobbying activities outside the legal framework.

It should be remembered that not only the legal provision on lobbying or transparency[509] are significant for improving participation and trust in the EU lawmaking. Much depends on the internal ethical codes and factual behaviors of the officials. Therefore, higher standards should be demanded from European civil society toward the EU institutions.

§3.04 CONCLUSION

As J.-C. Juncker warned in 2014 in his opening speech as the President of the Commission, "this will be the last-chance Commission .... Either we will succeed in bringing our citizens closer to Europe, or we will fail."[510] Accordingly, the main goal of the EU in recent years has been to make the EU closer to its citizens. This can be achieved by involving the representatives of civil society more broadly in the EU lawmaking and requires further developments. First, the scope of NGOs taking part in

508. For instance, as reported, J.-C. Juncker met with 18 business lobbyists but not one NGO. See J. Crisp, *Juncker met 18 business lobbyists in 2015, but not one green NGO*, available at: https://www.euractiv.com/section/climate-environment/news/juncker-met-18-business-lobbyists-in-2015-but-not-one-green-ngo/ (on February 9, 2019). See also the list of the biggest lobbying entities at the EU level in *7,000 and counting...* See also M. Schirdewan, *Why Brussels Toxic Lobbying Culture Must End*, available at: https://euobserver.com/opinion/144093 (on February 9, 2019).

509. As such provisions do not exclude risk of "transparency corruption." For more see A. Classen, *Interessenvertretung...*, pp. 256-257, J. D'Angelo, *The Evolution of Transparency Corruption*, Harvard University 2017, available at: http://bit.do/ej72y (on February 9, 2019).

510. *Time for action—Statement in the European Parliament plenary session ahead of the vote on the College*, J.-C. Juncker's speech of 22.10.2014, available at: http://europa.eu/rapid/press-release_SPEECH-14-1525_en.htm (on February 9, 2019).

consultation process at the EU level should be wider, and, second, the EU institutions should not expect that NGOs will always be adherents of their policies.[511]

NGOs can influence the EU lawmaking in a "grassroot" manner through the instruments of access to documents and the European Citizens' Initiative. While the former one can generally contribute to enhancing transparency in the lawmaking process, the latter one is designed to bring certain issues to the EU agenda. Even though both of these measures face noticeable shortcomings in practice, their application and recent outcomes can contribute to an even greater impact of European civil society on the EU lawmaking.

NGOs also engage in regular contacts with the EU institutions. This chapter discussed the frameworks of relations between third sector organizations and the Commission, the EP, the Council and the CJEU. The most structural form of dialogue is available within the Commission. Still, it is doubtful to what extent the views presented by the interested NGOs are taken into consideration by the officials. Other EU institutions provide a rather limited scope of cooperation with the representatives of civil society. This is especially noticeable in the case of the Council which does not envisage any formal channels of contacts with NGOs.

In order to reinforce their influence on the EU lawmaking, NGOs increasingly get involved in lobbying activities. However, the present rules of lobbying at the EU level are voluntary and leave room for possible misuses. Also, despite the obvious beneficial role of NGOs in advocating for the interests of European civil society and providing more input and output legitimacy to the EU institutions, their democratic potential is restricted as lobbying is practically limited to the biggest organizations.

Many institutional innovations regarding NGOs participation, described in the previous paragraphs, can certainly make the EU "closer to citizens." Nevertheless, it should be observed that the sole fact that NGOs engage in deliberation during the lawmaking, both on the national and the EU level, does not make the decisions of the institutions cooperating with such organizations democratically legitimated. Perhaps the most important factor concerns the fact to what extent the recommendations presented by grassroot organizations are examined and taken into consideration.[512] This, however, vastly depends on nonlegal factors.

511. A. von Bogdandy, *The European...*, p. 326.
512. In this respect, the "citizens forums" on the future of Europe, proposed by the French President E. Macron and initiating in 2018 will be interesting to observe. See, to this extent, the "Bringing the EU forward in 2018" declaration available at: http://www.governo.it/sites/governo.it/files/documenti/documenti/Notizie-allegati/governo/DeclarationIVEUSouthSummit.pdf (on February 9, 2019). See also E. Maurice, *Macron to "Rebuild" EU with Citizens Conventions*, available at: https://euobserver.com/political/138941 (on February 9, 2019). In line with this idea, in May 2018, the EESC conducted special consultations with 80 EU citizens selected from all Member States on the future of Europe. See 100 citoyens européens réunis à Bruxelles pour discuter du futur de l'Europe, available at: https://www.touteleurope.eu/actualite/reportage-100-citoyens-europeens-reunis-a-bruxelles-pour-discuter-du-futur-de-l-europe.html (on February 9, 2019).

CHAPTER 4
NGOs as Entities Acting in the Collective Interest of European Civil Society

This chapter will focus on the influence of the EU law on NGOs as subjects acting in the collective interest. This issue has two dimensions: national and European. In the national dimension, the EU law opens, in some spheres, the possibility for NGOs to act in the shared public interest, for instance by creating a path to the local decision-making procedures, providing access to information or encouraging them to raise awareness on certain issues. Also, there are cases where the EU law enables the third sector entities to file an "altruistic complaint" as a means of giving expression to the collective interest. In the EU dimension, the opportunities for NGOs to issue proceedings before the CJEU in the collective interest are, in fact, limited. However, these organizations still have possibilities to act as representatives of civil society in order to ensure the proper enforcement of the EU law. These measures result from the general provisions of the Treaties.

Both of the above-presented dimensions are vastly influenced by the Convention on Access to Information, Public Participation in Decision-Making and Access to Justice in Environmental Matters done at Aarhus, Denmark, on June 25, 1998[1] (which will be further referred to as "the Aarhus Convention"). This international agreement was a big step in enhancing the role of NGOs in environmental matters. However, the implementation of the Aarhus Convention at the EU level was problematic in several aspects. This issue will be thoroughly discussed in the following parts of this chapter.

§4.01 LEGITIMACY IN ACTING FOR THE COLLECTIVE INTEREST

The ensuing paragraphs will discuss the rules deriving from the EU law which can be used by NGOs as actors operating in the collective interest at the national and the EU

1. Available at: http://www.unece.org/fileadmin/DAM/env/pp/documents/cep43e.pdf (on February 9, 2019).

level. This subject matter encompasses both general rules, available for all private law entities, and specific legislations for NGOs.

[A] National Level

To begin with, a few general remarks considering the relations between national law and the EU law should be pointed out. First, if an NGO is a party in national court or administrative proceedings, it can benefit from the general rules of applying the EU law. Most notably, it can invoke the principles of primacy[2] and direct effect of the EU law.[3] It can also lodge a nonbinding request to the Court to initiate a reference for a preliminary ruling to the CJEU.[4] Moreover, if it is directly affected by an infringement of the EU law by a Member State, it can bring an action for damages.[5]

Second, the general rule concerning the application of the EU law in Member States is that, unless the procedural issues are directly regulated in the EU primary or

2. Also referred to as the principle of supremacy. According to this principle, when there is conflict between the EU law and the law of Member States, EU law prevails and the norms of national law have to be set aside. See e.g. C-6/63 *Costa v. ENEL*, ECLI:EU:C:1964:66, C-106/77 *Amministrazione delle Finanze dello Stato v. Simmenthal SpA*, ECLI:EU:C:1978:49, C-106/89 *Marleasing SA v. La Comercial Internacional de Alimentacion SA*, ECLI:EU:C:1990:395.
3. Without going into details and differences between specific acts of the EU law, it should be reminded that in order to produce direct effect, the obligation deriving from the EU law must be precise, clear and unconditional, not calling for additional measure, either national or European (see, to this extent, e.g. C-26/62 *van Gend en Loos*, ECLI:EU:C:1963:1). For specific conditions on the direct effect of directives see e.g. C-91/92 *Faccini Dori*, ECLI:EU:C:1994:292). Consequently, wherever the provisions of a directive appear, as far as their subject matter is concerned, to be unconditional and sufficiently precise, those provisions may be relied upon by an individual against any authority of a Member State where that state either has failed to implement the Directive in national law by the end of the period prescribed or has failed to implement it correctly (C-103/88 *Fratelli Costanzo v. Comune di Milano*, ECLI:EU:C:1989:256; see also e.g. C-118/94 *Associazione Italiana per il WWF and others*, ECLI:EU:C:1996:86, C-435/97 *WWF and others*, ECLI:EU:C:1999:418, C-201/02 *D. Wells*, ECLI:EU:C:2004:12, C-127/02 *Waddenzee*, ECLI-:EU:C:2004:482, C-213/03 *Syndicat professionnel coordination des pêcheurs de l'étang de Berre et de la région v. Électricité de France (EDF)*, ECLI:EU:C:2004:464). Furthermore, the direct effect of an environmental Directive was envisaged in, e.g. C-72/95 *Kraaijevels*, ECLI:EU:C:1996:404.
4. As an example, see C-422/16 *Verband Sozialer Wettbewerb eV v. TofuTown.com GmbH* (ECLI: EU:C:2017:458); see also A. Kastelik-Smaza, *Pytania prejudycjalne do Trybunału Sprawiedliwości Unii Europejskiej a ochrona praw jednostki*, Warsaw 2010, pp. 27 et seq.
5. The EU law confers a right to reparation where three conditions are met: the rule of law infringed must be intended to confer rights on individuals; the breach must be sufficiently serious; and there must be a direct causal link between the breach of the obligation resting on the state and the damage sustained by the injured parties (see C-46/93 and C-48/93 *Brasserie du Pêcheur*, ECLI:EU:C:1996:79, para. 51; for more information see e.g. M. Kawczyńska, *Pozaumowna odpowiedzialnosć odszkodowawcza Unii Europejskiej*, Warsaw 2016, pp. 243 et seq.). Yet, an NGO acting in the common good sphere cannot successfully claim reparation as it does not directly suffer any damage. For more see e.g. J.H. Jans, H.H.B. Vedder, *European Environmental Law After Lisbon*, Groningen 2012, p. 208, N. Półtorak, *Odpowiedzialność odszkodowawcza państwa w prawie wspólnot europejskich*, Kraków 2002, p. 248. However, some scholars hold that such an action should be possible in cases where redressing the damage is impossible or would be ineffective in the given factual situation. This should especially apply to environmental issues (see B. Iwańska, *Koncepcja "skargi zbiorowej" w prawie ochrony środowiska*, Warsaw 2013, pp. 530-532). Yet, in this context it should be also acknowledged that environmental damages are very often hard to assess (B. Iwańska, *Koncepcja...*, p. 532).

secondary law, Member States possess the so-called procedural autonomy.[6] In other words, Member States remain competent to independently legislate on procedural issues as long as this possibility has not been preempted by the EU.[7] This gives each Member State freedom to use its own solutions in applying the EU law in the absence of specific EU procedural rules preempting this discretion[8] and is sometimes referred to as the model of "delegated execution of law."[9] That said, it must be stated that the EU law does not provide for any general *actio popularis*,[10] understood as a measure that can be used by any individual in order to protect the collective interest[11] at the national level.

Still, if the EU law confers a certain right at the national level to an individual, it must be safeguarded by an action which is adopted according to the principles of equivalence and effectiveness. The principle of equivalence requires the same remedies and procedural rules to be available to claims based on the EU law as are extended to analogous claims of a purely domestic nature. The principle of effectiveness, or effective judicial protection, obliges Member State courts to ensure that national remedies and procedural rules do not render claims based on the EU law impossible in practice or excessively difficult to enforce.[12]

A good example of practical significance of these principles for NGOs acting in the collective interest is the case C-115/09 *Bund für Umwelt und Naturschutz Deutschland, Landesverband Nordrhein-Westfalen eV v. Bezirksregierung Arnsberg.*[13] The basis for the judgment was a remedy admitted to NGOs under Article 10a of Directive 85/337.[14] According to this norm, Member States shall ensure that, in accordance with the relevant national legal system, members of the public concerned:[15]

6. K. Kowalik-Bańczyk, *Procedural Autonomy of Member States and the EU Rights of Defence in Antitrust Proceedings*, Yearbook of Antitrust and Regulatory Studies 2012, p. 215, N. Półtorak, *The Impact of the Jurisprudence of the European Court of Justice on National Remedies*, Centrum Europejskie Natolin/EUI Research Laboratory Vol. 22/2005, pp. 36-39, M. Kawecki, *Reforma ochrony danych osobowych. Współpraca administracyjna w świetle ogólnego rozporządzenia o ochronie danych osobowych*, Warsaw 2017, p. 65.
7. K. Kowalik-Bańczyk, *Procedural...*, p. 218.
8. See e.g. C-158/80 *Rewe*, ECLI:EU:C:1981:163.
9. N. Półtorak, *Ochrona uprawnień wynikających z prawa Unii Europejskiej*, Warsaw 2010, p. 22, N. Półtorak, *European Union Rights in National Courts*, Alphen aan den Rijn 2015, pp. 30-37.
10. However, the latter parts of this chapter will discuss specific legal measures in environmental issues which take the form of *action popularis* in some countries.
11. See J. Law (ed.), *A Dictionary of Law*, Oxford 2015, p. 33. For more information see also e.g. B. Iwańska, *Koncepcja...*, p. 327.
12. See e.g. C-432/05 *Unibet*, ECLI:EU:C:2007:163.
13. ECLI:EU:C:2011:289.
14. Presently Directive 2003/35/EC of the EP and of the Council of 26 May 2003 providing for public participation in respect of the drawing up of certain plans and programs relating to the environment and amending with regard to public participation and access to justice Council Directives 85/337/EEC and 96/61/EC—Statement by the Commission, Official Journal L 156, 25.6.2003.
15. According to Art. 1 (2) of the Directive, "the public concerned" means: the public affected or likely to be affected by, or having an interest in, the environmental decision-making procedures referred to in Art. 2(2); for the purposes of this definition, nongovernmental organizations promoting environmental protection and meeting any requirements under national law shall be deemed to have an interest.

(a) having a sufficient interest, or
(b) alternatively maintaining the impairment of a right, where administrative procedural law of a Member State requires this as a precondition,

have access to a review procedure before a court of law or another independent and impartial body established by law to challenge the substantive or procedural legality of decisions, acts or omissions subject to the public participation provisions of this Directive.

The CJEU stated that nongovernmental organizations can rely before courts on the infringement of the rules of national law deriving from Article 6 of the Habitats Directive[16] in an action contesting a decision authorizing projects "likely to have significant effects on the environment" for the purposes of Article 1 (1) of Directive 85/337. They can do so even where national procedural law does not permit it, on the grounds that the rules relied on protect only the interests of the general public and not the interest of individuals.[17] Thus, although it is for the Member States to determine what rights can give rise, when infringed, to an action concerning the environment, they cannot, when making this determination, deprive environmental organizations which fulfill the conditions laid down in Article 1 (2) of that Directive[18] of the opportunity of playing the role granted them both by Directive 85/337 and the Aarhus Convention.[19]

As a result, although the national legislature is entitled to limit the scope of individual public law rights whose infringement may be relied on by an individual in legal proceedings contesting one of the decisions, acts or omissions referred to in Article 10a of Directive 85/337, such a limitation cannot be applied as such to environmental protection organizations without disregarding the objectives of the last sentence of the third paragraph of Article 10a. As it is clear from that provision, those organizations must be able to rely on the same rights as individuals. Therefore, it would be contrary to the objective of giving the public concerned wide access to justice and at odds with the principle of effectiveness if such organizations were not also allowed to rely on the impairment of the EU environmental law solely on the grounds that those rules protect the public interest. This very largely deprives those organizations of the possibility of verifying compliance with the rules of that branch of law, which, for the most part, address the public interest and not merely the protection of the interests of individuals as such. It follows that the concept of "impairment of a right" cannot depend on conditions which only other physical or legal persons can fulfill, such as the condition of being a more or less close neighbor of an installation or of suffering in one way or another the effects of the installation's operation. More generally, it follows that the last sentence of the third paragraph of Article 10a of Directive 85/337 should be read as meaning that the "rights of being impaired" which

16. Council Directive 92/43/EEC of 21 May 1992 on the conservation of natural habitats and of wild fauna and flora, Official Journal L 206, 22.7.1992.
17. Para. 59 in C-115/09.
18. I.e., referring to the notion of "the public concerned."
19. Para. 44 in C-115/09.

the environmental protection organizations are supposed to enjoy must necessarily include the rules of national law implementing the EU environmental law and the rules of the EU environmental law having direct effect.[20] In other words, once the EU law confers NGOs a special right of protecting the collective interest, it must be safeguarded by a national remedy which fulfills the conditions of effectiveness in the domestic law.

As a result, NGOs, like any other legal persons, are entitled to benefit from the main principles of the EU law. In general, they are provided with these rights without any limitations when they act for their own behalf and only in the scope of the given entitlement when they enforce the collective interest. Both possibilities, especially with regard to the right to invoke,[21] can be very beneficial in terms of the so-called *private enforcement* of the EU law,[22] particularly in the community-relevant spheres like the environment.

Apart from the general principles of the EU law, diverse acts of secondary law oblige Member States to introduce specific measures for NGOs in order to enable them to act in the public interest. These primarily include:

(1) Regulation (EU) No 2016/679 of the EP and of the Council of April 27, 2016, on the protection of natural persons with regard to the processing of personal data and on the free movement of such data, repealing Directive 95/46/EC (General Data Protection Regulation—GDPR);[23]

---

20. Para. 45-48 in C-115/09.
21. N. Półtorak, *Ochrona uprawnień...*, pp. 194-211, M. Szpunar, *Odpowiedzialność podmiotu prywatnego z tytułu naruszenia prawa wspólnotowego*, Warsaw 2008, p. 262.
22. B. Iwańska, *Koncepcja...*, p. 348.
23. Official Journal L 119/1, 4.5.2016: according to Art. 80:

 (1) the data subject shall have the right to mandate a not-for-profit body, organisation or association which has been properly constituted in accordance with the law of a Member State, has statutory objectives which are in the public interest, and is active in the field of the protection of data subjects' rights and freedoms with regard to the protection of their personal data to lodge the complaint on his or her behalf, to exercise the rights referred to in Articles 77, 78 and 79 on his or her behalf, and to exercise the right to receive compensation referred to in Article 82 on his or her behalf where provided for by Member State law.
 (2) Member States may provide that any body, organisation or association referred to in par. 1 of this Article, independently of a data subject's mandate, has the right to lodge, in that Member State, a complaint with the supervisory authority which is competent pursuant to Article 77 and to exercise the rights referred to in Articles 78 and 79 if it considers that the rights of a data subject under this Regulation have been infringed as a result of the processing.

 Moreover, the general prohibition of processing personal data revealing racial or ethnic origin, political opinions, religious or philosophical beliefs, or trade union membership, and the processing of genetic data, biometric data for the purpose of uniquely identifying a natural person, data concerning health or data concerning a natural person's sex life or sexual orientation does not apply to a foundation, association or any other not-for-profit body with a political, philosophical, religious or trade union aim and on condition that the processing relates solely to the members or to former members of the body or to persons who have regular contact with it in connection with its purposes and that the personal data are not disclosed outside that body without the consent of the data subjects (Art. 6 (2) (d)).

(2) Regulation (EU) No 1303/2012 of the EP and of the Council of December 17, 2013, laying down common provisions on the European Regional Development Fund, the European Social Fund, the Cohesion Fund, the European Agricultural Fund for Rural Development and the European Maritime and Fisheries Fund and laying down general provisions on the European Regional Development Fund, the European Social Fund, the Cohesion Fund and the European Maritime and Fisheries Fund and repealing Council Regulation (EC) No 1083/2006;[24]

(3) Directive 2014/67/EU of the EP and of the Council of May 15, 2014, on the enforcement of Directive 96/71/EC concerning the posting of workers in the framework of the provision of services and amending Regulation (EU) No 1024/2012 on administrative cooperation through the Internal Market Information System (the IMI Regulation);[25]

(4) Directive 2006/54/EC of the EP and of the Council of July 5, 2006, on the implementation of the principle of equal opportunities and equal treatment of men and women in matters of employment and occupation;[26]

(5) Directive 2013/11/EU of the EP and of the Council of May 21, 2013, on alternative dispute resolution for consumer disputes and amending Regulation (EC) No 2006/2004 and Directive 2009/22/EC;[27]

24. Official Journal L 347/320, 20.12.2013; according to Art. 5 (1), for the Partnership Agreement and each program, each Member State shall in accordance with its institutional and legal framework organize a partnership with the competent regional and local authorities. The partnership shall also include the following partners: (a) competent urban and other public authorities, (b) economic and social partners and (c) relevant bodies representing civil society, including environmental partners, nongovernmental organizations and bodies responsible for promoting social inclusion, gender equality and nondiscrimination; See also, to this extent, Commission Delegated Regulation (EU) No 240/2014 on the European code of conduct on partnership in the framework of the European Structural and Investment Funds, Official Journal L 74/1, 14.3.2014.
25. Official Journal L 159/11, 28.5.2014; according to Art. 11 (3), Member States shall ensure that trade unions and other third parties, such as associations, organizations and other legal entities which have, in accordance with the criteria laid down under national law, a legitimate interest in ensuring that this Directive and Directive 96/71/EC are complied with, may engage, on behalf or in support of the posted workers or their employer, and with their approval, in any judicial or administrative proceedings with the objective of implementing this Directive and Directive 96/71/EC and/or enforcing the obligations under this Directive and Directive 96/71/EC.
26. Official Journal L 204/23, 26.7.2006; according to Art. 17 (2), Member States shall ensure that associations, organizations or other legal entities which have, in accordance with the criteria laid down by their national law, a legitimate interest in ensuring that the provisions of this Directive are complied with, may engage, either on behalf or in support of the complainant, with his/her approval, in any judicial and/or administrative procedure provided for the enforcement of obligations under this Directive.
27. Official Journal L 165/63, 18.6.2013; for instance, according to Art. 15 (4), the Commission and the Member States shall take accompanying measures to encourage consumer organizations and professional organizations, at Union and at national level, to raise awareness of ADR entities and their procedures and to promote ADR take-up by traders and consumers. Those bodies shall also be encouraged to provide consumers with information about competent ADR entities when they receive complaints from consumers.

(6) Directive 2008/52/EC of the EP and of the Council of May 21, 2008, on certain aspects of mediation in civil and commercial matters;[28]
(7) Council Directive 2004/81/EC of April 29, 2004, on the residence permit issued to third-country nationals who are victims of trafficking in human beings or who have been subject of an action to facilitate illegal immigration, who cooperate with the competent authorities;[29]
(8) Council Directive 2000/78/EC of November 27, 2000, establishing a general framework for equal treatment in employment and occupation;[30]
(9) Council Directive 2000/43/EC of June 29, 2000, implementing the principle of equal treatment between persons irrespective of racial or ethnic origin;[31]
(10) Directive 2008/96/EC of the EP and of the Council of November 19, 2008, on road infrastructure safety management.[32]

These acts of law award NGOs with various competences at national level. They vary from "hard" (the possibility of lodging a complaint in the name of a natural person concerned) to quite "soft" ones (promoting certain issues in the public). As it has already been mentioned, the EU law does not provide for any *actio popularis*, understood as a measure to complain against a breach of the primary or secondary law

28. Official Journal L 136/3, 24.5.2008; according to Art. 4 (1), Member States shall encourage, by any means which they consider appropriate, the development of, and adherence to, voluntary codes of conduct by mediators and organizations providing mediation services, as well as other effective quality control mechanisms concerning the provision of mediation services.
29. Official Journal L 261/19, 6.8.2004, according to Art. 5, when the competent authorities of the Member States take the view that a third-country national may fall into the scope of this Directive, they shall inform the person concerned of the possibilities offered under this Directive. Member States may decide that such information may also be provided by a nongovernmental organization or an association specifically appointed by the Member State concerned. According to Art. 12 (1), the third-country nationals concerned shall be granted access to existing programs or schemes, provided by the Member States or by nongovernmental organizations or associations which have specific agreements with the Member States, aimed at their recovery of a normal social life, including, where appropriate, courses designed to improve their professional skills, or preparation of their assisted return to their country of origin. Member States may provide specific programs or schemes for the third-country nationals concerned.
30. Official Journal L 303, 2.12.2000; for instance, according to Art. 9 (2), Member States shall ensure that associations, organizations or other legal entities which have, in accordance with the criteria laid down by their national law, a legitimate interest in ensuring that the provisions of this Directive are complied with, may engage, either on behalf or in support of the complainant, with his or her approval, in any judicial and/or administrative procedure provided for the enforcement of obligations under this Directive.
31. Official Journal L 180, 19.7.2000; for instance, according to Art. 7 (2), Member States shall ensure that associations, organizations or other legal entities, which have, in accordance with the criteria laid down by their national law, a legitimate interest in ensuring that the provisions of this Directive are complied with, may engage, either on behalf or in support of the complainant, with his or her approval, in any judicial and/or administrative procedure provided for the enforcement of obligations under this Directive. According to Art. 12, Member States shall encourage dialogue with appropriate nongovernmental organizations which have, in accordance with their national law and practice, a legitimate interest in contributing to the fight against discrimination on the grounds of racial and ethnic origin with a view to promoting the principle of equal treatment.
32. Official Journal L 319, 29.11.2008; according to Art. 11 (3), where appropriate, relevant nongovernmental organizations, active in the field of safety and management of road infrastructures, may be consulted on matters related to technical safety aspects.

without the necessity to demonstrate a proper and direct legal interest. The above-listed acts do not construct any general legal remedies as well. However, although Member States in general do not envisage instruments of *actio popularis* in their legal systems either,[33] the implementation of these directives in some countries contributed to a stronger legitimacy of NGOs in both civil[34] and administrative proceedings.[35]

---

33. With the exception of Portugal (and to a large extent of Slovenia, Spain, Romania and Latvia) which will be discussed in the following paragraphs of this chapter.
34. For instance, Directive 2008/52/EC and Directive 2002/73/EC of the European Parliament and of the Council of 23 September 2002 amending Council Directive 76/207/EEC on the implementation of the principle of equal treatment for men and women as regards access to employment, vocational training and promotion and working conditions (Official Journal L 269, 5.10.2002) were implemented to the Polish Code of Civil Procedure (*Kodeks postępowania cywilnego*) in Art. 61: § 1. Nongovernmental organizations may, within the scope of their statutory duties, bring actions on behalf of a natural person, subject to his written consent, in matters concerning:

    (1) maintenance benefits;
    (2) environmental protection;
    (3) consumer protection;
    (4) industrial property protection;
    (5) protection of equality and nondiscrimination by directly or indirectly differentiating the rights and obligations of citizens in an unjust manner.
    § 2. In the cases referred to in § 1, nongovernmental organizations may, within the scope of their statutory duties and subject to a written consent of a natural person, join the individual in pending proceedings.
    § 3. Subject to the written consent of an entrepreneur who is a natural person, the nongovernmental organization of which the entrepreneur is a member may bring an action on his behalf or join him in pending proceedings in a dispute with another entrepreneur concerning claims arising from the economic activities being pursued.
    § 4. A complaint or letter whereby a nongovernmental organization joins a natural person in proceedings shall be accompanied by the natural person's written consent.

    Even though some prerogatives were attributed to NGOs earlier (i.e., in the scope of maintenance benefits), the Directive was an indubitable basis for further procedural rights. For more see e.g. P. Grzegorczyk, *Komentarz do art. 61* in: *Kodeks postępowania cywilnego. Komentarz. Tom I. Postępowanie rozpoznawcze*, T. Ereciński (ed.), Warsaw 2016, lex.pl.
35. For instance, Directive 96/71/EC, Directive 2003/35/EC and Directive 2014/67/EU were implemented to the Polish Code of Administrative Procedure (*Kodeks postępowania administracyjnego*) in Art. 31: § 1. Social organization can in a case involving another person occur with the request:

    (1) of the opening of proceedings;
    (2) release her to participate in the procedure, if this is justified by the statutory objectives of the Organization and when the reasons for the public interest.
    § 2. Public administration, recognizing the request of the social organization for justified, decides to initiate proceedings ex officio or to admit your organization to participate. In order not to initiate the procedure or admission to participate in the procedure of social organization's for the complaint.
    § 3. Social organization participates in the proceedings on the rights of the parties.
    § 4. Public administration, by bringing proceedings in a case involving another person, it shall inform the social organization, if it considers that it may be interested in participating in this proceeding because of its statutory objectives, and when speaking for the public interest.
    § 5. Social organization, which does not participate in the proceedings on the rights of the parties, may with the consent of the public authority to submit to it its views on, expressed in the resolution or statement of its statutory authority.

    Likewise, the former example, the EU law contributed to stronger procedural rights of NGOs, exceeding the prerogatives envisaged expressly in the Directive. See also A. Wróbel,

It seems that labor law is the subject matter in which the value of contribution of the third sector organizations is highly appreciated. Still, environmental protection is the sphere where the role of NGOs is mostly emphasized. The importance of public participation in decision-making, consultations and access to justice led to the development of "environmental democracy."[36] Even though this term is mainly attributed to the implications of the Aarhus Convention, it should be remembered that the EU passed numerous acts of law dealing with the position of NGOs as subjects acting in the collective environmental interest before the implementation of this significant international agreement.

Without going into details of "environmental democracy" at the EU level, which will be extensively discussed in the subsequent parts of this chapter, the role of NGOs in environmental protection is emphasized in the following acts of secondary law:

(1) Directive 2010/75/EU of the EP and of the Council of November 24, 2010, on industrial emissions (integrated pollution prevention and control);[37]
(2) Directive 2004/35/EC of the EP and of the Council of April 21, 2004, on environmental liability with regard to the prevention and remedying of environmental damage;[38]
(3) Directive 2003/35/EC of the EP and of the Council of May 26, 2003, providing for public participation in respect of the drawing up of certain plans and programs relating to the environment and amending with regard to public

Komentarz do art. 31 in: *Kodeks postępowania administracyjnego. Komentarz*, M. Jaśkowska, A. Wróbel (eds), Warsaw 2013, lex.pl.

36. See e.g. J. Ebbesson, *A Modest Contribution to Environmental Democracy and Justice in Transboundary Contexts: The Combined Impact of the Espoo Convention and Aarhus Convention*, Review of European, Comparative & International Environmental Law Vol. 20/2011, pp. 248 et seq.
37. Official Journal L 334/17, 17.12.2010; for instance, according to Art. 13 (1), in order to draw up, review and, where necessary, update BAT reference documents, the Commission shall organize an exchange of information between Member States, the industries concerned, nongovernmental organizations promoting environmental protection and the Commission. Pursuant to Art. 25 (3), what constitutes a sufficient interest and impairment of a right shall be determined by Member States, consistently with the objective of giving the public concerned wide access to justice. To this end, the interest of any nongovernmental organization promoting environmental protection and meeting any requirements under national law shall be deemed sufficient for the purpose of para. 1(a). Such organizations shall also be deemed to have rights capable of being impaired for the purpose of para. 1(b).
38. Official Journal L 143, 30.4.2004; according to Art. 12 (1), Natural or legal persons:
    (a) affected or likely to be affected by environmental damage; or
    (b) having a sufficient interest in environmental decision-making relating to the damage; or
    (c) alternatively, alleging the impairment of a right, where administrative procedural law of a Member State requires this as a precondition;

    shall be entitled to submit to the competent authority any observations relating to instances of environmental damage or an imminent threat of such damage of which they are aware of and shall be entitled to request the competent authority to take action under this Directive.

    What constitutes a "sufficient interest" and "impairment of a right" shall be determined by the Member States.

    To this end, the interest of any nongovernmental organization promoting environmental protection and meeting any requirements under national law shall be deemed sufficient for the purpose of subparagraph (b). Such organizations shall also be deemed to have rights capable of being impaired for the purpose of subparagraph (c).

participation and access to justice Council Directives 85/337/EEC and 96/61/EC—Statement by the Commission;[39]

(4) Directive 2001/18/EC of the EP and of the Council of March 12, 2001, on the deliberate release into the environment of genetically modified organisms and repealing Council Directive 90/220/EEC—Commission Declaration (GMO Directive);[40]

(5) Directive 2001/42/EC of the EP and of the Council of June 27, 2001, on the assessment of the effects of certain plans and programs on the environment (SEA Directive);[41]

(6) Directive 2003/87/EC of the EP and of the Council of October 13, 2003, establishing a scheme for greenhouse gas emission allowance trading within the Community and amending Council Directive 96/61/EC (Emissions Trading Scheme Directive—ETS);[42]

(7) Directive 2002/49/EC of the EP and of the Council of June 25, 2002, relating to the assessment and management of environmental noise—Declaration by the Commission in the Conciliation Committee on the Directive relating to

39. Official Journal L 156, 25.6.2003; for instance, according to Art. 2 (3), Member States shall identify the public entitled to participate for the purposes of para. 2, including relevant nongovernmental organizations meeting any requirements imposed under national law, such as those promoting environmental protection. See Art. 10, already mentioned in the context of case C-115/09.

40. Official Journal L 106, 17.4.2001; for instance, according to Art. 9 (1), Member States shall, without prejudice to the provisions of Arts. 7 and 25, consult the public and, where appropriate, groups on the proposed deliberate release. In doing so, Member States shall lay down arrangements for this consultation, including a reasonable time period, in order to give the public or groups the opportunity to express an opinion. (2) Without prejudice to the provisions of Art. 25:

    - Member States shall make available to the public information on all part B releases of GMOs in their territory.
    - the Commission shall make available to the public the information contained in the system of exchange of information pursuant to Art. 11.

41. Official Journal L 197, 21.7.2001, for instance, according to Art. 6 (2), the authorities referred to in para. 3 and the public referred to in para. 4 shall be given an early and effective opportunity within appropriate time frames to express their opinion on the draft plan or program and the accompanying environmental report before the adoption of the plan or program or its submission to the legislative procedure. (3) Member States shall designate the authorities to be consulted which, by reason of their specific environmental responsibilities, are likely to be concerned by the environmental effects of implementing plans and programs. (4) Member States shall identify the public for the purposes of para. 2, including the public affected or likely to be affected by, or having an interest in, the decision-making subject to this Directive, including relevant nongovernmental organizations, such as those promoting environmental protection and other organizations concerned.

42. Official Journal L 275, 25.10.2003; according to Art. 3 (f), "the public" means one or more persons and, in accordance with national legislation or practice, associations, organizations or groups of persons; Pursuant to Art. 11 (1), for the three-year period beginning January 1, 2005, each Member State shall decide upon the total quantity of allowances it will allocate for that period and the allocation of those allowances to the operator of each installation. This decision shall be taken at least three months before the beginning of the period and be based on its national allocation plan developed pursuant to Art. 9 and in accordance with Art. 10, taking due account of comments from the public.

the assessment and management of environmental noise (Noise Directive);[43]

(8) Council Directive 92/43/EEC of May 21, 1992, on the conservation of natural habitats and of wild fauna and flora (Habitats Directive);[44]

(9) Directive 2000/60/EC of the EP and of the Council of October 23, 2000, establishing a framework for Community action in the field of water policy (Water Framework Directive);[45]

(10) Directive 2012/18/EU of the EP and of the Council of July 4, 2012, on the control of major accident hazards involving dangerous substances, amending and subsequently repealing Council Directive 96/82/EC.[46]

As it can be seen, the EU law does envisage some rights for NGOs as advocates of the public interest at national level. Having in mind the "procedural autonomy" principle, these recognitions are not meaningless. It is doubtless that the most

43. Official Journal L 189, 18.7.2002; according to Art. 3 (v): "the public" shall mean one or more natural or legal persons and, in accordance with national legislation or practice, their associations, organizations or groups. Pursuant to Art. 10 (1), Member States shall ensure that the strategic noise maps they have made, and where appropriate adopted, and the action plans they have drawn up are made available and disseminated to the public in accordance with relevant Community legislation, in particular Council Directive 90/313/EEC of 7 June 1990 on the freedom of access to information on the environment(13), and in conformity with Annexes IV and V to this Directive, including by means of available information technologies.

44. Official Journal L 206, 22.7.1992; according to Art. (3), any plan or project not directly connected with or necessary to the management of the site but likely to have a significant effect thereon, either individually or in combination with other plans or projects, shall be subject to appropriate assessment of its implications for the site in view of the site's conservation objectives. In the light of the conclusions of the assessment of the implications for the site and subject to the provisions of para. 4, the competent national authorities shall agree to the plan or project only after having ascertained that it will not adversely affect the integrity of the site concerned and, if appropriate, after having obtained the opinion of the general public.

45. Official Journal L 327, 22.12.2000; according to Art. 14 (1), Member States shall encourage the active involvement of all interested parties in the implementation of this Directive, in particular in the production, review and updating of the river basin management plans. Member States shall ensure that, for each river basin district, they publish and make available for comments to the public, including users:
    (a) a timetable and work program for the production of the plan, including a statement of the consultation measures to be taken, at least three years before the beginning of the period to which the plan refers;
    (b) an interim overview of the significant water management issues identified in the river basin, at least two years before the beginning of the period to which the plan refers;
    (c) draft copies of the river basin management plan, at least one year before the beginning of the period to which the plan refers.

    On request, access shall be given to background documents and information used for the development of the draft river basin management plan.

46. Official Journal L 197/1, 24.7.2012; according to Art. 15 (6) Where general plans or programs are being established relating to the matters referred to in points (a) or (c) of para. 1, Member States shall ensure that the public is given early and effective opportunities to participate in their preparation and modification or review using the procedures set out in Art. 2(2) of Directive 2003/35/EC of the European Parliament and of the Council of 26 May 2003 providing for public participation in respect of the drawing up of certain plans and programs relating to the environment. Member States shall identify the public entitled to participate for the purposes of this paragraph, including relevant nongovernmental organizations meeting any relevant requirements imposed under national law, such as those promoting environmental protection.

important sphere of acknowledgment is attributed to environmental protection. Further remarks on this issue will be presented in the subsequent parts of this chapter.

[B] EU Level

The following paragraphs will be focused on the inquiries concerning if, how and under what circumstances NGOs can file complaints against acts of the EU law and, therefore, contribute to the common good of European civil society. These issues deal especially with the possibility of instituting proceedings before the CJEU but also with other more "conciliatory" means.

[1] Action for Annulment

The main opportunity for individuals to bring an action against acts undertaken at the EU level is provided in Article 263 paragraph 4 of the TFEU. Accordingly, any natural or legal person may, under the conditions laid down in the first and second paragraphs,[47] institute proceedings against an act addressed to that person or which is of direct and individual concern to them, and against a regulatory act which is of direct concern to them and does not entail implementing measures. The actions of individuals are brought to the General Court (which until 2009 was known as the CFI—Court of First Instance) and appeals are brought to the Court of Justice.[48]

It is quite obvious that this remedy can be used by NGOs if they are a direct addressee of the EU act of law. However, it is important to outline the borders of using Article 263 of the TFEU as a means of protecting collective interests at the EU level. In this respect, the proper understanding of "direct and individual concern" is crucial. This is also important due to the fact that the Treaties, just like most national legal systems, do not envisage any designatum of an *actio popularis*.

First of all, it should be mentioned that according to the settled case law, in an action brought under Article 263 of the TFEU, the Court has no jurisdiction to rule on the lawfulness of a measure adopted by a national authority.[49] It is also settled case law that this position cannot be altered by the fact that the measure forms part of an EU decision-making procedure, where it is clear from the division of powers in the fields between the national authorities and the EU institutions that the measure adopted by the national authority is binding on the EU decision taking authority and therefore determines the terms of the EU decision to be adopted.[50] However, in respect to these remarks, it should be remembered that the EU institutions are often not bound with the decisions of the Member States authorities. Article 4 (5) of Regulation 1049/2001,

47. I.e., on the grounds of lack of competence, infringement of an essential procedural requirement, infringement of the Treaties or of any rule of law relating to their application or misuse of powers.
48. See Art. 256 (1) of the TFEU.
49. C-64/05 P, *IFAW Internationaler Tierschutz-Fonds gGmbH* (ECLI:EU:C:2007:802), para. 91; see also e.g. C-97/91 *Oleificio Borelli v. Commission*, ECLI:EU:C:1992:491, para. 9.
50. Para. 10 in C-97/91.

which has been presented in the previous chapter,[51] can provide an example of this issue. The aim of this article was not aimed at establishing division between two powers, one national and the other one of the EU, with different powers.[52] This provision only creates a decision-making procedure the sole object of which is to determine whether access to a document should be refused under one of the substantive exceptions listed in Article 4 (1)-(3) of the Regulation. Therefore, from the point of view of the person concerned, the Member State's intervention does not affect the EU nature of the decision that it is subsequently addressed to him by the institution in reply to the request he had made for access to a document in its possession.[53] Thus, the decision taken by the EU institution in this sphere can be subject to the action of annulment based on Article 263 of the TFEU.

It is consistently significant to point out that under Article 78 (3) of the Rules of Procedure of the General Court, an application made by a legal person governed by private law shall be accompanied by a recent proof of that person's existence (extract from the register, firms or associations or any other official document). As the General Court settled in T-168/13 *European Platform Against Windfarms (EPAW)*,[54] an applicant is a legal person under the EU judicial system if, at the latest by the expiry period prescribed for proceedings to be instituted, it has acquired legal personality in accordance with the law governing its constitution.[55] Moreover, the proof is also not established by the applicant's inclusion in the Transparency Register of the EU. The inclusion on that register is not subject to the existence of legal personality on the part of the body concerned.[56] It means that an applicant must be a registered entity with legal personality. In contrast, an action cannot be brought by civic movements or other civil society groups which are not legal persons.

The biggest considerations arise from the interpretation of "direct and individual concern." This issue actualizes when an individual wishes to bring action against an act of law which is not directly addressed to him. It is important to notice that this remedy does not encompass only decisions. In C-358/89 *Extramet*[57] and C-309/89 *Codorniu*[58] the CJEU accepted that general acts of law, including regulations, may be challenged by individual applicants, since the fact that an act is of general application does not prevent it from being of direct and individual concern to some of the subjects concerned.[59] It means that not the form of the act but its content prejudges the

51. According to which a Member State may request the institution not to disclose a document originating from that Member State without its prior agreement.
52. Para. 93 in C-64/05 P.
53. Para. 94 in C-64/05 P.
54. ECLI:EU:T:2014:47.
55. Para. 23 in T-168/13; see also C-50/84 *Bensider and Others v. Commission*, ECLI:EU:C:1984:190, paras. 7 and 8.
56. Para. 19 in T-168/13.
57. ECLI:EU:C:1992:257.
58. ECLI:EU:C:1994:197.
59. In these cases the subjects concerned were the traders.

opportunity of bringing an action by an individual before the CJEU. Still, nonbinding acts of law cannot be challenged under Article 263 of the TFEU in general.[60]

According to the CJEU, persons other than the addresses may claim that a decision is of direct concern to them only if that decision (or other act of law having an effect like a decision) affects them by reason of certain attributes which are peculiar to them, or by reason of factual circumstances which differentiate them from all other persons and thereby distinguish them individually in the same way as the person addressed.[61] This reasoning is often referred to as the "Plaumann test."[62]

In case law, this interpretation translates to the admissibility of actions brought by associations or other NGOs in three situations:[63]

(1) where they represent, in accordance with the powers conferred to them by their statutes,[64] the interests of persons[65] who, for their part, would have the standing to take action;[66]
(2) where they are individually identified by reason of the impact on their interests as an association or as a group, particularly because their position of negotiator has been affected by the act whose annulment is sought;[67]
(3) where a legal provision expressly grants them a number of powers of a procedural nature.[68]

60. See, to this extent, e.g. T-670/14 *Milchindustrie-Verband eV and Deutsher Raiffeisenverband eV v. European Commission*, ECLI:EU:T:2015:906.
61. See, to this extent, i.a. Case C-198/91 *Cook v. Commission*, ECLI:EU:C:1993:197, para. 20, C-225/91 *Matra v. Commission*, ECLI:EU:C:1993:239, para. 14, C-260/05 P *Sniace v. Commission*, ECLI:EU:C:2007:700, para. 53.
62. Since it was first established by the CJEU in Cases 25-62 *Plaumann & Co. v. Commission of the European Economic Community*, ECLI:EU:C:1963:17.
63. See, to that effect e.g. T-189/08 *Forum 187 v. Commission*, ECLI:EU:T:2010:99, para. 58; see also T-122/96 *Federolio v. Commission*, ECLI:EU:T:1997:142, T-196/03 *EFfCI v. Parliament*, ECLI-:EU:T:2004:355, T-170/04 *FederDoc and Others*, ECLI:EU:T:2005:257, T-38/98 *Associazione Nazionale Bieticoltori (ANB), Francesco Coccia and Vincenzo Di Giovine v. Council of the European Union*, ECLI:EU:T:1998:281.
64. K. Lenaerts, I. Maselis, K. Gutman, *EU Procedural...*, p. 348.
65. I.e., in cases where their members are each individually concerned by the contested act of law; for more see M. von Wolferen, *The Limits to the CJEU's Interpretation of Locus Standi. A Theoretical Framework*, Journal of Contemporary European Research Vol. 12/2016, p. 924.
66. I.e., members of the organization should be directly and individually concerned by the contested act of law; see T-381/11 *Europäischer Wirtschaftsverband der Eisen- und Stahlindustrie (Eurofer) ASBL*, ECLI:EU:T:2012:273, para. 26. However, if only some members of the organization are directly and individually concerned by the contested decision, the situation is more complex as the CJEU refused to accept that collective organizations representing their members qualify as directly and individually concerned themselves. For instance, the CJEU refused to hear two cases where work councils complained against decisions of the Commission allowing mergers to proceed (T-96/92 *Comité Central d'Entreprise de la Société Générale des Grandes Sources v. Commission*, ECLI:EU:T:1995:77, T-12/93 *Vittel v. Commission*, ECLI:EU:T:1993:35). The same attitude was applied by the CJEU in a case where a works council complained against a decision condemning state aid (T-189/97 *Comité d'entreprise de la Société Française de Production v. Commission*, ECLI:EU:T:1998:38).
67. See e.g. T-447/93-449/93 *AITEC and Others v. Commission*, ECLI:EU:T:1996:174, para. 62.
68. See e.g. C-67/85-70/85 *Van der Kooy and Others v. Commission*, ECLI:EU:C:1988:38, paras. 21-24, C-313/90 *Comité International de la Rayonne et des Fibres Synthétiques and others v.*

This clarification does not resolve all problems dealing with NGOs acting as proponents of collective interest at the EU level as it seems somewhat strict. Consequently, NGOs sought many ways to loosen the binding doctrine of "direct and individual concern" in cases of organizations acting as public advocates.

Perhaps the most significant judgment in this subject matter was issued in C-321/95 *Stichting Greenpeace Council (Greenpeace International) and Others v. Commission*.[69] The case was based on the following facts. The appellants (Greenpeace and other entities) brought an appeal against the order of the CFI in case T-585/93[70] in so far as it declared inadmissible their action for annulment of the Commission's decision allegedly taken between March 7, 1991, and October 29, 1993, to disburse to the Kingdom of Spain EUR 12 million pursuant to Decision C (91) 440 concerning financial assistance provided by the European Regional Development Fund for the construction of two power stations in the Canary Islands (Gran Canaria and Tenerife).[71] First, the appellants argued that the decision was unlawful because the enterprise that received the funding (*Unelco*) had failed to undertake an environmental impact assessment study in accordance with Council Directive 85/337/EEC and, second, that the declaration of environmental impact issued by the Canary Islands Commission for Planning and the Environment (*Cumac*) was contrary to the provisions of the Directive. Moreover, Greenpeace asked the Commission for full disclosure of all information relating to measures it had taken with regard to the construction of the two power stations in accordance with Article 7 of Council Regulation (EEC) No 2052/88 of June 24, 1988, on the tasks of the Structural Funds and their effectiveness and on coordination of their activities between themselves and with the operations of the European Investment Bank and the other existing financial instruments.[72] The Director-General of DG XVI replied as follows: "I regret to say that I am unable to supply this information since it concerns the internal decision making procedures of the Commission ... but I can assure you that the Commission's decision was taken only after full consultation between the various services concerned."[73]

The CFI stated that an association formed for the protection of the collective interests of a category of persons could not be considered to be directly and individually concerned for the purposes of the fourth paragraph of Article 173 of the Treaty (presently Article 263 of the TFEU), by a measure affecting the general interests of that

Commission of the European Communities, ECLI:EU:C:1993:111, T-481/93 and T-484/93 *Exporteurs in Levende Varkens and Others v. Commission*, ECLI:EU:T:1995:209, para. 64.

69. ECLI:EU:C:1998:153.
70. ECLI:EU:T:1995:147.
71. Para. 1 in C-321/95.
72. Which provided: (1) Measures financed by the Structural Funds or receiving assistance from the EIB or from another existing financial instrument shall be in keeping with the provisions of the Treaties, with the instruments adopted pursuant thereto and with Community policies, including those concerning the rules on competition, the award of public contracts and environmental protection. (2) Without prejudice to the Financial Regulation, the provisions referred to in Art. 3 (4) and (5) shall lay down harmonized rules for strengthening checks on structural operations. They shall be adjusted to reflect the special nature of the financial operations concerned. The procedures for carrying out checks on operations undertaken by the EIB shall be as set out in its Statute.
73. Paras. 10-11 in C-321/95.

category, and was therefore not entitled to bring an action for annulment where its members could not do so individually.[74] Then it went on to observe that special circumstances, such as the role played by an association in a procedure which led to the adoption of an act within the meaning of Article 174 of the Treaty (presently Article 191 of the TFEU), might justify treating as admissible an action brought by an association whose members were not directly and individually concerned by the contested measure.[75] However, the CFI came to the conclusion that the exchange of correspondence and the discussions which Greenpeace had with the Commission concerning the financing of the project for the construction of two power stations in the Canary Islands did not constitute special circumstances of that kind since the Commission did not, prior to the adoption of the contested decision, initiate any procedure in which Greenpeace participated. Nor was Greenpeace in any way the interlocutor of the Commission with regard to the adoption of the contested decision.[76]

The appellants argued that the environmental associations should be recognized as having *locus standi* where their objectives concern mainly environmental protection and one or more of their members are individually concerned by the contested Community (EU) decision, and where, regardless, their primary objective is environmental protection and they can demonstrate a specific interest in the question at issue. Thus, Article 173 (presently Article 263 of the TFEU) should not be interpreted restrictively. Its wording does not expressly require belonging on an exhaustive list of subjects in order to be individually concerned by a Community (EU) act. It should be rather interpreted in such a way as to safeguard fundamental environmental interests and protect individual environmental rights effectively.[77]

Therefore, the appellants proposed a different interpretation of the fourth paragraph of Article 173 of the Treaty (presently Article 263 of the TFEU). In order to determine whether a particular applicant is individually concerned by a Community (EU) act involving violations of Community (EU) environmental obligations, that applicant should be required to demonstrate that:

(a) he has personally suffered (or is likely to suffer) some actual or threatened detriment as a result of the allegedly illegal conduct of the Community (EU) institution concerned, such as violation of his environmental rights or interference with his environmental interests;
(b) the detriment can be traced to the act challenged; and
(c) the detriment is capable of being redressed by a favorable judgment.[78]

The appellants contented that they satisfy these three conditions. As regards the first condition, they stated that they had submitted statements describing the detriment which they have suffered as a result of the Commission's acts. As regards the second

74. Para. 14 in C-321/95.
75. Para. 15 in C-321/95.
76. Para. 16 in C-321/95.
77. Paras. 25-26 in C-321/95.
78. Para. 23 in C-321/95.

condition, they pointed out that, by disbursing the funds under Decision C (91) 440 for the projects in breach of Community (EU) environmental law, the Commission directly contributed to the detriment caused to their interests since the Spanish authorities had no discretion as to the use to which those funds were to be put. As regards the third condition, the appellants considered that if the CFI had annulled the contested decision, the Commission would not have continued to finance work on the construction of the power stations which then have probably been suspended until completion of the environmental impact procedure.[79]

In the opinion of the Advocate General Cosmas,[80] environmental protection is a matter of general interest. Conservation of the environment is a legal interest theoretically shared by all natural persons. Thus, it has a communal dimension. Furthermore, the more significant the intervention in or impingement on the environment is, the greater the number of persons affected thereby.[81] However, the argumentation of the appellants has no support in existing case law as the *locus standi* conditions cannot but be the same in all cases, irrespective of the subject matter of the dispute, meaning that the applicant must be individually affected by the act which he contests.[82] Moreover, the relaxation by the Court of the criteria of admissibility could be abused and lead to aberrant consequences. Natural persons without *locus standi* under the fourth paragraph of Article 173 of the Treaty (presently Article 263 of the TFEU) could circumvent that procedural impediment by setting up an environmental association. Moreover, while the number of citizens of the EU, however high it may be, remains limited, the number of environmental associations capable of being created is, at least in theory, infinite. But, even if that obstacle could be overcome, for example by conferring *locus standi* only on associations constituted prior to adoption of the contested measure, account would have to be taken of the fact that, within the EU, the number of legal persons which have as their object the protection and conservation of the environment is particularly high. If the Court was ultimately to follow the proposal of the appellant associations, in the future every measure of a Community (EU) institution concerning the environment or having an impact on it could be expected, on each occasion, to form the subject matter of proceedings brought by a plethora of environmental associations.[83]

This opinion seems, at least partially, misguided. The *locus standi* cannot be assessed by the possible number of subjects that could institute proceedings before the Court. In contrast, such an evaluation is entirely subjective and not objective. Moreover, the complaint possibility of individuals cannot be linked with the internal organization of the CJEU. Additionally, the fears of overloading the General Court was rightly rejected by the Advocate General Jacobs in a different case.[84]

79. Para. 24 in C-321/95.
80. ECLI:EU:C:1997:421.
81. Para. 102 in C-321/95.
82. Paras. 103, 116 in C-321/95.
83. Para. 117 in C-321/95.
84. In his opinion in Case C-50/00 P *UPA*, ECLI:EU:C:2002:197, Advocate General Jacobs noted: the fears of overloading the Court of First Instance seem exaggerated since the time limit in Art.

However, the Court of Justice dismissed the appeal and shared the main arguments of the CFI and the Advocate General. In particular, it stated that where the specific situation of the applicant was not taken into consideration in the adoption of the act, which concerns him in a general and abstract fashion and, in fact, like any other person in the same situation, the applicant is not individually concerned by the act. The same applies to associations which claim to have *locus standi* on the basis of the fact that the persons whom they represent are individually concerned by the contested decision.[85] It also confirmed that the applicant could claim that the decision was of individual concern to him only if that decision affected him by reason of certain attributes of a particular nature, or by reason of factual circumstances which differentiate him from all other persons, and thereby distinguishing him individually in the same way as the person addressed. For an individual to be directly affected, the measure challenged must directly produce effects on his legal, not factual, position and leave no discretion to the addresses of that measure, who are entrusted with implementation, that being a purely automatic matter flowing solely from the EU law without the intermediation of other rules.[86]

The *Greenpeace* judgment has been widely criticized by the commentators who have rightly pointed out that the rigid Plaumann test to which the CJEU so firmly clings is singularly inapt to accommodate the protection of environmental interests which are, by their very nature, collective and diffuse, and therefore almost never concern any particular person in a way that an individual is "differentiated from all other persons."[87] This admissibility test in principle cannot be satisfied by an NGO. An organization formed for the protection of the collective interest of a category of persons could not be considered to be directly and individually concerned by a measure affecting the general interests of that category.[88]

Other difficulties with the *Greenpeace* ruling pointed out by the doctrine include:[89]

230(5) EC and the requirement of direct concern will prevent an insuperable increase of the caseload; there are procedural means to deal with a more limited increase of cases.

85. Paras. 27 and 28 in C-321/95.
86. Which is a repetition of the Plaumann test; see also, to this extent, R. Mastroianni, A. Pezza, *Striking the Right Balance: Limits on the Right to Bring an Action under Article 263 (4) of the Treaty on the Functioning of the European Union*, American University International Law Review Vol. 30/2015, pp. 764-765.
87. M. Pallemaerts, *Access to Environmental Justice at EU Level. Has the "Aarhus Regulation" Improved the Situation* in: *Aarhus Convention at Ten. Interactions and Tensions Between Conventional International Law and EU Environmental Law*, M Pallemaerts (ed.), Groningen 2011, p. 300.
88. D. Obradovic, *EU Rules...*, p. 173.
89. N. Gerard, *Case Law Analysis. Access to Justice in Environmental Matters—A Case of Double Standard? Greenpeace and Others v. Commission of the European Union*, Journal of Environmental Law Vol. 8/1996, pp. 149-157, N. Gerard, *Case Law Analysis. Access to the European Court of Justice: A Lost Opportunity. Stichting Greenpeace Council (Greenpeace International) and others v. Commission*, Journal of Environmental Law Vol. 10/1998, pp. 331-346, Ch. Hilson, *Community Rights and Wrongs: Greenpeace Before the Court of Justice. Case C-321-95 P, Stichting Greenpeace Council (Greenpeace International) and others v. Commission*, Environmental Law Review Vol. 52/1999, pp. 52-58, F. de Lange, *Beyond Greenpeace. Courtesy of the Aarhus Convention*, Yearbook of European Environmental Law Vol. 3/2003, pp. 227-248, S. Schikhof, *Direct and Individual Concern in Environmental Cases: The Barriers to Prospective Litigants*,

(1) not taking into account the direction of the EU law development, i.e. the rising role of the collective interest protection;
(2) leaving many acts of the EU law outside the judiciary control as there are no individuals with proper "direct and individual concern" to bring an action against them before the CJEU, whereas these acts can undermine the collective interest;
(3) not taking into account that the Commission should be put under extensive control in their actions undertaken in the spheres of the collective interest;
(4) an implicit acknowledgment that national measures (including preliminary references) can be an equivalent to the lack of remedies against certain acts of the EU law for the representatives of the collective interest.[90]

Although some of these reasons may seem a bit farfetched,[91] it is obvious that the *Greenpeace* case contributed to a very strict understanding of "direct and individual concern." In fact, this rigid judicature has not been relaxed ever since.[92] Still, the reasoning of NGOs wishing to ease this interpretation was further developed.

One line of argumentation was focused on their significant role in the decision-making procedures. Thus, it was claimed that once an organization took part in these processes, it should be then treated as directly and individually concerned by the final outcome.[93] However, according to the case law of the CJEU, already depicted in the *Greenpeace* case, the sole fact of taking part in the decision-making procedures is not enough. For instance, in T-60/96 *Merck and Others v. The Commission*,[94] the CFI stated

EELR Vol. 7/1998, D.L. Torrens, *Locus Standi for Environmental Associations under EC Law—Greenpeace—A Missed Opportunity for the ECJ*, Review of European Community & International Environmental Law Vol. 8/1999, pp. 336-346, R. Williams, *Enforcing European Environmental Law: Can the European Commission be Held to Account?*, Yearbook of European Environmental Law Vol. 2/2002, pp. 276-278, C. Zengerling, *Greening International Jurisprudence. Environmental NGOs Before International Courts, Tribunals and Compliance Committees*, Leiden 2013, pp. 65-66, M. Eliantonio, *Towards an Ever Dirtier Europe? The Restrictive Standing of Environmental NGOs Before the European Courts and the Aarhus Convention*, Croatian Yearbook of European Law and Policy Vol. 7/2011, pp. 73-76.

90. Even though such procedure is, in principle, not a judicial remedy for individuals, rather a means of cooperation between national courts and the CJEU when an action is brought before national courts; see e.g. C-354/04 P *Gestoras Pro Amnistía, Juan Mari Olano Olano and Julen Zelarain Errasti*, ECLI:EU:C:2007:115.
91. See e.g. T. Tridimas, S. Poli, *Locus Standi of Individuals under Article 230(4): The Return of Euridice* in: *Continuity and Change in EU Law: Essays in Honour of Sir Francis Jacobs*, A. Arnull, P. Eeckhout, T. Tridimas (eds), Oxford 2008, pp. 70 et seq.
92. See further cases, including: T-117/94 *Associazione Agricoltori della Provincia die Rovigo a.o. v. Commission*, ECLI:EU:T:1995:37, T-219/95 *R Danielsson et al. v. Commission*, ECLI-:EU:T:1995:219.
93. This argument was first raised by WWF-UK in T-461/93 *An Taisce—The National Trust for Ireland and World Wide Fund for Nature v. Commission of the European Communities*, ECLI:EU:T:1997:26.WWF considered itself to be individually concerned by the contested decision, not only because it was actively and strongly involved in the procedure which led to the adoption of the contested decision but also because of its direct and active involvement in environmental matters, which distinguishes it from other persons and obligations (para. 27). However, the CFI contested the litigated decision without examining the *locus standi* of the organization (para. 40).
94. ECLI:EU:T:1997:81.

that the fact that a person participates in one way or another in the process leading to the adoption of a Community (EU) act does not distinguish him individually in relation to the act in question unless the relevant Community (EU) legislation has laid down specific procedural guarantees for such a person.[95] Likewise, in C-355/08 P *WWF-UK*,[96] the CJEU emphasized that the fact that a person is involved in the procedure leading to the adoption of a Community (EU) measure is capable of distinguishing that person individually in relation to the measure in question only if the applicable Community (EU) legislation grants him certain procedural guarantees in his own right.[97] Moreover, it was noted that where such procedural rights are conferred on an entity composed of a number of members, only the entity expressly named in the Community (EU) provision conferring those rights may be regarded as individually concerned for the purposes of the fourth paragraph of Article 263 of the TFEU and not its members as individuals.[98] Thus, individual persons cannot exercise the right attributed to the organization as a whole, even if they are its members.

Furthermore, in C-150/06 P *Arizona Chemical*,[99] the Court of Justice approved the reasoning of the CFI,[100] in which it emphasized the fact that when the Commission and the Working Group draft proposals to be submitted to the Regulatory Committee, they take account of the information and data provided by the interlocutors for the purposes of the classification or declassification of substances, likewise does not suffice to make the preliminary assessment of individual concern.[101] Moreover, according to the case law concerning acts or decisions drafted in several stages, in principle only measures definitively laying down the position of the institution concerned on the conclusion of that procedure may be the subject of an action for annulment so that intermediate measures which serve to prepare for the final decision are excluded.[102] The duty of diligence in the decision-making procedure is essentially an objective procedural guarantee arising from an absolute and unconditional obligation of the Community (EU) institution to the drafting of an act of general application and not the exercise of any individual act. Therefore, the subjects concerned cannot rely on the duty of diligence in the context of a procedure resulting in the adoption of measures of general application in the same way as they may rely on procedural guarantees in the

95. Para. 73 in T-60/96; see also e.g. T-339/00 *Bactria Industriehygiene-Service Verwaltungs GmbH and Others*, ECLI:EU:T:2002:107, para. 51, T-291/04 *Enviro Tech Europe Ltd and Enviro Tech International, Inc. v. European Commission*, ECLI:EU:T:2011:760, para. 67.
96. ECLI:EU:C:2009:286.
97. Para. 23 in C-355/08 P.
98. Para. 43; see also T-264/03 *Schmoldt and Others v. Commission*, ECLI:EU:T:2004:157 paras. 41 and 42, T-122/96 *Federolio v. Commission*, ECLI:EU:T:1997:142, para. 69.
99. ECLI:EU:C:2007:164.
100. T-369/03, ECLI:EU:T:2005:458.
101. Para. 60 in Case T-369/03.
102. Para. 64 in Case T-369/03; see also e.g. T-175/96 *Berthu v. Commission*, ECLI:EU:T:1997:72, para. 44 and T-123/03 *Pfizer v. Commission*, ECLI:EU:T:2004:167. The action for annulment in the latter case was held to be admissible not on the basis of the duty of diligence as a procedural guarantee protecting the applicants but on the basis of other criteria, including procedural guarantees expressly laid down by the legislation in question so that the applicants were considered to be individually concerned by the contested regulation.

context of a procedure resulting in the adoption of an administrative act of individual application.[103]

Consequently, according to the CJEU, an NGO had to play a special role in a procedure which led to the adoption of an act in order to meet the admissibility test from Article 263 of the TFEU. Also, an NGO could be individually concerned if it participated in the procedure initiated by the Commission prior to the adoption of the impugned decision.[104] However, it is unlikely that the Commission's current practice of issuing an online invitation addressed to the public in general and not to particular parties to participate in the impact assessment consultations would be considered to qualify as a procedure, participation in which will guarantee standing to NGO to challenge the EU acts in order to protect their participation rights. Moreover, it is doubtful whether an obligation imposed upon the EU institutions to provide "early and effective opportunities for the public to participate during the preparation, modification or review"[105] of certain decisions would be interpreted by the CJEU as a provision endowing NGOs with individual procedural rights within the meaning of the case law.[106]

Another line of argumentation toward enhancing the admissibility of actions brought by advocates of the public interest focused on transposing the understanding of "direct and individual concern" from national laws to the EU level. For instance, in T-236/04 and T-241/04 *European Environmental Bureau (EEB) and Stichting Natuur en Milieu v. Commission*,[107] the applicants claimed essentially that the approach in Directive 2004/35[108] is consistent with prevailing legal practice in a number of Member States, including the Netherlands, according to which associations may bring civil proceedings before the national courts because they are directly and individually concerned in the light of their statutes, their specific situation and their actual activities, including effective protection of the interests in question. More specifically, in the Dutch legal system, Natuur en Milieu was considered to be directly and individually concerned by breaches of legal rules protecting environmental and wildlife interests. Furthermore, the applicants claimed that they were individually concerned because they pursue their activities in the field of environmental protection and conservation of nature, including wildlife, in the context of Directive 92/43 and that, in that capacity, the EEB had a special consultative status with the Commission and other European institutions. Moreover, Natuur en Milieu had a similar status with the Netherlands authorities.[109]

---

103. Para. 86 in Case T-369/03.
104. D. Obradovic, *EU Rules...*, p. 175.
105. As provided in Art. 9 (1) of Regulation (EC) No 1367/2006 of the European Parliament and of the Council of 6 September 2006 on the application of the provisions of the Aarhus Convention on Access to Information, Public Participation in Decision-Making and Access to Justice in Environmental Matters to Community institutions and bodies, Official Journal L 264/13, 25.9.2006.
106. D. Obradovic, *EU Rules...*, p. 175.
107. ECLI:EU:T:2005:426.
108. I.e., Directive 2004/35/CE of the EP and of the Council of 21 April 2004 on environmental liability with regard to the prevention and remedying of environmental damage.
109. Paras. 44 and 45 in Cases T-236/04 and T-241/04.

Still, the CFI noted that the standing on the applicants in some of the legal systems of the Member States is irrelevant for the purposes of determining whether they have the standing to bring an action for annulment of a Community (EU) act pursuant to Article 230 of the Treaty (presently Article 263 of the TFEU).[110] In addition, it is clear that the contested provisions affect the applicants in their objective capacity as entities whose purpose is to protect the environment in the same manner as any other person in the same situation. That capacity is not by itself sufficient to establish that the applicants were individually concerned by the contested decisions.[111] What is also worth mentioning is the remark of the CFI that the Community (EU) law, as it now stands, does not provide for a right to bring a class (collective) action before the Community (EU) courts.[112]

Further propositions put forward by Advocate General Jacobs in C-50/00 P *UPA*[113] and the ruling of the CFI in T-177/01 *Jégo-Quéré*[114] for relaxing the individual and direct concern requirements and replacing them by alternative standing rules similar to those operating at the national level, such as "a substantial adverse effect upon the applicant's interest" and "impairment of a right or the imposition of obligation" respectively, were rejected by the Court of Justice.[115]

Nevertheless, the Treaty of Lisbon[116] introduced a possibility of instituting proceedings by individuals against "regulatory acts" which are of direct concern to

---

110. Para. 62 in Cases T-236/04 and T-241/04.
111. Para. 56 in Cases T-236/04 and T-241/04.
112. Para. 63 in Cases T-236/04 and T-241/04.
113. Advocate General Jacobs proposed to recognize that an applicant is individually concerned by a Community measures where the measure has, or is liable to have, a substantial adverse effect on his interests. In his opinion:

> there are no compelling reasons to read into the notion of "individual concern" a requirement that an individual applicant seeking to challenge a general measure must be differentiated from all others affected by it in the same way as the addressee' (par. 59 of the opinion). In par. 45-48 he observed: "There is no compelling reason to read into the notion of individual concern, within the meaning of the fourth paragraph of Article 230 EC, a requirement that an individual applicant seeking to challenge a general measure must be differentiated from all others affected by it in the same way as an addressee. In those circumstances, and having regard to the fact that the Treaty established a complete system of legal remedies and procedures designed to permit the Community judicature to review the legality of measures adopted by the institutions, the strict interpretation, applied until now, of the notion of a person individually concerned according to the fourth paragraph of Article 230 EC, must be reconsidered. Consequently, in order to ensure effective judicial protection for individuals, a natural or legal person is to be regarded as individually concerned by a Community measure of general application that concerns him directly if the measure in question affects his legal position, in a manner which is both definite and immediate, by restricting his rights or by imposing obligations on him. The number and position of other persons who are likewise affected by the measure, or who may be so, are of no relevance in that regard."

114. ECLI:EU:T:2002:112.
115. See C-50/00 P *UPA*, ECLI:EU:C:2002:462, C-263/02 P *Jégo-Quéré*, ECLI:EU:C:2004:210.
116. Still, even the intergovernmental conference which led to the Amsterdam Treaty acknowledged that "it may be asked, however, whether the right to bring an action under Art. 173 of the EC Treaty (presently Art. 263 of the TFEU), which individuals enjoy only in regard to acts of direct and individual concern to them, is sufficient to guarantee for them effective judicial protection

them and which do not entail implementing measures.[117] However, this new notion raised many doubts as it was not defined anywhere in the Treaty, nor was it referred to in any other provision. The CJEU explained that the concept of "regulatory act" provided for in the fourth paragraph of Article 263 of the TFEU did not encompass legislative act, i.e. regulations, directives and decisions adopted by legislative procedure (Article 289 (1) of the TFEU).[118]

Although this new complaint possibility awoke hopes for a broader inclusion of individuals in proceedings issued to the CJEU against the EU acts of law,[119] the sad ascertainment must be the fact that it changed hardly anything. In order to bring an action against a regulatory act, it still needs to be of "direct concern" to the complainant and, as mentioned in the previous paragraphs, the understanding of this condition has not really changed for years. Moreover, the implementing measures are common in the EU acts of law dealing with the public good.[120] For instance, a great part of the EU environmental measures is adopted in the form of directives, which, regardless of their legislative or nonlegislative nature, by definition entail implementing measures.[121] Additionally, all decisions which are adopted by legislative procedure constitute "legislative acts" and cannot, therefore, be challenged under the new wording in Article 263 of the TFEU.[122] That is why no NGO has yet been granted standing under Article 263 of the TFEU against decisions or other acts of law not addressed directly to

against possible infringements of their fundamental rights arising from the legislative activity of the institutions." (see M. Andenas, F. Jacobs, *European Community Law in English Courts*, Oxford 1998, p. 20).

117. For specific definition of "act which does not entail implementing measures" see C-456/13 P *T&L Sugars Ltd*, ECLI:EU:C:2015:284. According to the CJEU, this expression seems to include any measure that gives effect or only applies a regulatory act at the EU or national level, irrespective of whether the implementing authority enjoys any discretion on the content of that measure; for more see R. Mastroianni, A. Pezza, *Striking...*, p. 761.
118. C-583/11 P *Inuit Tapiriit Kanatami and Others*, ECLI:EU:C:2013:625, para. 61, T-382/15 *Greenpeace Energy and Others v. Commission*, ECLI:EU:T:2016:589, para. 148.
119. See e.g. A. Türk, *Judicial Review in EU Law*, London 2009, pp. 167-169.
120. For instance, where regulations and decisions are used in the environmental field, they tend to entail a considerable number of implementing measures such as the designation of national competent authorities, the issuing of permits by national authorities and the monitoring of respect for the provisions by the national authorities; see M. Eliantonio, *Towards...*, p. 82. Moreover, the broad interpretation adopted by the CJEU in Case C-456/13 P for the term "implementing measure" in most cases prevents individuals from challenging EU acts that are detrimental to their interests; see R. Mastroianni, A. Pezza, *Striking...*, p. 761. Furthermore, as Advocate General Wathelet pointed out in his Opinion delivered in Case C-132/12 P *Stichting Woonpunt v. Commission*, ECLI:EU:C:2013:335, even simple formalities, such as a publication, notification, confirmation or recall, even if merely optional, might be considered "implementing measures" and therefore obstruct individuals' direct access to the European Courts.
121. M. Eliantonio, *Towards...*, p. 82.
122. Furthermore, in the case of adoption by way of a nonlegislative procedure, many decisions could still not be challenged in court under Art. 263 of the TFEU, because they would either not qualify as regulatory acts because of a lack of general application, or because they need implementing measures at the EU or Member State level; for more see M. Eliantonio, *Towards...*, p. 82.

them.[123] As it will be further discussed, this strict interpretation of *locus standi* conditions before the CJEU has not even been altered after the implementation of the Aarhus Convention.

In the discussed proceedings against acts of the EU law instituted by NGOs, the argumentation of the Commission was largely oriented at the interpretation of the principle of judicial protection. Therefore, it argued that this rule did not enter into play every time an individual seeks to challenge an act of general application directly before the EU judicature. Respectively, according to the Commission, the Treaty has established a complete system of remedies which enables individuals to challenge acts of general application through proceedings before national courts (which may request preliminary rulings from the CJEU). Moreover, where rules of national law, exceptionally, prevent an individual from challenging a measure of general application before the national courts or from obtaining a preliminary ruling from the CJEU on the alleged illegality of that measure, the solution is not to modify the system of remedies laid down in the Treaty, or to adopt a *contra legem* interpretation of Article 263 of the TFEU but to change those rules of national law in order to ensure that the principle of effective judicial protection is respected and that the Member State in question complies with its duty of cooperation.[124]

Although this argumentation may appear convincing, it still seems that the principle of effective judicial protection requires that applicants have access to a court which is competent to grant remedies capable of protecting them against the effect of unlawful measures. National courts, in particular, are not competent to declare measures of the EU law invalid.[125] Moreover, while the system of judicial review in the national courts of Member States and the requests for preliminary ruling are a significant element for ensuring consistent application and proper implementation of the EU law in Member States, it cannot be a basis for generally denying members of the public access to the EU Courts to challenge decisions, acts and omissions by EU institutions and bodies.[126]

As it can be seen, the reasoning of the CJEU makes it practically impossible for NGOs to bring actions in the collective interest as the understanding of "direct and individual concern" under the Plaumann test is very strict. As for now, there appear to be no chances to loosen this attitude, following at least some of the arguments

123. Apart from the discussed cases, actions were dismissed in e.g.: C-583/11 P *Inuit Tapiriit Kanatami and Others*, T-382/15 *Greenpeace Energy and Others v. Commission*, ECLI-:EU:T:2016:589, T-670/14 *Milchindustrie-Verband eV, Deutshcer Raiffeisenverband eV v. European Commission*, ECLI:EU:T:2015:906, T-296/12 *The Health Food Manufacturers' Associations and Others v. European Commission*, ECLI:EU:T:2015:375, T-334/12 *Plantavis GmbH, NEM, Verband mittelständischer europäischer Hersteller und Distributoren von Nahrungsergänzungsmitteln & Gesundheitsprodukten eV v. European Commission*, ECLI:EU:T:2015:376, T-381/11 *Europäischer Wirtschaftsverband der Eisen- und Stahlindustrie (Eurofer) ASBL v. European Commission*, ECLI:EU:T:2012:273, T-296/12 *The Health Food Manufacturers' Association and Others v. European Commission*, ECLI:EU:T:2015:375.

124. See e.g. paras. 28-31 in C-50/00 P.

125. See paras. 41-44 of the opinion of Advocate General Jacobs in C-50/00 P.

126. See the Aarhus Convention compliance case ACCC/C/2008/32 (European Union).

presented above. Therefore, the only certain possibility for an NGO to launch proceedings before the CJEU is the case when it is a direct addressee of the contested act of law.[127] Nevertheless, decisions addressed to NGOs are extremely rare.[128]

The foregoing conclusion leads to the need for searching other remedies for NGOs at the EU level.

[2] Actions for Failure to Act

An individual can also bring an action to the CJEU on the grounds of Article 265 paragraph 3 of the TFEU. Accordingly, any natural or legal person may, under the conditions laid down in the preceding paragraphs,[129] complain to the Court that an institution, body, office or agency of the Union has failed to address to that person any act other than a recommendation or an opinion.

According to the settled case law, the action for failure to act against an EU institution or body can be brought to the CJEU only by an individual who would be directly and individually concerned by the act of law which was not issued against an existing legal obligation.[130] In other words, an individual may bring proceedings before the CJEU under Article 265 paragraph 3 of the TFEU only for a reason that an institution has declined, in breach of the EU law, to adopt the decision of which those persons are the potential addressees or which they could challenge in annulment proceedings according to Article 263 of the TFEU.[131]

As a result, NGOs acting as advocates of the collective interest cannot successfully bring an action for failure to act against the EU institutions or bodies. In any case, they would have to prove that if the institution issued the act of law, they would be directly and individually concerned with it. This is why, although there is no statistics concerning the actual use of the discussed provision by NGOs, it can be assumed that the practical significance of this remedy for the third sector organizations is even more limited than Article 263 of the TFEU. Thus, the formal requirements and the actual proceedings before the CJEU will not be further examined.

127. M. Pallemaerts, *Access...*, p. 293.
128. See e.g. M. Pallemaerts, *Access...*, p. 294.
129. I.e., should the European Parliament, the European Council, the Council, the Commission or the European Central Bank, in infringement of the Treaties, fail to act, the Member States and the other institutions of the Union may bring an action before the Court of Justice of the European Union to have the infringement established. This Article shall apply, under the same conditions, to bodies, offices and agencies of the Union which fail to act. The action shall be admissible only if the institution, body, office or agency concerned has first been called upon to act. If, within two months of being so called upon, the institution, body, office or agency concerned has not defined its position, the action may be brought within a further period of two months.
130. See e.g. 15/70 *Chevalley v. Commission*, ECLI:EU:C:1970:109, para. 6, T-395/04 *Air One v. Commission*, ECLI:EU:T:2006:123, para. 25.
131. T-13/94 *Century Oils Hellas v. Commission* (ECLI:EU:T:1994:77), paras. 13 and 14, T-191/00 *Edlinger v.. Commission*, ECLI:EU:T:2001:183, para. 20, T-334/02 *VSTKSAP v. Commission*, ECLI:EU:T:2003:323, para. 44, See also K. Scheuring, *Komentarz do art. 265* in: *Traktat... t. III.*, lex.pl.

[3] Complaints to the Commission

According to Article 17 (1) *in principio* of the TEU, the Commission shall promote the general interest of the Union and take appropriate initiatives to that end. It shall ensure the application of the Treaties and of measures adopted by the institutions pursuant to them. It shall oversee the application of Union law under the control of the Court of Justice of the European Union. Within this context, Article 258 of the TFEU defines the role of the Commission as "the guardian of the Treaties." Thus, it is obliged to control the execution of the EU law by Member States and undertake actions against infringements. Accordingly, if the Commission considers that a Member State has failed to fulfill an obligation under the Treaties, it shall deliver a reasoned opinion on the matter after giving the state concerned the opportunity to submit its observations.[132] If the state concerned does not comply with the opinion within the period laid down by the Commission, the latter may bring the matter before the CFEU.[133]

Infringements may be detected by the Commission's own investigations or brought to its attention by complaints from members of the public, including NGOs. If the complaint is admissible and feasible, the Commission can initiate the "EU Pilot"[134] procedure within the administrative phase. At this stage, the complainant has certain prerogatives which will be discussed in the following paragraphs. Yet, this part of analysis will not concentrate on the judicial phase of infringement proceedings as, in essence, the possible role of NGOs is not different from any other proceedings before the CJEU, as it was discussed in the previous chapter.

The prerogatives of complainants at the administrative phase of infringement proceedings were not regulated for a long time. This deficiency was the basis for the European Ombudsman own-initiative inquiry of October 13, 1997.[135] By recalling the principle of good administration, the Ombudsman encouraged the Commission to develop procedural rights applicable to complainants under the provision of Article 258 of the TEC (presently Article 263 of the TFEU) without, however, reducing its established margin of discretion in infringement proceedings. Consecutive expectations were published by the European Ombudsman in 2001.[136] An individual informed the Commission about a possible breach of the Community (EU) public procurement law in the case concerning the Metro project in Thessaloniki, Greece. The Ombudsman acknowledged that the Commission did not provide the complainant with adequate reasons for its decisions to close the file and give him a fair opportunity to be heard before the conclusion of the investigation, which was incompatible with the EUChFR and the right of good administration.[137] In consequence, it was argued that a clear and

132. The so-called administrative phase.
133. The so-called judicial phase; for more information see e.g. N. Półtorak, *Komentarz do art. 258* in: *Traktat… t. III*, lex.pl.
134. Which is an informal dialogue between the Commission and the Member State concerned on issues related to potential noncompliance with the EU law, prior to launching a formal infringement procedure. For more information see: http://ec.europa.eu/internal_market/scoreboard/performance_by_governance_tool/eu_pilot/index_en.htm (on February 9, 2019).
135. 303/97/PD.
136. In Case 995/98/OV.
137. Art. 41 of the EUChFR states:

transparent code of procedural provisions in infringement allegations should be adopted, in a manner comparable to the existing acts applicable to, for example, competition actions.[138] In response, the Commission issued a Communication which combined the internal procedural rules regulating the infringement complaints.[139] Presently, these proceedings are described in the Communication of the Commission to the Council and the EP: updating the handling of relations with the complainant in respect of the application of Union Law of April 2, 2012.[140] In fact, this version was amended due to another own initiative of the European Ombudsman.[141] Although this act of law is nonbinding and constitutes nonjusticiable commitments for the Commission, which may be only relied upon before the European Ombudsman (as an example of "maladministration"—a subject matter which will be further discussed in this chapter) and not the CJEU,[142] it still contributed for a better handling of complaints dealing with infringements of the EU law by Member States.[143]

According to the Communication, "complaint" shall mean any written approach made to the Commission pointing to the measures, absence of measure or practices of a Member State contrary to Union law. "Complainant" shall mean any person or body who files a complaint with the Commission.[144] Anyone may file a complaint with the Commission free of charge against a Member State about any measure (law, regulation or administrative action), absence of measure or practice by a Member State which

---

1. Every person has the right to have his or her affairs handled impartially, fairly and within a reasonable time by the institutions and bodies of the Union.
2. This right includes:
   a) the right of every person to be heard, before any individual measure which would affect him or her adversely is taken;
   b) the right of every person to have access to his or her file, while respecting the legitimate interests of confidentiality and of professional and business secrecy;
   c) the obligation of the administration to give reasons for its decisions.
3. Every person has the right to have the Union make good any damaged caused by its institutions or by its servants in the performance of their duties, in accordance with the general principles common to the laws of the Member States.
4. Every person may write to the institutions of the Union in one of the languages of the Treaties and must have an answer in the same language.

138. See Decision of the European Ombudsman on complaint 995/98/OV against the European Commission, available at: https://www.ombudsman.europa.eu/en/cases/decision.faces/en/1088/html.bookmark (on February 9, 2019). In fact, according to Art. 7 (2) of Council Regulation (EC) No 1/2003 of 16 December 2002 on the implementation of the rules on competition laid down in Arts. 81 and 82 of the Treaty (Official Journal L 001, 4.1.2003), natural persons and legal persons who show a legitimate interest can lodge a complaint to the Commission in cases of infringements of the EU competition rules. Such complaints can also be submitted by NGOs.
139. See Commission Communication to the European Parliament and the European Ombudsman on relations with the complainant in respect of infringements of community law (COM(2002) 0141 final), Official Journal 244, 10.10.2002.
140. COM(2012) 154 final,
141. I.e., due to the own-initiative inquiry OI/2/2011/OV of 18 April 2011. For more information see also A. Tsadiras, *Guarding the Guardian: "Article 258 TFEU complaints" Before the European Ombudsman*, International Review of Administrative Sciences Vol. 81/2015, pp. 621-639.
142. In particular, if the Commission does not respond to the complaint, it cannot be subject to an action under Art. 265 of the TFEU; see also K. Scheuring, *Komentarz...*, lex.pl.
143. See e.g. A. Tsadiras, *Guarding...*, p. 638.
144. Para. 1. Definitions and scope.

they consider incompatible with Union law. Complainants do not have to demonstrate a formal interest in bringing proceedings, neither do they have to prove that they are principally and directly concerned by the measure, absence of measure or practice complained of.[145] As a result, there is no need for the complainant to prove any direct or individual concern. This is perfectly understandable as the subject bringing a complaint is not per se a party in the EU Pilot procedure. His task is primarily to inform the Commission about the possible infringement and, if necessary, to provide supplementary data to fully examine the case. Therefore, it is absolutely possible for NGOs to act in the collective interest and bring an action even if they are not by any means affected by the potential infringement of the EU law by a Member State. Moreover, it is conceivable that an NGO informs the Commission about an infringement of a Member State even if it has a registered office in another country.

As a general rule, all complaints brought to the Commission should be registered and duly examined. In order to be registered in the application,[146] complaints must be submitted in writing, by letter, fax or e-mail. They shall be written in one of the official languages of the Union.[147] The Commission provides for a form of a complaint,[148] which can be used to inform about the possible infringement but which is not obligatory. In fact, it is designed for natural persons only as it does not envisage the basic information attributed to legal entities.[149] Still, the introduction of this form should be praised as it seems quite intuitive and does not require any specific legal knowledge to fulfill. In this way, the Commission clearly opens the complaint possibility for a wide range of individuals.

Nevertheless, correspondence shall not be investigable as a complaint by the Commission and shall therefore not be recorded if:

- it is anonymous, fails to show the address of the sender or shows an incomplete address;
- it fails to refer, explicitly or implicitly, to a Member State to which the measures of practice contrary to Union law may be attributed;
- it denounces the acts or omissions of a private person or body unless the measure or complainant reveals the involvement of public authorities or alleges their failure to act in response to these acts or omissions;
- it fails to set out a grievance;
- it sets out a grievance with regard to which the Commission has adopted a clear, public and consistent position, which shall be communicated to the complainant;
- it sets out a grievance which clearly falls outside the scope of Union law.[150]

145. Para. 2. General principles.
146. I.e., in CHAP ("Complaint handling/Accueil des plaignants").
147. Para. 5. Methods of submitting a complaint.
148. Available at: https://ec.europa.eu/info/system/files/complaint-form_en_2.docx; however, a different form in envisaged in cases of state aid complaints (which is available at: http://ec.europa.eu/competition/forms/download_en.html [on February 9, 2019]).
149. I.e., company name or its seat address.
150. Para. 3. Recording of complaints.

As it was pointed out in the doctrine, three issues concerning this list require particular attention.[151] First, the European Ombudsman consistently holds that the grounds justifying nonregistration of infringement complaints is exhaustive.[152] Second, the exception list must be understood restrictively as it constitutes derogations from the general principle of recording all incoming complaints.[153] Third, according to the reasoning of the European Ombudsman, the good administration principle does not necessarily require that registration of infringement correspondence must be completely liberalized and other possible exceptions are not a priori excluded. Therefore, the list can be expanded upon publication in an amended Communication.[154]

The Commission should issue an acknowledgment of all complaints[155] which is a reactive obligation derived from the European Code of Good Administrative Behaviour.[156] In cases where the Commission decides not to register the application, it shall notify the author about that effect and explain its reasons. Consequently, the Commission will also inform the complainant about any possible alternative forms of redress, such as recourse to national courts, the European Ombudsman, a national ombudsman or any other national or international complaints procedure.[157] Although the time frame of 15 days is not binding, the European Ombudsman appears to expect the Commission to communicate the decision of nonregistration "at an early stage" and preferably "when it first responses to the complainant's correspondence."[158]

The Communication also sets a proactive obligation to keep the complainant informed about the undertaken measures and any essential developments during the pending infringement procedure. Accordingly, following registration, a complainant can be examined further in cooperation with the Member State concerned. The Commission will inform the complainant thereof in writing. If subsequently infringement proceedings are launched on the basis of a complaint, the Commission will contact complainants and inform them in writing of each procedural step (formal notice, reasoned opinion, referral to the Court or closure of the case).[159]

As a general rule, the Commission will investigate complaints with a view to arriving at a decision to issue a formal notice or to close the case within not more than one year from the date of registration of the complaint. Where the limit is exceeded, the Commission will inform the complainant in writing upon his request.[160] In the

151. A. Tsadiras, *Guarding...*, pp. 624-625.
152. See e.g. Decision in Case 446/2007/WP.
153. See e.g. Decision in Case OI/3/2009/MHZ.
154. *Ibid.*
155. Still, an interesting finding of the European Ombudsman is that it is willing to abstain from further inquiries if the Commission recognized its failure to respond to the complainant's communication and eventually rectifies its omission. For more details see e.g. Decision in Case 3255/2005/IP.
156. Office for Official Publications of the European Communities, 2000, available at: https://www.ombudsman.europa.eu/en/resources/code.faces#/page/1 (on February 9, 2019); see Art. 14.
157. Para. 4. Acknowledgment of receipt.
158. E.g., Decision in Case 80/2009/BU.
159. Para. 7. Communication with complainants.
160. Para. 8. Time limit for investigating complaints.

European Ombudsman comprehension, the Commission is expected to provide reasonable, adequate and specific explanations for the passage of the prescribed time limit.[161]

After investigating the complaint, the Commission may either issue a formal notice opening proceedings against the Member State in question or close the case definitively. This decision is limited only to the margin of discretion of the Commission.[162] Unless there are exceptional circumstances requiring urgent measures, where it is envisaged that no further action shall be taken on a complaint, the Commission will give the complainant prior notice thereof in a letter setting out the grounds on which it is proposing that the case should be closed and inviting the complainant to submit any comments within a period of four weeks.[163] The Commission's decisions of infringement cases are also published within one week of their adoption on the Secretariat General's Internet site.[164]

Unfortunately, the statistics demonstrate that the complaints to the Commission are used quite rarely and not more 25%-30% of them actually lead to initiating the EU Pilot procedure.[165] It seems that the most significant reason for it is the lack of proper knowledge among the EU citizens and national NGOs. The Commission seldom informs about the discussed complaint possibility in terms of widening participatory democracy in the EU.[166] Still, it seems that NGOs remain an active part among the

161. Factors which can be considered in determining the justified character of the delay include: the size and importance of the file; the factual, legal and technical complexity of the issues involved; the frequency, length and relevance of correspondence and exchange of information between the Commission; the complainants and the Member States concerned; the volume of related complaints and concomitant pressure for prioritization; the onus of translating the requisite documentation; the need to take a uniform approach on the questions raised and solve them simultaneously in all the Member States; the necessity and duration of awaiting the outcome of pending judicial proceedings and legislative processes at the EU and national level. For more information see A. Tsadiras, *Guarding...*, p. 630.
162. Para. 9. Outcome of the investigation of complaints; Still, it is important to note that the evaluation of the European Ombudsman in reference to the Commission's discretion in these cases varies. One the one hand, there are instances where the Ombudsman acknowledged the Commission's latitude of appreciation under Art. 258 of the TFEU. On the other hand, there are cases when the Ombudsman appears to be on the verge of substituting his own judgments for that of the Commission; see also A. Tsadiras, *Guarding...*, p. 634.
163. Para. 10. Closure of the case.
164. Para. 11. Publicising infringement decisions.
165. The number of complaints in the last few years is as follows: 2012—3141, 2013—3505, 2014—3715, 2015—3450, 2016—3783. In 2016 a total of 790 (20%) led to EU Pilot procedure, in 2015—881 (25.5%), in 2014—1208 (32.5%). The subject matter of the complaints is divided thusly: "Other"—948, "Justice and consumers"—919, "Employment"—679, "Internal market, industry, entrepreneurship and SMEs"—483, "Taxation and customs"—406, "Environment"—348. The most common complaints in 2016 were issued against Italy (753), Spain (424) and France (325). There is no specific information concerning the number of complaints brought by NGOs. For more details see Report from the Commission. Monitoring the application of European Union law 2016 Annual Report Brussels, 6.7.2017 COM(2017) 370 final.
166. See K.L. Scheppele, *Enforcing the Basic Principles of EU Law Through Systemic Infringement Actions* in: *Reinforcing Rule of Law Oversight in the European Union* C. Closa, D. Kochenov (eds), New Jersey 2016, pp. 129-130.

complainants[167] as their complaints concerning alleged breach of EU law are often well organized and thoroughly discussed by the public opinion.[168]

Furthermore, environmental issues seem to attract much attention of the European Ombudsman in its dealings with individual infringement complaints brought to the Commission. The conducted inquiries complaints resulted in three draft recommendation and one special report of the European Ombudsman.[169] The conclusions underlined the readiness of the Ombudsman to treat grievances in the area of law where the EU Courts are limited due to considerable *locus standi* restraints in a forceful manner.[170]

As it was apparent in this part of analysis, the issues of complaint possibilities to the Commission and complaints to the European Ombudsman often interpenetrate. The main reason for this is that any failure to act from the Commission's side cannot be a basis of proceedings before the CJEU. Yet, as it was also noticeable, the influence of the European Ombudsman may be quite significant in improving relations between individuals and the EU institutions.[171] Hence, complaints to the Ombudsman should be presented in a more detailed way.

[4] Complaints to the European Ombudsman

The European Ombudsman was established in the Maastricht Treaty[172] in order to oversee the cases of "maladministration" of the EU institutions and bodies, excluding the CJEU when acting in its judicial role. According to Article 228 (1) of the TFEU, a European Ombudsman, elected by the European Parliament, shall be empowered to receive complaints from any citizen of the Union or any legal person residing or having its registered office in a Member State concerning instances of maladministration in the activities of the Union institutions, offices or agencies, with the exception of the Court of Justice of the European Union acting in its judicial role. He or she shall examine such complaints and report on them. In accordance with his duties, the Ombudsman shall conduct inquiries for which he finds groups, either on his own initiative or on the basis of complaints submitted to him directly or through a Member of the European Parliament, except where the alleged facts are or have been subject of legal proceedings. Where the Ombudsman establishes an instance of maladministration, he shall refer the matter to the institution, body, office or agency concerned, which shall have a period of three months in which to inform him of its views. The Ombudsman shall

167. Even though there is no official statistics dealing with this subject matter.
168. As an example see a joint complaint of numerous NGOs in the Białowieza Forest District Case, available at: http://bit.do/ej8VN (on February 9, 2019).
169. A. Tsadiras, *Guarding...*, p. 636.
170. C. Harlow, *Citizen Access to Political Power in the European Union*, Working Paper No. 2, European University Institute 1999.
171. P. Kostandinova, *Improving...*, pp. 1089-1090.
172. For the grounds of establishing the European Ombudsman in the EU system see e.g. K. Heede, *European Ombudsman: Redress and Control and the Union Level*, The Hague 2002, pp. 10-16. However, the EP addressed the concept already in 1979 when it adopted a resolution on the appointment of a "Community Ombudsman"; for more see L.C. Reif, *The Ombudsman, Good Governance and the International Human Rights System*, Dordrecht 2004, p. 371.

then forward a report to the European Parliament and the institution, body, office or agency concerned. The person lodging the complaint shall be informed of the outcome of such inquiries. The Ombudsman shall submit an annual report to the European Parliament on the outcome of his inquiries.

The European Ombudsman deals with cases of "maladministration" of the EU institutions or bodies. In contrast, he cannot investigate complaints against institutions and authorities of Member States (national, regional or local), even if they relate to matters of application of the EU law. In practice, if appropriate, the European Ombudsman refers such complaints to a national ombudsman.[173] As far as the notion of "maladministration" is concerned, the office of the Ombudsman describes it as "poor or failed administration. This occurs if an institution fails to act in accordance with the law, fails to respect the principles of good administration or violates human rights. Some examples are: administrative irregularities, unfairness, discrimination, abuse of power, failure to reply, refusal of information or unnecessary delay."[174]

The procedure of lodging a complaint is outlined in Decision of the EP on the regulations and general conditions governing the performance of the Ombudsman's duties[175] (later referred to as "the European Ombudsman's Statute"). According to its Article 2, the complaint must allow the person lodging the complaint and the object of the complaint to be identified. The person lodging the complaint may request that his complaint remain confidential. A complaint shall be made within two years of the date on which the facts on which it is based came to the attention of the person lodging the complaint and must be preceded by the appropriate administrative approaches to the institutions and bodies concerned. The Ombudsman may advise the person lodging the complaint to address it to another authority.

Naturally, a complaint can be brought by an NGO, as long as it resides or has its registered office in a Member State. Unlike in the CJEU procedures and likewise the infringement procedures within the Commission, a complainant does not need to present any individual or direct concern by the alleged maladministration in order to successfully lodge a complaint to the European Ombudsman. Therefore, in bringing complaints to the European Ombudsman, NGOs can act freely in the collective interest. In fact, the Ombudsman regularly underlines the importance of NGOs in pointing out possible instances of maladministration in the EU institutions.[176]

173. L. C. Reif, *The Ombudsman...*, p. 375. See also, to this extent, Art. 5 (1) of the European Ombudsman's Statute.
174. See: http://bit.do/ej8XH (on February 9, 2019).
175. Adopted by Parliament on March 9, 1994 (Official Journal L 113, 4.5.1994) and amended by its decisions of 14 March 2002 (Official Journal L 92, 9.4.2002) and 18 June 2008 (Official Journal L 189, 17.7.2008).
176. See the Ombudsman's press release of 28.1.2008, "NGOs can help EU institutions do their job better," available at: https://www.ombudsman.europa.eu/en/press/release.faces/en/236/html.bookmark (on February 9, 2019).

According to the European Ombudsman's Internet site,[177] complaints can be sent by mail or e-mail. A paper form and an electronic form are available online.[178] Although both of them are very easy to follow and they require even less information than the forms provided by the Commission in the infringement procedure,[179] the paper form is available only to natural persons.[180] Still, the forms are not obligatory and complaints can be brought in any other written forms, as long as they contain basic information about the alleged maladministration.

According to Article 2 (6) of the European Ombudsman's Statute, complaints submitted to the Ombudsman shall not affect time limits for appeals in administrative or judicial proceedings. Thus, although there is a clear border between the proceedings carried out by the European Ombudsman and the judicial processes, a complainant can still take the matter to the CJEU or other tribunals as long as this route is taken after the complaint is heard by the Ombudsman and not beforehand.[181] Still, it is important to remember that the Ombudsman cannot intervene in cases before the courts (both before the CJEU and other national or international courts or tribunals) and cannot question the soundness of a court ruling.[182]

The Ombudsman shall, as soon as possible, inform the person lodging the complaint of the action he has taken on it (Article 2 (9) of the European Ombudsman's Statute). However, this action can consist of various steps. Usually, after the complaint is deemed admissible, the Ombudsman informs the institution or body concerned and asks it to give a preliminary opinion on the matter. When this opinion is received, a copy is normally sent to the complainant who can comment on it. After that, the Ombudsman either decides to continue the investigation as there is preliminary evidence of maladministration or closes the inquiry. In fact, the European Ombudsman developed an informal practice of encouraging the concerned institution or body to try to reach a settlement directly with the complainant.[183] However, if there has been no informal resolution and practices of maladministration have been found out, the Ombudsman usually examines the possibility of a "friendly" solution with the institution or body to end the maladministration and satisfy the complainant.[184] In this matter, the Ombudsman may submit a proposal for such a settlement which is often accepted. If this settlement is not obtained, the case can be closed due to the fact that there is no feasible manner of correcting the maladministration and it has no general

177. See: https://www.ombudsman.europa.eu/atyourservice/couldhehelpyou.faces#howtocomplain (on February 9, 2019).
178. See: https://www.ombudsman.europa.eu/atyourservice/interactiveguide.faces (on February 9, 2019).
179. The complaint form provided by the European Ombudsman consists of just two pages.
180. As it does not envisage information concerning, e.g. company name or its seat address.
181. L. C. Reif, *The Ombudsman...*, p. 376.
182. N. Vogiatzis, *The European Ombudsman and Good Administration in the European Union*, London 2017, p. 50.
183. L. C. Reif, *The Ombudsman...*, p. 377.
184. *Ibid.*

implication. Otherwise, the Ombudsman can make a report with draft recommendations. The institution or body concerned is then required to respond within three months with a detailed opinion.[185]

Although the EU institutions and bodies are not obliged to follow the recommendations issued by the European Ombudsman (since he has no "strict" competences to, for example, impose sanctions), recurrent accidents of similar cases of maladministration can lead to launching a further investigation, followed by a special report addressed to the EP. In typical cases, the European Ombudsman can encourage the EU institutions to ameliorate their internal modes of administration in two ways. First, he can issue critical remarks with specific recommendations. Second, he can follow up the cases where critical remarks were made and investigate if the particular institution complied with them.[186]

As far as practice is concerned, it can be noted that a steady number of about 1,500-2,100 complaints are brought to the European Ombudsman each year.[187] In 2017, there were 2,181 complaints[188] and 433 inquiries[189] were opened on the basis of complaints.[190] The most common subject matters raised in the complaints include:[191]

(1) failure to obtain access to documents,[192]
(2) transparency in EU decision-making,[193]
(3) the execution of the Commission's function as a "guardian of the Treaties,"
(4) the way of admitting funding, tenders and grants,
(5) issues of hiring and human resource management.

This list depicts a valid statement—the complaint to the European Ombudsman is indeed a consequence of the strict understanding of *locus standi* preconditions under Article 263 of the TFEU. The first four issues are particularly relevant to NGOs acting as

185. See also Art. 3 (1)—(8) of the European Ombudsman Statute.
186. P. Kostandinova, *Improving...*, p. 1082.
187. However, this tendency has been recently on the increase. I.e. in 2017 there were 2,181 complaints; in 2016—1,169; in 2015—1,239; in 2014—1,427; in 2013—1,665; in 2012—1,720; for more information see European Ombudsman. Annual Report 2017 (available at: https://www.ombudsman.europa.eu/en/annual/en/94827 [on February 9, 2019]), p. 34.
188. Most from Spain—410, Germany—234, Poland—144, France—124; for more information see European Ombudsman..., p. 26.
189. I.e., 19.8% of all complaints.
190. A total of 14 inquiries were the own initiative of the European Ombudsman; see European Ombudsman..., p. 34.
191. See P. Kostandinova, *Improving...*, pp. 1087-1088. See also European Ombudsman..., pp. 7-18.
192. The amount of complaints concerning access to documents resulted in launching a "fast-track" procedure in February 2018. Under the new system the European Ombudsman will be able to take a decision within two months of receiving the complaint. Access to documents decisions can be prioritized in this way as—unlike other complaints alleging maladministration—the institution will in general have already fully outlined its reasons for its decision when the Ombudsman receives the complaint.

For more information see Ombudsman launches "fast-track" complaint procedure for access to documents, Press release No 3/2018 of 3.2.2018, available at: https://www.ombudsman.europa.eu/press/release.faces/en/89910/html.bookmark [on February 9, 2019].
193. See also P. Teffer, *Transparency Complaints Keep the EU Ombudsman Busy*, available at: https://euobserver.com/institutional/138003 (on February 9, 2019).

advocates of the collective interest at the EU level as in this way they can correct administration practices of the EU institutions without having to prove any direct or individual concern. Actually, in the matter of access to documents, some NGOs often choose to lodge a complaint to the European Ombudsman instead of bringing an action before the CJEU as the former case may be successfully resolved much sooner.[194]

[5] Contractual and Noncontractual Liability of the EU

In some cases, NGOs can claim compensation for contractual and noncontractual damages which they suffered from the conduct of the EU institutions. However, in order to do so, they need to be affected by the damage directly. Therefore, they cannot bring an action to redress public damages.

The EU institutions and bodies can conclude contracts which give rise to liability on the part of the Union. However, the CJEU does not always have jurisdiction in disputes arising from these contracts. An action for damages can be brought before the CJEU only if a prorogation clause provides so. In other words, the contract to which the EU is a party must contain a clause providing for the jurisdiction of the CJEU in the event of a dispute. In the absence of such a clause, the national courts will have jurisdiction in disputes arising from the contract.[195] As far as NGOs are concerned, this form of liability can theoretically occur for instance in cases of dispute resolutions related to grant contracts.[196]

Nevertheless, the EU is obliged to compensate for damage for which it is responsible, even if it was not related to any contract. Such damage may, for example, be caused by a servant of the EU in the performance of their duties. It may also result from the legislative activities of the EU institutions. The noncontractual liability of the EU complies with uniform rules which have been developed by the case law of the CJEU.[197] Actions may be brought by individuals (and Member States) who have suffered damage and wish to obtain compensation. The deadline for acting is five years from the date on which the damage occurred. The actions brought by individuals are examined by the General Court.[198]

The CJEU shall recognize the liability of the EU when three conditions are met:

194. B. Driessen, *Transparency...*, pp. 141 et seq.
195. Cf. Art. 272 of the TFEU.
196. Cf. Art. 201 (2) (i) and (j) of the "Financial Regulation" (which will be discussed in the fifth chapter). According to these provisions, the grant agreement should at least include i.a. the applicable law which shall be Union law, complemented, where necessary, by national law and the choice of the competent court or arbitration tribunal to hear disputes.

   Cf. also Art. 40 (4) of General Conditions for Service Contracts for External Actions Financed by the European Union or by the European Development Fund (available at: http://bit.do/ej83o [on February 9, 2019]):

   If the amicable settlement procedure and, if so requested, the conciliation procedure fails, each party may refer the dispute to the decision of either a national jurisdiction or arbitration, as specified in the Special Conditions.
197. See e.g. C-6/90 and C-9/90 *Francovich*, ECLI:EU:C:1991:428, C-46/93 *Brasserie du Pêcheur*, ECLI:EU:C:1996:79.
198. Cf. Art. 256 (1) of the TFEU.

(1) the claimant has suffered damage,
(2) the EU institutions or their agents have acted illegally under the EU law,
(3) there is a direct and causal link between the damage suffered by the claimant and the illegal act of the European institutions or their agents.[199]

Nevertheless, the nature of relations between the EU institutions and NGOs results in a rare number of noncontractual liability of the EU.[200] It seems that one of the sparse cases of such an opportunity is when an NGO is a direct addressee of an act of the EU law.[201]

As it has already been notified in the remarks dealing with the complaint possibilities at national level, an NGO cannot claim compensation for a public damage, for example inflicted to the environment. The reason for this statement is that an organization cannot directly prove that it suffered an individual damage.[202] Therefore, there is no causal link and according to the premises of the settled case law such an action would have to be dismissed.[203]

[6] Other Possibilities

The above discussed legal institutions do not exhaust the full list of actual complaint possibilities for NGOs at the EU level. Other opportunities of advocating for the public interest by the representatives of civil society include:

(1) Petitions to the EP—which may present either an individual request, a complaint or observation concerning the EU law or an appeal to adopt a position on a specific matter.[204] Thus, a complaint is just one of the possible contents of a petition as this institution forms a broader mechanism of dialogue between the EP and the EU citizens. That is why this instrument has already been discussed in Chapter 3 as an example of the relations between the EU institutions and European civil society.
(2) "Lighten the load"—allows to send comments to the Commission[205] about existing EU rules and initiatives. Selected comments are then forwarded to the REFIT platform (Regulatory Fitness and Performance Program), which was established in 2015. The aim of REFIT is to simplify EU law, remove unnecessary burdens and adapt existing legislation without compromising

199. See e.g. C-198/03 P *CEVA Santé Animale*, ECLI:EU:C:2005:445.
200. See e.g. C-331/05 P *Internationaler Hilfsfonds eV*, ECLI:EU:C:2007:390.
201. Cf. A.-K. Lindblom, *Non-Governmental...*, p. 264.
202. See e.g. J.H. Jans, H.H.B. Vedder, *European Environmental...*, p. 208, N. Półtorak, *Odpowiedzialność...*, p. 248
203. Yet, different arguments are also presented in the doctrine; for more see e.g. B. Iwańska, *Koncepcja...*, p. 532.
204. See e.g. http://www.europarl.europa.eu/atyourservice/en/20150201PVL00037/Petitions (available on February 9, 2019].
205. Via the form available at: https://ec.europa.eu/info/law/better-regulation/lighten-load/suggestions/add (on February 12, 2019).

policy objectives.[206] The European Commission annually presents an overview of the results of the simplification measures. Although the platform is partly composed of the representatives of civil society (i.e., members of the EESC), REFIT focuses mainly on simplifying legislation in the area of entrepreneurship.[207] What is more, the REFIT recommendations are purely advisory and have no direct impact on the EU legislation.

(3) Interventions within the proceedings conducted by the CJEU—which, obviously, do not constitute a direct complaint institution but are rather a legal form of presenting views in cases which can be relevant to the public interest. It can also be treated by NGOs as a substitute of taking a direct part in the proceedings before the CJEU as a complainant, due to the strict interpretation of Article 263 of the TFEU.[208] Still, interventions, just like petitions to the EP, should be treated as a means of dialogue with the representatives of the European civil society and, therefore, they have also been thoroughly discussed in Chapter 3.

(4) Nonlegal actions,[209] understood as public campaigns (including those launched online), social movements,[210] petitioning[211] and other means of influencing both the EU institutions and the European public opinion[212] in order to advocate for matters important for the collective interest[213] or, more generally speaking, to bring substantial issues to the EU agenda.[214] Although these mechanisms can be very beneficial,[215] their nature is entirely factual and not legal. That is why this book does not cover these instruments of social lobbying.[216]

206. For more information see: https://ec.europa.eu/info/law/law-making-process/evaluating-and-improving-existing-laws/refit-making-eu-law-simpler-and-less-costly/refit-platform_en (on February 12, 2019).
207. According to the annual reports available at: https://bit.ly/2KjEuBA (on February 9, 2019).
208. See R. Mastroianni, A. Pezza, *Striking...*, pp. 778-779.
209. Which may, however, include quasi-legal measures like presenting position papers in the public discussion; for an example see: http://bit.do/egYAX.
210. Including also, e.g. demonstrations, blockages or sabotages; see, to this extent, e.g. D. Glasberg, D. Shannon, *Political Sociology: Oppression, Resistance and the State*, Thousand Oaks 2011, pp. 149-153.
211. Including online petitioning, "capable of swiftly mobilising millions of citizens to pressure decision-makers on matters as diverse as trade agreements, civil liberties, and consumer issues," see A. Alemanno, *Lobbying...*, pp. 6-12.
212. E.g., by "naming and shaming." See, to this extent, J.C. Franklin, *Human Rights Naming and Shaming: International and Domestic Processes* in: *The Politics of Leverage in International Relations. Name, Shame and Sanction*, H.R. Friman (ed.), London 2015, pp. 43 et seq.
213. See e.g. A. Prakash, M.K. Gugerly, *Advocacy Organizations and Collective Action: An Introduction* in: *Advocacy Organizations and Collective Action*, A. Prakash, M.K. Gugerly (eds), Cambridge 2010, pp. 1-28.
214. See e.g. S. Breiteneder, *Power to Grassroots! Die Ablehnung des ACTA-Abkommes durch das Europaische Parlament*, in: *Lobbying in der Europäischen Union. Zwischen Professionalisierung und Regulierung*, D. Dialer, M. Richter (eds), Wiesbaden 2014, pp. 113 et seq.
215. See e.g. A. Alemanno, *Lobbying...*, London 2017, pp. 68-105.
216. For more information see e.g. A. Alemanno, *Lobbying...*, pp. 106 et seq., E. Chamlee-Wright, V.H. Storr, *Social Capital, Lobbying and Community-Based Interest Groups*, Public Choice Vol. 10/2011, pp. 149-167.

[7] *Summary*

Noticeably, the complaint possibilities available for NGOs at the EU level seem quite narrow. Of course, the third sector organizations may use all the legal instruments available to individuals in order to exert their individual rights. However, the paths for bringing actions in the collective interest are seemingly reduced. This assertion can be expressed on the grounds of the strict understanding of Article 263 of the TFEU which makes it nearly impossible to bring an action in the collective interest as the complainant must always prove the premises of individual and direct concern.[217] This leaves a significantly wide range of the EU acts of law outside the judiciary control of the CJEU because there is hardly any individual and direct addressee. Of course, the "privileged" applicants[218] can bring actions against any acts of law but, still, it would be beneficial to somehow involve the social dimension of judiciary control more deeply, for instance, by extending the *locus standi* on the interested NGOs. Therefore, the arguments put forward by the applicants in the *Greenpeace* case should be reconsidered. However, it seems that the loosening of the understanding of Article 263 of the TFEU could be quite problematic without the Treaties being modified.[219]

This is the reason why the other complaint opportunities—to the Commission and the European Ombudsman—should not be neglected. Clearly, these measures are not substitutes for judicial proceedings as their nature is "soft" in principle. Moreover, the complainant is rather an "informant" on the possible breaches of the EU law and is not a direct party in the consecutive procedures. Still, both of these instruments are well organized and make a valuable contribution to the engagement of NGOs as public advocates at the EU level. Furthermore, once a proceeding is started, an organization gains an essential "partner" in controlling the Member States or other EU institutions. Undoubtedly, the institutional position and actual power of both the Commission and the European Ombudsman are incomparably stronger than those of individual organizations. As a result, it should be highly recommended to all actors acting at the EU level to make use of these complaint possibilities as often as possible.

§4.02 THE AARHUS CONVENTION AND THE SPECIAL ROLE OF NGOs IN ENVIRONMENTAL PROTECTION

The Aarhus Convention was signed on June 25, 1998, and entered into force on October 30, 2001.[220] The EU has been a party to the Convention since May 2005.[221] The

217. With exception of the cases where members of the NGO are each individually concerned by the contested act of law.
218. I.e., Member States, the EP, the Council and the Commission; cf. Art. 263 para. 2 of the TFEU.
219. M. von Wolferen, *The Limits...*, p. 930. However, according to a different argument: "nothing in Article 263 suggests that if an applicant is to prove individual concern vis-à-vis a measure of general application, then the person needs to prove that he is differentiated from all other persons in the same way as an addressee. In other words, the Plaumann formula is not contained in the Treaties, but is the European Courts' interpretation of the phrase 'individual concern'"; see M. Eliantonio, *Towards...*, p. 80.
220. See: http://ec.europa.eu/environment/aarhus/ (on February 9, 2019).

agreement establishes a number of rights of the public (including individuals and NGOs) with regard to environmental protection. The parties to the Convention are required to make the necessary provision so that public authorities will contribute to these rights to become effective.[222]

The core of the Aarhus Convention is the need to preserve the environment which is understood as a public and common good.[223] The doctrine evaluates the Aarhus Convention as the most comprehensive and ambitious effort to establish international legal standards in the field of individual environmental rights to date and an instrument which has had a considerable impact on national systems of environmental law and administrative practices in many countries of Europe and beyond, as well as at the level of the institutions of the EU.[224] Respectively, the ultimate aim of the Convention is to increase the openness and democratic legitimacy of government policies on environmental protection and to develop "responsible environmental citizenship." The latter notion can be described as a way of deepening the awareness of the citizens by giving them the means to access information, to assert their interest by participating in the decision-making process, to monitor the decisions of the public bodies and to take legal actions to protect their environment.[225] As a result, the Aarhus Convention improves the environmental democracy which demands the government to be more transparent, accountable and involving people in decisions that affect the quality of their lives and the environment.[226] Whereas the Convention states sustainable development as one of its primary goals,[227] the broad acknowledgment of public participation is legitimated by extending the aim of environmental assessment beyond the usual approach of a cost-benefit analysis tool to be used in conjunction with instruments of the positive economy.[228] In this sphere, the Aarhus Implementation

221. On the grounds of the Council Decision No 2005/370/EC of 17 February 2005 on the conclusion, on behalf of the European Community, of the Convention on access to information, public participation in decision-making and access to justice in environmental matters, Official Journal L 124, 17.5.2005.
222. See: http://ec.europa.eu/environment/aarhus/ (on February 9, 2019).
223. For further details see B. Iwańska, *Koncepcja...*, Warsaw 2013, ss. 37 et seq. See also J.B. Quilligan, *Why Distinguish Common Goods from Public Goods?* in: *Wealth of the Commons. A World Beyond Market & State*, D. Bollier, S. Helfrich (eds), Amherst 2012, pp. 45-48.
224. M. Pallemaerts, *Introduction* in *Aarhus Convention at Ten. Interactions and Tensions between Conventional International Law and EU Environmental Law*, M Pallemaerts (ed.), Groningen 2011, p. 3.
225. *Ibid.*, p. 4.
226. G. Bándi, *The Three Pillars of Environmental Democracy in a European Perspective* in: *Environmental Democracy and Law*, G. Bándi (ed.), Groningen 2014, pp. 39-44, M. Mason, *Environmental Democracy: A Conceptual Approach*, Abingdon 1999, pp. 21-23; see also D. Weaver, *The Aarhus Convention and Process Cosmopolitanism*, International Environmental Agreements: Politics, Law and Economics 2017, pp. 1-15, S. Jodoin, S. Duyck, K. Lofts, *Public Participation and Climate Governance: An Introduction*, Review of European, Comparative & International Environmental Law Vol. 24/2015, pp. 117-122.
227. In its Art. 3 (3).
228. F. La Camera, *Economy, Ecology and Environmental Democracy* in: *Aarhus Convention at Ten. Interactions and Tensions between Conventional International Law and EU Environmental Law*, M Pallemaerts (ed.), Groningen 2011, p. 27.

Guide[229] notes that "there is no set formula for public participation, but at a minimum it requires effective notice, adequate information, proper procedures and appropriately taking account of the outcome of the public participation. The level of public involvement in a particular process depends on a number of factors, including the expected outcome, its scope, who and how many will be affected, whether the result settles on a national, region or local level, and so on. In addition, different persons may have different status in connection with participation on a particular matter."[230]

A general assumption of the Aarhus Convention can be encapsulated in a statement that the environment cannot defend itself but needs to be represented, for example, by active citizens or NGOs.[231] This is the ground for conferring certain rights to the public concerned with environmental issues. The parties to the Convention voiced this special role of the representatives of civil society as in the preamble they refer to the further recognition of the importance of the respective roles that individual citizens, nongovernmental organizations and the private sector can play in the environmental protection[232] and to the concern that effective judicial mechanisms should be accessible to the public, including organizations, so that its legitimate interests are protected and the law is enforced.[233]

The Convention distinguishes the notions of "the public" and "the public concerned." While the former one means one or more natural or legal persons, and, in accordance with national legislation or practice, their associations, organizations or groups (Article 2 (4), the latter one means the public affected or likely to be affected by, or having an interest in, the environmental decision-making; for the purposes of this definition, nongovernmental organizations promoting environmental protection and meeting any requirements under national law shall be deemed to have an interest (Article 2 (5)). As it will be demonstrated in the following paragraphs, some of the rights established by the Convention are attributed especially to "the public concerned." Moreover, as a general principle, each party shall provide for appropriate recognition of and support to associations, organizations or groups promoting environmental protection and ensure that its national legal system is consistent with this obligation (Article 3 (4)).

229. Available at: https://www.unece.org/env/pp/implementation_guide.html; However, according to the CJEU (see, to this extent, C-182/10 *Marie-Noëlle Solvay and Others v. Région wallonne*, ECLI:EU:C:2012:82), "it is permissible to take the Implementation Guide for that Convention into consideration, but that Guide has no binding force and does not have the normative effect of the provisions of that Convention." Also, while that guide may be regarded as an explanatory document, which may be taken into consideration, if appropriate, along with other relevant material for the purpose of interpreting the Aarhus Convention, the indications contained therein have no binding force and do not have the normative effect of the provisions of that Convention (C-673/13 P *European Commission v. Stichting Greenpeace and PAN Europe*, ECLI:EU:C:2016:889, para. 59; see also C-279/12 *Fish Legal and Shirley*, EU:C:2013:853, para. 38 and the case law cited).

230. Implementation Guide, p. 119.

231. Opinion of Advocate General Kokott in C-260/11 *The Queen, on the application of David Edwards and Lilian Pallikaropoulos v. Environment Agency and Others*, ECLI:EU:C:2012:645, para. 42.

232. See the Preamble to the Convention.

233. *Ibid.*

The Aarhus Convention is based on three pillars:[234]

(1) the right to environmental information—the right of everyone to receive environmental information that is held by public authorities. This includes information on the state of the environment but also on policies or measures taken or on the state of human health and safety where this can be affected by the state of the environment. Applicants are entitled to obtain this information within one month of the request and without having to say why they require it. In addition, public authorities are obliged to actively disseminate environmental information to their possession;[235]
(2) the right of public participation in environmental decision-making—provides for arrangements by public authorities to make the public affected and environmental NGOs to comment, for example, on proposals for projects affecting the environment or plans and programs relating to the environment and take the comments into due account in decision-making, as well as information is to be provided on the final decisions and the reasons for it;[236]
(3) the right of access to justice—the right to review procedures to challenge public decisions that have been made without respecting the two aforementioned rights of environmental law in general.[237]

The subsequent parts of this chapter will focus on the detailed presentation of these pillars and their implementation in the EU legal system. Unfortunately, there is no general, uniform regulation or directive dealing with the transposition of the Aarhus Convention at the national level. In contrast, there is a relatively diverse set of conditions, articulated in various acts of law.[238] Furthermore, the implementation of the Aarhus Convention at the EU level is not complete. Consequently, many difficulties arise therefrom.

[A] Access to Environmental Information

According to Article 2 (3) of the Convention, "environmental information" means any information in written, visual, aural, electronic or any other form on:

(a) the state of elements of the environment, such as air and atmosphere, water, soil, land, landscape and natural sites, biological diversity and its components, including genetically modified organisms and the interaction among these elements;
(b) factors, such as substances, energy, noise and radiation, and activities or measure, including administrative measures, environmental agreements,

234. See: http://ec.europa.eu/environment/aarhus/ (on February 9, 2019).
235. Arts. 4-5 of the Convention.
236. Arts. 6-8 of the Convention.
237. Art. 9 of the Convention.
238. G. Bándi, *The Three...*, p. 56.

policies, legislation, plans and programs,[239] affecting or likely to affect the elements of the environment listed above, and cost-benefit and other economic analyzes and assumptions used in environmental decision-making;

(c) the state of human health and safety, conditions of human life, cultural sites and built structures, inasmuch as they are or may be affected by the state of the elements of the environment or, through these elements, by the factors or measures referred to above.

In this sphere, according to Article 4 (1), each Party shall ensure that, subject to the following paragraphs of this article,[240] public authorities, in response to a request for environmental information, make such information available to the public, within the framework of national legislation, including, where requested and subject to subparagraph (b) below, copies of the actual documentation containing or comprising such information:

(a) without an interest having to be stated;
(b) in the form requested unless:
   (i) it is reasonable for the public authorities to make it available in another form, in which case reasons shall be given for making it available in that form; or
   (ii) the information is already publicly available in another form.

Access to environmental information is not unconditional and is subject to certain exceptions laid down in the Convention. For the purposes of this chapter, these exemptions will be divided into "formal" and "substantive." Thus, whereas the first ones do not require an in-depth material analysis of the request, the latter ones demand such an investigation.

The "formal" exceptions are envisaged in Article 4 (3) of the Convention. Accordingly, a request for environmental information may be refused if:

(a) the public authority to which the request is addressed does not hold the environmental information requested;
(b) the request is manifestly unreasonable or formulated in too general a manner; or
(c) the request concerns material in the course of completion or concerns internal communications of public authorities where such an exemption is provided for in national law or customary practice, taking into account the public interest served by disclosure.

239. According to the CJEU, the notion "plans and programmes" can cover normative acts adopted by law or regulation (see C-290/15 *Patrice D'Oultremont and Others v. Région wallonne*, ECLI:EU:C:2016:816, para. 52).

240. In particular, the environmental information referred to in para. 1 above shall be made available as soon as possible and at the latest within one month after the request has been submitted, unless the volume and the complexity of the information justify an extension of this period up to two months after the request. The applicant shall be informed of any extension and of the reasons justifying it (Art. 4 (2)).

Article 4 (4) of the Convention regulates the "substantive" exemptions of access to environmental information. Respectively, a request for environmental information might be refused if the disclosure adversely affected:

(a) the confidentiality of the proceedings of public authorities, where such confidentiality is provided for under national law;
(b) international relations, national defense or public security;
(c) the course of justice, the ability of a person to receive a fair trial or the ability of a public authority to conduct an inquiry of a criminal or disciplinary nature;
(d) the confidentiality of commercial and industrial information, where such confidentiality is protected by law in order to protect a legitimate economic interest. Within this framework, information on emissions which is relevant for the protection of the environment shall be disclosed;
(e) intellectual property rights;
(f) the confidentiality of personal data and/or files relating to a natural person where that person has not consented to the disclosure of the information to the public, where such confidentiality is provided for in national law;
(g) the interests of a third party which has supplied the information requested without that party being under or capable of being put under a legal obligation to do so and where that party does not consent to the release of the material; or
(h) the environment to which the information relates, such as the breeding sites of rare species.

The aforementioned grounds for refusal shall be interpreted in a restrictive way, taking into account the public interest served by disclosure and taking into account whether the information requested relates to emissions into the environment.

The notion "may" used in the above-presented catalogs means that the exemptions are not obligatory. Thus, the states, while implementing the Convention to their legal systems, can limit the possible exceptions of access to environmental information to only some of the cases mentioned in the catalogs.[241] In contrast, they cannot establish new exemptions, which are not envisaged in Article 4 (3) and (4) of the Convention.

The Convention also deals with the duty of dissemination of environmental information. Consequently, according to Article 5 (2), each Party shall ensure that, within the framework of national legislation, the way in which public authoritarian make environmental information available to the public is transparent and that it is effectively available.[242] Pursuant to Article 5 (5), the dissemination should particularly apply to:

241. For more see e.g. R. Hallo, *Access to Environmental Information. The Reciprocal Influences of EU Law and the Aarhus Convention* in: *Aarhus Convention at Ten. Interactions and Tensions between Conventional International Law and EU Environmental Law*, M Pallemaerts (ed.), Groningen 2011, pp. 63-65.
242. I.a., by:

(a) legislation and policy documents, such as documents on strategies, policies, programs and action plans relating to the environment, and progress reports on their implementation, prepared at various levels of government;
(b) international treaties, conventions and agreements on environmental issues; and
(c) other significant international documents on environmental issues, as appropriate.

Moreover, according to Article 5 (3), each Party shall ensure that environmental information progressively becomes available in electronic databases which are easily accessible to the public through telecommunication networks.

[1] National Level

It is said[243] that the first pillar of the Aarhus Convention was heavily influenced by Council Directive 90/313/EEC of June 7, 1990, on the freedom of access to information on the environment.[244] After the implementation of the Convention by the EU and its Member States, it was replaced by Directive 2003/4/EC of the EP and of the Council of January 28, 2003, on public access to environmental information and repealing Council Directive 90/313/EEC.[245] Moreover, it should be mentioned that apart from the Aarhus Convention, access to environmental information in some Member States[246] is also regulated by the Council of Europe Convention on Access to Official Documents,[247] which, however, was not ratified by the EU as a whole.

The environmental documents at national level are made available upon request. According to Article 3 (1) of Directive 2003/4, Member States shall ensure that public authorities are required, in accordance with the provisions of the Directive, to make

---

(a) providing sufficient information to the public about the type and scope of environmental information held by the relevant public authorities, the basic terms and conditions under which such information is made available and accessible, and the process by which it can be obtained;
(b) establishing and maintaining practical arrangements, such as:
  (i) publicly accessible lists, registers or files;
  (ii) requiring officials to support the public in seeking access to information under this Convention; and
  (iii) the identification of points of contact; and
(c) providing access to the environmental information contained in lists, registers or files as referred to in subparagraph (b) (i) above free of charge.

243. For more see e.g. G. Bándi, *The Three...*, pp. 56 et seq.
244. Official Journal L 158, 23.6.1990.
245. Official Journal L 156, 25.6.2003; Moreover, some directives directly refer to the provisions of Directive 2003/4. For instance, see Art. 6 (3) of Directive 2011/92/EU of the European Parliament and of the Council of 13 December 2011 on the assessment of the effects of certain public and private projects on the environment Text with EEA relevance, Official Journal L 26, 28.1.2012.
246. I.e., in Belgium, Estonia, Finland, Hungary, Lithuania, Slovenia and Sweden (as at February 9, 2019).
247. CETS No 205, available at: https://www.coe.int/en/web/conventions/full-list/-/conventions/treaty/205 (on February 9, 2019).

available environmental information held by or for them to any applicant at his request and without his having to state an interest. Apparently, this provision makes it very easy for the advocates of public interest to request for documents concerning environmental issues.

Pursuant to Article 3 (2) the timescale for reply is set out as follows:

(a) as soon as possible or, at the latest, within one month of the receipt of the request by the public authority;
(b) within two months after the receipt of the request by the public authority if the volume and the complexity of the information is such that one-month period cannot be complied with. In such cases, the applicant shall be informed as soon as possible, and in any case before the end of the one-month period, of any such extension and reasons for it.

In general, the request should be free of charge (Article 5 (1) of Directive 2003/4). However, according to Article 5 (2), public authorities may make a charge for supplying any environmental information but such charge shall not exceed a reasonable amount.[248]

Article 4 of the Directive reflects the "formal" (paragraph (1)) and the "substantive" (paragraph (2)) exceptions to access to environmental information envisaged in the Aarhus Convention, although some premises were subject to minor clarifications.[249] The Directive also deploys the requirement of dissemination of environmental

248. A charge which does not exceed a reasonable amount within the meaning of Art. 5(2) of Directive 2003/4 is a charge which:

(i) is set on the basis of objective factors that are known and capable of review by a third party;
(ii) is calculated regardless of who is asking for the information and for what purpose;
(iii) is set at a level that guarantees the objectives of the right of access to environmental information upon request and thus does not dissuade people from seeking access or restrict their right of access; and
(iv) is no greater than an amount that is appropriate to the reason why Member States are allowed to make this charge (i.e., that a member of the public has made a request for the supply of environmental information) and directly correlated to the act of supplying that information.

In particular, a charge of a "reasonable amount" under Art. 5(2) of Directive 2003/4 is to be based on the costs actually incurred in connection with the act of supplying environmental information in response to a specific request. That will include the costs of staff time spent on searching for and producing the information requested and the cost of producing it in the form requested (which may vary). However, it is not permissible for such a charge also to seek to recover overheads such as heating, lighting or internal services. While part of such overheads might indeed be attributable to the process of putting in place the conditions that enable an authority to give access to environmental information upon request, they (like the costs of maintaining and giving access to registers and lists of environmental information) are not incurred solely in connection with the supply of information in response to a specific request (C-71/14 *East Sussex County Council v. Information Commissioner*, ECLI:EU:C:2015:656, paras. 27-45).

249. I.e., Art. 4 (2) (d) of the Directive adds "including the public interest in maintaining statistical confidentiality and tax secrecy" to "the confidentiality of commercial or industrial information

information.[250] Furthermore, Article 8 (1) establishes the "quality principle." Thus, Member States shall, as far as it is within their power, ensure that any information, which is compiled by them or on their behalf, is up to date, accurate and comparable.

In its Article 6, the Directive also establishes appeal procedures, both administrative and judiciary. Hence, Member States shall ensure that any applicant who considers that his request for information has been ignored, wrongfully refused (whether in full or in part), inadequately answered or otherwise unlawfully dealt with, has access to a procedure in which the acts or omissions of the public authority concerned can be reconsidered by that or another public authority or reviewed administratively by an independent and impartial body established by law. Any such procedure shall be expeditious and either free of charge or inexpensive. In addition, Member States shall ensure that an applicant has access to a review procedure before a court of law or another independent and impartial body established by law, in which the acts or omissions of the public authority concerned can be reviewed and whose decisions may become final. Member States may furthermore provide that third parties incriminated by the disclosure of information may also have access to legal recourse.

It seems that the scope of access to environmental information at national level is very wide.[251] In practice, however, there were many problems with the implementation of Directive 2003/4[252] and with the interpretation of its certain provisions.[253] Still,

---

where such confidentiality is provided for by national or Community law to protect a legitimate economic interest" laid down in the Convention.

250. According to Art. 7 (1) *in principio*, Member States shall take the necessary measures to ensure that public authorities organize the environmental information which is relevant to their functions and which is held by or for them, with a view to its active and systematic dissemination to the public, in particular by means of computer telecommunication and/or electronic technology, where available. According to Art. 7 (2), the information to be made available and disseminated shall be updated as appropriate and shall include at least:
    (a) texts of international treaties, conventions or agreements, and of Community (the EU), national, regional or local legislation, on the environment or relating to it;
    (b) policies, plans and programs relating to the environment;
    (c) progress reports on the implementation of the items referred to in (a) and (b) when prepared or held in electronic form by public authorities;
    (d) the reports on the state of the environment;
    (e) data or summaries of data derived from the monitoring of activities affecting, or likely to affect, the environment;
    (f) authorizations with a significant impact on the environment and environmental agreements or a reference to the place where such information can be requested or found;
    (g) environmental impact studies and risk assessments concerning the environmental elements referred.
251. For more see e.g. P. Szkudlarek, *Prawo do informacji w konwencji z Aarhus*, Kwartalnik Prawa Publicznego Vol. 3/2003, pp. 175 et seq.
252. For instance, infringement proceeding was initiated on this ground against Poland; for more information (including arguments of the Commission) see e.g. B. Draniewicz, *Uprawnienia organizacji ekologicznych w postępowaniach wymagających udziału społeczeństwa*, Monitor Prawniczy Vol. 1/2011, pp. 13-16.
253. For example, in the German judicature it was noticed that the system introduced by the Directive does not envisage a far-reaching protection of confidential information. In case of information which can be considered as business secret, it is assumed that there is a justified interest of the company in nondiffusion of the information concerning restricted knowledge in the field of technology and commerce. Furthermore, the ministry during the legislative procedure is released from the duty of giving proper information to the public; for more see W.

the transposition of the first pillar of the Aarhus Convention to the legal systems of EU Member States undoubtedly contributed to the growth of NGOs significance.[254] This improvement was perhaps not solely grounded on access to information per se but also on the reinforcement of this right with an accessible review procedure. These two interpenetrating prerogatives contributed to an increasingly proactive role of the third sector actors in the distribution of environmental information which is often vitally important to the local or national communities. Nevertheless, it should be also emphasized that access to environmental information is often misused by commercial entities and "bogus" organizations.[255]

[2] EU Level

The first pillar of the Aarhus Convention is generally implemented at the EU level by the already discussed Regulation 1049/2001 regarding public access to EP, Council and Commission documents. In fact, Article 3 of Regulation (EC) No 1367/2006 of the EP and of the Council of 6 September 2006 on the application of the provisions of the Aarhus Convention on Access to Information, Public Participation in Decision-Making and Access to Justice in Environmental Matters to Community institution and bodies[256] states that Regulation 1049/2001 shall apply to any request by an applicant for access to environmental information held by Community (EU) institutions and bodies without discrimination as to citizenship, nationality or domicile and, in the case of a legal person, without discrimination as to where it has its registered seat or an effective center of its activities. This means that the general provisions on access to the EU documents by NGOs apply to the first pillar of the Aarhus Convention as well. Most importantly, the EU documents dealing with environmental issues are made available upon request.[257] Moreover, Regulation 1367/2006 also envisages special provisions on collection and dissemination of environmental information.[258] The disseminated information should be very easily reproducible and accessible by computer

Durner, *Obowiązek informacyjny w niemieckim prawie ochrony środowiska* (supplementary to Monitor Prawniczy Vol. 21/2013, pp. 37-38).

254. E.g. B. Draniewicz, *Uprawnienia...*, pp. 12 et seq.
255. As the research conducted in 2006 in the Environmental Protection Inspectorate in Cologne (Germany) indicates, about 80% of all request were really motivated by "industrial espionage" and not by environmental protection; for more see W. Durner, *Obowiązek...*, p. 38.
256. Official Journal L 264, 25.9.2006.
257. Cf. Art. 3 of Regulation 1367/2006.
258. According to Art. 4 (2), in addition to the documents listed in Art. 12(2) and (3) and in Art. 13(1) and (2) of Regulation (EC) No 1049/2001, the databases or registers shall include the following:
    (a) texts of international treaties, conventions or agreements, and of Community legislation on the environment or relating to it, and of policies, plans and programs relating to the environment;
    (b) progress reports on the implementation of the items referred to under (a) where prepared or held in electronic form by Community institutions or bodies;
    (c) steps taken in proceedings for infringements of Community law from the stage of the reasoned opinion pursuant to Art. 226(1) of the Treaty;
    (d) reports on the state of the environment as referred to in para. 4;

telecommunications or by other electronic means.[259] Also, Article 5 (1) of Regulation 1367/2006 states that Community (EU) institutions and bodies shall, insofar as is within their power, ensure that any information that is compiled by them, or on their behalf, is up-to-date and comparable.

However, there are certain differences between the provisions of Regulation 1049/2001 and the requirements of the Aarhus Convention, particularly as far as the allowed exceptions are concerned. It appears that the exemptions provided in Regulation 1049/2001 and the Convention cross over in some cases.[260] Yet, Regulation 1367/2006 does not explain all the differences. According to its Article 6 (1) and (2), as regards Article 4 (2) first and third indents of Regulation 1049/2001,[261] with the exception of investigations, in particular those concerning possible infringements of Community (EU) law, an overriding public interest in disclosure shall be deemed to exist where the information relates to emissions into the environment. As regards the other exceptions set out in Article 4 of Regulation 1049/2001, the grounds for refusal shall be interpreted in a restrictive way, taking into account the public interest served by disclosure and whether the information requested relates to emissions into the environment. In addition to the exceptions set out in Article 4 of Regulation 1049/2001, Community (EU) institutions and bodies may refuse access to environmental information where disclosure of the information would adversely affect the protection of the environment to which the information relates, such as the breeding sites of rare species. Nevertheless, both the CJEU and the EU Ombudsman have found that the practice of the Commission is not always in compliance with the requirements of Regulation 1049/2001 when evaluating requests for environmental information, especially with reference to applying provisions on exceptions to access to documents.[262]

(e) data or summaries of data derived from the monitoring of activities affecting, or likely to affect, the environment;
(f) authorizations with a significant impact on the environment, and environmental agreements, or a reference to the place where such information can be requested or accessed;
(g) environmental impact studies and risk assessments concerning environmental elements, or a reference to the place where such information can be requested or accessed.

259. See Art. 4 (1) para. 3 of Regulation 1367/2006.
260. E.g., in C-60/15 P *Saint-Gobain Glas*, ECLI:EU:C:2017:540, the CJEU stated that Art. 4 (4) (a) of the Aarhus Convention provides that a request for environmental information may be refused where disclosure of that information would adversely affect the confidentiality of the proceedings of public authorities, where such confidentiality is provided for under national law, and not the entire administrative procedure at the end of which those authorities hold their proceedings which is in accordance with Art. 4 (3) of Regulation 1049/2001 (para. 81).
261. I.e., the institutions shall refuse access to a document where disclosure would undermine the protection of: commercial interests of a natural or legal person, including intellectual property and the purpose of inspections, investigations and audits.
262. For example, respecting deadlines or inadequate or too extensive application of refusal reasons, weighing up the interests at stake or a clear demonstration of no overriding public interest when refusing the access to information, see e.g. T-120/10 *ClientEarth, BirLife International v. European Commission*, ECLI:EU:T:2011:646, T-449/10 *ClientEarth and Others v. Commission*, ECLI:EU:T:2011:647, T-362/08 *IFAW Internationaler Tierschutz-Fonds gGmbH v. European Commission*, ECLI:EU:T:2011:6, T-36/04 *Association de la presse internationale ASBL (API) v. Commission of the European Communities*, ECLI:EU:T:2007:258; see also E. Kružíková, *Implementation of Public Participation Principles. Experience of the EU* in: *Environmental Democracy and Law*, G. Bándi (ed.) Groningen 2014, p. 144, see also S. Wolf, *Access to EU*

The compatibility between the exceptions set out in Regulation 1049/2001 and the Aarhus Convention was evaluated by the CJEU in the case C-612/13 P *ClientEarth*.[263] ClientEarth, a company limited by guarantee[264] under English law, one of whose objects is protection of the environment, claimed that Article 4 (1) and (4) (c) of the Aarhus Convention should be directly applicable to the institutions of the EU,[265] even though these exceptions are not directly envisaged by Regulation 1049/2001 as the EU signed the Convention and has to abide its provisions. In general, the CJEU can undertake an examination of the alleged incompatibility of an act of the EU law with the provisions of an international agreement to which the Union is a party only where (1) the nature and the broad logic of that agreement do not preclude it and (2) those provisions appear, as regards to their content, to be unconditional and sufficiently precise.[266] However, the Court of Justice[267] stated that the Regulation makes no express reference to the Aarhus Convention and does not implement a particular obligation stemming from that Convention.[268] Moreover, the reference in Article 4 (1) of the Aarhus Convention to national legislation indicates that this international agreement was manifestly designed with the national legal orders in mind, and not to the specific legal features of institutions of regional and economic integration, such as the EU, even where those institutions can sign and accede to the Aarhus Convention.[269] It is for that reason that the Community (the EU) made a declaration upon signing the Convention, which was annexed to Decision 2005/370. In this declaration, it was stated that "the Community (the EU) institutions will apply the Convention within the framework of their existing and future rules on access to documents and other relevant rule of Community (EU) law in the field covered by the Convention."[270] Therefore, Article 4 (1) and (4) of the Aarhus Convention cannot be put forward in order to assess the legality of Article 4 (2) of Regulation 1049/2001.[271]

The main thesis deriving from this judgment can be summed up that Regulation 1049/2001 is not fully compatible with the Aarhus Convention because it does not need to be. Article 4 of the Convention is not directly applicable to the EU institutions. Still, it should be recalled that the case law of the CJEU recognized that the exceptions to the right of access to documents must be always interpreted and applied strictly. This

Environmental Information: EU compliance with Aarhus Convention, ERA Forum Vol. 14/2013, pp. 475 et seq.

263. ECLI:EU:C:2015:486.
264. An alternative type of corporation in the British and Irish law, used primarily by NGOs that require legal personality; for more see e.g. A. Sienicka, *Formy prawne przedsiębiorstw społecznych w Anglii i Walii*, Ekonomia Społeczna Teksty 2006, pp. 4-5, available at: http://konsultacje.ngo.pl/files/kuj-pom.ngo.pl/public/SES/biblioteka/autorskiesienicka.pdf (on February 9, 2019).
265. Para. 28 in C-612/13 P.
266. See C-344/04 *IATA and ELFAA*, ECLI:EU:C:2006:10, para. 39, C-308/06 *Intertanko and Others*, ECLI:EU:C:2008:312, para. 45, C-366/10 *Air Transport Association of America and Others*, ECLI:EU:C:2011:864, para. 54.
267. Following the reasoning of the General Court in T-111/11, ECLI:EU:T:2013:482.
268. Para. 37 in C-612/13 P.
269. Para. 40 in C-612/13 P.
270. Para. 41 in C-612/13 P.
271. Para. 43 in C-612/13 P.

statement was developed partly by employing the Aarhus Convention in an indirect manner.[272]

These remarks lead to a conclusion that access to environmental information at the EU level is treated like other documents held by the EU institutions. It means that NGOs or other applicants cannot derive any special rights in cases of requests for environmental information. Yet, they can benefit from all the general prerogatives and standards of inquiring the EU documents.

[B] Public Participation in Environmental Decision-Making

It is important to emphasize that the Aarhus public participation pillar relates to administrative acts with potential significant effects on the environment, while it does not cover measures of a legislative nature.[273] It is also fair to say that the Convention provides a framework in which members of the public have more power where they have particularized interests with respect to matters which directly affect their lives and well-being and progressively less direct power and influence as matters become more abstract and general.[274] However, NGOs (especially "environmental" NGOs), as opposed to other legal persons and natural persons, will generally fall into the category of the "public concerned," meaning a larger set of participation prerogatives.[275]

According to Article 6 (2) of the Aarhus Convention, the public concerned shall be informed, either by public notice or individually as appropriate, early in an environmental decision-making procedure, and in an adequate, timely and effective manner, *inter alia*, of:

(a) the proposed activity and the application on which a decision will be taken;
(b) the nature of possible decisions or the draft decision;
(c) the public authority responsible for making the decision;

---

272. See e.g. para. 48 in T-111/11.
273. J. Jendrośka, *Public Participation in Environmental Decision-Making. Interaction Between the Convention and EU Law and Other Key Legal Issues in Its Implementation in the Light of the Opinions of the Aarhus Convention Compliance Committee* in: *Aarhus Convention at Ten. Interactions and Tensions between Conventional International Law and EU Environmental Law*, M Pallemaerts (ed.), Groningen 2011, p. 95..
274. *Ibid.*, p. 97.
275. This statement was properly developed by Advocate General Sharpston in Case C-263/08 *Djurgården*, ECLI:EU:C:2009:421. In her opinion, she affirmed that "unlike natural persons, nongovernmental organizations promoting environmental protection *always* have the status of 'the public concerned' provided that, in accordance with Article 1 (2) [of Directive 85/337/EEC], they comply with 'any requirement under national law'." The root cause of this assertion is that "nongovernmental organizations promoting environmental protection give expression to the collective interest." Because they "represent a number of different parties and interests, they protect general objectives." This gives them the requisite "collective dimension." They also "contribute specialized knowledge which helps to distinguish important cases form cases of lesser significance." They "speak with one voice on behalf of many, with a level of technical specialization which is often not available to the individual. By so doing, they can rationalize the way in which the various conflicting interests are voiced and placed before the authorities" (see paras. 42-65).

(d) the envisaged procedure, including, as and when this information can be provided:
  (i) the commencement of the procedure;
  (ii) the opportunities for the public to participate;
  (iii) the time and venue of any envisaged public hearing;
  (iv) an indication of the public authority from which relevant information can be obtained and where the relevant information has been deposited for examination by the public;
  (v) an indication of the relevant public authority or any other official body to which comments or questions can be submitted and of the time schedule for transmittal of comments or questions; and
  (vi) an indication of what environmental information relevant to the proposed activity is available.

e) the fact that the activity is subject to a national or transboundary environmental impact assessment procedure.

The public participation in the administrative proceedings is stipulated by certain rules. According to them:

- the public participation procedures shall include reasonable time frames for the different phases, allowing sufficient time for informing the public and for the public to prepare and participate effectively during the environmental decision-making (Article 6 (3));
- the public participation should be provided at an early stage when all options are open and effective public participation can take place (Article 6 (4));[276]
- the prospective applicants should be encouraged to identify the public concerned, to enter into discussions and to provide information regarding the objectives of their application before applying for a permit (Article 6 (5));
- the competent public authorities should give to the public concerned access for examination, upon request where so required under national law, free of charge and as soon as it becomes available, to all information relevant to the decision-making (without prejudice to the right of parties to refuse to disclose certain information, Article 6 (6));
- the public is allowed to submit, in writing or, as appropriate, at a public hearing or inquiry with the applicant, any comments, information, analyzes or opinions that it considers relevant to the proposed activity (Article 6 (7));
- in the final decision, due account should be taken of the outcome of the public participation (Article 6 (8));[277]

276. This condition is an attempt to address the problem of public participation coming too late during the decision-making process which is said to be one of the key shortcomings of the traditional mechanisms of public participation. It is also important stress out that he requirement of "early public participation" does apply not only to the entire chain of decision-making procedures but also to each of them. See also J. Jendsośka, *Public...*, pp. 133-135.

277. The requirement of "due account":

- when the decision has been taken by the public authority, the public should be promptly informed of the decision in accordance with the appropriate procedures; the text of the decision along with the reasons and considerations on which the decision is based (Article 6 (9)).

Furthermore, the Convention sets out requirements concerning more general measures of public concern. Thus:

- each Party shall make appropriate practical and/or other provisions for the public to participate during the preparation of plans and programs relating to the environment[278] within a transparent and fair framework, having provided the necessary information to the public (Article 7);[279]
- each Party shall strive to promote effective public participation at an appropriate stage, and while options are still open, during the preparation by public authorities of executive regulations and other generally applicable legally binding rules that may have a significant effect on the environment (Article 8).[280]

In contrast to the first pillar of the Aarhus Convention, the EU law does not adopt a coherent and holistic approach in prescribing the requirements for conducting the EU and national level consultations on environmental issues with interest groups.[281] A rich mosaic of legal solutions in various acts indicates that the requirements arising from the second pillar of the Convention will be presented concisely, focusing mainly on the possible problems of NGO participation in environmental matters.

- does not amount to the right of veto accorded to the public;
- is not meant to give any special status to the local community living nearby the project;
- cannot be considered as a requirement to accept all the comments, reservations or opinions submitted; see e.g. Report of the 24th meeting of the Compliance Committee, ECE/MP.PP/C.1/2009/4, para. 28.

278. According to the doctrine, "it is neither necessary nor possible to provide a rigorous distinction between the plans and programmes"—see J. Jendrośka, *Public...*, p. 115.
279. As confirmed by the Compliance Committee, the "Convention does not establish a precise boundary between Article 6-type decisions and Article 7-type decisions" (ACCC/C/8 (Armenia), para. 28). Therefore, the Committee considers that this must be determined on a conceptual basis, taking into account the legal effect of each decision (ACCC/C/16 (Lithuania), para. 57).
280. To this end, the following steps should be taken:
    (a) Time frames sufficient for effective participation should be fixed;
    (b) Draft rules should be published or otherwise made publicly available; and
    (c) The public should be given the opportunity to comment, directly or through representative consultative bodies.
    The result of the public participation shall be taken into account as far as possible.
281. J. Jendrośka, *Public...*, p. 151. This is perhaps one of the reasons why the right of citizens to participate is often considered a bureaucratic burden that should be reduced. See F. La Camera, *Economy...*, p. 22.

[1] National Level

The public participation pillar of the Aarhus Convention is transposed in the following directives:

(1) Integrated Pollution Prevention and Control Directive (2010/75/EU);[282]
(2) Directive 2003/35/EC providing for public participation in respect of the drawing up of certain plans and programs relating to the environment and amending with regard to public participation and access to justice Council Directives 85/337/EEC and 96/61/EC—Statement by the Commission;[283]
(3) GMO Directive (2001/18/EC);[284]
(4) Strategic Environmental Assessment (SEA) Directive (2001/42/EC);[285]
(5) Emissions Trading Scheme Directive (ETS) (2003/87/EC);[286]

282. According to Art. 4 (1), Member States shall ensure that the public concerned are given early and effective opportunities to participate in the following procedures:
(a) the granting of a permit for new installations;
(b) the granting of a permit for any substantial change;
(c) the granting or updating of a permit for an installation where the application of Art. 15 (4) is proposed;
(d) the updating of a permit or permit conditions for an installation in accordance with Art. 21 (5) (a).
The procedure set out in Annex IV shall apply to such participation.
283. See the added Annex V—Public participation in decision-making in Directive 2003/35/EC.
284. According to Art. 9 (1), Member States shall, without prejudice to the provisions of Arts. 7 and 25, consult the public and, where appropriate, groups on the proposed deliberate release. In doing so, Member States shall lay down arrangements for this consultation, including a reasonable time period, in order to give the public or groups the opportunity to express an opinion.
285. See Art. 6:

> (1) The draft plan or program and the environmental report prepared in accordance with Article 5 shall be made available to the authorities referred to in paragraph 3 of this Article and the public.
> (2) The authorities referred to in paragraph 3 and the public referred to in paragraph 4 shall be given an early and effective opportunity within appropriate time frames to express their opinion on the draft plan or program and the accompanying environmental report before the adoption of the plan or program or its submission to the legislative procedure.
> (3) Member States shall designate the authorities to be consulted which, by reason of their specific environmental responsibilities, are likely to be concerned by the environmental effects of implementing plans and programs.
> (4) Member States shall identify the public for the purposes of paragraph 2, including the public affected or likely to be affected by, or having an interest in, the decision-making subject to this Directive, including relevant nongovernmental organizations, such as those promoting environmental protection and other organizations concerned.
> (5) The detailed arrangements for the information and consultation of the authorities and the public shall be determined by the Member States.

286. According to Art. 15 (1), without prejudice to Council Directive 90/313/EEC of 7 June 1990 on the freedom of access to information on the environment (14), Member States shall take the necessary measures to ensure that applications for permits for new installations or for substantial changes are made available for an appropriate period of time to the public, to enable it to comment on them before the competent authority reaches its decision.

(6) Noise Directive (2002/49/EC);[287]
(7) Habitats Directive (92/43/EEC);[288]
(8) Water Framework Directive (2000/60/EC);[289]
(9) Directive 2011/92/EU on the assessment of the effects of certain public and private projects on the environment;[290]
(10) Directive 2012/18/EU on the control of major accident hazards involving dangerous substances, amending and subsequently repealing Council Directive 96/82/EC.[291]

---

287. According Art. 8 (7), Member States shall ensure that the public is consulted about proposals for action plans, given early and effective opportunities to participate in the preparation and review of the action plans, that the results of that participation are taken into account and that the public is informed on the decisions taken. Reasonable time frames shall be provided allowing sufficient time for each stage of public participation.

 If the obligation to carry out a public participation procedure arises simultaneously from this Directive and any other Community legislation, Member States may provide for joint procedures in order to avoid duplication.

288. According to Art. 22, in implementing the provisions of this Directive, Member States shall: (a) study the desirability of reintroducing species in Annex IV that are native to their territory where this might contribute to their conservation, provided that an investigation, also taking into account experience in other Member States or elsewhere, has established that such reintroduction contributes effectively to reestablishing these species at a favorable conservation status and that it takes place only after proper consultation of the public concerned.

289. See Art. 14:

 (1) Member States shall encourage the active involvement of all interested parties in the implementation of this Directive, in particular in the production, review and updating of the river basin management plans. Member States shall ensure that, for each river basin district, they publish and make available for comments to the public, including users:
 a) a timetable and work program for the production of the plan, including a statement of the consultation measures to be taken, at least three years before the beginning of the period to which the plan refers;
 b) an interim overview of the significant water management issues identified in the river basin, at least two years before the beginning of the period to which the plan refers;
 c) draft copies of the river basin management plan, at least one year before the beginning of the period to which the plan refers.
 On request, access shall be given to background documents and information used for the development of the draft river basin management plan.
 (2) Member States shall allow at least six months to comment in writing on those documents in order to allow active involvement and consultation.

290. According to Art. 6 (4), the public concerned shall be given early and effective opportunities to participate in the environmental decision-making procedures referred to in Art. 2(2) and shall, for that purpose, be entitled to express comments and opinions when all options are open to the competent authority or authorities before the decision on the request for development consent is taken.

 According to Art. 6 (6), reasonable time frames for the different phases shall be provided, allowing sufficient time for informing the public and for the public concerned to prepare and participate effectively in environmental decision-making subject to the provisions of this Article.

291. According to Art. 15:

 1. Member States shall ensure that the public concerned is given an early opportunity to give its opinion on specific individual projects relating to:
 (a) planning for new establishments pursuant to Article 13;

Most of these acts of law have already been mentioned in this chapter as examples of the EU secondary law which admit additional rights to NGOs at national

---

(b) significant modifications to establishments under Article 11, where such modifications are subject to obligations provided for in Article 13;
(c) new developments around establishments where the siting or developments may increase the risk or consequences of a major accident pursuant to Article 13.

2. With regard to the specific individual projects referred to in paragraph 1, the public shall be informed by public notices or other appropriate means, including electronic media where available, of the following matters early in the procedure for the taking of a decision or, at the latest, as soon as the information can reasonably be provided:
(a) the subject of the specific project;
(b) where applicable, the fact that a project is subject to a national or transboundary environmental impact assessment or to consultations between Member States in accordance with Article 14(3);
(c) details of the competent authority responsible for taking the decision, from which relevant information can be obtained and to which comments or questions can be submitted, and details of the time schedule for transmitting comments or questions;
(d) the nature of possible decisions or, where there is one, the draft decision;
(e) an indication of the times and places where, or means by which, the relevant information will be made available;
(f) details of the arrangements for public participation and consultation made pursuant to paragraph 7 of this Article.
3. With regard to the specific individual projects referred to in paragraph 1, Member States shall ensure that, within appropriate time frames, the following is made available to the public concerned:
(a) in accordance with national legislation, the main reports and advice issued to the competent authority at the time when the public concerned was informed pursuant to paragraph 2;
(b) in accordance with the provisions of Directive 2003/4/EC of the European Parliament and of the Council of 28 January 2003 on public access to environmental information, information other than that referred to in paragraph 2 of this Article which is relevant for the decision in question and which only becomes available after the public concerned was informed in accordance with that paragraph.
4. Member States shall ensure that the public concerned is entitled to express comments and opinions to the competent authority before a decision is taken on a specific individual project as referred to in paragraph 1 and that the results of the consultations held pursuant to paragraph 1 are duly taken into account in the taking of a decision.
5. Member States shall ensure that when the relevant decisions are taken, the competent authority shall make available to the public:
(a) the content of the decision and the reasons on which it is based, including any subsequent updates;
(b) the results of the consultations held before the decision was taken and an explanation of how they were taken into account in that decision.
6. Where general plans or programs are being established relating to the matters referred to in points (a) or (c) of paragraph 1, Member States shall ensure that the public is given early and effective opportunities to participate in their preparation and modification or review using the procedures set out in Article 2(2) of Directive 2003/35/EC of the European Parliament and of the Council of 26 May 2003 providing for public participation in respect of the drawing up of certain plans and programs relating to the environment.
Member States shall identify the public entitled to participate for the purposes of this paragraph, including relevant nongovernmental organizations meeting any relevant requirements imposed under national law, such as those promoting environmental protection.
This paragraph shall not apply to plans and programs for which a public participation procedure is carried out under Directive 2001/42/EC.
7. The detailed arrangements for informing the public and consulting the public concerned shall be determined by the Member States.

level.[292] However, as far as the participation conditions are concerned, only a few of the abovementioned directives[293] directly refer to NGOs as "obligatory" partners in the decision-making procedures. Still, in some cases, Member States bear more responsibility for ensuring adequate participation of interest groups in consultations than the EU institutions, even than the Commission.[294] In general, national authorities are required to make special efforts in order to ensure the participation of interest groups in consultations. For instance, Directive 2003/35 instructs Member States to develop detailed arrangements for both informing and consulting the public concerned for the purpose of fulfilling the Aarhus requirements and it stipulates that those arrangements can, for example, take the form of written submissions or public inquiries.[295]

Perhaps the biggest controversy concerning the transposition of the second pillar of the Aarhus Convention in the EU secondary law is the actual number of these acts of law and their differentiation. There is no one environmental participation directive and no set of uniform rules of consultations. The reason for these inconveniences is that many of the environmental directives had been passed earlier than the Aarhus Convention was adopted by the EU. It should be remembered that the EU had been in the vanguard of environmental legislation for years and many provisions of the Aarhus Convention, including those on participation, were based on the already existing standards in the EU law.[296] Moreover, it should also be emphasized that the EU approach to environmental protection is rather branch-oriented and not sectorial, which is obviously linked to the shared competences of the EU in environment.[297] It is why there are many EU acts of law concentrating on the chosen environmental issues and certain provisions on consultation are attached to them. Naturally, in the spheres not encompassed by the EU competences, Member States should envisage their own measures of implementing the second pillar of the Aarhus Convention. Moreover, even in the spheres where the EU law is present, they can introduce a wider scope of participation mechanisms.[298] That said, the existing patchwork of legal solutions leads to many problems in establishing a set of participation requirements at national level. The most important ones are the following:

(1) Some directives (especially the "older" ones) are very laconic. This means that in most cases a great level of flexibility in the scope of implementation is

Reasonable time frames for the different phases shall be provided, allowing sufficient time for informing the public and for the public concerned to prepare and participate effectively in environmental decision-making subject to the provisions of this Article.

292. With the exemption of Directive 2004/35/EC.
293. I.e., Directives 2003/35/EC and 2001/42/EC.
294. D. Obradovic, *EU Rules...*, pp. 163-164.
295. Cf. Art. 6 (5) of the Directive; see also D. Obradovic, *EU Rules...*, p. 154.
296. D. Obradovic, *EU Rules...*, pp. 151-156.
297. *Ibid.*, p. 155.
298. As the Directives very often envisage a minimum standard for participation (referred to "at least").

given to Member States. In practice, this may lead to discrepancies in the privileges of NGOs as participants in the environmental decision-making.[299]

(2) Even where the directives are specific, they are often not coherent between one another. This particularly concerns the approach of setting time frames of public participation.[300]

(3) It is questionable if all of the requirements established in the directives are in accordance with the provisions of the Aarhus Convention. For instance, there are cases of apparent limitations to the participation obligation.[301] Many concerns raised on the grounds of not providing "early participation, when all options are open and effective." In fact, this led to amendments in a few directives.[302]

(4) There is a disparity in promoting proactive attitudes to the environmental protection in general. For instance, the Water Framework Directive not only prescribes the consultation of the public but also requires the Member States to "encourage the active involvement of all interested parties in national decision-making on issues covered by the Directive" (see Article 14 (1)). It seems that such provisions would be beneficial and should be included in other directives as well.

As a result, NGOs willing to take part in the decision-making procedures at national level cannot rely on one EU framework of environmental participation. These sets of standards may differ from one Member State to another. However, although there are voices in the doctrine that recommend the introduction of one directive encompassing the participation methods in all EU-related spheres of environmental law,[303] it seems that in practice it would be hardly possible. Even though some differences in the directives have little explanation,[304] most of them are in fact justified. The decisions taken in various spheres related to environmental issues have different

299. See e.g. J. Ebbesson, *The EU and the Aarhus Convention: Access to Information, Public Participation in Decision-Making and Access to Justice in Environmental Matters*, the EP briefing of June 2016, available at: http://www.europarl.europa.eu/RegData/etudes/BRIE/2016/571357/IPOL_BRI(2016)571357_EN.pdf (on February 9, 2019), pp. 7-8.

300. E.g., according to Art. 14 of the Water Framework Directive, Member States shall allow at least six months to comment in writing on those documents in order to allow active involvement and consultation, while other Directives, for instance the SEA Directive, refers to "appropriate time."

301. E.g., it is questionable what is the character of the wording "where appropriate" in Art. 9 (1) of the GMO Directive (Member States shall, without prejudice to the provisions of Arts. 7 and 25, consult the public and, where appropriate, groups on the proposed deliberate release).

302. See, to this extent, e.g. ACCC/C/17 (European Community). In this case, the communicant alleged "that EIA Directive and IPPC Directive fail to comply with the Convention because they fail to provide for 'early participation, when all options are open and effective public participation can take place' on account of the fact that the participation may take place after the construction has commenced." It further maintained that "any public participation that is envisaged after the construction of an installation can by no means be considered as 'early public participation, when all options are open and effective public participation can take place'" (para. 29).

303. See e.g. D. Obradovic, *EU Rules...*, pp. 182-185.

304. *Ibid.*, pp. 183-184.

impact, affect diverse subjects and require particular proceedings, for instance with reference to issuing prior plans or programs.[305] Accordingly, an "uninformed" set of participation rules would anyway have to be blurred and susceptible to broad interpretation. Therefore, it appears that only the general participation rules[306] in environmental matters could be harmonized in one directive which, as a matter of fact, would still be very advantageous.[307]

[2] EU Level

The second pillar of the Aarhus Convention is implemented at the EU level by Article 9 of Regulation 1367/2006. According to this provision:

(1) Community (EU) institutions and bodies shall provide, through appropriate practical and/or other provisions, early and effective opportunities for the public to participate during the preparation, modification or review of plans or programs relating to the environment when all options are still open. In particular, where the Commission prepares a proposal for such a plan or program which is submitted to other Community institutions or bodies for decision, it shall provide for public participation at that preparatory stage (paragraph (1)).

(2) Community (EU) institutions and bodies shall identify the public affected or likely to be affected by, or having an interest in, a plan or program of the type referred to in paragraph 1, taking into account the objectives of the Regulation (paragraph (2)).

(3) Community (EU) institutions and bodies shall ensure that the public referred to in paragraph (2) is informed, whether by public notices or another appropriate means, such as electronic media where available, of:

  (a) the draft proposal, where available;

  (b) the environmental information or assessment relevant to the plan or program under preparation, where available; and

  (c) practical arrangements for participation, including:
   - the administrative entity from which the relevant information may be obtained;
   - the administrative entity to which comments, opinions or questions may be submitted; and
   - reasonable time frames allowing sufficient time for the public to be informed and to prepare and participate effectively in the environmental decision-making process (paragraph (3)).

305. See e.g. J. Jendrośka, *Obowiązek powiadamiania społeczeństwa w nowych przepisach o ocenie oddziaływania przedsięwzięcia na środowisko*, Prawo i Środowisko Vol. 1/2009, pp. 56-57.
306. I.e., concerning entities that should be informed about the decision-making and documents that should be made available prior to the actual participation.
307. D. Obradovic, *EU Rules...*, p. 185.

(4) A time limit of at least eight weeks shall be set for receiving comments. Where meetings or hearings are organized, prior notice of at least four weeks shall be given. Time limits may be shortened in urgent cases or where the public has already had the opportunity to comment on the plan or program in question (paragraph (4)).
(5) In taking a decision on a plan or program relating to the environment, Community (EU) institutions and bodies shall take due account of the outcome of the public participation. Community (EU) institutions and bodies shall inform the public of that plan or program, including its text, and of the reasons and considerations upon which the decision is based, including information on public participation (paragraph (5)).

A breach of these provisions can comprise an infringement of an essential procedural requirement for the purposes of actions brought before the CJEU under Article 263 of the TFEU[308] or be an example of maladministration and form basis for a complaint to the European Ombudsman. They could also be undermined in the internal review procedure which will be thoroughly discussed in the following paragraphs. The consultations concerning environmental matters with the Commission should also fulfill the General Principles of 2002 and the Guidelines of 2017 which were discussed in the previous chapter. The Commission claims that its objective in instituting the General Principles and the Guidelines was not to establish procedural rights, the respect of which would be subject to judicial control and review[309] and, indeed, it seems that their breach cannot be a direct basis for an action before the CJEU.[310] However, it appears that in environmental matters they should be generally raised in an auxiliary way as they do not vastly differ from the provisions of Regulation 1367/2006. Respectively:

(1) The Regulation, the General Principles and the Guidelines provide an obligation of "early participation" in the decision-making.
(2) Both standards impose an obligation to identify the possible partners in the consultation process. However, the General Principles and the Guidelines form a narrower precondition as they pertain to "target groups"[311] and not to the broader notion of "the public affected."

308. E.g., in some cases, the submission by a relevant party (both a Member State, see e.g. T-432-434/93 *Socurté STEC v. Commission of the European Communities*, ECLI:EU:T:1995:43; and an individual, see e.g. Case 17-74 *Transocean Marine Paint v. Commission*, ECLI-:EU:C:1974:106) of its comments prior to the adoption of the decision can be an essential procedural requirement. If the party is deprived of this right, it can be perceived as an infringement of an essential procedural requirement. See also e.g. K. Lenaerts, I. Maselis, K. Gutman, *EU Procedural...*, pp. 355 et seq., K. Scheuring, *Komentarz...*, lex.pl/el.
309. European Governance: Preparatory Work for the White Paper 2002, Luxembourg 2001, p. 73.
310. Nevertheless, nonbinding acts of law like Communications can, in some cases, be subject to litigation before the CJEU—see e.g. C-366/88, *French Republic v. Commission of the European Communities*, ECLI:EU:C:1990:348, C-325/91, *French Republic v. Commission of the European Communities*, ECLI:EU:C:1993:245, C-57/95 *French Republic v. Commission of the European Communities*, ECLI:EU:C:1997:164.
311. Which are defined as subjects:

(3) The General Principles and the Regulation specify the time frame for consultations as "at least 8 weeks." The Guidelines extend this period to 12 weeks.
(4) The General Principles and the Guidelines do not require to take due account of the outcome of the public participation. However, the Guidelines oblige the Commission to "analyze" the received feedback.
(5) The Regulation and the Guidelines set a requirement of providing the public in an open manner with "consultation documents," e.g. with the draft proposals or other environmental information or assessment relevant to measures under preparation. In matters not related to the environment, this kind of openness often relies on the policy of the specific institution. Working papers can also be acquired on the basis of Regulation 1049/2001.[312]

It occurs that the provisions of Regulation 1367/2006, the General Principles and the Guidelines are alike. However, the Regulation has a binding nature and applies to all EU institutions and bodies. Therefore, the breach of its requirements can be challenged more easily.[313] Also, the Regulation provisions seem easier to follow.[314] These assertions mean that the implementation of the second pillar of the Aarhus Convention at the EU level should be generally evaluated positively, even though it did not change much in the practice of the EU institutions.[315]

[C] Access to Justice

Access to justice is believed to be crucial for environmental protection, as environmental law tends to suffer from an enforcement deficit due to several varying reasons—from the inability to the unwillingness for national governments to implement the legislation in a sufficient manner, and the fact that the majority of environmental law does not confer rights on individuals or NGOs that could be invoked in court.[316] Furthermore, access to justice for members of the public should always be effective, which includes more factors than just standing preconditions. A crucial question in this context is to what they are entitled when they are allowed to challenge an environmental decision in the Court.[317]

- those affected by the policy;
- those who will be involved in implementation of the policy; or
- bodies that have stated objectives giving them a direct interest in the policy.

312. I.e., by requests to the EU documents.
313. Also in complaints to the European Ombudsman (as a case of maladministration).
314. Cf. e.g. L. Hallstrom, *Eurocratising Enlargement? EU Elites and NGO Participation in European Environmental Policy*, Environmental Politics Vol. 13/2004, p. 192, E. Fasoli, *Legal Standing of NGOs in Environmental Disputes in Europe* in: *International Courts and the Development of International Law. Essays in Honour of Tullio Trevez*, N. Boschiero, T. Scovazzi, C. Pitea, Ch. Ragni (eds), The Hague 2013, pp. 346-347.
315. See also, D. Obradovic, *EU Rules...*, pp. 157 et seq.
316. C. Zengerling, *Greening...*, pp. 2 et seq.
317. J. Darpö, *Effective Justice? Synthesis Report of the Study on the Implementation of Articles 9.3 and 9.4 of the Aarhus Convention in the Member States of the European Union*, p. 16, available

The Aarhus Convention reinforces the provisions granted to the public by introducing three different types of remedies. Accordingly:

(1) Each Party shall, within the framework of its national legislation, ensure that any person who considers that his or her request for information under Article 4 has been ignored, wrongfully refused, whether in part or in full, inadequately answered, or otherwise not dealt with in accordance with the provisions of that article, has access to a review procedure before a court of law or another independent body established by law (Article 9 (1)).

(2) Each Party shall, within the framework of its national legislation, ensure that members of the public concerned:

(a) having a sufficient interest; or

(b) alternatively, maintaining impairment of a right, where the administrative procedural of a party requires this as a precondition

have access to a review procedure before a court of law and/or another independent and impartial body established by law, to challenge the substantive and procedural legality of any decision, act or omission subject to the provision of Article 6 and, where so provided for under national law and without prejudice to paragraph (3), of other relevant provision of the Convention.

What constitutes a sufficient interest and impairment of a right shall be determined in accordance with the requirements of national law and consistently with the objective of giving the public concerned wide access to justice within the scope of the Convention.

To this end, the interest of any nongovernmental organization meeting the requirements referred to in Article 2 (5) shall be deemed sufficient for the purpose of subparagraph (a) above. Such organizations shall also be deemed to have rights capable of being impaired for the purpose of subparagraph (b) above.

The provisions of this paragraph shall not exclude the possibility of a preliminary review procedure before an administrative authority and shall not affect the requirement of exhaustion of administrative review procedures prior to recourse to judicial review procedures, where such a requirement exists under national law (Article 9 (2)).

(3) In addition and without prejudice to the review procedures referred to in paragraphs (1) and (2), each Party shall ensure that, where they meet the criteria, if any, laid down in its national law, members of the public have access to administrative or judicial procedures to challenge acts and omissions by private persons and public authorities which contravene provisions of its national law relating to the environment (Article 9 (3)).

---

at: http://ec.europa.eu/environment/aarhus/pdf/synthesis%20report%20on%20access%20to%20justice.pdf (on February 9, 2019).

In short, Article 9 of the Aarhus Convention establishes three types of remedies for members of the public in environmental matters:

(1) to protect access to information rights (in paragraph (1));
(2) to protect public participation rights (in paragraph (2));
(3) to uphold laws related to the environment in general (in paragraph (3)).

The implementation of these complaint possibilities in the EU law raised many difficulties and was not fully executed. The reasons and consequences of this deficiencies will be further discussed in the following paragraphs. In this regard, the direct effect of the Convention will be also considered. Such an effect is possible when, regard being to its wording and to the purpose of the agreement, the provision contains a clear and precise obligation which is not subject, in its implementation or effects, to the adoption of any subsequent measure.[318]

It should be also kept in mind that the implementation of the third pillar of the Aarhus Convention in the EU legal system (especially with reference to the conditions of effective *locus standi*) should be read together with proper Treaty norms on access to justice, i.e. Article 19 (1) of the TEU[319] and Article 47 of the EUChFR,[320] as well as Article 6 of the ECHR.[321]

Article 9 (2) provides standing to those members of the "public concerned" who either have "sufficient interest" or maintain an "impairment of a right." These alternatives are meant to include both the right-based legal systems[322] and those who are interest-based.[323] Still, NGOs have a special status in bringing an action before the

318. See e.g. C-63/99 *Głoszczuk*, ECLI:EU:C:2001:488, para. 30 and C-171/01 *Wählergruppe Gemeinsam*, ECLI:EU:C:2003:260, para. 54.
319. The Court of Justice of the European Union shall include the Court of Justice, the General Court and specialized courts. It shall ensure that in the interpretation and application of the Treaties the law is observed.
Member States shall provide remedies sufficient to ensure effective legal protection in the fields covered by Union law.
320. Everyone whose rights and freedoms guaranteed by the law of the Union are violated has the right to an effective remedy before a tribunal in compliance with the conditions laid down in this Article.
Everyone is entitled to a fair and public hearing within a reasonable time by an independent and impartial tribunal previously established by law.
Everyone shall have the possibility of being advised, defended and represented. Legal aid shall be made available to those who lack sufficient resources in so far as such aid is necessary to ensure effective access to justice.
321. According to Art. 6 of ECHR, everyone has the right to access to national courts to "challenge an act interfering with his rights." As explained by the European Court of Human Rights, such right may be subject to limitations only if they:
(1) do not impair the very essence of the right; and
(2) pursue a legitimate aim in a proportionate manner; see also M. von Wolferen, *The Limits...*, p. 927.
322. I.e., based on the concept of *recours objectif*, see J. Hage, A. Waltermann, B. Akkermans, *Introduction to Law*, Cham 2014, p. 224.
323. I.e., based on the concept of *recours subjectif*, see J. Hage, A. Waltermann, B. Akkermans, *Introduction...*, p. 224.

court (or other equivalent body) under Article 9 (2) as they do not have to prove sufficient interest. The sole indication of the statutory aims should be sufficient for deeming their actions admissible.[324] As it was rightly clarified by Advocate General Sharpston in case C-263/08 *Djurgården-Lilla Värtans Miljöskyddsförening,*[325] "the authors of the Aarhus Convention decided to strengthen the role of nongovernmental organizations promoting environmental protection. That formula was adopted in an attempt to steer a middle course between the maximalist approach of the *actio popularis* and the minimalist idea of the right of an individual action available only to parties having a direct interest at stake. Giving special standing for nongovernmental organizations reconciles these two positions."[326] As a result, the specific role of environmental NGOs shall be taken as a kind of assistance in representing community interests and also as means and methods to channel public opinion and public knowledge, even in the judicial procedures.[327]

In contrast to Article 9 (2), Article 9 (3) provides standing to those "members of the public" which meet the criteria established in national law. This wording theoretically allows for an institution of *actio popularis*, even though the Aarhus Convention does not expressly require such a solution.[328] Neither does it require abstract norm control, a procedural solution which is quite common in the EU Member States.[329]

Consequently, the Aarhus Convention sets up the environment as a public good that should be protected by mechanisms of the objective legal order. Thus, the established complaint possibilities should be considered as "altruistic,"[330] "fiduciary"[331] and part of the wider issue of public interest litigation (PIL).[332]

The Aarhus Convention also provides effectiveness measures, certain facilitations and information requirements concerning access to justice. Therefore:

(1) The procedures referred to in paragraphs (1), (2) and (3) shall provide adequate and effective remedies, including injunctive reliefs as appropriate,

324. J. Darpö, *Effective...*, p. 14.
325. ECLI:EU:C:2009:631.
326. Para. 63 of the opinion in C-263/08.
327. G. Bándi, *The Three...*, p. 8.
328. See e.g. Commission recommendation "on common principles for injunctive and compensatory collective redress mechanisms in the Member States concerning violations of rights granted under Union Law" C(2013) 3539, available at: http://ec.europa.eu/justice/newsroom/civil/news/130611_en.htm (on February 9, 2019).
329. Even though the possibility of abstract norm control exists in many Member States, it cannot be regarded generally as a requirement under EU law—or required by the European Convention of Human Rights for that matter (see, to this extent, e.g. judgments of the European Court of Human Rights in cases *Norris v. Ireland, Klass v. Germany* or *Västberga taxi v. Sweden*).
330. B. Iwańska, *Koncepcja...*, p. 350, see also Ch. Calliess, *Europäische Vorgaben für die umweltrechtliche Verbandsklage* EurUP 2003, p. 12.
331. B. Iwańska *Koncepcja...*, p. 346.
332. See e.g. M.M. Kenig-Witkowska, *Międzynarodowe prawo ochrony środowiska*, Warsaw 2011, pp. 76 et seq., L. Krämer, *Public Interest Litigation in Environmental Matters Before European Courts*, Journal of Environmental Law Vol. 8/1996, pp. 13-14; see also S. Cummings, L. Trubek, *Globalizing Public Interest Law*, UCLA Journal of International Law and Foreign Affairs Vol. 13/2008, pp. 8-10, C. Halpern, J. Cunningham, *Reflections on the New Public Interest Law: Theory and Practice at the Center for Law and Social Policy*, Georgetown Law Journal Vol. 59/1995, pp. 1095-1116.

and be fair, equitable, timely and not prohibitively expensive. Decisions under this Article shall be given or recorded in writing. Decisions of courts, and whenever possible of other bodies, shall be publicly accessible (Article 9 (4)).

(2) In order to further the effectiveness of the provisions of this Article, each Party shall ensure that information is provided to the public on access to administrative and judicial review procedures and shall consider the establishment of appropriate assistance mechanism to remove or reduce financial and other barriers to access to justice (Article 9 (5)).

(3) Each Party shall endeavor to ensure that officials and authorities assist and provide guidance to the public in seeking access to information, in facilitating participation in decision-making and in seeking access to justice in environmental matters (Article 3 (2)).

Furthermore, the Convention provides the third sector organizations with certain *quasi-instruments* of access to justice at the international level which are described in the doctrine as PIL-like litigation methods.[333] Respectively, NGOs may take part as observers in the meetings of the parties of the Aarhus Convention (Article 10 (5))[334] or can decide to report the violation of their Aarhus rights before the Aarhus Convention Compliance Committee.[335] Accordingly, the parties regularly address issues of compliance, on the basis of the Committee's reports. At the Committee's recommendation, they adopt decisions on general issues of compliance and also decisions on compliance by individual parties. The compliance mechanism may be triggered in four ways:

(1) a party may make a submission about compliance by another party,
(2) a party may make a submission concerning its own compliance,
(3) the secretariat may make a referral to the Committee,
(4) members of the public may make communications concerning a party's compliance with the Convention.[336]

333. See e.g. Ch. Schall, *Public Interest Litigation Concerning Environmental Matters Before Human Rights Courts: A Promising Future Concept?*, Journal of Environmental Law Vol. 20/2008, p. 451.

334. According to Art. 10 (5), any nongovernmental organization, qualified in the fields to which this Convention relates, which has informed the Executive Secretary of the Economic Commission for Europe of its wish to be represented at a meeting of the parties shall be entitled to participate as an observer unless at least one-third of the parties present in the meeting raise objections.

335. Art. 15 of the Aarhus Convention on review of compliance requires the Meeting of the Parties to establish "optional arrangements of a non-confrontational, non-judicial and consultative nature for reviewing compliance with the provisions of the Convention." Following this obligation, the Meeting of the Signatories established a Working Group to prepare such a mechanism. At its first session (in October 2002), the Meeting of the Parties adopted Decision I/7 on review of compliance and elected the first Compliance Committee; for more see: https://www.unece.org/env/pp/ccbackground.html (on February 9, 2019).

336. See also e.g. V. Koester, *The Compliance Committee of the Aarhus Convention—An Overview of Procedures and Jurisprudence*, Environmental Policy and Law Vol. 37/2007, pp. 83-96, V. Koester, *Review of Compliance Committee under the Aarhus Convention: A Rather Unique Compliance Mechanism*, Journal of European Environmental & Planning Law No. 1/2005, pp.

In fact, the fourth possibility is the most common path of initiating a compliance procedure[337] which demonstrates that NGOs remain vigilant in environmental matters also at international level.

[1] National Level

The transposition of the third pillar of the Aarhus Convention by the EU instruments at national level is quite complex:

(1) Article 9 (1) of the Convention is reiterated by Article 6 of Directive 2003/4 on public access to environmental information.[338]
(2) Article 9 (2) of the Convention is reflected in the following directives:
   (a) Integrated Pollution Prevention and Control Directive (2010/75/EU) —Article 25.[339]
   (b) Directive 2003/35/EC providing for public participation in respect of the drawing up of certain plans and programs relating to the environment

---

31-44, R. Lanceiro, *The Review of Compliance with the Aarhus Convention of the European Union* in: *Global Administrative Law*, E. Chiti, B.G. Mattarella (eds), New York 2011, pp. 359-382.

337. T. Weber, *Die Umsetzung der Aarhus-Konvention beim direkten Vollzug von Unionsrecht*, Journal für Rechtspolitik Vol. 20/2012, p. 147.

338. (1) Member States shall ensure that any applicant who considers that his request for information has been ignored, wrongfully refused (whether in full or in part), inadequately answered or otherwise not dealt with in accordance with the provisions of Arts. 3, 4 or 5 has access to a procedure in which the acts or omissions of the public authority concerned can be reconsidered by that or another public authority or reviewed administratively by an independent and impartial body established by law. Any such procedure shall be expeditious and either free of charge or inexpensive.
(2) In addition to the review procedure referred to in paragraph 1, Member States shall ensure that an applicant has access to a review procedure before a court of law or another independent and impartial body established by law, in which the acts or omissions of the public authority concerned can be reviewed and whose decisions may become final. Member States may furthermore provide that third parties incriminated by the disclosure of information may also have access to legal recourse.
(3) Final decisions under para. 2 shall be binding on the public authority holding the information. Reasons shall be stated in writing, at least where access to information is refused under this Article.

See also Art. 23 (a) of Directive 2012/18/EU.

339. (1) Member States shall ensure that, in accordance with the relevant national legal system, members of the public concerned have access to a review procedure before a court of law or another independent and impartial body established by law to challenge the substantive or procedural legality of decisions, acts or omissions subject to Art. 24 when one of the following conditions is met:
   (a) they have a sufficient interest;
   (b) they maintain the impairment of a right, where administrative procedural law of a Member State requires this as a precondition.
(2) Member States shall determine at what stage the decisions, acts or omissions may be challenged.
(3) What constitutes a sufficient interest and impairment of a right shall be determined by Member States, consistently with the objective of giving the public concerned wide access to justice.

and amending with regard to public participation and access to justice Council Directives 85/337/EEC and 96/61/EC—Statement by the Commission—Article 15a.[340]

(c) Directive 2004/35/EC on environmental liability with regard to the prevention and remedying of environmental damage[341]—Article 13.[342]

To this end, the interest of any nongovernmental organization promoting environmental protection and meeting any requirements under national law shall be deemed sufficient for the purpose of para. 1(a).

Such organizations shall also be deemed to have rights capable of being impaired for the purpose of para. 1(b).

(4) Paras. 1, 2 and 3 shall not exclude the possibility of a preliminary review procedure before an administrative authority and shall not affect the requirement of exhaustion of administrative review procedures prior to recourse to judicial review procedures, where such a requirement exists under national law.

Any such procedure shall be fair, equitable, timely and not prohibitively expensive.

(5) Member States shall ensure that practical information is made available to the public on access to administrative and judicial review procedures.

340. Member States shall ensure that, in accordance with the relevant national legal system, members of the public concerned:
(a) having a sufficient interest; or
(b) alternatively, maintaining the impairment of a right, where administrative procedural law of a Member State requires this as a precondition have access to a review procedure before a court of law or another independent and impartial body established by law to challenge the substantive or procedural legality of decisions, acts or omissions subject to the public participation provisions of this Directive.

Member States shall determine at what stage the decisions, acts or omissions may be challenged.

What constitutes a sufficient interest and impairment of a right shall be determined by the Member States, consistently with the objective of giving the public concerned wide access to justice. To this end, the interest of any nongovernmental organization meeting the requirements referred to in Art. 2(14) shall be deemed sufficient for the purpose of subpara. (a) of this Article. Such organizations shall also be deemed to have rights capable of being impaired for the purpose of subpara. (b) of this Article.

The provisions of this Article shall not exclude the possibility of a preliminary review procedure before an administrative authority and shall not affect the requirement of exhaustion of administrative review procedures prior to recourse to judicial review procedures, where such a requirement exists under national law.

Any such procedure shall be fair, equitable, timely and not prohibitively expensive.

In order to further the effectiveness of the provisions of this Article, Member States shall ensure that practical information is made available to the public on access to administrative and judicial review procedures.

341. Which, however, can be perceived as a legislation independent of the Aarhus provisions as it does not refer to the Convention, nor does it implement the second pillar. See, to this extent, P. Wennerås, *The Enforcement of EC Environmental Law*, Oxford 2007, p. 91.

342. (1) Natural or legal persons:
(a) affected or likely to be affected by environmental damage;
(b) having a sufficient interest in environmental decision-making relating to the damage; or
(c) alleging the impairment of a right, where administrative procedural law of a Member State requires this as a precondition shall have access to a court or other independent and impartial public body competent to review the procedural and substantive legality of the decisions, acts or failure to act of the competent authority under this Directive.

(d) Directive 2011/92/EU on the assessment of the effects of certain public and private projects on the environment—Article 11.[343]

(3) Article 9 (3) and (4) are presently not transposed by any EU act of law, which, however, does not mean that their implementation to the domestic legal systems of Member States is completely left out of the scope of the EU law.

The first two paths of access to justice are quite evident as Article 9 (1) and (2) of the Aarhus Convention is an amplification of the Convention's first two pillars.[344] That said, the provisions mentioned in the first two points above are a more or less express reiteration of requirements established in Article 9 (1) and (2) of the Aarhus Convention. As a result, once an individual's rights of access to environmental documents or public participation in environmental matters are breached, proper infringement procedures should be provided. In fact, requests for documents and public participation can be utilized as "gate-openers" for access to justice as in the doctrine they are sometimes referred to as "indirect *actio popularis*" or "multi-stage *actio popularis*."[345]

---

(2) This Directive shall be without prejudice to any provisions of national law which regulate access to justice and those which require that administrative review procedures be exhausted prior to recourse to judicial proceedings.

343. (1) Member States shall ensure that, in accordance with the relevant national legal system, members of the public concerned:
(a) having a sufficient interest; or
(b) alternatively, maintaining the impairment of a right, where administrative procedural law of a Member State requires this as a precondition have access to a review procedure before a court of law or another independent and impartial body established by law to challenge the substantive or procedural legality of decisions, acts or omissions subject to the public participation provisions of this Directive.
(2) Member States shall determine at what stage the decisions, acts or omissions may be challenged.
(3) What constitutes a sufficient interest and impairment of a right shall be determined by the Member States, consistently with the objective of giving the public concerned wide access to justice. To that end, the interest of any nongovernmental organization meeting the requirements referred to in Art. 1 (2) shall be deemed sufficient for the purpose of point (a) of para. 1 of this Article. Such organizations shall also be deemed to have rights capable of being impaired for the purpose of point (b) of para. 1 of this Article.
(4) The provisions of this Article shall not exclude the possibility of a preliminary review procedure before an administrative authority and shall not affect the requirement of exhaustion of administrative review procedures prior to recourse to judicial review procedures, where such a requirement exists under national law.
Any such procedure shall be fair, equitable, timely and not prohibitively expensive.
(5) In order to further the effectiveness of the provisions of this Article, Member States shall ensure that practical information is made available to the public on access to administrative and judicial review procedures.

See also Art. 23 (b) of Directive 2012/18/EU.

344. Cf. e.g. para. 38 in C-263/08 *Djurgården-Lilla Värtans Miljöskyddsförening*, ECLI:EU:C:2009:631: "participation in an environmental decision-making procedure under the conditions laid down in Articles 2(2) and 6(4) of Directive 85/337 is separate and has a different purpose from a legal review, since the latter may, where appropriate, be directed at a decision adopted at the end of that procedure. Therefore, participation in the decision-making procedure has no effect on the conditions for access to the review procedure."

345. J. Darpö, *Effective...*, p. 14.

Still, it is troublesome why not all EU provisions on public participation are equipped with access to justice instruments. Although this problem exceeds the subject matter of this book,[346] it should be remembered that even if Article 9 (2) is not fully transposed in the directives,[347] it has to be thoroughly implemented by Member States in their legal systems.

Article 9 (3) of the Convention is presently not regulated by any directive. Nevertheless, its implementation in a way falls into the sphere of the EU law. This issue was elaborated by the CJEU in case C-240/09 *Lesoochranárske zoskupenie VLK*.[348] The reference to the Court of Justice was made in proceedings between Lesoochranáske zoskupenie VLK ("zoskupenie"), an association established in accordance with Slovak law, whose objective was the protection of the environment, and the Ministry of the Environment of the Slovak Republic. The case concerned the association's request to be a "party" in the administrative proceedings relating to the grant of derogations to the system of protection for species such as the brown bear, access to protected countryside areas or the use of chemical substances in such areas.[349] The preliminary reference dealt primary with the question if it is possible to recognize Article 9 (3) of the Aarhus Convention as having the direct effect of an international treaty in a situation where the EU acceded to this agreement but has not yet adopted Community (EU) legislation in order to transpose it into Community (EU) law.[350]

According to the Court of Justice, in Decision 2005/370, the Community (EU) stated that the legal instruments in force do not cover fully the implementation of the obligations resulting from Article 9 (3) of the Convention as they relate to administrative and judicial procedures to challenge acts and omissions by private persons and public authorities other than the institutions of the Community (EU). Consequently, Member States are responsible for the performance of these obligations at the time of approval of the Convention and will remain so until the Community (EU), in the exercise of its powers, adopts provisions of Community (EU) law covering the implementation of those obligations.[351] However, it cannot be inferred that the implementation of Article 9 (3) of the Aarhus Convention does not fall within the scope of the EU law because a specific issue which has not yet been subject to the EU legislation may fall within the scope of the EU law if it relates to a field covered by it in large measure.[352]

346. This leads to an unfavorable phenomenon which is quite common among the Member States; i.e. the access to justice possibilities are much wider in procedures for public participation than in other kinds of decision-making procedures on environmental matters. See e.g. J. Darpö, *Effective...*, p. 27.
347. Nevertheless, the general tendency is to include access to justice provisions in the new EU Directives. See e.g. Art. 16 of the Proposal for a Directive of the EP and of the Council on the quality of water intended for human consumption (recast) of 1.2.2018, COM(2017) 753 final.
348. ECLI:EU:C:2011:125.
349. Para. 2 in C-240/09.
350. Para. 23 in C-240/09.
351. Para. 39 in C-240/09.
352. Para. 40 in C-240/09. Moreover, in that connection, it is irrelevant that Regulation 1367/2006 only concerns the institutions of the EU and cannot be regarded as the adoption by the EU of provisions implementing the obligations which derived from Art. 9 (3) of the Aarhus Convention with respect to national administrative or judicial proceedings (para. 41).

Nevertheless, the CJEU stated that the provisions of Article 9 (3) of the Aarhus Convention do not contain any clear and precise obligation capable of directly regulating the legal position of individuals since only members of the public who meet the criteria, if any, laid down by national law are entitled to exercise the rights provided for in Article 9 (3), that provision is subject, in its implementation or effects, to the adoption of a subsequent measure.[353]

On that basis, the detailed procedural rules governing actions for safeguarding an individual's rights under the EU law must be no less favorable than those governing similar domestic actions (principle of equivalence) and must not make it in practice impossible or excessively difficult to exercise rights conferred by the EU law (principle of effectiveness). Therefore, if the effective protection of the EU environmental law is not to be undermined, it is inconceivable that Article 9 (3) of the Aarhus Convention be interpreted in such a way as to make it in practice impossible or excessively difficult to exercise rights conferred by the EU law. It is for the Court to interpret, to the fullest extent possible, the procedural rights relating to the conditions to be met in order to bring administrative or judicial proceedings in accordance with the objectives of Article 9 (3) of the Aarhus Convention and the objective effective judicial protection of the rights conferred by the EU law in order to enable an environmental protection organization to challenge before a court a decision taken following administrative proceedings liable to be contrary to the EU environmental law.[354]

In conclusion, the CJEU stated that Article 9 (3) of the Aarhus Convention cannot be applied directly. Still, due to the fact that it is a part of the EU law, it has to be interpreted in a broad sense so that the conferred remedy is effective.[355] This general remark is applicable to all procedural actions attributed to individuals in the EU law.[356] However, as observed in C-661/15 *Protect Natur-, Arten- und Landschaftsschutz Unweltorganisationen*[357] if such a compliant interpretation were to be found impossible, then it would be for the Court to disapply, in the proceedings before it, the rule of national procedural law which limits the *locus standi* of an NGO, exercising its right of access to justice deriving from the Aarhus Convention and the secondary acts of the

353. Para. 45 in C-240/09.
354. Paras. 48-51 in C-240/09.
355. The reasoning which has already been discussed in previous paragraphs of this chapter on basis of Case C-115/09 *Bund für Umwelt und Naturschutz Deutschland* which concerned the measures attributed by Directive 2003/35. To this extent see also the opinion of Advocate General Sharpston in this case (ECLI:EU:C:2010:773). In para. 72 of the opinion she observed: "Furthermore, if the German Government were correct, whether an environmental NGO had *locus standi* to bring an action would depend in part on chance. Imagine two lakes, fairly alike in flora and fauna. The first is in the wilderness, in a remote corner of a large tract of land under the general control of the local authority (which will also consider any planning request). Not a soul lives nearby. The second is near a few houses. Under the German Government's interpretation, an environmental NGO could have *locus standi* to challenge a decision authorizing a construction project bordering on the second lake (if it alleged that the householders' rights were or could be impaired) but not the first. That surely cannot be the intent of the EIA Directive. Access to justice cannot be made dependent on extraneous factors, such as the precise location of the project that an environmental NGO fears may cause damage to the environment."
356. For more see e.g. N. Półtorak, *European...*, pp. 45 et seq.
357. ECLI:EU:C:2017:753.

EU law.[358] Even though the implementation of Article 9 (3) of the Convention is left to Member States, the words "criteria, if any, laid down in its national law" in Article 9 (3) of the Aarhus Convention cannot allow to impose criteria so strict that it would be effectively impossible for environmental organizations to contest the actions or omissions that are the subject of that provision.[359] Still, the discussed provision leaves a wide scope of recognition,[360] its transposition differs across particular states and can be generally evaluated as "inconsistent."[361] This converts to various procedural positions of NGOs as Article 9 (3) of the Convention, in contrast to Article 9 (2), does not directly refer to the conditions of their legal standing. Accordingly, following a rights-based approach, the implementation can lead to a very wide understanding of *locus standi* (which practically contributes to the instruments of *actio popularis* in environmental matters) or, following an interest-based approach (or the protective norm theory, i.e. *Schutznormtheorie*), can introduce a strict understanding of access to justice.

The construction of *actio popularis* is known in Portugal and, to a large extent, in Slovenia, Spain, Romania and Latvia.[362] In those legal systems, anyone who participates in the decision-making procedure in environmental matters is allowed to challenge that decision in court.[363] Similarly, according to the Greek Council of State, *locus standi* in environmental cases has been broadened to such an extent that it can be described as *quasi-actio popularis*.[364] The conditions are also comparable in Ireland and Romania (and in some instances in Croatia and Finland). In those legal systems anyone can initiate enforcement actions in case of breach of environmental law. Furthermore, the opportunity to launch private prosecution in the UK can be characterized as a form of *action popularis*.[365]

The interest-based approach is implemented at least to some extent in other countries. In the most rigorous forms, which applies in Germany and Austria, it means that in order to bring an action before the administrative court, the applicant has to

358. See para. 55 in C-661/15.
359. Para. 48 in C-661/15.
360. See also G. Garçon, *Limits of NGO Rights to Invoke Access to Justice under the Aarhus Convention*, European Journal of Risk Regulation Vol. 6/2015, pp. 461-468.
361. For instance, there are diverging tendencies among Member States as to the means available for access to justice according to Art. 9 (3) of the Aarhus Convention. In most countries, administrative decisions can be contested both through administrative procedures and through the courts. Sometimes, the administrative remedies must be exhausted before utilizing judicial review. Administrative remedies usually consist of appeals to the authority that issued the contested decision or to a body that is hierarchically superior. In other countries, some administrative appeal is made to special tribunals which are equipped with technical experts of their own; see J. Darpö, *Effective...*, p. 11.
362. Report on Access to Justice in Environmental Matters, Justice and Environment. European Network of Environmental Law Organizations 2010, available at: http://www.justiceandenvironment.org/_files/file/2010/05/JE-Aarhus-AtJ_Report_10-05-24.pdf (on February 9, 2019).
363. J. Darpö, *Effective...*, p. 12.
364. *Ibid.*
365. *Ibid.*, p. 13.

present that the decision or omission concerns his individual or public law right.[366] A similar approach can also be attributed to the Polish legal system.[367]

Although there is no common approach to the implementation of the Aarhus Convention in Member States, its general outcomes can be evaluated positively. Essentially, the possibilities of challenging environmental decisions have been enhanced in many ways, for instance by relaxing the *locus standi* conditions[368] or establishing new possibilities of NGOs to bring an action to the Court.[369] In many cases these developments can be attributed to the pressure of the Commission or the Compliance Committee of the Aarhus Convention. The case law of the CJEU has also played a significant role in increasing access to justice in many Member States.[370] Nevertheless, an opposite tendency in some spheres is also noticeable. It mainly concerns large-scale, nationwide projects[371] which are commonly resolved at the highest level of the administration and approved according to a centralized "plan."[372] The means of challenging such policy decisions before courts are often weak or nonexistent.[373]

The Commission acknowledges that environmental NGOs play an important role in ensuring compliance with the obligations of the EU environmental law and enjoy a broad right to protect the environment which national courts need to uphold.[374] In fact, the implementation of the third pillar of the Aarhus Convention[375] in most Member States led to establishing standing for NGOs by criteria in express legislation. However, the respective preconditions alter. That is why there are strong reasons for establishing deliberate principles also at the EU level.[376] The clearest situation is in those countries which provide instruments of *actio popularis*. As access to justice is wide, there is little reason to define specific standing criteria for NGOs. Yet, in other countries the *locus standi* premises are not always so apparent. In this aspect, it should be once again

366. Report on Access..., J. Darpö, *Effective...*, p. 14.
367. Cf. B. Iwańska, *Koncepcja...*, p. 534. For instance, according to the general provisions in the Polish Law (i.e., Art. 50 § 1 of the Law on Proceedings Before Administrative Courts, *Prawo o postępowaniu przed sądami administracyjnymi*): entitled to bring an action is anyone who has a legal interest, the public prosecutor, the Ombudsman, the Ombudsman on the rights of the child and a social organization in terms of its statutory activities and in matters relating to the legal interests of other persons, where it took part in the administrative proceedings.
368. I.e., Belgium, Bulgaria, Estonia, Denmark, Greece, Ireland, Luxembourg, Sweden, Slovenia, Slovakia; see J. Darpö, *Effective...*, p. 10, N. de Sadeleer, G. Roller, M. Dross, *Access to Justice in Environmental Matters. Final Report 2002*, ENV.A.3/ETU/2002/0030, pp. 21-24.
369. I.e., Austria, the Czech Republic, France, Hungary, Lithuania, Malta, Poland, Romania; see J. Darpö, *Effective...*, p. 10, N. de Sadeleer, G. Roller, M. Dross, *Access...*, pp. 21-24.
370. J. Darpö, *Effective...*, p. 10.
371. I.e., nuclear power station, offshore activities, infrastructural projects and other activities considered to be of vital public interest.
372. J. Darpö, *Effective...*, p. 10.
373. For instance, in the case of Slovenia law. In other countries, e.g. Belgium, Denmark, Greece, Ireland, Spain, the Netherlands, Romania, Sweden, the United Kingdom, these opportunities are rather weak. See Report on Access...; see also N. de Sadeleer, G. Roller, M. Dross, *Access...*, p. 25, J. Darpö, *Effective...*, p. 10.
374. Communication from the Commission of 28.4.2017. Commission Notice on Access to Justice in Environmental Matters, C(2017) 2616 final, p. 13.
375. Meaning Art. 9 (1) of the Convention and the specific provisions of the EU Directives.
376. N. de Sadeleer, G. Roller, M. Dross, *Access...*, p. 35.

reiterated that the conditions of access to justice should be effective in order to be rendered admissible. As the CJEU stated in case C-263/08 *Djurgården-Lilla Värtans Miljöskyddsförening*,[377] it is true that the acts of the EU law[378] implementing the Aarhus Convention leave to national legislatures the task of determining the conditions which may be required in order for a nongovernmental organization which promotes environmental protection to have a right of appeal under the conditions set out above, but the national rules thus established must, first, ensure "wide access to justice" and, second, render effective the provisions of the appropriate measures on judicial remedies.[379] Furthermore, it is settled case law that access to justice in environmental matter for members of the public should also be either free of charge or be free of "prohibitively expensive means."[380]

The most common requirements set up in national procedural laws for NGOs wishing to obtain *locus standi* in environmental matters include:

(1) prior registration and recognition[381] (which is seen in the doctrine as the most obvious criterion);[382]
(2) statutory prerequisites dealing with the organization's:
    (a) established aims,[383]

377. ECLI:EU:C:2009:631.
378. The judgment was focused on the provisions of Directive 835/337.
379. Para. 45 in C-263/08.
380. See also C-260/11, *David Edwards, Lilian Pallikaropoulos*, ECLI:EU:C:2013:221: "The requirement, under the fifth paragraph of Article 10a of Council Directive 85/337/EEC of 27 June 1985 on the assessment of the effects of certain public and private projects on the environment and the fifth paragraph of Article 15a of Council Directive 96/61/EC of 24 September 1996 concerning integrated pollution prevention and control, as amended by Directive 2003/35/EC of the European Parliament and of the Council of 26 May 2003, that judicial proceedings should not be prohibitively expensive means that the persons covered by those provisions should not be prevented from seeking, or pursuing a claim for, a review by the courts that falls within the scope of those articles by reason of the financial burden that might arise as a result. Where a national court is called upon to make an order for costs against a member of the public who is an unsuccessful claimant in an environmental dispute or, more generally, where it is required—as courts in the United Kingdom may be—to state its views, at an earlier stage of the proceedings, on a possible capping of the costs for which the unsuccessful party may be liable, it must satisfy itself that that requirement has been complied with, taking into account both the interest of the person wishing to defend his rights and the public interest in the protection of the environment" (para. 35). In the context of that assessment, "the national court cannot act solely on the basis of that claimant's financial situation but must also carry out an objective analysis of the amount of the costs. It may also take into account the situation of the parties concerned, whether the claimant has a reasonable prospect of success, the importance of what is at stake for the claimant and for the protection of the environment, the complexity of the relevant law and procedure, the potentially frivolous nature of the claim at its various stages and the existence of a national legal aid scheme or a costs protection regime" (para. 42). By contrast, "the fact that a claimant has not been deterred, in practice, from asserting his claim is not of itself sufficient to establish that the proceedings are not prohibitively expensive for him" (para. 43).
381. I.e., in Austria, Finland, France, Denmark, Greece, Hungary, Lithuania, Luxembourg, Italy, Latvia, Poland, Romania, Slovenia, Slovakia, see J. Darpö, *Effective...*, p. 14, N. de Sadeleer, G. Roller, M. Dross, *Access...*, p. 27.
382. B. Iwańska, *Koncepcja...*, p. 331.
383. This criterion is sometimes replaced or complemented with a requirement for activity in an expressly names field of law. Occasionally, the statutes have been read quite narrowly by the

(b) nonprofit goals,[384]
(c) length of existence,[385]
(d) numeric criteria,[386]
(e) geographic criteria,[387]
(f) "democratic" criteria.[388]

(3) prior participation in decision-making and exhaustion of existing administrative appeals.[389]

In order to complete the proper understanding of effective access to justice of NGOs in environmental matters, a few remarks should also be made on the basis of the Compliance Committee's case law. Thus:[390]

---

courts, and the NGO has only been allowed to challenge issues that are expressly mentioned in them (for instance, in the Netherlands); for more see J. Darpö, *Effective...*, p. 14, N. de Sadeleer, G. Roller, M. Dross, *Access...*, p. 23.

384. Used in Austria, Belgium, Germany, Poland and Slovenia, see *Report...*

385. Varying between one year (in Sweden and Ireland in some cases), two years (in Spain and Hungary), three years (in Austria, Belgium, France, Denmark, Luxembourg and Sweden) and even five years (in Cyprus and Slovenia); see J. Darpö, *Effective...*, pp. 14-15.

386. Existing in Slovenia and Sweden (30 and 100 members, respectively). However, this limitation can raise concerns dealing with the EU principle of effectiveness in access to court. See, to this extent C-263/08 *Djurgården-Lilla Värtans Miljöskyddsförening*, ECLI:EU:C:2009:631: "It is conceivable that the condition that an environmental protection association must have a minimum number of members may be relevant in order to ensure that it does in fact exist and that it is active. However, the number of members required cannot be fixed by national law at such a level that it runs counter to the objectives of Directive 85/337 and in particular the objective of facilitating judicial review of projects which fall within its scope. In that connection, it must be stated that, although Directive 85/337 provided that members of the public concerned who have a sufficient interest in challenging projects or have rights which may be impaired by projects are to have the right to challenge the decision which authorizes it, that Directive in no way permits access to review procedures to be limited on the grounds that the persons concerned have already been able to express their views in the participatory phase of their decision-making procedure" (paras. 47-48).

387. Meaning that "if the activities of the NGO according to its statutes are confined to one region, it is not allowed to appeal decisions in another. For instance, in Italy, the organization is required to show that it has been active in 5 out of 20 regions. The same goes for Slovenia, where NGOs must have been active in the whole of the country's territory in order to be recognized" see J. Darpö, *Effective...*, p. 14, Cf. Report on Access..., N. de Sadeleer, G. Roller, M. Dross, *Access...*, p. 27.

388. For instance, in Estonia, ad hoc groups must show that the organization represents a significant percentage of the inhabitants of the affected area. In Sweden, an alternative to the numeric criterion is that the NGO can show that it has "support from the public"; see J. Darpö, *Effective...*, p. 15.

Openness and democratic structure is also used as a criterion in Germany and Italy, thus excluding well-known, international NGOs from standing in environmental cases; see J. Darpö, *Effective...*, p. 15, *Report...*

389. Understood this way, only those who have raised their voices in the participatory stage of the decision-making procedure are allowed to challenge the final outcome in court (Austria, Latvia, Denmark, Hungary, Ireland, the Netherlands, Slovenia, Slovakia). In some of these countries, this prerequisite is read narrowly, only allowing those issues that were objected to in the participatory stage to be challenged in court (Austria, Denmark, Ireland, the Netherlands); see J. Darpö, *Effective...*, p. 15, N. de Sadeleer, G. Roller, M. Dross, *Access...*, pp. 21-23.

390. See also B. Iwańska, *Koncepcja...*, pp. 364-365.

- while the Convention does not prevent a party from applying general criteria, it does prohibit a too restrictive access to justice for environmental organizations, i.e. such criteria that effectively bar most, if not all, organizations from challenging certain acts of law relating to environment;[391]
- access to justice—interpreted together with the preamble of the Convention—should be aimed at providing the public and environmental organizations with effective judicial instruments;[392]
- a too strict approach to the criteria of *locus standi* of NGOs in environmental matters cannot be redressed by complaint possibilities of the national Ombudsman;[393]
- an introduction to the national law of a requirement of proving "direct and individual concern" for the purposes of gaining *locus standi* in national environmental proceedings is not per se contrary to Article 9 (3) of the Aarhus Convention as long as this condition does not lead to the exclusion of a vast majority of members of the public that could be entitled to contest the acts and omissions in environmental matters.[394]

In order to harmonize the *locus standi* criteria the Commission issued in 2003 a proposal for a directive on access to justice in environmental matters.[395] Its aim was to furnish rules concerning judicial and administrative review procedures to challenge acts and omissions by public authorities. The justification for this act of law, unquestionably accurate, was presented as follows: "the lack of enforcement of environmental law is too frequent due to the fact that legal standing is limited to persons directly affected by the infringement. A way of improving enforcement is hence to ensure that representative associations seeking to protect the environment have access to administrative or judicial procedures in environmental matters. Practical experience gained from granting legal standing to environmental nongovernmental organizations indicates that this can enhance the implementation of environmental law."[396]

The Directive would be applicable to "environmental proceedings" understood as administrative or judicial proceedings in environmental matters,[397] other than criminal proceedings, before a judicial authority or another independent and impartial

391. ACCC/C/2008/32 (European Union), ACCC/C/2006/18 (Denmark).
392. ACCC/C/2008/32 (European Union), ACCC/C/2006/18 (Denmark), ACCC/C/2010/48 (Austria).
393. ACCC/C/2010/48 (Austria). Furthermore, actions brought to independent public authorities deprived of judiciary competences cannot be considered as measures of access to appeal procedures. If they were, then it would have to be considered as a limitation to access to justice; see also N. Półtorak, *Ochrona uprawnień...*, pp. 169-170.
394. ACCC/C/2008/32 (European Union).
395. COM(2003) 624 final.
396. See point 1.1. General considerations of the Explanatory memorandum.
397. According to Art. 2 (1) (g) of the proposal, "Environmental law" means Community (EU) legislation and legislation adopted to implement Community (EU) legislation which have as their objective the protection or the improvement of the environment, including human health and the protection or the rational use of natural resources, in areas such as: (i) water protection, (ii) noise protection, (iii) soil protection, (iv) atmospheric pollution, (v) town and country planning and land use, (vi) nature conservation and biological diversity, (vii) waste management, (viii) chemicals including biocides and pesticides, (ix) biotechnology, (x) other

body established by law to review acts and omissions of public authorities (Article 2 (1) (f)). The Directive did not differentiate between access to a judicial authority or another independent and impartial body as it aimed at the legally binding effect of decisions emanating from the authority in question. Thus, Member States would be able to decide before which body these proceedings could be brought.

Under the provisions of the proposed Directive, access to justice would be appropriate for "members of the public" and "qualified entities." The prerogatives of these subjects were designed in a different manner.

According to Article 2 (1) (b) of the proposal, a "member of the public" means one or more natural or legal persons, and their associations, organizations or groups. As it can be seen, this definition is very wide as it encompasses not only registered NGOs but other entities without legal personality as well. Article 4 establishes the criteria for determining which members of the public have legal standing in administrative or judicial proceedings, including interim relief measures, against acts and omissions of public authorities aimed at by the Directive. According to the Directive, members of the public must have a sufficient interest in the related administrative act or omission, or maintain the impairment of a right, where the administrative procedural law of the Member State concerned requires this as a precondition to obtaining access to review procedures. Under the terms of the proposal, members of the public meeting the criteria above have access to review proceedings challenging both the procedural and substantive legality of administrative acts or omissions in breach of environmental law. However, with the establishment of these conditions, the Commission decided not to opt for the possibility of a general right of legal standing for every natural person as it found that the generalized requirement of *actio popularis* is incompatible with the principle of subsidiarity, in the light of the fact that the Aarhus Convention leaves the possibility of laying down criteria under national law.[398]

A "qualified entity" is defined in Article 2 (1) (c) of the proposal. Accordingly, this notion means any association, organization, group whose objective is protection of the environment and which is recognized according to the prescribed procedure. Under the proposed Directive, "qualified entities" obtain legal standing without the need of proving a sufficient interest or maintaining the impairment of a right.[399] Although the conditions of *locus standi* are extensive, the Directive also in this extent cannot be seen as attributing *actio popularis* for NGOs because they still need to fulfill certain prerequisites. According to Article 8 of the proposal, apart from having protection of the environment as their statutory objective, a "qualified entity":

---

emissions, discharges and releases in the environment, (xi) environmental impact assessment, (xii) access to environmental information and public participation in decision-making.

398. See point 6. Detailed Explanation of the Proposal.

399. In Art. 9, regarding the process of recognizing the qualified entities, the proposal provides for a mixed approach combining the possibility of a preliminary procedure and (ad hoc) case-by-case recognition. The possibility of these two procedures has the advantage of providing effectiveness and flexibility. Certain environmental organizations may choose advance recognition, whereas others may prefer to choose ad hoc recognition. Member States may decide at their discretion to provide for an advance or an ad hoc recognition procedure. Should a Member State decide for advance recognition, it shall also ensure that access to an expeditious ad hoc recognition is available.

(a) must be an independent and non-profit-making legal person;
(b) must have an organizational structure which enables it to ensure the adequate pursuit of its statutory objectives;
(c) must have been legally constituted and worked actively for environmental protection, in conformity with its statutes, for a period to be fixed by the Member State in which it is constituted, but not exceeding three years;
(d) must have its annual statement of account certified by a registered auditor for a period to be fixed by each Member State.[400]

It seems understandable that the privileged legal standing of qualified entities requires a clear definition of the qualifying characteristics. As a result, the proposal applies an evaluation procedure for the activity of these entities. The legal standing is conditioned upon the subject of the procedure being a statutory and geographically relevant activity of the entity concerned. Moreover, the proposal incorporates the possibility of having access to environmental proceedings in transboundary cases. Thus, an entity recognized in one Member State may have recourse to environmental proceedings in another Member State to challenge a breach of environmental law provided it falls within its statutory and geographical area of activities.[401]

Furthermore, to overcome obstacles that prevent access to justice and in line with Article 9 (4) of the Aarhus Convention, Article 10 of the proposed Directive foresees the establishment of effective and adequate proceedings that must be fair, equitable, timely and not prohibitively expensive. In order to give appropriate legal certainty and transparency, decisions under the terms of the proposal shall be given in writing to the public and whenever possible shall be publicly accessible.

The proposal was eventually withdrawn in 2014,[402] and no new recommendations for a complex implementation of the third pillar of the Aarhus Convention at national level have been issued since then. In fact, the Commission presently claims that existing requirements stemming from the EU secondary law and international commitments, as interpreted by the CJEU, already provide a coherent framework for access to justice in environmental matters.[403] Yet, it is obvious that a common legal framework would be beneficial to harmonize the conditions of *locus standi* in all Member States. This statement applies particularly to Article 9 (3) of the Aarhus Convention due to a basic uncertainty about the requirements of this provision.[404] The practical guidelines concerning this subject matter issued by the Commission in 2017[405] are a positive step, but they definitely do not clarify all the doubts dealing with the implementation of access to justice provisions.

400. Those criteria are the same as the ones used in Art. 11 of Regulation 1367/2006, except for the time criterion, which requires NGOs to have been active for at least two years.
401. See point 6. Detailed Explanation of the Proposal, Art. 5.
402. Official Journal C 153, 21.5.2014.
403. See Commission Notice..., p. 60.
404. I.e., dealing with issues what measures are needed, what kind of decisions are covered, what kind of body (administrative or judicial) should undertake the review, what kind of review is needed, etc.
405. See Commission Notice..., pp. 18 et seq.

As a result, it seems that the main measure to control the efficiency of implementing means of access to justice in environmental matters is to use infringement proceedings in accordance with Article 258 of the TFEU. This is the most persuasive way to ensure that Member States fulfill the conditions established by the case law of the CJEU.[406]

[2] EU Level

The transposition of Article 9 of the Aarhus Convention at the EU level is quite convoluted and raises many concerns:

(1) Article 9 (1) of the Convention is provided by general complaint possibilities in cases of access to documents. Therefore, a refusal or a partial access to information can be subject to an action brought by the interested individual under Article 263 of the TFEU to the General Court or comprise an example of maladministration for the purposes of a complaint to the European Ombudsman. These possibilities have been thoroughly discussed in the previous chapter.

(2) While the abovementioned directives providing participation in environmental matters explicitly envisage that Member States should enable NGOs to have access to a review procedure for the purpose of protecting their Aarhus rights, such guarantee is not provided at the EU level.[407] In relation to contributing access to justice in terms of public participation in environmental decision-making as required by Article 9 (2) of the Convention, the Commission considers that decision-making covered by Article 6 of the Convention is generally at Member State level.[408] Still, as it has been already signaled in the previous paragraphs of this chapter, a glaring breach of the second pillar of the Aarhus Convention by the EU institutions can comprise an infringement of an essential procedural requirement for the purposes of actions brought before the CJEU under Article 263 of the TFEU or can be an example of maladministration and form basis for a complaint to the European Ombudsman. Yet, what has also been emphasized above, it would be extremely difficult for an NGO to bring an action before the CJEU as it is practically impossible to fulfill the preconditions of "direct and individual concern" if the complaining subject is not a direct addressee of the contested act. The sole fact of taking part in the decision-making procedure (without any specific rights conferred to the interested individual in this process) does not change anything in such a strict understanding of Article 263 of the

406. J. Darpö, *Effective...*, p. 24.
407. D. Obradovic, *EU Rules...*, pp. 171-172.
408. See T. Crossen, V. Niessen, *NGO Standing in the European Court of Justice—Does the Aarhus Convention Open the Door?*, Review of European, Comparative & International Environmental Law Vol. 16/2007, p. 334.

TFEU.[409] Thus, the compatibility of the *locus standi* conditions under Article 263 of the TFEU (and the so-called Plaumann test) with Article 9 (2) of the Convention raises many concerns as the latter one allows a wide access to justice for individuals solely on the grounds of "a sufficient interest" or "impairment of a right."[410] Nevertheless, the Commission considers that the procedure provided in Regulation 1367/2006 to implement the requirements of Article 9 (3) of the Convention can also be applicable for cases related to environmental participation.[411]

(3) Article 9 (3) of the Aarhus Convention is transposed in Article 10-12 of Regulation 1367/2006. These provisions will be the center point of analysis in the following paragraphs.

Regulation 1367/2006 establishes "internal review" as a new measure of access to justice in environmental matters at the EU level. This instrument seems to resemble "requests for retrial" which exist in some national administrative procedures.[412] However, contrary to these instruments, internal review is attributed only to NGOs. The legal doctrine evaluates that internal review procedure was designed not only as an administrative review procedure in its own right, through which the qualified NGOs could force the EU institutions and bodies to reconsider their acts or omissions, but also as a stepping-stone to enable the same NGOs to seek judicial review by the EU judicature of the institution's response to the request for internal review if they consider it unsatisfactory.[413] In particular, NGOs wishing to initiate internal review procedure do not have to justify that they are directly and individually concerned by the contested decision, contrary to actions brought before the CJEU under Article 263 of the TFEU. The internal review eligibility criteria are focused on the objectives and activities pursued by NGOs intending to call upon the EU institutions for the purpose of protecting their Aarhus rights.[414]

According to Article 10 (1) of the Regulation, any nongovernmental organization which meets the set out criteria is entitled to make a request for internal review to the Community (EU) institution or body that has adopted an administrative act under environmental law or, in case of an alleged administrative omission, should have adopted such an act. This kind of request must be made in writing and within a time limit not exceeding six weeks after the administrative act was adopted, notified or published, whichever is the latest, or, in the case of an alleged omission, six weeks after the date when the administrative act was required. The request shall state the grounds

409. See the previously discussed judgments of the CJEU, especially in Case C-321/95.
410. For more see M. Eliantonio, *Towards...*, p. 78. However, it can be argued that the conditions of access to justice under Art. 9 (2) of the Aarhus Convention apply only to Member States as this provision refers to "the framework of national legislation." This would be the same reasoning as the one implemented in the case of access to documents under Regulation 1049/2001 and its compliance with the Convention.
411. D. Obradovic, *EU Rules...*, pp. 171-172.
412. For example, in Art. 127 of the Polish Code of Administrative Procedure (*Kodeks postępowania administracyjnego*); see also B. Iwańska, *Koncepcja...*, p. 453.
413. M. Pallemaerts, *Access...*, p. 309.
414. D. Obradovic, *EU Rules...*, p. 174.

for the review. The Community (EU) institution or body shall consider any such request, unless it is clearly unsubstantiated. The Community (EU) institution or body shall state its reasons in a written reply as soon as possible, but not later than 12 weeks after receipt of the request (Article 10 (2)).[415] Where the Community (EU) institution or body is unable, despite exercising due diligence, to act in accordance with paragraph (2), it shall inform the nongovernmental organization, which made the request as soon as possible and at the latest within the period mentioned in that paragraph, of the reasons for its failure to act and when it intends to do so. In any event, the Community (EU) institution or body shall act within 18 weeks from receipt of the request (Article 10 (3)).

As it can be seen, the subject of internal review procedure is limited only to "administrative acts" and "alleged administrative omissions." These notions are defined as follows:

- "administrative act" means any measure of individual scope under environmental law, taken by a Community (EU) institution or body, and having legally binding and external effects (Article 2 (1) (g));
- "administrative omission" means any failure of a Community (EU) institution or body to adopt an administrative act (Article 2 (1) (h)).

Although not the legal form but the substance of an act should be decisive in determining whether or not it qualifies as an "administrative act,"[416] it always needs to have an individual (and not general) scope in order to be qualified for internal review procedure. Such an act is most likely to be an act of the Commission.[417] Furthermore, it seems that administrative acts that were adopted not directly "under the environmental law" but which directly influence the environment can also be subject to internal review procedure.[418]

In order to make a request for internal review, an NGO is subject to certain conditions laid down in Article 11 (1) of the Regulation. Thus, the interested organization is obliged to prove that:

(a) it is an independent non-profit-making[419] legal person[420] in accordance with a Member State's national law or practice;[421]

415. It seems that this time period has an instructional character. See, to this extent, internal review of Commission Decision C(2009) 2560 of 7 April 2009 on the notification by the Netherlands of a postponement for attaining the deadline for the limit values for NO_2 and an exemption from the obligation to apply the limit values for PM_{10} (decision not published in the OJ). However, the contravention of the prescribed time period may be subject of a complaint to the European Ombudsman.
416. M. Pallemaerts, *Access...*, p. 284.
417. *Ibid.*, pp. 291-292.
418. T. Crossen, V. Niessen, *NGO...*, pp. 335-336.
419. Which means that the organization should be not for profit.
420. Which excludes third sector actors that do not have legal personality (for instance, not registered social movements).
421. However, it is possible for an NGO registered in one Member State to lodge a request for internal review in a case concerning a different Member State; see, to this extent, internal

(b) it has the primary stated objective of promoting environmental protection in the context of environmental law;
(c) it has existed for more than two years and is actively pursuing the objective referred to under (b);
(d) the subject matter in respect of which the request for internal review is made is covered by its objectives and activities.

These preconditions mean that individual citizens and civil society groups active in environmental area but whose prime objective is not the protection of the environment are left out from the scope of internal review procedure.[422] The organization bringing a request for internal review is also subject to other formal requirements,[423]

review by the European Commission of the decision taken on February 17, 2014 on the notification by the Republic of Poland of a transitional national plan referred to in Art. 32 of Directive 2010/75/EU of the European Parliament and of the Council on industrial emissions.

422. Still, both individuals and civil groups whose prime objective is not the protection of the environment can participate in the EU level consultations, see also D. Obradovic, *EU Rules...*, p. 167.

423. Commission Decision of 13 December 2007 laying down detailed rules for the application of Regulation (EC) No 1367/2006 of the European Parliament and of the Council on the Aarhus Convention as regards requests for the internal review of administrative acts (2008/50/EC), Official Journal L 13, 16.1.2008.

According to its Art. 1, any nongovernmental organization which submits a request for internal review of an administrative act or omission as referred to in Art. 10 of Regulation (EC) No 1367/2006 shall:

1. specify the administrative act or alleged administrative omission whose review is sought and the provisions of environmental law which it considers not to have been complied with;
2. state the grounds on which that request is made;
3. provide the relevant information and documentation supporting those grounds;
4. specify the name and contact details of one person empowered to represent the nongovernmental organization vis-à-vis third parties for the purpose of making the request for internal review in the case at issue;
5. provide evidence of its entitlement to make the request in accordance with Article 3.

According to Art. 3 (1) of the decision, any nongovernmental organization which submits a request for internal review of an administrative act or omission as referred to in Art. 10 of Regulation (EC) No 1367/2006 shall provide evidence that it meets the criteria set out in Art. 11 (1) of that Regulation, in form of the documents listed in the Annex to this Decision.

Where any of those documents cannot be provided for reasons not attributable to the nongovernmental organization, that organization may provide evidence in form of any other equivalent documentation.

The Annex to the decision lists the documents which are to be provided under Art. 3 (1):

1. Statute or bylaws of the nongovernmental organization, or any other document fulfilling the same role under national practice, in respect of those countries where national law does not require or provide for a nongovernmental organization to adopt statute or bylaws.
2. Annual activity reports of the nongovernmental organization of the last two years.
3. In respect of nongovernmental organizations established in countries where the fulfillment of such procedures is a prerequisite for a nongovernmental organization to obtain legal personality, copy of the legal registration with the national authorities (public registry, official publication, or any other relevant document).
4. Where relevant, documentation that the nongovernmental organization has previously been acknowledged by a Community institution or body as being entitled to make a request for internal review.

which may cause some practical problems.[424] The request should be sent by mail, fax or e-mail to the department responsible for the application of the provision on the basis of which the administrative act was adopted, or in respect of which the administrative omission is alleged.[425]

Regulation 1367/2006 establishes a two-stage right of access to justice in environmental matters.[426] Internal review procedure was conceived not only as a means of providing easy access to an administrative procedure for selected "members of the public," but also by indirectly giving those same legal persons meeting the Regulation's criteria for entitlement access to the existing judicial review procedures provided in Articles 263 and 265 of the TFEU.[427] According to Article 12 (1) of the Regulation, the nongovernmental organization which made the request for internal review pursuant to Article 10 may institute proceedings before the Court of Justice in accordance with the relevant provisions of the Treaty. Where the Community (EU) institution or body fails to act in accordance with Article 10 (2) or (3), the nongovernmental organization may institute proceedings before the Court of Justice in accordance with the relevant provisions of the Treaty (Article 12 (2)). As this provision refers to the Treaty, it should be emphasized that it does not establish any other, "supplementary" possibility of bringing an action before the CJEU. Moreover, a lack of response or an insufficient response from the EU institution can be subject of "maladministration" in the complaint to the European Ombudsman.

The application of Article 12 of the Regulation with reference to Article 263 of the TFEU raises some questions. The first one is attributed to the subject of actions brought under the Treaty provisions after internal review. In other words, should the organization make a complaint against the decision of the EU institution (either the "first one" which was contested or the "second one" issued as a result of the internal review procedure) or should it contest the "written reply?"[428]

---

424. This concerns mainly the requirement of annual reports from the preceding two years. For more see P. Staszczyk, *Organizacje pozarządowe a dostęp do wymiaru sprawiedliwości w sprawach środowiskowych—wybrane zagadnienia* in: *Inteligentna i zrównowaznona gospodarka sprzyjająca właczeniu społecznemu—wyzwania dla systemów prawnych Unii Europejskiej i państw członkowskich*, S. Dudzik, B. Iwańska, N. Półtorak (eds), Warsaw 2017, p. 299.
425. See Art. 3 (1) of the Annex to Detailed rules for the application of Regulation (EC) No 1367/2006 of the European Parliament and of the Council on the application of the provisions of the Aarhus Convention on Access to Information, Public Participation in Decision-Making and Access to Justice in Environmental Matters to Community institutions and bodies to the Commission Decision of 20 April 2008 amending its Rules of Procedure as regards detailed rules for the application of Regulation (EC) No 1367/2006 of the European Parliament and of the Council on the application of the provisions of the Aarhus Convention on Access to Information, Public Participation in Decision-Making and Access to Justice in Environmental Matters to Community institution and bodies (2008/401/EC, Euratom), Official Journal L 140, 30.5.2008.
426. B. Pirker, *Access to Justice in Environmental Matters and the Aarhus Convention's Effects in the EU Legal Order: No Room for Nuanced Self-executing Effect?*, Review of European Community & International Environmental Law Vol. 25/2016, p. 86.
427. M. Pallemaerts, *Access...*, p. 289.
428. B. Iwańska, *Koncpejca...*, p. 454, J.H. Jans, H.H.B. Vedder, *European Environmental...*, pp. 217-218.

The case law of the General Court follows the second possibility. In T-177/13 *TestBioTech*[429] it argued that where there has been a decision to reject a request for internal review made as unfounded, the NGO to which that decision is addressed may bring an action for annulment against the decision, as provided for in the first situation covered by the fourth paragraph of Article 263 of the TFEU. By contrast, if the institution or the body in request decides to adapt the authorization covered by the request for internal review, the adapting measure may, where applicable, be the subject of a new request for internal review, provided that the conditions laid down in Article 10 of the Regulation are met. However, an NGO that made the request for internal review of an administrative act under Article 10 of the Regulation cannot require, at the end of internal review, that any specific measure be taken by the institution or body concerned. Thus, the choice of measures to be adopted following an internal review is entirely discretionary.[430] Moreover, the doctrine adds that the "written reply" does not automatically guarantee the admissibility of the action for annulment insofar as it is directed against the underlying measure. Therefore, the Court can apply the classical test of "direct and individual concern" to judge the admissibility of that action.[431]

The second question deals with the issue whether NGOs, which have unsuccessfully availed themselves of the internal review procedure, still have access to judicial review under Article 263 of the TFEU. It seems that the introduction of internal review procedure changed nothing in the complaint possibilities of NGOs before the CJEU. In particular, if the request in internal review procedure is considered inadmissible by the EU institution, the organization can still bring an action against the primary decision before the CJEU, provided that it fulfills all the requirements, including the two-month time period of launching proceedings by individuals.[432] As a result, the action under Article 263 of the TFEU and the request for internal review do not exclude each other. Still, it should be remembered that the understanding of the "direct and individual concern" requirements remain strict. In particular, the special status attributed to NGOs in the Aarhus Convention cannot automatically provide for circumstances of "individual concern" by the contested act of the EU law.[433] As a reminder, it means that the applicant can claim that the decision was of individual concern to him only if the decision affected him by reason of certain attributes of a particular nature, or by reason of factual circumstances which differentiate him from all other persons, and thereby distinguish him individually in the same way as the person addressed. For an individual to be directly affected, the measure challenged must directly produce effects on his legal, not factual, position and leave no discretion to the addresses of that measure who are entrusted with implementation, that being a purely automatic matter

429. ECLI:EU:T:2016:736.
430. Paras. 53-55 in T-177/13.
431. M. Pallemaerts, *Access...*, p. 296.
432. See, to this extent, T-565/14 *European Environmental Bureau (EEB) v. European Commission*, ECLI:EU:T:2015:559, T-685/14 *European Environmental Bureau (EEB) v. European Commission*, ECLI:EU:T:2015:560.
433. See, to this extent, T-236/04 *European Environmental Bureau (EEB) and Stichting Natuur en Milieu v. Commission of the European Communities*, ECLI:EU:T:2005:426.

flowing solely from the EU law without the intermediation of other rules.[434] However, this test has never been found to be fulfilled in any action for annulment brought by a member of the public, whether an NGO or individual seeking to enforce the EU environmental law.[435] In fact, the admissibility test in principle is hardly possible to be satisfied by any NGO. An organization formed for the protection of the collective interest of a category of persons could not be considered to be directly and individually concerned by a measure affecting the general interests of that category.[436]

The final issue deals with the scope of internal review procedure and its compatibility with Article 9 (3) of the Aarhus Convention. As discussed, internal review procedure is attributed solely to administrative acts and omissions of individual scope. Yet, the Convention does not limit access to justice only to individual acts of law and allows bringing actions against general acts of law as well. Consequently, it should be considered if Article 9 (3) could be directly applicable at the EU level.[437] This problem was subject to the CJEU ruling in joined cases C-401/12 P—C/403/12 P *Vereniging Milieudefensie and Stichting Stop Luchtverontreiniging Utrecht*.[438]

By the decision at issue, the Commission rejected the request for internal review procedure brought by Vereiniging Milieudefensie and Stichting Stop Luchtverontreiniging Utrech, an environmental association and a foundation governed by the Dutch law. The Commission found that the request was inadmissible on the grounds that the undermined decision[439] was not a measure of individual scope and that it could therefore not be considered an "administrative act."[440] The General Court annulled the decision at issue.[441] According to its judgment, Regulation 1367/2006 was adopted to meet the EU's international obligations under Article 9 (3) of the Aarhus Convention. The term "acts" is not defined by the Convention. Pursuant to well-established case law and Article 31 of the Vienna Convention of May 23, 1969, on the Law of Treaties,[442] an international treaty must be construed by reference to the terms in which it is framed and in the light of its objectives. Consequently, it must be held that an internal review procedure which covered only measures of individual scope would be very limited since acts adopted in the field of the environment are mostly acts of general

434. See also e.g. C-404/96 P *GlencoreGrain v. Commission*, ECLI:EU:C:1998:196, para. 41, C-486/01 P *National Front v. Parliament*, ECLI:EU:C:2004:394, para. 34, C-417/04 P *Regione Siciliana v. Commission*, ECLI:EU:C:2006:282, para. 28.
435. M. Pallemaerts, *Access...*, p. 298.
436. D. Obradovic, *EU Rules...*, p. 173.
437. The question also deals with the problem if Art. 9 (3) can serve as a reference criterion for the purposes of the review of legality. Provisions of international law that might serve such a criterion must necessarily include sufficiently clear, intelligible and precise elements. Nevertheless, it is important to point out that such a provision may be mixed in nature. If it is possible to isolate parts of the content of that provision which satisfy that requirement, it must be possible to conduct the review of legality; see e.g. Opinion of Advocate General Jääskinen in joined Cases C-401/12 P-C-403/12 P, ECLI:EU:C:2014:310, paras. 70-79.
438. ECLI:EU:C:2015:4.
439. I.e. Decision C(2009) 2560 final.
440. Para. 12 in C-401/12 P-C/403/12 P.
441. T-396/09, ECLI:EU:T:2012:301.
442. Available at: http://legal.un.org/ilc/texts/instruments/english/conventions/1_1_1969.pdf (on February 9, 2019).

application. Therefore, in the light of the objectives and purpose of the Aarhus Convention, such limitation is not justified.[443]

During the proceedings before the Court of Justice, the NGOs argued that the General Court vitiated the judgment by error of law in refusing to recognize the direct effect of Article 9 (3) of the Aarhus Convention, at least in so far as it provides that "acts" which infringe national environmental law must be subject to a right of appeal and, consequently, in refusing to assess the legality of Article 10 (1) of Regulation 1367/2006 in the light of Article 9 (3) of the Convention.[444]

The Court of Justice confirmed the previous assessment established in case C-240/09 *Lesoochranárske zoskupenie*[445] that Article 9 (3) does not contain sufficiently precise obligation capable of directly regulating the legal position of individuals.

443. According to the General Court, it emerges from the sixth and eighth recitals in the preamble to the Aarhus Convention that the authors of that Convention, "[r]ecognising that adequate protection of the environment is essential to human well-being and the enjoyment of basic human rights, including the right to life itself," consider that, "to be able to assert this right and observe this duty, citizens must have access to information, be entitled to participate in decision-making and have access to justice in environmental matters, [...] acknowledging in this regard that citizens may need assistance in order to exercise their rights." Moreover, the tenth recital to the Aarhus Convention states that "in the field of the environment, improved access to information and public participation in decision-making enhance the quality and the implementation of decisions, contribute to public awareness of environmental issues, give the public the opportunity to express its concerns and enable public authorities to take due account of such concerns." In addition, Art. 1 of the Aarhus Convention, which is entitled "Objective," provides that "[i]n order to contribute to the protection of the right of every person of present and future generations to live in an environment adequate to his or her health and well-being, each Party shall guarantee the rights of access to information, public participation in decision-making, and access to justice in environmental matters in accordance with the provisions of this Convention." Furthermore, it must be held that an internal review procedure which covered only measures of individual scope would be very limited, since acts adopted in the field of the environment are mostly acts of general application. In the light of the objectives and purpose of the Aarhus Convention, such limitation is not justified. Also, as regards the terms in which Art. 9(3) of the Aarhus Convention is framed, it should be noted that, under those terms, the Parties to that Convention retain a certain measure of discretion with regard to the definition of the persons who have a right of recourse to administrative or judicial procedures and as to the nature of the procedures (whether administrative or judicial). Under Art. 9(3) of the Aarhus Convention, only "where they meet the criteria, if any, laid down in [the] national law, [may] members of the public have access to administrative or judicial procedures." However, the terms of Art. 9(3) of the Aarhus Convention do not offer the same discretion as regards the definition of the "acts" which are open to challenge. Accordingly, there is no reason to construe the concept of "acts" in Art. 9(3) of the Aarhus Convention as covering only acts of individual scope. Lastly, so far as the wording of the other provisions of the Aarhus Convention is concerned, it should be noted that, under Art. 2(2) of that Convention, the concept of "public authority" does not cover "bodies or institutions acting in a judicial or legislative capacity." Accordingly, the possibility that measures adopted by an institution or body of the European Union acting in a judicial or legislative capacity may be covered by the term "acts," as used in Art. 9(3) of the Aarhus Convention, can be ruled out. That does not mean, however, that the term "acts" as used in Art. 9(3) of the Aarhus Convention can be limited to measures of individual scope. There is no correlation between measures of general application and measures taken by a public authority acting in a judicial or legislative capacity. Measures of general application are not necessarily measures taken by a public authority acting in a judicial or legislative capacity (paras. 63-67 in T-396/09).

444. Para. 29 in C-401/12 P-C/403/12 P.

445. Which, however, was based on the possible direct effect of Art. 9 (3) of the Aarhus Convention at national level.

Moreover, this provision is not unconditional since only members of the public who "meet the criteria, if any, laid down in ... national law" are entitled to exercise the rights provided for in Article 9 (3), which means that provision is subject, in its implementation or effects, to the adoption of a subsequent measure.[446] It cannot be considered that by adopting the Regulation 1367/2006, which concerns only the EU institutions and deals only with one of the remedies available to individuals for ensuring compliance with the EU environmental law, the EU intended to implement the full scope of obligations deriving from Article 9 (3) of the Aarhus Convention.[447] It follows that Article 9 (3) of the Aarhus Convention cannot be relied on in order to assess the legality of Regulation 1367/2006.[448]

Although this reasoning was also confirmed by judgment in C-404/12 and C-405/12 P *Stichting Natuur en Milieu*[449] and T-12/17 *Mellifera eV, Vereinigung für wesensgemäße Bienenhaltung*,[450] it is still subject to criticism in the doctrine. It was argued that the thinking of the CJEU concerning the potential direct effect of Article 9 (3) of the Aarhus Convention at the EU level was "insufficiently nuanced."[451] Accordingly, in the *Lesoochranárske zoskupenie* case the domestic courts were given the difficult and far-reaching task of finding a consistent interpretation with the Aarhus Convention's requirements to effectively enforce the limits of Article 9 (3) even against the domestic legislature.[452] Some scholars called the reasoning in these rulings "judicial subsidiarity"[453] as they go against the grain of the principle of procedural autonomy.[454] The transposition of the logic presented by the CJEU on the EU level would mean that the institutions such as the Commission should be obliged to implement Article 9 (3) in order to give it full effect, perhaps alongside broadening the scope of internal review to general acts of law as well. Simultaneously, such a perception could be the basis for loosening the strict understanding of "direct and individual concern" by the CJEU.[455]

These assertions were the main reasons why Regulation 1367/2006 met criticism in the doctrine.[456] It was indicated that it hardly brought any improvements to the legal standing of NGOs at the EU level as the scope of the Regulation was too restrictive.

---

446. Para. 55 in C-401/12 P-C/403/12 P.
447. Para. 60 in C-401/12 P-C/403/12 P.
448. Para. 61 in C-401/12 P-C/403/12 P.
449. ECLI:EU:C:2015:5, see paras. 44-52.
450. ECLI:EU:T:2018:616, see paras. 78-88.
451. J. Pirker, *Access...*, p. 89; see also A. Knade-Plaskacz, *Dostęp do wymiaru sprawiedliwości w sprawach dotyczących środowiska—transpozycja trzeciego filaru Konwencji z Aarhus do prawa Unii Europejskiej*, Przegląd Prawa Ochrony Środowiska Vol. 1/2014, p. 227.
452. J. Pirker *Access...*, p. 90.
453. S. Bogojević, *Judicial Protection of Individual Applicants Revisited: Access to Justice through the Prism of Judicial Subsidiarity*, Yearbook of European Law Vol. 34/2015, p. 5; cf. G.A. Bermann, *Taking Subsidiarity Seriously: Federalism in the European Community and the United States*, Columbia Law Review Vol. 94/1994, p. 331.
454. Cf. R. Ortlep, R.J.G.M. Widdershoven, *Judicial Protection* in: *Europeanisation of Public Law*, J.H. Jans, S. Prechal, R.J.G.M Widdershoven (eds), Groningen 2015, pp. 443-445.
455. R. Lanceiro, *The Review...*, pp. 379-381.
456. See e.g. A.M. Keessen, *European Administrative Decisions: How the EU Regulates Products on the Internal Market*, European Administrative Series Vol. 2/2009, pp. 151-153, J.H. Jans, *Did Baron von Munchausen ever visit Aarhus? Some Critical Remarks on the Proposal for a*

Unfortunately, it can be stated that the doctrinal considerations dealing with internal review are perhaps too theoretical as the actual application of the procedure is quite limited. A relatively high number of publications does not transpose to practice.[457] As the statistics indicates, internal review is very seldom used by NGOs. There have been only 38 requests for internal review to the Commission so far,[458] which were submitted as presented in Table 4.1.[459]

Table 4.1 The Number of Requests for Internal Review under the Provisions of Regulation 1367/2006

2007[1]	*2008*	*2009*	*2010*	*2011*	*2012*	*2013*	*2014*	*2015*	*2016*[2]
2	3	3	2	1	6	4	7	6	4

[1] Regulation 1367/2006 entered into force on June 28, 2007.

[2] There has been no data for 2017 or 2018 so far.

None of the requests led to an actual change of the contested decision. A vast majority of them (30%-79%) were deemed inadmissible. In most cases the reason for such a response was based on the strict understanding of "administrative act" as an act of individual scope.[460] A few requests (6%-14%)[461] were considered admissible but

Regulation on the Application of the Provisions of the Aarhus Convention to EC Institutions and Bodies in: *Reflections on 30 Years of EU Environmental Law: A High Level of Protection?*, R. Macrory (ed.), Groningen 2005, pp. 475-490.

457. For more see P. Staszczyk, *Organizacje...*, pp. 302-304.
458. Even though the actual number of the lodged requests is higher. This is due to the fact that if they deal with the same issue, they are joined into one proceeding.
459. Based on the official data published by the Commission at: http://ec.europa.eu/environment/aarhus/requests.htm.
460. Although there were also cases of lack of legal personality (see internal review of Commission Directive 2010/77/EU of 10 November 2010 amending Council Directive 91/414/EEC as regards the expiry dates for inclusion in Annex I of certain active substances) and of exceeding the prescribed time limit to sending a request (see internal review by GIET (Groupe International d'Études Transdisciplinaire) of the Commission Implementing Decision (EU) 2015/2279 of 4.12.2015 authorizing the placing on the market of products containing, consisting of, or produced from genetically modified maize NK603 × T25 (MON-ØØ6Ø3-6 × ACS-ZMØØ3-2) pursuant to Regulation (EC) No 1829/2003 of the European Parliament and of the Council (notified under document C(2015) 8581)).
461. I.e.:

    - internal review of Commission Decision 2007/701/EC of 24 October 2007 authorizing the placing on the market of products containing, consisting of, or produced from genetically modified maize NK603xMON810 (MON-00603-6xMON-00810-6) pursuant to Regulation (EC) No 1829/2003 of the European Parliament and of the Council (notified under document number C(2007) 5140), Commission Decision 2007/702/EC of 24 October 2007 authorizing the placing on the market of products containing, consisting of, or produced from genetically modified maize 59122 (DAS-59122-7) pursuant to Regulation (EC) No 1829/2003 of the European Parliament and of the Council (notified under document number C(2007) 5141), Commission Decision 2007/703/EC of 24 October 2007 authorizing the placing on the market of products containing, consisting of, or produced from genetically modified maize 1507xNK603 (DAS-01507-1xMON-00603-6) pursuant to

unfounded in terms of substance. Moreover, two requests[462] were deemed partially inadmissible and partially unfounded. On the grounds of Article 263 of the TFEU, 16 responses of the Commission (42%) were challenged before the General Court.[463] However, none of the actions was successful for the applying NGOs.

Regulation (EC) No 1829/2003 of the European Parliament and of the Council (notified under document number C(2007) 5142);

- internal review of Commission Decision 2010/135/EU of 2 March 2010 concerning the placing on the market, in accordance with Directive 2001/18/EC of the European Parliament and of the Council, of a potato product (*Solanum tuberosum L.* line EH92-527-1) genetically modified for enhanced content of the amylopectin component of starch and Commission Decision 2010/136/EU of 2 March 2010 authorizing the placing on the market of feed produced from the genetically modified potato EH92- 527-1 (BPS-25271-9) and the adventitious or technically unavoidable presence of the potato in food and other feed products under Regulation (EC) No 1829/2003 of the European Parliament and of the Council (GMO authorization);
- internal review of the Commission Implementing Decision 2012/347/EU of 28 June 2012 authorizing the placing on the market of products containing, consisting of, or produced from genetically modified soybean MON 87701 × MON 89788 (MON-877Ø1-2 × MON-89788-1) pursuant to Regulation (EC) No 1829/2003 of the European Parliament and of the Council;
- internal review by Greenpeace European Unit of the Commission Decision C(2015) 363 of 30.1.2015 recognizing *Le Commerce du Bois* as a monitoring organization under Regulation (EU) No 995/2010 laying down the obligations of operators who place timber and timber products on the market;
- internal review by ClientEarth of Commission Implementing Decision C(2016) 3549 granting an authorization for uses of bis(2-ethylhexyl) phthalate (DEHP) under Regulation (EC) No 1907/2006 of the European Parliament and of the Council of 16 June 2016;
- internal review by ClientEarth e.a. of Commission Decision C(2016) 5644 granting an authorization for uses of lead sulfochromate yellow and lead chromate molybdate sulfate red of 2.5.2017.

462. I.e.:

- internal review by GeneWatch UK and TestBiotech e.V. of the Commission Implementing Decision (EU) 2015/686 of 24 April 2015 authoring the placing on the market of products containing, consisting of, or produced from genetically modified soybean MON 87769 (MON-87769-7) pursuant to Regulation (EC) No 1829/2003 of the European Parliament and the Council (notified under document C(2015) 2757), the Commission Implementing Decision (EU) 2015/696 of 24 April 2015 authoring the placing on the market of products containing, consisting of, or produced from genetically modified soybean MON 87705 (MON-87705-6) pursuant to Regulation (EC) No 1829/2003 of the European Parliament and the Council (notified under document C(2015) 2770), the Commission Implementing Decision (EU) 2015/698 of 24 April 2015 authoring the placing on the market of products containing, consisting of, or produced from genetically modified soybean 305423 (DP-305423-1) pursuant to Regulation (EC) No 1829/2003 of the European Parliament and the Council (notified under document C(2015) 2773);
- internal review by TestBiotech e.V. of the Commission Implementing Decision (EU) 2015/687 of 24 April 2015 authoring the placing on the market of products containing, consisting of, or produced from genetically modified oilseed rape MON 88302 (MON-88302-9) pursuant to Regulation (EC) No 1829/2003 of the European Parliament and the Council (notified under document C(2015) 2759).

463. And only one judgment of the General Court was appealed before the Court of Justice (the already discussed Cases C-401/12 P-C/403/12 P *Vereniging Milieudefensie and Stichting Stop Luchtverontreiniging Utrecht*).

It appears that contrary to many prior predictions,[464] Regulation 1367/2006 and the introduction of internal review procedure did not "open" any new doors in terms of access to justice for NGOs acting in the collective interest at the EU level. Noticeably, the EU institutions do not adequately promote the accessibility of internal review and do not dispel all the practical doubts dealing with the requests. For instance, even though the Commission published a document called "Access to information, public participation and access to justice in environmental matters at Community level—A Practical Guide,"[465] it did not clarify the most significant issues arising in the process of preparing a request.[466] The Practical Guide is rather a simple repetition of proper provisions of Regulation 1367/2006 and the abovementioned decisions. As a matter of fact, this document has not even been updated since the Treaty of Lisbon.

Yet, the most significant problem with internal review is its scope. Although the organizations requesting for internal review do not have to prove their "direct and individual concern" by the challenged act of law, the limitation of this legal instrument to "administrative acts" makes it rather ineffective. Despite the presented case law of the CJEU, this limitation raises obvious doubts concerning the compatibility of Regulation 1367/2006 with Article 9 (3) of the Aarhus Convention. In fact, in March 2017, the Aarhus Convention Compliance Committee found that the EU was breaching the Convention by preventing the members of the public from challenging the EU institutions' environmental decisions in court.[467] Specifically, the Committee stated that neither the EU Regulation 1367/2006 nor the jurisprudence of the CJEU implemented or complied with the obligation established under the Convention.[468] Although the Committee did not state it directly, it seems that these critical remarks are based on the narrow scope of internal review procedure and, to some extent, on the strict premises of *locus standi* for individuals under Article 263 of the TFEU.[469] The ruling of the Compliance Committee was eventually accepted by the Council[470] but so far there have been no following decisions on how to apply it. It seems that the most desirable change would be to expand internal review procedure on general acts of the EU

464. Cf. T. Crossen, V. Niessen, *NGO...*, pp. 339-340.
465. Which was issued on the basis of Art. 7 of Decision 2008/401/EC; the Practical Guide is available at: http://ec.europa.eu/environment/aarhus/pdf/guide/AR%20Practical%20Guide%20EN.pdf (on February 9, 2019).
466. For more see P. Staszczyk, *Organizacje...*, p. 303.
467. See also F. Simon, *EU Slapped for Breaching Aarhus Convention on Access to Environmental Justice*, available at: http://bit.do/ej9H5 (on February 9, 2019).
468. See the press release of the Council of the European Union: *Aarhus Convention: Council adopts EU's positions for the forthcoming meeting of the parties*, available at: http://bit.do/eg4gU (on February 9, 2019).
469. This incompatibility was, however, stated directly in a different case. In a report issued in 2011, the Compliance Committee considered that the conditions under Art. 263 of the TFEU, as interpreted by the CJEU, were too restrictive for natural and legal persons to challenge an act before the ECJ. Moreover, according to the Committee's opinion, the preliminary ruling procedure neither met the requirements of access to justice under Art. 9 of the Aarhus Convention nor compensated for the strict conditions imposed by the CJEU (see Report of the Compliance Committee, Findings and Recommendations with regard to Communication ACCC/C/2008/32, European Union). Unfortunately, this case did not have any implications.
470. Even though the Commission had attempted to overturn the Council's decision; see F. Simon, *EU slapped...*

environmental law (at least to some extent). Even though such an amendment could raise some concerns,[471] it would definitely make the procedure more effective and, to a certain degree, would provide a remedy for the strict understanding of Article 263 of the TFEU in terms of bringing an action in the collective interest.

[D] Summary

The overall implementation of the Aarhus Convention should be evaluated positively. Its three pillars directly provided specific rights for members of the public, most notably for NGOs, in environmental matters.[472] Yet, it appears that the transposition of the Convention had different implications on the national and the EU level.

Doubtlessly, the Aarhus Convention at the national level contributed to a more proactive role of NGOs in the sphere of environmental law. This phenomenon can be most noticeably observed in court proceedings. Although the Convention does not require an introduction of *actio popularis*, it appears that environmental matters are the core of actions brought before the courts by NGOs acting in the collective interest.[473] Moreover, the Aarhus Convention provided general minimum standards of access to documents and participation in environmental decision-making which were not common in all Member States.[474] Still, it should be emphasized that the EU law deals with the transpositions of the Convention at the national level only to some extent (the transposition of other obligations deriving from the Aarhus Convention is left to Member States). In this area, the EU legislative is very fragmented and often not coherent. Therefore, it would be very expedient to create a common framework of general rules, especially in the sphere of access to justice and the general rules of public participation.

As far as the EU level is concerned, it can be generally stated that the implementation of the Aarhus Convention did not, in fact, change much:

(1) Access to documents was already provided by Regulation 1049/2001.
(2) The rules on public participation resemble the General Principles and Guidelines.
(3) The introduction of internal review has not led to any modifications of the challenged acts of law so far. It seems that if the procedure were not limited only to cases of "administrative acts," the outcomes of this new legal measure would be much more satisfactory.

Accordingly, some amendments would be most welcome. As the biggest concerns deal with the transposition of the third pillar of the Aarhus Convention, it would

471. For example, dealing with the question which EU institution should be competent to examine the requests for internal review in cases where the undermined act of law was issued jointly.
472. See also J. Jabłoński, *Dostęp do wymiaru sprawiedliwości w sprawach ochrony śwodowiska w świetle standardów prawa międzynarodowego*, Prawo i Srodowisko Vol. 3/2001, pp. 87 et seq.
473. E. Fasoli, *Legal...*, p. 338.
474. See e.g. E. Morgera, *An Update on the Aarhus Convention and Its Continued Global Relevance*, Review of European, Comparative & International Environmental Law Vol. 14/2005, p. 138.

be advantageous to expand the scope of internal review to at least some general acts of law dealing with environmental issues as well. Even though Regulation 1367/2006 does not directly relate to the premises of access to the CJEU by members of the public, it should be once again emphasized that the understanding of the conditions of NGO *locus standi* remains strict and forms a difficulty in bringing actions in the collective interest. Unfortunately, even though these remarks were also presented by the Aarhus Convention Compliance Committee, the amplification of access to justice in environmental matters at the EU level is rather unlikely in the nearest future.

§4.03 CONCLUSION

The analysis carried out in this chapter proved that the EU law envisages some special measures for NGOs acting in the collective interest. Apart from that, they can obviously benefit from all the general rules of the EU law, including specific rights attributed to individuals. The "legal tools" which may be used by NGOs can be found both at the national and the EU levels.

In certain spheres, the EU law grants particular rights to NGOs acting at the national level. Most notably, these means are related to environmental matters. In fact, some EU provisions on environmental participation[475] were a role model for remedies conceded in the Aarhus Convention. Furthermore, these specific rights seem to "spillover" to other fields as well. For instance, NGOs are subject to certain privileges in the new General Data Protection Regulation.

Two general remarks can be made in the context of rights attributed to NGOs at the national level. First, it should be remembered that the remedies ascribed by the EU law to individuals must be always effective. As a result, Member States are obliged to ensure that national remedies and procedural rules do not render claims based on the EU law impossible in practice or excessively difficult to enforce. Second, although the rights attributed by the EU law to NGOs can be limited in their scope, practice indicates that these prerogatives are not rarely broadened by Member States and they contribute to a better protection of the collective interest.

NGOs wishing to act in the public interest at the EU level can, in particular, lodge complaints to the Commission and the European Ombudsman. Even though these means have a "soft" nature, they can still have strong input on the EU agenda. One reason for this statement is that if the reasons presented in the complaint are credible, the whole procedure is "intercepted" by the proper EU institution which obviously has a more powerful position in the EU system than any NGO. The second reason is that the complaint possibilities to the CJEU are in fact limited. There is no *actio popularis* at the EU level and in issuing proceedings NGOs, like any other individuals, have to prove "direct an individual concern" by the challenged act of law. Even though they can also bring actions against acts directly addressed to them and against regulatory acts which are of direct concern to them and do not entail implementing measures, the fact is that the actions brought by NGOs are seldom admissible. Decisions are rarely addressed

475. E.g. Directive 85/337/EEC.

directly to the third sector organizations, and in the case of regulatory acts, the organizations still have to prove "direct concern." Moreover, an NGO can, theoretically speaking, successfully bring an action before the CJEU when it acts explicitly in the name of its members who are directly and individually concerned by the act at stake. Yet, the strict understanding of the premises of "direct and individual concern" makes it practically impossible for any NGO to act in the collective interest. In fact, none of the actions brought by various organizations in the collective interest was deemed admissible. As discussed, such strict understanding of the *locus standi* conditions was subject to much criticism in the legal literature. The propositions of loosening the presently binding interpretation were put forward by Advocate General Jacobs in C-50/00 P *UPA* and the ruling of the CFI in T-177/01 *Jégo-Quéré* but, unfortunately, were not accepted by the Court of Justice. Therefore, the rise of public interest litigation as a response to the growth of the EU into a legal order that goes beyond mere economic origins is still cumbersome.[476]

The picture of the rights attributed to NGO as advocates of the collective interest should be also complemented by the Aarhus Convention. This international agreement was doubtlessly a cornerstone in bolstering the role of NGOs in environmental matters. However, as it was evaluated in the previous paragraphs of this chapter, the Convention had a stronger influence on the national level. In particular, the implementation of the Aarhus Convention at the EU level is not complete. Moreover, many provisions deriving from the Convention had existed before in the EU law. Nevertheless, as suggested above, the proper transposition of this international agreement requires some amendments, both at the national and the EU levels.

476. M. von Wolferen, *The Limits...*, p. 930.

CHAPTER 5
The EU Law and the Cross-Border Activities of NGOs: Selected Aspects

The activity of NGOs at the European level does not limit itself to contacts with the EU institutions. Perhaps the most important sphere in developing European civil society is related to the daily cross-border activities and collaborations. The following chapter deals with the selected aspects of this inquiry.

Accordingly, it is significant to examine the CJEU case law and to observe to what extent NGOs can be exposed to the EU provisions on economic activities or free movement of capital. It should also be mentioned that the Commission has already proposed two regulations dealing with pan-European forms of NGO legal status. However, they did not encompass the vast variety of functions closely linked to not-for-profit actions of the third sector. Most notably, they did not provide sufficient norms on volunteering, public benefit purposes or crowdfunding. The subsequent part of analysis would not be complete without mentioning grant possibilities from the EU budget and the problems arising therefrom. In this aspect, a special legal form of political foundations shall also be distinguished as it is often confused with other third sector entities.

§5.01 THE CJEU CASE LAW ON NGO ACTIVITY

The CJEU case law provided many interesting indications dealing with the NGOs actions. Thus, it determined limits between "nonprofit" and "economic" activities in support for application of the EU labor and competition law. Additionally, while referencing to free movement of capital, it contributed to a special tax treatment for charity entities in Member States.

[A] "Economic Activity" and the Nondiscriminatory Principle

As a general rule, NGOs are not covered by the EU freedom of establishment.[1] Article 54 of the TFEU states that companies or firms formed in accordance with the law of a Member State and having their registered office, central administration or principal place of business within the Union shall be treated, for the purposes of this chapter,[2] in the same way as natural persons who are nationals of Member States. However, the notion "companies or firms" means companies or firms constituted under civil or commercial law, including cooperative societies, and other legal persons governed by public or private law, safe for those which are non-profit-making. The latter one generally excludes associations, foundations and other legal forms of NGOs as their primary objects are not targeted at profit-making. However, this statement does not mean that third sector organizations are forbidden to engage to some extent in economic activity and therefore benefit from the right of establishment.[3] Also, this does not signify that NGOs are completely precluded from the economic regulations and obligations. In practice, the CJEU adopted a functional approach toward NGO activity. Thus, it found entities operating in the nonprofit matter to be subject, in specific cases, to the EU law in areas ranging from labor law to competition law.

In C-29/91 *Sophie Redmond Stichting v. Hendrikus Bartol*,[4] the CJEU ruled that under the Directive on the transfer of undertaking,[5] the EU labor law requirements applied to a Dutch NGO financed entirely by the government.[6] The Court found out that functionally there was nothing to prevent the application of the Directive to nonprofit organizations on the transfer of their employees.[7]

As far as the EU competition law is concerned, the CJEU stated that it did not apply to organizations that primarily perform social functions and engage in non-profit-making activities of a noncommercial nature.[8] In order to be subject to the competition provisions, an organization has to be found an "undertaking" which means it engages

1. See e.g. E. Skibińska, *Komentarz do art. 58* in: *Traktat o funkcjonowaniu Unii Europejskiej. Komentarz, t. I. Art. 1-89*, D. Miąsik, N. Półtorak, A. Wróbel (ed.), Warsaw 2012, lex.pl. The freedom of establishment is, however, a fundamental right. See S. Biernat, A. Wasilewski, *Wolność gospodarcza w Europie*, Kraków 2000, pp. 197-202.
2. I.e., Title IV Free movement of persons, services and capital. Chapter 2 Right of establishment.
3. Broad definition: see, to that effect, Cases 2/74 *Reyners* (ECLI:EU:C:1974:68), para. 21 and C-55/94 *Gebhard*, ECLI:EU:C:1995:411, para. 25.
4. ECLI:EU:C:1992:144.
5. I.e., the previously binding Council Directive 77/187/EEC of 14 February 1977 on the approximation of the laws of the Member States relating to the safeguarding of employees' rights in the event of transfers of undertakings, businesses or parts of undertakings or businesses.
6. In his opinion, Advocate General Van Gerven, ECLI:EU:C:1992:144, acknowledged that never before had the Court been called upon to consider the application of this Directive to nonprofit organizations.
7. Para. 30 in Case C-29/91.
8. The Commission interpreted the case law as meaning that internal market and competition rules generally do not apply to "noneconomic activities" (as opposed to "economic activities") of organizations such as trade unions, political parties, churches and religious societies, consumer associations, learned societies, charities and relief and aid organizations—see Commission Notice on the notion of State aid as referred to in Art. 107(1) of the Treaty on the Functioning of the European Union, Official Journal, C 262/1, 19.7.2016.

in an "economic activity" regardless of its legal form, status or the manner in which it is financed. Nevertheless, the case law of the CJEU applies a wide test in this dimension. It is sufficient to be found an "undertaking" once an entity engages itself in an "economic activity" consisting in offering goods or services on the market.[9] For instance, in C-244/94 *Fédération Française des Sociétés d'Assurance,*[10] the CJEU observed that the sole fact that an NGO is not-profit-making or that it seeks only noncommercial objectives is irrelevant for the purposes of defining it as an "undertaking" for the purposes of the application of the EU competition law.[11] In consequence, NGOs are not generally exempted from the EU provisions applying to for-profit entities.[12] Such an approach also leads to the extension of the state aid rules to tax benefits in some instances. For example, in C-222/04 *Ministero dell'Economia e delle Finanze,*[13] the CJEU pointed out potential tax implications for NGOs that are subject to the competition rules.[14] Essentially, it observed that tax exemptions granted to such organizations might be treated as state aid which is incompatible with the EU law.[15]

Another notable aspect deals with Article 18 of the TFEU on the prohibition of discrimination on the basis of nationality. This legal norm provided the CJEU with an indirect and limited means of reviewing national laws that discriminated against certain member-based nonprofit associations. In C-172/98 *The Commission v. Kingdom of Belgium,*[16] the Commission questioned the compatibility of two Belgian laws with the EU law. Under the law of 1919, the conferral of legal personality on an international association pursuing "philanthropic, religious, scientific, artistic or pedagogical objectives" required at least one member with Belgian citizenship on the executive organ. Likewise, the law of 1921 concerning non-profit-making associations

9. See also J. Blicharz, *Skutki implementacji dyrektywy usługowej UE na działalność trzeciego sektora w Polsce—analiza prawna*, Trzeci Sektor Vol. 15/2008, pp. 63 et seq.
10. C-244/94 *Fédération Française des Sociétés d'Assurance, Société Paternelle-Vie, Union des Assurances de Paris-Vie and Caisse d'Assurance et de Prévoyance Mutuelle des Agriculteurs v. Ministère de l'Agriculture et de la Pêche*, ECLI:EU:C:1995:392.
11. See also Cases C-180/98-C-184/98 *Pavlov Stichting Pensioenfonds Medische Specialisten*, ECLI-:EU:C:2000:428.
12. See O. Breen, *EU Regulation of Charitable Organizations: The Politics of Legally Enabling Civil Society*, The International Journal of Not-for-Profit Law Vol. 10/2008, available at: http://www.icnl.org/research/journal/vol10iss3/special_3.htm (on February 9, 2019).
13. C-222/04 *Ministero dell'Economia e delle Finanze vs. Cassa di Risparmio di Firenze SpA, Fondazione Cassa di Risparmio di San Miniato, Cassa di Risparmio di San Miniato SpA*, ECLI:EU:C:2006:8.
14. The preliminary reference case concerned Italian foundations of banking origin, created by statute to be the controlling shareholding in companies engaged in banking activity upon the privatization of Italian public sector credit institutions (para. 7 in Case C-222/04). The question was whether these foundations could be subject to the EU rules on competition, even though they were assigned objects of social benefit (para. 60 in Case C-222/04). To this issue, the Court distinguished between a foundation that simply makes grants to nonprofit organizations and a foundation acting directly to pursue public interest or social assistance aims, using the national legislature's authorization to undertake necessary or opportune financial, commercial, real estate and asset operations (para. 105 in Case C-222/04). Whereas the former was not an undertaking, the latter had to be viewed as one because it was capable of offering goods or services on the market in competition with other operators, for example in fields like scientific research, education, art or health (para. 122 in Case C-222/04).
15. Para. 124 in C-222/04.
16. ECLI:EU:C:1999:335.

and institutions promoting the public interest required that three-fifths of the members should be Belgian citizens in order to qualify for legal personality against third parties.[17] The CJEU stated that these two laws breached the nondiscriminatory principle as they made the legal personality of an association contingent on the presence of Belgian citizens in the organization or its governing structures.[18] In other words, the freedom of establishment should be enjoyed by all EU citizens who wish to form associations in Belgium. However, it is important to emphasize that this assertion dealt with the freedom of establishment of citizens as natural persons and not of associations as legal persons.[19] It followed that given its membership element, a nonprofit association could not be discriminated against in terms of establishment in a Member State. To do so would indirectly discriminate against citizens of the EU on the basis of their nationality. Nevertheless, this case concerned only associations—entities with membership as an inseparable feature. In contrast, foundations are not based on membership but rather on their capital. This obviously reduces the applicability of Article 18 of the TFEU with reference to freedom of establishment in some cases dealing with NGOs.[20]

Furthermore, the CJEU articulated that the nondiscriminatory rule does not restrain Member States from imposing a "nonprofit" requirement in some spheres of service providing. In C-70/95 *Sodemare and Others v. Regione Lombardia*,[21] the Court stated that a Member State may, in the exercise of the powers it retains to organize its social security system, consider that the admission of private operators to that system as providers of social welfare services is to be made subject to the condition that they are non-profit-making.[22] Moreover, the fact that it is impossible for profit-making companies to participate autonomously in the running of a statutory social welfare system of a Member State by concluding contract which entitles them to be reimbursed by the public authorities for the costs of providing social welfare services is not liable to place profit-making companies from other Member States in a less favorable factual or legal situation than profit-making companies in the Member State in which they are established.[23] Thus, the nonprofit premise to conduct social service in national law cannot be regarded as contrary to provisions on freedom to provide services.[24]

As it can be seen, the sole fact that an entity is an NGO is not sufficient for any differences in its legal treatment. This statement entrails both rights and obligations. However, special treatment may arise if an organization pursues charity or public benefit purposes. Particularly, this concerns the benefits of free movement of capital, provided by Article 63 of the TFEU..

17. Para. 3 in C-172/98.
18. Para. 13 in C-172/98.
19. I.e., the right which is at present referred to in Art. 54 of the TFEU.
20. For more see O. Breen, *EU Regulation...*
21. ECLI:EU:C:1997:301.
22. Para. 32 in C-70/95.
23. Para. 33 in C-70/95.
24. I.e., at present referred to in Arts. 56-62 of the TFEU.

[B] Free Movement of Capital

The CJEU case law confirmed that nonprofit organizations enjoy the same rights under the Treaties as for-profit entities in the scope of free movement of capital between Member States.[25] Moreover, it assured that there were some exceptions in their free right to establishment. This resulted in a basis for new tax exemptions in cross-border charity in the EU. Most notably, in C-386/04 *Centro di Musicologia Walter Stauffer v. Finanzamt München für Körperscharften*,[26] the CJEU determined that although freedom of establishment of the foundation was not applicable to the Italian-based foundation because its residence in Germany was not a permanent one (even though the services additional to the building of the foundation were provided by a German agent), the organization enjoyed the benefits of free movement of capital.

In the discussed case, the CJEU was asked whether German corporation tax applied to commercial property in Munich owned by an Italian charitable foundation, when comparable property owned by German charities was exempt. The Stauffer Foundation, which was established in Italy, endowed scholarships for the young Swiss to study the history of music in Cremona, Italy. Under the German tax law, the foundation pursued recognized charitable objectives. Moreover, the German legislation did not require that the pursuit of such objectives benefit only the German nationals. As a result, the Italian foundation should be exempt from corporation tax. However, because the foundation seat and management were in Italy, its rental income in Germany was subject to tax. The German Federal Finance Court (*Bundesfinanzhof*) asked in a preliminary reference whether this approach was compatible with the Treaty's provisions on freedom of establishment and free movement of capital.[27]

The German government[28] argued that the conditions under which Member States conferred charitable status on a foundation, which entailed the grant of tax benefits and other privileges, varied from one state to the other, according to each state's conception of public utility and the scope given by it to the concept of "charitable purposes." It followed that a foundation which met the requirement imposed by Italian law was in comparable situation to a foundation which met the requirements imposed by the German law since it was highly likely that the requirements applicable in each Member State concerning the conferring of charitable status were different.[29] Consequently, a German foundation contributed to German society and benefited the state budget by relieving the state of some responsibilities. In contrast, the charitable activities of Stauffer Foundation had no benefits for the German people.

The CJEU found this argument only partially acceptable. First of all, it expounded that the provisions regulating the freedom of establishment were inapplicable to the

25. For more see also T. von Hippel, *Tax Benefits for Foreign-Based Charities: Key Challenges of the Non-discrimination Rule of the European Court for Justice*, ERA Forum Vol. 10/2009, pp. 281 et seq.
26. ECLI:EU:C:2006:568.
27. Para. 13 in C-386/04.
28. Together with the government of the United Kingdom.
29. Para. 35 in C-386/04.

Stauffer Foundation. However, the Court did not state that on the grounds that nonprofit NGOs in general can ever avail themselves of the establishment provisions. Instead, the CJEU noted that "establishment" should be understood very broadly. Hence, it stated that the right of establishment allowed a Community (EU) national to participate, on a stable and continuous basis, in the economic life of a Member State other than his state of origin and to profit therefrom, so contributing to economic and social interpretation within the Community in the sphere of activities as self-employed persons. Thus, NGOs are not automatically excluded from the scope of the right of establishment if a specific organization actively contributes to economic and social integration in the EU.[30] However, the Stauffer Foundation could not rely on this conclusion as it did not have a secured presence in Germany for the purposes of pursuing its activities because a German property management agent handled the services ancillary to the leasing of its Munich property.[31]

Yet, the CJEU found that the provision on the free movement of capital could be used in this case. The Court stated that this freedom forbad any restrictions on capital movements between Member States, including investments in real estate on a national territory by a nonresident.[32] As a result, as the German tax exemption applied only to charitable organizations established in Germany, the exemption in principle discriminated against charitable organizations established in other Member States and constituted an obstacle to the freedom.[33] The CJEU noted that while Member States were entitled to require a sufficiently close link between foundations upon which they confer charitable status for the purposes of granting certain tax benefits and the activities pursued by those foundations, in this case it was irrelevant whether such a link existed.[34]

According to the CJEU, an organization recognized as a charity[35] within its Member State of origin is not automatically entitled to the same status in other Member States. This means that there is no automatic recognition of the special treatment conferred to an organization (with reference to its public purpose status) in one Member State. However, a Member State cannot deny the right to equal treatment on the grounds that an NGO[36] is established in another state if it meets three conditions:[37]

(1) it holds a charitable status in one Member State,
(2) it satisfies the requirements for a charitable status in a second Member State,
(3) it promotes the same public interests (the matter that should be evaluated by the authorities of the second Member State).

30. See also, to this extent C-70/95 *Sodemare.*
31. Para. 23 in C-386/04.
32. See also C-35/98, *Verkooijen,* ECLI:EU:C:2000:294, para. 59, C-136/00 *Danner,* ECLI:EU:C:2002:558, para. 56.
33. Para. 27 in C-386/04.
34. Para. 37 in C-386/04.
35. Or, in other legal systems (e.g., in Poland), a public benefit entity.
36. The judgment dealt with a foundation but it is justified to extrapolate it to other NGOs as well.
37. Para. 40 in C-386/04.

This statement led the CJEU to a conclusion that the requirement of German establishment in the *Stauffer* case could only be sustained if it was justified by overriding reasons in the general interest (e.g., the promotion of culture, training and education, the need for effective fiscal supervision, the need to ensure the cohesion of the national tax system, the need to protect the basis of tax revenue or the fight against crime).[38] The CJEU noted that Germany faced obvious difficulties whether a foreign charitable NGO fulfilled its public benefit requirements or in monitoring the management of the organization. However, these difficulties were of a "purely administrative nature."[39] As for the public benefit requirement, the national tax authority could require that the organization produced evidence to support its claim or it could call upon tax authorities in other Member States to validate the required information. As for the fight against crime, the Court held that a foundation established in another Member State could not of itself give rise to an assumption of criminal activity. Therefore, barring tax exemptions on this basis was also disproportionate.[40]

The judgment in the *Stauffer* case is very significant in respect of NGOs foreign fundings. According to the CJEU, a charitable NGO (i.e., an organization dealing with the public benefit purposes listed by a Member State) which enjoys tax exemptions in one Member State cannot be discriminated on the basis of its nonresident status.[41] In consequence, the judgment means that the denial of tax benefits with reference to national requirements for charitable or public purpose status should be thoroughly justified. Previously, a Member State could make equal tax reliefs conditional to:

(a) a requirement that an organization has its seat in this Member State,
(b) varying requirements of national laws on charity or public benefit purposes.[42]

It seems that the outcome of the *Stauffer* case raised more concern on the NGO cross-border activity. As a result, the Commission investigated various national tax regimes in areas dealing with tax exemptions for charity NGOs.[43] In fact, some countries changed their tax laws in order to fulfill the nondiscriminatory requirements established by the CJEU in the *Stauffer* case.[44]

38. Para. 43 in C-386/04.
39. Para. 48 in C-386/04.
40. Para. 61 in C-386/04
41. O. Breen, *EU Regulation...*
42. For more see O. Breen, *EU Regulation...*; P. Bater, *The Tax Treatment of Cross-Border Activities*, International Bureau of Fiscal Documentation (Amsterdam) No 121/2001, p. 121.
43. E.g. Belgium, the UK, Ireland, Poland, and Portugal.
44. S. Heidenbauer, *Charity Crossing Borders. The Fundamental Freedom' Influence on Charity and Donor Taxation in Europe*, Alphen aan den Rijn 2011, p. 42. In this matter, a good example is Art. 26 of the Polish Act on Income Tax from Natural Persons (*Ustawa o podatku dochodowym od osób fizycznych*) which was amended and now states:

 1.Basis for calculation of the tax, subject to article 22. 29-30 c, art. 30e. 30F, income is determined in accordance with article 8. 9, art. 24 paragraph 1. 1, 2, 3b-3e, 4-4e and 6 or article. paragraph 24B. 1 and 2, or article. 25, after deduction of amounts:

 9) donations provided for the purposes of: (a)) referred to in Article 1. 4 of the act on public benefit activities, the organizations referred to in article 1. 3 paragraphs 1 and 2. 2 and 3

Another significant judgment was issued in C-318/07 *Hein Persche v. Finanzamt Ludenscheid*.[45] The preliminary reference dealt with the question whether the free movement of capital applied where a national of a Member State donated goods to a body based in a different Member State, when the goods were recognized as charitable by that Member State law. Again, the core of this inquiry related to tax issues.

In his tax return for 2003, H. Persche claimed an exceptional deductible expense of a gift of bed linen, towels, zimmer frames and toy cars for children, which he made to a Portuguese NGO—Centro Popular de Lagoa in a total value of EUR 18,180. The center led a retirement home and was situated in the area where the appellant in the main proceeding owned a house.[46] By its assessment for 2003, the Finanzamt refused the deduction claimed. It also rejected, as unfounded, the objection lodged against the assessment by the appellant in the main proceedings. The appeal which H. Persche brought before the District Court in Münster (*Fianzgericht Münster*) was also unsuccessful. The appellant subsequently lodged an appeal on a point of law before the Bundesfinanzhof which referred to the Court for a preliminary ruling dealing with the scope of the free movement of capital.[47]

By the first question, the national court asked whether, where a taxpayer claimed in a Member State, the deduction for tax purposes of gifts to bodies established and recognized as charitable in another Member State, such gifts came within the compass of the provision of the EC Treaty relating to the free movement of capital, even if they were made in kind in the form of everyday consumer goods. The CJEU stated that such gifts were within the compass of the provisions of the Treaty.[48]

By its second and third questions, the national court asked whether the free movement of capital precluded legislation of a Member State which allowed the benefit of a deduction for tax purposes only for gifts made in favor of charitable bodies established in that state. This doubt was referred to the fact that the tax authorities of that Member State had to be able to verify the taxpayer's declarations and could not require to act in breach of the principle of proportionality.[49]

The CJEU declared that the German legislation providing the deduction for tax purposes to charitable bodies situated in Germany, while excluding that tax advantage for gifts to bodies established and recognized as charitable in another Member State, constituted a restriction of the freedom.[50] It added that while it was lawful for a

of this act, or equivalent organizations referred to in the regulations governing public benefit activities other than those in force in the Republic of Poland a Member State of the European Union or another country belonging to the European economic area, the public benefit activities in the sphere of public tasks, carrying out these objectives, subject to the provisions of paragraph 2. 6E, b), c) religious donations by honorary blood donors in accordance with article 4. 6 of the act of 22 August 1997 on public service (Journal of laws No. 106, item 681, with further amendments), in the amount of money equivalent for taken blood specific provisions issued pursuant to article 12. 11 (1). 2 of this act, in the amount of donations, but not more than the amount representing 6% of income.

45. ECLI:EU:C:2009:33.
46. Para. 12 in C-318/07.
47. Para. 14 in C-318/07.
48. Para. 25 in C-318/07.
49. Para. 31 in C-318/07.
50. Paras. 37 and 39 in C-318/07.

Member State to restrict the grant of tax advantages pursuing certain of its charitable purposes,[51] a Member State could not restrict the benefit of such advantages to bodies established in that state whose activities were capable of absolving it of some of its responsibilities.[52]

Admittedly, the CJEU noted that by encouraging taxpayers, with the prospect of a tax deduction for gifts made to bodies recognized as charities, a Member State encouraged such bodies to develop charitable activities for which, in most cases, it would or could take responsibility. Therefore, it is conceivable that national legislation providing a deduction for tax purposes of gifts for the benefit of charities could encourage such bodies to substitute themselves for the public authorities in assuming certain responsibilities and that such assumption could lead to a reduction of the expenses of the Member State concerned capable of compensating, at least partly, for its decreased tax revenues resulting from the right to deduct gifts.[53] However, it did not follow that a Member State could introduce a difference in treatment, in respect of the deduction for tax purposes of gifts, between national bodies recognized as being charitable and those established in another Member State.[54] Conversely, it was permissible for a Member State to apply a difference in treatment between national bodies recognized as charitable and those established in other Member States if the latter bodies pursued objectives other than those advocated by their own legislation.

The CJEU also confirmed that where a body recognized as having charitable status in one Member State satisfied the requirements imposed for that purpose by the law of another Member State and where its object was to promote the very same interests of the general public, so that it would be likely to be recognized as having charitable status in the latter Member State, it could not be denied the right to equal treatment solely on the grounds that it was not established in that Member State.[55]

A different problem arose in C-25/10 *Missionswerk Werner Heukelbach eV v. the Belgian State*.[56] The reference was made in proceedings concerning the tax authority[57] refusal to apply at a reduced rate the succession duties payable by the organization in respect of a legacy which it had received. Missionswerk was a religious association with its seat in Germany. By a holograph will dated November 5, 2003, it was named as residuary legatee by Mrs. Renardie who resided in Belgium throughout her life and died there.[58] However, the tax authority did not apply the reduced rate for succession duties provided for bodies with a center of operation either in Belgium or in the Member State in which, at the time of death, the deceased actually resided or had his place of work, or in which he or she had previously actually resided or had his or her place of work.

51. In this matter see para. 57 in C-386/04.
52. Para. 44 in C-318/07.
53. Para. 45 in C-318/07.
54. Para. 46 in C-318/07.
55. Para. 49 in C-318/07.
56. ECLI:EU:C:2011:65.
57. I.e. *Administration de l'enregistrement et des domaines*.
58. Para. 7 in C-25/10.

According to the Belgian government, such a difference in tax treatment was justified since, in relation to the objective sought by the Belgian legislation, non-profit-making organizations like Missionswerk were not in a situation which was objectively comparable to that of bodies whose center of operations was in Belgium. Thus, the Belgian government claimed that Member States were entitled to require, for the purposes of granting certain tax benefits, a sufficiently close link between non-profit-making bodies and the activities in which they were engaged and to determine which interests of the community at large they wished to promote by granting tax benefits to those bodies.[59]

The CJEU did not agree with this argumentation. It stated that, in general, it was lawful for a Member State to require, for the purposes of granting certain tax advantages, that there is a sufficiently close link between the bodies which that Member State recognized as pursuing some of its charitable purposes and the activities pursued by those bodies. However, a Member State could not grant such advantages only to bodies which were established in its territory and whose activities were capable of relieving that state of some responsibilities.[60] In particular, the possibility that a Member State may have been relieved of some of its responsibilities did not mean that it was free to introduce any difference in treatment between national bodies recognized as pursuing charitable purposes on the one hand and bodies established in another Member State recognized as pursuing charitable purposes on the other hand, provided that they reflect the same objectives as the legislation of the former Member States. Thus, where a body recognized as pursuing charitable purposes in one Member State satisfied the conditions laid down for that purpose in the legislation of another Member State and where its object was to promote the very same interests of the community at large so that it would be likely to be recognized in the latter Member State as pursuing charitable purposes—a matter which was for the national authorities of that Member State, including its courts, to determine—the authorities of the latter Member State could not deny that body the right to equal treatment solely on the grounds that it was not established in the territory of that Member State.[61] It was also held that the need to prevent the reduction of tax revenues was neither among the objectives stated in Article 65 of the TFEU nor an overriding reason in the public interest capable of justifying a restriction on the freedom instituted by the Treaty.[62] Hence, according to the CJEU, Article 63 of the TFEU precludes legislation of a Member State which reserves application of succession duties at the reduced rate to non-profit-making bodies which have their center of operations in that Member State or in the Member State in which, at the time of death, the deceased actually resided or had his place of work, or in which he had previously resided or had his place of work.

Conclusively, in C-10/10 *European Commission v. The Republic of Austria*,[63] the CJEU dealt with tax exemptions related to donations. The Austrian tax deductions

59. Para. 27 in C-25/10.
60. Para. 30 in C-25/10.
61. Para. 33 in C-25/10.
62. Para. 31 in C-25/10.
63. ECLI:EU:C:2011:399.

entailed, for taxpayers making gifts to research and teaching institutions established in Member States other than the Republic of Austria, a greater tax burden than for taxpayers making gifts to the national institutions. The CJEU stated that while the Member States were free to define the objectives in the public interest that they wished to promote by granting tax advantages to private or public bodies which pursued those objectives in a disinterested manner and complied with the requirements relating to their implementation, they had to exercise that discretion in accordance with the EU law.[64] It followed that the sole criterion capable of distinguishing between taxpayers making gifts to institutions whose seat is in Austria and those making gifts to corresponding institutions established in other Member States was, in fact, the place of establishment of the recipient of the gift. Such a criterion, by definition, cannot be a valid criterion for assessing the objective comparability of the situations or, consequently, for establishing an objective difference between them.[65]

Insofar as the Republic of Austria relied on the objective of promoting national education and training, even assuming that such an objective could constitute an overriding reason in the public interest capable of justifying a restriction of the free movement of capital, a restrictive measure had to comply with the principle of proportionality in order to be justified. In this respect, according to the CJEU, the Republic of Austria did not put forward any argument to show that the objective it pursued in this field could not be achieved without the contested legislation or by applying less restrictive measures regarding the possibility of choosing the recipients for the gifts a taxpayer wished to make.[66] It can be summarized that for national tax legislation which distinguishes between gifts to national institutions and those to institutions established in other Member States, to be regarded as compatible with the Treaty provisions on the free movement of capital, the difference in treatment must concern situations which are not objectively comparable or must be justified by an overriding reason in the public interest.[67]

Most recently, in July 2017, the Commission decided to initiate infringement proceedings against Hungary for its new law on foreign-funded NGOs. In December 2017 the matter was brought before the CJEU.[68] The new Hungarian law introduced an obligation for certain categories of NGOs[69] receiving annual foreign funding above HUF 7,200,000 (about EUR 24,000) to register and label themselves in all their publications, websites and press material as "organizations supported from abroad," and to report specific information about the funding they receive from abroad to the Hungarian authorities.[70] What was rightly emphasized by the Commission is the fact that this law institutes an unjustified and disproportionate restriction to the free movement of

64. In this matter see para. 48 in C-386/04.
65. Para. 34 in C-25/10.
66. Para. 38 in C-10/10.
67. Para. 40 in C-10/10.
68. The European Commission Press release of 7 December 2017—Infringements—European Commission refers Hungary to the Court of Justice for its NGO Law.
69. E.g. Church, sport and ethical minorities organizations are excluded from the scope of this law.
70. The European Commission Press release of 13 July 2017—Infringements—Hungary: Commission launches procedure for law on foreign-funded NGOs.

capital as registration, reporting and publicity requirements foreseen by the law are discriminatory and create an administrative and reputational burden for the "foreign-funded" NGOs.[71] Such measures can have a dissuasive effect on the funding from abroad and will make it difficult for the concerned organizations to receive it.[72] Also, what was not stated clearly enough by the Commission is that the new law does not introduce any new field of transparency with regard to the subject organizations as all information, concerning their funding as well, is published in annual reports. Thus, it seems that the main object of the new law is to somehow "stigmatize" some NGOs as "foreign" and, in this way, to reduce their credibility.[73] Apart from movement of capital, the Commission has claimed that the new law is also at odd with:

- the EUChFR, in particular with the right to freedom of association, as it could prevent NGOs from raising funds and would restrict their ability to carry out their works;
- the right to protection of private life and of personal data as it does not strike a fair balance between transparency interests and the right of donors and beneficiaries to protect their personal data (in particular this relates to the requirement to provide the Hungarian authorities with the exact amounts of transactions and detailed information about donors, which are then to be made public by the authorities).[74]

Therefore, it seems that the new law will be found incompatible with the EU law. However, further legal proposals on "stigmatizing" foreign-funded NGOs have also been proposed in Hungary.[75] Similar developments are also proceeded in Romania.[76] All of these proposals should be evaluated negatively not only in the light of the free movement of capital but also due to the fact they attempt to falsely take away civil society's confidence in the third sector organizations.[77]

71. Press release of 13 July 2017.
72. See also *Hungarian NGO Funding Law in Breach of EU Fundamental Freedoms and Charter Right; Legal Opinion by J. Simor and A. Welsh,* Matrix Chambers 22.6.2017, available at: http://bit.do/ej94S (on February 9, 2019).
73. In this aspect, First Vice President of the Commission, T. Timmermans, noted: "Civil society is the very fabric of our democracies and therefore should not be unduly restricted in its works," see Press release of 13 July 2017.
74. Press release of 13 July 2017.
75. See *Hungary's Government Strengthens its Anti-NGO Smear Campaign,* Human Rights Watch opinion of 20.1.2018, available at: http://bit.do/ej95K (on February 9, 2019). In January 2019 the Commission sent a reasoned opinion to Hungary concerning "Stop Soros laws," i.e. legislation that criminalizes asylum activities and residence applications, restricts the right to request asylum and establishes restrictions for NGOs helping asylum seekers. See the European Commission Press release of 24 January 2019—Asylum: Commission takes next step in infringement procedure against Hungary for criminalizing activities in support of asylum applicants.
76. See Opinion on the Romanian Draft Law 140/2017 on Associations and Foundations as adopted by the Senate on November 20, 2017. Opinion prepared by the Expert Council of the Conference of INGOs of the Council of Europe, CONF/EXP(2017)3.
77. I. De Jesus Butler, *Participatory...*

[C] Summary

Although NGOs are not encompassed by Article 54 of the TFEU, they are not generally excluded from specific provisions, ranging from labor law to competition law, if they undertake particular activities. In certain instances, NGOs can also benefit from the nondiscriminatory principle. Furthermore, NGO activity can be subject to the free movement of capital. A few remarks can be made based on the case law on this issue. First, the CJEU does not preclude NGOs from provisions on economic activity. This concerns both rights and obligations that can be attributed according to the EU law. Second, although the CJEU does not establish a principle of automatic recognition of charity or public benefit status in the EU, it does state that an NGO cannot be treated differently in the context of free movement of capital on the grounds that it was grounded in another Member State. It results in the requirement of nondiscriminatory treatment of any EU-based charity organization with regard to tax law.[78] Third, the CJEU case law emphasizes that public benefit purposes of an organization cannot be seen as national only. Thus, if an organization operates in one Member State but primarily contributes to charity actions in another Member State, it cannot be discredited in the former one only because it does not have a sufficiently "close link" to its community. It seems that in this sphere the CJEU sees the "European community" as a whole. Therefore, although Member States can constitute a catalog of their public benefit purposes, they cannot limit their influence only to the national borders. This observation appears very relevant in the context of developing European civil society.

§5.02 REGULATION PROPOSALS

The EU company law was based on two concepts.[79] The first one was to harmonize the law of Member States by adopting harmonized rules. This attitude achieved some success but it was difficult to harmonize widely different legal systems, for example when they reflect different national attitudes to issues such as management of the company or worker involvement. The second approach was to construct a whole new system of the EU company law that coexist alongside the individual company laws of Member States.

Although the idea of a European company statute began in the 1960s, the concept of a uniform tool in the third sector is relatively recent.[80] The EU institutions' interest in this subject matter was predominantly linked to the initiation of internal market in the early 1990s. So far, there have been two proposals for European NGO statutes. In both cases, the approach of creating a uniform legal environment was adopted. This is perhaps one of the reasons why neither of the proposed regulations came into force.

78. Cf. P. Bater, *Introduction: International Tax Issues Relating to Nonprofit Organizations and Their Supporters* in: *The Tax Treatment of NGOs. Legal, Ethical and Fiscal Frameworkes for Promoting NGOs and Their Activities*, P. Bater, F. Hondius, P. Kessler Lieber (eds), The Hague 2004, p. 14.
79. H. Koster, *EU Legal Entities—New Options?*, European Company Law Vol. 12/2015, p. 5.
80. R. Rossi, *The Proposal for a European Foundation Statute and Its Influence on Italian Legislation*, International Journal of Not-for-Profit Law Vol. 16/2014, p. 24.

The doctrine names three advantages of the proposed statutes.[81] First, the new instruments would be beneficial for enhancing the collaboration practices between NGOs from different states in various joint activities and co-funded projects. Second, the proposed regulations would reassure that the pan-European NGOs enjoy the freedom of establishment for all activities that contribute to the common objectives of the EU. Third, the statutes would ease the giving and receiving of gifts and grants across borders. However, the latter argument is partially obsolete with the already discussed developments in the CJEU case law.

[A] European Association Statute

The initial Regulation on European Association (EA) Statute was proposed in 1991.[82] It was a part of the Community (EU) package on *économie sociale*.[83] This package, vastly based on French law, also comprised proposals of statutes for cooperatives[84] and mutual societies.[85] It was supposed to create the basis for European entities that would involve in economic activity but at the same time would have other "engaged" purposes, e.g. increasing solidarity on the labor market, protecting the environment or fighting against social exclusion and discrimination.[86] The preamble of the proposal stressed out that like cooperatives and mutual societies, associations became important in all European countries at the end of the previous century, in response to the needs of particular groups of people, especially the poorest. They took different shapes depending on the traditions of the country and the particular circumstances of the time. The legal mechanisms adopted were not the same from one century to another. Cooperatives, mutual societies and associations are different forms, but in practice they may amount to much the same thing.[87]

The doctrine noted that the general legal basis for establishing the EA could be found in the antidiscrimination principle on the grounds of nationality, embedded on the freedom of establishment which should provide a legal instrument to enable third sector bodies to operate transnationally.[88] This foundation could provide the European Statute of Association with an instrument against discrimination toward nonprofit entities. Thus, the background of the proposed statute was to enable associations to

81. For more see O. Breen, *EU Regulation...*
82. Final version of 5 March 1992, COM(91) 273 final—SYN 386.
83. See e.g. J. Restakis, *Defining the Social Economy—The BC Context*, BC Social Economy Roundtable 2006, available at: http://www.msvu.ca/socialeconomyatlantic/pdfs/DefiningSocialEconomy_FnlJan1906.pdf, February 9, 2019.
84. COM(91) 273 final—SYN 389.
85. COM(91) 273 final—SYN 391.
86. C.R.M. Versteegh, *Civil...*, p. 5, S. McLaughlin, *Unlocking Company Law*, Abingdon 2013, p. 54.
87. See explanatory memorandum—Statute for a European Association, para. 4.
88. T. von Hippel, T. Vahlpahl, *The European Foundation Statute—As Things Currently Stand*, Trust & Trustees, Vol. 6/2013, p. 511, J. Kendall, L. Fraisse, *The European Statute of Association: Why an Obscure but Contested Symbol in a Sea of Indifference and Skepticism?*, TSEP working paper 11, 2005. The Center for Civil Society, London School of Economics and Political Science, London, UK, available at: http://eprints.lse.ac.uk/29018/1/11TSEP.pdf (on February 9, 2019).

take advantage of the single market in the same ways as companies can.[89] According to the proposal, the completion of the internal market means that there must be full freedom of establishment for all activities which contribute to the objectives of the Community (EU), irrespective of the form taken by the body which carries them on.[90]

[1] Project Scope

As already noted above, domestic association law is not subject of harmonization through the proposed Regulation and the EA would be a new form of transnational organization that could operate in all Member States. Nevertheless, the proposal has many flaws. It appears that the majority of articles deal with issues of rather minor importance. Thus, a large part of the proposed Regulation copes with internal procedures in a very protracted and detailed way (for instance, Articles 11-14 on the general meeting). As a result, it is often hard to follow. This was arguably one of the reasons for its failure as the key to success for regulations is their availability and comprehensibility.[91]

Although the proposal copes with associations, the principal idea was to discipline both associations and foundations in a unique regulation. The preamble of the revised proposal for a Council Regulation on the Statute for a European Association published in 1993[92] is explicit in referring to both of these legal forms as it emphasizes that "the introduction of a European form of organization should enable all associations and foundations to operate outside their own national borders." The proposal affirms the role of both legal forms of the third sector organizations as they:[93]

- help to promote the general interest to develop many and various activities in fields such as education, culture, social work or development aid;
- are entities to which have been irrevocably allotted goods, rights and resources for carrying out work which is of public interest;
- are entities which act without the main intention of securing a profit and which operate in accordance with their own principles, which are different from those applying to other businesses;
- play a full part in the life of the economy, by engaging on a regular basis in some economic activity, as their main activity or a secondary one;
- are hampered by legal and administrative difficulties in the Community (EU) which should be eliminated in a market without frontiers;

89. J. Cremers, *The European Association* in: *A Decade of Experience with the European Company*, J. Cremers, M. Stollt, S. Vitols (eds), Brussels 2013, p. 256.
90. See *Voluntary organisations: proposed EC statutes: European cooperative society; European mutual society; European association and accompanying Directives regarding the involvement of employees. A consultative document issued by the Treasury of Great Britain*, available at: https://archive.org/details/op1279308-1001.
91. Cf. O. Breen, *The European Foundation Statute Proposal: Striking the Balance Between Supervising and Supporting European Philanthropy?*, Nonprofit Policy Forum Vol. 1/2014, p. 31.
92. As presented by the Commission, COM(93) 285 final.
93. See preamble to the Regulation on the statute for an FE.

- are a form of organization generally recognized in all Member States, with an adequate legal instrument capable of facilitating the development of their transnational activities;
- exemplify a People's Europe in that they help and encourage individuals to play an active role in the life of the Community (EU) and it is fitting that natural persons should also be able to establish a European association *ab initio*.

Yet, the proposal does not envisage the possibility that the third sector organizations could conduct their cross-border activities in the legal form of a foundation. Even if foundations were the only subjects wishing to ground a European legal entity, the legal form of such a body would have to be of an association.

According to Article 1 (1) of the proposal, a European Association (EA) shall be a permanent body whose members pool their knowledge or their activities either for a purpose in the general interest as understood in the legal system of the Member State in which the EA has its registered office or in order, directly or indirectly, to promote the trade or professional interests of its members. Thus, the Regulation designates the EA to freely determine its objects, provided they are compatible with the public policy of the Member State in which it has its seat and, implicitly (as it is to function across borders), with the objectives of the Community (EU).[94] Moreover, the organization is not prevented from carrying on economic activities. Neither are there any limitations as to the extent of the conducted economic activities or to their profitability.[95] However, the profits from any economic activity carried out by the EA should be devoted exclusively to the pursuit of its objects and may not be divided among its members.[96] Hence, the EA fulfills the requirements to be qualified as a not-for-profit NGO. Moreover, the EA's liability is limited to its assets.[97]

Article 2 of the proposal forms the EA's legal personality which is to be acquired on the day of registration in the register designated by the Member State in which the EA has its registered office.[98] An EA's legal personality entitles in particular to perform any of the following acts, provided they are necessary for the pursuit of its objects:

(a) to conclude contracts and to perform other acts,
(b) to acquire movable and immovable property,
(c) to receive donations and legacies,

94. J. Cremers, *The European...*, p. 256.
95. Direct quote of Art. 1 (2): subject to the application at national level of the legal and administrative rules governing the carrying on of an activity or the exercise of a profession, the EA shall be free to determine the activities necessary to pursuit its objects, provided they are compatible with the objectives of the Community, Community public policy and the public policy of the Member States. It shall pursue them in accordance with the principles which derive from its character as a grouping of persons and shall be managed in a disinterested fashion.
The profits from any economic activity carried out by the EA shall be devoted exclusively to the pursuit of its objects and may not be divided among the members.
96. Explanatory memorandum, remarks to Art. 1.
97. For more information see e.g. R. Märkle, M. Alber, *Der Verein im Zivil- und Steuerrecht*, Munich 2017, pp. 7 et seq.
98. I.e., registered by proper national institution, e.g. in Poland by National Court Register (*Krajowy Rejestr Sądowy*).

(d) to employ staff,
(e) to be a party to legal proceedings.

Article 3 (1) and (2) list two ways of forming an EA. First, an EA can be formed directly either by at least two of the legal entities listed in the Annex to the Regulation,[99] which are formed under the law of a Member State in accordance with the laws, regulations and administrative provisions in force, and have their registered offices in at least two Member States, or by a minimum of 21 natural persons who are nationals of and resident in at least two Member States. This figure of 21 takes account of the minimum conditions laid down by the Greek law on associations.[100] Reasonably, the EESC Assembly found that "the minimum requirement of 21 natural persons is too high,[101] particularly as this threshold was set to take account of only one country's law."[102] Therefore, it proposed that an EA might have been formed from a minimum of seven natural persons.[103] Second, an EA could be formed by conversion of a domestic association if the converting association has an establishment in a Member State other than that in which it has its registered office and can show that it is carrying a genuine cross-border activity. However, in this case the European character of the newly formed EA cannot be fictitious and there must be a genuine and substantial presence of members of different nationalities. Such a conversion into an EA shall not result in the association being wound up or in the creation of a new legal person.

According to Article 3 (3) the statue of an EA must include:

- its name, preceded or followed by the abbreviation "EA";
- a precise statement of its objects;
- the name, address, occupation and nationality of the founder members, where there are natural persons;
- the name, objects and registered offices of the founder members, where these are legal entities;
- the address of the EA's registered office;
- the conditions and procedures for the admission, expulsion and resignation of members;
- the rights and obligations of members and the different categories of member if any, and the rights and obligations of members in each category;
- the powers and responsibilities of the executive committee and the extent of its authority to represent the EA in dealings with third parties;

99. I.e., Annex: Legal Entities Mentioned in Art. 3; the list makes it impossible for mutual and cooperatives to form an EA. Thus, the proposed Regulation would cement the line between the different organizational forms within the *economie sociale*.
100. See Statutes for the European Cooperative, Mutual and Non-profit Sectors. Opinion issued by the EESC, Catalogue No: ESC-92-009-EN.
101. It seems that there is a tendency in the EU Member States to soften the requirements dealing with minimum number of founding members. In this matter, a good example is the Polish Law on Association (*Prawo o stowarzyszeniach*) which in 2016 was amended in this way that an association can be founded by 7 natural persons, whereas previously it had to be at least 15 persons.
102. See Statutes...
103. *Ibid.*

- provisions governing the appointment and removal of the members of the executive committee;
- the majority and quorum requirements;
- the conditions for the initiation of proceedings on behalf of the EA under Article 34;[104]
- the grounds for winding up.

In comparison to national laws on associations,[105] it seems that the above-presented catalog is excessively casuistic. For example, the need to reveal the occupation of all founder members seems entirely senseless as it is not any point of reference to their reliability, nor is it any indicator to the organization's aims.[106] As for the obligation to disclose addresses of the founder members, it raises questions if it is compatible with the data protection principles.[107] This issue is relevant as the statute would have to be disclosed to the general public.

Regarding the EA's registered office, according to Article 4, it must be situated within the EU[108] and be in the same place as its central administration. Pursuant to Article 5 (1), it can be transferred to another Member State without the EA being wound

104. Dealing with Proceeding on behalf of the EA.
105. E.g., Art. 2 of the Belgian Law on Non-Profit Associations, International Non-Profit Associations and Foundations (*Loi sur les associations sans but lucratif, les associations internationaes sans but lucrative et les fondations*), although also very detailed (especially in reference to the details on the founders), seems to list only the most important parts of a statue:

    (1) the name, surname, residence, date and place of birth of each founder, or, where it is a legal person, the name, the legal form and the address of the head office;
    (2) the name and address of the registered office of the association and as the judicial district which it depends;
    (3) the minimum number of members. It cannot be less than three;
    (4) the designation specifies the purposes for which it is incorporated;
    (5) the conditions and formalities for admission and exit of members;
    (6) the powers and mode of convocation of the General Assembly as well as the manner in which its resolutions are brought to the attention of members and third parties;
    (7) (a) the mode of appointment, termination of functions and removal of Directors, the extent of their powers and the way to exercise by acting either individually or jointly, or in college, as well as the duration of their mandate;
    (b) where appropriate, the mode of appointment, termination of functions and revocation of persons authorized to represent the association in accordance with Art. 13, para. 4, the scope of their powers and how to exercise them, acting either individually or jointly, or in college;
    (c) where appropriate, the mode of appointment, termination of functions and revocation persons delegated the daily management of the association in accordance with Art. 13 bis, para. 1, the scope of their powers and how to exercise them, acting either individually or jointly, either in college;
    (d) where appropriate, the method of appointment of Auditors.
    (8) the maximum amount of contributions or payments by members;
    (9) the destination of the heritage of the association in the event of dissolution, which must be assigned to an end disinterested;
    (10) the duration of the association when it is not unlimited.

106. See Statutes…
107. Cf. e.g. S. Zhan, S.-Y. Tang, *Understanding the Implications of Government Ties for Nonprofit Operations and Functions*, Public Administration Review Vol. 76/2016, pp. 589 et seq.
108. Obviously, the term "Community" is used in the proposal.

up. It seems that this provision does not pay sufficient attention to the needs of the tax authorities to be able to monitor such transfers. It could also result in abuses leading to tax evasion or law shopping.[109] Yet, the Regulation does not exclude the national tax authorities from enacting provisions mandating the control and taxation provisions they deem necessary upon transferal of registered offices and EAs out of their jurisdiction.[110]

As stated in Article 6 (1), EAs are to be governed first and foremost by the Regulation and, where the Regulation expressly so authorizes, by the rules of the EA. Where the Regulation is silent on a particular point, the principles of freedom of choice and freedom of contract have full play, subject to compliance with the binding provisions of the law applying to associations in the Member State in which the EA has its registered office. Furthermore, it should be noted that in addition to the rules applicable to EAs on the basis of the Regulation and the law governing associations and foundations in the state in which the EA would have its registered office, other norms of the EU and national law would be also applicable, including social and labor law, intellectual, industrial and commercial property law, bankruptcy law, etc.[111]

The Regulation directly articulates a nondiscriminatory rule in Article 6 (3). According to this provision, in each Member State and subject to the express provisions of this Regulation, an EA shall have the same rights, powers and obligations as one of the legal entities set out in the Annex and formed under the law of the Member State in which the EA has its registered office. As far as finances are concerned, the same principle is expressed in Article 41. Accordingly, an EA may avail itself of all forms of financing under the most favorable conditions as those applying to the EA's founding entities in the state in which it has its registered office and in the Member States in which it has its establishments. The nondiscriminatory rule should be interpreted in a restrictive manner. Its objective is not that the EA may avail itself of the rights it has in its country of registration in all other states. The EA should simply not be discriminated against when it operates in any other Member State.[112] However, it is not clear whether the forms of financing referred to in Article 41 include both subsidies and the possibility of an EA appealing to the public generosity.[113]

Registration and disclosure requirements are established in Article 7. Thus, the founder members shall draw up the statutes of the EA in accordance with the provisions for the formation of associations laid down by the law of the state in which the EA has its registered office. The statutes must at least be in writing and signed by the founder members. In those Member States, whose legislation does not provide for any precautionary supervision, whether administrative or judicial, at the time of

109. See H. Murpy, A. Kellow, *Forum Shopping in Global Governance: Understanding States, Business and NGOs in Multiple Arenas*, Global Policy Vol. 4/2013, pp. 139 et seq.
110. See O. Gjems-Onstad, *The Proposed European Association—A symbol in Need of Friends?*, Voluntas: International Journal of Voluntary and Nonprofit Organizations Vol. 6/1995, p. 7.
111. Explanatory memorandum, remarks to Art. 6.
112. As for the extent of nondiscriminatory rule in reference to associations see also e.g. opinion of Advocate General Kokott in Case C-106/14 *Fédération des entreprises du commerce et de la distribution (FCD) and Fédération des magasins de bricolage et de l'aménagement de la maison (FMB) v. Ministre de l'écologie, du développement durable et de l'énergie*, ECLI:EU:C:2015:93.
113. O. Glems-Onstad, *The Proposed...*, p. 14.

formation, the statutes shall be adopted by notarial act. Member States shall designate the register in which EAs must be registered and shall determine the rules governing it.[114] They shall also lay down the procedures for filling the EAs statues.[115]

The following documents and particulars concerning an EA should be disclosed (Article 7 (4)):

(a) the statutes of the EA, any amendments to them, and the complete text of the statutes in its up-to-date form;
(b) the opening or closing of any establishment;[116]
(c) the appointment, termination of office and particulars of the persons who either as a body constituted pursuant to law or as members of any such body:
  - are authorized to represent the EA in dealings with third parties and in legal proceedings;
  - take part in the administration, supervision or control of the EA.
(d) the balance sheet and the profit and loss account for each financial year; the document containing the balance sheet shall give particulars of the persons who are required by law to certify it;
(e) any proposal to transfer the registered office (as referred to in Article 5 (2));
(f) the winding-up and liquidation of the EA and the decision to continue the EA's activities taken under Article 42;[117]
(g) any declaration of nullity of the EA by a court;
(h) the appointment of liquidators, particulars of such liquidators and their respective powers, the termination of their office;
(i) the conclusion of the liquidation of the EA and the removal of the EA from the register.

Whenever an EA is formed or liquidated, a notice to that effect must be published for information purposes in the Official Journal of the European Communities (of the EU, Article 9 *in principio*). This type of information is important in view of the fact that the activities of an EA are by definition transnational. According to the proposal, such publication will not, however, have any legal consequences. Only disclosure pursuant to Article 8 of the proposal is valid against third parties. Respectively, Member States shall ensure that the documents and particulars concerning an EA are published in the appropriate official gazette in the Member State[118] in which the EA has its registered office and shall determine by which persons the disclosure of formalities are to be carried out. Disclosure shall be effected by publications either of an extract or of a

114. I.e., by the rules governing the national register, e.g. in the Polish case—the National Court Register.
115. Moreover, no EA may be registered until the measures provided in Directive supplementing the Statute for a European Association with regard to the involvement of employees have been adopted.
116. This notion should be understood not like in the context of "freedom of establishment" but rather as a synonym of "company."
117. I.e., dealing with winding up by the general meeting.
118. I.e., an official journal for public and private entities, e.g. in Poland—Court and Commercial Gazette (*Monitor Sądowy i Gospodarczy*).

reference to the entry in the register. Member States shall also ensure that anyone may consult the documents in the register and may obtain a copy of the whole or any part, by post if requested. As it can be seen, the proposal emphasizes the need to run the EA in a very transparent way.

As for internal organization of an EA, the proposal envisaged two obligatory bodies: the general meeting and the executive committee. Both are a standard for association laws in EU Member States.[119] The first one of them is a forum for all members of the organization and the other one is the principal governing body.

According to Article 11, the general meeting is to decide on matters for which it has sole responsibility under the Regulation and on matters for which the executive committee does not have sole responsibility. Pursuant to Article 13, general meetings may be convened at any time by the executive committee either on its own initiative or at the request of at least 25% of the members. The internal rules may set a lower proportion. Members should be given sufficient time to prepare to attend the general meeting or to arrange to be represented there, bearing in mind that an increasing number may be resident outside the country in which the EA has its registered office, and that too short a period of notice would prevent them from attending. The arrangements for the appointment of proxies or for the amendment of the agenda by a minority of members is not allowed unless sufficient time is given. The Regulation therefore lays down a period of one month.[120] A general meeting must be held at least once a year, not later than six months after the end of the EA's financial year. This requirement is dictated by the need to approve the annual accounts. The principle applied to the members' voting rights is that of "one member, one vote."

The notice calling the general meeting does not give its members enough precise information on certain decisions to be taken by it. Therefore, in Article 16 the proposal provides for a rule of greater openness—certain documents must be made available to any member at least one month before the meeting is held. Most importantly, this obligation concerns the annual accounts and the Auditors' report.

The executive committee is described in Articles 22-35 of the proposal. The main aim of this body is to manage the EA. It consists of at least three members, with the maximum number fixed by the statues. The member or members of the executive committee shall have the power to represent the EA in dealings with third parties and in the legal proceedings. The functions of the members of the executive committee can be performed only by natural persons. The admission of legal entities as members of the executive committee is conditional on their designating a natural person as their representative.[121] However, no one may be appointed a member of the executive committee who has been disqualified by a judicial or administrative decision (and who has been reinstated in his personal rights) or whose activities have been declared incompatible under the law of the state in which the EA has its registered office. All members of the executive committee are to have the same rights and obligations. One of the main obligations of committee members is the obligation not to divulge

119. See P. Suski, *Stowarzyszenia i fundacje*, Warsaw 2011, p. 200.
120. Explanatory memorandum, remarks to Art. 13.
121. Explanatory memorandum, remarks to Art. 26.

confidential information. The Regulation also makes it very clear that the executive committee is to act in the interest of the EA, its members and its employees.

To ensure that the members of the executive committee can be held accountable for their acts, it is considered appropriate to establish the principle that they can be appointed only for a specific period at a time. This period is not to exceed six years. They may be reappointed.

A decision of the executive committee shall be required to authorize any of the following operations:

(a) closing or transferring a large establishment or a substantial part of such an establishment;
(b) substantially reducing, extending or altering the activities of the EA;
(c) making substantial organizational changes within the EA;
(d) establishing cooperation with other legal entities which is both long-term and of importance to the activities of the EA, or terminating such cooperation;
(e) raising loans in respect to operations in excess of a ceiling laid down in the statutes, issuing securities and assuming or guaranteeing liabilities of a third party;
(f) acquiring movable or immovable property.

The statute of the EA may provide that the need of authorization shall apply to other operations. Member States may also specify other categories of operation for which authorization is required.

The executive committee has the power of representing the EA. Where the authority to represent the EA in dealings with third parties is conferred on two or more members, those persons shall exercise that authority collectively. However, the statutes of the EA may provide that the EA shall be validly bound either by each of the members acting individually or by two or more of them acting jointly. Acts performed by the members of the governing body of the EA shall bind the EA vis-à-vis third parties even where the acts in question are not in accordance with the objects of the EA, providing they do not exceed the powers conferred to them by the law or which the law allows to be conferred on it. However, Member States may provide that the EA shall not be bound where such acts are outside the objects of the EA if it proves that the third party knew that the act was outside those objects or could not in view of the circumstances have been unaware of it. Disclosure of the statutes shall not of itself be sufficient proof thereof.[122]

The members of the executive committee are to be liable for loss or damage sustained by the EA as a result of breach of the obligations attaching to their functions. Where the executive committee is composed of more than one member, all the members shall be jointly and severally liable for loss or damage sustained by the EA. However, a member may be relieved of liability if he can prove that he is not in breach of the obligations attaching to his functions. Liability will be incurred only if the EA has

122. Explanatory memorandum, remarks to Art. 29 (3).

suffered damage. Therefore, there has to be a causal link, the act done and the damage suffered.[123]

Specific financial provisions were established in Articles 36-40. Most notably, the EA must draw up a budget for the forthcoming financial year. As regards the drawing up, auditing and disclosure of its annual accounts and its consolidated accounts if any, the EA is to be subject to the law of the state in which it has its registered office giving effect to the Fourth Council Directive (78/660/EEC) of July 25, 1978, on annual accounts, the Seventh Council Directive (83/349/EEC) of June 13, 1983, on consolidated accounts, the Eight Council Directive (84/253/EEC) of June 13, 1983, of April 10, 1984, on the approval of persons responsible for carrying out the statutory audits of accounting documents and Council Directive 89/48/EEC of December 21, 1988, on a general system for the recognition of higher education diplomas awarded on completion of professional education and training of at least three years' duration. These rules are to lay down the form of audit of the accounts and supervision of the EA.[124]

The Regulation on the statute for an EA was proposed alongside the Council Directive supplementing the Statute for a European Association with regard to the involvement of employees.[125] The Directive was drafted in opposition to the Directive supplementing the statute for a European company (SE) with regard to the involvement of employees[126] in order to avoid any distortion between the EA and the SE. Thus, in view of the nature of the EA, a simplified procedure is provided for. It consists of:

- referring to national provisions concerning employee participation in those Member States where they exist and if the Member State concerned wishes to apply them;
- harmonizing the arrangements concerning the information and consulting of employees, notably as regards the minimum areas covered.[127]

According to its Article 1, the Directive coordinates the laws, regulations and administrative provisions of the Member States concerning the involvement of employees in the EA. No EA may be registered until a participation model or, in the absence of thereof, an information and consultation system has been chosen in accordance with the provisions of the Directive. Article 2 states that the laws, governing regulations and administrative provisions of the participation of employees in the Member State supervisory or administrative boards of national companies may be made applicable to an EA whose registered office is in its territory.

However, Member State may choose not to enact such rules for the participation of employees. In this case, it may instead enact rules for information and consultation with employees according to the requirements stated in Articles 3-4 of the Directive. A basic component of these provisions is that the employees are to be involved from the

123. According Art. 33 of the proposal, see also explanatory memorandum, remarks to Art. 33.
124. Explanatory memorandum, remarks to Arts. 36-40.
125. COM(91) 273 final—SYN 387.
126. Council Directive 2001/86/EC of 8 October 2001 supplementing the Statute for a European company with regard to the involvement of employees, Official Journal L 294, 10.11.2001.
127. See explanatory memorandum on the Council Directive Supplementing the Statute for a European Association with Regard to the involvement of employees.

outset.[128] According to Article 3 (1), before an EA is registered, an agreement has to be made in writing between the executive committee of the founder entities and the representatives of the employees of these entities regarding the procedures for consulting and information. If an EA is formed by natural persons, procedures for informing and consulting the employees have to be laid out in accordance with the Directive and approved by the general meeting called upon to approve the formation of the EA (Article 3 (2)). If the EA has fewer than 50 employees, the representatives of the governing boards and the employees may decide upon simplified information and consultation agreements (Article 4 (3)).

[2] Remarks on the Proposal

Due to the lack of legislative progress,[129] the proposal for the statute for the EA was eventually withdrawn in 2006.[130] In retrospect, it seems that there were two major reasons for the failure of the proposal. First, it raised many controversies among Member States. Second, it did not include any strong incentives for the representatives of civil society. Therefore, the stakeholders did not advocate strongly for the regulation, and it simply lacked sufficient support.[131]

The national association laws, as it was noted above, were not directly influenced by the proposed regulation. Therefore, an apparent harmonization in spite of significant legal differences may be confusing. The newly established EAs could be inclined to choose the most liberal legal systems for their statutory seats.[132] It would not only be legal but, in fact, facilitated by the Regulation.[133] This disorientation might be bypassed if the Regulation had not avoided many relevant aspects. For instance, the Regulation does not deal with tax issues. Therefore, all operations dealt with by the EA would be restricted by the domestic tax legislations. It is possible that an EA would have to generate various sets of accounts to meet the requirements of different Member

128. See Statutes...
129. See G.-J. Vossestein, *Modernization of European Company Law and Corporate Governance*, Alphen aan den Rijn 2010, pp. 250-251, C.R.M. Versteegh, *Civil Society and Civil Society Organisations in the Institutional and Legal Framework of the European Union* in: *Civil Society in Europe. Minimum Norms and Optimum Conditions of Its Regulation*, T.J. van der Ploeg, W.J.M. van Veen, C.R.M. Versteegh (eds), Cambridge 2017, p. 62.
130. Official Journal C 64, 17.3.2006. In spite of the fact that the Commission foresaw its adoption in its 2003 Action Plan for Company Law and Corporate Governance—a modern legal framework for more engaged shareholders and sustainable companies, COM(2012) 0740 final.
131. O. Gjems-Onstad, *The Proposed...*, p. 7; see also J. Kendall, L. Fraisse, *The European...*
132. As a result, it would reinforce the need for the creation of European Supervisory Authority Enforcement network maintained centrally (preferably by the Commission) which would identify and facilitate contact between the appropriate Member State bodies tasked with a role in the Regulation of FEs. For more detailed information see O. Breen, *The...*, pp. 36-37.
133. E.g. through the procedure of transferring the registered office from one Member State to another.

States.[134] Obviously, this signifies that EAs would take tax legislations into consideration while deciding on their "host" Member State. Nevertheless, the Regulation could be also advantageous for raising awareness on the existing shortcomings in this matter.

It is arguable whether the proposal would actually be a significant legal development in comparison to the Convention on Recognition of the Legal Personality of International Non-Governmental Organizations.[135] Certainly, the EAs would be attributed with a "European" feature. Still, the same objective can be achieved by implementing the notions "European" or "Europe" in the names of the associations.[136] Nevertheless, the most significant advantage of the Regulation would be the fact that the newly established EAs could operate in any Member State without having to incorporate or found itself in a new legal regime.[137] Currently such a requirement is common among different states.

As it can be noticed, the proposal was flawed on many levels. Its provisions appeared excessively detailed. They were too complex in matters relating to internal procedures within the EA but, at the same time, left too much room for possible misuses in tax evasion. It appears, however, that the Regulation would be most advantageous for small and medium organizations as the costs of registration or compliance with legal prerequisites in different Member States are most burdensome for them.[138]

Regardless of its weaknesses, the failure of adopting the proposal is a missed opportunity in reaching European civil society. It seems clear that through establishing the EAs, NGOs might have made themselves a more visible part of the transnational activity in the EU. A newly formed statute could help some organizations to perform more efficiently across borders. Enacting the EA Regulation would perhaps not be a very significant contribution to the daily needs of NGOs. Still, it would make a symbolic move in the right direction.[139]

Although the proposal for the statute for the EA is not at present on the official agenda in the EU legislature, it seems that the EU institutions did not forget the idea of creating a legal form for pan-European associations. In 2011, the EP issued a declaration on establishing European statutes for mutual societies, associations and foundations.[140] In this document, the EP noted that there is a need to create a "level playing

134. A. Perri, E. Kuti, *Into the European Community: Impacts of Future Membership on Hungary's Non-profit Sector*, Journal of European Social Policy Vol. 3/1993, p. 273; there even are different sets of accounting rules applying to different types of NGOs in one county. A good example is a "micro" entity in the Polish Act on Accounting (*Ustawa z dnia 29 września 1994 r. o rachunkowości*) which is subject to a less demanding standard of accounting management.
135. Which has already been discussed in Chapter 1; according to Art. 2 (1) of the Convention, "the legal personality and capacity, as acquired by an NGO in the party in which it has its statutory office, shall be recognized as of right in the other Parties."
136. See O. Gjems-Onstad, *The Proposed...*, p. 7.
137. I.e., in the form of a branch of its mother organization.
138. O. Gjems-Onstad, *The Proposed...*, p. 3.
139. J. Kendall, L. Fraisse, *The European...*, A. Perri, *European Competition Law and the Non-profit Sector*, Voluntas Vol. 3/1992, p. 215.
140. P7_TA(2011)0101; Also in 2011, the EESC conducted a public hearing entitled "Towards a Statute of the European Association—a report" is available at: http://civic-forum.eu/wp-content/uploads/2015/06/sea_hearing_report.pdf (on February 9, 2019).

field" that provides associations, mutual societies and foundations with instruments and opportunities equivalent to those available to other organizational legal structures, thereby giving a European dimension to their organization and activities. It also called the Commission to take the necessary steps to introduce proposals for statutes for associations, mutual societies and foundations, to propose a feasibility study and an impact assessment for the statutes for associations and mutual societies, and to complete the impact assessment for the statute for foundations in due course.

[B] European Foundation Statute

For years, the attention devoted to the foundations at the EU level was relatively low. One of the main reasons of this issue was certainly a wide diversity of national legal traditions across Europe.[141] However, even though the number of foundations in the EU is still significantly lower than associations, their number has grown notably in the last years.[142] This resulted in many problems concerning their cross-border activities and legal obstacles that raise operating costs.[143] The growing popularity of this legal form of the third sector organizations,[144] as well as the failure of the proposal for the statute for the EA led to considerations on the need of creating a pan-European legal form of foundations.

In this aspect, four scenarios were considered by the Commission. The first one, called "baseline scenario" was focused on the ongoing initiatives in order to support cross-border activities.[145] However, it would have a rather limited outcome due to the fact that Member States could still establish different tax regimes for domestic and foreign foundations, leading to an actual discrimination. The second alternative was to inform foundations about their prerogatives in cross-border relations. Additionally, a "European quality charter" could be introduced in order to enhance the trustworthiness in the cross-border activities of foundations. However, obviously, such a soft law

141. Since the idea of a European Foundation was first presented in 2001 by Klaus J. Hopt, it has received growing attention from legal scholars and, since 2003, from the European Commission, which first launched a feasibility study on such a Statute. See K. J. Hopt, T. von Hippel, *The European Foundation: A New Legal Approach*, Cambridge 2006, p. 21, H. Surmatz, *Towards a European Framework for foundations in Europe*, ERA Forum Vol. 7/2006, pp. 398-410.
142. See e.g. L. T. McGill, *Number of Registered Public Benefit Foundations in Europe Exceeds 141.000. A 2015 report*, Foundation Center, available at: http://bit.do/ekacs (on February 9, 2019).
143. R. Rossi, *The Proposal...*, p. 24.
144. Explanatory memorandum: 1.1. Foundations play an important role in the EU, particularly in civil society. Through their various activities in numerous areas, they contribute to the fundamental values and objectives of the Union, such as respect for human rights, the protection of minorities, employment and social progress, protection and improvement of the environment or the promotion of scientific and technological advance. In this context, they make a substantial contribution to achieving the ambitious goals of smart, sustainable and inclusive growth set by the Europe 2020 strategy. They also enhance and facilitate a more active involvement of citizens and civil society in the European project. Nonetheless, the exercise of their activities encounters various obstacles across the EU.
145. R. Rossi, *The Proposal...*, pp. 24-25.

instrument would have a very limited impact.[146] The third choice would be to harmonize the national laws on foundations, with or without considering the fiscal aspects of their activities. This harmonization would include registration requirements, minimum assets or aspects of their internal governance. Although this process would have a rather limited outcome, the Commission still found out that it would encounter difficulties in compromising on harmonized definitions.[147] Finally, the Commission reached the conclusion that a general Statute for a European Foundation with automatically applied nondiscriminatory tax treatment would be the most appropriate option as it would most efficiently remove cross-border obstacles for foundations and donors and facilitate the efficient channeling of funds for public benefit purposes.[148]

The proposal for the Council Regulation on the Statute for a European Foundation (FE) was issued in 2012.[149] It seems that two issues of particular concern gave rise to the Member States' eventual disquiet[150]—namely the proposed definition of public benefit purposes and the provision for automatic and universal tax exemption for European Foundations.[151]

Whereas the proposal for the statute for the EA did not envisage any provisions on tax issues, the primary aim of the Regulation on the FE was not to further develop the cross-border philanthropy in Europe but to remove existing obstacles which denied foundations the profits of a common market enjoyed by their for-profit counterparts.[152] This solution was based on the Commission's feasibility study that considered five different models to overcome the legal barriers of cross-border activity within the EU.[153] The authors recommended "the European Foundation Model with additional tax exemptions" as their preference, on the grounds that: "such a European Foundation would mean the most expectable costs reduction effects .... The potential cost reduction could add to EUR 91 million up to EUR 101.7 million (EUR 138 million up to EUR 178.7 million, minimum capital included). The approach would create the most far-reaching incentive for funding transnational European causes, and would have the greatest potential to foster science and research funding, as well as other causes of European interest. It would also lead to a shared concept of a European public good, even though such a concept may only be feasible for a limited list of purposes mentioned in European Treaties, such as the goal to promote R&D[154] and the competitiveness associated therewith."[155] It followed that with an estimated 110,000

146. *Ibid.*, p. 25.
147. *Ibid.*, p. 26.
148. *Ibid.*, p. 25.
149. COM(2012) 035 final—2012/0022 (APP).
150. See e.g. the position of the Polish government on the proposal available at: https://bip.ms.gov.pl/pl/dzialalnosc/projekty-aktow-prawnych/prawo-unii-europejskiej/download,1724,0.html.
151. O. Breen, *European Non-Profit Oversight: The Case for Regulating from the Outside In*, Chicago-Kent Law Review Vol. 91/2016, p. 107.
152. O. Breen, *European...*, p. 107.
153. *Feasibility Study on a European Foundation Statute—Final Report*, University of Heidelberg, Center for Social Investment and Max Planck Institute for Comparative and International Private Law, 2009, available at: http://bit.do/eg4vZ (on February 9, 2019).
154. I.e., Research & Development.
155. See *Feasibility...*

foundations in operating with assets in excess of EUR 1.4 billion in Europe alone, over 67% of these bodies were engaged in international activity, giving rise to a further growth in cross-border activity.[156] Foundations operating in more than one jurisdiction encountered additional costs (and often difficulties) in establishing, registering and operating outside their home territory.[157] According to the study, the estimated costs of these legal barriers amounted to between EUR 140 million and EUR 249 million per year.[158]

Further rationales for the proposal were presented in its preamble.[159] Thus, it was noted that public benefit purpose entities, through their activities in numerous areas, contributed to the fundamental values and objectives of the Union such as respect for human rights, protection of minorities, employment and social progress, the protection, conservation and improvement of the environment or the promotion of scientific and technological advances. However, the legal framework in which these entities carry out their activities in the Union is based on national laws, without harmonization at Union level. In addition, there are substantial differences between civil and tax laws across Member States. Such differences make cross-border operation of public benefit purpose entities costly and cumbersome. As a result, cross-border channeling of funds to public benefit purposes remains largely underexploited.[160] That is why the FE should promote public benefit purposes only, understood as benefiting a broadly defined group of beneficiaries. Since activities of public benefit purpose entities focus on areas that are important for European citizens and European economy, such scope would bring the highest social, economic and environmental benefits.[161]

What is particularly interesting in the preamble is that it references to "European citizens." It seems, therefore, that the proposal was seen as one of the main tools in further developing European civil society.

---

156. However, this statement is very questionable and the *Feasibility Study* does not provide for a proper review of Central and Eastern Europe in this matter. Consequently, only 10% of Polish NGOs declare international activity according to the report issued by Klon Jawor (*Polskie organizacje pozarządowe 2015*), available at: http://fakty.ngo.pl/files/fakty.ngo.pl/public/kondycja_2015/KondycjaNGO2015.pdf (on February 9, 2019).
157. This is party the reason why there is hardly any branch offices of foreign foundations registered in Poland, see e.g. H. Cioch, *Komentarz do art. 19* in: *Ustawa o fundacjach. Komentarz*, H. Cioch, A. Kidyba (eds), Warsaw 2007, Lex/el., P. Staszczyk, *Ustawa o fundacjach...*, pp. 130-131.
158. *Feasibility...*
159. Explanatory memorandum of the FE statute noted that foundations cannot channel funds efficiently on a cross-border basis in the EU. When they decide to operate across borders, foundations have to spend part of the resources they collect on legal advice and administrative requirements laid down by the different national laws. Thus, the initiative for a European Foundation designed a new form intended to facilitate foundations' establishment and operation in the single market. It should allow foundations to more efficiently channel private funds to public benefit purposes on a cross-border basis in the EU. This, in turn, should result—for instance, due to lower costs for foundations—in more funding being available for public benefit purpose activities and therefore, should have a positive impact on European citizens' public good and the EU economy as a whole.
160. Points 1 and 2 of the preamble to the Regulation proposal.
161. Point 7 of the preamble to the Regulation proposal.

[1] *Project Scope*

The proposal of the Regulation does not provide any formal definition of a "European Foundation" or even of a "foundation."[162] It seems that this omission was made on purpose as there is no definite answer in the legal systems of the EU Member States to the question what constitutes a foundation.

In civil law legal regimes, foundations are not based on membership, as opposed to associations. Thus, while associations are formed by a plurality of subjects, foundations are created through a unilateral act in the form of a deed, testamentary disposition or written declaration.[163] This invokes the traditional separation between *universitas personae* and *universitas bonorum* under Roman law.[164] However, some civil law countries distinguish "commercial foundations"[165] which in many cases resemble associations. Nevertheless, such a distinction between an association as entities with members and foundations without members is not so simple in all common law countries. Some legal systems provide foundation structures that are more or less similar to associations (i.e., foundations with "*quasi-membership*").[166] In civil law regimes there is no corresponding difference between nonprofit foundations and associations. For instance, a charitable trust in the United Kingdom does not have a membership or legal personality. Still, a charitable company, just like any other company, must always have a membership of at least one person (though these

162. An interesting approach in the doctrine was presented by K. Hopt and T. von Hippel. Art. 1.1. of their proposal gives a general definition of the European Foundation containing four basic criteria, the first three of which are usually found in the different jurisdictions.

    A foundation is a distinct organization ("separately constituted and independently managed bodies with their own governing board") with its own legal status (cf. Art. 2):

    - A foundation is deemed to have an endowment and/or a source of income ("irrevocably provided with valuable goods, rights or other sources and/or having an income at their disposal"),
    - A foundation has no membership,
    - A foundation must promote a public benefit purpose (cd. Art. 1.2) (K. Hopt, T. von Hippel in: *The European*..., p. 29).

    Moreover, according to *Feasibility*... a foundation:

    - is an independent organization (generally with its own legal personality), which has not formal membership;
    - is supervised by a state supervisory authority;
    - serves a public benefit purpose (in some Member States: any lawful purpose), for which a founder has provided an endowment and determined the foundation's purpose and statutes.
163. R. Rossi, *The Proposal*..., p. 28.
164. Examples are Bulgaria, Belgium, the Czech Republic, Estonia, France, Greece, the Netherlands, Germany, Slovenia, Sweden and Switzerland—for more see K. Hopt, T. von Hippel, *The European*..., p. 36.
165. Envisaged by the Danish Act on Commercial Foundations (*Lov om erhervsdrivende fonde*).
166. I.e., in the Netherlands, Sweden, Denmark, Bulgaria. Moreover, in Italy there is a separate legal form of a "participatory foundation.'"

members may also be its directors).[167] The main difficulty is that in common law foundations are less a legal concept and more a descriptive label.[168] Usually, charitable companies (companies limited by guarantee) and charitable trusts are the legal vehicles of choice in common law countries when it comes to cross-border philanthropy.[169] Both of these legal forms fall outside the scope of the proposed Regulation. Moreover, some civil law and common law legal systems[170] envisage a separate subject of "private foundations" (as opposed to nonprofit foundations). These entities can be set up only by an individual, a family or a group of individuals for a purpose such as philanthropy or other legal economic object and they do not generally solicit funds from the public.[171]

This diversity seems to have influenced the effectiveness of the statute for the European Foundation which, from the very beginning, was seemingly limited to civil society actors active in some EU Member State and, therefore, it did not receive efficient support from the charity support.[172]

Instead of defining a "foundation," Article 2 of proposal provides a definition of a "public benefit purpose entity." This organization should be understood as a foundation with public benefit purpose and/or similar public benefit purpose corporate body without membership formed in accordance with the law of one of the Member States. Moreover, Article 25 states that the name of the FE shall include the abbreviation "FE" and only the FE may use this abbreviation in its name. The FE shall have a cross-border character with activities or a statutory objective of carrying out activities in at least two Member States (Article 6). Practically speaking, the FE statute would be reserved for large organizations as the proposal sets a requirement of minimum assets of EUR 25,000 (Article 7 (2)).[173] This obligation seems quite troublesome[174] because in most EU Member States minimal assets for establishing a foundation are not regulated.[175] In other countries, instead of a minimum asset requirement, there are stricter

167. K. Hopt, T. von Hippel, *The European...*, p. 36.
168. H. Cioch, *Prawo fundacyjne*, Warsaw 2011, p. 29.
169. P. Staszczyk, *Problemy podatkowe w międzynarodowych działaniach organizacji pozytku publicznego na tle prawa Unii Europejskiej*, Trzeci Sektor Vol. 32/2014, p. 84.
170. E.g. the USA, the Netherlands, Austria or Sweden.
171. K. Hopt, T. von Hippel, *The European...*, p. 3B. Hopkins, *Private Foundation Law Made Easy*, Hoboken 2008, p. 31.
172. O. Breen, *EU Regulation...*
173. *Ibid.*, p. 112. .
174. The CoR proposed an even higher requirement. In its opinion on "The Statute for a European Foundation" (2013/C 17/13, Official Journal C 17/81, 19.1.2013), it states that it understands the desire to strike a balance between the requirements of national law in the various Member States regarding the minimum level of assets required for a foundation and the aim of facilitating the creation of FEs throughout the EU. The Committee is, however, keen to ensure that donors and the public have adequate guarantees regarding the financial soundness of FEs. It calls for the minimum level of assets required for registration of an FE to be increased to EUR 50,000 instead of EUR 25,000, which it considers to be too low. It also suggests that if the capital falls below EUR 25,000, the FE should be dissolved by law (point 23).
175. Examples are France, Estonia, Romania, Latvia, the Netherlands or Poland. In some cases, like in Poland, a foundation may, however, be dissolved by Court Order if it lacks the means to achieve its purpose and there are no prospects of their future acquisition. Also, a charity in the common law countries needs no founding assets or endowment; for more see K. Hopt, T. von Hippel, *The European...*, p. 36.

audit obligations for bigger organizations.[176] The liability of the FE shall be limited to its assets (Article 8) as such a limited liability is an inherent characteristic of foundations as legal entities.[177]

According to Article 5 (1), the FE shall be a separately constituted entity for a public benefit purpose. Pursuant to the second paragraph of this norm, the FE shall serve the public interest at large. It may be created only for the following purposes, to which its assets shall be irrevocably dedicated:

(a) arts, culture or historical preservation;
(b) environmental protection;
(c) civil or human rights;
(d) elimination of discrimination based on gender, race, ethnicity, religion, disability, sexual orientation or any other legally prescribed form of discrimination;
(e) social welfare, including prevention or relief of poverty;
(f) humanitarian or disaster relief;
(g) development aid and development cooperation;
(h) assistance to refugees or immigrants;
(i) protection of, and support for, children, youth or elderly;
(j) assistance to, or protection of, people with disabilities;
(k) protection of animals;
(l) science, research and innovation;
(m) education and training;
(n) European and international understanding;
(o) health, well-being and medical care;
(p) consumer protection;
(q) assistance to, or protection of vulnerable and disadvantaged persons;
(r) amateur sports;
(s) infrastructure support for public benefit purposes.

This list, forming a catalog of "public benefit purposes" for the first time at the EU level, raises some concerns. First, the proposed catalog is closed. Meanwhile, the early working papers on the FE statute proposed an "open-ended catalog." It was argued that "the great value of the foundation sector in society is its ability to further innovation, to allow imaginative public-spirited individuals to address the needs of society in new ways." Thus, the premise of the catalog should be flexible to support such innovation.[178] Second, the catalog entirely omits religious purposes.[179] In this aspect, even

176. E.g. Spanish Law 50/2002 on Foundations (*Ley 50/2002 de Fundaciones*).
177. B. Hopkins, *Private...*, p. 31.
178. K. Hopt, T. von Hippel, *The European...*, p. 43.
179. However, this purpose was included in the proposal presented by K. Hopt and T. von Hippel (see K. Hopt, T. von Hippel, *The European...*, p. 42). During the legislation procedure other propositions appeared as well. For instance, the CoR proposed "the defense of victims of violence of all kinds" as one of the public benefit purposes.

though some countries, following a policy of secularism,[180] exclude these tasks from their catalogs,[181] most EU Member States consider the promotion of religion as a public benefit purpose.[182] Third, the use of the descriptor "public benefit purpose" may cause confusion for common law countries, as the catalog is closer to the civil law understanding of the essential tests for public benefit.[183]

Moreover, the sole fact of establishing the catalog of public benefit purposes in the proposal does not mean that a registered FE would always be treated as a public benefit entity in all EU Member States. Although in some legal systems the actual and continuous exercising of public benefit purposes "automatically" leads to acknowledgment of such a status,[184] other countries require a special registration for obtaining the

180. E.g., in France. For more see e.g. T.J. Gunn, *Religion and Law in France: Secularism, Separation and State Intervention*, Drake Law Review Vol. 57/2009, pp. 949 et seq.
181. K. Hopt, T. von Hippel, *The European...*, p. 43.
182. Such a possibility is provided, e.g. in Polish and Latvian Law. According to Art. 2 (2) of the Polish Public Benefit and Volunteer Work Act (*Ustawa o działalnosci pozytku publicznego i o wolontariacie*), public benefit activities may be conducted by: (1) legal persons and agencies operating on the basis of the provisions of the state to the Catholic Church in the Republic of Poland, of the relation to other churches and religious societies, and about the guarantees of freedom of conscience and religion, if their statutory objectives include activities of public benefit. According to Art. 3 of the Latvian Public Good Organization Law (*Sabiedriskā labuma organizāciju likums*), public benefit organizations are association and foundations that Charter, Constitution or bylaws of the specified purpose is a public good, as well as the activities of religious organizations and their institutions (religious organizations), which carried out the public good if these associations, foundations and religious organizations granted public good organizations and if they used their income pursuant to this law, in Arts. 11 and 12 under certain restrictions.

    However, Art. 5 of the proposal also names other public benefit purposes what are absent in some EU Member States. For instance, neither the advancement of human rights nor the advancement of amateur sports are deemed charitable in Ireland.
183. E.g., in England and Wales: for an organization to be a charity, each of its purposes must be for the public benefit. The Charities Act of 2011 calls this the "public benefit requirement." The public benefit requirement has two aspects:

    (1) The "benefit aspect"—To satisfy this aspect:
    - a purpose must be beneficial—this must be in a way that is identifiable and capable of being proved by evidence where necessary and which is not based on personal views;
    - any detriment or harm that results from the purpose (to people, property or the environment) must not outweigh the benefit—this is also based on evidence and not on personal views.

    (2) The "public aspect"—To satisfy this aspect the purpose must:
    - benefit the public in general, or a sufficient section of the public—what is a "sufficient section of the public" varies from purpose to purpose;
    - not give rise to more than incidental personal benefit—personal benefit is "incidental" where (having regard both to its nature and to its amount) it is a necessary result or by-product of carrying out the purpose.

    In general, for a purpose to be a charitable purpose it must satisfy both the benefit and the public aspects. However, charities for the relief (and in some cases the prevention) of poverty need only to satisfy the benefit aspect.
184. E.g., in Germany, see P. Staszczyk, *Problemy...*, p. 80.

status of a "public benefit organization," "charity" etc.[185] In other words, in order to acquire this position, the FE would still have to fulfill specific national requirements and be registered by a respective institution in some countries.

According to Article 3 of the proposal, the FE shall be governed by the Regulation and the statutes of the FE. In matters that are not, or are only partly, regulated by the Regulation and/or the statutes of the FE, the FE shall be governed by the following rules:

(a) the provisions adopted by Member States in order to ensure the effective application of this Regulation;
(b) for matters not covered by point (a), the provisions of the national law applicable to public benefit purpose activities.

Moreover, pursuant to Article 4, information concerning the FE shall be disclosed in accordance with the applicable national law in such a way that it is easily accessible to the public.

As a result, like in the EA case, there would be not one but many FE laws.[186] However, because the FE proposal deals with tax treatment (and national supervisory authority), which was one of the biggest omissions in the EA proposal, this situation would not be harmful and would have limited effects in terms of law shopping among EU Member States.

Article 10 of the proposal states that the FE has full legal capacity in all Member States. Thus, unless restricted by its statutes, the FE shall have all rights necessary to pursue its activities, including the right to own movable and immovable property, to make grants, to raise funds, to receive and hold donations of any kind, including shares and other negotiable instruments, inheritances and gifts "in kind" from any lawful source including the third countries. Where necessary for the pursuance of its activities, the FE shall have the right of establishment in any Member State. The FE may act in pursuit of its purpose in any lawful manner allowed by its statutes which is consistent with its public benefit purpose and is in allowance with the Regulation. Also, unless restricted by its statutes, the FE may carry out activities in any third country. The latter provision seems to be rather a declaration than a strict norm. Conducting activities by an FE in a third country (outside the EU)[187] would depend on the possibility of its recognition in the given state.

Pursuant to Article 11, the FE has the capacity and is free to engage in trading or other economic activities provided that any profit is exclusively used in pursuance of its public benefit purpose(s). However, economic activities unrelated to the public benefit

185. E.g., in Poland a registration in National Court Register is required; in the UK a register is run by the Charity Commission, see P. Staszczyk, *Problemy...*, p. 80.
186. According to the EESC opinion on the Proposal for a Council Regulation on the Statute for a European Foundation (INT/645 EESC-2012-1211): at Union level there is no possible way to harmonize the legal frameworks in which the public benefit purpose entities carry out their activities in the EU. Some estimated 50+ laws govern the formation and operations of foundations across the EU (point 2.1).
187. E.g., in the form of "branch offices."

purpose of the FE are allowed up to 10% of the annual net turnover of the FE provided that the results from unrelated activities are presented separately in the accounts. This provision is quite interesting as in many EU Member States economic activity is allowed only as a means of exercising the organization's public benefit purpose.[188] It seems that the FE can be profit oriented in other spheres as well, provided that the profit does not exceed 10% of the annual overall revenue.[189] This makes the FE a *not-for-profit* but not a *nonprofit* organization.[190]

Article 12 envisages four methods of establishing an FE:

1. testamentary disposition of any natural person, as provided for in Article 17,
2. notarial deed or written declaration of any natural and/or legal person(s) or public body(ies) in accordance with the applicable national law, as provided for in Article 13,
3. merger of public benefit purpose entities legally established in one or more Member States, as provided for in Articles 14, 15 and 16,
4. conversion of a national public benefit purpose entity legally established in a Member State, into the FE, as provided for in Articles 17 and 18.

It is not clear whether an FE can be formed as a result of merger between associations (or between a foundation and an association) or conversion of an association. As the list in Article 12 refers only to "public benefit purpose entities," it seems that such situations are permissible. However, in both cases, the organization would have to reestablish itself as the character of foundations differs vastly from associations (which was discussed in the foregoing paragraphs).

The FE shall be set up for an indefinite period of time or, where expressly laid down in its statutes, for a specified period of time of not less than two years. Moreover, according to Article 36, the FE may transfer its registered office from one Member State to another one. Such transfer shall not result in the winding up of the FE or the creation of a new legal entity or affect any right or obligation existing before the transfer. However, the FE shall not transfer its registered office where it is the subject of the use of supervisory powers, when it is in dissolution or if proceeding for winding-up, insolvency or similar proceedings have been brought against it or where the transfer is against the statutes of the FE or would jeopardize the fulfillment of the purpose of the FE. Also, the transferal opportunity is not unconditional. Thus, the governing board of the FE shall submit a transfer proposal to the competent authority of the home Member

188. E.g., in the Polish Public Benefit and Volunteer Work Act (*Ustawa o działalności pożytku publicznego i o wolontariacie*)—see Art. 20 (1) pp. 2 and 3.
189. Which could possibly lead to a "professionalization" of some NGOs, especially in those countries where the third sector is not yet fully developed. In this matter see also P. Staszczyk, *Ustawa o fundacjach...*, pp. 17 et seq.
190. A *nonprofit* organization can be described as not undertaking any profit-oriented activities at all. In contrast, a *not-for-profit* organization can undertake profit-oriented activities but, in general, only to cover its expenses (e.g., organizational and legal). For more see e.g. H. Cioch, *Prawo...*, p. 26.

State.[191] Similar preconditions are envisaged in the case of cross-border mergers.[192] Nevertheless, these provisions do not give any indications as to what should be understood as a "competent authority." It seems that this notion concerns the national institution which is responsible for carrying the respective registry.

The requirements concerning the statutes of the FE are established in Article 19 (1). Accordingly, the statute shall include at least:

(a) the names of the founders;
(b) the name of the FE;
(c) the address of the registered office;
(d) a description of its public benefit purposes;
(e) the assets at the time of formation;
(f) the financial year of the FE;
(g) the number of members of the governing board;
(h) rules on the appointment and dismissal of the governing body;
(i) the bodies of the FE other than the governing board and their functions, where applicable;
(j) the procedure for amending the statutes;
(k) the specified period of time the FE shall exist for if it is not established for an indefinite period of time;
(l) the distribution of net assets after winding up;
(m) the date when the statutes were adopted.

This catalog seems less casuistic than in the case of the EA Regulation,[193] especially in reference to information considering the founders. In fact, the above-listed

191. According to Art. 37 (2) of the proposal, the transfer proposal shall include at least the following particulars:

- the name of the FE, the address of its registered office in the home Member State, the information necessary to identify the registry referred to in Art. 22(1) and the number of the FE in that registry;
- the proposed name of the FE and the address of its intended registered office in the host Member State;
- the amended statutes of the FE, where appropriate;
- the proposed timetable for the transfer;
- a report explaining and substantiating the legal and economic aspects of the proposed transfer and explaining the implications of the transfer for creditors and employees of the FE.

192. According to Art. 15 (2) of the proposal, the request for a merger shall include the decision of the governing board referred to in Art. 14(2) and the common draft terms of merger containing at least the following particulars:

- the name and address of each of the merging public benefit purpose entities;
- the name and address of the intended registered office for the FE;
- the proposed statutes of the FE;
- the forms of protection of the rights of creditors and employees of the merging entities.

193. Still, the proposal issued by K. Hopt and T. von Hippel was even more simplistic. According to Art. 3.6. of the proposal, the statutes of the European Foundation shall determine:

requirements are very similar to the ones set in national foundation laws in the EU Member States.[194]

Article 20 of the proposal makes it clear that the FE, in contrast to the association, is a stable entity with a constant (although not immovable or perpetual) purpose.[195] The proposal accurately distinguishes the common changes to the statute (Article 20 (1)) from those changes that affect its purpose. The latter one, according to Article 20 (2), may only be changed if the current purpose has been achieved or cannot be achieved or where the current purpose(s) has clearly ceased to provide a suitable and effective method of using the assets. In any case, the decision to change the purpose must be adopted unanimously by the governing board and approved by the supervisory authority.

FEs shall be registered in one Member State. For this purpose, each Member State has to designate a registry and notify the Commission hereof (Articles 21-22).

The Regulation lists governing board as the only obligatory body of the FE.[196] The organization can also establish managing directors and other bodies (most notably of supervisory nature) in their statutes.

"Governing board" is not provided with any legal definition in the proposal. It should be seen as an analog institution to the "executive committee" in the EA proposal. Its main purpose is to "govern" the organization (Article 27 (1)). Article 33 of the Regulation envisages that the governing board, as well as any other person that the governing board has authorized and is under its instructions, may represent the FE in relations with third parties and in legal proceedings. This body should consist of at least three persons. Members of the governing board shall have full legal capacity and not be disqualified under laws of any Member State or a judicial or administrative decision in any Member State from serving as a board member (Article 28 (1)). This means that the admission of legal entities as members of the governing boards is conditional on their designating a natural person as their representative.

Pursuant to Article 29, the governing board, apart from its governing and representative duties, has two functions:

(1) to take responsibility for the proper administration, management and conduct of the FE's activities;
(2) to ensure compliance with the statutes of the FE, the Regulation and the applicable national law.

(a) the name of the foundation, followed by the abbreviation FE;
(b) the public benefit purpose;
(c) the address of the one and only registered foundation office; and
(d) the process for appointing members of Board of Directors (and, where applicable, the Board of Directors).

194. See *Comparative Highlights of Foundation Laws: The Operating Environment for Foundations in Europe 2015*, a report from European Foundation Centre, available at: http://bit.do/ekagn (on February 9, 2019).

195. R. Rossi, *The Proposal...*, p. 28.

196. Which is a standard in other Member States; for more information see *Comparative...*

Members of the governing board shall act in the best interest of the FE and its public benefit purpose and observe a duty of loyalty in the exercise of their responsibilities.

As envisaged in Article 30, in the field of its competences, the governing board may nominate one or more managing directors to be responsible for the day-to-day management of the FE. Managing directors shall act in the best interest of the FE and its public benefit purpose and observe a duty of loyalty in the exercise of their responsibilities.

As the proposal deals with large organizations, specific transparency and accountability requirements are also provided. Therefore, according to Article 34, the FE shall keep full and accurate records of all financial transactions. In particular, the foundation should draw up an annual activity report containing at least information on the activities of the FE, description of the way the public benefit purposes, for which the FE has been established, have been promoted during the given financial year and a list of the grants distributed, taking into account the right of privacy of the beneficiaries. Moreover, an annual account should be made. This document has to be audited by one or more persons approved to carry out statutory audits in accordance with the national rules adopted pursuant to Directive 2006/43/EC of the EP and of the Council[197] and be duly approved by the governing board, together with the opinion submitted by the person responsible for auditing the accounts and the activity report. This document should be also disclosed, together with the annual activity reports.

In order to promote the rights of employees of the FE, Article 38 creates an obligation to establish a European Works Council representing the employees of the FE.[198] The objective of this institution is to constitute a platform for the employees and volunteers of the FE to be informed and consulted at Union level on the situation, evolution, organization and employment matters of the FE.

The most controversial part of the proposal, apart from establishing the catalog of public benefit purposes, is the tax treatment provisions of the FEs. According to Article 49, with respect to income and capital gains taxes, gift and inheritance taxes, property and land taxes, registration taxes, stamp duties and similar taxes, the Member State where the FE has its registered office shall subject the FE to the same tax treatment as is applicable to public benefit purpose entities established in that Member State. Member States other than those in which the FE has its registered office shall subject the FE to the same tax treatment as is applicable to public benefit purpose entities established in those Member States. For these purposes, the FE shall be regarded as equivalent to public benefit purpose entities established pursuant to the law of the Member States concerned.

197. Official Journal L 157/87, 9.6.2006.
198. Where the total number of employees employed within the Union by the FE and its offices reaches or exceeds 50 and at least 10 in each of at least two Member States (para. 1); the FE with up to 200 employees—on the request of at least 20 of its employees in at least two Member States or representatives of those employees; the FE with more than 200 employees—on the request of at least 10% of its employees in at least two Member States or representatives of those employees (para. 2); representatives of volunteers engaged in formal volunteering activities in the FE for a sustained period shall be given an observer status (para. 3).

This provision forms the basis for universal tax-exempt status of the FEs by virtue of their establishment.[199] In other words, the sole existence of an FE would be sufficient to be considered as an equivalent tax-exempt domestic charity without any further national inquiry being conducted.[200] Hence, the Regulation reverses the burden of proof that up until now has been laid on the foreign charity to prove its tax equivalent status to the tax authority of the host Member State.

Moreover, Articles 50 and 51 deal with the donors and beneficiaries of the FE. Accordingly, any natural or legal person donating to the FE within or across the borders shall be subject with respect to income, gift, transfer, registration taxes, stamp duties and similar taxes to the same treatment that is applicable to donations made to public benefit purpose entities established in the Member State where the donor is resident for tax purposes. The FE receiving the donation shall be regarded as equivalent to public benefit purpose entities established pursuant to the law of the Member State where the donor is resident for tax purposes. With reference to beneficiaries of the FE, they shall be treated with respect to the grant or other benefits received, as if they were given by a public benefit purpose entity established in the Member State in which the benefit is resident for tax purposes.

It is noticeable that the tax provisions in the proposal are an aftermath of the CJEU case law presented in the previous parts of this chapter (*Stauffer*, *Hein Persche*, *Missionswerk* and *European Commission v. The Republic of Austria* cases). Still, the automatic acceptance of tax legitimacy by virtue of the FE label proved to be extremely controversial among Member States with the fear that a host tax authority would be forced to grant tax relief to an FE registered in another Member State but active in the host country without having the ability to scrutinize the latter's purposes in the same way as it would scrutinize a domestic charity applying under national law.[201] This is the main reason why the unpublished, later version of the proposal of 2013 did not include tax exemptions at all.[202]

A skeptical attitude toward such an encompassment of tax provision was also demonstrated by the CoR and the EESC in their opinions on the proposal. The CoR presented reservations concerning the automatic extension to FEs of the tax treatment applicable to national public interest entities, on account of the significant disparities between Member States in terms of the conditions for granting these national favorable tax regimes.[203] The EESC argued that the FE should be granted standard nonprofit status (i.e., "automatic" in all EU Member States) in full respect of the competence and practice of the tax authorities of the Member State where the FE is tax liable, to determine its tax treatment in accordance with applicable tax regulations at the national level. While Member States cannot discriminate against FEs vis-à-vis national public benefit foundations, which is contrary to the CJEU case law, they still have the leeway to choose which tax regime applies. Member States should also specify what tax

199. O. Breen, *European...*, p. 111.
200. *Ibid.*
201. *Ibid.*
202. H. Koster, *EU Legal...*, p. 6, K. Hopt, T. von Hippel, *The European...*, p. 28.
203. See the CoR opinion, point 19.

regime will apply to FEs, when several regimes for not-for-profit organizations can be found in their jurisdiction.[204]

Of course, a situation of misusing the position of the FE is conceivable. For instance, an FE, having its registered office in one Member State, could benefit from incomes from other countries with perhaps stricter tax regulations. This likelihood, apart from the possibility of conducting economic activities unrelated to the public benefit purposes up to 10% of the annual net turnover of the FE, could lead to troubling tax abuses.[205] Yet, it does not seem that Member States would be completely defenseless in the struggle to avoid the possible corruptions. As it was argued in the doctrine,[206] Member States could always use FATF regulations (the Financial Action Task Force)[207] in order to fight against money laundering, terrorist financing and other related threats to the integrity of the international financial system.[208] A structural tool against misuses was also provided by the Regulation itself.

In order to avoid the possibilities of tax treatment abuses (and other breaches of law),[209] the proposal envisages that each Member State shall designate a supervisory authority for the FEs. In particular, according to Article 46, this institution shall ensure

---

204. See the EESC opinion, point 3.8.
205. See. R. Godlewski, P. Staszczyk, *Projekt rozporządzenia w sprawie statutu fundacji europejskiej—szansa dla rozwoju działalności pozytku publicznego w Unii Europejskiej*, Finanse Komunalne No 6/2015, p. 13.
206. See remarks by D. Brakman Reiser, *Nonprofit Oversight under Siege: Introduction*, Chicago-Kent Law Review Vol. 843/2016, pp. 850 et seq.
207. An intergovernmental body established in 1989 by the Ministers of its Member jurisdictions, see for more details see: http://www.fatf-gafi.org/about/ (on February 9, 2019).
208. VIII Special Recommendations issued by the FATF provide that counties should review the adequacy of laws and regulations that relate to entities that could be abused for the financing of terrorism. Nonprofit organizations are particularly vulnerable and countries should ensure that they cannot be misused:

    (i) by terrorist organizations posing as legitimate entities;
    (ii) to exploit legitimate entities as conduits for terrorist financing, including for the purpose of escaping asset freezing measures; and
    (iii) to conceal or obscure the clandestine diversion of funds intended for legitimate purposes to terrorist organizations.

    The application of these recommendations should not, however, entail, e.g.:

    - requiring prior government approval to receive international funding;
    - capping the amount of international funding that a CSO is allowed to receive;
    - requiring that international funding be routed through government-controlled entities;
    - prohibiting CSOs from receiving international funding from specified donors;
    - constraining international funding through the overly broad application of counterterrorism and anti-money laundering measures, imposing onerous reporting requirements on the receipt of international funding (see D. Rutzen, *Aid Barriers and the Rise of Philanthropic Protectionism*, International Journal of Not-for-Profit Law Vol. 17/2015, pp. 1 et seq.).

209. In this matter, as it was argued in the doctrine, "the emergence of an informed understanding that better articulation of transparency and accountability standards at a national level can provide a solid basis for the growth of public benefit organizations for the betterment of civil society," O. Breen, *The European...*, p. 11.

that the governing board acts in accordance with the statutes of the FE, the Regulation and the applicable national law. In this manner, it has the following powers:

(a) where the supervisory authority has reasonable grounds to believe that the governing board of the FE is not acting in accordance with the statutes of the FE, the Regulation or the applicable national law, to inquire into the affairs of that FE and, for that purpose, to require the directors and employees of the FE as well as its auditor(s) to make available of all necessary information and evidence;
(b) where there is evidence of financial impropriety, serious mismanagement or abuse, to appoint an independent expert to inquire into the affairs of the FE at the expense of the FE;
(c) where there is evidence that the governing board has not acted in accordance with the statutes of the FE, the Regulation or the applicable national law, to issue warnings to the governing board and to order the governing board to comply with the statutes of the FE, the Regulation and the applicable national law;
(d) to dismiss a member of the governing board or where provided for in the applicable national law, to propose the dismissal to a competent court;
(e) to decide to wind up the FE or, where provided for in the applicable national law, to propose the winding up of the FE to a competent court.

Moreover, what is relevant to cross-border activities of the FEs, the supervisory authority of a Member State where the FE has its registered office and the supervisory authorities of Member States where the FE carries out its activities shall cooperate with each other. In this aspect, the supervisory authorities shall provide each other with all relevant information in the event of infringements or suspected infringements by the FE of its statutes, the Regulation or the applicable national law. On request of the supervisory authority of a Member State where the FE carries out its activities, the supervisory authority of the Member State where the FE has its registered office shall investigate suspected infringements by that FE. The supervisory authority of the Member State where the FE has its registered office shall inform the tax authorities of that Member State as soon as it starts an inquiry into suspected irregularities.[210] It shall also inform those tax authorities of those inquiries as well as about any warnings issued or sanctions imposed. The registry as well as the supervisory authority of the Member State where the FE has its registered office shall make available to the tax authority of any Member State, on its request, any documents or information concerning the FE (Articles 47-48).

It seems that these provisions could minimalize the possibility of tax misuses by the FEs.[211] However, it must be borne in mind that the actual cooperation between

210. However, there is no requirement to inform other tax agencies notwithstanding that host Member States' tax treatment of an FE may also be affected.
211. See also B. Weitemeyer, *Fundatio Europaea—Risk of Abuse by Tax Shopping?*, ERA Forum Vol. 14/2013, pp. 277 et seq.

supervisory authorities could be also varied. Noticeably, in many cases of cross-border services between different EU Member States institutions, some of them tend to be more "liberal" and enable more ease for private entities.[212]

Conclusively, the FE may be dissolved in two ways:

(1) by conversion of the FE into a public benefit purpose entity under national law, as provided for in Articles 41 and 42;
(2) by winding up the FE, as provided for in Articles 43 and 44.

The governing board of the FE may decide to wind up the FE in one of the following cases:

(a) the purpose of the FE has been achieved or cannot be achieved;
(b) the time for which it was set up has expired;
(c) it has lost all its assets.

Although the two latter occurrences are clear, the first one requires a short commentary. Thus, it should be reminded that in practice many (if not most) statutory purposes of foundations have an abstract nature. This is the example of aims worded as "promoting environmental protection," "helping the socially excluded," "pursuing for equal racial rights." Such aims cannot be definitely achieved.[213] However, if an FE has such abstract purposes, it cannot be wound up on this premise. This possibility only deals with specifically proclaimed aims that are subsequently deemed as impossible.[214]

[2] Remarks on the Proposal

The FE was designed as a pan-European legal form. As a result, the proposal took the form of a regulation on the basis of Article 352 of the TFEU.[215] It was argued that it was the legal basis for the existing European legal forms in the field of company law, i.e. the European Company, the European Economic Interest Grouping and the European Cooperative Society. Moreover, the CJEU confirmed in C-436/03 *European Company v. Council of the European Union*[216] on the European Cooperative Society that Article 352

212. See e.g. G. Baber, *The Free Movement of Capital and Financial Services: An Exposition?*, Cambridge 2014, p. 536.
213. P. Staszczyk, *Ustawa o fundacjach...*, p. 119.
214. See also K. Hopt, T. von Hippel, *The European...*, p. 267.
215. According to its para. (1), if action by the Union should prove necessary, within the framework of the policies defined in the Treaties, to attain one of the objectives set out in the Treaties, and the Treaties have not provided the necessary powers, the Council, acting unanimously on a proposal from the Commission and after obtaining the consent of the European Parliament, shall adopt the appropriate measures. Where the measures in question are adopted by the Council in accordance with a special legislative procedure, it shall also act unanimously on a proposal from the Commission and after obtaining the consent of the European Parliament.
216. ECLI:EU:C:2006:277.

of the TFEU was the correct legal basis.[217] However, the chosen Treaty provision meant that the Council should have adopted the proposed act of law unanimously. Yet, an agreement could not have been reached because of the basically different views presented by Member States. Even though the Italian presidency tried to achieve consensus in the second half of 2014,[218] the Commission withdrew the proposal in March 2015 due to the lack of progress on the statute.[219]

Although the FE statute appears as a significant improvement from the EA association (on account of fixing the main problems presented by the doctrine) and would be a substantial step forward from the Convention on Recognition of the Legal Personality of International Non-Governmental Organizations, it cannot be stated that it was flawless. Following the opinions issued by the CoR and the EESC, it can be summarized that:

(1) while the FE should be able to pursue economic activities related to its public benefit mission, the notion of unrelated economic activities may be more difficult to define. Thus, it might be clearer to allow the FE to undertake only indirect unrelated economic activities through another legal entity[220] or, taking a stricter approach, to define the limits of economic activities in which the FEs could be engaged more clearly and inextricably link them with the organization's public interest tasks; therefore, any profit would be used only in pursuance of the public benefit purpose;[221]
(2) the term "public benefit" is troublesome as it is understood differently in the EU Member States. Thus, it could be replaced by "public interest" which would reduce the risk of confusion with tax law or public concepts used in certain states with regard to grating foundations (or associations) a particular tax status or treatment under national law;[222]
(3) the proposal should establish some basic rules concerning the inner supervisory bodies of the FE. For instance, procedures for auditing and publishing the reports on the activities of FEs could be clarified and made more specific. Also, it would be desired to clearly state that no person may at the same time be a member of both the governing board and the supervisory body.[223]

Although in 2015 the Commission stated that it would further consider, together with the foundation sector and other stakeholders, other possibilities, including

217. Explanatory memorandum to the proposal, para. (3.1).
218. S. Jung, *Need for a New Approach in European Company Law?—The European Foundation as a Turning Point*, Trust & Trustees Vol. 6/2015, p. 625.
219. Official Journal C 80, 7.3.2015.
220. The EESC opinion, point 4.6.
221. The CoR opinion, point 22.
222. The CoR opinion, point 21.
223. The CoR opinion, point 27.

nonlegislative ones, which could be used in order to facilitate the activity of foundations across the EU,[224] the failure of the FE statute should be estimated as a lost opportunity. The proposal was a great chance to ease the cross-border activities of European Foundations. Most significantly, the statutes would enable some NGOs to enjoy the freedom of establishment for all activities that contribute to the objectives of the EU.[225] It could also establish an interesting tool for national activities.[226] Possibly, the withdrawal was too premature. It seems that with clearer provisions on tax treatment and public benefit purposes, the Regulation could eventually enter into force.[227] In this matter, a lack of communication (and involvement) between the EU institutions, Member States and, unfortunately, NGOs lied at the heart of the second unsuccessful attempt to regulate a pan-European legal form of the third sector organizations.

[3] European Political Foundations

To systematize the possibility of conducting cross-border activities in the EU by NGOs, a few remarks on European political foundations (informally referred to as "Eurofoundations") should be made. These entities should not be confused with third sector organizations as they have utterly different aims. According to Article 1 (4) of Regulation (EU, EURATOM) No 1141/2014 of the EP and of the Council of October 22, 2014, on the statute of European political parties and European political foundations,[228] a European political foundation is an entity which is formally affiliated with a European political party, which is registered with the Authority[229] in accordance with the conditions and procedures laid down in the Regulation and which through its activities, within the aims and fundamental values pursued by the Union, underpins and complements the objectives of the European political party by performing one or more of the following tasks:

(a) observing, analyzing and contributing to the debate on European public policy issues and on the process of European integration;
(b) developing activities linked to European public policy issues, such as organizing and supporting seminars, training, conferences and studies on such issues between relevant stakeholders, including youth organizations and other representatives of civil society;
(c) developing cooperation in order to promote democracy, including in the third countries;

224. Letter from the Commission to the EESC from January 2015, see *European Foundation Statute state of play. EESC—Social Economy Category meeting 26 February 2015*, presentation available at: http://www.eesc.europa.eu/resources/docs/european-foundation-centre.pdf.
225. O. Breen, *EU Regulation...*
226. See. R. Godlewski, P. Staszczyk, *Projekt...*, pp. 10-12.
227. See O. Breen, *The European...*, pp. 38 et seq.
228. Official Journal L 317, 4.11.2014.
229. The Authority for European political parties and European political foundations was established for the purpose of registering, controlling and imposing sanctions on these entities.

(d) serving as a framework for national political foundations, academics and other relevant actors to work together at European level.

Accordingly, European political foundations are research and advocacy organizations closely linked to (but independent from) European political parties. Their purpose is to act as platforms aiming at developing forward-looking ideas and concepts for their respective political family and providing a forum where those ideas can be widely debated.[230] Each European political party can have only one formally affiliated European political foundation. Yet, every European political party and the affiliated European political foundation shall ensure a separation between their respective day-to-day management, governing structures and financial accounts. According to Article 2 (1) of the Regulation, a European political foundation can be registered only upon the following conditions:

- it must be affiliated with a European political party registered in accordance with the conditions and procedures laid down in the Regulation;
- it must have its seat in a Member State as indicated in its statutes;
- it must observe, in particular in its program and its activities, the values on which the Union is founded, as expressed in Article 2 of the TEU, namely respect for human dignity, freedom, democracy, equality, the rule of law and respect for human rights, including rights of persons belonging to minorities;
- its objectives must complement the objectives of the European political party with which it is formally affiliated;
- its governing body must be composed of members from at least one-quarter of the Member States;
- it must not pursue profit goals.

European political foundations have a pan-European legal form. According to Articles 12 and 13 of the Regulation, they have legal personalities and enjoy legal recognition and capacity in all Member States. Likewise, the requirements concerning its internal organization seem quite demanding.[231]

---

230. S. Hix, Ch. Lord, *Political Parties in the European Union*, New York 1997, p. 4.
231. According to Art. 5 (1) of the Regulation, the statutes of a European political foundation shall comply with the applicable law of the Member State in which it has its seat and shall include provisions covering at least the following:

- its name and logo, which must be clearly distinguishable from those of any existing European political party or European political foundation;
- the address of its seat;
- a description of its purpose and objectives, which must be compatible with the tasks listed in point (4) of Art. 2;
- a statement, in conformity with point (f) of Art. 3 (2), that it does not pursue profit goals;
- the name of the European political party with which it is directly affiliated and a description of the formal relationship between them;
- a list of its bodies, specifying for each of its powers, responsibilities and composition and including the modalities for the appointment and dismissal of the members and managers of such bodies;

Since 2008, the EP has been awarding annual operating grants for the European political foundations. The grant can cover up to 85% of the eligible expenditure of a foundation, while the rest should be covered by its own resources (e.g., membership fees or donations).[232] The grant can be used to cover expenses directly linked to the activities set out in the foundation's program of activities (including meeting and conferences, publications, studies and advertisements or administrative, personnel and travel costs).[233] However, the grant cannot be used, among others, to meet expenditure such as campaign costs for referenda and elections, direct or indirect funding of national parties, election candidates and national political foundations. To support financial transparency, external restrictions are rigidly restricted.[234] In particular, European political foundations (like European political parties) shall transmit a list of all donors with their corresponding donations, indicating both the nature and the value of the individual donations at the time of the submission of their annual financial statements.

In spite of these restraints, the European public opinion is sometimes disturbed by misuses conducted by European political foundations. The most common example is financing national parties through European political foundations in an indirect manner (e.g., by paying for political conventions or meetings that serve to promote certain candidates and politicians).[235] As the discussed entities are commonly called "Eurofoundations," they may give a misleading impression of being connected with "normal," grassrooted foundations. Thus, although European political foundations lead significant research in various fields of knowledge and they promote the European

- its administrative and financial organization and procedures, specifying in particular the bodies and offices holding the powers of administrative, financial and legal representation and the rules on the establishment, approval and verification of annual accounts;
- the internal procedure for amending its statutes;
- the internal procedure to be followed in the event of its voluntary dissolution as a European political foundation.

232. For specific funding principles see Arts. 17-22 of the Regulation.
233. See *European Parliament Contracts and Grants*, available at: http://www.europarl.europa.eu/contracts-and-grants/en/20150201PVL00101/Political-parties-and-foundations (on February 9, 2019).
234. According to Art. 20 (1) of the Regulation, European political parties and European political foundations may accept donations from natural or legal persons up to a value of EUR 18,000 per year and per donor. Pursuant to para. (4), they shall not accept any of the following:

   - anonymous donations or contributions;
   - donations from the budgets of political groups in the EP;
   - donations from any public authority from a Member State or a third country or from any undertaking over which such a public authority may exercise, directly or indirectly, a dominant influence by virtue of its ownership of it, its financial participation therein or the rules which govern it;
   - donations from any private entities based in a third country or from individuals from a third country who are not entitled to vote in elections to the EP.

235. See e.g. W. Cieśla, *EU Fraud Case Sheds Light on Danish and Polish Politics*, https://euobserver.com/investigations/136112 (on February 9, 2019), H. Cooper, *Polish Minister Faces Call to Quit over Party Funding*, http://www.politico.eu/article/eu-funding-scandal-threatens-to-engulf-polish-government/ (on February 9, 2019).

integration in many ways, they should always be differentiated from representatives of European civil society, just like the political foundations are generally treated as bodies not acting in the scope of public benefit purposes at the national level.[236]

[C] Summary

A common argument against a pan-European legal form for NGOs is that the EU law should not harmonize areas where the legal traditions of the Member States are different.[237] Although this assertion seems more than questionable, one of the biggest problems with passing the statutes for European NGOs was, undoubtedly, finding the proper and efficient legal basis. As it was rightly noted in the literature,[238] the use of Article 352 of the TFEU as legislative ground for the regulation proposals on European third sector organizations proved to be controversial. This legal norm, while providing the broader basis for the EU action, requires unanimity within the Council for the successful passage of any regulation, which showed to be a certain difficulty with 28 Member States involved. Other possible legal basis, Article 114 of the TFEU,[239] has the advantage of requiring only a qualified majority vote within the Council, but it is more limited in its use since it only applies to a narrower range of Council measures, meaning "measures for the approximation of the provisions laid down by law, regulation or administrative action in Member States which have their object the establishment and functioning of the internal market." Accordingly, the absence of an optimal Treaty basis for acts of law on nonprofit activity may appear as one of the reasons for the lack of a proactive legislative agenda in this matter in the past.[240]

Although the proposals for the statutes for EA and FE failed, the EU institutions undertook other measures that could possibly be used by NGOs in their cross-border activities:

(1) In 1993 (along with the EA statutes), the Commission presented a proposal for a Regulation on European Mutual Society.[241] It was specified as "an autonomous association of persons (legal entities or natural persons) united voluntarily, whose primary purpose is to satisfy their common needs and not to make profits or provide a return on capital." This new form of cross-border legal person was to be managed according to solidarity principles among members participating in corporate governance. The

236. E.g., according to Art. 3 (4) p. 5, the foundations set up by political parties are excluded from the scope of Polish Public Benefit and Volunteer Work Act (*Ustawa o działalności pozytku publicznego i o wolontariacie*).
237. J. Kendall, L. Fraisse, *The European Statue of Association: Why an Obscure but Contested Symbol in a Sea of Indifference and Skepticism?*, Third Sector European Policy Working Papers. London School of Economics and Political Science, No. 11/2005, p. 8. See also C.R.M. Versteegh, *Civil...*, p.
238. O. Breen, *Through the Looking Glass: European Perspectives on Non-profit Vulnerability, Legitimacy and Regulation*, Brooklyn Journal of International Law Vol. 36/2011, p. 956.
239. O. Breen, *Through...*, p. 956.
240. *Ibid.*
241. COM(91) 273 final—SYN 390.

Commission withdrew the proposal in 2006[242] due to the lack of interest in the majority of Member States. However, it is worth noticing that recently the EP has expressed interest in reactivating the legislative procedure on a new statute for a European Mutual Society.[243]

(2) Another instrument that could theoretically be used by NGOs in their European activities is the Statue for a European Cooperative Society (SCE). In particular, an SCE may be formed by five or more natural persons and companies and firms within the meaning of the second paragraph of Article 48 of the TFEU and other legal bodies governed by public or private law, formed under the law of a Member State, resident in, or governed by, the law of at least two different Member States or by companies and firms within the meaning of the second paragraph of Article 48 of the TFEU and other legal bodies governed by public or private law formed under the law of a Member State which are governed by the law of at least two different Member States (see Article 2 (1) of the Council Regulation (EC) No 1435/2003 of July 22, 2003, on the Statute for a European Cooperative Society (SCE)).[244] It seems that associations and foundations fall into the scope of the notion "other legal bodies governed by public or private law." However, the involvement of NGOs in SCEs seems troublesome as the principal object of this European entity is related to economic activity. Other aims, including social activities, have a rather subsidiary relevance.[245] It is why cooperative societies in domestic legal systems are often outside the scope of public benefit entities.[246] Accordingly, Article 1 (3) of the Regulation states that an SCE shall have as its principal object the satisfaction of its members' needs and/or the development of their economic and social activities, in particular the conclusion of agreements with them to supply goods or services or to execute work of the kind that the SCE carries out or commissions. An SCE may also have as its objects the satisfaction of its members' needs by promoting their participation in economic activities, in one or more SCEs and/or national cooperatives.

(3) According to Article 4 (1) (a) of the Council Regulation (EEC) No 2137/85 of July 25, 1985, on the European Economic Interest Grouping (EEIG),[247] this entity is open to companies or firms within the meaning of the second paragraph of Article 58 (presently Article 54) of the TFEU and other legal bodies governed by public or private law, which have been formed in

242. Official Journal C 64, 17.3.2006.

243. See the EP resolution of 14 March 2013 with recommendations to the Commission on the Statute for a European mutual society (2012/2039(INL)) and *A Statute for European mutual societies An assessment accompanying the European Parliament's Legislative own-Initiative Report* of 2013, available at: http://www.europarl.europa.eu/RegData/etudes/etudes/join/2013/494461/IPOL-JOIN_ET(2013)494461_EN.pdf (on February 9, 2019).

244. Official Journal L 207, 18.8.2003.

245. See D. Cracogna, A. Fici, H. Henry, *International Handbook of Cooperative Law*, Heidelberg 2013, p. 142.

246. H. Anheier, S. Toepfer, *International Encyclopedia of Civil Society*, New York 2010, p. 1257.

247. Official Journal L 199/1, 31.7.1985.

accordance with the law of a Member State and which have their registered statutory office and central administration in the EU. The allowed purposes of the EEIG are to coordinate different tasks of the participants. They concern, for example, research, marketing and distribution. However, only economic activities may be facilitated through the EEIG. Also, as it has already been discussed in the previous paragraphs of this chapter, NGOs do not, in principle, fall into the scope of Article 54 of the TFEU. It is why NGO participation in an EEIG is a rather theoretical possibility.[248]

(4) The fourth hypothetical possibility for NGOs to conduct cross-border activity in a harmonized legal form is utilizing Council Regulation (EC) No 2157/2001 of October 8, 2001, on the Statute for a European Company (SE).[249] However, the *Societas Europaea* is profit oriented and can be established only in order to pursue economic activities.[250] Also, as a general rule stated in Article 2 of the Regulation, a European company may be formed only by national public and private limited-liability companies.[251] Article 2 (3) refers to companies and firms within the meaning of the second paragraph of Article 48 of the TFEU as entities that may form a subsidiary SE by subscribing its shares, but, as it has already been discussed above, NGOs are mainly excluded from the scope of this provision. Thus, a European company cannot serve as a vehicle for pan-European activity of the third sector organizations.

To sum up, at present there is no good legal tool for NGOs to conduct their activities in one legal form in all EU Member States. In fact, national laws are also not very helpful as they usually do not provide the possibility of acknowledging the legal personality of foreign third sector organizations without some kind of prior registration[252]

248. P. Bater, *Introduction...*, p. 20.
249. Official Journal L 294/1, 10.11.2001.
250. See e.g. H. Zimmer, *Einmal SE, immer SE?, Zum Bestandsschutz einer Societas Europaea bei fehlerhafter Gründung*, Wirtschaftsrechtliche Blätter Vol. 11/2008, pp. 518 et seq.
251. According to Annex I and Annex II to the Regulation.
252. E.g. According to Art. 7 of the Spanish Law 50/2002 on Foundations (*Ley 50/2002 de Fundaciones*):

> 1. Foreign foundations intending to carry out his activities in a stable way in Spain, should keep a delegation in Spanish territory which will be their home for the purposes of this act, and register at the competent register of foundations based on the territorial area in which mainly develop their activities.
> 2. The foreign foundation seeking registration must demonstrate before the corresponding register of foundations which has been validly constituted in accordance with their personal law.
> Registration may be refused when the circumstance referred to in the preceding paragraph is not accredited as well as weekends are not of general interest in accordance with Spanish legislation.
> 3. The foreign foundations that fail to comply with the requirements laid down in this article may not be used the designation of "Foundation."
> 4. The delegations in Spain of foreign foundations shall be subject to the protectorate that corresponds according to the geographical area in which mainly develop their activities being implementing the legal regime envisaged for the Spanish foundations.

or recognition.[253] In fact, most legal systems do not envisage any status for "foreign" NGOs[254] at all. Some legal systems provide a special status of "open branch offices" for foreign organizations.[255] However, this institution resolves hardly any problems as these "foreign" types of entities are not equipped with legal capacity.[256] Only the Belgian system[257] establishes the legal form of "international non-profit associations and foundations" which, still, have to be registered under the requirements of national law.[258]

This mosaic of legal resolutions is the main reason why large, international NGOs are forced to register national organizations as "representatives," "dependent" on the

253. E.g., the Romanian Law No. 21 of 6 February 1924 for Legal Entities—Associations and Foundations (*lege nr. 21 din 6 februarie 1924 pentru Persoanele juridice—Asociații și Fundații*) envisages a special procedure of recognition of foreign organizations.
254. E.g., they are not regulated in the German Formation and Activities of Foundations Act (*Gesetz über die Bildung und Tätigkeit von Stiftungen*), the Polish Law on Associations (*Prawo o stowarzyszeniach*) or the Latvian Associations and Foundations Act (*Biedrību un nodibinājumu likums*).
255. E.g., pursuant to Art. 19 of the Polish Law on Foundations (*Ustawa o fundacjach*):

   1. Foreign foundations sited abroad may open branch offices on the territory of the Republic of Poland.
   2. The opening of the branch office referred to in Paragraph I requires a permit, which is tantamount to approval of the commencement of the activities specified in the permit. The permit is granted by the minister proper with regard to the scope of his activities and the purposes for which said branch office is opened.
   3. The permit may be granted if the opening of the branch office is intended to promote the accomplishment of the objectives referred to in Article 1. If the branch office is also to engage in economic activity, the provisions of Article 5, Paragraph 5, first sentence, apply accordingly.
   4. The branch office is obligated to adhere to the laws binding on the territory of the Republic of Poland.
   5. The minister proper with regard to the scope of his activities and the purposes for which the branch office is opened may revoke the permit if the branch office does not adhere to the terms specified in the permit or markedly violates the laws binding on the territory of the Republic of Poland or the interests of the state.
   6. If the branch office or the foundation it represents impairs the security or other important interests of the state, the proper minister may suspend its permit. Such suspension entails—until a ruling on the revocation of the permit is issued—an immediate cessation of the activities specified in the permit without payment of any compensation therefor.
   7. Matters concerning the economic activity of the branch office of a foundation are moreover governed by separate regulations governing the conduct of economic activity on the territory of the Republic of Poland by representations of foreign entities.

256. See P. Staszczyk, *Ustawa o fundacjach...*, p. 130; in consequence, such an open branch office cannot be a public benefit purpose entity (and is not even perceived as an NGO) as according to Art. 3 (2) of the Polish Public Benefit and Volunteer Work Act (*Ustawa o działalności pozytku publicznego i o wolontariacie*), Nongovernmental organizations are: (1) other than units of the public finance sector, within the meaning of the act on public finance, (2) not aimed to make a profit—legal persons or organizational units not having a legal personality, which separate the law recognizes the legal capacity, including foundations and associations, subject to the provisions of paragraph.
257. It is arguable because many international organizations (including the EU institutions) have their headquarters in Brussels.
258. As provided by the Belgian Law on Non-Profit Associations, international Non-Profit Association and Foundations (*Loi sur les associations sans but lucratif, les associations internationales sans but lucratif et les fondations*).

"mother" organization to operate in various countries.[259] However, this procedure often raises problems—for instance, with transparency in mutual relations or financial reliance. In this matter, the failure of regulations on European associations and foundations seems to be even more burdensome.

§5.03 THE EU FUNDING FOR NGOs

Even though the term "nongovernmental organization" suggests full independence from governments,[260] many NGOs depend heavily on government financing.[261] This remark is valid also at the EU level as the European grants for NGOs are very attractive. However, with only a few organizations which claim that they will not ever accept funding from governments or any IGOs,[262] the issue of the EU funding raises many concerns dealing with its scope and requirements. In fact, even some NGOs often denounce the relationship between the EU institutions and third sector organizations as "problematic."[263] Therefore, the omission of this aspect would result in an incomplete analysis on the prospects for European civil society.

The following paragraphs will concentrate only at the possibility of obtaining funding by NGOs at the EU level (i.e., from the EU institutions). In contrast, it will not handle with national grants opportunities,[264] even if the funds themselves derive from the EU budget (i.e., Cohesion Fund or European Social Funds). The reason for this distinction is that the distribution of the latter ones, as a practical effect of the subsidiarity principle,[265] is determined by national authorities.[266]

259. P. Zaleski, *Global Non-governmental Administrative System: Geosociology of the Third Sector* in: *Civil Society in the Making*, D. Gavin, P. Gliński (eds), Warsaw 2006, pp. 131 et seq.
260. For specific information on sources of financing of NGOs in various countries see e.g. M. Gumkowska, *Skąd organizacje na świecie mają pieniądze*, available at: http://fakty.ngo.pl/wiadomosc/2089714.html.
261. P. Zaleski, *Global...*, p. 128. For the reasons why governments funds NGOs see e.g. R. Burger, I. Dasgupta, T. Owens, *Why Pay NGOs to Involve the Community?*, Annals of Public and Cooperative Economics Vol. 86/2015, pp. 7 et seq. In contrast, for the possible threats see e.g. K. AbouAssi, *Get Money Get Involved? NGO's Reactions to Donor Funding and Their Potential Involvement in the Public Policy Processes*, International Society for Third-Sector Research Vol. 25/2014, pp. 968 et seq.
262. An example being Greenpeace (see *Greenpeace International Annual Report 2015*, available at: http://www.greenpeace.org/international/Global/international/publications/greenpeace/2016/2015-Annual-Report-Web.pdf (on February 9, 2019), p. 24), see also S.J. Gilbert, *The Value of Environmental Activists*, Harvard Business School HBS Cases, available at: http://hbswk.hbs.edu/item/the-value-of-environmental-activists (on February 9, 2019).
263. See *The Central Role of European Governments in NGO Funding*, a report issued by NGO Monitor, available at: http://bit.do/ekaCb (on February 9, 2019).
264. According to the Commission, approximately 80% of EU-funding sources for NGOs are managed by EU countries themselves. See *Funding opportunities for NGOs*, available at: http://bit.do/ekaC5 (on February 9, 2019).
265. See e.g. S. Luc, *Zasada pomocniczości w polityce gospodarczej Unii Europejskiej*, Prace i Materiały Instytutu Rozwoju Gospodarczego SGH 2012, p. 156.
266. More specifically, basing on the multiannual Financial Framework 2014-2020. This funding takes a form of shared management (managed jointly by the EU and Member State).

[A] Legal Basis

General provisions on grants possibilities at the EU level are envisaged by Regulation (EU, Euratom) No 2018/1046 of the EP and of the Council of July 18, 2018, on the financial rules applicable to the general budget of the Union amending Regulations (EU) No 1296/2013, (EU) No 1301/2013, (EU) No 1303/2013, (EU) No 1304/2013, (EU) No 1309/2013, (EU) No 1316/2013, (EU) No 223/2014, (EU) No 283/2014 and Decision No 541/2014/EU and repealing Regulation (EU, Euratom) No 966/2012[267] (Financial Regulation). According to its Article 2 (33), grants are financial contributions by way of donation. Pursuant to Article 180 (1), they may be awarded to finance any of the following:

(1) an action intended to help achieve a Union policy objective ("action grants");
(2) the functioning of a body which has an objective forming part of, and supporting, a Union policy ("operating grants").

Grants can have various forms[268] and are distributed within numerous programs.[269] They shall be subject to principles of "equal treatment," "transparency," "cofinancing," "noncumulative award and no double financing," "nonretroactivity" and "no-profit" (Article 188). Pursuant to Article 197 (2) grant applications shall be eligible if submitted by the following:

(1) legal persons;
(2) natural persons, in so far as this is required by the nature of characteristics of the action or the objective pursued by the applicant;
(3) entities which do not have legal personality under the applicable national law, provided that their representatives have the capacity to undertake

267. Official Journal L 193/1, 30.7.2018.
268. Art. 125 (1) of the Regulation names:

1. financing not linked to the costs of the relevant information based on:
   (a) the fulfillment of conditions set out in sector-specific rules or Commission decisions, or
   (b) the achievement of results measured by reference to previously set milestones or through performance indicators;
2. reimbursement of a specified proportion of the eligible costs,
3. reimbursement on the basis of unit costs,
4. lumps sums,
5. flat-rate financing,
6. a combination of the forms referred to in points (1) to (5).

269. E.g.:

(1) Horizon 2020.
(2) Erasmus +.
(3) European Fund for Strategic Investments (EFSI).
(4) Development and cooperation programs.
(5) European Structural and Investment Funds (ESIF).
(6) European Agriculture Guarantee Fund.

> legal obligations on behalf of the entities and that the entities offer guarantees for the protection of the financial interests of the Union equivalent to those offered by legal persons. In particular the applicant shall have a financial and operational capacity equivalent to that of a legal person. The representatives of the applicant shall prove that those conditions are satisfied.

NGOs are naturally included in the scope of possible grant receivers in the second point of the cited norm. The third point opens up the possibility of applying for EU funds by social movements which are not registered as NGOs. The Regulation does not provide any specific rules on NGOs (or social movements) as grant applicants. However, it applies additional rules for recipients of the EU funding. The main principle is that they must not be in an excluding situation which is specified in Article 136 (1) of the Regulation.[270] Understanding and application of these criteria is often not clear and requires legal expertise in many cases.[271] Still, NGOs are generally not covered by the "no-profit principle" established in Article 192 (1) of the Regulation. According to this principle, grants shall not have the purpose or effect of producing any profit within

---

270. The excluding situations are i.a.:

    (1) the person or entity is bankrupt, subject to insolvency or winding-up procedures; its assets are being administered by a liquidator or by a court; it is in an arrangement with creditors; its business activities are suspended; or it is in any analogous situation arising from a similar procedure provided for under Union or national law;
    (2) it has been established by a final judgment or a final administrative decision that the person or entity is in breach of its obligations relating to the payment of taxes or social security contributions in accordance with the applicable law;
    (3) it has been established by a final judgment or a final administrative decision that the person or entity is guilty of grave professional misconduct by having violated applicable laws or regulations or ethical standards of the profession to which the person or entity belongs, or by having engaged in any wrongful conduct which has an impact on its professional credibility where such conduct denotes wrongful intent or gross negligence;
    (4) it has been established by a final judgment that the person or entity is guilty of any of the following: fraud, corruption, conduct related to a criminal organization, money laundering or terrorist financing, terrorist offences or offences linked to terrorist activities, child labor;
    (5) the person or entity has shown significant deficiencies in complying with main obligations in the implementation of a legal commitment financed by the budget which has:
        (i) led to the early termination of a legal commitment;
        (ii) led to the application of liquidated damages or other contractual penalties; or
        (iii) been discovered by an authorising officer, OLAF or the Court of Auditors following checks, audits or investigations.
    (6) it has been established by a final judgment or final administrative decision that the person or entity has committed an irregularity within the meaning of Article 1(2) of Council Regulation (EC, Euratom) No 2988/95 (52);
    (7) it has been established by a final judgment or final administrative decision that the person or entity has created an entity in a different jurisdiction with the intent to circumvent fiscal, social or any other legal obligations in the jurisdiction of its registered office, central administration or principal place of business;
    (8) it has been established by a final judgment or final administrative decision that an entity has been created with the intent referred to in point (7).

271. Cf. U. Güb, *European Governance: Views from the UK on Democracy, Participation and Policy-Making in the EU*, London 2002, p. 134.

the framework of the action or the work program of the beneficiary. However, according to Article 192 (3) it shall not apply to:

(1) actions the objective of which is the reinforcement of the financial capacity of a beneficiary, or actions which generate an income to ensure their continuity after the period of Union financing provided for in the grant decision or agreement;
(2) study, research or training scholarships paid to natural persons;
(3) actions implemented by nonprofit organizations;
(4) grants in the form referred to in the first subparagraph of Article 125 (1) (a);
(5) low value grants.

Grants are ordinarily awarded upon calls for proposals which is an aftermath of the "transparency" principle. However, the current Regulation lists some major exceptions from this rule in Article 195.[272]

Specific grant possibilities which are relevant in terms of the topic of this book are provided by Council Regulation (EU) No 390/2014 of April 14, 2014, establishing the "Europe for Citizens" program for the period 2014-2020.[273] The subject responsible for the development and running of this program is the Commission's Directorate-General for Communication. On the one hand, it manages the budget[274] and defines objectives, strategies and priority areas of action for the program.[275] On the other hand, in order to bring the information on the Europe for Citizens Program closer to its stakeholders and provide them with guidance and support, the Commission established the Europe for Citizens Contact Point. These national structures are responsible for ensuring targeted,

---

272. I.e. grants may be awarded without a call for proposals in the following cases:
    (a) for the purposes of humanitarian aid, emergency support operations, civil protection operations or crisis management aid;
    (b) in other exceptional and duly substantiated emergencies;
    (c) to bodies with a de jure or de facto monopoly or to bodies designated by Member States, under their responsibility, where those Member States are in a de jure or de facto monopoly situation;
    (d) to bodies identified by a basic act, within the meaning of Article 58, as beneficiaries or to bodies designated by Member States, under their responsibility, where those Member States are identified by a basic act as beneficiaries;
    (e) in the case of research and technological development, to bodies identified in the work program referred to in Article 110, where the basic act expressly provides for that possibility, and on condition that the project does not fall under the scope of a call for proposals;
    (f) for activities with specific characteristics that require a particular type of body on account of its technical competence, its high degree of specialisation or its administrative powers, on condition that the activities concerned do not fall within the scope of a call for proposals;
    (g) to the EIB or the EIF for actions of technical assistance.
273. Official Journal L 115/3 17.4.2015.
274. According to Art. 12 (1) of the Regulation, the complete budget amounts to EUR 185,468,000.
275. See Europe for Citizens—Programme Guide—version valid as of 2017, European Commission, Directorate-General for Migration and Home Affairs, Education, Audiovisual and Culture Executive Agency, available at: Education, Audiovisual and Culture Executive Agency, available at: https://eacea.ec.europa.eu/sites/eacea-site/files/2017_programme_guide_en.pdf (on February 9, 2019), p .10.

effective grassroot dissemination of practical information on the implementation, its activities and funding opportunities.[276]

The Regulation can be described as an "executive" tool for achieving the goals described in the TFEU as the preambles of both of these acts refer to founding "an ever closer Union."[277] Hence, the preamble to the Regulation in the fourth paragraph notes that in order to bring Europe closer to its citizens and to enable them to participate fully in the construction of an ever closer Union, a variety of actions and coordinated efforts through transnational and Union level activities are required. This assertion can be explained that the accomplishment of founding "an ever closer Union" is determined not only by the EU institutions or Member States but also, if not foremost, by the citizens and their organizations that correspond with the values of the EU, provided that they are equipped with proper funds. In this matter, according to Article 2 (1), under the overall aim of bringing the Union closer to citizens, the general objectives of the Program are the following:[278]

- to contribute to citizens' understanding of the Union, its history and diversity;
- to foster European citizenship and to improve conditions for civic and democratic participation at the Union level.

The second component of the program is especially significant in terms of this book as its aim is to provide support for all activities that cover civic participation in the broadest sense with a particular focus on the activities directly linked to the Union policies, with a view to concretely participate in the Union policy-making process.[279] It also covers projects and initiatives that develop opportunities for mutual understanding, intercultural learning solidarity, societal engagement and volunteering at the Union level.[280] These objectives can be funded by two sorts of grants:[281]

276. Europe..., p. 10.
277. In the Preamble to the TFEU it reads i.a.: "DETERMINED to lay the foundations of an ever closer union among the peoples of Europe."
278. Specific aims of the program are presented on its official webpage (http://ec.europa.eu/citizenship/europe-for-citizens-programme/) as follows:
    (a) to contribute to citizens' understanding of the EU, its history and diversity;
    (b) to foster European citizenship and to improve conditions for civic and democratic participation at the EU level;
    (c) to raise awareness of remembrance, common history and values;
    (d) to encourage democratic participation of citizens at the EU level, by developing citizens' understanding of the EU policy-making process and, by promoting opportunities for societal and intercultural engagement and volunteering at the EU level.
279. Europe..., p. 18.
280. I.e.:
    - promotion of societal engagement and solidarity—activities able to promoting debate/campaigns/actions on the themes and common interest in the larger framework of the rights and responsibilities of the Union citizens and making the link to the European political agenda and policy making process;
    - gathering of opinions—activities aiming at gathering the individual opinions of the citizens on a specific topic to be yearly defined, favoring bottom-up approach (including the use of societal network, webinars, etc.) and media literacy;

(1) action grants which can be granted for projects, i.e. for actions with a limited lifetime during which proposed specific activities are implemented;
(2) operating grants which provide financial support for costs required for the proper conduct of the usual and permanent activities of an organization, i.e. staff costs, the cost of internal meetings, information and dissemination, travel costs arising from the implementation of the work program, rental payments, depreciation and other costs directly linked to the organization's work program.

The grant program is aimed precisely at NGOs[282] with legal personality and "operational capacity."[283] The latter requirement means that the applicant must show the necessary competencies and motivation to carry out the proposed project. This capacity is assessed on the basis of the applicants' experience in managing projects in the field concerned. Moreover, in requests exceeding EUR 60,000 the applicant is obliged to submit a "declaration on honor."[284] As a rule, the program is open to subjects from all EU Members States, as well from acceding and candidate countries, potential candidate countries and the EFTA countries.[285]

Other grant possibilities for NGOs at the EU level include:

(1) The Creative Europe program;[286]
(2) Horizon 2020;[287]
(3) some projects in the Connecting Europe Facility;[288]
(4) thematic or regional programs managed by the Commission's department dealing with international cooperation and development (DEVCO);[289]

- volunteering—activities promoting solidarity among the Union citizens and beyond (Europe..., p. 21).

281. Europe..., p. 8.
282. However, according to Art. 6 of the Regulation, the program is also open to all stakeholders promoting European citizenship and integration, in particular local and regional authorities organizations, twinning committees, European public policy research organizations (think tanks), civil society organizations (including survivors' associations) and cultural, youth, educational and research organizations.
283. Europe..., p. 15.
284. *Ibid.*, p. 14.
285. The applications are evaluated according to four criteria:

- consistency with the objectives of the program and program strand—30%;
- quality of the activity plan of the project—35%;
- dissemination—15%;
- impact and citizen involvement—20% (see Europe..., pp. 16-17).

286. See: https://eacea.ec.europa.eu/creative-europe_en (on February 9, 2019).
287. See: https://ec.europa.eu/programmes/horizon2020/ (on February 9, 2019).
288. See: https://ec.europa.eu/digital-single-market/connecting-europe-facility (on February 9, 2019).
289. See: https://ec.europa.eu/europeaid/about-funding_en (on February 9, 2019).

(5) humanitarian aid and civil protection activities through the Commission's department dealing with humanitarian aid and civil protection (ECHO).[290]

The first three of these opportunities are not directly aimed at NGOs. Therefore, they will not be discussed in detail. The latter two are, in turn, generally designed for foreign-based organizations, and they do not contribute to the development of European civil society. Nevertheless, some problems arising from these grant possibilities will be presented in the subsequent paragraphs of this chapter.

As a side note, it should be mentioned that NGOs are one of the focal points in the EEA Grants and Norway Grants which are the financial contributions of Norway, Iceland and Liechtenstein toward the reduction of economic and social disparities in the European Economic Ares (EEA) and the strengthening of bilateral relations.[291] "Culture, civil society, good governance, fundamental rights and freedoms" are named as one of the priority sectors for specific allocations[292] in both of them. Moreover, 10% of the total of the country-specific allocations in the EEA Grants shall be set aside for a fund for civil society,[293] whereas in the Norway Grants a special emphasis lies on cooperation with civil society and cross-border cooperation with neighboring third countries.[294] Due to the fact that precise conditions for these funding opportunities are agreed upon between the donors and interested countries, and that they are not per se a part of the EU funds, they will not be further analyzed.[295] Still, it is worth mentioning that they often play a significant role in the daily functioning of NGOs in the EU and can, in fact, be a major argument in the debate on the state of the rule of law in certain Member States.[296]

[B] Remarks on the Present EU Funding System

The Commission does not provide for any accurate analysis of funding allocated to individual NGOs or NGOs in general. The study conducted by the EP in 2010[297] identified significant shortcomings in the way the Commission records grant funding. These shortcomings seem to remain up until today as they are repeated in the EP study

290. See: http://ec.europa.eu/echo/funding-evaluations/funding-for-humanitarian-aid_en (on February 9, 2019).
291. See the preamble to the Agreement between the European Union, Iceland, the Principality of Liechtenstein and the Kingdom of Norway on an EEA Financial Mechanism 2014-2021, Official Journal L 141/3, 28.5.2016 (EEA Grants Agreement).
292. Art. 3 (1) of the EEA Grants Agreement and Art. 3 (1) of the Agreement between the Kingdom of Norway and the European Union on a Norwegian Financial Mechanism for the period 2014-2021, Official Journal L 141/11, 28.5.2016 (Norway Funds Agreement).
293. See Art. 3 (2) (b) of the EEA Grants Agreement.
294. Art. 3 (2) (c) of the Norway Funds Agreement.
295. However, it is worth mentioning that they are distributed party by the national authorities and partly by the selected NGOs (i.e., the social part of funds).
296. See e.g. A. Eriksson, *Norway Defends NGOs in Hungary and Poland*, available at: https://euobserver.com/social/137818 (on February 9, 2019).
297. Financing of Non-governmental Organizations (NGOs) from the EU budget. Study 2010, available at: http://www.europarl.europa.eu/meetdocs/2009_2014/documents/cont/dv/5_study_/5_study_en.pdf (on February 9, 2019).

of 2016[298] and, to large extent, in the European Court of Auditors Special Report of 2018.[299] The most important remarks are that:

- the Commission does not use any NGO classification, but rather the term "not-for-profit," which includes many types of organizations;
- the Commission's data does not reflect redistribution of grant funding between consortium partners.[300]

Analysis reveals a complex web of interconnected NGOs linked through membership of numerous overlapping networks that address many different issues. NGOs that do not receive the EU funding directly may nevertheless benefit indirectly from the EU funding through memberships in networks that receive the EU grants.[301] Hence, it is often difficult to identify which organization in a network or consortium is undertaking which activity or how funds flow between them in relation to those activities. It seems that the Commission has inadvertently contributed to this complexity, for example, by setting requirements that grant applicants must have partners in all or most Member States.[302] Additionally, monitoring and control procedures for the funding of NGOs active in the spheres of, e.g. environmental, social or health policy and development aid seem to be ineffective as individual Directorates-General apply different guidelines for grant funding laid down in the Financial Regulation. This often leads to a lack of traceability of the funds granted.[303]

Moreover, NGOs receiving the EU funds provide varying levels of transparency. It is rather unclear if this is due to the Commission's visibility rules or the way in which NGOs apply them. For instance, some NGOs acknowledge the EU support on each webpage. The others provide limited, seemingly haphazard acknowledgment of the EU funding on their websites or in their publications.[304] Therefore, it is often rather difficult to link actual NGO activities and outputs to the specific EU grants as they are often presented without any reference to the specific EU-funded actions.[305] In this matter, the Financial Transparency System (FTS—an obligatory database for all beneficiaries from the EU budget),[306] individual departments of the Commission and

298. Democratic Accountability and Budgetary Control of Non-Governmental Organizations Funded by the EU Budget. Study 2016, available at: http://bit.do/ekaT9 (on February 9, 2019). The study was followed by a Draft Report on budgetary control of financing NGOs from the EU budget of 16.3.2017, 2015/2345(INI).
299. Transparency of EU funds implemented by NGOs: more effort needed. A Special Report of the European Court of Auditors of 18.12.2018, available at: http://bit.do/eHWuA (on February 10, 2019).
300. Democratic..., p. 11.
301. E.g., in the form of sub-granting; see Transparency of EU..., pp. 34-39.
302. Democratic..., p. 97.
303. The EP Draft Report on budgetary control of financing NGOs from the EU budget (2015/2345(INI)), p. 4.
304. Democratic..., p. 12.
305. Cf. Transparency of EU..., pp. 50 et seq.
306. The basic requirement for the Commission to publish this information on beneficiaries of EU funds is given in Art. 35 of the Financial Regulation applicable to the general budget of the Union (the Commission shall make available, in an appropriate and timely manner, information on recipients, as well as the nature and purpose of the measure financed from the budget,

NGO annual reports[307] are not helpful either as NGOs provide various levels of detail in their documents.[308] The FTS itself lacks clear and unified organizational typology, which is hampering analysis at policy and operational levels. It deplores the fact that data concerning NGOs in the FTS cannot be sufficiently analyzed.[309] It is also frequently not clear where further information can be found.

In addition, the EP report emphasizes a high concentration of the EU funding among just a couple of beneficiaries. Recently, almost 60% of the funding available under the EU's environmental, social, health and human rights programs have been allocated to just 20 NGOs.[310] As a result, smaller organizations are practically excluded from funding at the EU level. Therefore, the EP calls on the Commission to improve its control and diversity procedures. The report also requests the Commission to introduce requirements for NGOs to publish the details of the lobbying contacts they have with EU officials and MEPs on annual basis. Thus, the report calls for "harmonized rules" to apply on any grants awarded by the EU, suggesting no double standards should apply in the way funds are allocated and controlled.[311]

The actual limitation of the EU funding to the largest NGOs strengthens the "NGOization"[312] of the third sector at the EU level. It means that many organizations lack proper legitimization from the grassroot civil society (in whose name they should perform their actions). Hence, they conduct their own policies, very often similar to

---

where the latter is implemented directly in accordance with point (a) of Art. 58 (1), and information on recipients as provided by the entities, persons and Member States to which budget implementation tasks are entrusted under other methods of implementation. The obligation set out in the first subparagraph shall also apply to the other institutions with regard to their recipients).

307. Most of the beneficiaries limit themselves to the most basic information required, meaning:

- who receives the funds;
- subject, i.e. the purpose of the expenditure;
- where the beneficiary is located;
- amount and type of expenditure;
- which responsible department awarded the funding;
- which part of the EU budget it comes from;
- which year the amount was booked in the accounts.

308. Democratic..., p. 97.
309. One of the main problems is also associated with keyword searches. For instance, the terms of Polish limited "liability company" are names variously as "spółka zoo," "spółka z ograniczona odpowiedzialnością" or "sp(zoo)."
310. In 2010 NGOs received EUR 1.5 billion in grants, of which almost 70% (EUR 1.12 billion) went to just 273 NGOs, amounting to an average of EUR 1.5 million for each NGO. In 2015 almost 60% of the funding available under the EU's environmental, social, health and human rights programs was allocated to just 20 NGOs. Moreover, it is not possible to precisely identify the top 50 NGO recipients of EU funding using existing, publicly available databases (such as the Financial Transparency System); for more information see Democratic..., p. 9.
311. Democratic..., pp. 82-83.
312. See e.g. E. Korolczuk, *Kłopot z „NGOizacją." Debata o społeczeństwie obywatelskim w Polsce a rzeczywistość*, Polityka Społeczna No. 5-6/2011, pp. 37 et seq., B. Koch, V. Buth, *Der Spagat der europäischen Zivilgesellschaft zwischen Professionalität und Bürgernähe* in *Die Entzauberung...*, pp. 167 et seq.

those of the biggest enterprises.[313] This results in a "vicious circle": the biggest NGOs sustain a structural dialogue with the EU institutions; therefore, they are most likely to be invited to formal or informal consultations, and they have the best "know-how" to obtain the EU grants.[314] On the one hand, this leads to a threat of "sponsor effect,"[315] meaning that NGOs which often depend on the EU funding will be more likely to support the policies of the EU institutions and, thus, make the whole consultation process ineffective.[316] On the other hand, it follows that it is hard to "break through" for smaller NGOs at the EU level and to perform their actions effectively.[317] As a side note, it is very interesting how this matter will be affected by "Brexit" as one of the biggest beneficiaries of the EU funding are British NGOs.[318]

Without going into details, it should be noted that foreign-based NGOs are among the biggest beneficiaries of the EU grants.[319] This form of financing can be even facilitated by the EU in some cases.[320] Undoubtedly, external funding plays a very

313. T. Grosse, *Europeizacja organizacji obywatelskich w Polsce—wyzwania*, Trzeci Sektor No. 27/2012, pp. 18 et seq.; see also A. Graff, *Urzędasy, bez serc, bez ducha. Organizacje pozarządowe—spojrzenie z wewnątrz*, Gazeta Wyborcza No. 4/2011, p. 19.
314. A common argument is also that the EU grants (and national grants as well) are often "too easy" to obtain. Thus, they are a much more effortless way of funding NGO activity in comparison to, e.g. collecting membership fees or conducting public collections of money; see e.g. M. Łojkowska, *Węgierskie NGO pod presją. Co czeka nas w Polsce [an interview with J. Celichowski]*, available at: http://wiadomosci.ngo.pl/wiadomosc/2084407.html (on February 9, 2019).
315. T. Grosse, *Europeizacja...*, p. 19.
316. S.A. Hewlett, K. Peraino, L. Sherbin, K. Sumberg, *The Sponsor Effect: Breaking Through the Last Glass Ceiling*, Harvard Business Review Research Report 2010, p. 7.
317. See e.g. V. Marinov, M. Assenova, E. Dogramadijeva, *Key Problems and Gaps in the EU Funds Absorption for Heritage Attractions Development: The Case of Bulgaria*, Almatourism. Journal of Tourism, Culture and Territorial Development Vol. 7/2017, pp. 187 et seq.
318. Among 20 biggest beneficiaries of EU grants for NGOs, 6 were of British origin, see *Democratic...*, p. 24.
319. NGOs operating in external relations received the EU funding of EUR 1.2 billion in 2015. More than 90% of the monies were allocated under the "Global Europe" heading, referring to EU aid and emergency funding for development counties. Other budget headings were much smaller—around 4% was allocated under "Sustainable growth within natural resources," almost 4% under "Security and citizenship" and less than 0.5% under "Smart and inclusive growth."
320. See Article 156 of the Financial Regulation:

    1. The Commission may, in accordance with point (c)(ii) of the first subparagraph of Article 62(1), implement the budget indirectly with international public-sector organizations set up by international agreements ('international organizations') and with specialised agencies set up by such organizations. Those agreements shall be transmitted to the Commission as part of the assessment carried out by the Commission in accordance with Article 154(3).
    2. The following organisations shall be assimilated to international organizations:
       (a) the International Committee of the Red Cross;
       (b) the International Federation of National Red Cross and Red Crescent Societies.
    3. The Commission may adopt a duly justified decision assimilating a non-profit organization to an international organization provided that it satisfies the following conditions:
       (a) it has legal personality and autonomous governance bodies;
       (b) it has been established to perform specific tasks of general international interest;
       (c) at least six Member States are members of the non-profit organization;
       (d) it is provided with adequate financial guarantees;

significant role in the EU foreign policy.[321] It appears that the new tendency in the EU strategy is to promote "soft edge" democracy promotion which involves developing grassroot structures.[322] What has not been fully researched in this field is the financial support of various NGOs acting in counties which are at war or which are rather unstable. In this way the EU supports distinct individuals or parties without making it official and therefore without exposing itself to possible negative consequences in the international relations.[323] It seems there is a consensus among the EU institutions to keep a certain level of secrecy in this field.[324] Even though the majority of this external

(e) it operates on the basis of a permanent structure and in accordance with systems, rules and procedures which can be assessed in accordance with Article 154(3).

4. Where international organisations implement funds under indirect management, verification agreements concluded with them shall apply.

Still, according to Article 41 (3) (g) as regards funding to international organizations, The Commission shall attach to each draft budget a working document containing:

- a summary of all contributions, with a breakdown per Union program or fund and per international organization;
- a statement of reasons explaining why it is more efficient for the Union to fund those international organizations rather than to act directly.

321. For more information see e.g. L. Davis, EU *Foreign Policy, Transitional Justice and Mediation. Principle, Policy and Practice*, Abingdon 2014, pp. 174 et seq., P. Müller, *The Role of Law in EU Foreign Policy-Making: Legal Integrity, Legal Spillover and the EU Policy of Differentiation Towards Israel*, Journal of Common Market Studies Vol. 55/2017, pp. 871-888.

322. M. Kurki, *Governmentality and EU Democracy Promotion: The European Instrument for Democracy and Human Rights and the Construction of Democratic Civil Societies*, International Political Sociology Vol. 5/2011, p. 349.

323. See, to this extent, the allegations of the Ministry of Strategic Affairs and Public Diplomacy in The Money Trail. The Millions Given by EU Institutions to NGOs with Ties to Terror and Boycotts against Israel. An In-Depth Analysis, available at: http://bit.do/ekB9A (on February 9, 2019). See also *Whitewashing "Resistance"—Human Rights Funding to Organizations Blurring the Lines Between Violence and Nonviolence*, NGO Monitor report of 2017, available at: http://bit.do/ekB92 (on February 9, 2019).

324. A good example is the Case T-17/10 *G. Steinberg v. European Commission*, ECLI:EU:T:2012:625 which concerned access to information considering EU's financial support to NGOs operating in Israel and, possibly, Palestine. On October 23, 2008, Mr. Gerald Steinberg, the President of NGO Monitor, a nongovernmental organization with its headquarters in Jerusalem (Israel) requested access from the European Commission to a series of documents relating to funding decisions for grants to Israeli and Palestinian NGOs under the "Partnership for Peace" (PfP) program and the European Instrument for Democracy and Human Rights (EIDHR). Mr. Steinberg based his request on the provisions of Regulation No 1049/2001 regarding public access to European Parliament, Council and Commission documents (paras. 18-19). The applicant submitted that, in any event, "the process by which tens of millions of Euros in public funds are provided to NGOs and civil society organizations concerned in the Arab-Israeli conflict creates an 'overriding public interest in disclosure" (para. 59). Both the Commission and the Court stated that the requested documents concern NGOs operating in or carrying out activities in Israel and/or the Occupied Palestinian Territory. As that region is unstable, in the grip of great tension and presents a very tense security situation, with the risks of violent confrontations or even of armed conflicts, the Israeli and Palestinian NGOs carry out their activities in extremely difficult conditions. The situation is particularly complex for the Palestinian NGOs because the Palestinian Authority of the West Bank and of the Gaza Strip expressly forbids any cooperation between them and the Israeli NGOs. The implementation of any projects covered by the PfP or the EIDHR by Palestinian NGOs may be therefore perceived by some radical groups as collaboration with Israel (para. 81). As a result, the activities of the

funding is not objectionable, in practice there are cases where it is questioned if the funding actually goes into the right hands.[325] The EP Draft Report strongly suggests to legally reject any funding for organizations which "demonstrably disseminate untruths and/or whose objectives are contrary to the fundamental values of the European Union, democracy, human rights and/or strategic commercial and security policy objectives of the European Union institutions."[326] In this document, the EP calls on the Commission to reject funding for NGOs that oppose the "strategic commercial and security objectives" of the EU[327] and states that the way EU taxpayer money is used to fund NGOs should be "comprehensively and credibly documented."[328]

To sum up, it seems that the present grant funding system (especially in the matter of its transparency) is flawed. In consequence, a single, centralized system for recording and managing all grant funding should be introduced. It would enhance transparency and analysis by eliminating variations that currently occur between different schemes existing in the Commission. The new system should record not only forecast commitments but also actual disbursements.[329] Furthermore, in order to understand how much funding individual NGOs receive, it seems highly recommended to record how grant funds are actually redistributed between all project partners. Hence, rather than relying on grant beneficiaries to inform the Commission of changes in their situation with regard to the exclusion criteria, it may be advisable for the Commission to proactively review the status of the largest beneficiaries as a matter of course.[330]

As far as the visibility of being a beneficiary of the EU funds is concerned, a couple of suggestions have also been made.[331] Therefore, it has been recommended to introduce:

NGOs in question would attract a high risk of hostile attention which could result in threats to the moral or psychical integrity of the various persons concerned and thus disturb public security, with the result that it was necessary to blank out certain detailed information on the projects in question in the requested documents (para. 83).

325. See e.g. G. Paravicini, H. Cooper, *Mystic Money Man Behind Brussels Activists*, available at: https://www.politico.eu/article/ayman-jallad-ayman-jallad-mystic-money-man-behind-brussels-activists-ngo-funding/ (on February 9, 2019).

326. The EP Draft..., p. 5. This remark is also relevant in the context of the international counterterrorism provisions. See, to this extent, *Risk of Terrorist Abuse in Non-profit Organisations*, FATF Report, June 2014, available at: http://www.fatf-gafi.org/media/fatf/documents/reports/Risk-of-terrorist-abuse-in-non-profit-organisations.pdf (on February 9, 2019).

327. The EP Draft..., p. 5, see also B. Wirtz, *EU Funded Lobbying Is Expensive and Undemocratic*, available at: https://euobserver.com/opinion/139093 (on February 9, 2019).

328. See also S. Michalopoulos, *Parliament Report Opens "Pandora's Box" of EU Funded NGOs*, available at: https://www.euractiv.com/section/politics/news/parliament-report-opens-pandoras-box-of-eu-funded-ngos/ (on February 9, 2019).

329. Democratic..., p. 92.

330. *Ibid.*, p. 99.

331. *Ibid.*, p. 98.

(1) a requirement to display a standard, highly recognizable "EU-funded" logo[332] in a prominent position on each webpage of all[333] beneficiaries;
(2) a webpage linked to the abovementioned logo showing all EU funding this entity has received in the last five years;
(3) links to other EU-funded project websites;
(4) links to publicly available information on the Commission's systems relating to actions listed on the webpage (e.g., the FTS).

Other criticisms deal with the present complexity of legal provisions on the EU-funding opportunities.[334] Some stakeholders stress out that there is a need for greater consistency in the way that information about overarching rules is presented and some of this information could benefit from simplification (e.g., the already mentioned exclusion criteria). Also, redundant duplication of information between documents should ideally be eliminated.[335] Likewise, the simplification of funding regulations could lead to a broader disposal of EU grants, therefore hampering the "NGOization" at the EU level. The current Financial Regulation follows these demands, at least to some extent, by introducing the possibility of awarding grants without calls for proposals in clearly named cases (as noted in previous paragraphs). The outcomes of this form of financing are yet to be assessed. It is crucial that those "simplified" procedures will always be used only according to strict and transparent practices.[336]

The complexity of relationships between NGOs funded by the Commission and the complication of the actions they undertake pose significant challenges regarding accountability and transparency not just to the EU, but to civil society in general. Doubtlessly, there is a need to review how this is ensured and to consider new tools and approaches at the EU level. For instance, the emergence of a new and innovative approach to NGO funding increasingly releases NGOs from the transparency and accountability requirements imposed by large institutional donors, and this implies that their activities are not subject to such intensive, systematic monitoring. This includes, for example, organizations that are funded mainly through multiple, small public donations that exist primarily on the Internet and operate across multiple jurisdictions.[337] It seems there is a need to encourage such organizations to enhance their transparency and accountability. At the same time, there is a need to develop new approaches to a society to monitor their activities.[338] Therefore, there is an urgency of

332. According to Art. 201 (2) (h) of the Financial Regulation, the grant agreement should include provisions governing the visibility of the Union financial support, except in duly justified cases where public display is not possible or appropriate. Nevertheless, transparency problems may arise in cases of sub-grants.
333. Including consort partners within the funded project.
334. See Final conclusions and recommendations of the High Level Group on Simplification for post 2020, available at: http://ec.europa.eu/regional_policy/en/information/publications/reports/2017/esif-simplification-hlg-proposal-for-policymakers-for-post-2020 (on February 9, 2019).
335. Democratic..., p. 99.
336. Cf. *EU Funding for NGOs. Value for Money?*, NGO Monitor 2016, available at: http://www.ngo-monitor.org/nm/wp-content/uploads/2016/02/Value-for-money-Part-I-Final-1.pdf (on February 9, 2019), pp. 7-8.
337. Democratic..., p. 12.
338. *Ibid.*, p. 99.

strong pressure on beneficiaries of all kinds of funding (including EU funding) to be transparent, in order to track how much money (and exactly from whom) they obtained, how it was spent and how it was appraised.

Finally, due to the already discussed national legislative proposals that could hamper NGO activity in some Member States and in order to strengthen the independence of organizations promoting the EU values from governmental funding, some activists,[339] alongside the EP[340] and the EESC[341] advocate for a new EU fund designed especially for those "threatened" NGOs.[342] This initiative should be evaluated very positively and hopefully will eventually be included in the new budgetary framework.[343] However, it is significant to emphasize that even in this case such a grant possibility should not be the only (or major) source of funding for the subject NGOs. The third sector organizations should enjoy a vast scope of independence from the central authorities in all instances, especially when it comes to funding.

[C] Summary

The EU grants are a significant source of financing for NGOs. Even though the majority of these amounts are allocated at the national level, some funds are distributed specifically at the EU level. Still, numerous problems are related to the present legal framework and practice of this form of funding. First, it appears that the EU grants are in fact limited to a rather limited scope of beneficiaries. On the one hand, this practically leaves most of organizations outside this opportunity of obtaining funds. On the other hand, it means that there is a real danger of "NGOization" at the EU level. It means that NGOs which are financed by the EU funds often pursue, in fact, the policies of the EU institutions and not the grassroot civil society. Second, the distribution of the EU grants often lacks transparency. This is especially noticeable in the sphere of funds in the EU external actions. Also, the actual beneficiaries of the EU funding are not always easy to distinguish. Third, it seems that the existing provisions on the EU grant

339. I. De Jesus Butler, *Two Proposals to Promote and Protect European Values Through the Multiannual Financial Framework: Conditionality of EU Funds and a Financial Instrument to Support NGOs*, Civil Liberties Union for Europe, pp. 16 et seq., available at: http://bit.do/eka9L (on February 9, 2019).

340. European Parliament resolution on the need to establish a European Values Instrument to support civil society organizations which promote fundamental values within the European Union at local and national levels (2018/2619(RSP)).

341. See Financing of civil society is essential for democracy, the EESC own initiative of 20.10.2007, available at: https://www.eesc.europa.eu/en/news-media/news/financing-civil-society-essential-democracy (on February 9, 2019).

342. The present proposal on "Rights and Values Programme" has three specific objectives:

 (1) to promote equality and rights;
 (2) to promote citizens engagement and participation in the democratic life of the Union;
 (3) to fight violence.

343. It was officially announced by the Commission on 30.5.2018. See The European Commission Press release of 30 May 2018—The Commission is proposing a new Justice, Rights and Values Fund, simplifying the existing programs in this field.

possibilities are too complex and should be simplified in order to reach wider groups of potential recipients.

As a result, it is very significant to increase transparency in the process of granting and spending the EU grants. Furthermore, new funds should be advantageous. This especially concerns the funding for NGOs which promotes the EU values or are treated in a discriminatory way in their countries of origin. Nevertheless, it is always important to emphasize that NGOs by definition ought to stay independent of central authorities, including the EU institution. This autonomy primarily concerns financial issues.

§5.04 POSSIBLE AREAS OF EU LEGISLATION

The preceding parts of this book analyzed the existing norms and regulations of the EU law that could be applied by NGOs. This scope of rules can be perceived as quite limited and often not conforming with serious problems facing the organizations operating at the EU level. Thus, the following paragraphs will concentrate on a summary of issues that could possibly be regulated by the EU law in order to facilitate the daily cross-border activities of the third sector.[344]

[A] Enhancing Philanthropy and Public Benefit Purposes

Due to the fact that the EA and the FE proposals were unsuccessful and in order to enhance NGO activity in the EU, it might be most advantageous for the EU institutions to abandon the arduous plans of introducing regulations on new pan-European legal forms for the third sector entities and concentrate on less ambitious but more practical issues in terms of enhancing cross-border philanthropy. Such approach could include provisions on:

(1) cross-border transfer of registered seats of NGOs;
(2) cross-border merger issues;
(3) prohibitions of restrictions on foreign funding;
(4) reassurance of tax incentives in line with the case law of the CJEU.[345]

These actions would not require a legal form of regulation but could be encompassed in a directive, leaving a considerate range of discretion for the Member States while implementing proper national legislations. It is a significant remark as an EU regulation on any NGO activity seems to remain a remote prospect. The sole fact that a regulation governs nonprofit or not-for-profit actors appears to be a matter of

344. Of course, there are also numerous possible initiatives that could be beneficiary for the development of European civil society in general. In this aspect, see e.g. K. Niklewicz, *Weeding Out Fake News. An Approach to Social Media Regulation*, Wilfried Martens Centre for European Studies 2017, available at: http://bit.do/ekbco (on February 9, 2019).

345. For more information see O. Breen, *Enlarging the Space for European Philanthropy*, A DAFNE/EFC study of 18.1.2018, available at: http://bit.do/ekCop (on February 9, 2019).

little, if any, importance. It is when the focus of the regulation is upon the activities of nonprofits that difficulties arise in terms of the EU competences and the EU consensus, as proved by the experience of the EA and the FE.[346] It appears that at present the normative case for civil society and public benefit in the EU takes a pluralistic approach and is maintained at the national level.[347] Another suggestion in the area of providing certain incentives for NGOs in the EU law is the use of enhanced cooperation of the interested Member States.[348] However, it seems that this concept would further differentiate the position of NGOs in various countries and thus is not worthy of support.

An even more demanding task would be to introduce a number of incentives for NGOs that could be attributed an EU status of public benefit (public interest) entities. Such notion applies to a special status given to certain third sector organizations which are active in the spheres of specific social interest. The concept was first used in the English Statute of Charitable Uses of 1601. It was designed to list charitable activities and their sources with simultaneous means against misuses.[349] In general, public benefit (public interest) purpose does not need to serve the whole society. In contrast, it can be aimed only at the good of a smaller community.[350] Still, it cannot be oriented solely on the benefit of the organization's direct members.[351]

The EU Member States provide for a wide variety of legal forms dealing with public benefit purposes, ranging from an altruistic purpose[352] to a purpose in conformity with charity law.[353] For example, in the Netherlands and Germany, the acquisition of public benefit status is determined by the objectives and activities of the organization and is provided by supervising authorities.[354] In other countries like Belgium, the United Kingdom, Poland and Hungary, NGOs may qualify to a specific law that grants them the status of public benefit organizations.[355] In some cases, this status translates into ascribed privileges or benefits which are the subject matter of special laws on the promotion of public benefit purposes.[356] Such benefits may include fiscal privileges or tax exemptions, including, e.g. income tax, VAT reliefs or incentives for the organizations' donors.[357] However, in some legal systems, economic purposes are not allowed

346. O. Breen, *EU Regulation...*
347. L. Versteegh, *Civil...*, p. 13.
348. O. Breen, *Enlarging...*
349. J. Garton, *Public Benefit in Charity Law*, Oxford 2013, p. vii, C.R.M. Versteegh, *Civil...*, p. 9.
350. K. Hopt, T. von Hippel, *The European...*, 43, P. Staszczyk, *Ustawa o działalności pożytku publicznego i o wolontariacie*, Warsaw 2013, p. 78.
351. J. Garton, *Public...*, p. 4, P. Staszczyk, *Ustawa o działalności...*, pp. 78-79.
352. E.g. in Belgium.
353. E.g. in the UK.
354. D. Moore, K. Hadzi-Miceva, N. Bullain, *A Comparative Overview of Public Benefit Status in Europe*, The International Journal of Not-for-Profit Law Vol. 11/2008, available at: http://www.icnl.org/research/journal/vol11iss1/special_1.htm (on February 9, 2019).
355. D. Moore, K. Hadzi-Miceva, N. Bullain, *A Comparative...*
356. E.g. in Poland all associations and foundations may apply for a status of public benefit organization according to the rules and procedures listed in the Public Benefit and Volunteer Work Act (*Ustawa o działalności pożytku publicznego i o wolontariacie*), particularly in reference to its Art. 20.
357. L. Versteegh, *Civil...*, p. 10.

or are permitted only under special conditions for public benefit organization pursuing public benefit purposes .[358]

As it was already noted, the catalog of public benefit purposes was first introduced at the EU level in the proposal for the statute for the FE. To remind, an FE could only be an organization that undertook at least one of the public benefit purposes listed in the proposed Regulation. Yet, the acknowledgment of a public benefit entity at the EU level could lead to a more ambitious objective, imposing certain obligations on the EU institutions or creating a possibility of partnership agreements. In this matter, a good example would be the Polish Public Benefit and Volunteer Work Act (*Ustawa o działalności pożytku publicznego i o wolontariacie*). According to its Article 5 (2), the cooperation between public administration and bodies carrying out activities in the sphere of public tasks can take place particularly in the forms of:

(1) entrusting NGOs with the performance of public benefit tasks;
(2) reciprocal feedback concerning all planned activities;
(3) consulting NGOs on draft normative acts in areas relating to their statutory activity;
(4) consulting draft normative acts concerning public tasks;
(5) setting up joint advisory and initiative teams composed of representatives of NGOs and representatives of relevant public administration authorities;
(6) agreement on carrying out a local initiative;
(7) partnership agreements set out in distinguished laws.[359]

Binding public benefit entities at the EU level with some of these privileges would undoubtedly boost NGOs in general. In such a case, it would be important to undertake public benefit tasks EU wide as it would entail significant rights, including the right to be consulted. This prerogative, in contrast to the general rule set out in Article 11 of the TEU, would be also itemized and would have to be strictly abided by the EU institutions. Ideally, the introduction of the public benefit purposes at the EU level would eventually lead to the possibility of entrusting NGOs with certain competences of the EU institutions[360] and to the creation of legal basis of partnership agreements, especially in social matters.[361] In fact, such a solution would be beneficial to both parties. On the one hand, it would in a way resolve the problem of the "managing

358. E.g. in Romania public benefit, NGOs may directly carry out economic activities that are "closely connected to the main purpose of the organization" and in Lithuania those that are "necessary to achieve its purposes/closely related to its operational goals"; for more information see *Legal Regulations of Economic Activities of Civil Society Organisations*, European Center for Not-for-Profit Law 2015, available at: http://ecnl.org/wp-content/uploads/2015/07/ECNL-Economic-Activities.pdf (on February 9, 2019).
359. I.e. Act on the Rules for Conducting Development Policy (*Ustawa o zasadach prowadzenia polityki rozwoju*).
360. Such procedures already take place but to a very limited extent. For instance, NGOs can host Europe Direct Information Centres (which is a European information network designated by the Commission) in the EU Member States. See e.g. http://bit.do/ekbgL (on February 9, 2019).
361. Cf. J. Zeitlin, *Towards a Stronger OMC in a More Social Europe 2020: A New Governance Architecture for EU Policy Coordination* in: *Europe 2020: Towards a More Social Europe?*, E. Marlier (ed.), Brussels 2010, p. 253.

deficit" ("staff deficit")[362] of the EU institutions, especially of the Commission.[363] On the other hand, it could also be beneficial for the involvement process of NGOs as they would have to take greater responsibility for the quality of executing the EU law. This might in turn result in a "better law" because more subjects would be engaged in identifying its flaws.[364]

[B] Crowdfunding

The Commission describes "crowdfunding" as a channel of financing, which can be used in many ways.[365] It is regularly used by NGOs in order to raise funds for their activities in a grassroot manner.[366] Donations can be collected from people, which would qualify as donation-based crowdfunding if collected for a specific project during a specified time period promoted through Internet and social media.[367] However, crowdfunding campaigns can also offer contributors something in exchange. Therefore, one may refer to reward-based or presales crowdfunding when contributors get in return something symbolic, like the opportunity to participate in the cultural experience they finance (e.g., being offered special CDs, DVDs or Blu-rays) or a product that was developed and produced with the funds raised.[368] All of these forms of crowdfunding can also be described as "crowd sponsoring."[369]

Crowdfunding is currently regulated only in some Member States' legal systems.[370] As an example, the Belgian crowdfunding law creates a specific status for equity and debt crowdfunding platforms (referred to as "alternative financing platforms") and prescribes operating requirements for both alternative financing platforms and regulated entities (credit institutions and investment firms) that engage in alternative financing activities.[371] Moreover, the crowdfunding law modifies existing law legislation in order to render effective various tax benefits for investment in start-up companies. Rewards and donation-based platforms are not within the scope of this

362. H. Kassim, *Revisiting the "Management Deficit": Can the Commission (Still Not) Manage Europe?* in: *Multi-Level Governance: The Missing Linkages (Critical Perspectives on International Public Sector Management. Vol. 4*, E. Ongaro (ed.), Bingley 2015, pp. 41 et seq.
363. I.e. this institution is often perceived as having a too limited personnel for so many competences.
364. B. Kohler-Koch, *The Three...*, p. 53.
365. Communication of the Commission to the EP, the Council, the EESC and the CoR—Unleashing the potential of Crowdfunding in the European Union, 27.3.2014, COM(2014) 0172 final; see also e.g. G.A. Gabison, *Understanding Crowdfunding and Its Regulations. How Can Crowdfunding Help ICT Innovation?*, available at: http://publications.jrc.ec.europa.eu/repository/bitstream/JRC92482/lbna26992enn.pdf (on February 9, 2019).
366. Even though crowdfunding is also often subject to criticism as, e.g. a means of "privatization masquerading as democracy." See e.g. A. Minton, *Civic Crowdfunding Is Privatization Masquerading as Democracy*, available at: http://bit.do/ekbhZ (on February 9, 2019).
367. Communication of 27.3.2014.
368. *Ibid.*
369. *Ibid.*
370. I.e. in Austria, Belgium, Spain, Finland, France, UK, Italy, Germany and Portugal.
371. The Belgian Law Organizing the Recognition and Supervision of Crowdfunding and Various Provisions in Finance (*Loi organisant la reconnaissance et l'encadrement du crowdfunding et portant des dispositions diverses en matière de finances*).

law.[372] Other countries do not provide any specified laws on crowdfunding. Thus, in those legal systems beneficiaries, donors and platform administrators rely on at least a couple of national acts of law.[373]

In March 2018, the Commission issued proposal for a Regulation on European crowdfunding services providers.[374] However, it omits the "social" or "charity" aspects of crowdfunding and focuses on the organizational issues of crowdfunding platforms. The main objective of the proposal is to facilitate the development of the European FinTech.[375] Thus, it defines "crowdfunding service" as "means of matching the business funding interest of investors and project owners through the use of a crowdfunding platform" (Article 3 (1) (a) of the proposal). Consequently, the impact of the proposed regulation on philanthropic crowdfunding would be rather small and would not eliminate the numerous legal and tax problems in different Member States. However, it could provide greater legal certainty in fund-raising by creating an obligation of authorizing all crowdfunding service providers operating in the EU and covering them with the supervision of the European Securities and Markets Authority. This, in turn, could also help crowdfunding in the EU to be more transboundary. Nowadays many collections are more state concentrated.[376]

[C] Volunteer Work

In general, volunteer work is considered as an altruistic activity where an individual or a group provides services for nonfinancial gain to benefit another person, group or organization.[377] It is estimated that more than 100 million EU citizens are volunteers.[378] Despite this popularity, the EU law provides for a limited scope of norms on cross-border (i.e., among the EU Member States) volunteer work. Different traditions and social, economic and cultural factors lead to various architectures of the volunteer sector and the lack of a clear legal and regulatory framework are considered a key challenge for volunteer work across borders (and for the coordinating NGOs).[379] Many Member States do not provide for any clear legal status of volunteers or regulatory

372. See Chapter 2 of the Belgian Law on crowdfunding.
373. P. Staszczyk, *Crowdfunding a prawo polskie—kilka wątpliwości*, Trzeci Sektor Vol. 38/2016, pp. 69 et seq.
374. Proposal for a Regulation of the EP and of the Council on European Crowdfunding Service Providers (ECSP) for Business, COM(2018) 113 final.
375. See The European Commission Press release of 8.3.2018 - FinTech: Commission takes action for a more competitive and innovative financial market.
376. Commission Staff Working Document. Crowdfunding in the EU Capital Markets Union, SWD(2016) 154 final, p. 4; Although there are a few crowdfunding platforms operating at the EU level (e.g., Crowdfunding International https://www.crowdfundinginternational.eu), they operate under national laws.
377. J. Wilson, *Volunteering*, Annual Review of Sociology Vol. 26/2000, p. 215.
378. According to the preamble of the Volunteer Charter, European Charter on the Rights and Responsibilities of Volunteers, issued by the European Youth Forum, available at: https://www.youthforum.org/assets/2014/04/volunteering-charter-en.pdf (on February 9, 2019).
379. Mobility of Young Volunteers Across Europe, A Study by the Public Policy and Management Institute, available at: http://cor.europa.eu/en/documentation/studies/Documents/Mobility-of-young-volunteers-%20across-Europe/EN.pdf (on February 9, 2019), pp. 62 et seq.

framework of the volunteer organizations.[380] Moreover, regulatory framework (if in place)[381] vary in scope and in their definitions of volunteers and volunteer organizations, which also contributes to a lack of legal certainty. From the cross-border perspective in volunteer work across the EU, the unclear legal status can have implications with regard to, e.g. setting up residence, welfare benefit provisions or taxation of any income volunteers receive in the form of stipends or grants.[382]

[1] Legal Framework: European Solidarity Corps

Volunteer work was in the center of numerous acts of binding and nonbinding nature at the EU level, including:

(a) Decision No 1719/2006/EC of the EP and of the Council of November 15, 2006, establishing the Youth in Action program for the period 2007 to 2013;[383]

---

380. Belgium, Cyprus, the Czech Republic, Hungary, Italy, Latvia, Luxembourg, Malta, Poland, Portugal, Romania and Spain adopted specific laws on volunteering. Yet, the extent to which they apply to volunteers, volunteer organizations and the voluntary sector also differ. For instance, the Polish Public Benefit and Volunteer Work Act (*Ustawa o działalnosci pozytku publicznego i o wolontariacie*) refers to NGOs in the regulations concerning volunteer work, especially as beneficiaries of volunteering. Thus, according to its Art. 42, volunteers shall, on terms and conditions set out in this Chapter, provide services to support the following:

    (1) nongovernmental organizations and other entities defined in Article 3, para 3 in relation to their statutory activity, in particular in the field of public benefit work, with the exception of business activity they may engage in;
    (2) public administration authorities, with the exception of business activity they may engage in;
    (3) organizational units reporting to public administration authorities or supervised by the same, with the exception of business activity they may engage in—hereinafter referred to as "the beneficiaries."

    Provisions laid out in this chapter shall also apply as appropriate to volunteers providing services to support international organizations in the territory of the Republic of Poland, unless provisions of international agreements provide otherwise.

    Moreover, a member of an association may also provide services, as a volunteer, for the association they are a member of.

    However, the Czech Law on Volunteer Service and on Amendments to Certain Laws (*zákon o dobrovolnické služběě a o změěněě něěkterých zákonůů*) does not name NGOs specific as possible recipients of volunteer work. There are only specific regulations dealing with foreign (sending or receiving) organizations.
381. For instance, in the Polish Public Benefit and Volunteer Work Act (*Ustawa o działalności pozytku publicznego i o wolontariacie*) (Art. 2, point 3), it states under the term "volunteer" shall mean a natural person who provides services voluntarily and without remuneration, under the provisions hereof. According to its Art. 43, a volunteer shall be duly qualified and conform to all requirements appropriate for the type and scope of services provided, whenever separate legal provisions provide for the obligation to have such qualifications and to fulfill relevant conditions.
382. Cross-Border Volunteering. Cost of Non-Europe Report, The EP Research Service Study 2015, p. 61.
383. Official Journal L 327, 24.11.2006.

(b) Decision No 1904/2006/EC of the EP and of the Council of December 12, 2006, establishing the period 2007 to 2013 the program "Europe for Citizens" to promote active European citizenship;[384]
(c) Council Decision 2010/37/EC of November 27, 2009, on the European Year of Voluntary Activities Promoting Active Citizenship;[385]
(d) Council resolution of November 27, 2007, on voluntary activities of young people (14427/1/2007);
(e) Resolution of the Council and the Representatives of the Governments of the Member States, meeting within the Council of May 16, 2007, on implementing the common objectives for voluntary activities of young people;[386]
(f) Council recommendation of November 20, 2008, on the mobility of young volunteers across the EU;[387]
(g) Council conclusions of October 3, 2011, on the role of voluntary activities in social policy (14552/2011);
(h) Council conclusions of November 29, 2011, on the role of voluntary activities in sport in promoting active citizenship;[388]
(i) Communication of September 20, 2011, from the Commission to the EP, the Council, the EESC and CoR entitled "EU Policies and Volunteering: Recognizing and promoting cross-border voluntary activities in the EU."[389]

In the latter one, the Commission has noticed that volunteering is closely linked to its general political objective of reinforcing citizenship and putting citizens at the heart of the EU policy-making. Therefore, volunteering can complement citizens' entitlements to rights and promote their active participation in society. This is particularly the case for cross-border volunteering, which has the potential for intercultural learning and the development of a European identity.[390]

Yet, acts on volunteer work at the EU level do not include the vast scope of its possibilities in cross-border relations. In contrast, they are mostly aimed at youths (which is one of the means of fighting unemployment among young people). This was the main purpose of the European Voluntary Service for Young People (EVS) program.[391] More precisely, the program objectives were named as follows:[392]

(a) to encourage a spirit of initiative, creativity and solidarity among young people so as to enable them to become actively integrated into society and to contribute to the attainment of the objectives of the program;

384. Official Journal L 378, 27.12.2006.
385. Official Journal L 17/43, 22.1.2010.
386. Official Journal C 241, 20.9.2008.
387. Official Journal C 319, 13.12.2008.
388. Official Journal C 372, 20.12.2011.
389. COM(2011) 0568.
390. Communication of 20 September 2011, point 2.2.
391. Established by Decision No 1686/98/EC of the EP and the Council of 20 July 1998, Official Journal L 214, 31.7.1998.
392. See Art. 2 (2) of the Decision.

(b) to step up participation by young people legally resident in a Member State in long-term or short-term transnational activities of benefit to the community, within the Community or in third countries, in particular those with which the Community has concluded cooperation agreements;
(c) to promote recognition of the value of informal educational experience acquired in a European context;
(d) to facilitate access to the program for all young people.

The volunteer work legal scheme is presently complemented by the possibility of volunteering in the third countries citizens as a result of Directive (EU) 2016/801 of the EP and of the Council of May 11, 2016, on the conditions of entry and residence of third-country nationals for the purposes of research, studies, training, voluntary service, pupil exchange schemes or educational projects and au pairing.[393] According to Article 2 (1) of the Directive, it shall apply to third-country nationals who apply to be admitted or who have been admitted to the territory of a Member State for the purpose of research, training or voluntary service in the EVS. Member States may also decide to apply the provisions of the Directive to third-country nationals who apply to be admitted for the purpose of a pupil exchange scheme or educational project, voluntary service other than European Voluntary Service or au pairing.

Following the "Bratislava Roadmap"[394]—a plan to fight youth unemployment and to create more opportunities for young people in the EU—in December 2016, J.-C. Juncker in his State of the Union[395] announced the transformation of the EVS to the European Solidary Corps as a part of broader policy agenda geared toward a stronger inclusion of young people in the society. The legal basis for this transformation was introduced by Regulation (EU) 2018/1475 of the EP and of the Council laying down the legal framework of the European Solidarity Corps and amending Regulations (EU) No 1288/2013, (EU) No 1293/2013 and Decision No 1313/2013/EU.[396] The aim of this new mechanism is to contribute to "strengthening cohesion, solidarity and democracy in Europe, with particular effort to the promotion of social inclusion" (Article 1 (1)).

According to the Regulation, with the launch of the European Solidarity Corps, participants have the opportunity to be placed with a project either for volunteering or for a traineeship, an apprenticeship or a job for a period between 2 and 12 months.[397] The program is fully funded by the EU budget and open to young people aged from 17 to 30. Participants are be able to engage in a broad range of activities such as education, health, social integration, assistance in the provision of food, shelter construction, reception, support and integration of migrants and refugees, environmental protection or prevention of natural disasters.[398]

393. Official Journal L 132, 21.5.2016, pp. 21-57.
394. Confirmed by Bratislava Summit of 16 September 2016 by the Heads of State and Government of 27 Member States.
395. For more information https://ec.europa.eu/commission/state-union-2016_en.
396. Official Journal L 250/1, 4.10.2018.
397. The European Commission Press release of 7 December 2016—Investing in Europe's youth: Commission launches European Solidarity Corps.
398. Explanatory memorandum to the proposal of the Regulation.

The program is open not only to individual persons but also to "participating organizations".[399] Their role was explicitly emphasized in the explanatory memorandum. It was noted that addressing solidarity and building social, economic and civic cohesion requires a rich tissue of dynamic organizations (private and public, profit and nonprofit). In this context, there is a need to cater better for the needs of such organizations, especially those working at the grassroot level with the most disadvantaged communities. Organizations creating and offering solidarity placements need support, in terms of resources, ensuring appropriate training and preparation for volunteers, trainees or workers, as well as activity in a European context. In this matter, organizations also need clear and simple rules.[400] As a result, as indicated in point 16 of the Regulation's preamble, young people and organizations participating in the European Solidarity Corps should feel that they belong to a community of individuals and entities committed to enhancing solidarity across Europe and beyond.

"Volunteering" is defined in Article 2 (6) of the Regulation. Thus, it means a solidarity activity that takes the form of a voluntary unpaid activity for a period of up to twelve months and that provides young people with the opportunity to contribute to the daily work of organizations in solidarity activities to the ultimate benefit of the communities within which the activities are carried out. It takes place either in a country other than the country of residence of the participant (cross-border) or in the country of residence of the participant (in-country). It does not substitute traineeships or jobs and, therefore, is in no case equated with employment.[401] Volunteers are to participate in "solidarity activities" understood as high-quality temporary activity that does not interfere with the functioning of the labor market which addresses important societal challenges to the benefit of a community or society as a whole, thereby contributing to the achievement of the objectives of the European Solidarity Corps. They take place in a broad range of areas, such as environmental protection, climate

399. I.e. according to Art. 13 (1) of the Regulation, the European Solidarity Corps shall be open to the participation of public or private entities, whether nonprofit or profit-making, provided that they offer activities that correspond to the definition of solidarity activity within this Regulation and that they have received a quality label. In line with Regulation (EU, Euratom) 2018/1046, the grants shall not have the purpose or effect of producing a profit. Moreover, each "participating organization" need to adhere to the European Solidarity Corps Charter, setting out the rights and responsibilities during all stages of the solidarity experience; for more information see: https://europa.eu/youth/solidarity_en (on February 9, 2019).

400. In this matter see also e.g. *Best Practices in Volunteer Management: An Action Planning Guide for Small and Rural Nonprofit Organizations*, Canadian Volunteerism Initiative 2005, available at: http://bit.do/eg4Jm (on February 9, 2019), p. 26, M.-C. Pantea, *Young People in Cross-National Volunteering: Perceptions of Unfairness*, Journal of Social and Personal Relationships Vol. 30/2013, pp. 128-129.

401. Still, the European Solidarity Corps also envisage job opportunities. According to Art. 2 (9) of the Regulation, a "job" means a solidarity activity, undertaken for a period of between three and twelve months, that is paid by the participating organization employing the participant, either in a country other than the country of residence of the participant (cross-border) or in the country of residence of the participant (in-country). When the duration of the employment contract exceeds twelve months, financial support to participating organisations offering jobs shall not exceed twelve months. Such jobs shall include a learning and a training component and be based on a written employment contract which respects all the terms and conditions of employment as defined in the national law, applicable collective agreements, or both, of the country in which the job is being carried out.

change mitigation and greater social inclusion but does not include activities that are part of curricula in formal education, vocational education and training systems and activities for emergency response (Article 2 (1)).

[2] Shortcomings in the EU Law

Although the previous EVS program and the current European Solidarity Corps are clearly beneficial for volunteering in the EU, they are very vague when it comes to harmonizing and simplifying the cross-border activities of NGOs organizing volunteer work. Also, they do not resolve all the problems concerning volunteers, especially in cases when they are not eligible for these schemes (not all volunteers are young people entering the labor market) or when the volunteer work is not related to any "solidarity activity" as defined in the abovementioned Regulation. Furthermore, the European Solidarity Corps are, in fact, organized by the EU itself, and there is a lack of space for a more grassroot orientation. In this respect, a study of industrialized countries by John Hopkins University[402] and the experience of the European Year 2011 remain partially up-to-date. Basing on these inquiries, the Commission identified the potential obstacles of volunteering,[403] in particular across borders, as the following:

- lack of a clear legal framework: almost one in five Member States does not have a clear legal framework and clear rules for volunteers and volunteering;[404]
- lack of national strategies for promoting voluntary activities;
- financial constraints: volunteering, while freely given, is not cost-free. Organizations based on voluntary activity often face a lack of sustainable funding and competition for available funds is fierce;
- mismatch between supply and demand: the increasing trend to professionalize the volunteering sector causes a certain mismatch between the needs of volunteering organizations and the aspirations of new volunteers. Volunteers are available for short-term projects while organizations need people to make long-term commitments;
- lack of recognition: skills that are gained through volunteering activities are not always sufficiently recognized or given credit;
- tax obstacles: Member States apply different tax treatments to volunteers' income/allowances and the reimbursement of the expenses sustained during their service. Consequently, volunteers and organizations may encounter tax obstacles when operating across borders;

402. L.M. Salamon, S.W. Sokolowski, M.A. Haddock, H.S. Tice, *The State of Global Civil Society and Volunteering. Latest Findings from the Implementation of the UN Nonprofit Handbook*, John Hopkins University 2013, available at: http://ccss.jhu.edu/wp-content/uploads/downloads/2013/04/JHU_Global-Civil-Society-Volunteering_FINAL_3.2013.pdf (on February 9, 2019).
403. Communication of 20 September 2011, point 1.2.
404. Thus, it seems that the provisions of the Polish Public Benefit and Volunteer Work Act (*Ustawa o działalności pozytku publicznego i o wolontariacie*) is a praiseworthy exception among the EU Member States.

- insufficient data: better comparable data on volunteering in the Member States can help identify best practices and improve policy-making.

Furthermore, the EP study of 2015[405] concluded that the costs associated with barriers to cross-border volunteering in the EU amounted to an estimated average of around EUR 65 million per year. These barriers could be overcome through EU actions and are mainly linked to:[406]

(1) lack of legal recognition of volunteer status (with regard to access to services linked to legal residence status and loss of social security and unemployment benefit);
(2) diversity in recruitment and lack of information on volunteer opportunities;
(3) lack of uniform recognition of skills acquired;
(4) lack of adequate training and predeparture preparation for cross-border volunteers.

The EP proposed the following possible actions to reduce these barriers:[407]

(1) widening the scope of the proposal for a Regulation on the Statute for a European Foundation;
(2) proposal for a Council Regulation setting up a European Statute for Associations;
(3) recommendation on a voluntary code through a Commission Communication;
(4) a "stakeholder engagement plan"—the establishment of a European Commission Steering or an Advisory Committee on cross-border volunteering issues or a European Parliament Intergroup.

The first two solutions seem to be currently unattainable. In the meantime, the proposal for a Regulation on the FE has been withdrawn. However, what is striking is the fact that the EP invoked the statute for an EA, although it has not been on the EU agenda for years. Perhaps this can be seen as an indication that this idea is not definitely abandoned after all. As for the other recommendations, the third one is interesting but due to its unbinding character it would obviously have a limited outcome for the voluntary sector. The fourth one should be perceived as an invitation for further developments and, therefore, looks most likely to happen in the nearest future.

405. Cross-Border..., p. 7.
406. *Ibid.*, p. 12.
407. *Ibid.*, p. 27.

[D] Summary

There are numerous matters that could be regulated by the EU law in order to facilitate the cross-border activities of NGOs. The preceding paragraphs focused on three issues. First, a directive could be introduced to promote cross-border philanthropy. Such an act of law could concentrate on merger or tax incentives. An even more ambitious action would be to introduce an EU legislation on public benefit that could result in admitting certain organizations with particular privileges. Also, the introduction of the benefit purposes at the EU level could eventually lead to the possibility of entrusting NGOs with specific competences of the EU institutions. Second, an EU act of law on various aspects of crowdfunding would contribute to an easier and more effective grounds for raising funds across borders. Yet, such legislation should primarily concentrate on tax issues. Third, even though there is a considerable number of acts on European volunteer work, they are quite limited in their scope. Also, there is lack of a clear legal framework on volunteering and NGOs coordinating such efforts in trans-boundary relations. An EU act of law could regulate these shortcomings.

Additionally, one could distinguish other spheres of potential EU legislation that would be beneficial for European civil society. For instance, this remark refers to means of combating fake news at the EU level. Unfortunately, it appears that the proposed acts of law will not be passed in a foreseeable future.

§5.05 CONCLUSION

This chapter demonstrated that the EU legal acts on NGOs cross-border activities are in fact limited in their scope and number. It can be summarized that the main privileges derive from the CJEU developments on freedom of capital movement and, in a limited way, on freedom of establishment. These prerogatives concern tax exemptions and an interdiction to treat a public benefit organization differently only on the grounds that it was registered in another Member State.

Two major proposals on NGO statutes—i.e., statute for a European Association and a European Foundation—were on the EU agenda but were eventually withdrawn. Their scope and applicability were dubious in many points, but they would definitely provide for a better and a more "user-friendly" legal environment for the third sector organizations operating in more than one EU Member States. Perhaps the chosen measure was the biggest problem. Maybe a regulation was a too controversial legal instrument for this subject matter, and the EU institutions should have proposed a directive comprising just the most demanded issues, e.g. the general recognition of legal personality of certain NGOs in all EU Member States. This would abolish the burdensome obligation of registration in countries in which an organization wishes to function. Yet, it should be reminded that the failure of these proposals was also an effect of feeble interest from NGOs themselves. The third sector hardly advocated for adopting these regulations.[408]

408. O. Breen, *European...*

Even though the majority of EU grants are distributed by national authorities, the direct EU funding is a valuable source for NGOs. However, the current allocation of funds by the EU institutions raise many questions and unfortunately contribute to the discussion on "NGOization" and "sponsor effect." The EU funds are also practically reduced to a limited scope of organizations. Moreover, the legal provisions on the EU grants seem quite complex, and they further limit the funding opportunities for smaller NGOs. To reduce these criticisms, an amendment to make the system more transparent and open is necessary. Additionally, new funds could be advantageous. Specifically, a tool of financing NGOs which promote the EU values or are treated in a discriminatory way in their countries of origin should be established.

There are numerous subject matters that could be embodied in the EU law in order to facilitate the cross-border activities of NGOs. Three of them have been discussed in this chapter: enhancing philanthropy and public benefit purposes, crowd-funding and volunteer work. Because much emphasis has been recently laid on volunteer work, perhaps the most desired action would be to facilitate the legal surroundings of organizations which are engaged in such cross-border endeavors. Also, much depends on how relatively new instruments (like crowdfunding) will be used internationally in practice and if necessary EU action arises. Other fields (i.e., public benefit purposes) are likely to be regulated only if a consensus is achieved between the EU institutions, Member States and stakeholders. Nevertheless, it appears that the possibility of passing acts of law on these issues remains a distant future. Unfortunately, this remark also refers to other potential civil society-relevant spheres of law.

Concluding Remarks

The following concluding remarks are divided into two parts. First, the main findings of this book will be presented. Second, the implications arising therefrom will be discussed. In this way, the major chances and risks for shaping European civil society and the role of NGOs in this process will be encapsulated.

I FINDINGS

(1) Even though there is no general consensus concerning the definition of "nongovernmental organizations," this notion is commonly used at the national and international level. NGOs are included in the institutional systems of various IGOs in order to "democratize" their decision-making procedures. However, different IGOs provide diversified "modes" of cooperation with the representatives of civil society. These modes include direct involvement, formal relations with selected NGOs which gain "consultative" or "participatory" status, informal consultations or a particular institution within the framework of an IGO which is designed to represent the voices of NGOs.

(2) European civil society understood as an organized aggregate of individuals that manifests its will and advocates for the collective interests in transboundary, European relations, is possible. Even though its basis might appear feeble due to the lack of a strong European identity, at its core, it is a legal community, shaped by the EU law and the jurisprudence of the CJEU. In fact, the concept of European civil society and the role of the representatives of civil society have been emphasized in the theory of European integration, particularly in neofunctionalism, constructivism, sociological approaches and multilevel governance (MLG). In order to strengthen European civil society, three issues are crucial: transparency, advocacy and cooperation.

(3) NGOs may act as a "transmission belt" between grassroot, national civil societies and an emerging European public sphere. First, NGOs can give voice to citizens' concerns and channel them into the deliberative process of the EU. Second, they can make internal decision-making of the EU more transparent to the wider public. Third, NGOs can provide a stronger output legitimacy for the EU institutions. In this way, the democratic deficit of the EU could be considerably diminished.

(4) The issue of involving NGOs and enabling civil society at the EU level has been present in the considerations of the EU institutions for a long time. The emergence of NGOs as proper partners in lawmaking and the "social dialogue" was primarily an outcome of the new competences attributed to the EU. Subsequently, the need of a "civil dialogue" with the representatives of civil society was also recognized in other dimensions. The White Paper on European Governance of 2001 remains the most distinct document on reasons, means and implications of engaging NGOs, and civil society in general, at the EU level.

(5) Four main Treaty bases for social participation can be distinguished at the EU level: Article 2 of the TEU, Article 12 of the EUChFR (Article 11 of the ECHR), Article 11 of the TEU and Article 152 of the TFEU. While the first two articles can be perceived as general rules of the EU law, the latter ones refer directly to "representative associations" and "social partners," thus engaging the role of NGOs and the representatives of civil society in the EU system.

(6) The official arena of NGO participation in the EU constitutional system is the EESC which was designed to articulate the voices of the organized civil society. Additionally, the CoR can be also perceived as a channel of social participation. Still, the actual role of these institutions in the lawmaking is rather weak. Therefore, the most influential NGOs tend to operate on their own at the EU level, frequently forming platforms, meta-platforms and other means of ad hoc cooperation.

(7) There are two main legal tools of civil participation in the EU lawmaking: access to documents and the European Citizens' Initiative. The main objective of access to documents is to ensure transparency of the EU institutions and to make their decisions more accountable and understandable to the public. The ECI is designed as a measure of proposing subjects to the EU agenda by European civil society. Both of these tools, although not free from weaknesses, are regularly used by NGOs.

(8) Despite the introduction of Article 11 of the TEU after the Treaty of Lisbon, the practice of particular institutions in their contacts with the interested NGOs remains ambiguous. The Commission seems to be the most open as it is the only EU institution that provides substantive framework for consultation requirements. Still, the dialogue with civil society usually takes form of online consultations which are often criticized as an "illusion of participation." Other EU institutions envisage noticeably fewer possibilities for NGO participation. The EP provides the possibility of forming

Intergroups and can be addressed with petitions which, unfortunately, can produce rather "soft" outcomes. The Council provides no legal framework for NGO participation or any official consultations. As a result, much depends on practices of specific Member States missions in Brussels. Finally, even though NGOs cannot present amicus curiae briefs in proceedings before the CJEU, they can intervene in the proceedings under certain conditions.

(9) Due to the fact that official consultation tools provided by particular EU institutions remain rather opaque, NGOs, like other stakeholders, often engage in lobbying activities. However, the current legal framework for lobbying at the EU level raises many concerns. It only covers the Commission and the EP and has a voluntary character. There is also a large loophole for possible misuses of unregistered lobbying.

(10) The complaint possibilities available for NGOs at the EU level are quite narrow. The conditions of Article 263 of the TFEU are understood very strictly by the CJEU. This makes it nearly impossible to bring an action in the collective interest as the complainant must prove the premises of individual and direct concern. Still, other complaint opportunities—to the Commission and the European Ombudsman—are present in the EU legal system. Yet, these measures are not substitutes for judicial proceedings as their nature is "soft" in principle.

(11) Some acts of the EU secondary law provide certain additional rights for NGOs as advocates of the collective interest at the national level. These prerogatives are particularly attributed to environmental issues, but they have been increasingly included in other spheres of law as well, e.g. in the new data protection provisions.

(12) The Aarhus Convention has established a number of rights of the public with regard to the environment. The Convention provides specific preconditions on access to environmental information, public participation in environmental decision-making and access to justice. Still, it appears that the transposition of the Convention had different implications on the national and the EU level. At the national level, it contributed to a more proactive role of NGOs in the sphere of environmental law. Although the Convention did not require an introduction of *actio popularis*, it appears that environmental matters are the core of actions brought before the courts by NGOs acting in the collective interest. Moreover, the Aarhus Convention provided general minimum standards of access to documents and participation in environmental matters which were not common in all Member States. The implementation of the Convention at the EU level had a lesser impact. Access to documents was already envisaged in the EU law and the rules on public participation did not differ from the previously binding provisions. The Aarhus Convention did not change the strict understanding of the *locus standi* conditions under Article 263 of the TFEU, and the introduction of internal review has not led to any modifications of the challenged acts of law so far.

(13) The EU law can be very relevant in the daily activities of NGOs. Although they are not encompassed by Article 54 of the TFEU, they are not generally excluded from specific provisions, ranging from labor law to competition law, if they undertake particular activities. Furthermore, NGO activity can be subject to the free movement of capital.

(14) Two legislative proposals on pan-European legal statutes of NGOs were proposed by the Commission but were eventually withdrawn. The first one concerned the European Association and the other one dealt with the European Foundation. Even though these proposals had noticeable drawbacks, they would have doubtlessly contributed to a better legal framework for NGO activity across borders. Presently, there is no good legal tool for such organizations to conduct their operations in one legal form in all EU Member States. In fact, national laws are not very helpful as they usually do not provide the possibility of acknowledging the legal personality of foreign third sector organizations without some kind of prior registration or recognition.

(15) The EU grants are a significant source of financing for NGOs. Even though the majority of these amounts are allocated at the national level, some funds are distributed specifically at the EU level. Still, it seems that these grants are often limited to a rather limited scope of beneficiaries.

II IMPLICATIONS

(1) In order to reinforce the belief in the future of European integration, the EU needs to put even more attention to the prerequisites of democracy and transparency. It means that the EU institutions should not only monitor those values in Member States but also, primarily, strengthen their own democratic standards. It is safe to say that in order to maintain the EU project, the EU institutions need to be more open and transparent in comparison to national authorities. Only in this way could the democratic deficit be diminished.

(2) NGOs do have instruments to execute the demands of democracy and transparency at the EU level. Most notably, they can take part in consultations, request access to the EU documents or initiate a European Citizens' Initiative. In this way, they contribute to shaping European civil society. Still, these EU prerogatives of NGOs could be wider and more effective.

(3) The EU institutions, particularly the Commission, often declares the will of broader inclusion of the representatives of civil society in the decision-making procedures. Still, these declarations hardly ever transpose into any acts of law or even into practical changes. Although these pronouncements remain very important in political terms, the EU institutions should get

them passed as means of mere wishful thinking and concentrate on real measures to amplify civil participation at the EU level.

(4) Some amendments in the EU constitutional system would be desired. In particular, the EESC, the institution which was designed to be the voice of civil society in the EU, does not fulfill its role. Its consultative competences are often too weak to actually influence the EU lawmaking. Therefore, it would be beneficial if these prerogatives were broadened. At least, there should be an obligation to duly consider the recommendations of the EESC in some cases of legislative procedures, e.g. while proceeding on acts of law related to social policy or environmental protection.

(5) It appears that Article 11 of the TEU should be equipped with more powerful measures of civil inclusion in the EU lawmaking. The Commission, the EP and the Council should establish clear rules of civil participation. In particular, such rules should provide the obligation of conducting consultation. It would be also beneficial if those provisions took the form of regulation with regard to the obligations of the Commission. In this way, their potential breach would be easier to challenge before the CJEU. Furthermore, it would be favorable to introduce clear preconditions of evaluating online consultations. Particularly, it would be perhaps a good idea to impose an obligation on the Directorates-General to evaluate each online consultation in order to present the reasons why certain opinions were taken into consideration and why the others were not.

(6) In order to enhance transparency in the EU lawmaking it is essential to introduce an obligatory Transparency Register. It should also encompass the Council. It seems to be the only way to protect the EU lawmaking from unofficial lobbying. It would also be recommended to reduce other expressions of "secret lawmaking," particularly in relation to "trilogue" meetings. Furthermore, it would be beneficial to introduce the obligation of publishing "footnotes" of each amendment submitted in the legislative procedure.[1] In this way, the interests underlying each proposal would be easily identifiable. As a result, it would enshrine transparency in the lawmaking.

(7) Even though the recent proposals of amending the European Citizens' Initiative should be assessed very positively, perhaps it would be advantageous to reconsider this instrument in full. The ECIs which have been submitted so far have produced limited effects. Possibly, the situation would have been different if the ECI had not been a mere agenda-setting instrument. Therefore, it would be advantageous to request a specific legislative proposal in the ECI procedure which would then be voted on by the Commission or the EP.

(8) The possibility of bringing actions in the collective interest before the CJEU under Article 263 of the TFEU is hardly attainable. The main reason for this

1. See also P. Leino, *On Knowledge as Power: Transparency of EU Law-Making Procedures*, available at: http://eulawanalysis.blogspot.com/2016/01/on-knowledge-as-power-transparency-of.html (on February 9, 2019).

is the strict understanding of the conditions of direct and individual concern. Therefore, it would be favorable to "loosen" these *locus standi* preconditions in line with, for instance, the judgment of the CFI in T-177/01 *Jégo-Quéré*. Still, such change of the case law of the CJEU would be questionable without amending the Treaties.

(9) There are spheres that could be regulated by the EU law in order to unleash the potential of European civil society and the daily cross-border activities of NGOs. The subject matters of potential EU legislature include incentives for philanthropy, public benefit purposes, crowdfunding and volunteer work.

(10) NGOs operate in various legal environments in EU Member States. This issue is closely related to the national legislative traditions and understanding of different types of the third sector organizations. Thus, it would be advantageous if NGOs could operate in a harmonized legal sphere in the EU. Perhaps the proposed statutes of the European Association and the European Foundation were too ambitious. Still, maybe some provisions on recognition of foreign NGOs could be regulated in the form of a directive. Such a harmonization would be also recommended in the field of access to justice in environmental matters. Presently, this issue is very diversified and is not easy to follow in the EU directives and, consequently, in the implementing acts of national law.

(11) In the face of risks of violation of the financial and political autonomy of NGOs in certain Member States, establishing a special EU fund for organizations promoting the rule of law deserves an approval. Nevertheless, it should be emphasized that no third sector organization should make its activities dependent only on the EU or national grants and needs to seek independent sources of financing as well.

(12) NGOs can play a significant role in shaping European civil society. Yet, it should be remembered that their democratic legitimacy is limited as they are not in any way elected and they do not represent the vast scope of European grassroot movements or all EU citizens. For this reason, the organizations acting at the EU level ought to comply with high standards of transparency and openness themselves. In other words, the future of European civil society does not depend solely on the EU law but also on the accountability of its advocates.

(13) Additionally, other nonlegal factors are crucial in shaping European civil society. For instance, in order to establish European public sphere, it is essential for the national media to regularly report on the EU-relevant issues. Otherwise, Brussels will remain a distant and abstract place where law is rather imposed than passed in a democratic manner.

Bibliography

1. LITERATURE

A Decade of Experience with the European Company, J. Cremers, M. Stollt, S. Vitols (ed.), Brussels 2013.

A Dictionary of Law, J. Law (ed.), Oxford 2015.

Aarhus Convention at Ten. Interactions and Tensions Between Conventional International Law and EU Environmental Law, M Pallemaerts (ed.), Groningen 2011.

AbouAssi K., *Get Money Get Involved? NGO's Reactions to Donor Funding and Their Potential Involvement in the Public Policy Processes*, International Society for Third-Sector Research Vol. 25 (2014).

Adamski D., *Access to Documents, Accountability and the Rule of Law—Do Private Watchdogs Matter?*, European Law Journal Vol. 20/2014.

Advocacy Organizations and Collective Action, A. Prakash, M.K. Gugerly (ed.), Cambridge 2010.

Ahmed S., *The Impact of NGOs on International Organizations: Complexities and Considerations*, Brooklyn Jorunal of International Law Vol. 36/2011.

Alemanno A., *Lobbying for Change: Find Your Voice to Create a Better Society*, London 2017.

Alemanno A., Stefan O., *Openness at the Court of Justice of the European Union: Toppling a Taboo*, Common Market Law Review Vol. 1/2014.

Alemanno A., *Unpacking the Principle of Openness in EU Law, Transparency, Participation and Democracy*, European Law Review Vol. 39/2014.

Alexander T., *Practical Politics. Lessons in Power and Democracy*, London 2016.

Almer J., Rotkirch M., *European Governance—An Overview of the Commission's Agenda for Reform*, Stockholm 2004.

Andenas M., Jacobs F., *European Community Law in English Courts*, Oxford 1998.

Anheier H., Toepfe S.r, *International Encyclopedia of Civil Society*, New York 2010.

Arab Revolutions and Beyond. The Middle East and Reverberations in the Americas, S. Alnasseri (ed.), New York 2016.

Aristotle, *The Politics*, London 2000.

Armstrong B.A., *Rediscovering Civil Society: The European Union and the White Paper on Governance,* European Law Journal Vol. 8/2002.

Aston J.D., *The United Nations Committee on Non-governmental Organizations: Guarding the Entrance to a Politically Divided House,* European Journal of International Law Vol. 12/2001.

Baber G., *The Free Movement of Capital and Financial Services: An Exposition?,* Cambridge 2014.

Balme R., Chabenet D., *European Governance and Democracy: Power and Protest in the EU,* Plymouth 2008.

Bannister F., Conolly R., *The Trouble with Transparency: A Critical Review of Openness in e-Government,* Policy & Internet Vol. 3/2011.

Baratta R., *Rule of Law "Dialogues" Within the EU: A Legal Assessment,* Hague Journal on the Rule of Law Vol. 8/2016.

Barcik J., Wentkowska A., *Prawo Unii Europejskiej,* Warsaw 2014.

Barcz J., *Inicjatywa obywatelska—aspekty prawne i instytucjonalne,* Europejski Przegld Sdowy Vol. 10/2011.

Barcz J., Jasińki F., Łazowski A., Podstawa K., *Fundamental Rights Protection in the European Union,* Warsaw 2009.

Bartholomeusz L., *The Amicus Curiae Before International Courts and Tribunals,* Non-State Actors and International Law Vol. 5/2005.

Bater P., *The Tax Treatment of Cross-Border Activities,* International Bureau of Fiscal Documentation (Amsterdam) No 121/2001.

Bermann G.A., *Taking Subsidiarity Seriously: Federalism in the European Community and the United States,* Columbia Law Review Vol. 94/1994.

Bernard N., *Multilevel Governance in the European Union,* The Hague 2002.

Berthoud O., *NGOs: Somewhere Between Compassion, Profitability and Solidarity,* Envio Digital Vol. 241/2001.

Bertrand Ch., *La démocratie participative dans le système institutionnel de l'Union européenne,* Siècles. Cahiers du Centre d'histoire "Espaces et Cultures" Vol. 37/2013.

Between Autonomy and Dependence. The EU Legal Order under the Influence of International Organisations, R.A. Wessel, S. Blockmans (ed.), The Hague 2013.

Beyers J., De Bruycker I., *Lobbying Makes (Strange) Bedfellows: Explaining the Formation and Composition of Lobbying Coalitions in EU Legislative Politics,* Political Studies Vol. 10/2017.

Biernat S., *Europejskie prawo administracyjne i europeizacja krajowego prawa administracyjnego (zarys problematyki),* Studia prawno-europejskie Vol. VI/2002.

Biernat S., Wasilewski A., *Wolność gospodarcza w Europie,* Kraków 2000.

Biernat T., *Wspólnota prawa. O osobliwościach systemu europejskiego,* Toruń 2002.

Birkinshaw P., *Freedom of Information and Openness: Fundamental Human Rights?,* Law Review Vol. 58/2006.

Blicharz J., *Skutki implementacji dyrektywy usługowej UE na działalność trzeciego sektora w Polsce—analiza prawna,* Trzeci Sektor No 15/2008.

Bogojević S., *Judicial Protection of Individual Applicants Revisited: Access to Justice Through the Prism of Judicial Subsidiarity*, Yearbook of European Law Vol. 34/2015.

Bokajło W., *Społeczeństwo obywatelskie*, Wrocław 2001.

Borkowski P.J., *Polityczne teorie integracji międzynarodowej*, Warsaw 2007.

Börzel T., Rosse Th., *Governance Without a State: Can It Work?*, Regulation & Governance Vol. 4/2010.

Bouwen P., *The Logic of Access to the European Parliament: Business Lobbying in the Committee on Economic and Monetary Affairs*, Journal of Common Market Studies Vol. 42/2004.

Bouza Garcia L., *Participatory Democracy and Civil Society in the EU*, London 2015.

Brakman Reiser D., *Nonprofit Oversight under Siege: Introduction*, Chicago-Kent Law Review Vol. 843/2016.

Bräutigam D., Segarra M., *Difficult Partnership: The World Bank, States and NGOs*, Latin American Politics and Society Vol. 4/2007.

Bredt S., *Prospects and Limits of Democratic Governance in the EU*, European Law Journal Vol. 17/2011.

Breen O., *EU Regulation of Charitable Organizations: The Politics of Legally Enabling Civil Society*, The International Journal of Not-for-Profit Law Vol. 10/2008.

Breen O., *European Non-profit Oversight: The Case for Regulating from the Outside In*, Chicago-Kent Law Review Vol. 91/2016.

Breen O., *The European Foundation Statute Proposal: Striking the Balance Between Supervising and Supporting European Philanthropy?*, Nonprofit Policy Forum Vol. 1/2014.

Brett R., *The Role and Limits of Human Rights NGOs at the United Nations*, Political Studies Vol. 1/1995.

Broscheid A., Coen D., *Lobbying Activity and Fora Creation in the EU: Empirically Exploring the Nature of the Policy Good*, Journal of European Public Policy Vol. 14/2007.

Brownlie I., Brookfield F.M., *Treaties and Indigenous Peoples*, Oxford 1990.

Buijze A., *The Principle of Transparency in EU Law*, Vianen 2013.

Bunea A., *Designing Stakeholder Consultations: Reinforcing or Alleviating Bias in the European Union System of Governance?*, European Journal of Political Research Vol. 11/2016.

Bunea A., *Estimating Interest Groups' Policy Positions Through Content Analysis: A Discussion of Automated and Human-Coding Text Analysis Techniques Applied to Studies of EU-Lobbying*, European Political Science Vol. 10/2016.

Bunea A., Thomson R., *Consultations with Interest Groups and the Empowerment of Executives: Evidence from the European Union*, Governance: An International Journal of Policy, Administration and Institutions Vol. 28/2015.

Burger R., Dasgupta I., Owens T., *Why Pay NGOs to Involve the Community?*, Annals of Public and Cooperative Economics Vol. 86/2015.

Burley A.-M., Mattli W., *Europe Before the Court: A Political Theory of Legal Integration*, International Organization Vol. 47/1993.

Cali B., *International Law for International Relations*, Oxford 2010.

Calliess Ch., *Europäische Vorgaben für die umweltrechtliche Verbandsklage* EurUP 2003.

Casier L., Fraser R., Halle M., Wolfe E., *Shining a Light on Fossil Fuel Subsidies at the WTO: How NGOs Can Contribute to WTO Notification and Surveillance*, World Trade Review Vol. 13/2014.

Challenges of Good Governance in the European Union, R. Grzeszczak (ed.), Baden-Baden 2016.

Chamlee-Wright E., Storr V.H., *Social Capital, Lobbying and Community-Based Interest Groups*, Public Choice Vol. 10/2011.

Charmovitz S., *Nongovernmental Organizations and International Law*, American Journal of International Law Vol. 100/2006.

Cheneval F., Schimmerfenning F., *The Case for Democracy in the European Union*, Journal of Common Market Studies Vol. 51/2013.

Chesterman S., Johnstone I., Malone D.M., *Law and Practice of the United Nations*, Oxford 2016.

Chou M., *From Crisis to Crisis: Democracy, Crisis and the Occupy Movement*, Political Studies Review Vol. 13/2015.

Christiansen Th., Kirchner E., *Committee Governance in the European Union*, Manchester 2000.

Cichowski R., *The European Court and Civil Society: Litigation, Mobilization and Governance*, Cambridge 2007.

Cioch H., *Prawo fundacyjne*, Warsaw 2011.

Citizen Participation in Multi-level Democracies, C. Fraenkel-Haeberle, S. Kropp, F. Palermo, K.-P. Sommermann (ed.), Leiden 2015.

Civil Society and International Governance. The Role of Non-state Actors in Global and Regional Regulatory Frameworks, D. Armstrong, V. Bello, J. Gilson, D. Spini (ed.), Abingdon 2011.

Civil Society in Europe. Minimum Norms and Optimum Conditions of Its Regulation, T.J. van der Ploeg, W.J.M. van Veen, C.R.M. Versteegh (ed.), Cambridge 2017.

Civil Society in the Making, D. Gavin, P. Gliński (ed.), Warsaw 2006.

Civil Society Participation in European and Global Governance, J. Steffek, J. Kissling, P. Nanz (ed.), New York 2008.

Civil Society, International Courts and Compliance Bodies, T. Treves, M. Frigessi di Rattalma, A. Tanzi, Al. Fodella, C. Pitea, Ch. Ragni (ed.), The Hague 2005.

Classen A., *Interessenvertretung in der Europaischen Union. Zur RechtmaBigkeit politischer Einflussnahme*, Wiesbaden 2014.

Cliquennois G., Champetier B., *The Economic, Judicial and Political Influence Exerted by Private Foundations on Cases Taken by NGOs to the European Courts of Human Rights: Inklings of a New Cold War?*, European Law Journal Vol. 22/2016.

Colombo A., *The Principle of Subsidiarity and European Citizenship*, Milan 2004.

Comparative Corporate Governance of Non-profit Organizations, K.J. Hopt, T. von Hippel (ed.), Cambridge 2012.

Continuity and Change in EU Law: Essays in Honour of Sir Francis Jacobs, A. Arnull, P. Eeckhout, T. Tridimas (ed.), Oxford 2008.

Corporate Governance und Korruption. Wirtschaftliche und moralökonomische Perspektiven der Bestechung und ihrer Bekämpfung, D. Aufderhelde, M. Dabrowski, K. Hofmann (ed.), Berlin 2005.

Cottrell P., Nance M., Trubek D., *"Soft Law," "Hard Law" and European Integration: Toward a Theory of Hybridity*, New York 2005.

Cracogna D., Fici A., Henry H., *International Handbook of Cooperative Law*, Heidelberg 2013.

Craig P., de Burca G., *The European Court of Justice*, Oxford 1999.

Craig P., de Burca G., *The Evolution of EU Law*, Oxford 2011.

Craig P., *EU Administrative Law*, Oxford 2018.

Crespy A., *Deliberative Democracy and the Legitimacy of the European Union: A Reappraisal of Conflict*, Political Studies Vol. 62/2014.

Cross J., *Striking a Pose: Transparency and Position Taking in the Council of the European Union*, European Journal of Political Research Vol. 52/20.

Crossen T., Niessen V., *NGO Standing in the European Court of Justice—Does the Aarhus Convention Open the Door?*, Review of European, Comparative & International Environmental Law Vol. 16/2007.

Cuesta Lopez V., *The Lisbon Treaty's Provisions on Democratic Principles: A Legal Framework for Participatory Democracy*, European Public Law Vol. 1/2010.

Cullen P., *The Platform of European Social NGOs: Ideology, Division and Coalition*, Journal of Political Ideologies Vol. 15/2010.

Cummings S., Trubek L., *Globalizing Public Interest Law*, UCLA Journal of International Law and Foreign Affairs Vol. 13/2008.

Curtin D., Hofman H., Mendes J., *Constitutionalising EU Executive Rule-Making Procedures: A Research Agenda*, European Law Journal Vol. 19/2013.

Curtin D., *Judging EU Secrecy*, Cahiers de Droit Européen Vol. 2/2012.

Curtin D., Mendes J., *Transparence et participation: Des principes démocratiques pour l'administration de l'Union européenne*, l'E.N.A. Revue française d'administration publique Vol. 1/2011.

Czaputowicz J., *Administracja publiczna. Wyzwania w dobie integracji europejskiej*, Warsaw 2008.

Czech Yearbook of International Law 2014. The Role of Governmental and Nongovernmental Organizations in the 21st Century, A.J. Belohlavek, N. Rozehnalova, F. Cerny (ed.), New York 2014.

Czerw J., *Dostęp do informacji publicznej w Polsce*, Przegląd Prawa Publicznego Vol. 11/2013.

Dahl R., *On Democracy*, Yale 1999.

Daske H., Hail L., Leuz, Ch. Verdi R., *Adopting a Label: Heterogeneity in the Economic Consequences Around IAS/IFRS Adoptions*, Journal of Accounting Research Vol. 51/2013.

Davis J., *Justice Across Borders. The Struggle for Human Rights in U.S. Courts*, Cambridge 2008.

Davis L., *EU Foreign Policy, Transitional Justice and Mediation. Principle, Policy and Practice*, Abingdon 2014.

De Jesus Butler I., *Non-governmental Organisation Participation in the EU Law-Making Process: The Example of Social Non-governmental Organisations at the Commission, Parliament and Council,* European Law Journal Vol. 5/2008.

de Lange F., *Beyond Greenpeace. Courtesy of the Aarhus Convention,* Yearbook of European Environmental Law Vol. 3/2003.

De Schutter O., *Europe in Search of Its Civil Society,* European Law Journal Vol. 8/2002.

de Tocqueville A, *Democracy in America,* Washington 2004.

Deacon B., *The Social Protection and Global Social Governance: Towards Policy Synergy and Cooperation Between International Organizations,* International Social Security Review Vol. 3-4/2013.

Deficyt demokracji w Unii Europejskiej, K.A. Wojtaszczyk, J. Szymańska (ed.), Warsaw 2014.

Delanty G., *Inventing Europe: Idea, Identity, Reality,* London 1995.

Delreux T., *Concluding Early Agreements in the EU: A Double Principal-Agent Analysis of Trilogue Negotiations,* Journal of Common Market Studies Vol. 2/2018.

Democracy and the Role of Associations: Political, Structural and Social Contexts, S. Rossleutshcer (ed.), Abingdon 2005.

Democratic Legitimacy in the European Union and Global Governance, B. Pérez de las Heras (ed.), Cham 2017.

Demokracja bezpośrednia. Wymiar globalny i lokalny, M. Marczewska-Rytko, A. Piasecki (ed.), Lublin 2010.

Der Staat im Recht. Festschrift für Eckhart Klein zum 70. Geburtstag, M. Breuer, A. Epiney, A. Haratsch, S. Schmahl, N. Weiß (ed.), Berlin 2013.

Developments of International Law in Treaty Making, R. Wolfrum, V. Röben (ed.), Berlin 2005.

DeWiel B., *A Conteptual History of Civil Society: From Greek Beginnings to the Ends of Marx,* Past Imperfect Vol. 6/1997.

Die Entzauberung partizipativer Demokratie. Zur Rolle der Zivilgesellschaft bei der Demokratisierung von EU-Governance, B. Kohler-Koch, Ch. Quittkat (ed.), Frankurt am Mein 2011.

Die EU und der Prozess ihrer Legitimation: Legitimationsgrundlagen der Europäischen Union, F. Cheneval (ed.), Hamburg 2007.

Die Europäische Demokratie in guter Vergassung?, K. Hofmann, K. Naumann (ed.), Baden-Baden 2010.

Dingwerth K., Blauberger M., Schneider Ch., *Postnationale Demokratie. Eine Einführung am Beispiel von EU, WTO und UNO,* Wiesbaden 2011.

Dougan M., *What Are We to Make of the Citizens' Initiative?,* Common Market Law Review Vol. 6/2011.

Draniewicz B., *Uprawnienia organizacji ekologicznych w postępowaniach wymagających udziału społeczeństwa,* Monitor Prawniczy Vol. 1/2011.

Driessen B., *Transparency in EU Institutional Law: A Practitioner's Handbook,* London 2008.

du Vall M., *Electronic Civil Disobediance (ECD) jako jedna ze współczesnych form obywatelskiego nieposłuszeństwa,* Państwo i Społeczeństwo Vol. 2/2010.

Duszka-Jakimko H, *Globalisation and Its Impact on Civil Society: Philosophical, Legal and Sociological Aspects*, Wrocław Review of Law, Administration & Economic Vol. 1/2011.

Ebbesson J., *A Modest Contribution to Environmental Democracy and Justice in Transboundary Contexts: The Combined Impact of the Espoo Convention and Aarhus Convention*, Review of European, Comparative & International Environmental Law Vol. 20/2011.

Eising R., *Clientelism, Committees, Pluralism and Protests in the European Union: Matching Patterns?*, West European Politics Vol. 31/2008.

Eising R., *The Access of Business Interests to EU Institutions: Towards Elite Pluralism?*, Journal of European Public Policy Vol. 14/2007.

El-Agraa A.M., *The European Union. Economics and Politics*, Cambridge 2011.

Eliantonio M., *Towards an Ever Dirtier Europe? The Restrictive Standing of Environmental NGOs Before the European Courts and the Aarhus Convention*, Croatian Yearbook of European Law and Policy Vol. 7/2011.

Eliott M., Thomas R., *Public Law*, Oxford 2014.

Environmental Democracy and Law, G. Bándi (ed.), Groningen 2014.

EU Civil Society. Patterns of Cooperation, Competition and Conflict, H. Johansson, S. Kalm (ed.), Basingstoke 2015.

Europäische Identität: Voraussetzungen und Strategien, J. Nida-Rümelin, W. Weidenfeld (ed.), Baden-Baden 2007.

Europäische Zivilgesellschaft. Konzepte, Akteure, Strategien, M. Knodt, B. Finke (ed.), Wiesbaden 2005.

Europe 2020: Towards a More Social Europe?, E. Marlier (ed.), Brussels 2010.

Europe in Change. Committee Governance in the European Union, T. Christiansen, E. Kirchner (ed.), Manchester 2000.

European Integration Theory, A. Wiener, Th. Diez (ed.), Oxford 2009.

European Union. Power and Policy-Making, J. Richardson, S. Mazey (ed.), Abingdon 2015.

Europeanisation of Public Law, J.H. Jans, S. Prechal, R.J.G.M Widdershoven (ed.), Groningen 2015.

Euroscepticism: Images of Europe Among Mass Publics and Political Elites, D. Fuchs, R. Magni-Berton, A. Roger (ed.), Leverkusen 2009.

EUV/AEUV. Das Verfassungsrecht der Europäischen Union mit Europäischer Grundrechtekarta. Kommentar, Ch. Calliess, M. Ruffert (ed.), Munich 2011.

Fahley E., *The Actors of Postnational Rule-Making*, London 2015.

Fashoyin T., *Coopération tripartite, dialogue social et développement national*, Revue international du Travail Vol. 4/2004.

Ferrand B., *Lobbying and Lawmaking in the European Union: The Development of Copyright Law and the Rejection of the Anti-Counterfeiting Trade Agreement*, Oxford Journal of Legal Studies Vol. 35/2015.

Fligstein N., Polyakova A., Sandholz W., *European Integration, Nationalism and European Identity*, Journal of Common Market Studies Vol. 50/2012.

Forschung zu Zivilgesellschaft, NPOs und Engagement. Quo vadis?, A.E. Zimmer, R. Simsa (ed.), Wiedbaden 2014.

Fox G., Roth B., *Democratic Governance and International Law*, Cambridge 2010.

Franzius C., Preuß U., *Die Zukunft der europäischen Demokratie*, Baden-Baden 2012.

Freeden M., *Civil Society and the Good Citizen: Competing Conceptions of Citizenship in Twentieth-Century Britain*, Oxford 2003.

Freiberg S., *Nowy traktat o Unii Europejskiej*, Warsaw 2015.

Furtak F., *Nichtregierungsorganisationen (NGOs) im politischen System der Europäischen Union*, Munich 2008.

Gaitanides Ch., Grözinger G., *Diversity in Europe*, Baden-Baden 2015.

Garçon G., *Limits of NGO Rights to Invoke Access to Justice under the Aarhus Convention*, European Journal of Risk Regulation Vol. 6/2015.

Garton J., *Public Benefit in Charity Law*, Oxford 2013.

Geddes A., *Lobbying for Migrant Inclusion in the European Union: New Opportunities for Transnational Advocacy?*, Journal of European Public Policy Vol. 7/2000.

Gehring T., *Integrating Integration Theory. Neofunctionalism and International Regimes*, Florence 1995.

Geiger A., *EU Lobbying Handbook*, Brussels 2012.

Geiger Ch., Kahn D.-E., Kotzur M., *Commentary on the TEU/TFEU*, Oxford 2014.

Gerard N., *Case Law Analysis. Access to Justice in Environmental Matters—A Case of Double Standard? Greenpeace and Others v. Commission of the European Union*, Journal of Environmental Law Vol. 8/1996.

Gerard, N. *Case Law Analysis. Access to the European Court of Justice: A Lost Opportunity. Stichting Greenpeace Council (Greenpeace International) and Others v. Commission*, Journal of Environmental Law Vol. 10/1998.

Gillespie A., *Facilitating and Controlling Civil Society in International Environmental Law*, Review of European, Comparative & International Environmental Law Vol. 15/2006.

Gjems-Onstad O., *The Proposed European Association—A Symbol in Need of Friends?*, Voluntas: International Journal of Voluntary and Nonprofit Organizations Vol. 6/1995.

Glasberg D., Shannon D., *Political Sociology: Oppression, Resistance and the State*, Thousand Oaks 2011.

Global Administrative Law, E. Chiti, B.G. Mattarella (ed.), New York 2011.

Głogowski P., Maurer, *The European Citizens' Initiative—Chances, Constraints and Limits*, Vienna 2013.

Godlewski R., Staszczyk P., *Projekt rozporządzenia w sprawie statutu fundacji europejskiej—szansa dla rozwoju działalności pożytku publicznego w Unii Europejskiej*, Finanse Komunalne Vol. 6/2015.

Governance and Civil Society in the European, C. Ruzza. V. Della Sala (ed.), Manchester 2007.

Governing Europe under a Constitution, H.J. Blanke, S. Mangiameli (ed.), London 2006.

Greenwood J., *Interest Representation in the European Union*, London 2011.

Grigorescu A., *Democratic Intergovernmental Organisations?*, Cambridge 2015.

Grosse T., *Dialog Społeczny a dialog w Unii Europejskiej*, Trzeci Sektor Vol. 4/2006.

Grosse T., *Europeizacja organizacji obywatelskich w Polsce—wyzwania*, Trzeci Sektor Vol. 27/2012.

Grosse T., *Komisja Europejska wobec trzeciego sektora na przykładzie strategii lizbońskiej*, Trzeci Sektor Vol. 20/2009.

Grzeszczak R., *The Concept and Practice of Good Governance in the European Union*, World Academy of Science, Engineering and Technology. International Journal of Social, Behavioral, Economic, Business and Industrial Engineering Vol. 9/2015.

Güb U., *European Governance: Views from the UK on Democracy, Participation and Policy-Making in the EU*, London 2002.

Gunn T.J., *Religion and Law in France: Secularism, Separation and State Intervention*, Drake Law Review Vol. 57/2009.

Haas E., *Beyond the Nation State: Functionalism and International Organisation*, Colchester 2008.

Habermas J., *The Crisis of the European Union. A Response*, Cambridge 2013.

Hage J., A. Waltermann, B. Akkermans, *Introduction to Law*, Cham 2014.

Hallstrom L., *Eurocratising Enlargement? EU Elites and NGO Participation in European Environmental Policy*, Environmental Politics Vol. 13/2004.

Halpern C., Cunningham J., *Reflections on the New Public Interest Law: Theory and Practice at the Center for Law and Social Policy*, Georgtown Law Journal Vol. 59/1995.

Harlow C., *Citizen Access to Political Power in the European Union*, Working Paper No 2, European University Institute 1999.

Hartlapp M., Metz J., Rauh C., *Which Policy for Europe? Power and con ict inside the European Commission*, Oxford 2014.

Heede K., *European Ombudsman: Redress and Control and the Union Level*, The Hague 2002.

Heidenbauer S., *Charity Crossing Borders. The Fundamental Freedom' Influence on Charity and Donor Taxation in Europe*, Alphen aan den Rijn 2011.

Herausforderung Europa: Wege zu einer europäischen Identität M. Delgado, M. Lutz-Bachmann (ed.), Munich 1995.

Hewlett S.A., Peraino K., Sherbin L., Sumberg K., *The Sponsor Effect: Breaking Through the Last Glass Ceiling*, Harvard Business Review Research Report 2010.

Hieber T., *Die Europaische Bürgerinitiative nach dem Vertrag von Lissabon*, Tübingen 2014.

Hillebrandt M.Z., Curtin D., Meijer A., *Transparency in the EU Council of Ministers: An Institutional Analysis*, European Law Journal Vol. 20/2014.

Hilson Ch., *Community Rights and Wrongs: Greenpeace Before the Court of Justice. Case C-321-95 P, Stichting Greenpeace Council (Greenpeace International) and others v. Commission*, Environmental Law Review Vol. 52/1999.

Hirst P., *Associative Democracy. New Forms of Economic and Social Governance*, Oxford 1994.

Hix S., Lord Ch., *Political Parties in the European Union*, New York 1997.

Hofmann H., Rowe G., Turk A., *Administrative Law and Policy of the European Union*, Oxford 2011.

Hönnige Ch., Panke D., *The Committee of the Regions and the European Economic and Social Committee: How Influential are Consultative Committees in the European Union?*, Journal of Common Market Studies Vol. 3/2013.

Hopkins B., *Private Foundation Law Made Easy*, Hoboken 2008.

Hopt K.J., von Hippel T., *The European Foundation: A New Legal Approach*, Cambridge 2006.

Howard P., *New Media Campaigns and the Managed Citizen*, New York 2005.

Huber M., *Principles, Tasks, and Problems of the Red Cross in International Law*, Geneva 1946.

Iglesias Sanchez S., *Fundamental Rights and Citizenship of the Union at a Crossroads: A Promising Alliance or a Dangerous Liaison?*, European Law Journal Vol. 4/2014.

Inteligentna i zrównoważnona gospodarka sprzyjająca włączeniu społecznemu—wyzwania dla systemów prawnych Unii Europejskiej i państw członkowskich, S. Dudzik, B. Iwańska, N. Półtorak (ed.), Warsaw 2017.

International Courts and the Development of International Law. Essays in Honour of Tullio Trevez, N. Boschiero, T. Scovazzi, C. Pitea, Ch. Ragni (ed.), The Hague 2013.

Iwańska B., *Koncepcja "skargi zbiorowej" w prawie ochrony środowiska*, Warsaw 2013.

Jabłoński J., *Dostęp do wymiaru sprawiedliwości w sprawach ochrony śwodowiska w świetle standardów prawa międzynarodowego*, Prawo i Środowisko Vol. 3/2001.

Jacobs M., *Precedents and Case-Base Reasoning in the European Court of Justice*, International Journal of Constitutional Law Vol. 3/2014.

Jaeger H.-M., *"Global Civil Society" and the Political Depolitization of Global Governance*, International Political Sociology Vol. 1/2007.

Jans J.H., Vedder H.H.B., *European Environmental Law After Lisbon*, Groningen 2012.

Jaskulski A., *Federalizm europejski początków integracji i doby kryzysu gospodarczego*, Rocznik Integracji Europejskiej Vol. 6/2012.

Jendrośka J., *Obowiązek powiadamiania społeczeństwa w nowych przepisach o ocenie oddziaływania przedsięwzięcia na środowisko*, Prawo i Środowisko Vol. 1/2009.

Jodoin S., Duyck S., Lofts K., *Public Participation and Climate Governance: An Introduction*, Review of European, Comparative & International Environmental Law Vol. 24/2015.

Jones E., Menon A., Weatherill S., *Oxford Handbook of the European Union*, Oxford 2014.

Joos K., *Lobbying in the New Europe*, Weinheim 2011.

Jordan A., *The European Union: An Evolving System of Multi-level Governance... or Government?*, Policy & Politics Vol. 29/2001.

Jung S., *Need for a New Approach in European Company Law?—The European Foundation as a Turning Point*, Trust & Trustees Vol. 6/2015.

Juris J.S., *Reflections on #Occupy Everywhere: Social Media, Public Space and Emerging Logics of Aggregation*, American Ethnologist. Journal of the American Ethnological Society Vol. 39/2012.

Kaasch A., Martens K., *Actors and Agency in Global Social Governance*, Oxford 2015.

Karolewski I.P., *Citizenship and Collective Identity in Europe*, Abingdon 2010.

Karolewski I.P., *Pathologies of Deliberation in the EU*, European Law Journal Vol. 1/2011.

Kastelik-Smaza A., *Pytania prejudycjalne do Trybunału Sprawiedliwości Unii Europejskiej a ochrona praw jednostki*, Warsaw 2010.

Kawczyńska M., *Pozaumowna odpowiedzialnosć odszkodowawcza Unii Europejskiej*, Warsaw 2016.

Kawecki M., *Reforma ochrony danych osobowych. Współpraca administracyjna w świetle ogólnego rozporządzenia o ochronie danych osobowych*, Warsaw 2017.

Kawka I., *Zasady dobrego rządzenia w prawie Unii Europejskiej. Sektory infrastrukturalne*, Kraków 2011.

Keessen M., *European Administrative Decisions: How the EU Regulates Products on the Internal Market*, European Administrative Series Vol. 2/2009.

Keller B., *Social Dialogues—The State of the Art a Decade after Maastricht*, Industrial Relation Journal Vol. 5/2003.

Kendall J., Fraisse L., *The European Statue of Association: Why an Obscure But Contested Symbol in a Sea of Indifference and Skepticism?*, Third Sector European Policy Working Papers. London School of Economics and Political Science Vol. 11/2005.

Kenig-Witkowska M., Łazowski A., Ostrihansky R., *Prawo instytucjonalne Unii Europejskiej*, Warsaw 2011.

Kenig-Witkowska M.M., *Międzynarodowe prawo ochrony środowiska*, Warsaw 2011.

Kilanowski M., *Ku wolnosci jako odpowiedzialności. Dewey, Rorty I Habermas o nowej jakości demokracji*, Toruń 2013.

Kirsch A., *Demokratie und Legitimation in der Europäischen Union*, Baden-Baden 2008.

Klüwer H., *Lobbying in the European Union*, Oxford 2013.

Knade-Plaskacz A., *Dostęp do wymiaru sprawiedliwości w sprawach dotyczących środowiska—transpozycja trzeciego filaru Konwencji z Aarhus do prawa Unii Europejskiej*, Przegląd Prawa Ochrony Środowiska Vol. 1/2014.

Kodeks postępowania administracyjnego. Komentarz, M. Jaśkowska, A. Wróbel (ed.), Warsaw 2013.

Koenig C., *Observer Status for the International Committee of the Red Cross at the United Nations: A Legal Viewpoint*, International Review of the Red Cross Vol. 280/1991.

Koester V., *Review of Compliance Committee under the Aarhus Convention: A Rather Unique Compliance Mechanism*, Journal of European Environmental & Planning Law Vol. 1/2005.

Koester V., *The Compliance Committee of the Aarhus Convention—An Overview of Procedures and Jurisprudence*, Environmental Policy and Law Vol. 37/2007.

Kohler Koch B., Finke B., *The Institutional Shaping of EU-Society Relations: A Contribution to Democracy via Participation?*, Journal of Civil Society Vol. 3/2007.

Kohler-Koch B., Quittkat Ch., *De-Mystification of Participatory Democracy: EU Governance and Civil Society*, Oxford 2013.

Kohler-Koch B., *The Three Worlds of European Civil Society—What Role for Civil Society for What Kind of Europe?*, Policy and Society Vol. 28/2009.

Konopacki S., *Dylematy federalizmu europejskiego*, Studia Europejskie Vol. 3/1988.

Konopacki S., *Neofunkcjonalistyczna teoria integracji politycznej Ernsta Haasa i Leona Lindberga*, Studia Europejskie Vol. 3/1998.

Konstytucja Rzeczypospolitej Polskiej. Komentarz, M. Haczkowska (ed.), Warsaw 2014.

Korkea-Aho M., *"Mr Smith Goes to Brussels": Third Country Lobbying and the Making of EU Law and Policy*, Cambridge Yearbook of European Legal Studies Vol. 18/2016.

Kornobis-Romanowska D., *Europejska Konwencja Praw Człowieka w systemie prawa Wspólnot Europejskich*, Warsaw 2001.

Korolczuk E., *Kłopot z "NGOizacją." Debata o społeczeństwie obywatelskim w Polsce a rzeczywistość*, Polityka Społeczna Vol. 5-6/2011.

Kostakopoulou D., *Ideas, Norms and European Citizenship: Explaining Institutional Change*, Modern Law Review Vol. 68/2005.

Kostandinova P., *Improving the Transparency and Accountability of EU Institutions: The Impact of the Office of the European Ombudsman*, Journal of Common Market Studies Vol. 5/2015.

Koster H., *EU Legal Entities—New Options?*, European Company Law Vol. 12/2015.

Kovar R., Simon D., *La citoyennété européenne*, Cahiers de droit européen Vol. 3-4/1993.

Kowalik-Bańczyk K., *Procedural Autonomy of Member States and the EU Rights of Defence in Antitrust Proceedings*, Yearbook of Antitrust and Regulatory Studies 2012.

Krämer L., *Public Interest Ligitation in Environmental Matters Before European Courts*, Journal of Environmental Law Vol. 8/1996.

Kranenborg H., Voermans W., *Access to Information in the European Union: A Comparative Analysis of EC and Member State Legislation*, Amsterdam 2005.

Krastev I., *After Europe*, Philadelphia 2017.

Krawiec G., *Europejskie prawo administracyjne*, Warszawa 2009.

Kubin T., *Legitymizacja system instytucjonalnego Unii Europejskiej*, Katowice 2014.

Kurczewska U., Molęda-Zdziech M., *Lobbing w Unii Europejskiej—zarys problematyki*, Studia Europejskie Vol. 2/1999.

Kurki M., *Governmentality and EU Democracy Promotion: The European Instrument for Democracy and Human Rights and the Construction of Democratic Civil Societies*, International Political Sociology Vol. 5/2011.

Kurpas S., Brügemann M., Meyer Ch., *The Commission White Paper on Communication. Mapping a Way to a European Public Sphere*, CEPS Policy Brief Vol. 101/2006.

Kutay A., *How Does the European Commission Create a European Civil Society with Words? A Discourse Theoretical Inquiry*, Journal of Common Market Studies Vol. 55/2017.

Kutay A., *Limits of Participatory Democracy in European Governance*, European Law Journal Vol. 21/2015.

Lang S., *NGOs, Civil Society and the Public Sphere*, Cambridge 2012.

Lanor Ch., *The Legal Status of National Red Cross and Red Crescent Societies*, International Review of the Red Cross Vol. 840/2000.

Lavelle K., *Legislating International Organizations*, Washington 2011.

Leininger A., *Direct Demoracracy in Europe: Potentials and Pitfalls*, Global Policy Vol. 6/2015.

Leino P., *Just a Little Sunshine in the Rain: The 2010 Case Law of the European Court of Justice on Access to Documents*, Common Market Law Review Vol. 48/2011.

Lenaerts K., Maselis I., Gutman K., *EU Procedural Law*, Oxford 2014.

Lincoln J., *Transitional Justice, Peace and Accountability*, London 2011.

Lindblom A.-K., *Non-governmental Organisations in International Law*, Cambridge 2008.

Lobbying in der Europäischen Union. Zwischen Professionalisierung und Regulierung, D. Dialer, M. Richter (ed.), Wiesbaden 2014.

Lobbying the European Union: Institutions, Actors and Issues, D. Coen, J. Richardson (ed.), Oxford 2009.

Lobbying. Strukturen. Akteure. Strategien, R. Kleinfeld, A. Zimmer, U. Willems (ed.), Berlin 2007.

Luc S., *Zasada pomocniczości w polityce gospodarczej Unii Europejskiej*, Prace i Materiały Instytutu Rozwoju Gospodarczego SGH 2012.

Luchetta G., *Impact Assessment and the Policy Cycle in the EU*, European Journal of Risk Regulation Vol. 3/2012.

Lundberg E., *Changing Balance: The Participation and Role of Voluntary Organisations in the Swedish Policy Process*, Scandinavian Political Studies Vol. 35/2012.

Mahoney C., *The Power of Institutions: State and Interest Group Activity in the European Union*, European Union Politics Vol. 5/2014.

Märkle P., Alber M., *Der Verein im Zivil- und Steuerrecht*, Munich 2017.

Marks G., Hooghe L., *Multi-level Governance and European Integration*, London 2011.

Martens K., *NGOs and the United Nations*, New York 2005.

Martens K., *NGOs in the United Nations System: Evaluating Theoretical Approaches*, Journal of International Development Vol. 18/2006.

Marxsen Ch., *Open Stakeholder Consultations at the European Level—Voice of the Citizens?*, European Law Journal Vol. 2/2015.

Mastroianni R., Pezza A., *Striking the Right Balance: Limits on the Right to Bring an Action Under Article 263 (4) of the Treaty on the Functioning of the European Union*, American University International Law Review Vol. 30/2015.

Mather J.D., *The Court of Justice and the Union Citizen*, European Law Journal Vol. 11/2005.

Mayer F., Palmowski J., *European Identities and the EU—The Ties That Bind the Peoples of Europe*, Journal of Common Market Studies Vol. 3/2004.

Mazey S., Richardson J., *Lobbying in the European Community*, Oxford 1993.

McCann M.W., *Rights at Work: Pay Equity Reform and the Politics of Legal Mobilization*, Chicago 1994.

McLaughlin S., *Unlocking Company Law*, Abingdon 2013.

Medes J., *Participation in EU Rule-Making*, Oxford 2011.

Mendes J., *Delegated and Implementing Rule Making: Proceduralisation and Constitutional Design*, European Law Journal Vol. 19/201.

Mendes J., *Participation and the Role of Law after Lisbon: A Legal View on Article 11*, Common Market Law Review Vol. 6/2011.

Menéndez A.J., *The European Democratic Challenge: The Forging of a Supranational Volonté Générale*, European Law Journal Vol. 3/2009.

Menkes J., Wasilkowski A., *Organizacje międzynarodowe. Prawo instytucjonalne*, Warsaw 2010.

Menkes M., *Governance gospodarczy—stadium prawnomiędzynarodowe*, Warsaw 2016.

Meyer D., Whittier N., Robnett B., *Social Movements. Identity, Culture and the State*, Oxford 2002.

Meyer J., *Charta der Grundrechte der Europäischen Union*, Baden-Baden 2014.

Migdał J.S., *State in Society: Studying How States and Societies Transform and Constitute One Another*, Cambridge 2001.

Mitchell T., *The Limits of the State: Beyond Statist Approaches and Their Critics*, American Political Science Review Vol. 85/1988.

Moffitt B., *Transnational Populism? Representative Claims, Media and the Difficulty of Constructing a Transnational People*, Journal of the European Institute for Communication and Culture Vol. 24/2017.

Mollers Ch., *Multi-Level Democracy*, Ratio Juris Vol. 3/2011.

Moore D., Hadzi-Miceva K., Bullain N., *A Comparative Overview of Public Benefit Status in Europe*, The International Journal of Not-for-Profit Law Vol. 11/2008.

Moreno-Jiménez J.-M., Polasek W., *e-democracy and Knowledge. A Multicriteria Framework for the New Democratic Era*, Journal of Multi-Criteria Decision Analysis Vol. 12/2004.

Morgera E., *An Update on the Aarhus Convention and Its Continued Global Relevance*, Review of European, Comparative & International Environmental Law Vol. 14/2005.

Moro G., *Citizens in Europe. Civic Activism and the Community Democratic Experiment*, Rome 2012.

Moroń D., *Organizacje pozarządowe—fundament społeczeństwa obywatelskiego*, Wrocław 2012.

Muchlinski P., *Multinational Enterprises & The Law*, Oxford 2007.

Müller P., *The Role of Law in EU Foreign Policy-Making: Legal Integrity, Legal Spillover and the EU Policy of Differentiation Towards Israel*, Journal of Common Market Studies Vol. 55/2017.

Multi-legel Governance w Unii Europejskiej, J. Ruszkowski, L. Wojnicz (ed.), Szczecin 2013.

Multi-level Governance: The Missing Linkages (Critical Perspectives on International Public Sector Management. Vol. 4, E. Ongaro (ed.), Bingley 2015.

Murpy H., Kellow A., *Forum Shopping in Global Governance: Understanding States, Business and NGOs in Multiple Arenas*, Global Policy Vol. 4/2013.

Musiał-Karg M., *Instytucje demokracji bezpośredniej w procesie integracji europejskiej—od referendum ogólnonarodowego do europejskiej inicjatywy obywatelskiej*, Rocznik Integracji Europejskiej Vol. 6/2012.

Nakano S., *Maastricht Social Protocol Revisited: Origins of the European Industrial Relations System*, Journal of Common Market Studies Vol. 5/2014.

Narody wobec Europy. Negocjowanie tożsamości, J. Mikułowski-Pomorski (ed.), Kraków 2002.

Nelson P., *The Varied and Conditional Integration of NGOs in the Aid System: NGOs and the World Bank*, Journal of International Development Vol. 18/2006.

Neshkova M.I., *The Impact of Subnational Interests on Supranational Regulation*, Journal of European Public Policy Vol. 8/2010.

NGOs in International Law: Efficiency in Flexibility?, P.-M. Dupuy, L. Vierrucci (ed.), Cheltenham 2008.

Non-state Actors and Human Rights, P. Alston (ed.), Oxford 2006.

Non-state Actors as New Subjects of International Law, R. Hofmann (ed.), Berlin 1999.

Noortmann M., Ryngaert C., *Non-state Actor Dynamics in International Law. From Law-Takers to Law-Makers*, Oxford 2015.

Norris P., *Democratic Deficit: Critical Citizens Revisited*, Cambridge 2011.

Obradovic D., *Civil Society and the Social Dialogue in European Governance*, Yearbook of European Law Vol. 24/2005.

Ochrona praw jednostki, B. Drzewiecka, K. Malinowska, P. Pszczółkowski, A. Siejka (ed.), Warsaw 2003.

Ochrona praw obywatelek i obywateli Unii Europejskiej. 20 lat—osiągnięcia i wyzwania na przyszłość, G. Baranowska, A. Bodnar, A. Gliszczyńska-Grabias (ed.), Warsaw 2015.

Odumosu I., *Revisiting NGO Participation in WTO and Investment Dispute Settlement: From Procedural Arguments to (Substantive) Public Interest Considerations*, Canadian Yearbook of International Law Vol. 44/2007.

Olivo U.M., *Evolution of the Term Non Governmental Organization (NGO)*, Revista Venezoelana de Analisis de Coyuntura Vol. XIII/2007.

Opening EU Governance to Civil Society—Gains and Challenges, B. Kohler-Koch, D. De Biévre, A. Maloney (ed.), Mannheim 2008 (The CONNEX Report Series No 5).

Organ J., *Decommissioning Direct Democracy?, A Critical Analysis of Commission Decision-Making on the Legal Admissibility of European Citizens. Initiative Proposals*, European Constitutional Law Review Vol. 10/2014.

Ozcurumez S., Hoxha J., *Conditional Deliberation: The Case of Joint Parliamentary Committees in the EU*, Journal of Common Market Studies Vol. 3/2015.

Pallas Ch., *Transnational Civil Society and the World Bank. Investigating Civil Society's Potential to Democratize Global Governance*, London 2013.

Panke D., *Lobbying Institutional Key Players: How States Seek to Influence the European Commission, the Council Presidency and the European Parliament*, Journal of Common Market Studies Vol. 50/2012.

Pantea M.-C., *Young People in Cross-National Volunteering: Perceptions of Unfairness*, Journal of Social and Personal Relationships Vol. 30/2013.

Participatory Governance. Political and Societal Implications, J.R. Grote, B. Gbikpi (ed.), Cham 2002.

Parvin P., *Democracy Without Participation: A New Politics for a Disengaged Era*, Res Publica Vol. 24/2018.

Patek A., Rydel J., Węc J.J., *Najnowsza historia świata 1945-1995. Tom I 1945-63*, Kraków 1997.

Pech L., *Rule of Law as a Guiding Principle of the European Union's External Action*, The Hague 2012.

Pedraza-Farina L., *Conceptions of Civil Society in International Lawmaking and Implementation: A Theoretical Framework*, Michigan Journal of International Law Vol. 34/2013.

Peers S., Hervey T., Kenner J., Ward A., *The EU Charter of Fundamental Rights*, Baden-Baden 2014.

Peeters M., Nóbrega S., *Climate Change-Related Aarhus Conflicts: How Successful Are Procedural Right in EU Climate Law*, Review of European, Comparative & International Environmental Law Vol. 23/2014.

Perez-Solorzano N., Smismans S., *Representativeness: A Tool to Structure Interest Intermediation in the European Union?*, Journal of Common Market Studies Vol. 3/2012.

Perri A., *European Competition Law and the Non-profit Sector*, Voluntas Vol. 3/1992.

Perri A., Kuti E., *Into the European Community: Impacts of Future Membership on Hungary's Non-profit Sector*, Journal of European Social Policy Vol. 3/1993.

Peters A., *Elemente einer Theorie der Verfassung Europas*, Berlin 2011.

Petrażycki L., *Wstęp do nauki polityki prawa*, Warsaw 1968.

Pichler A.J., Kaufmann B., *The European Citizens' Initiative: Into New Democratic Territory*, Oxford 2010.

Pietrzyk-Reeves D., *Idea społeczeństwa obywatelskiego*, Wrocław 2004.

Pijnenburg B., *EU Lobbying by Ad Hoc Coalitions: An Exploratory Case Study*, Journal of European Public Policy Vol. 5/1998.

Pikuła Ł., *Aksjologia Unii Europejskiej w świetle źródeł, wykładni i instytucji*, Toruń 2015.

Pilakos A., *Les Conditions d'Exercice du Droit de Petition*, Cahiers droit européen 1993.

Pirker B., *Access to Justice in Environmental Matters and the Aarhus Convention's Effects in the EU Legal Order: No Room for Nuanced Self-executing Effect?*, Review of European Community & International Environmental Law Vol. 25/2016.

Politikberatung und Lobbying in Brüssel, S. Dagger, M. Kambeck (ed.), Wiesbaden 2007.

Półtorak N., *European Union Rights in National Courts*, Alphen aan den Rijn 2015.

Półtorak N., *Ochrona uprawnień wynikających z prawa Unii Europejskiej*, Warsaw 2010.

Półtorak N., *Odpowiedzialność odszkodowawcza państwa w prawie wspólnot europejskich*, Kraków 2002.

Półtorak N., *The Impact of the Jurisprudence of the European Court of Justice on National Remedies*, Centrum Europejskie Natolin/EUI Research Laboratory Vol. 22/2005.

Prasad M., *The Role of Non-governmental Organisations in the New Human Rights Procedures for Human Rights Complaints*, International Law & Politics Vol. 5/1975.

Preuß U., *Transformacja europejskiego państwa narodowego szansa na powstanie europejskiej opinii publicznej?*, Nowa Europa. Przegląd Natoliński Vol. 5/2007.

Quittkat Ch., *The European Commission's Online Consultations: A Success Story?*, Journal of Common Market Studies Vol. 49/2011.

Qureshi A., *Extraterritorial Shrimps, NGOs and the WTO Appellate Body*, International and Comparative Law Quarterly Vol. 48/1999.

Randi G., *Environmental Democracy and Law*, Groningen 2014.

Ratner S, Goodin R., *Democratizing International Law*, Global Policy Journal Vol. 2/2012.

Reflections on 30 Years of EU Environmental Law: A High Level of Protection?, R. Macrory (ed.), Groningen 2005.

Reif L.C., *The Ombudsman, Good Governance and the International Human Rights System*, Dordrecht 2004.

Reimann K., *A View from the Top: International Politics, Norms and the Worldwide Growth of NGOs*, International Studies Quarterly Vol. 50/2006.

Reinforcing Rule of Law Oversight in the European Union C. Closa, D. Kochenov (ed.), New Jersey 2016.

Rethinking Democracy and the European Union, E.O. Eriksen, J.E. Fossum (ed.), Devon 2012.

Riemann F., *Die Transparenz der Europäischen Union. Das neue Recht auf Zugang zu Dokumenten von Parlament, Rat un Kommission*, Berlin 2003.

Ripinsky S., van den Bossche P., *NGO Involvement in International Organizations*, London 2007.

Risse T., *"Let's Argue!" Communicative Action in World Politics*, International Organization, Vol. 1/2000.

Rosamond B., *Theories of European Integration*, New York 2010.

Rosenberg G., *The Hollow Hope: Can Courts Bring About Social Change?*, Chicago 1991.

Ross G., *Jacques Delors and European Integration*, Cambridge 1995.

Rossi I., *Legal Status of Non-governmental Organizations in International Law*, Antwerp 2010.

Rossi R., *The Proposal for a European Foundation Statute and Its Influence on Italian Legislation*, International Journal of Not-for-Profit Law Vol. 16/2014.

Rulemaking by the European Commission. The New Systems for Delegations of Powers, C.F. Bergstrom, D. Ritleng (ed.), Oxford 2016.

Rutzen D., *Aid Barriers and the Rise of Philanthropic Protectionism*, International Journal of Not-for-Profit Law Vol. 17/2015.

Sanchez Salgado R., *Europeanizing Civil Society. How the EU Shapes Civil Society Organizations*, London 2015.

Sarat A., Scheingold S., *Cause Lawyering: Political Commitments and Professional Responsibilities*, Oxford 1998.

Schall Ch., *Public Interest Litigation Concerning Environmental Matters Before Human Rights Courts: A Promising Future Concept?*, Journal of Environmental Law Vol. 20/2008.

Schiek D., *Economic and Social Integration. The Challenge for EU Constitutional Law*, Cheltenham 2013.

Schikhof S., *Direct and Individual Concern in Environmental Cases: The Barriers to Prospective Litigants*, EELR Vol. 7/1998.

Schlotmann M., *Interessenvertretung bei der Europaischen Kommission*, Frankfurt am Mein 2005.

Schmachl S., Breuer M., *The Council of Europe. Its Laws and Policies*, Oxford 2016.

Schmidt V., *Democracy and Legitimacy in the European Union Revisited: Input, Output and "Throughput,"* Political Studies Vol. 61/2013.

Schmidt V., *Democracy in Europe: The EU and National Polities*, Oxford 2006.

Schneider R., *Petitionen zum Europaischen Parlament mit Berücksichtigung des Bürgeauftragten*, Frankfurt am Mein 2009.

Scicluna N., *Politization Without Democratization: How the Eurozone Crisis in Transforming EU Law and Politics*, International Journal of Constitutional Law Vol. 12/2014.

Seligman A, *The Idea of Civil Society*, New Jersey 1992.

Servais J.-M., *International Labour Organization (ILO)*, Alphen aan den Rijn 2011.

Setala M., Schiller T., *Citizens' Initiative in Europe. Procedures and Consequences of Agenda-Setting by Citizens*, London 2012.

Shepherd L.J., *Power and Authority in the Production of United Nations Security Council Resolution 1325*, International Studies Quarterly Vol. 2/2008.

Shielding Humanity, Ch. Jalloh, O. Elias (ed.), Leiden 2015.

Shore C., *"European Governance" or Governality? The European Commission and the Future of Democratic Governments*, European Law Journal Vol. 17/2011.

Shore C., *"Government Without Statehood?" Anthropological Perspectives on Governance and Sovereignty in the European Union*, European Law Journal Vol. 6/2006.

Sikora A., *Sankcje finansowe w razie niewykonania wyroków Trybunału Sprawiedliwości Unii Europejskiej*, Warsaw 2011.

Slotboom M., *Participation of NGOs Before the WTO and EC Tribunals: Which Court is the Better Friend?*, World Trade Review Vol. 5/2006.

Smismans S., *European Civil Society: Shaped by Discourses and Institutional Interests*, European Law Journal Vol. 9/2003.

Sobotta Ch., *Transparenz in den Rechtsetzungsverfahren der Europäischen Union*, Frankfurt am Main 2000.

Socjologia. Lektury, P. Sztompka, M. Kucia (ed.), Kraków 2005.

Staszczyk P., *Crowdfunding a prawo polskie—kilka wątpliwości*, Trzeci Sektor Vol. 38/2016.

Staszczyk P., *Problemy podatkowe w międzynarodowych działaniach organizacji pożytku publicznego na tle prawa Unii Europejskiej*, Trzeci Sektor Vol. 32/2014.

Staszczyk P., *Ustawa o działalności pożytku publicznego i o wolontariacie*, Warsaw 2013.

Staszczyk P., *Ustawa o fundacjach. Komentarz praktyczny*, Warsaw 2015.

Sternberg E., *NGOs v. Civil Society: Reflections on the Illiberal, the Illegitimate and the Unaccountable*, IEA Economic Affairs Vol. 10/2010.

Stillman G., *Global Standard NGOs: The Essential Elements of Good Practice*, Geneva 2007.

Stoecker F.W., *NGOs und die UNO. Die Einbindung von Nichtregierungsorganisationen (NGOs) in die Strukturen der Vereinten Nationen*, Frankfurt am Mein 2000.

Stroup S., Murdie A., *There's No Place Like Home: Explaining International NGO Advocacy*, The Review of International Organizations Vol. 7/2012.

Stroup S., Wong W., *The Agency and Authority of International NGOs*, Perspectives on Politics Vol. 14/2016.

Sudre F., *Droit européen et international des droits de l'homme*, Paris 2016.

Surmatz H., *Towards a European Framework for foundations in Europe*, ERA Forum Vol. 7/2006.

Suski P., *Stowarzyszenia i fundacje*, Warsaw 2011.

Szabados M., *"Precedents" in EU Law—The Problem of Overruling*, ELTE Law Journal Vol. 1/2015.

Szacki J., *Ani książę, ani kupiec: Obywatel. Idea społeczeństwa obywatelskiego w myśli współczesnej*, Kraków 1997.

Szawiel T., *Tożsamości polskie a Europa*, Nowa Europa. Przegląd Natoliński Vol. 5/2007.

Szazi E., *NGOs: Legitimate Actors of International Law*, Leiden 2012.

Szkudlarek P., *Prawo do informacji w konwencji z Aarhus*, Kwartalnik Prawa Publicznego Vol. 3/2003.

Szpunar M., *Odpowiedzialność podmiotu prywatnego z tytułu naruszenia prawa wspólnotowego*, Warsaw 2008.

Tallberg J., Dellmuth L., Agne H., Duit A., *NGOs Influence in International Organizations: Information, Access and Exchange*, Oxford 2015.

Tankebe J., Liebling A., *Legitimacy and Criminal Justice*, Oxford 2013.

The Actors of Postnational Rule-Making. Contemporary Challenges of European and International Law, E. Fahey (ed.), Abingdon 2016.

The Changing Role of Law in the Age of Supra- and Transnational Governance, R. Nickel, A. Greppi (ed.), Baden-Baden 2014.

The Conscience of the World, P. Willets (ed.), Oxford 1996.

The EU Economic and Social Model in the Global Crisis. Interdisciplinary Perspectives, D. Schiek (ed.), Abingdon 2013.

The European Citizens' Initiative—Into New Democratic Territory, J.W. Pichler, B. Kaufmann (ed.), Wien-Graz 2010.

The European Commission, D. Spence (ed.), London 2006.

The Institutions of the European Union, J. Peterson, M. Shackleton (ed.), Oxford 2002.

The Politics of Leverage in International Relations. Name, Shame and Sanction, H.R. Friman (ed.), London 2015.

The Regional Dimension of the European Union: Towards a Third Level in Europe?, C. Jeffery (ed.), London 1997.

The Tax Treatment of NGOs. Legal, Ethical and Fiscal Frameworked for Promoting NGOs and Their Activities, P. Bater, F. Hondius, P. Kessler Lieber (ed.), The Hague 2004.

Torrens D.L., *Locus Standi for Environmental Associations under EC Law—Greenpeace—A Missed Opportunity for the ECJ*, Review of European Community & International Environmental Law Vol. 8/1999.

Towards a European Legal Culture, G. Helleringer, K. Purnhagen (ed.), Baden-Baden 2014.

Traktat o funkcjonowaniu Unii Europejskiej. Komentarz, t. I. Art. 1-89, D. Miąsik, N. Półtorak, A. Wróbel (ed.), Warsaw 2012.

Traktat o funkcjonowaniu Unii Europejskiej. Komentarz, t. III. Art. 223-358, D. Kornobis-Romanowska, J. Łacny, A. Wróbel (ed.), Warsaw 2012.

Treisman D., *Causes of Corruption: A Cross-National Study*, Journal of Public Economics Vol. 76/2000.

Trenz H.-J., *European Civil Society: Between Participation, Representation and Discourse*, Policy and Society Vol. 28/2009.

Tsadiras A., *Guarding the Guardian: "Article 258 TFEU Complaints" Before the European Ombudsman*, International Review of Administrative Sciences Vol. 81/2015.

Türk A., *Judicial Review in EU Law*, London 2009.

Unia Europejska. Prawo instytucjonalne i gospodarcze, A. Łazowski (ed.), Warsaw 2005.

Unity and Diversity in International Law, A. Zimmermann, R. Hofmann (ed.), Berlin 2006.

Uruena R., *No Citizens Here: Global Subjects and Participation in International Law*, Leiden 2009.

Ustawa o fundacjach. Komentarz, H. Cioch, A. Kidyba (ed.), Warsaw 2007.

van Amersfoort P., *European Civil Society*, Asia Europe Journal Vol. 3/2005.

Van Bossche P., *NGO Involvement in the WTO: A Comparative Perspective*, Journal of Economic International Law Vol. 11/2008.

van den Bossche P., Zdouc W., *The Law and Policy of the World Trade Organization*, Cambridge 2013.

van Ginneken W., *Zivilgesellschaft und sozialer Basisschutz*, Internationale Revue für Soziale Sicherheit Vol. 3-4/2014.

van Huijstee M., Glasbergen P., *Business-NGO Interactions in Multi-Stakeholder Context*, Business and Society Review Vol. 3/2010.

van Schendelen R., *More Machiavelli in Brussels: The Art of Lobbying the EU*, Amsterdam 2010.

Vedder A., *NGO Involvement in International Governance and Policy: Sources and Legitimacy*, Leiden 2007.

Verhoeven A., *The European Union in Search of a Democratic and Constitutional Theory*, The Hague 2002.

Versteegh C.R.M., *Civil Society under the Treaty of Lisbon: Relationship Between National Public Benefit Organizations and European Union Policy?*, Nonprofit Policy Forum Vol. 2/2011.

Vetulani-Cęgiel A., *Lobbing w procesie kształtowania prawa autorskiego w Unii Europejskiej*, Warsaw 2014.

Victor J.N., *Financing Friends: How Lobbyists Create a Web of Relationships Among Members of Congress*, Interest Groups & Advocacy Vol. 5/2016.

Vigoda-Gado E., *Revitalizing Democracy? New Avenues for Citizen Participation in the Era of Information Technology*, Public Administration Review Vol. 4/2007.

Vogiatzis N., *The European Ombudsman and Good Administration in the European Union*, London 2017.

von Bogdandy A., *The European Lesson for International Democracy: The Significance of Articles 9-12 EU Treaty for International Organization*, The European Journal of International Law Vol. 23/2012.
von Hippel T., *Tax Benefits for Foreign-Based Charities: Key Challenges of the Non-discrimination Rule of the European Court for Justice*, ERA Forum Vol. 10/2009.
von Hippel T., Vahlpahl T., *The European Foundation Statute—As Things Currently Stand*, Trust & Trustees, Vol. 6/2013.
von Hoecke M., *Methodologies of Legal Research: Which Kind of Method for What Discipline?*, Oxford 2011.
von Wolferen M., *The Limits to the CJEU's Interpretation of Locus Standi. A Theoretical Framework*, Journal of Contemporary European Research Vol. 12/2016.
Vossestein G.-J., *Modernization of European Company Law and Corporate Governance*, Alphen aan den Rijn 2010.
Walter S., *EU Citizens in the European Public Sphere*, Wiesbaden 2017.
Warleigh A., *"Europeanizing" Civil Society: NGOs as Agents of Political Socialization*, Journal of Common Market Studies Vol. 39/2001.
Wealth of the Commons. A World Beyond Market & State, D. Bollier, S. Helfrich (ed.), Amherst 2012.
Weaver D., *The Aarhus Convention and Process Cosmopolitanism*, International Environmental Agreements: Politics, Law and Economics 2017.
Weber T., *Die Umsetzung der Aarhus-Konvention beim direkten Vollzug von Unionsrecht*, Journal für Rechtspolitik Vol. 20/2012.
Węc J.J., *Spór o kształt ustrojowy Wspólnot Europejskich i Unii Europejskiej w latach 1950-2010: między ideą ponadnarodowości a współpracą międzyrządową. Analiza politologiczna*, Kraków 2012.
Weitemeyer B., *Fundatio Europaea—Risk of Abuse by Tax Shopping?*, ERA Forum Vol. 14/2013.
Wennerås P., *The Enforcement of EC Environmental Law*, Oxford 2007.
Wessels W., *The European Council*, London 2016.
Wilczyński P., *Pomocniczość jako zasada udziału podmiotów niepublicznych w realizacji zadań administracji publicznej*, Acta Universitatis Lodziensis. Folia Iuridica Vol. 69/2009.
Williams R., *Enforcing European Environmental Law: Can the European Commission Be Held to Account?*, Yearbook of European Environmental Law Vol. 2/2002.
Wilson J., *Volunteering*, Annual Review of Sociology Vol. 26/2000.
Wolf S., *Access to EU Environmental Information: EU Compliance with Aarhus Convention*, ERA Forum Vol. 14/2013.
Wolkenstein F., *Demoicracy, Transnational Partisanship and the EU*, Journal of Common Market Studies Vol. 2/2018.
Woods L., Watson P., *Steiner & Woods EU Law*, Oxford 2014.
Wright S., *A Virtual European Public Sphere? The Futurum Discussion Forum*, Journal of European Public Policy Vol. 14/2007.
Współczesne koncepcje ochrony wolności i praw podstawowych, A. Bator, M. Jabłoński, M. Maciejewski, K. Wójtowicz (ed.), Wrocław 2013.

Yanacopulos H., *International NGO Engagement, Advocacy, Activism. The Faces and Spaces of Change*, London 2016.

Zengerling C., *Greening International Jurisprudence: Environmental NGOs Before International Courts, Tribunals, and Compliance Committees*, Leiden 2013.

Zhan S., Tang S.-Y., *Understanding the Implications of Government Ties for Nonprofit Operations and Functions*, Public Administration Review Vol. 76/2016.

Zimmer H., *Einmal SE, immer SE?, Zum Bestandsschutz einer Societas Europaea bei fehlerhafter Gründung*, Wirtschaftsrechtliche Blätter Vol. 11/2008.

Związkowe przedstawicielstwo pracowników zakładu pracy, Z. Hajn (ed.), Warsaw 2012.

2. ONLINE SOURCES

www.amicus-ecj.eu.
www.assemblee-nationale.fr.
www.ardi-ep.eu.
www.asktheeu.org.
www.concordeurope.org.
www.crowdfundinginternational.eu.
www.digitallibrary.un.org.
www.ec.europa.eu.
www.edf-feph.org.
www.eeb.org.
www.eesc.europa.eu.
www.enar-eu.org.
www.esango.un.org.
www.euobserver.com.
www.euractiv.com.
www.europa.eu.
www.europarl.europa.eu.
www.ilo.org.
www.liberties.eu.
www.minority-safepack.eu.
www.ombudsman.europa.eu.
www.powerbase.info.
www.thegoodlobby.eu.
www.touteurope.eu.
www.unece.org.
www.worldbank.org.
www.wto.org.

"Bringing the EU forward in 2018" declaration, available at: http://www.governo.it/sites/governo.it/files/documenti/documenti/Notizie-allegati/governo/DeclarationIVEUSouthSummit.pdf.

Aiginger K., *Juncker's missing scenario: Empower the member states*, available at: http://www.euractiv.com/section/future-eu/opinion/junckers-missing-scenario-empower-the-member-states/.

Alemanno A., *Legal Opinion on the Proposed Inter-institutional Agreement for a Mandatory Transparency Register in the European Union*, HEC Paris Research Paper No. LAW-2017-1218, available at: https://papers.ssrn.com/sol3/papers.cfm?abstract_id=2996619.

An ECI That Works! Learning from the First Two Years of the European Citizens' Initiative, Alfter 2014, available at: http://ecithatworks.org.

Barbière C., Flausch M., *Les rencontres entre eurodéputés et lobbyistes sortent de l'ombre*, available at: https://bit.ly/2Sv7iA0.

Best Practices in Volunteer Management: An Action Planning Guide for Small and Rural Nonprofit Organizations, Canadian Volunteerism Initiative 2005, available at: http://bit.do/eg4Jm.

Breen O., *Enlarging the Space for European Philanthropy*, A DAFNE/EFC study of 18.1.2018, available at: http://bit.do/ekCop.

Bursting the Brussels Bubble, A study by LobbyControl, Berlin 2010, available at: https://www.lobbycontrol.de/wp-content/uploads/bursting-the-brussels-bubble.pdf.

Can Civic Tech Save Democracy? How Technology Is Renewing Civic Engagement, L'Atelier BNP Paribas Report, available at: https://atelier.bnpparibas/uploads/file/20171208-Civic-Tech-Study-LAtelier-BNPParibas-NA.pdf.

Cieśla W., *EU Fraud Case Sheds Light on Danish and Polish Politics*, https://euobserver.com/investigations/136112.

Comparative Highlights of Foundation Laws: The Operating Environment for Foundations in Europe 2015, a Report from European Foundation Centre, available at: http://www.efc.be/publication/comparative-highlights-of-foundation-laws-the-operating-environment-for-foundations-in-europe-2015/.

Confessore N., *Cambridge Analytica and Facebook: The Scandal and the Fallout So Far*, New York Times 4.4.2018, available at: http://bit.do/ekUXY.

Cooper H., Hervey G., Bauvir E., Antypas I., *Big East-West Skew in Record EU Lobbying bonanza*, available at: http://bit.do/ekUX7.

Cooper H., *Polish Minister Faces Call to Quit over Party Funding*, http://bit.do/ekUYd.

D'Angelo J., *The Evolution of Transparency Corruption*, Harvard University 2017, available at: http://bit.do/ekx8f.

Darpö J., *Effective Justice? Synthesis Report of the Study on the Implementation of Articles 9.3 and 9.4 of the Aarhus Convention in the Member States of the European Union*, available at: http://bit.do/ekx8i.

De Jesus Butler I., *Participatory Democracy under Threat: Growing Restrictions on the Freedoms of NGOs in the EU*, Civil Liberties for Europe. August 2017, available at: http://bit.do/eg9By.

De Jesus Butler I., *Two Proposals to Promote and Protect European Values Through the Multiannual Financial Framework: Conditionality of EU Funds and a Financial Instrument to Support NGOs*, Civil Liberties Union for Europe, available at: http://bit.do/ekx8n.

de Sadeleer J.N., Roller G., Dross M., *Access to Justice in Environmental Matters. Final Report 2002*, ENV.A.3/ETU/2002/0030.

Democratic Accountability and Budgetary Control of Non-governmental Organisations Funded by the EU Budget. Study 2016, available at: http://bit.do/ekUYj.

Ebbesson J., *The EU and the Aarhus Convention: Access to Information, Public Participation in Decision-Making and Access to Justice in Environmental Matters*, the EP Briefing of June 2016, available at: http://bit.do/ekx8E.

Enabling Civil Society: Practical Aspects of Freedom of Association, Public Interest Law Initiative, New York 2003, available at: http://www.pilnet.org/public-interest-law-resources/30-enabling-civil-society-practical-aspects-of-freedom-of.html.

Eriksson A., *Norway Defends NGOs in Hungary and Poland*, available at: https://euobserver.com/social/137818.

EU Funding for NGOs. Value for Money?, NGO Monitor 2016, available at: http://www.ngo-monitor.org/nm/wp-content/uploads/2016/02/Value-for-money-Part-I-Final-1.pdf.

European Parliament Contracts and Grants, available at: http://www.europarl.europa.eu/contracts-and-grants/en/20150201PVL00101/Political-parties-and-foundations.

Feasibility Study on a European Foundation Statute—Final Report, University of Heidelberg, Centre for Social Investment and Max Planck Institute for Comparative and International Private Law, 2009, available at: http://bit.do/eg4vZ.

Financing of Non-governmental Organisations (NGOs) from the EU Budget. Study 2010, available at: http://bit.do/ekx8Q.

Funding Opportunities for NGOs, available at: https://ec.europa.eu/info/funding-tenders/how-eu-funding-works/who-eligible-funding/funding-opportunities-ngos_en.

Gabison G.A., *Understanding Crowdfunding and Its Regulations. How Can Crowdfunding Help ICT Innovation?*, available at: http://bit.do/ekx82.

Giuliani J.D., *La bonne gouvernance*, available at: http://www.jd-giuliani.eu/fr/article/cat-4/33_La-bonne-gouvernance.html.

Graff A., *Urzędasy, bez serc, bez ducha. Organizacje pozarządowe—spojrzenie z wewnątrz*, Gazeta Wyborcza 6.1.2011, available at: http://bit.do/ekCJx.

Greenpeace International Annual Report 2015, available at: http://bit.do/ekynY.

Guérot U., *Now the EU Needs to Hand Power to Its Citizens. Here's Why*, The Guardian 7.2.2018, available at: https://www.theguardian.com/commentisfree/2018/feb/07/european-union-power-citizens-republic.

Guide on Access to EU Documents. Accessing Information from the European Union, AccessInfo 2013, available at: http://bit.do/ekUYH.

Guillaume S., Hübner D., *EU Parliament Should Befriend Transparency*, available at: https://euobserver.com/opinion/138363.

Hersh D., *The Problem with Participatory Democracy Is the Participants*, New York Times 29.6.2017, available at: http://bit.do/ekUYN.

Hooghe L., Marks G., *Types of Multi-level Governance*, available at: http://bit.do/ekU3e.

Hungarian NGO Funding Law in Breach of EU Fundamental Freedoms and Charter Right; Legal Opinion by J. Simor and A. Welsh, Matrix Chambers 22.6.2017, available at: http://bit.do/ekx89.

Hungary Asked Kremlin Lobbyist to Airlift Oettinger to Budapest, http://www.euractiv.com/section/public-affairs/news/hungary-asked-kremlin-lobbyist-to-airlift-oettinger-to-budapest.

Hungary's Government Strengthens Its Anti-NGO Smear Campaign, Human Rights Watch opinion of 20.1.2018, available at: https://www.hrw.org/news/2018/01/20/hungarys-government-strengthens-its-anti-ngo-smear-campaign.

Kavrakova A., *Revising the ECI: How to Make It "Fit for Purpose,"* available at: https://www.euractiv.com/section/politics/opinion/revising-the-eci-how-to-make-it-fit-for-purpose/.

Kendall J., Fraisse L., *The European Statute of Association: Why an Obscure but Contested Symbol in a Sea of Indifference and Skepticism?*, TSEP working paper 11, 2005. The Centre for Civil Society, London School of Economics and Political Science, London, UK, available at: http://eprints.lse.ac.uk/29018/1/11TSEP.pdf.

Kerschen N., Sweeney M., *Participation Democracy and European Governance in Social Policy*, Working paper series FVeP 26, available at: http://bit.do/ekx9e.

King T., *Juncker's White Paper: More Style than Substance*, available at: https://www.politico.eu/article/junckers-white-paper-more-style-than-substance/.

Leal-Arcas R., *Essential Elements of the Rule of Law Concept in the EU*, Queen Mary University of London, School of Law Legal Studies Research Paper No 180/2014, available at: http://bit.ly/2lrpszc

Legal Regulations of Economic Activities of Civil Society Organisations, European Center for Not-for-Profit Law 2015, available at: http://ecnl.org/wp-content/uploads/2015/07/ECNL-Economic-Activities.pdf.

Leino P., *On knowledge as power: Transparency of EU Law-Making Procedures*, available at: http://eulawanalysis.blogspot.com/2016/01/on-knowledge-as-power-transparency-of.html.

Lobbying the EU Institutions Library Briefing Library of the European Parliament 18/06/2013, available at: http://bit.do/ekx9q.

Lobbyists, Governments and Public Trust, Volume 2. A report of the OECD, available at: http://bit.do/ekx9z.

Łojkowska M., *Węgierskie NGO pod presją. Co czeka nas w Polsce [an interview with J. Celichowski]*, available at: http://wiadomosci.ngo.pl/wiadomosc/2084407.html.

Lowe K., Suter K., *The Trouble with Referendums*, available at: http://bit.do/ekx9W.

Maurice E., *Macron to "Rebuild" EU with Citizens Conventions*, available at: https://euobserver.com/political/138941.

Mayer F., *Europa als Rechtsgemeinschaft*, Humboldt-Universität Berlin, Working Paper 8/05, Berlin 2005, http://whi-berlin.de/documents/whi-paper0805.pdf.

McGill L.T., *Number of Registered Public Benefit Foundations in Europe Exceeds 141.000. A 2015 Report*, Foundation Center, available at: http://bit.do/ekx9g.

Michalopoulos S., *Parliament Report Opens "Pandora's Box" of EU funded NGOs*, available at: http://bit.do/ekx92.

Minton A., *Civic Crowdfunding Is Privatization Masquerading as Democracy*, available at: http://bit.do/ekx95.

Mobility of Young Volunteers Across Europe, A Study by the Public Policy and Management Institute, available at: http://bit.do/ekyad.

More Initiative for Europe's Citizens. Future of Democracy, Bertelsmann Stiftung 02.2018, available at: http://bit.do/ekyah.

NGO Participation Arrangements at the UN and in Other Agencies of the UN System, http://bit.do/ekyaj.

NGOs Blocked from Delivering Statement, International Service for Human Rights, available at: https://www.ishr.ch/news/ngo-committee-ngos-blocked-delivering-statement.

NGOs Demand Timmermans Make Good on Mandatory Lobbying Register, available at: http://bit.do/ekyaq.

Nielsen N., *Secret Law Making Takes over Brussels*, available at: https://euobserver.com/institutional/136630.

Niklewicz K., *Weeding Out Fake News. An Approach to Social Media Regulation*, Wilfried Martens Centre for European Studies 2017, available at: http://bit.do/ekyav.

Nyst C., *Data Protection Standards for Civil Society Organisations*, A Study of European Center for Not-for-Profit Law (ECNL), available at: http://bit.do/ekyaA.

Organ J., *Signs of Life for EU "Citizens" Initiative*, available at: https://euobserver.com/opinion/137858.

Ortiz I., Burke S., Berrada M., Cortes Saenz H., *World Protests 2006–2013*, Initiative for Policy Dialogue. Working Paper #274, available at: http://bit.do/ekyaC.

Panichi J., Aries Q., *Beat the Betraymont. Five Easy Ways to Skirt the EU Lobbying Rules*, available at: http://www.politico.eu/article/know-your-eu-lobbying-loopholes/.

Paravicini G., Cooper H., *Mystic Money Man Behind Brussels Activists*, available at: http://bit.do/ekyaH.

Peñarubba M., *Times of Change: The Public Consultation on the European Citizens' Initiative*, available at: http://bit.do/ekyaP.

Pothier F., *Why Europe Needs US-Style Primaries*, available at: https://www.politico.eu/article/europe-needs-us-style-primaries-spitzenkandidaten/.

ReNEUAL Model Rules on EU Administrative Procedure (ReNEUAL 1.0), available at: http://www.reneual.eu/index.php/projects-and-publications/reneual-1-0.

Report of Klon Jawor (*Polskie organizacje pozarządowe 2015*), available at: http://fakty.ngo.pl/files/fakty.ngo.pl/public/kondycja_2015/KondycjaNGO2015.pdf.

Report on Access to Justice in Environmental Matters, Justice and Environment. European Network of Environmental Law Organizations 2010, available at: http://bit.do/ekyaS.

Restakis J., *Defining the Social Economy—The BC Context*, BC Social Economy Roundtable 2006, available at: http://bit.do/ekyaV.

Sadurski W., *How Democracy Dies (in Poland): A Case Study of Anti-Constitutional Populist Backsliding*, Sydney Law School Legal Studies Research Paper No 18/01, available at: http://ssrn.com/abstract=3103491.

Salamon L.M., Sokolowski S.W., Haddock M.A., Tice H.S., *The State of Global Civil Society and Volunteering. Latest Findings from the Implementation of the UN Nonprofit Handbook*, John Hopkins University 2013, available at: http://bit.do/ekyaY.

Schirdewan M., *Why Brussels Toxic Lobbying Culture Must End*, available at: https://euobserver.com/opinion/144093.

Schmidt V.A., *The Eurozone's Crisis of Democratic Legitimacy: Can the EU Rebuild Public Trust and Support for European Economic Integration?*, European Commission Discussion Paper 015/2015, available at: https://ec.europa.eu/info/sites/info/files/dp015_en.pdf.

Silva M., *The Biggest Loophole in the Commission's Lobby Transparency Efforts*, available at: http://bit.do/ekya2.

Simon F., *EU Slapped for Breaching Aarhus Convention on Access to Environmental Justice*, available at: http://bit.do/ekya6.

Smismans S., *"Civil Society" in European Institutional Discourses*, Paper presented to the ECPR Joint Sessions on March 22–27, 2002, Torino, available at: http://bit.do/ehatT.

Staszczyk P., *Zielone światło dla reformy Europejskiej inicjatywy obywatelskiej*, available at: http://bit.do/eH4he.

Successful ECIs Must Be Given a Fair Chance of Having a Political Impact. The Commission Proposal on ECI Revision and What Is Crucially Missing, available at: http://bit.do/ekybd.

Świeboda P., Zerka P., *Aktywność polskich organizacji pozarządowych na szczeblu europejskim. Ekspertyza przygotowana na zlecenie Urzędu Komitetu Integracji Europejskiej*, Warsaw 2009, available at: http://bit.do/ekybf.

Teffer P., *EU "Must Lift Lid" on Secretive "Deal-Making,"* available at: https://euobserver.com/institutional/134340.

Teffer P., *EU Embassies "Shockingly" Opaque about Lobbyists*, available at: https://euobserver.com/institutional/144092.

Teffer P., *Missing: Paper Trail of EU Meetings with Big Tech*, available at: https://euobserver.com/institutional/144082.

Teffer P., *Transparency Complaints Keep the EU Ombudsman Busy*, available at: https://euobserver.com/institutional/138003.

The Central Role of European Governments in NGO Funding, a Report Issued by NGO Monitor, available at: http://bit.do/ekybm.

Timmermans F., *Make Lobbying in the EU Truly Transparent*, available at: http://bit.do/eH3QB.

van den Boschee P., *NGO Involvement in the WTO: A Lawyer's Perspective on a Glass Half-Full or Half-Empty*, Maastricht 2006, available at: http://bit.do/ekybq.

Voluntary Organisations: Proposed EC Statutes: European Cooperative Society; European Mutual Society; European Association and Accompanying Directives Regarding the Involvement of Employees. A Consultative Document Issued by the Treasury of Great Britain, available at: https://archive.org/details/op1279308-1001.

Whitewashing "Resistance"—Human Rights Funding to Organizations Blurring the Lines Between Violence and Nonviolence, NGO Monitor report of 2017, available at: http://bit.do/ekB92.

Wirtz B., *EU Funded Lobbying Is Expensive and Undemocratic*, available at: https://euobserver.com/opinion/139093.

World Bank—Civil Society Engagement. Fiscal Report 2010-2012, http://bit.do/ekybt.

Zalan E., Maurice E., *Transparency Is Key EU Tactic in Brexit Talks*, available at: https://euobserver.com/uk-referendum/137444.

3. OTHER

Berg C., *How to launch a European Citizens' Initiative?*, a presentation during The Good Lobby Advocacy School, 23.6.2017 in Brussels.

European Foundation Statute State of Play. EESC—Social Economy Category Meeting on 26 February 2015, presentation available at: http://bit.do/ekUY9.

Joint complaint of NGOs in the Białowieża Forest District Case, available at: http://bit.do/ekybA.

Table of Cases

1. The CJEU

2. Cases Before the European Ombudsman

3. Cases Before the Aarhus Compliance Committee

4. Internal Reviews Procedures Before the European Commission

Table of Legislation

1. International Law

2. EU Law

(a) Primary Law

Treaty on European Union (consolidated version), Official Journal C 326, 26.10.2012, 5, 7, 39, 41–43, 57, 68, 70–73, 77–82, 85, 86, 91, 97, 98, 103, 114, 116, 117, 119, 120, 127, 136, 152, 198, 234, 308, 330, 342, 345

Treaty on the Functioning of the European Union (consolidated version), Official Journal C 326, 26.10.2012, 5, 31, 42, 68, 70, 80–82, 84–87, 89, 103–106, 112, 113, 145, 148, 150, 159, 184–189, 192–199, 202, 203, 207, 209, 210, 231, 249, 250, 253, 254, 259–261, 266, 268, 274, 277, 305, 306, 310–312, 318, 342–345

The Charter of Fundamental Rights of the European Union, Official Journal C 326, 26.10.2012, 42, 73, 81, 85, 104, 145, 198, 234, 276, 342

The Maastricht Treaty, Official Journal C 191, 29.7.1992, 56, 57, 83, 91, 101, 145, 203

The Amsterdam Treaty, Official Journal C 191, 29.7.1992, 58, 59, 129, 194

The Treaty of Nice, Official Journal C 080, 10.3.2001, 67

The Treaty of Lisbon, Official Journal C 206, 17.12.2007, 42, 43, 68, 69, 70, 77, 78, 82, 86, 97, 100, 102, 116, 135, 194, 260, 342

(b) Secondary Law

Commission Decision of 13 December 2007 laying down detailed rules for the application of Regulation (EC) No 1367/2006 of the EP and of the Council on the Aarhus Convention as regards requests for the internal review of administrative acts (2008/50/EC), Official Journal L 13, 16.1.2008, 252

Commission Regulation (EC) No 773/2004 of 7 April 2004 relating to the conduct of proceedings by the Commission pursuant to Articles 81 and 82 of the EC Treaty, Official Journal L 123, 27.4.2004, 114

Council Decision (EU) No 2016/1859 of 13 October 2016 on the Tripartite Social Summit for Growth and Employment and repealing Decision 2003/174/EC, Official Journal L 284, 28.10.2016, 83

Council Decision 2003/174/EC of 6 March 2003 establishing a Tripartite Social Summit for Growth and Employment, Official Journal L 070, 14.3.2003, 83

Council Decision 2010/37/EC of 27 November 2009 on the European Year of Voluntary Activities Promoting Active Citizenship, Official Journal L 17/43, 22.1.2010, 334

Council Decision No 2005/370/EC of 17 February 2005 on the conclusion, on behalf of the European Community, of the Convention on access to information, public participation in decision-making and access to justice in environmental matters, Official Journal L 124, 17.5.2005, 211

Commission Delegated Regulation (EU) No 240/2014 on the European code of conduct on partnership in the framework of the European Structural and Investment Funds, Official Journal L 74/1, 14.3.2014, 178

Directive 2013/11/EU of the EP and of the Council of 21 May 2013 on alternative dispute resolution for consumer disputes and amending Regulation (EC) No 2006/2004 and Directive 2009/22/EC, Official Journal L 165/63, 18.6.2013, 178

Directive 2014/67/EU of the EP and of the Council of 15 May 2014 on the enforcement of Directive 96/71/EC concerning the posting of workers in the framework of the provision of services and amending Regulation (EU) No 1024/2012 on administrative cooperation through the Internal Market Information System, Official Journal L 159/11, 28.5.2014, 178, 180

Directive 90/313/EEC of 7 June 1990 on the freedom of access to information on the environment, Official Journal L 158, 23.6.1990, 183, 216, 225

Regulation (EC) No 1049/2001 of the EP and of the Council of 30 May 2001 regarding public access to European Parliament, Council and Commission documents, Official Journal L 145, 31.5.2001, 104, 114, 160, 219, 324

Regulation (EC) No 1107/2006 of the EP and of the Council of 5 July 2006 concerning the rights of disabled persons and persons with reduced mobility when travelling by air, Official Journal L 204, 26.7.2006, 144

Regulation (EC) No 1367/2006 of the EP and of the Council of 6 September 2006 on the application of the provisions of the Aarhus Convention on Access to Information, Public Participation in Decision-Making and Access to Justice in Environmental Matters to Community institution and bodies, Official Journal L 264, 25.9.2006, 193

Regulation (EU, EURATOM) No 1141/2014 of the EP and of the Council of 22 October 2014 on the statute of European political parties and European political foundations, Official Journal L 317, 4.11.2014, 307

Regulation (EU) No 2016/679 of the EP and of the Council of 27 April 2016 on the protection of natural persons with regard to the processing of personal data and on the free movement of such data, repealing Directive 95/46/EC (General Data Protection Regulation—GDPR, Official Journal L 119/1, 4.5.2016, 177

Regulation (EU) No 211/2011 of the EP and of the Council on the citizens' initiative, Official Journal L 65/1, 11.3.2011, 117

Regulation (EU) No 1303/2012 of the EP and of the Council of 17 December 2013 laying down common provisions on the European Regional Development Fund, the European Social Fund, the Cohesion Fund, the European Agricultural Fund for Rural Development and the European Maritime and Fisheries Fund and laying down general provisions on the European Regional Development Fund, the European Social Fund, the Cohesion Fund and the European Maritime and Fisheries Fund and repealing Council Regulation (EC) No 1083/2006, Official Journal L 347/320, 20.12.2013, 178

Regulation (EU, Euratom) No 2018/1046 of the EP and of the Council of July 18, 2018 on the financial rules applicable to the general budget of the Union amending Regulations (EU) No 1296/2013, (EU) No 1301/2013, (EU) No 1303/2013, (EU) No 1304/2013, (EU) No 1309/2013, (EU) No 1316/2013, (EU) No 223/2014, (EU) No 283/2014, and Decision No 541/2014/EU and repealing Regulation (EU, Euratom) No 966/2012, Official Journal L 193/1, 30.7.2018, 315

Regulation (EU) 2018/1475 of the EP and of the Council laying down the legal framework of the European Solidarity Corps and amending Regulations (EU) No 1288/2013, (EU) No 1293/2013 and Decision No 1313/2013/EU, Official Journal L 250/1, 4.10.2018, 335

3. National Law

Belgian Law on Non-Profit Associations, International Non-Profit Associations and Foundations, 1921 (*Loi sur les associations sans but lucratif, les associations internationaes sans but lucrative et les fondations*), 282, 313

Belgian Law Organizing the Recognition and Supervision of Crowdfunding and Various Provisions in Finance, 2016 (*Loi organisant la reconnaissance et l'encadrement du crowdfunding et portant des dispositions diverses en matière de finances*), 331

British Charities Act, 2011, 296

Constitution of the Republic of Poland, 1997 (*Konstytucja Rzeczpospolitej Polskiej*), 84

Czech Law on Volunteer Service and on Amendments to Certain Laws, 2002 (*zákon o dobrovolnické službě a o změně některých zákonů*), 333

Danish Act on Commercial Foundations, 2014 (*Lov om erhervsdrivende fonde*), 293

German Formation and Activities of Foundations Act, 1990 (*Gesetz über die Bildung und Tätigkeit von Stiftungen*), 313

Hungarian Act CLVI on Public Benefit Organizations, 1997 (*évi CLVI. törvény a közhasznú szervezetekről*), 7

Latvian Associations and Foundations Act, 2003 (*Biedrību un nodibinājumu likums*), 313

Latvian Public Good Organization Law, 2004 (*Sabiedriskā labuma organizāciju likums*), 296

Polish Act on Income Tax from Natural Persons, 1991 (*Ustawa o podatku dochodowym od osób fizycznych*), 271

Polish Code of Administrative Procedure, 1960 (*Kodeks postępowania administracyjnego*), 180, 250

Polish Code of Civil Procedure, 1964 (*Kodeks postępowania cywilnego*), 180

Polish Law on Accounting, 1994 (*Ustawa o rachunkowości*), 289

Polish Law on Associations, 1989 (*Prawo o stowarzyszeniach*), 313

Polish Law on Foundations, 1984 (*Ustawa o fundacjach*), 313

Polish Law on Proceedings Before Administrative Courts, 2002 (*Prawo o postępowaniu przed sądami administracyjnymi*), 343

Polish Law on Public Benefit and Volunteer Work, 2003 (*Ustawa o działalności pożytku publicznego i o wolontariacie*), 296, 298, 310, 313, 330, 333, 337

Polish Law on the Rules for Conducting Development Policy, 2006 (*Ustawa o zasadach prowadzenia polityki rozwoju*), 330

Polish Law on Trade Unions, 1991 (*Ustawa o związkach zawodowych*), 85

Romanian Law for Legal Entities—Associations and Foundations, 2000 (*lege nr. 21 pentru Persoanele juridice—Asociaţii şi Fundaţii*), 313

Spanish Law 50/2002 on Foundations, 2002 (*Ley 50/2002 de Fundaciones*), 295, 312

4. Internal Law

Agreement between the European Parliament and the European Commission on the transparency register for organisations and self-employed individuals engaged in EU policy-making and policy implementation, Official Journal L 277, 19.9.2014, 156

Code of Conduct for Members of the European Parliament with respect to financial interests and conflicts of interest of 2011, available at: http://bit.do/ekx5d, 165

Commission Decision of 25 November 2014 on the publication of information on meetings held between Members of the Commission and organisations or self-employed individuals, 2014/839/EU, Euratom, Official Journal L 343/22, 28.11.2014, 165

Commission Decision of 31 January 2018 on a Code of Conduct for the Members of the European Commission, C(2018) 700, 165

Decision 94/90/ECSC, EC, Euratom on public access to Commission documents, Official Journal L 46/58, 18.2.1994, 101

Decision of the Court of Justice of the European Union of 11 October 2016 concerning public access to documents held by the Court of Justice of the European Union in the exercise of its administrative functions (2016/C 445/03), Official Journal C 445/3, 30.11.2016, 105

Decision of the EP on the regulations and general conditions governing the performance of the Ombudsman's duties (the European Ombudsman's Statute), Adopted by Parliament on 9 March 1994, Official Journal L 113, 4.5.1994, p. 15 and amended by its decisions of 14 March 2002, Official Journal L 92, 9.4.2002, p. 13 and 18 June 2008, Official Journal L 189, 17.7.2008, 204

Decision of the European Economic and Social Committee of 1 July 2003 on public access to European Economic and Social Committee documents (2003/603/EC), Official Journal C 205/19, 14.8.2003, 105

Provisional Rules of Procedure of the UN Security Council of 1983, S/96/Rev.7, 19

Rules of Procedure of the General Court of 4 March 2015, Official Journal L 105, 23.4.2015, as amended on 13 July 2016, Official Journal L 217, 12.8.2016 and on 11 and 31 July 2018, Official Journal L 240, 25.9.2018, 150

Rules of Procedure of the Court of Justice of 25 September 2012, Official Journal L 265, 29.9.2012, as amended on 18 June 2013, Official Journal L 173, 26.6.2013 and on 19 July 2016, Official Journal L 217, 12.8.2016, 150

Rules Governing the Establishment of Intergroups. Decision of the Conference of Presidents of the EP of 16 December 1999, available at: http://bit.do/ekymC, 143

Statute of the International Court of Justice, 26.5.1945, 20

The consolidated version of Protocol (No 3) on the Statute of the Court of Justice of the European Union, annexed to the Treaties, as amended by Regulation (EU, Euratom) No 741/2012 of the European Parliament and of the Council of 11 August 2012, Official Journal L 228, 23.8.2012, 150

The CoR Rules of Procedure of 2014, Official Journal L 65/41, 5.3.2014, 91

The Council Decision 93/731/EC on public access to its documents, Official Journal L 340/43, 31.12.1993, 101

The EESC Rules of Procedure of 2010, Official Journal L 324/52, 9.12.2010, 87

The Rules of Ethics for Advocates and the Dignity of the Profession (Code of Ethics for Advocates, *Zbiór Zasad Etyki Adwokackiej i Godności Zawodu (Kodeks Etyki Adwokackiej)*), adopted by the Polish Bar Council on 10.10.1998 (Resolution No 2/XVIII/98), as amended by Resolution No 32/2005 of the Polish Bar Council of 19.11.2005 and resolutions of the Polish Bar Council Nos 33/2011–54/2011 of 19.11.2011, available at: http://bit.do/ekx7J, 167

The Rules of Procedure of the EP of 2017, available at: http://bit.do/ekx7u, 142–147

5. Non-binding Acts of Law, Legal Proposals, Official Reports, Opinions, Press Releases and Other Provisions

Access to information, public participation and access to justice in environmental matters at Community level—A Practical Guide of the Commission, available at: http://bit.do/ekxRs, 260

Annex to Detailed rules for the application of Regulation (EC) No 1367/2006 of the European Parliament and of the Council on the application of the provisions of the Aarhus Convention on Access to Information, Public Participation in Decision-making and Access to Justice in Environmental Matters to Community institutions and bodies to the Commission Decision of 20 April 2008 amending its Rules of Procedure as regards detailed rules for the application of Regulation (EC) No 1367/2006 of the European Parliament and of the Council on the application of the provisions of the Aarhus Convention on Access to Information, Public Participation in Decision-making and Access to Justice in Environmental Matters to Community institution and bodies (2008/401/EC, Euratom), Official Journal L 140, 30.5.2008, 253

"Better Regulation Toolbox" of 2015, SWD(2015) 111, 134

"Better Regulation Guidelines," SWD (2017), 350, 134

Challenges facing civil society organisations working on human rights in the EU. Report of the European Union Agency for Fundamental Rights, Luxembourg: Publications Office of the European Union 2017, available at: http://fra.europa.eu/en/publication/2018/challenges-facing-civil-society-orgs-human-rights-eu, 2

The CJEU 2017 Annual Report on Judicial Activity, available at https://curia.europa.eu/jcms/upload/docs/application/pdf/2018-04/_ra_2017_en.pdf, 106

Commission Staff Working Document "Better Regulation Guidelines," SWD(2017) 350, 80, 134

Commission Staff Working Document "Crowdfunding in the EU Capital Markets Union," SWD(2016) 154 final, 332

Commission's EU Citizenship Report 2010 "Dismantling the obstacles to EU citizens' rights" COM(2010) 602 final, 68

Commission's Notice on Access to Justice in Environmental Matters of 28.4.2017, C(2017) 2616 final, 243

Investigation of informal trilogue negotiations since the Lisbon Treaty—Added value, lack of transparency and possible democratic deficit. Study by the EESC of 2017, available at: http://bit.do/ekxHu, 102

The letter of the European Ombudsman to the President of the European Concil entitled Administration of the European Council (SI/8/2017/KR), 170

The Millions Given by EU Institutions to NGOs with Ties to Terror and Boycotts against Israel. An In-Depth Analysis of 2018, The Ministry of Strategic Affairs and Public Diplomacy of the State of Israel, available at: http://bit.do/ekB9A, 324

Openness, Transparency and the Right of Access to Documents in the EU. In-depth analysis for the PETI Committee 2016, available at: http://bit.do/ekxGu, 110

Opinion of the Economic and Social Committee on "European Governance — a White Paper" of 27.5.2002, COM(2001) 428 final, Official Journal C 125, 65

Opinion on the Romanian Draft Law 140/2017 on Associations and Foundations as adopted by the Senate on 20.11.2017. Opinion prepared by the Expert Council of the Conference of INGOs of the Council of Europe, CONF/EXP(2017)3, 276

The position of the Polish government on the proposal for the Statute for a European Foundation, available at: https://bip.ms.gov.pl/pl/dzialalnosc/projekty-aktow-prawnych/prawo-unii-europejskiej/download,1724,0.html, 291

Proposal for a Council Decision on the determination of a clear risk of a serious breach by the Republic of Poland of the rule of law, COM(2017) 835 final, 72

Proposal for a Council Directive on implementing the principle of equal treatment between persons irrespective of religion or belief, disability, age or sexual orientation, COM(2008) 426 final, 141

Proposal for a Council Regulation (EEC) on the Statute for a European Association, COM(91) 273 final SYN 386, 278

Proposal for a Council Regulation (EEC) on the Statute for a European mutual society, COM(91) 273 final SYN 391, 310

Proposal for a Council Regulation (EEC) on the Statute for a European cooperative society, COM(91) 273 final SYN 389, 278

Proposal for a Directive of the EP and of the Council on access to justice in environmental matters, COM(2003) 624 final, 246

Proposal for a Directive of the EP and of the Council on the quality of water intended for human consumption (recast), COM(2017) 753 final, 240

Proposal for a Interinstitutional Agreement on a mandatory Transparency Register, COM(2016) 627 final, available at: https://ec.europa.eu/transparency/regdoc/rep/1/2016/EN/1-2016-627-EN-F1-1.PDF, 169

Proposal for a Regulation of the EP and of the Council on the European citizens' initiative, 2017/0220 (COD), 123

Proposal for a Regulation of the EP and of the Council on European Crowdfunding Service Providers (ECSP) for Business, COM(2018) 113 final, 332

Proposal for the Council Regulation on the Statute for a European Foundation (FE), COM(2012) 035 final, 291

Proposal for the Treaty Establishing a Constitution for Europe, available at: http://bit.do/ekxFz

EUROPEAN MONOGRAPH SERIES

1. Lammy Betten (ed.), *The Future of European Social Policy,* 1991 (ISBN 90-654-4585-4).
2. Annemarie Loman, Kamiel Mortelmans, Harry H.G. Post & Stewart Watson, *Culture and Common Law: Before and After Maastricht,* 1992 (ISBN 90-654-4638-9).
3. John A.E. Vervaele, *Fraud against the Community: The Need for European Fraud Legislation,* 1994 (ISBN 90-654-4634-6).
4. Philip Raworth, *The Legislative Process in the European Community,* 1993 (ISBN 90-654-4690-7).
5. Jules Stuyck, *Financial and Monetary Integration in the European Economic Community,* 1993 (ISBN 90-654-4718-0).
6. Jules Stuyck & A.J. Vossestein (eds), *State Entrepreneurship, National Monopolies and European Community Law,* 1993 (ISBN 90-654-4773-3).
7. Jules Stuyck & A. Looijestijn-Clearie (eds), *The European Economic Area EC-EFTA,* 1994 (ISBN 90-654-4815-2).
8. Rosita B. Bouterse, *Competition and Integration: What Goals Count?,* 1995 (ISBN 90-654-4816-0).
9. René Barents, *The Agricultural Law of the EC: An Inquiry into the Administrative Law,* 1994 (ISBN 90-654-4867-5).
10. Nicholas Emiliou, *Principles of Proportionality in European Law: A Comparative Study,* 1996 (ISBN 90-411-0866-1).
11. Eivind Smith, *National Parliaments as Cornerstones of European Integration,* 1996 (ISBN 90-411-0898-X).
12. Jan H. Jans, *European Environmental Law,* 1996 (ISBN 90-411-0877-7).
13. Síofra O'Leary, *The Evolving Concept of Community Citizenship: From the Free Movement of Persons to Union Citizenship,* 1997 (ISBN 90-411-0878-5).
14. Laurence W. Gormley (ed.), *Current and Future Perspectives on EC Competition Law,* 1983 (ISBN 90-411-0691-X).
15. Simone White, *Protection of the Financial Interests of the European Communities: The Fight against Fraud and Corruption,* 1998 (ISBN 90-411-9647-1).
16. Morten P. Broberg, *Broberg on the European Commission's Jurisdiction to Scrutinise Mergers,* 4th Edition, 2013 (ISBN 978-90-411-3339-7).
17. Doris Hildebrand, *The Role of Economic Analysis in the EC Competition Rules: The European School,* 2nd Edition, 2002 (ISBN 90-411-1706-7).
18. Christof R.A. Swaak, *European Community Law and the Automobile Industry,* 1999 (ISBN 90-411-1140-9).

19. Dorthe Dahlgaard Dingel, *Public Procurement: A Harmonization of the National Judicial Review of the Application of European Community Law,* 1999 (ISBN 90-411-1161-1).
20. John A.E. Vervaele (ed.), *Compliance and Enforcement of European Community Law,* 1999 (ISBN 90-411-1151-4).
21. Martin Trybus, *European Defence Procurement Law: International and National Procurement Systems as Models for a Liberalized Defence Procurement Market in Europe,* 1999 (ISBN 90-411-1167-0).
22. Helen Staples, *The Legal Status of Third Country Nationals Resident in the European Union,* 1999 (ISBN 90-411-1277-4).
23. Damien Geradin (ed.), *The Liberalization of State Monopolies in the European Union and Beyond,* 1999 (ISBN 90-411-1264-2).
24. Katja Heede, *European Ombudsman: Redress and Control at Union Level,* 2000 (ISBN 90-411-1413-0).
25. Ulf Bernitz & Joakim Nergelius (eds), *General Principles of European Community Law,* 2000 (ISBN 90-411-1402-5).
26. Michaela Drahos, *Convergence of Competition Laws and Policies in the European Community,* 2002 (ISBN 90-411-1562-5).
27. Damien Geradin (ed.), *The Liberalization of Electricity and Natural Gas in the European Union,* 2001 (ISBN 90-411-1560-9).
28. Gisella Gori, *Towards an EU Right to Education,* 2001 (ISBN 90-411-1670-2).
29. Brendan P.G. Smith, *Constitution Building in the European Union,* 2001 (ISBN 90-411-1695-8).
30. Friedl Weiss & Frank Wooldridge, *Free Movement of Persons within the European Community,* 2nd Edition, 2007 (ISBN 978-90-411-2545-3).
31. Ingrid Boccardi, *Europe and Refugees: Towards an EU Asylum Policy,* 2002 (ISBN 90-411-1709-1).
32. John A.E. Vervaele & André Klip (eds), *European Cooperation Between Tax, Customs and Judicial Authorities,* 2001 (ISBN 90-411-1747-4).
33. Wouter P.J. Wils, *The Optimal Enforcement of EC Antitrust Law: Essays in Law and Economics,* 2002 (ISBN 90-411-1757-1).
34. Damien Geradin (ed.), *The Liberalization of Postal Services in the European Union,* 2002 (ISBN 90-411-1780-6).
35. Nick Bernard, *Multilevel Governance in the European Union,* 2002 (ISBN 90-411-1812-8).
36. Jill Wakefield, *Judicial Protection through the Use of Article 288(2) EC,* 2002 (ISBN 90-411-1823-3).
37. Sebastiaan Princen, *EU Regulation and Transatlantic Trade,* 2002 (ISBN 90-411-1871-3).
38. Amaryllis Verhoeven, *The European Union in Search of a Democratic and Constitutional Theory,* 2002 (ISBN 90-411-1872-1).
39. Paul L.C. Torremans, *Cross Border Insolvencies in EU, English and Belgian Law,* 2002 (ISBN 90-411-1888-8).

40. Malcolm Anderson & Joanna Apap (eds), *Police and Justice Cooperation and the New European Borders*, 2002 (ISBN 90-411-1893-4).
41. Christin M. Forstinger, *Takeover Law in EU and USA: A Comparative Analysis*, 2002 (ISBN 90-411-1919-1).
42. Antonio Bavasso, *Communications in EU Antitrust Law: Market Power and Public Interest*, 2003 (ISBN 90-411-1974-4).
43. Fiona G. Wishlade, *Regional State Aid and Competition Policy in the European Union*, 2003 (ISBN 90-411-1975-2).
44. Gareth Davies, *Nationality Discrimination in the European Internal Market*, 2003 (ISBN 90-411-1998-1).
45. René Barents, *The Autonomy of Community Law*, 2003 (ISBN 90-411-2251-6).
46. Gerhard Dannecker & Oswald Jansen (eds), *Competition Law Sanctioning in the European Union*, 2004 (ISBN 90-411-2100-5).
47. Nauta Dutilh (ed.), *Dealing with Dominance: The Experience of National Competition Authorities*, 2004 (ISBN 90-411-2211-7).
48. Stefaan van den Bogaert, *Practical Regulation of the Mobility of Sportsmen in the EU Post Bosman*, 2005 (ISBN 90-411-2327-X).
49. Katalin Judit Cseres, *Competition Law and Consumer Protection*, 2005 (ISBN 90-411-2380-6).
50. Philipp Kiiver, *The National Parliaments in the European Union: A Critical View on EU Constitution Building*, 2006 (ISBN 978-90-411-2452-4).
51. Alexander Turk, *The Concept of Legislation in European Community Law*, 2006 (ISBN 978-90-411-2472-2).
52. Dimitrios Sinaniotis, *The Interim Protection of Individuals before the European and National Courts*, 2006 (ISBN 978-90-411-2498-2).
53. M. Holoubek & D. Damjanovic, M. Traimer (eds), *Regulating Content: The European Regulatory Framework for the Media and Related Creative Sectors*, 2006 (ISBN 978-90-411-2597-2).
54. Anneli Albi & Jacques Ziller (eds), *The European Constitution and National Constitutions: Ratification and Beyond*, 2006 (ISBN 978-90-411-2524-8).
55. Gustavo E. Luengo, *Regulation of Subsidies and State Aids in WTO and EC Law: Conflicts in International Trade Law*, 2007 (ISBN 978-90-411-2547-7).
56. Eniko Horvath, *Mandating Identity: Citizenship, Kinship Laws and Plural Nationality in the European Union*, 2007 (ISBN 978-90-411-2662-7).
57. Rass Holdgaard, *External Relations Law of the European Community: Legal Reasoning and Legal Discourses*, 2007 (ISBN 978-90-411-2604-7).
58. Jill Wakefield, *The Right to Good Administration*, 2007 (ISBN 978-90-411-2697-9).
59. Dimitry Kochenov, *EU Enlargement and the Failure of Conditionality: Pre- accession Conditionality in the Fields of Democracy and the Rule of Law*, 2008 (ISBN 978-90-411-2696-2).
60. Despina Mavromati, *The Law of Payment Services in the EU: The EC Directive on Payment Services in the Internal Market*, 2008 (ISBN 978-90-411-2700-6).

61. Anne Meuwese, *Impact Assessment in EU Lawmaking,* 2008 (ISBN 978-90-411-2720-4).
62. Ulf Bernitz, Joakim Nergelius & Cecilia Cardner (eds), *General Principles of EC Law in a Process of Development,* 2008 (ISBN 978-90-411-2705-1).
63. Johan van de Gronden (ed.), *The EU and WTO Law on Services: Limits to the Realisation of General Interest Policies within the Services Markets?,* 2008 (ISBN 978-90-411-2809-6).
64. Alina Tryfonidou, *Reverse Discrimination in EC Law,* 2009 (ISBN 978-90-411-2751-8).
65. Mikael Berglund, *Cross-Border Enforcement of Claims in the EU: History Present Time and Future,* 2014 (ISBN 978-90-411-4564-2).
66. Theodore Konstadinides, *Division of Powers in European Union Law: The Delimitation of Internal Competence between the EU and the Member States,* 2009 (ISBN 978-90-411-2615-3).
67. Mattias Derlén, *Multilingual Interpretation of European Union Law,* 2009 (ISBN 978-90-411-2853-9).
68. René Barents, *Directory of EU Case Law on the Preliminary Ruling Procedure,* 2009 (ISBN 978-90-411-3150-8).
69. Yan Luo, *Anti-dumping in the WTO, the EU and China: The Rise of Legalization in the Trade Regime and Its Consequences,* 2010 (ISBN 978-90-411-3207-9).
70. Patrick Birkinshaw & Mike Varney (eds), *The European Union Legal Order after Lisbon,* 2010 (ISBN 978-90-411-3152-2).
71. Thomas Gr. Papadopoulos, *EU Law and Harmonization of Takeovers in the Internal Market,* 2010 (ISBN 978-90-411-3340-3).
72. Bas van Bockel, *The* Ne Bis In Idem *Principle in EU Law,* 2010 (ISBN 978-90-411-3156-0).
73. Veljko Milutinović, *The 'Right to Damages' under EU Competition Law: From* Courage v. Crehan *to the White Paper and Beyond,* 2010 (ISBN 978-90-411-3235-2).
74. Amandine Garde, *EU Law and Obesity Prevention,* 2010 (ISBN 978-90-411-2706-8).
75. Leonard Besselink, Frans Pennings & Sacha Prechal (eds), *The Eclipse of the Legality Principle in the European Union,* 2011 (ISBN 978-90-411-3262-8).
76. Sacha Garben, *EU Higher Education Law: The Bologna Process and Harmonization by Stealth,* 2011 (ISBN 978-90-411-3365-6).
77. Dimitry Kochenov (ed.), *EU Law of the Overseas: Outermost Regions, Associated Overseas Countries and Territories, Territories Sui Generis,* 2011 (ISBN 978-90-411-3445-5).
78. Pablo Ibáñez Colomo, *European Communications Law and Technological Convergence: Deregulation, Re-regulation and Regulatory Convergence in Television and Telecommunications,* 2012 (ISBN 978-90-411-3829-3).
79. Elise Muir, *EU Regulation of Access to Labour Markets: A Case Study of EU Constraints on Member State Competences,* 2012 (ISBN 978-90-411-3823-1).
80. Tim Corthaut, *EU Ordre Public,* 2012 (ISBN 978-90-411-3232-1).

81. Oana Ştefan, *Soft Law in Court: Competition Law, State Aid and the Court of Justice of the European Union*, 2013 (ISBN 978-90-411-3997-9).
82. Francesco Rossi dal Pozzo, *Citizenship Rights and Freedom of Movement in the European Union*, 2013 (ISBN 978-90-411-4660-1).
83. Jens Hartig Danielsen, *EU Agricultural Law*, 2013 (ISBN 978-90-411-3280-2).
84. Ulf Bernitz, Xavier Groussot & Felix Schulyok (eds), *General Principles of EU Law and European Private Law*, 2013 (ISBN 978-90-411-4683-0).
85. Michelle Everson, Cosimo Monda & Ellen Vos (eds), *European Agencies in between Institutions and Member States*, 2014 (ISBN 978-90-411-2843-0).
86. Stefan Leible & Matthias Lehmann (eds), *European Contract Law and German Law*, 2014 (ISBN 978-90-411-2588-0).
87. Piero Leanza & Ondrej Pridal, *The Right to a Fair Trial: Article 6 of the European Convention on Human Rights*, 2014 (ISBN 978-90-411-4855-1).
88. Patrick J. Birkinshaw, *European Public Law: The Achievement and the Challenge*, 2014 (ISBN 978-90-411-4744-8).
89. George Cumming, *Expert Evidence Deficiencies in the Judgments of the Courts of the European Union and the European Court of Human Rights*, 2014 (ISBN 978-90-411-4123-1).
90. Vesna Rijavec, Tomaž Kerestes & Tjaša Ivanc (eds), *Simplification of Debt Collection in the EU*, 2014 (ISBN 978-90-411-4854-4).
91. Nina Półtorak, *European Union Rights in National Courts*, 2015 (ISBN 978-90-411-5863-5).
92. Kyriaki-Korina Raptopoulou, *EU Law and Healthcare Services: Normative Approaches to Public Health Systems*, 2015 (ISBN 978-90-411-5013-4).
93. Torsten Frank Koschinka & Piero Leanza, *Preliminary Injunctions: Germany, England/Wales, Italy and France*, 2015 (ISBN 978-90-411-5833-8).
94. Vesna Rijavec, Tomaž Kerestes & Tjaša Ivanc (eds), *Dimensions of Evidence in European Civil Procedure*, 2016 (ISBN 978-90-411-6662-3).
95. Stefan Leible (ed.), *General Principles of European Private International Law*, 2016 (ISBN 978-90-411-5955-7).
96. Patrick J. Birkinshaw & Andrea Biondi (eds), *Britain Alone!: The Implications and Consequences of United Kingdom Exit from the EU*, 2016 (ISBN 978-90-411-5832-1).
97. René Barents, *Remedies and Procedures before the EU Courts*, 2016 (ISBN 978-90-411-6614-2).
98. Luca Prete, *Infringement Proceedings in EU Law*, 2017 (ISBN 978-90-411-6900-6).
99. Robert van den Hoven van Genderen, *Privacy Limitation Clauses: Trojan Horses under the Disguise of Democracy*, 2017 (ISBN 978-90-411-8599-0).
100. Mariusz Krzysztofek, *Post-Reform Personal Data Protection in the European Union: General Data Protection Regulation (EU) 2016/679*, 2017 (ISBN 978-90-411-6237-3).
101. Gianni Lo Schiavo, *The Role of Financial Stability in EU Law and Policy*, 2017 (ISBN 978-90-411-8230-2).

102. Emmanuel Guinchard & Marie-Pierre Granger (eds), *The New EU Judiciary: An Analysis of Current Judicial Reforms*, 2017 (ISBN 978-90-411-6834-4).
103. Kirsten Henckel, *Cross-Border Transfers of Undertakings: A European Perspective*, 2017 (ISBN 978-90-411-9227-1).
104. Vesna Rijavec, Wendy Kennett, Tomaž Keresteš & Tjaša Ivanc, *Remedies Concerning Enforcement of Foreign Judgements: Brussels I Recast*, 2018 (ISBN 978-90-411-9416-9).
105. Albert Sanchez-Graells & Constant De Koninck, *Shaping EU Public Procurement Law: A Critical Analysis of the CJEU Case Law 2015–2017*, 2018 (ISBN 978-94-035-0160-4).
106. Andrea Biondi, Patrick J. Birkinshaw & Maria Kendrick, *Brexit: The Legal Implications*, 2019 (ISBN 978-90-411-9540-1).
107. Mariusz Krzysztofek, *GDPR: General Data Protection Regulation (EU) 2016/679: Post-Reform Personal Data Protection in the European Union*, 2019 (ISBN 978-94-035-0594-7).
108. Giovanni Bassani, *The Legal Framework Applicable to the Single Supervisory Mechanism: Tapestry or Patchwork?*, 2019 (ISBN 978-94-035-0872-6).
109. Piotr Staszczyk, *A Legal Analysis of NGOs and European Civil Society*, 2019 (ISBN 978-94-035-1251-8).